Adult
Teacher

The Word of Life Series of Adult Bible Lessons
Based on Outlines From the Evangelical Curriculum Commission

September 1984-August 1985

02-0446

WRITERS

FALL   Stanley M. Horton ● John Maempa
WINTER   W. Charles Harris ● Curtis Ringness ● Ron Held
SPRING   Kenneth D. Barney ● Beth Snodderly
SUMMER   Stanley M. Horton ● Gary Speer

CHURCH SCHOOL LITERATURE STAFF

NATIONAL DIRECTOR Hardy W. Steinberg
EDITOR Charles W. Ford
ASSOCIATE EDITOR Gary Leggett
BIBLE AND DOCTRINE EDITOR Zenas J. Bicket
ADULT EDITOR Kenneth D. Barney
ASSISTANT ADULT EDITOR Sherman N. Shell
SENIOR EDITORIAL ASSISTANT Viv Blakeney
EDITORIAL ASSISTANT James E. Erdmann

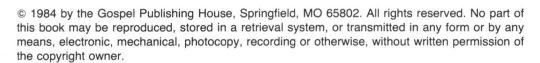

Library of Congress Catalog Number 77-77219
International Standard Book Number 0-88243-446-2
Printed in the United States of America

TABLE OF CONTENTS

Index of Scripture Texts, Volumes 1-7

Recommended Resources

The fall/84 theme is "Beyond the Natural World." The teacher will find the following books very helpful in advance preparation and classroom use:

GENERAL REFERENCE WORKS

The Packet of Adult Teaching Helps (PATH) contains teaching and learning aids especially designed to supplement the fall studies. Use with every study. Order #67 1175, $5.00.

The Wycliffe Bible Commentary by Charles F. Pfeiffer and Everett F. Harrison, editors. A phrase-by-phrase commentary on the whole Bible. Perhaps one of the best single-volume commentaries on the market. Order #03 WX 0881, $23.95.

SELECTED STUDY HELPS

Knowing God by J. I. Packer. This book discloses the nature and character of God and how to get to know Him. Use with study 1. Order #03 WX 1857, $6.95.

God in Three Persons by Carl Brumback. A Trinitarian answer to the Oneness or "Jesus Only" false doctrine. Use with study 7. Order #03 WX 1574, $4.95.

Genesis: Lessons About God and Man by T. M. Moore. A brief guide to the book of God's revelation to us about the universe, himself, man, sin, and redemption. Use with study 2. Order #03 WX 1521, $2.50.

What the Bible Teaches About What Jesus Did by F. F. Bruce. The works and ministry of Jesus traced through the Gospels. Use with study 4. Order #03 WX 0427, $3.95.

More Than a Carpenter by Josh McDowell. This is a straightforward book for skeptics of Jesus' deity and resurrection. Use with study 3. Order #03 WX 2063, $2.50.

The Spirit Himself by Ralph M. Riggs. This book is a study of the Person of the Holy Spirit. Use with study 5 and 6. Order #02 WX 0590, $4.95.

The Strategy of Satan by Warren W. Wiersbe. Satan exposed as a deceiver, destroyer, wicked ruler, and accuser. Use with study 8 and 9. Order #03 WX 2518, $2.95.

The Screwtape Letters by C. S. Lewis. A clever, lighthearted exposé of the way Satan tries to trip us Christians. Use with study 9. Order #03 WX 2439, $2.50.

Spiritual Dynamics by G. Raymond Carlson. A brief study of the Person and work of the Holy Spirit. Use with study 5 and 6. Order #02 WX 0894, $2.50.

Concerning Spiritual Gifts by Donald Gee. Another classic with penetrating insights into the gifts. The ministry of each is clearly outlined. Use with study 6. Order #02 WX 0486, $2.50.

What the Bible Says About the Holy Spirit by Stanley M. Horton. Written from a positive evangelical and Pentecostal viewpoint, this comprehensive volume examines every aspect of the Holy Spirit. Order #02 WX 0647, $4.95.

Charismata—A Fresh Look —by David Lim. A complete commentary on gifts of the Spirit from a Pentecostal viewpoint. Use with study 6. Order #03 WX 1251, $3.50.

How To Use Your Adult Teacher

It is imperative that you read the Adult Student quarterly during your advance study. Pay particular attention to the questions under "Applying the Word." Be ready to discuss any one of these questions during class time if a student brings it up. You may wish to integrate specific questions into your presentation for a given Sunday.

Wide and Narrow Columns

Instead of the two equal columns used in the past, your *Adult Teacher* now uses the format of a wide and narrow column. Each study contains the same information as before, but it has been rearranged.

The wide column contains the following: SEEING THE SCRIPTURES, SETTING THE SCENE, BIBLE COMMENTARY (including Scripture blocks), Guidelines for Living, LIVING THE TRUTH, and EVANGELISM OUTREACH.

On the first page of each study, the narrow column contains an overview of the study under the heading, PREPARING TO TEACH. This column shows the Study Text, Outline, Golden Text, Central Truth, and Learning Goals.

On the remaining pages, the narrow column includes: GETTING STARTED, Clarification, Teaching Tips, questions from the commentary, and the daily devotional guide.

Helps Where You Need Them

The commentary, application, and methodology sections are totally integrated so the teacher has what he needs at the point of use. The section headed, GETTING STARTED, is at the beginning—where it would be used. It contains suggestions for getting the students' immediate attention and providing a bridge to the Bible study that follows.

The "Clarification" section, which explains words or expressions in the study text that might be difficult to understand, is placed opposite the Scripture block to which it applies.

Each Teaching Tip is placed or referred to at the point where it would be used to help students get a better grasp of that part of the Bible Commentary. If a Teaching Tip calls for the use of PATH (Packet of Adult Teaching Helps), that information will be given. When you see the heading, "Question," in the narrow column, it is a question answered in the Bible Commentary at that point.

The guidelines for living are considered a part of the application, but are so closely related to the commentary that this section is inserted in the commentary. It is set off by a long, narrow bracket and by the heading, "Guideline for Living," followed by the number. This section should not be considered an interruption of the commentary. It is for the purpose of helping the teacher apply to daily life the Bible truth being studied.

The daily devotional guide is for the teacher's personal benefit. It is to help you get into the Word throughout the week, and hopefully you will find in the daily devotionals truths you will use in the lesson.

At the end of the study, "Living the Truth" is a summary of all the guidelines for living. "Evangelism Outreach" is actually a sub-head under "Living the Truth." It is a reminder to use the class not only as a time to nurture Christians but also to bring the unsaved to a decision for Christ.

Use It as a Tool

You will find more material in the *Adult Teacher* than you can use in any one session. Your own advance study will show you what to include and what to omit. You may sometimes develop activities of your own that will seem more suitable. The *Adult Teacher* is a tool, not a substitute for the Bible or personal preparation. Use this quarterly for the purpose for which it has been designed and your efforts will be rewarded.

EVALUATION
ADULT

Please respond to the questions below at the end of the quarter. Then remove, fold, tape, stamp, and return this form.

1. _____ Average Sunday school attendance.
2. _____ Average class attendance.
3. Did you find the following sections of the lesson format helpful? (Check one)

Yes	No	Didn't Use	
____	____	____	Setting the Scene
____	____	____	Learning Goals
____	____	____	Communicating Bible Truth
____	____	____	Clarification
____	____	____	Teaching Tips
____	____	____	Guidelines for Living
____	____	____	Living the Truth
____	____	____	Preparing for Next Week
____	____	____	Daily Devotional Guide

Is the general reaction of your class to the Adult Student favorable? ____YES ____No

Additional comments: (If appropriate, please indicate publication, item, and page number.)

Thank you,
The Editors

Fold

CHURCH SCHOOL LITERATURE DEPARTMENT
Gospel Publishing House
1445 Boonville Avenue
Springfield, MO 65802

Attention: Adult Section

Fold

BEYOND THE NATURAL WORLD

1 | THE NATURE OF GOD

PREPARING TO TEACH

Study Text
Leviticus 11:44, 45; Psalms 90:2; 102:24-27; 139:1-12; Jeremiah 32:17-19, 27; Ezekiel 39:7; John 3:16; 1 John 4:7-10, 16

Outline
I. God Is Eternal
   A. Without Beginning
   B. Without Ending
II. God Is Almighty
   A. Omniscient
   B. Omnipresent
   C. Omnipotent
III. God Is Holy
   A. God's Holy Name
   B. God's Holiness the Standard for Ours
IV. God Is Love
   A. God's Love Is Calvary Love
   B. A Love That Trusts

Golden Text: God is love; and he that dwelleth in love dwelleth in God, and God in him. 1 John 4:16

Central Truth: The Bible reveals that God is eternal, almighty, holy, and loving.

Learning Goals
1. To examine the magnitude of God's nature.
2. To appreciate the greatness of God.
3. To realize that God is our all-sufficient Source of wisdom, power, and righteousness.
4. To determine to align our lives with the nature and character of God.

SEEING THE SCRIPTURES

Psalm 139:1-12

1. O Lord, thou hast searched me, and known me.

2. Thou knowest my downsitting and mine uprising; thou understandest my thought afar off.

3. Thou compassest my path and my lying down, and art acquainted with all my ways.

4. For there is not a word in my tongue, but, lo, O Lord, thou knowest it altogether.

5. Thou hast beset me behind and before, and laid thine hand upon me.

6. Such knowledge is too wonderful for me; it is high, I cannot attain unto it.

7. Whither shall I go from thy Spirit? Or whither shall I flee from thy presence?

8. If I ascend up into heaven, thou art there: if I make my bed in hell, behold, thou art there.

9. If I take the wings of the morning, and dwell in the uttermost parts of the sea;

10. Even there shall thy hand lead me, and thy right hand shall hold me.

11. If I say, Surely the darkness shall cover me; even the night shall be light about me.

12. Yea, the darkness hideth not from thee; but the night shineth as the day: the darkness and the light are both alike to thee.

Jeremiah 32:17-19 17. Ah Lord God! behold, thou hast made the heaven and the earth by thy great power and stretched out arm, and there is nothing too hard for thee:

18. Thou showest loving-kindness unto thousands, and recompensest the iniquity of the fathers into the bosom of their children after them: The Great, The Mighty God, The Lord of hosts, is his name;

19. Great in counsel, and mighty in work: for thine eyes are open upon all the ways of the sons of men, to give every one according to his ways, and according to the fruit of his doings.

Ezekiel 39:7

7. So will I make my holy name known in the midst of my people Israel; and I will not let them pollute my holy name any more: and the heathen shall know that I am the Lord, the Holy One in Israel.

John 3:16

16. For God so loved the world, that he gave his only begotten Son, that whosoever believeth in him should not perish, but have everlasting life.

GETTING STARTED

From early days of childhood, most of us, if not all, have pondered the question, "What is God like?" Since no one has actually seen God, we have no objective image or impression by which we can formulate a likeness of Him.

God is imponderable. He is beyond what our finite mental faculties can comprehend. Yet we continue to ask, "What is God like?"

Launch this week's discussion by having the students share impromptu impressions of what they think God is like. This activity will simply stimulate thinking along the theme of the study content.

Clarification

Formed—brought to birth, brought forth.

World—continents.

Wax old—be worn out.

A vesture—clothes.

Change them—replace them.

Be changed—pass away, vanish.

Question.

What is the emphasis of Genesis 1:1?

TEACHING TIP 1

A number of God's attributes are covered in this week's discussion. There are other attributes important to God's nature that are not directly touched on but are included in the outline below. You may wish to reproduce the outline on an overhead transparency or write it on the chalkboard. As you discuss them, comment briefly on the attributes not covered in the commentary or simply list them for general information. Perhaps some students could be

SETTING THE SCENE

Someone once said, "I don't like to sing the song 'How Great Thou Art.' I don't feel I need to tell God how great He is. He already knows how great He is." If we think this, we miss the point. God's greatness calls for a response from us.

God has not left man to struggle in the darkness. In His grace He reaches down into the darkness and reveals himself in the written Word, the Bible, and in His Son our Lord Jesus Christ. Thank God for a dependable revelation that lets us know what God is like.

The universe itself makes us aware of God's greatness and power. Unfortunately, the minds of many are blinded by unbelief. However, they are without excuse, for God has revealed himself.

BIBLE COMMENTARY

I. God Is Eternal

Psalms 90:2; 102:24-27

Psalm 90:2. Before the mountains were brought forth, or ever thou hadst formed the earth and the world, even from everlasting to everlasting, thou art God. 102:24. I said, O my God, take me not away in the midst of my days: thy years are throughout all generations. 25. Of old hast thou laid the foundation of the earth: and the heavens are the work of thy hands. 26. They shall perish, but thou shalt endure: yea, all of them shall wax old like a garment; as a vesture shalt thou change them, and they shall be changed: 27. but thou art the same, and thy years shall have no end.

A. Without Beginning

Sometimes children ask the question, "Where did God come from?" In answer some have facetiously quoted Habakkuk 3:3: "God came from Teman." But this is simply a description of how the ancient Israelites looked across the wilderness toward Teman in Edom and saw the glory of God appear and then overspread the sky. The Bible's answer is that God always was. He is without beginning.

The words, "In the beginning," are emphasized. Ancient unbelievers supposed that the material world, or at least elements that make it up, are eternal, without beginning. When they spoke of creation in their myths, it was always creation out of something that was already there such as earth, air, fire, water, slime, or a giant's body. But the Bible teaches a real beginning, a creation out of nothing, a creation by God. It also teaches that God was not only there in the beginning, but before the beginning.

Deuteronomy 33:27 is a favorite. Here God is the true God from eternity past. The "everlasting arms" are "the arms of the Eternal One." (See also Habakkuk 1:12; Psalm 135:13; Isaiah 63:16, for example.)

assigned beforehand to comment on these attributes. A text such as Myer Pearlman's *Knowing the Doctrines of the Bible* would be a good study resource.

The Attributes of God
1. Active Attributes
   a. Omniscience
   b. Omnipresence
   c. Omnipotence
   d. Wisdom
   e. Sovereignty
2. Moral Attributes
   a. Holiness
   b. Righteousness
   c. Faithfulness
   d. Mercy
   e. Love
   f. Goodness

B. Without Ending

Not only was God before all things, but as the Psalmist says, "Even from everlasting to everlasting, thou art God." He was there in eternity past. He will always be there in eternity future, and when time is no more (Revelation 10:6).

The present heavens and earth will not last forever. They will be replaced just as worn-out clothes are replaced by brand-new ones. (See Revelation 20:11, where no place is found for the present earth and heavens. The word "new" in Revelation 21:1 and 2 Peter 3:13 usually means brand-new. Passages such as Ecclesiastes 1:4 either mean there will always be earth (though not necessarily the same one), or they are contrasting short-lived things with the longer enduring earth. Thus, we must interpret these passages in the light of Psalm 102:24-27, Isaiah 51:6, and Revelation 20:11.

Guideline for Living 1

What assurance do we gain from the fact of God's eternality?

In a continually changing world, it is reassuring to know there is One who is the same "yesterday, and today, and for ever." We find ultimate security in the One who changes not.

Our peace and assurance are eloquently stated in the opening phrase of Deuteronomy 33:27, "The eternal God is thy refuge, and underneath are the everlasting arms." It is because of God's changelessness that we can overcome fear of change in this life. We can know that His comfort, guidance, and providence will be there today, tomorrow, and forever.

II. God Is Almighty

Psalm 139:1-12; Jeremiah 32:17-19, 27

Psalm 139:1. O Lord, thou hast searched me, and known me. 3. Thou compassest my path and my lying down, and art acquainted with all my ways. 6. Such knowledge is too wonderful for me; it is high, I cannot attain unto it.

A. Omniscient

Not only is God eternal, He has all knowledge. He knows everything past, present, and future.

It only emphasizes how much more there is to know and how impossible it is for any one person to know it all. One scientist said that for every new fact discovered we know there are ten more out there yet to be discovered. In others words, what we know we are ignorant of is growing ten times faster than what we know we know, as far as the natural world is concerned.

Before the 200-inch telescope was placed on Mt. Palomar in California, some were predicting that the new telescope would be able to look around through a supposed curvature of space and see the earth's galaxy as it was long ago. But their mathematical model of the universe was too small. The new telescope brought into view multitudes of new galaxies that even Einstein hadn't dreamed of. Even today, it seems that only God knows what the universe is really like.

At the other end of the scale, *a Popular Science Yearbook* stated

Question.
What does Psalm 139:1-6 emphasize about God's knowledge?

Question.
Does this mean He predestines all that we do?

TEACHING TIP 3

Focus on the significance to our lives of God's omniscience by drafting the following outline on the chalkboard or overhead transparency. Ask various students to read aloud the Scripture verses listed.

God Knows . . .
1. Our frame—Psalm 103:14
2. Our hearts—Psalm 44:21; Luke 16:15
3. Our needs—Matthew 6:8; 10:29-31
4. Our path — Psalms 1:6; 37:23

Clarification

Hell—*sheol,* the place of the departed.

The sea—the west. That is, if I could go as fast as the dawn spreads from east to west, or if I could go with the speed of light.

Clarification

Lovingkindness—faithful, covenant-keeping love and loyalty.

a few years ago that the ultimate subatomic particle had been found, and now we knew all about the atom. The next year scientists found two more of these particles. It would seem that only God knows what the atom is really like.

He knows me, everything about me—my past, my present, my future. He knows what I think and plan even before those thoughts and intents are formulated in my brain.

Not at all. But He does press us hard before and behind. That is, He brings circumstances to bear to help us make the right choices. He lays His hand on us to try to fit us into His great will and plan so He can bless us. But whether we respond or not is up to us.

There is still a great deal of controversy about how God does this. But we can agree on verse 6. God knows more than we do and always will.

B. Omnipresent

Psalm 139:7. Whither shall I go from thy Spirit? Or whither shall I flee from thy presence? 8. If I ascend up into heaven, thou art there: if I make my bed in hell, behold thou art there. 9. If I take the wings of the morning, and dwell in the uttermost parts of the sea; 10. even there shall thy hand lead me, and thy right hand shall hold me.

What does Psalm 139:7-12 emphasize? First of all, that God is everywhere. David did not mean that he could on his own accord go up to heaven or down to the place of the departed. He is simply saying that if he could, he would find that God is there. There is no way anyone can go far enough or fast enough to get away from God.

Guideline for Living 2

What special consolation can the believer find in the fact of God's omnipresence?

We live in a lonely world. Despite more than 4 billion population, multitudes of people are desperately lonely, isolated from meaningful relationships with those around them. Alcohol, drugs, and illicit relationships are sought to compensate for dread of loneliness. Yet these can never provide happiness and contentment.

Although believers are not completely exempt from loneliness, it is a joy to know that God's presence is everywhere at all times. In times of separation from family, friends, and fellow believers, we can be assured that God is present to help in time of need.

David also emphasized that there is no place to hide. The wicked like to hide in the darkness. But there is no darkness with God. When He moves in, the darkest place will not hide anyone from the searchlight of His gaze. Darkness is only what seems dark to us. But darkness and light are both alike to Him. "God is light, and in him is no darkness at all" (1 John 1:5). Thus, where He is there is inexpressible light though we may not be able to see it. In the same way, spiritual darkness is only because of our own spiritual blindness.

C. Omnipotent

Jeremiah 32:17. Ah Lord God! behold, thou hast made the heaven and the earth by thy great power and stretched out arm, and there

Question.
What is the most obvious demonstration of the power of God?

is nothing too hard for thee: 18. thou showest lovingkindness unto thousands, and recompensest the iniquity of the fathers into the bosom of their children after them: The Great, the Mighty God, the Lord of hosts, is his name; 19. great in counsel, and mighty in work: for thine eyes are open upon all the ways of the sons of man, to give every one according to his ways, and according to the fruit of his doing. 27. Behold, I am the Lord, the God of all flesh: is there any thing too hard for me?

Jeremiah sees it as His work in creation. He made this great universe and everything in it. The Bible declares two things about God again and again. He alone is the Creator. He alone is the Redeemer. The New Testament shows that He accomplished both of these works through Jesus. (See John 1:3; 3:16.) It also shows we accept both of these things through faith (Ephesians 2:8; Hebrews 11:3).

We know that God has all power, so the work of creation was easy for Him. He carried out His plan of creation so that everything was good. Sin intervened. But He has another plan, the plan of redemption, and He has the power to carry out that too.

Guideline for Living 3
Power is one of the consuming passions of mankind. Nuclear technology has enabled scientists to tap energy resources almost beyond comprehension. A dreadful application is the development of nuclear weaponry capable of destroying entire cities. Then there are the great rocket engines capable of hurling tons of steel and payload into orbit. Yet these great examples of super power pale into insignificance before the Almighty God, Creator of heaven and earth. And what is the beautiful application of such power? God is able to change a life bound by the fierce grip of sin into one that is pure, holy, and righteous. What a powerful God we serve!

Question.
Who in this passage says there is nothing too hard for God?

Jeremiah says it in verse 17. God says it in verse 27. God said the same thing to Abraham and Sarah (Genesis 18:14). The Bible has many positive statements about God's unlimited power. In fact, the same word that is translated "to be hard" in these questions is usually translated "to be wonderful" or "to be marvelous" and a related form of the word speaks of God's wonderful or marvelous works. Take a concordance and you will find that these works are not only outstanding or extraordinary; they are supernatural. Thus there is nothing too hard, too difficult, too marvelous, too wonderful, or too supernatural for God.

Clarification
Sanctify yourselves—behave as people who have been consecrated (dedicated) to the service and worship of God.

Holy—separated to, dedicated to carrying out God's plan and purposes.

Creeping thing—small animal, reptile.

The heathen—the nations, the Gentiles.

III. God Is Holy
Leviticus 11:44, 45; Ezekiel 39:7.
Leviticus 11:44. I am the Lord your God: ye shall therefore sanctify yourselves, and ye shall be holy; for I am holy: neither shall ye defile yourselves with any manner of creeping thing that creepeth upon the earth. Ezekiel 39:7. So will I make my holy name known in the midst of my people Israel; and I will not let them pollute my holy name any more: and the heathen shall know that I am the Lord, the Holy One in Israel.

A. God's Holy Name

Throughout the Bible God is the Holy One. Isaiah, in connection with his call, saw a vision of God with seraphim chanting, "Holy, Holy, Holy" (Isaiah 6:3). God is holy in all that He is and does.

The root meaning of holiness is separation. God is separate from all that is sin, all that is evil. But that is not all. He showed His holiness also by bringing up the Israelites from Egypt. That is, God is separated to and dedicated to the carrying out of His covenants and promises. Because of His holiness He will not only judge sin, He will bring us into the blessings and inheritance He has promised.

B. God's Holiness the Standard for Ours

When we look around us, we see society in decay and decline. If we are to please God we must look above. We must see in Him the standard toward which we are to strive. Jesus said it in Matthew 5:48. Paul saw it in the revelation of God given us in Jesus (Ephesians 5:1, 2). Paul did not count himself to have attained final perfection in this life. But he pressed on toward the mark and he expected us to do the same (Philippians 3:12-15). What a contrast to those whose lack of holiness (dedication, consecration) allowed them to make a god of their belly and keep their mind on earthly things (Philippians 3:17-19).

TEACHING TIP 4

Depict the root meaning of God's holiness with the following sketch. Emphasize that this illustrates the appropriate separation of all believers from sin.

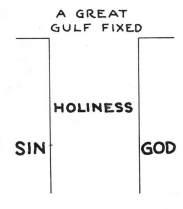

A GREAT
GULF FIXED

HOLINESS

SIN   GOD

TEACHING TIP 5

Ask the students to consider the following questions. Allow free discussion.
1. What standard of holiness should I strive to achieve?
2. Can a true state of holiness be gained in this life?
3. What are influences that may prevent me from living a holy life?

Guideline for Living 4

Holiness has always been an issue of concern in the Christian community, as it should be. Yet for some, holiness has been perceived as a list of stifling "don'ts" that restrict the believer's participation in various activities. Until this notion is corrected, it is difficult for the believer to understand Biblical holiness.

It is true that holiness essentially requires separation from sin. Yet it is far more than a list of regulations. Holiness is a state of being, a quality of life that results from an honest and open relationship between the believer and God. Holy living is nurtured and strengthened through careful attention to God's Word, an effectual prayer life, and regular worship and fellowship in God's house. When a close relationship exists between a believer and God, God's essential nature, which is holy, becomes part of the believer's nature. This is what gives him power to maintain his separation from the world.

IV. God Is Love

1 John 4:7, 10, 16; John 3:16

1 John 4:7. Beloved, let us love one another: for love is of God; and every one that loveth is born of God, and knoweth God. 10. Herein is love, not that we loved God, but that he loved us, and sent his Son to be the propitiation for our sins. 16. And we have known and believed the love that God hath to us. God is love; and he that dwelleth in love dwelleth in God, and God in him. John 3:16. For God so loved the world, that he gave his only begotten Son, that whosoever believeth in him should not perish but have everlasting life.

Clarification

Love—keep on loving. The Greek language has three words for love. The one used here is a high, holy, self-giving, faithful love, a love not dependent on sentimental feelings or on likes and dislikes.
Loveth—keeps on loving.

Is born—has been born. It is implied that this kind of love is impossible except for those who have been born of the Spirit.

Propitiation for—sin offering that pays the penalty and removes the guilt for.

We have known and believed—we have come to know and believe (and still believe and trust in).

Dwelleth in love—that is, makes this high, holy, faithful, Calvary love the constant expression of life and actions.

TEACHING TIP 6

Emphasize that love is the distinguishing characteristic of being a Christian. It is the hallmark of our faith. Ask the students to consider how effectively their lives reflect God's love by considering the statements on the "Is My Love Showing" work sheet in PATH. Distribute copies to the students. Allow time for discussion.

Daily Devotional Guide

M. Our God Is Great. Psalm 145:1-7

T. Our God Is Gracious. Psalm 145:8-16

W. Our God Is Righteous. Psalm 145:17-21

T. Our God Gives Strength. Isaiah 40:27-31

F. Our God Is Spirit. John 4:20-26

S. Our God Is Worthy. Revelation 4:6-11

A. God's Love Is Calvary Love

We see God's love in supreme demonstration when we look to Calvary. No other love has ever measured up to the love God showed when He sent His Son to save sinners (Romans 5:6-10). This is the love God asks us to show when we are commanded to love one another. Our neighbor needs more than the love we can give of ourselves. God is the true and only source of this love. Our neighbor needs to receive that love which comes through us when the Holy Spirit makes us channels of God's love.

This love has its source in God alone. No other religion offers anything like it. To the Hindu, the purest religion is to do neither good nor bad. To the Muslim, the purest religion is to submit to God in a fatalistic way without any regard for others. But our God gave His Son.

B. A Love That Trusts

Because we know God's love and have experienced it in a personal way, we come to have a wonderful confidence and trust in His love. Thus, we can declare that God is love. We can make His love the moving force of our lives. As we express His love in all we do, we then have further assurance that we live in God and God lives in us.

LIVING THE TRUTH

Why is a study of God's nature important? Because our duty as Christians is to become like Him. Of course, there are attributes that are possessed only by God. Yet every believer has the potential of appropriating the moral attributes of holiness, love, righteousness, mercy, and goodness. It is through careful study of God's Word that we discover those attributes. Then we must strive through the help of the Holy Spirit to become like God and be conformed to His image.

EVANGELISM OUTREACH

The initial step in understanding and becoming like God is to accept His Son, Jesus Christ, as Saviour. Be sensitive to any who may not have taken this first step. Be prepared to offer prayer and counsel following the class session.

THE WORKS OF GOD

SEEING THE SCRIPTURES

Genesis 1:1-5, 31

1. In the beginning God created the heaven and the earth.

2. And the earth was without form, and void; and darkness was upon the face of the deep. And the Spirit of God moved upon the face of the waters.

3. And God said, Let there be light: and there was light.

4. And God saw the light, that it was good: and God divided the light from the darkness.

5. And God called the light Day, and the darkness he called Night. And the evening and the morning were the first day.

31. And God saw every thing that he had made, and, behold, it was very good. And the evening and the morning were the sixth day.

Exodus 14:26-31

26. And the Lord said unto Moses, Stretch out thine hand over the sea, that the waters may come again upon the Egyptians, upon their chariots, and upon their horsemen.

27. And Moses stretched forth his hand over the sea, and the sea returned to his strength when the morning appeared; and the Egyptians fled against it; and the Lord overthrew the Egyptians in the midst of the sea.

28. And the waters returned, and covered the chariots, and the horsemen, and all the host of Pharaoh that came into the sea after them; there remained not so much as one of them.

29. But the children of Israel walked upon dry land in the midst of the sea; and the waters were a wall unto them on their right hand, and on their left.

30. Thus the Lord saved Israel that day out of the hand of the Egyptians; and Israel saw the Egyptians dead upon the seashore.

31. And Israel saw that great work which the Lord did upon the Egyptians: and the people feared the Lord, and believed the Lord, and his servant Moses.

Romans 6:23

23. For the wages of sin is death; but the gift of God is eternal life through Jesus Christ our Lord.

SETTING THE SCENE

When sinful human beings begin to think about God they come up with a variety of ideas. Some have made gods of natural objects and natural forces. They worshiped idols, birds, animals. But they were looking for gods they could manipulate. Others worshiped things they could not understand, such as the sun, stars, planets, storms. Others imagined a spirit of some kind in every tree, bush, and waterfall.

PREPARING TO TEACH

Study Text
Genesis 1:1 to 2:25; Exodus 6:6; 12:12; 14:19-31; 16:4-18; Joshua 10:12-15; Acts 5:1-11; Romans 3:21-26; 6:23; 2 Corinthians 5:18, 19

Outline
I. Creation
   A. God Works by a Plan
   B. God's Good Purpose
II. Miracles
   A. Miracles of Deliverance
   B. Miracles of Divine Provision
   C. Miracles Bring Victories
III. Judgment
   A. Judgment on God's Enemies
   B. Judgment in the House of God
IV. Salvation
   A. God's Gift
   B. The Ministry of Reconciliation

Golden Text:
By grace are ye saved through faith; and that not of yourselves: it is the gift of God. Ephesians 2:8

Central Truth:
God's works show His glory and His unchanging desire for man's ultimate good.

Learning Goals
1. To examine the works of God in Creation, miracles, judgment, and salvation.
2. To appreciate the fact that God is at work today in the affairs of men.
3. To give honor and praise to the God who does all things well.

Ask the students to brainstorm on a number of things that man worships in today's world. Sketch the following figure of a person.

Ask: "What does this suggest regarding man's need for God?" Point out that every human being has a void within that longs to worship something. Even primitive cultures that know nothing about the true God worship something—idols, animals, natural formations, etc. But only God can fill the void that is in each of us.

Clarification

In the beginning—emphatic, that is, in the furthest back beginning.

Created—Hebrew, *bara*, a word used only of God's unprecedented creative acts. (Compare Numbers 16:30 where "make a new thing" uses the same verb and means "create a creation.")

And the earth—rather, now the earth. The rest of the chapter is told from the point of view of the earth.

Void—empty of inhabitants. That is, God did not create the earth with people already on it. Notice that in the first three days that follow God gives the earth form. In the second three days He fills up the emptiness.

Moved—kept hovering. The verb is used elsewhere of a mother bird hovering over the young in its nest.

Firmament—expanse; that is, an atmosphere in which the clouds float.

Image—pattern.

Likeness—similarity; includes the potentialities placed in man that he could develop as he walked with God.

Still others made their god a great first cause who started or wound up the universe and left it to run by itself. This deistic view, of course, left them free to go their own way and do as they pleased. But the Bible reveals the true God who continues active in His universe and in our behalf.

Others speak of an impersonal "ground of being." Or they speak of an ultimate being, an *atman* or *brahma* that can't be said to exist or not exist, and who has no concern for us as individuals. The Bible reveals a personal God who loves us and cares about us—a God who shows His love in Christ.

BIBLE COMMENTARY

I. Creation

Genesis 1:1 through 2:25

Genesis 1:1. In the beginning God created the heaven and the earth. 2. And the earth was without form and void; and darkness was upon the face of the deep. And the Spirit of God moved upon the face of the waters. 26. And God said, let us make man in our image, after our likeness: and let them have dominion over the fish of the sea, and over the fowl of the air, and over the cattle, and over all the earth, and over every creeping thing that creepeth upon the earth. 31. And God saw everything that he had made, and, behold, it was very good. 2:7. And the Lord God formed man of the dust of the ground, and breathed into his nostrils the breath of life; and man became a living soul. 15. And the Lord God took the man, and put him into the garden of Eden to dress it and to keep it. 22. And the rib, which the Lord God had taken from man, made he a woman, and brought her unto the man.

A. God Works by a Plan

Verse 1 emphasizes that there was a real beginning where God created all things out of nothing. But as we look down through the chapter we notice that God is the One who is speaking, acting, creating, naming, and making judgments about His creation. The chapter is a revelation of God in action.

We see also a step-by-step sequence through the creation days leading up to a climax in the creation of man. Then we see correspondence between the first day, light, and the fourth day, lights or lightbearers; between the second day, the firmament or expanse with the clouds above and the ocean below; and the fifth day, the expanse creatures, birds to fly among the clouds and fish to swim in the sea; and between the third and sixth days, where dry land and vegetation prepare for animals and man. Then there is balance. Days one, two, four, and five have one major creative act each. Days three and six have two entirely distinct creative acts each.

This sort of thing does not happen by chance. When you have sequence, correspondence, balance, and climax, this can only mean that God worked by a plan. We do not have the space to deal with the theory of evolution here. Suffice it to say that the facts can be explained as well or better by a step-by-step creation where God reused patterns and allowed time in between for development.

Replenish—fill, as the same word is translated in Genesis 1:22.

Very Good—that is, perfectly suited to God's divine plan and purpose.

Formed—molded, like a potter.

Dust—moist earth; not dry dust.

Soul—individual, or person. Translated "creature" in Genesis 1:24.

Dress it—cultivate it.

A help meet for him—a helper as his counterpart or complement; like him mentally, physically, and spiritually.

One of his ribs—a piece of his side including bone, flesh, nerve tissue, etc.

Made he a woman—He proceeded to build into a woman. Implies close personal attention and care in a step-by-step creation.

Question.

What was God's primary concern in creation?

Question.

What are some of the things that show God's purpose was good?

Clarification

A wall—that is, the water rose as high walls at some distance on each side of them. The path was so wide that the Israelites could go across broadside and keep ahead of the Egyptians.

It is manna—"What is it?" Or, as we might say it, they called it a "what's it" because they did not know what it was.

Ajalon—Aijalon, "Hartville"; about 9 miles west of Gibeon. Notice the sun was in the east and the moon was in the west. It was morning and Joshua anticipated the time he would need.

Guideline for Living 1

What application do we see of God's planning in the affairs of man?

Anyone familiar with the Word of God can clearly see how God has guided and directed the affairs of mankind from the beginning of time. God has always had a plan for this world and its inhabitants. Throughout history, nations have risen and fallen, great men have come and gone, wars have been fought, pestilences of all kinds have swept the globe, and times of great awakening and revival have occurred. These events have not come about merely by chance. Each has been carefully planned by God Almighty. All have had their time and purpose in His master plan.

Yet it is not only in the broad events of history that we see the outworking of God's plans. Those who have accepted Jesus Christ as Saviour can look back and see how God has clearly opened and closed doors, made provision in time of need, and granted wisdom and guidance during times of decision. How heartening to realize that the One who orders the events of history is equally involved in directing the affairs of our individual lives. To God be the glory!

B. God's Good Purpose

In a sense He was preparing for man from the very beginning. He wanted a being created in His image who could walk in fellowship with Him.

At every step what He created was good and formed a beautiful balance in nature that prepared the earth to be a habitation for man. When He finished, He pronounced it all, including man—male and female—very good.

The second chapter gives more details of God's creation of the first man and woman. It emphasizes how God took personal care as He formed the man and then took the man's bone and flesh and built the woman. He also prepared a garden and gave them work to do in caring for it. Thus, they became fellow workers with the Lord.

II. Miracles
Exodus 14:19-31; 16:4-18; Joshua 10:12-25

Exodus 14:21 Moses stretched out his hand over the sea; and the Lord caused the sea to go back by a strong east wind all that night, and made the sea dry land, and the waters were divided. 30. Thus the Lord saved Israel that day out of the hand of the Egyptians; and Israel saw the Egyptians dead upon the seashore. 31. And Israel saw that great work which the Lord did upon the Egyptians: and the people feared the Lord, and believed the Lord, and his servant Moses. 16:12. I have heard the murmurings of the children of Israel: speak unto them, saying, At even ye shall eat flesh, and in the morning ye shall be filled with bread; and ye shall know that I am the Lord your God. 15. And when the children of Israel saw it, they said one to another, It is manna: for they wist not what it was. And Moses said unto them, This is the bread which the Lord hath given you to eat. Joshua 10:12. Then spake Joshua to the Lord in the day when the Lord delivered up the

Amorites before the children of Israel, and he said in the sight of Israel, Sun, stand thou still upon Gibeon; and thou, Moon, in the valley of Ajalon.

A. Miracles of Deliverance

Both the Greek and Hebrew have three separate words we translate "miracle." One means "an extraordinary, marvelous, supernatural wonder." Another means "a deed of mighty power." The third means "a sign," that is, "something that points to or reveals God's nature or plan." All of them show that God is a personal God who cares about us and who intervenes in the course of history, in the phenomena of nature, and in the affairs of individual men to work out His good purposes.

The deliverance of Israel out of Egypt through the sea is one of the greatest miracles in their history. Many miracles preceded it in connection with the plagues. In these God sometimes gave Pharaoh an advantage. For example, He let Pharaoh set the time when the plague of frogs would disappear. But the crossing of the sea and the destruction of Pharaoh's crack chariot troops is something Israel never forgot. God even sent a wind during the night so they wouldn't so much as get their feet muddy as they crossed. God was their Deliverer. He kept His promise.

B. Miracles of Divine Provision

God provided manna daily in the wilderness. Twice during the forty years He provided quail. Twice He provided water from the rock. God showed Israel that in spite of all their murmuring and complaining, He really cared about them. They could depend on Him for the provision of their needs. Even their shoes and clothes did not wear out during this time.

It lasted till they came to the Promised Land. Then they were able to live on the grain and other food they found there. God also instituted the Feast of Tabernacles (Booths) where they memorialized the 40 years in the wilderness and declared they were still as dependent on God as when He gave them manna and water from the rock.

Guideline for Living 2

Rick and Carol Rigenhagen and their son Dwight, home missionaries in Wainright, Alaska, were en route to Fairbanks in a small single-engine aircraft. Their final destination was Idaho where they were to itinerate. The sky had grown dark as they approached Fairbanks. About 60 miles outside the city, Rick was terrified as he watched the oil pressure drop to zero. Engine failure! Under normal circumstances it would only be moments before the engine would freeze and they would rapidly lose altitude.

There was no place to make an emergency landing. Only rugged mountain terrain lay below. Immediately, Carol began to cry out to God. Then a miracle happened. Amazed, Rick watched the oil pressure gauge slowly rise. The engine held steady. They flew safely into Fairbanks and landed before the engine failed. Commenting later on this incident, Rick said, "Any experienced mechanic will tell you it is impossible for oil pressure to be regained after it has dropped. Clearly this was a miracle of God."

But now the Rigenhagens were faced with a financial crisis. How

TEACHING TIP 2

We talk and hear a lot about the miracle-working God we serve. Yet for many believers, miracles are something that happened only in the Bible. Stress the fact that God still performs miracles today by contacting members of your class or in the general congregation who have experienced genuine miracles. Ask two or three to give brief testimonials or prerecord their testimonies on a cassette tape.

Discuss the following questions:

1. What is the purpose of a divine miracle?

2. Should I base my faith in God on miracles?

3. Why may we not be seeing a lot of miracles today?

Question.

How long did the manna last and what happened after it ceased?

were they to replace an airplane engine and still go on to Idaho? As before, they placed the situation in God's hands. In church services the very next day, God supplied each need through the generous giving of His people. Roundtrip commercial airfare to Idaho was given as well as an offer to completely repair the airplane. God had granted to the Rigenhagens a miracle of both deliverance and provision.

C. Miracles Bring Victories

Joshua needed more time to consolidate a God-given victory and conserve its results. So God gave him a double-length day to do it.

Never. Some folk suppose that miracles follow some sort of spiritual law. But miracles are always God's gracious provision to meet the needs of His people and fulfill His promise and plan. Many miracles involve God's timing, not ours. Many past miracles have never been repeated. Seldom are miracles repeated in exactly the same way. God sees things we cannot see. But the miracles in the Bible show we can trust Him and that He knows what is best.

III. Judgment
Exodus 6:6; 12:12; Acts 5:1-11

Exodus 6:6. Say unto the children of Israel, I am the Lord, and I will bring you out from under the burdens of the Egyptians, and I will rid you out of their bondage, and I will redeem you with a stretched out arm, and with great judgments. 12:12. For I will pass through the land of Egypt this night, and will smite all the firstborn in the land of Egypt, both man and beast; and against all the gods of Egypt I will execute judgment: I am the Lord. Acts 5:9. Then Peter said unto her, How is it that ye have agreed together to tempt the Spirit of the Lord? behold, the feet of them which have buried thy husband are at the door, and shall carry thee out. 11. And great fear came upon all the church, and upon as many as heard these things.

A. Judgment on God's Enemies

One of the great examples of a holy God's judgment is seen when God's mighty hand brings deliverance from the heavy hand of Pharoah.

Pharaoh was determined to destroy Israel, but he wanted to get as much work out of them as possible in the process. When Moses first came before him, he said, "Who is the Lord?" In other words, "Why should I obey the Lord? I have my own gods." The ten plagues each dealt with a god or something under the protection of the gods of Egypt, thus discrediting them. At the same time they built up the faith of the Israelites so they were willing to sprinkle the blood and eat the Passover in faith, expecting God's deliverance.

B. Judgment in the House of God

Those who know to do well and do it not must suffer severe judgment. For judgment must begin at the house of God (1 Peter 4:17). God does not always deal swiftly with such sin. However,

Question.
Did God ever do anything like that before or since?

Clarification
Burdens—forced labor.
Rid—rescue.
Firstborn—firstborn males.
Kept back part of the price—appropriated part of the price for his own benefit. "Kept back" is translated "purloined" in Titus 2:10. The Septuagint (Greek) translation (used by the Early Church) uses the same word of Achan's act of misappropriation (Joshua 7:1).
Being privy—sharing the secret knowledge and therefore the deceit.
Tempt—test, put to the test (in order to see what they could get away with).
Straightway—immediately. Sapphira's death was as sudden as her husband's.
Fear—a healthy fear which included an awe that inspired caution.
Church—assembly.

Question.
Why were the plagues of Egypt necessary?

TEACHING TIP 3
Focus on the mockery made of the Egyptian gods by reviewing the information sheet from PATH. You may wish to list each plague and the god mocked as you review the information. An alternate approach would be to give this sheet to a student a week be-

forehand and ask that he or she present the material to the class.

at the beginning of the history of the Church God wanted to let the people know that He cannot tolerate lies and selfish motives. Believers who give place to the devil as Ananias did are in just as much danger of the eventual judgment of God. We can be sure also that when Satan filled Ananias' heart there was no more room for the Holy Spirit. Thus Ananias, like Judas, went to the place he had chosen—the devil's hell. (See Teaching Tip 4.)

Clarification
By faith of Jesus—by faith in Jesus (as in Romans 3:22).
Redemption—release from sin.
Propitiation—mercy seat (Leviticus 16:14-16).

IV. Salvation
Romans 3:21-26; 6:23; 2 Corinthians 5:18, 19

Romans 3:24. Being justified freely by his grace through the redemption that is in Christ Jesus. 6:23. The wages of sin is death; but the gift of God is eternal life through Jesus Christ our Lord. 2 Corinthians 5:18. And all things are of God, who hath reconciled us to himself by Jesus Christ, and hath given to us the ministry of reconciliation.

A. God's Gift
Throughout the Bible we see God as our Creator and Redeemer. (See Teaching Tips 5 and 6.)

Nothing at all. Simple faith is the only requirement to receive salvation. Actually, since we have all sinned, none of us deserves to be justified, that is, pronounced not guilty. No matter how hard we work or how much good we do, we still cannot stand before God and say we are not guilty of any sin. So Jesus paid the price and set us completely free from sin and guilt. We could not possibly deserve this, so God gave it freely as a gift by grace. All who believe in Jesus receive it.

B. The Ministry of Reconciliation
Are we saved because we believe in Jesus? In a sense we are. But in a fuller sense we are saved because of what God did in Jesus. John 3:16 shows us it is because God gave His Son that we can have eternal life by believing in Jesus. Christ's death and the shedding of His blood on Calvary is the means of our salvation. Our faith becomes the door by which we enter into the blessings.

Question.
Since all are sinners is there anything we can do to deserve salvation?

TEACHING TIP 4
Hypocrisy and deception are not limited to the Early Church's example of Ananias and Sapphira. Perhaps there are ways in which believers today become caught up with these terrible vices. Explore some possible areas of concern by discussing the following questions:

1. Is it hypocrisy if our tithe is not 10 percent of our income?

2. Is it hypocrisy if our outward show of worship is not a true reflection of our relationship to God?

3. Is it hypocrisy if our daily lives do not reflect our profession of faith?

4. Is it hypocrisy if our service for God is done to bring attention to ourselves?

5. Is it hypocrisy to voice our concern for the lost and dying and then go our own way without another thought of their need?

Emphasize that although Ananias and Sapphira's deception was an overt act, there are many more subtle ways in

Guideline for Living 3
The beauty of salvation is in the complete transformation that takes place in the life of a believer. This is made possible because of the sinner's justification in the eyes of God. He is completely pardoned for his past transgressions. Someone has said that the term "justified" could be rendered "just-as-if-I'd" never sinned. So far as God is concerned, the slate is clean.

In addition to the wonderful work of justification, a new believer is also regenerated or given a new life in Jesus Christ. The imagery is given in Ephesians 4:22-24, which speaks of putting off the old man and putting on the new. Salvation brings freedom from sin, reconciliation to God, and a completely new life enriched by the presence of the Holy Spirit.

which we can be guilty of such a sin.

Question.

Does God have to be reconciled to the sinner?

Question.

Who is the rebel who needs to be reconciled?

TEACHING TIP 5

Ask a student to prepare a brief report on the development of God's plan of salvation. This should include a comparison of the Old Testament sacrificial system with the perfect once-for-all sacrifice of Jesus Christ.

Stress the fact that the Old Testament system of sacrifices covered only outward acts of sin and had no effect on the penitent's heart, whereas the sacrifice of Jesus Christ changes us within.

TEACHING TIP 6

Outline the process of salvation by displaying the overhead transparency from PATH. Highlight the "A B C" progression which is at the heart of the salvation process.

God hates sin, but His love always reaches out to the sinner. God is a good God and He has always wanted to bless mankind (Genesis 12:3). He has never wanted men to perish (2 Peter 3:9).

Sin in the Bible is basically rebellion. Man is the rebel. The sinner needs to be reconciled to God. God himself has provided that reconciliation through Christ. Our responsibility is to spread the good news.

LIVING THE TRUTH

We may stand in awe at God's works in creation, but this will not bring about a spiritual transformation in our lives. Creation displays God's greatness and wisdom, but Jesus had to come to earth to show God as a Father who longs to save every lost person. We read of many miracles in the Bible, but until we have experienced the personal miracle of the new birth, we cannot begin to understand God.

EVANGELISM OUTREACH

Perhaps there are some in your class who have not experienced a life-changing encounter with Jesus Christ. Ask the Holy Spirit to deal with their hearts and draw them to the point of making a decision for Christ.

Daily Devotional Guide
M. God Leads His People. Exodus 13:17-22
T. God Heals His People. Exodus 15:22-26
W. God Delivers His People. Joshua 24:2-13
T. God Provides for His People. Psalm 23:1-6
F. God Saves Those Who Believe. Ephesians 2:1-10
S. God Makes All Things New. Revelation 21:1-7

3 | THE PERSON OF CHRIST

PREPARING TO TEACH

Study Text

Matthew 1:21-23; 16:15, 16; Luke 1:31-35; John 1:1-3, 14-18, 45, 49; 13:1; 15:13; Romans 1:1-4; Galatians 4:4; Ephesians 5:25; Philippians 2:5-8; Hebrews 2:14; 4:15; 1 Peter 2:21-23

Outline

I. Son of God
  A. The Holy Son of God
  B. The Powerful Son of God
II. Son of Man
  A. The Virgin-Born Saviour
  B. Revealing God in the Human Sphere
III. Sinless Character
  A. Holy
  B. Loving
  C. Humble

Golden Text:
He saith unto them, But whom say ye that I am? And Simon Peter answered and said, Thou art the Christ, the Son of the living God. Matthew 16:15, 16

Central Truth:
Jesus Christ is God come in the flesh —truly God and truly man.

Learning Goals

1. To understand the character and nature of Jesus Christ.
2. To recognize that Jesus is indeed both God and man.
3. To appreciate Christ's purpose in coming to dwell among men.
4. To seek to pattern our lives after the character and nature of Jesus Christ.

SEEING THE SCRIPTURES

John 1:1-3, 14-18

1. In the beginning was the Word, and the Word was with God, and the Word was God.

2. The same was in the beginning with God.

3. All things were made by him; and without him was not any thing made that was made.

14. And the Word was made flesh, and dwelt among us, (and we beheld his glory, the glory as of the only begotten of the Father,) full of grace and truth.

15. John bare witness of him, and cried, saying, This was he of whom I spake, He that cometh after me is preferred before me; for he was before me.

16. And of his fulness have all we received, and grace for grace.

17. For the law was given by Moses, but grace and truth came by Jesus Christ.

18. No man hath seen God at any time; the only begotten Son, which is in the bosom of the Father, he hath declared him.

Philippians 2:5-8

5. Let this mind be in you, which was also in Christ Jesus:

6. Who, being in the form of God, thought it not robbery to be equal with God:

7. But made himself of no reputation, and took upon him the form of a servant, and was made in the likeness of men:

8. And being found in fashion as a man, he humbled himself, and became obedient unto death, even the death of the cross.

1 Peter 2:21-23

21. For even hereunto were ye called: because Christ also suffered for us, leaving us an example, that ye should follow his steps:

22. Who did no sin, neither was guile found in his mouth:

23. Who, when he was reviled, reviled not again; when he suffered, he threatened not; but committed himself to him that judgeth righteously.

SETTING THE SCENE

The Gospels show that Jesus is the Son of God in a unique sense. We never find Jesus teaching others to say, "Our Father," and including himself. We never see Jesus saying, "My Father," and including anyone else. This brought more opposition to Jesus than all His other teachings put together.

Unbelieving Jewish leaders wanted to kill Jesus when He opposed their legalistic way of keeping the Sabbath. They wanted even more to kill Him when they recognized that He was calling God, literally, His own Father (John 5:18). This same opposition

GETTING STARTED

Display two or three items that pertain to exacting measurements, patterns, or standards against which other items may be compared or checked. Some possible items may be a micrometer, ruler, clothes pattern, blueprint, a standard scale weight, etc. Ask: "What comparison may be drawn between these items and the Lord Jesus Christ?" Discussion should center on the fact that Jesus is our standard for Christian living. That is the whole purpose for examining His life, ministry, and teaching. Our desire must be to pattern our lives after the One in whom was no sin.

Clarification

Conceive—implies that God created the Y chromosomes and whatever else was necessary for a boy to be born. Thus God was literally the Father of Jesus.

The Highest—that is, God.

Overshadow—a word used of special manifestations of the presence of God.

Word—Greek, *logos;* used here to mean the embodiment, expression, and manifestation of the life, power, and love of God in a divine Person equal with God, the Lord Jesus Christ.

With God—with the God; implies an active intercommunion and living union between the Word and the Father. (See John 1:18; Genesis 1:26, "let us.")

Was God—was Deity. The article present in the preceding phrase is not present here. The Word is not "the" God, but He is God. He is included in the one Being of God. It should be noted that the word *God* in John 1:6, 12, 13, 18 does not have the article *the* either, though these verses refer to the Father, while John 20:28 does have the article though it refers to the Son.

dominated the thinking of the worldlings who opposed the spread of the Early Church. John did not deny that a personal antichrist is to come. But he recognized that the antichrist the Early Church had to deal with was any deceiver who denied that Jesus is the Son of God come in the flesh (1 John 4:3; 2 John 7).

Controversies concerning the person of Christ continued for centuries. But this antichristian world was and still is overcome by those who believe Jesus is the Son of God (1 John 5:4, 5).

BIBLE COMMENTARY

I. Son of God

Luke 1:31-35; John 1:1-3, 49; Romans 1:1-4

Luke 1:32. He shall be great, and shall be called the Son of the Highest; and the Lord God shall give unto him the throne of his father David: 35. And the angel answered and said unto her, The Holy Ghost shall come upon thee, and the power of the Highest shall overshadow thee: therefore also that holy thing which shall be born of thee shall be called the Son of God. John 1:1. In the beginning was the Word, and the Word was with God, and the Word was God. Romans 1:3. His Son Jesus Christ our Lord, which was made of the seed of David according to the flesh; 4. and declared to be the Son of God with power, according to the Spirit of holiness, by the resurrection from the dead.

A. The Holy Son of God

How do the four Gospels introduce us to Jesus? (See Teaching Tip 1.)

Matthew introduced Him as the descendant of David and of Abraham, that is, the heir of God's covenants and promises, the climax of the long history of God's dealings with Israel. Then Matthew goes on to tell how God persuaded Joseph to accept Mary because the Child in her womb was "of the Holy Ghost" (Matthew 1:20). That is, the male principle necessary for a son to be born came from the Holy Spirit.

Luke is even more specific when he records the words of the angel to Mary, explaining that Jesus would not only fulfill God's promise to David, but would be called the Son of the Highest. The Holy Spirit would overshadow her just as the Spirit hovered over the original ocean in preparation for the creative acts of Genesis 1. Then the power of God would do the work, creating in Mary's body whatever was necessary for the Saviour to be born.

Mark gives no details. He simply declares Jesus to be the Son of God.

John takes us back to the very beginning before anything was created. There in that past eternity the Son of God bore the title, "the Word," that is, the One through whom God reveals himself. He is the "express image" of God's person (Hebrews 1:3). He would do more than bring God's message. He would *be* God's message.

How does John relate "the Word" to God? (See Teaching Tip 2.)

1. The Word was with God. This means more than mere exis-

Which was made of—who was born of, who came from.

The Son of God with power—the powerful Son of God.

TEACHING TIP 1

Present the following brief outline overviewing the synoptic Gospels' portrait of Jesus Christ. Prepare the outline on an overhead transparency, a chart, or on the chalkboard.

Matthew
Jesus—the Messiah-King
Emphasis on Jesus' royalty and authority

Mark
Jesus—the Mighty Conqueror
Emphasis on Jesus' power over death and hell

Luke
Jesus—the Son of Man
Emphasis on Jesus as representative and Saviour of humanity

John
Jesus—the Son of God
Emphasis on Jesus as the incarnate Word of God

TEACHING TIP 2

It is important for the believer to recognize fully that Jesus Christ is indeed God the Son. John 1:1 clearly affirms this with three great statements. Ask the students to identify the statements and how they pertain to Christ's deity. This may be developed as follows:
1. "In the beginning was the Word"—eternal
2. "the Word was with God"—coexisted with the Father
3. "the Word was God"—Jesus is very God, or God in essence

tence alongside God. The Greek preposition translated "with" is not the ordinary word so translated. In fact, the same word used here is translated 539 times in the King James Version as "to," "unto," or "towards." It always implies mutual fellowship and intercommunication. Thus, as the Word with God, the Son was face-to-face with God in close personal fellowship, in a relationship that had no beginning and will have no end, for He is part of the very Being of God.

2. The Word was God. He was eternally and truly Deity. He shares the nature and being of God, yet with eternally separate identity and personality. He did not become God. He is God. He will always be God.

Guideline for Living 1

Suppose that a king with unlimited power rules the land. It is your privilege to be among his closest friends. Because of your unique relationship, you may at any time approach the king with a request which, if within reason, would be granted without hesitation. What a grand relationship that would be!

The fact is that such a relationship is not outside the realm of possibility. For those who know Jesus Christ as Saviour, it is a reality. He has unlimited power and resources to meet our every need. He is able to grant peace, love, security, and assurance to help make our lives even more blessed. What a joy to love and serve One who is all-sufficient!

B. The Powerful Son of God

Jesus took the disciples aside at Caesarea Philippi and asked them, "Whom say ye that I am?" Peter answered, "Thou art the Christ, the Son of the living God." Jesus then explained, "Flesh and blood hath not revealed it unto thee, but my Father which is in heaven." Through their contact with Jesus the disciples had come to know God in a new way. God was able to open their hearts and minds to the truth.

Guideline for Living 2

Jesus' question to His disciples, "Whom say ye that I am?" was no idle inquiry. It was purposely recorded so that we may consider our own response. Whom do we say Jesus is?

Peter's response, "Thou art the Christ, the Son of the living God," was a genuine, heartfelt acknowledgment of who Jesus is. Yet how often do we parrot such a statement without truly knowing or meaning what we have said? If we acknowledge Jesus as the Son of God, do our lives reflect it? When crises come our way, do we regard Jesus as our source of strength and comfort? When illness strikes, are we quick to rely upon His ability to mend our bodies? In times of great decision making, do we trust in Jesus' wisdom to guide us in the right path?

Such questions are important for us to consider from time to time. Only as we recognize Jesus as the Christ, the Son of the living God, can we benefit fully from His ability to help, guide, and sustain us day by day. As we accept and affirm His deity, there is nothing that can separate us from His love and care.

Question.

How did God publicly declare that Jesus is the Son of God?

Clarification

Jesus—"Jehovah [Hebrew, YHWH, the Lord] is salvation." The name imples both help and deliverance. It is His personal name and emphasizes His mission.

A virgin—the virgin. Mary was the virgin through whom God brought complete fulfillment to Isaiah 7:14. The Greek word used here can only mean "virgin." The Hebrew word in Isaiah 7:14 means a virgin of marriageable age and is never used in the Bible of anyone who was not a virgin.

Dwelt—tabernacled, as God dwelt with Israel in the wilderness (Revelation 21:3). Perhaps also a reference to the Shekinah (dwelling) cloud of glory (Exodus 40:34; 1 Kings 8:10, 11).

Glory—majestic power and might plus righteousness, goodness, holiness, love.

Truth—or reality (as opposed to the types and symbols of the Law).

The only begotten Son—rather, "God only begotten," as in some ancient manuscripts. Jesus is both God and only begotten (unique, one of a kind).

In the bosom—at a banquet table this would mean "at the right hand." This may be the meaning here. (See Hebrews 1:3.)

The fulness of the time—the completion of the (God-appointed) period of time.

Made of—born of, begotten by. Emphasizes his true humanity.

The power of death—the power or rule in death. Satan is not free to put death on us whenever he wishes, but he rules in the realm of death.

He did so at the baptism of Jesus in the Jordan. But that was not understood. Paul tells us in Romans that Jesus, who was descended from David (through Mary), was declared to be the powerful Son of God by His resurrection from the dead. This was accomplished by the Holy Spirit, who is the Spirit of holiness. This may also imply that death could not hold Jesus because He had no sin of His own. As the sinless Son of God He died for the sins of the world. Your sins and mine nailed Him to the cross.

II. Son of Man
Matthew 1:21-23; John 1:14-18; Galatians 4:4; Hebrews 2:14

Matthew 1:21. She shall bring forth a son, and thou shalt call his name Jesus: for he shall save his people from their sins. John 1:14. And the Word was made flesh, and dwelt among us, (and we beheld his glory, the glory as of the only begotten of the Father,) full of grace and truth. 18. No man hath seen God at any time; the only begotten Son, which is in the bosom of the Father, he hath declared him. Galatians 4:4. But when the fulness of the time was come, God sent forth his Son, made of a woman, made under the law. Hebrews 2:14. Forasmuch then as the children are partakers of flesh and blood, he also himself likewise took part of the same; that through death he might destroy him that had the power of death, that is, the devil.

A. The Virgin-Born Saviour

Matthew and Luke record the virgin birth of Jesus. Paul clearly implies it.

1. It shows us that God knows how to fulfill prophecy, and that He is faithful to do so even when it seems impossible in the natural.

2. It helps us to understand how Jesus who is truly and fully the Son of God is also fully and truly the Son of Man, fully and truly human. (See Teaching Tip 3.)

3. It lets us know that God does indeed intervene in the affairs of men and in the course of history to carry out His plan and bring us blessing.

Those who follow humanistic or materialistic philosophies have trouble with the virgin birth of Jesus because they are antisupernaturalists. They try to explain away the miracles of the Bible. But they cannot explain away the Virgin Birth as some mere accident or coincidence. Since mothers have only X chromosomes in their genes, if an ovum developed by some accidental stimulation it could only produce a girl. The virgin birth of Jesus required a miracle. But we who have been touched by the supernatural power of God as He has saved us and filled us with His Spirit have no trouble believing that God used Mary to bring us Jesus as the Son of Man. (See Teaching Tip 4.)

B. Revealing God in the Human Sphere

The whole Bible gives us a revelation of God. But the fullness of God's character and nature has been revealed in Jesus. As John says, "No man hath seen God at any time," that is, with physical eyes. God is Spirit (John 4:24) and He is infinite, filling the universe. Even with our best telescopes we cannot see all the stars.

TEACHING TIP 3

Divide the class into study groups of three or more. Give each group a copy of the "Character Sketch" relating to Jesus' deity and humanity found in PATH. Instruct the students to scan the various Scripture passages to determine what divine and human attributes or characteristics are indicated. These may be enumerated as follows:

GOD	MAN
Eternal	Made flesh
Omnipresent	Hungered
Omniscient	Thirsted
Omnipotent	Wearied
	Wept

Clarification

Which cannot be touched with the feeling of our infirmities—who is not able to sympathize with our weaknesses (such as timidity, weariness, weaknesses in judgment, and other frailties including sickness and disease).

Tempted like as we are, yet without sin—tempted in accordance to His likeness to us without committing any sin.

Guile—deceit, cunning, treachery, anything false (including the desire for personal revenge).

TEACHING TIP 4

Illustration: Planet Earth is positioned within the galaxy known as the Milky Way. It has been said that if we were to compare the entire North American continent to the Milky Way, earth in comparison would be no larger than a minute speck of dust deposited anywhere on the continent. When we add to that picture the fact that our galaxy is only one of many galaxies (some much larger) in the universe, we are quickly made aware of the smallness of our world and of ourselves.

In relation to this illustration, ask the students to consider the following questions:

How could we expect to see God? But Jesus, who is God and who is also the only begotten, the Son of Man, truly man, has declared Him. That is, Jesus has made Him known and in Jesus we see the explanation, interpretation, and description of what God is really like. In Jesus we see that God's glory is more than radiance. It is full of grace and reality, full of power, righteousness, holiness, goodness, and love.

Guideline for Living 3

While on earth in the flesh, Jesus was the true, perfect representation of God the Father. His life clearly reflected the Father's righteousness, holiness, goodness, and love. All that Jesus thought, said, and performed was in accord with the Father.

Is there a lesson for us in His example? Indeed there is. Just as Jesus faithfully reflected the character of His Father, so we who have been born into God's family should reflect His character. Jesus exhorts us in Matthew 5:16, "Let your light so shine before men, that they may see your good works, and glorify your Father which is in heaven." May our lives ever reflect the character of Him whom we serve.

III. Sinless Character

Hebrews 4:15; 1 Peter 2:21-23

Hebrews 4:15. We have not a high priest which cannot be touched with the feeling of our infirmities; but was in all points tempted like as we are, yet without sin. 1 Peter 2:22. Who did no sin, neither was guile found in his mouth.

A. Holy

Just as holiness is central to God's character (Isaiah 6:3), so we see that Jesus is above all else holy.

He was the only Man who ever lived a life totally free from sin. All of us have sinned and come short of the glory of God (Romans 3:23). We have all gone astray and turned to our own way (Isaiah 53:6). But in Jesus' sinlessness we see the glory of God revealed. In His sinless obedience we see the work of God accomplished. He always spoke His Father's words and did His Father's will (John 17:8; 14:24, 31).

Jesus was able to say, "Which of you convinceth me of sin?" (John 8:46). That is, Jesus challenged His opponents to point out any sin He had ever committed. No one was ever able to do that. He alone is holy to the full extent that God is holy. That is why the Bible can point to Him as our example. (See Teaching Tip 5.)

On the other hand, Jesus was not free from temptation. He felt what we feel, but without ever committing sin. He still feels for us and has compassion on us.

B. Loving

John 13:1; 15:13; Ephesians 5:25

John 13:1. Before the feast of the passover, when Jesus knew that his hour was come that he should depart out of this world

1. How does this affect our perspective regarding God's sending His Son to earth?

2. Should our minuteness cause us to have a greater appreciation for God's love and concern for His creation?

Focus on David's response to this matter by reading Psalm 8:3, 4.

Clarification

When Jesus knew—Jesus knowing (suggests His perfect foresight and His divine insight).

He loved them unto the end—He showed them His love to the uttermost, to the highest degree. What follows is a remarkable manifestation of that love.

TEACHING TIP 5

Ask the students to ponder and discuss the following questions:

1. Is it possible for you to live without sin?

2. What are influences that prompt you toward holy living?

3. What are influences that tempt you to sin?

4. What are you doing on a regular basis to live a stable, holy life?

5. Is it possible to live a victorious Christian life apart from daily devotion to God's Word and prayer?

Clarification

Thought it not robbery—did not think it something to be held on to.

Made himself of no reputation—emptied himself (of outward glory and privilege).

Question.

What spirit or attitude did Jesus show when he left heaven to come to earth?

Question.

How else did He humble himself?

unto the Father, having loved his own which were in the world, he loved them unto the end. 15:13. Greater love hath no man than this, that a man lay down his life for his friends. Ephesians 5:25. Husbands love your wives, even as Christ also loved the church, and gave himself for it.

What is the greatest example of love the world has ever seen? John 3:16 and Romans 5:8 speak of it as God's love in giving His Son to die for us "while we were yet sinners." In the verses of our study text we see also the love of Jesus for His own disciples, even for a sinful rebel like Judas. Jesus knew He was about to fulfill the typology of the Passover where the blood of a spotless lamb brought deliverance from the judgment of God and from the power of Egypt (a type of sin). But the pride of the disciples and the treachery of Judas did not lessen His love. He washed the feet of all of them, even the feet of Judas.

Then, in anticipation of the victory of the Resurrection and the forming of a new resurrection Body, the Church, He loved the Church and gave himself for it. What wife could not help loving a husband with a love like that!

Guideline for Living 4

The world often speaks of love. Yet it is portrayed as a sensual, hedonistic pursuit of pleasure and self-gratification. This is far from the kind of love expressed by Jesus Christ to us. His is a love that gives regardless of whether love is returned. Godly love is wholly unselfish, concerned primarily with the welfare of the one loved. We need to allow this quality of love to be developed in our lives as we relate to Christ and to those around us.

C. Humble

Philippians 2:5-8

Philippians 2:5. Let this mind be in you, which was also in Christ Jesus: 6. who, being in the form of God, thought it not robbery to be equal with God: 7. but made himself of no reputation, and took upon him the form of a servant, and was made in the likeness of men: 8. and being found in fashion as a man, he humbled himself, and became obedient unto death, even the death of the cross.

He left behind the radiance of divine glory and the praise of angels and took the form of an ordinary man. Not only did He become truly Man, there was no outward glory or anything else to distinguish His appearance from the other Jews of Galilee and Judea. He was still truly God, but His inner glory did not shine through except on the Mount of Transfiguration. For our sakes He took a humble place and came to serve us.

He humbled himself to the most shameful kind of death known, the cross kind of death! All this He did for us!

LIVING THE TRUTH

In Jesus Christ we find the flawless blueprint for living a victorious life. Our consuming passion ought to be to align ourselves so closely with this pattern that we reflect His character in all that we do, say, and think. This can be so if we are willing to search the Word and then live by its principles.

EVANGELISM OUTREACH

Perhaps there are some in your class who have little understanding of what living a Christlike life is all about. Take time to pray and counsel with any who may not know Jesus as their Saviour.

Daily Devotional Guide
M. A Miraculous Birth. Isaiah 7:10-14
T. A Growing Awareness. Luke 2:39-52
W. A Great Victory. Luke 4:1-15
T. A Superior Son. Hebrews 1:1-9
F. A Sinless Saviour. Hebrews 4:14 to 5:9
S. A Secure Salvation. 1 John 5:13-20

THE WORKS OF CHRIST

4

SEEING THE SCRIPTURES

Matthew 20:26-28

26. But it shall not be so among you: but whosoever will be great among you, let him be your minister;

27. And whosoever will be chief among you, let him be your servant:

28. Even as the Son of man came not to be ministered unto, but to minister, and to give his life a ransom for many.

Luke 19:10

10. For the Son of man is come to seek and to save that which was lost.

John 3:17; 10:10

17. For God sent not his Son into the world to condemn the world; but that the world through him might be saved.

10:10. The thief cometh not, but for to steal, and to kill, and to destroy: I am come that they might have life, and that they might have it more abundantly.

Acts 2:22; 10:38

22. Ye men of Israel, hear these words; Jesus of Nazareth, a man approved of God among you by miracles and wonders and signs, which God did by him in the midst of you, as ye yourselves also know.

10:38. God anointed Jesus of Nazareth with the Holy Ghost and with power: who went about doing good, and healing all that were oppressed of the devil; for God was with him.

Romans 5:6-8

6. For when we were yet without strength, in due time Christ died for the ungodly.

7. For scarcely for a righteous man will one die: yet peradventure for a good man some would even dare to die.

8. But God commendeth his love toward us, in that, while we were yet sinners, Christ died for us.

Colossians 1:21, 22

21. And you, that were sometime alienated and enemies in your mind by wicked works, yet now hath he reconciled

22. In the body of his flesh through death, to present you holy and unblamable and unreprovable in his sight.

SETTING THE SCENE

This week's study follows along very closely with the one we had last week. It is hard to separate the person of Christ from the works of Christ. He did what He did because He was and is who He is.

The prophet Isaiah gives us a key. He foresaw the Messiah as

PREPARING TO TEACH

Study Text

Matthew 8:23-27; 20:26-28; Mark 1:21-34; Luke 9:37-43; 19:10; John 3:17; 6:5-14; 10:10; Acts 2:22; 10:38; Romans 5:6-8; Colossians 1:21, 22; 1 Timothy 1:15

Outline

I. His Mission
   A. Sent To Serve
   B. Sent To Seek and To Save
II. His Miracles
   A. Miracles in Every Realm
   B. To God Be the Glory
III. His Atonement
   A. The Greatness of Our Need
   B. The Greatness of His Love

Golden Text:
God anointed Jesus of Nazareth with the Holy Ghost and with power: who went about doing good, and healing all that were oppressed of the devil; for God was with Him. Acts 10:38

Central Truth:
Christ came to reveal the Father and redeem man.

Learning Goals

1. To explore the works of Jesus Christ in reference to His mission, miracles, and atonement.
2. To understand how Jesus works in our lives today.
3. To recognize our need of a Saviour.
4. To determine to commit our lives in love and devotion to our Lord Jesus Christ.

Last week's study focused on the person, nature, and character of Jesus Christ. This week's study centers on the works of Jesus, or what He did while on earth and what He continues to do today. Direct thinking along this line by asking the students to respond to the question, "What makes Jesus Christ real today?" As volunteers respond, jot the comments on the chalkboard or overhead transparency.

Responses will probably include salvation, healing, providing, giving direction, etc. Note that these are all important works of Jesus that make Him real in our world today.

Clarification

Minister—serve. Jesus did not expect to be waited on while here on earth.

Was lost—is lost, perishing, headed for ruin and eternal death.

Faithful—trustworthy.

I am chief—emphatic.

God's suffering and anointed Servant. God called Israel as a nation to be His servant, but as a whole they were failing to serve Him. A godly remnant were indeed faithful to Him. But they did not have the power and they themselves needed to be redeemed. Thus, it would take the Messiah, the Christ, to be the One who would be God's Servant in the fullest sense. He would have the power to do God's work, the work of bringing redemption and deliverance to fallen mankind.

Acts 10:38 is another key verse. God anointed Jesus. He is the hoped-for Messiah or Anointed One. God gave Him power and authority. He used that power for good. Truly God was with Him.

BIBLE COMMENTARY

I. His Mission

Matthew 20:26-28; Luke 19:10; John 3:17; 10:10; 1 Timothy 1:15

Matthew 20:28. The Son of man came not to be ministered unto, but to minister, and to give his life a ransom for many. Luke 19:10. The Son of man is come to seek and to save that which was lost. John 3:17. God sent not his Son into the world to condemn the world; but that the world through him might be saved. 10:10. The thief cometh not, but for to steal, and to kill, and to destroy: I am come that they might have life, and that they might have it more abundantly. 1 Timothy 1:15. This is a faithful saying, and worthy of all acceptation, that Christ Jesus came into the world to save sinners; of whom I am chief.

A. Sent To Serve

Jesus was already on the way to the Cross when James and John began having visions of power and glory in the Kingdom. Using their mother they asked for the places beside Jesus in the Kingdom. This upset the other disciples. They were just as anxious for the best places as James and John were. Jesus called them aside and pointed out that it is the rulers of this world who want to show their power and play the tyrant. But the followers of Jesus become great by serving. They become chief or come into first place by becoming the servant, literally, the slave of others. In this we follow Jesus, for He came to serve and to give His life a ransom for many.

Guideline for Living 1

How does the world's ethic regarding service and leadership correspond with Jesus' teaching? It doesn't take much observation to find the answer.

Inconsistency in the world's application of Jesus' principles is often noticeable around election time. Political candidates sell themselves to the voting public on a platform of service. "Vote for me. I want to be your servant," is a common pledge. And although some candidates honestly desire to be servants, others seek office only for personal gain or status. The servant/leader concept has not really caught on in our society.

In the business world, the philosophy often is, "You don't earn power, wealth, and prestige; you take it—whatever the cost." Clearly the idea is to grab all you can while you can and cut down anyone who gets in your way.

Yet Jesus' servant/leader concept still lies at the root of true leadership and public respect. Think about it for a moment. What kind of business person do you appreciate most? What kind of politician do you respect? Naturally it is the one who is willing to go out of his or her way to serve you. We are glad to patronize and support such individuals. Why? Because they are operating by the principle of service to others. That gives them the prominence and status they deserve.

In our relations with those around us, we must always remember that genuine concern for others and willingness to serve will bring the leadership and respect we desire.

Question.
What are some of the ways Jesus gave himself in humble service?

Question.
What does it mean to be lost?

TEACHING TIP 1
Use the following sketch to focus on the truth that Jesus' sole purpose in coming to earth was to become a perfect sacrifice for our sins. Reproduce the sketch on the chalkboard or overhead transparency.

He walked the dusty roads of Palestine often without a place to lay His head (Luke 9:58). He taught and ministered to the people even when they crowded around and did not give Him time even to eat. Then when He took His disciples away for a rest, the crowd followed, and Jesus had compassion on them, taught them, and fed them (Mark 6:31-44). Jesus could be weary, but He never let that or anything else keep Him from serving others. Nor did He observe the limits ordinarily held by famous teachers. He served the children, the lepers, as well as the rich and powerful. Human need was all He took into account.

B. Sent To Seek and To Save

Great as the teaching ministry of Jesus was, He did not come primarily to be a teacher or an example. He came to die for lost humanity. Even when He was brought as a babe into the temple, the prophetic utterance of Simeon showed He was already living under the shadow of the Cross (Luke 2:30, 34, 35). (See Teaching Tip 1.)

It means one is perishing, dying, headed for ruin or destruction. The word is used of those lost at sea and about to perish in a storm. It is used of sheep gone astray who are an easy mark for the lion or bear. But it is used especially of those who are in the darkness of sin, cut off from the blessings and promise of God, and therefore lost to Him.

Why did Jesus say He came to give His life a ransom for many?

Jesus gave himself as an offering for sin. He fulfilled the entire sacrificial system of the law of Moses. He gave His life as the price for our ransom, our redemption. He is our Substitute. The *"many"* here is used simply in contrast to Christ as one. That is, only one Person hung on the Cross instead of many. Thus the word *"many"* includes the whole world, past, present, and future. (See John 3:16; Romans 5:18).

Why did Jesus speak of the thief in John 10:10? False messiahs have all been thieves. They take; they destroy. They cannot give

TEACHING TIP 2
In relation to the matter of reaching out to others, consider the following church growth statistics that indicate the effect of various methods of outreach. The percentages reveal the number of people won to Christ through the particular means of outreach used

Walked in	4.8 %
Crusade	0.3 %
Pastor	6.5 %
Relatives	14.8 %
Friends	48.2 %

Clarification
Amazed—a strong word. They were almost terrified in their astonishment.

What thing is this? what new doctrine is this—What is this? A new teaching! These were excited exclamations from the crowd.

Divers diseases—many different kinds of diseases.

Devils—demons. The Bible distinguishes between sickness and demon possession.

Faithless—unbelieving.

Tare him—convulsed him.

That prophet—that is, the Prophet promised by Moses (Deuteronomy 18:15, 18).

Miracles—powers, acts of God's mighty power.

Wonders—portents; omens of a startling, marvelous nature.

Signs—signs pointing to the supernatural, heavenly nature and power of Jesus.

Oppressed of the devil—exploited, dominated, ruled tyrannically by the devil (by Satan).

Question.
Some people today seem to

us salvation or new life because they themselves are under the judgment of God. But Jesus poured out His life freely that we might have life. Then He expects us to join Him in seeking others who are lost. The apostle Paul is a good example. Jesus sought him, saved him, healed him, taught him, and then sent him to seek others. (See Teaching Tip 2.)

The basic meaning of the word *sin* is, "to miss or fall short of the mark." The more he saw of the glory of God in Jesus, the more Paul realized that he still fell short. He had not yet attained. But because he was saved, he pressed on (Philippians 3:13, 14).

II. His Miracles
Matthew 8:23-27; Mark 1:21-34; Luke 9:37-43; John 6:5-14; Acts 2:22; 10:38

Matthew 8:27. The men marveled, saying, What manner of man is this, that even the winds and the sea obey him! Mark 1:27. They were all amazed, insomuch that they questioned among themselves, saying, What thing is this? what new doctrine is this? for with authority commandeth he even the unclean spirits, and they do obey him. Luke 9:42. As he was yet a coming, the devil threw him down, and tare him. And Jesus rebuked the unclean spirit, and healed the child, and delivered him again to his father. 43. And they were all amazed at the mighty power of God. John 6:11. Jesus took the loaves; and when he had given thanks, he distributed to the disciples, and the disciples to them that were set down; and likewise of the fishes as much as they would. 14. Then those men, when they had seen the miracle that Jesus did, said, This is of a truth that Prophet that should come into the world. Acts 2:22. Ye men of Israel, hear these words; Jesus of Nazareth, a man approved of God among you by miracles and wonders and signs, which God did by him in the midst of you, as ye yourselves also know. 10:38. God anointed Jesus of Nazareth with the Holy Ghost and with power: who went about doing good, and healing all that were oppressed of the devil; for God was with him.

A. Miracles in Every Realm
(See Teaching Tip 3.)

All four Gospels as well as the Book of Acts draw attention to the miracles of Jesus. During His ministry Jesus was known primarily as a teacher. At least 46 times in the four Gospels the word "Master" translates the Greek *didaskalos*, which is the ordinary Greek word for a teacher. But the miracles made the people realize Jesus was a Teacher come from God. Jesus himself recognized that these miracles were important as a witness to His teaching (John 10:38; 14:11).

Notice also that the New Testament uses three words to describe the miracles of Jesus. They are called powers because they demonstrate the mighty power of God. They are called wonders because of their startling, marvelous, supernatural character that let men know God was indeed working. They are called signs because they pointed to the nature and character of Jesus as the Son of God manifest in the flesh.

He accomplished the works of His Father in every realm. Notice

have a miracle ministry that specializes in a particular type of ministry. What can be said about the ministry of Jesus in this respect?

TEACHING TIP 3

Divide the class into study groups of three or more. Distribute a copy of the "Montage of Miracles" work sheet from PATH. Ask the students to examine the Biblical accounts of Jesus' miracles and list the miracle that occurred, its purpose (in light of Jesus' authority, ministry, etc.), and the result.

Use this work sheet to supplement the commentary regarding Jesus' miracle in every realm.

Question.

What effect did the miracles of Jesus have on the people who saw them?

the passages in our study text. In Matthew 8 Jesus rebuked the forces of nature. Not only did the wind cease, but the waves flattened out at once into a totally calm sea. The disciples had never seen anything like that before.

In Mark 1 we see Jesus first dealing with the spirit world and casting out a demon, an unclean spirit. Then we see Him touching Simon's wife's mother, a touch that not only drove out the fever but infused new strength into her so she was able to get up immediately and serve dinner to Jesus and His disciples. That evening many others were healed of all sorts of diseases. Jesus also cast out many demons. Thus Jesus brought healing to those who suffered from physical causes as well as to those who were oppressed by demons.

In Luke 9 we see Jesus dealing with unbelief as well as casting out a demon and then healing the boy of the effects of the demon's possession. Here is a case where long-term demon possession needed something more than just having the demon cast out. But Jesus was sufficient to meet the need.

In John 6 we see Jesus doing a creative miracle as He multiplies five little round barley loaves and two small fish to feed a crowd of 5,000 men plus possibly twice that number of women and children. This was an important miracle, for only God can create. All four Gospels record this one.

No wonder then that Acts 2:22 and 10:38 show us that the apostles in their preaching drew attention to the well-known miracles of Jesus. They continued to be a witness to Him as the Son of God and Saviour.

B. To God Be the Glory

Look again at the passages in our study text. The people marveled. They were amazed. They were filled with wonder, awe, and astonishment. But above all, they gave glory to God. They recognized that these miracles were indeed the mighty power of God. Jesus himself also drew attention to the fact that His works were really His Father's (John 9:4). The Gospels as well as the preaching of the apostles in Acts draw attention, not so much to what Jesus did, as to what God the Father did through Jesus. To God be the glory!

Guideline for Living 2

"If I could only see a miracle, I'd believe." Ever hear that comment? Maybe you have been inclined to think that way yourself sometimes. Certainly miracles do have an impact on those who witness them, but they do not guarantee acceptance and belief. The Children of Israel quickly forgot their God even after seeing His mighty intervention time and again.

Jesus' miracles did not always insure belief and commitment. His scathing rebuke, " 'Unless you people see miraculous signs and wonders, . . . you will never believe' " (John 4:48, *New International Version*) clearly revealed His concern over sign seeking. Jesus desires our belief in Him for who He is and not for what He does.

The central purpose of Jesus' miracles is spotlighted in John 20:31: "That ye might believe that Jesus is the Christ, the Son of

God; and that believing ye might have life through his name." Yet just two verses before this we read, "Blessed are they that have not seen, and yet have believed."

Clearly we must guard against the desire to see miracles as a basis for our faith and trust in Christ. Miracles are a result of such faith and are essentially intended to bring glory and honor to God the Father.

Clarification

Strength—moral strength, or strength of faith (to resist sin).

In due time—at the right (God-appointed) time. (See Galatians 4:4.)

Dare—have the courage.

Commendeth — continuously demonstrates, shows, brings out (by pointing to the Cross).

His love—His own love (emphatic), as demonstrated at Calvary and in contrast to any other love seen among mankind.

Question.

What is the essence of the good news, the gospel?

Question.

What was our condition that made it necessary for Jesus to come and die in our stead?

TEACHING TIP 4

Duplicate the following definition for atonement as expressed in *Knowing the Doctrines of the Bible* by Myer Pearlman.

"To atone for sin is to cover sin from God's sight so that it loses its power to provoke His wrath."

As the study discussion proceeds regarding man's need for atonement, use the following progression also outlined by Pearlman. Note that the sketches may help highlight each point. This outline may be developed on an overhead transparency or on the chalkboard.

III. His Atonement

Romans 5:6-8; Colossians 1:21, 22

Romans 5:6. When we were yet without strength, in due time Christ died for the ungodly. 7. For scarcely for a righteous man will one die: yet peradventure for a good man some would even dare to die. 8. But God commendeth his love toward us, in that, while we were yet sinners, Christ died for us. Colossians 1:21. And you, that were sometime alienated and enemies in your mind by wicked works, yet now hath he reconciled 22. in the body of his flesh through death, to present you holy and unblamable and unreprovable in his sight.

A. The Greatness of Our Need

We have already seen that the entire life of Jesus on earth was one long journey to the Cross. The four Gospels are not biographies in the ordinary sense of the word. They focus attention on the events that led to Calvary. They almost hurry us through the life and ministry of Jesus in order to bring us to that last week and to His death and resurrection. They are Gospels, accounts of the good news.

It is that Christ died for our sins, rose again for our justification, and is coming again for our glorification.

We were not only sinners, we were without moral strength. We were without the ability and without the faith necessary to resist sin.

Now it is true that some non-Christians seem to live good lives. But just let things go wrong, or let them feel threatened, and it is soon apparent how thin the veneer of civilization is.

Then the Bible says we were ungodly. The Greek means we did not give God the proper place in our life and worship. The Bible uses it of the people of Noah's time who were full of corruption and violence (2 Peter 2:5). But even though we might not have gone that far, we were in bad company, headed for the judgment of God (1 Timothy 1:9, 10), and were badly in need of the good news, the gospel.

We were also sinners, which means we were missing the mark, falling short of the glory of God, turning aside to our own ways instead of following the Lord.

Worse than that, our godlessness and sin were willful. We were alienated or estranged from God. Our wicked, unworthy deeds and acts had made us enemies of God in our minds. In other words, we put up mental barriers against the grace, love, and mercy of God. We were in a hopeless condition, unworthy of His love.

1. THE NECESSITY FOR THE ATONEMENT

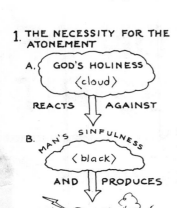

A. GOD'S HOLINESS ⟨cloud⟩

REACTS   AGAINST

B. MAN'S SINFULNESS ⟨black⟩

AND   PRODUCES

C. WRATH explosion & lightning

WHICH IS   AVERTED BY

D. THE ATONEMENT

Question.

What makes it possible for us to stand before a holy God?

B. The Greatness of His Love

To die for anyone else is almost unthinkable. Most of us want to do our best to preserve our own lives. But a mother or father who sees the good, the potential in their child, or a friend who has received tremendous good from another person might find the courage to die in an effort to save the other's life. But who would feel like dying for someone who had hurt us, mistreated us, robbed us, slandered us? This is even more unthinkable.

No wonder, then, that the Bible tells us God commends His love by demonstrating its greatness at the Cross. No greater love has ever been shown than the love that still flows from Calvary.

The God who loved us enough to send His beloved Son to die for us loves us enough to save us from the coming wrath and judgment. He loves us enough also to make every provision for us to make it all the way through to glory. As Romans 8:31, 32 shows us, God is for us. And "He that spared not his own Son, but delivered him up for us all, how shall he not with him also freely give us all things?" Then Romans goes on to show us that nothing in all creation can separate us from the love of God that is in Christ Jesus. Truly, this is good news!

> ### Guideline for Living 3
> "Oh, the love that drew salvation's plan!
> Oh, the grace that brought it down to man!
> Oh, the mighty gulf that God did span
> At Calvary."
> How eloquently these words of a familiar gospel hymn express the work of Christ's atonement for our sins. When we recognize that Jesus Christ, God in the flesh, gave himself freely as a sacrifice for our sins even in the face of scorn and ridicule, we cannot help but humbly bow in His name and give Him praise. How thankful we ought to be each day for Christ's ultimate act of love in the gift of himself for the redemption of our souls.

Not our own righteousness, not our own good works, but the death of Christ. His death on the cross accomplished for us all that was necessary to present us holy (consecrated, dedicated) and unblameable (blameless, without blemish or defect) and unreproveable in God's sight. The Bible adds only the condition that we continue in the faith, grounded and settled, and be not moved from the gospel.

LIVING THE TRUTH

Reflecting upon the beauty of Jesus' life and remembering that He was very man as well as very God, direct the students to conclude the session by singing, "To Be Like Jesus." Focus on the fact that Jesus serves as a perfect example of how we can live an overcoming, victorious Christian life each day. Follow through with brief sentence prayers of commitment by the class members.

EVANGELISM OUTREACH

Few study themes will give greater opportunity to encourage the unsaved to come to Christ than this one. Be responsive to the direction and moving of the Holy Spirit as He speaks to hearts.

5 | THE PERSON OF THE HOLY SPIRIT

Golden Text: Whither shall I go from thy Spirit? Or whither shall I flee from thy presence? Psalm 139:7

Central Truth: The Holy Spirit is a member of the Godhead—a divine Person and not a mere force or influence.

Learning Goals
1. To understand the person and character of God the Holy Spirit.
2. To recognize the deity of the Holy Spirit as the third Person of the Trinity.
3. To appreciate the fact that the Holy Spirit is fully able to guide and direct our lives.

SEEING THE SCRIPTURES

Psalm 139:7
7. Whither shall I go from thy Spirit? Or whither shall I flee from thy presence?

Matthew 28:19
19. Go ye therefore, and teach all nations, baptizing them in the name of the Father, and of the Son, and of the Holy Ghost.

John 7:37-39; 14:16, 17
37. In the last day, that great day of the feast, Jesus stood and cried, saying, If any man thirst, let him come unto me, and drink.
38. He that believeth on me, as the Scripture hath said, out of his belly shall flow rivers of living water.
39. (But this spake he of the Spirit, which they that believe on him should receive: for the Holy Ghost was not yet given; because that Jesus was not yet glorified.)
14:16. And I will pray the Father, and he shall give you another Comforter, that he may abide with you for ever;
17. Even the Spirit of truth; whom the world cannot receive, because it seeth him not, neither knoweth him: but ye know him; for he dwelleth with you, and shall be in you.

Acts 5:3, 4
3. But Peter said, Ananias, why hath Satan filled thine heart to lie to the Holy Ghost, and to keep back part of the price of the land?
4. While it remained, was it not thine own? and after it was sold, was it not in thine own power? why hast thou conceived this thing in thine heart? thou has not lied unto men, but unto God.

Romans 1:8, 8:2, 27
8. First, I thank my God through Jesus Christ for you all, that your faith is spoken of throughout the whole world.
8:2. For the law of the Spirit of life in Christ Jesus hath made me free from the law of sin and death.
27. And he that searcheth the hearts knoweth what is the mind of the Spirit, because he maketh intercession for the saints according to the will of God.

Ephesians 1:13; 4:30
13. In whom ye also trusted, after that ye heard the word of truth, the gospel of your salvation: in whom also, after that ye believed, ye were sealed with that Holy Spirit of promise.
4:30. And grieve not the Holy Spirit of God, whereby ye are sealed unto the day of redemption.

Ask: "When you think of the word *deity,* who comes to your mind first?" Encourage rapid responses.

Most likely a majority would respond with God the Father or Jesus Christ. We are sometimes slow to recognize the Holy Spirit as a person—the third Person of the Trinity. Why is this so? (You may want to discuss this question for a few moments.) Perhaps an important reason is that the Holy Spirit is often perceived as more of an experience than a Person. This week's study will help us better understand the personality and character of God the Holy Spirit.

Clarification

Teach—make disciples (students, learners) of; train them and inspire them to keep on learning more and more.

Into the name—implies into the worship and service of. The word "name" is singular because there is only one name or title each. (Compare Ruth 1:2 where the Hebrew uses the singular "name" of the two sons because only one name each is given.)

Holy Ghost—Holy Spirit. In the old English the terms *ghost* and *spirit* were used interchangeably. In today's English, *Spirit* gives the correct meaning.

Come upon—the same phraseology is used in Acts 1:8.

Holy thing—holy One, holy Child.

Question.

What are some of the attributes of Deity the Spirit has? That is, what characteristics show Him to be God?

TEACHING TIP 1

Develop the following outline as you discuss the various attributes of the Holy Spirit. You may wish to have students read

SETTING THE SCENE

During most of the history of the Church the Holy Spirit has been the neglected member of the Trinity. During the early centuries most of the Church fathers gave much of their time to studying and developing their understanding of the Person of Christ. That was right and proper, since the purpose of the Holy Spirit is to glorify Jesus and reveal Him. In time, however, the neglect of the Holy Spirit became almost disgraceful.

About the year 1660 one of the great Puritan writers Thomas Goodwin admitted that Christians of his day did not give the Holy Spirit the glory due Him. In fact, He was seldom even mentioned.

By the 19th century many were openly denying that the Holy Spirit is a real Person or that He is God. Others simply ignored the Holy Spirit and His work. Even in the first part of the present century when the Pentecostal revival had already begun, many churchmen were saying that the Holy Spirit was of no interest to them. Thank God, the Pentecostal revival has brought a change!

BIBLE COMMENTARY

I. Deity of the Holy Spirit

Psalm 139:7; Matthew 28:19; Luke 1:35; Acts 5:3, 4; Hebrews 9:14

Psalm 139:7. Whither shall I go from thy Spirit? Or whither shall I flee from thy presence? Matthew 28:19. Go ye therefore, and teach all nations, baptizing them in the name of the Father, and of the Son, and of the Holy Ghost. Luke 1:35. The angel answered and said unto her, the Holy Ghost shall come upon thee, and the power of the Highest shall overshadow thee: therefore also that holy thing which shall be born of thee shall be called the Son of God. Acts 5:3. Peter said, Ananias, why hath Satan filled thine heart to lie to the Holy Ghost, and to keep back part of the price of the land? 4. While it remained, was it not thine own? and after it was sold, was it not in thine own power? why hast thou conceived this thing in thine heart? thou hast not lied unto men, but unto God. Hebrews 9:14. How much more shall the blood of Christ, who through the eternal Spirit offered himself without spot to God, purge your conscience from dead works to serve the living God?

A. Divine Qualities

Again and again the Bible speaks of the Holy Spirit as the Spirit of God or the Spirit of the Lord.

The attributes of God we see revealed in the Bible include omnipresence (everywhere present), omnipotence (all powerful), and omniscience (knows everything). Though He will not go against His own nature, there is nothing that He cannot do. He is eternal, without beginning or ending. He always was, always is, and always will be God.

Our first passage, Psalm 139:7, means the Holy Spirit is om-

some of the supporting passages aloud.

God the Holy Spirit Is . . .

I. Omnipresent (present everywhere)
   Psalm 139:7
   John 14:7
   Acts 2:4
II. Omnipotent (all-powerful)
   Zechariah 4:6
   Psalm 104:30
III. Omniscient (all-knowing)
   Isaiah 40:13
   1 Corinthians 2:10, 11
IV. Eternal
   Hebrews 9:14
V. Supremely Good
   Nehemiah 9:20
VI. Loving
   2 Timothy 1:7
VII. Holy
   Revelation 15:4

nipresent. Wherever we can or might go in the universe, He is there. John 14:7 implies the same thing, since the Holy Spirit continues to be in believers wherever they go. So does Acts 2:4, where we see that they were all filled. In other words, He is everywhere present, but He also manifests His presence in special ways and in special relationships.

Note also that Zechariah 4:6 indicates the Spirit is all-powerful. So does Psalm 104:30. Isaiah 40:13 and 1 Corinthians 2:10, 11 indicate His omniscience. Hebrews 9:14 indicates His eternality. Psalm 143:10 and Nehemiah 9:20 show He is supremely good. He is also loving, as God is love (2 Timothy 1:7). Above all, He is the Holy Spirit, and He is holy in the same sense that God the Father is holy (Revelation 15:4).

B. Fully Divine

We must emphasize also that by saying the Holy Spirit has these attributes we mean more than saying the Holy Spirit is Godlike. We mean He is fully Deity. He is God, just as the Father is God, just as the Son is God.

The formula for baptism Jesus gave in Matthew 28:19 shows this. Luke 1:35 shows that the power of the Holy Spirit is the power of the Highest, that is, of God. Peter showed that when Ananias lied to the Holy Spirit he lied to God. Job 32:8, NIV, in a picturesque way calls the Holy Spirit the breath of the Almighty. Truly the Holy Spirit is God.

> ## Guideline for Living 1
>
> Ever hear statements like these?—"The Holy Spirit is such a wonderful thing!" "Have you received the Holy Spirit? It comes as such a beautiful experience!"
>
> What's wrong with these statements? Obviously it is a problem of identification. The Holy Spirit is *not* an "it" or a thing. The Holy Spirit is not an experience—He is a Person.
>
> We wouldn't think of referring to the Father or Jesus in the neuter. Yet we sometimes place the Holy Spirit in that category.
>
> Why is it so important to know the Holy Spirit as a Person? As a Person, He has the same divine qualities that are possessed by God the Father and God the Son. When we recognize His personality, we can more easily relate to Him on a personal basis. He is no longer just an experience or an "it," but a Person who loves us and cares for us and is able to abide with us always.

Clarification

Mind—way of thinking, mind-set, aim, aspiration.

Saints—dedicated ones, consecrated ones; includes all true believers.

Dividing—distributing, apportioning.

Severally—individually.

Grieve not—stop grieving or vexing.

Whereby ye are sealed—in whom you were sealed (as a sign of approval, acceptance.)

II. Personality of the Holy Spirit

Romans 8:27; 1 Corinthians 12:11; Ephesians 4:30

Romans 8:27. He that searcheth the hearts knoweth what is the mind of the Spirit, because he maketh intercession for the saints according to the will of God. 1 Corinthians 12:11. All these worketh that one and the selfsame Spirit, dividing to every man severally as he will. Ephesians 4:30. Grieve not the Holy Spirit of God, whereby ye are sealed unto the day of redemption.

Question.

What are the qualities that might be considered basic to show the Holy Spirit is a real Person?

Question.

How does Romans 8:27 show that the Spirit has mind, intelligence, and knowledge?

Question.

What is the most wonderful thing about the Spirit's intercession?

TEACHING TIP 2

Develop the following chart on the chalkboard or overhead transparency as the personal qualities of the Holy Spirit are discussed. You may wish to have the students read the various Scripture texts and determine what quality is highlighted.

Scripture Reference	Personal Quality
	Intellect
Romans 8:27	Has a mind
John 14:26	Guides us into all truth
Luke 12:12	Teaches us
	Will
2 Peter 1:20, 21	Anointed men to write God's Word
1 Corinthians 12:8-11	Gives gifts to Christians
John 16:13	Speaks to people
	Emotions
Romans 15:30	Can show love
Ephesians 4:30	Can be grieved or made sad

TEACHING TIP 3

Discuss the following questions in light of the Holy Spirit's feelings and affections:

1. In what ways may we grieve the Holy Spirit?

2. What did Paul mean when he exhorted the Thessalonians, "Quench not the Spirit"? (1 Thessalonians 5:19). How may we "quench" the Holy Spirit?

3. How important are our thought life, personal holiness, and attitudes toward the Holy Spirit?

Add to this discussion by citing Scripture passages that show how we may hinder the work of the Holy Spirit.

1. We can lie to Him (Acts 5:3, 4).

2. We can grieve Him (Ephesians 4:30).

A. The Mind of the Spirit

(See Teaching Tip 2.)

The basic qualities of a person are usually considered to be mind—including knowledge and intelligence, feeling—including affection and sensitivity, and will.

God who searches the heart knows what is in the mind of the Spirit. He knows the thoughts, aspirations, and desires of the Spirit for us. Then the Holy Spirit expresses these aims and aspirations as He intercedes for us.

He knows the mind and will of God, so He always prays in the will of God and in line with the character and nature of God. We know therefore that when the Spirit prays, the prayer will be answered positively.

We see the mind of the Spirit expressed also in that He speaks (Acts 8:29; 11:12; Revelation 2:7, 11). He calls (Acts 13:2). He sends (Acts 13:4). He forbids (Acts 16:6, 7). He invites (Revelation 22:17).

B. The Will of the Spirit

Most of the passages just mentioned also show that the Spirit has a will. This is specially stated in 1 Corinthians 12:11, where the gifts of the Spirit are distributed to individuals as the Spirit wills. We can be sure also that His will is not arbitrary. He knows what is best for the Body as well as what is best for the individual believer. He wants to build up the Body both spiritually and in numbers. His will can be resisted (Acts 7:51). But blessing comes as we respond and yield to the will of the Spirit.

C. The Spirit's Feeling and Affection

(See Teaching Tip 3.) The Holy Spirit can be grieved or vexed (Ephesians 4:30; Isaiah 63:10). He can be insulted or outraged (Hebrews 10:29). Impersonal things cannot react this way. For example, lightning may strike and cause damage, but there is no way the lightning can show grief over what is done.

Guideline for Living 2

God the Holy Spirit has much to offer us in our daily Christian experience. Yet we must ask ourselves, "Are we allowing the Holy Spirit to develop within us a fruitful, godly, and righteous character? Are we giving Him full rein in guiding us into all truth and shaping us into the image of our Lord and Saviour Jesus Christ?

How grieved the Holy Spirit must be when He looks upon the spiritual lethargy that grips so many. It is His desire to develop fruitfulness and godliness in our lives. This is not possible, however, until we are willing to yield fully to His power and influence. What blessing awaits the believer who submits fully to the Spirit's control!

The Holy Spirit also has feeling on the positive side of love and affection. Romans 15:30 speaks of the love of the Spirit.

Another interesting thing that points to the personality of the Spirit is the way John's Gospel refers to Him. In the Greek language the word for spirit (*pneuma*) is a neuter word. The laws of

3. We can quench His power (1 Thessalonians 5:19).

4. We can resist Him (Acts 7:51).

5. We can blaspheme His person (Matthew 12:31, 32).

Clarification

Wind—Greek, *pneuma*, which may mean "wind, breath, spirit, or Spirit." The identical word is also translated "Spirit" in John 3:8. New Testament Greek did not distinguish between capital and small letters. The translators do so on the basis of the context. But, since the word *sound* usually means "voice," some Bible scholars translate this: "The Spirit breathes where He wills, and you hear His Voice but do not know where He is coming from or where He is going."

That great day—that is, the eighth day of the Feast of Tabernacles.

He that believeth—the believer; he who keeps on believing and trusting with active commitment and obedience.

Belly—inner body where the heart is found. Some writers take it that the flow is from Christ's heart. His heart is indeed the ultimate source, but our hearts are the channels.

Flow—keep flowing abundantly.

Cloven tongues—tongues being broken up and distributed. Probably, what seemed to be a cloud of fire or ball of light appeared over the whole group and then broke apart with a flamelike tongue coming to rest on the head of each of them.

Question.

How did the wind come on the Day of Pentecost?

TEACHING TIP 4

Distribute copies of the work sheet from PATH. Instruct the students to fill in the information as you discuss the symbols of the Holy Spirit.

the language call for neuter pronouns to refer to it. Instead, John in passages such as 16:7, 8, 13, 14, uses masculine pronouns to refer to the Holy Spirit. This is his way of emphasizing that the Holy Spirit is indeed a Person.

III. Symbols of the Holy Spirit

John 3:8; Acts 2:2; John 7:38, 39; Isaiah 4:3, 4; Luke 3:16; Acts 2:3; Revelation 4:5; Matthew 3:16

John 3:8. The wind bloweth where it listeth, and thou hearest the sound thereof, but canst not tell whence it cometh, and whither it goeth: so is every one that is born of the Spirit. Acts 2:2. Suddenly there came a sound from heaven as of a rushing mighty wind, and it filled all the house where they were sitting. John 7:38. He that believeth on me, as the Scripture hath said, out of his belly shall flow rivers of living water. 39. (But this spake he of the Spirit, which they that believe on him should receive: for the Holy Ghost was not yet given; because that Jesus was not yet glorified.) Isaiah 4:4. When the Lord shall have washed away the filth of the daughters of Zion, and shall have purged the blood of Jerusalem from the midst thereof by the spirit of judgment, and by the spirit of burning. Luke 3:16. John answered, saying unto them all, I indeed baptize you with water; but one mightier than I cometh, the latchet of whose shoes I am not worthy to unloose: he shall baptize you with the Holy Ghost and with fire. Acts 2:3. There appeared unto them cloven tongues like as of fire, and it sat upon each of them. Revelation 4:5. Out of the throne proceeded lightnings and thunderings and voices: and there were seven lamps of fire burning before the throne, which are the seven Spirits of God. Matthew 3:16. Jesus, when he was baptized, went up straightway out of the water: and, lo, the heavens were opened unto him, and he saw the Spirit of God descending like a dove, and lighting upon him.

A. Wind

(See Teaching Tip 4.)

Wind is a frequent Biblical symbol of the Holy Spirit. The very word for *spirit* in both the Hebrew and the Greek can also mean "wind, breath," or "moving air." Genesis 1:2 pictures the Spirit of God gently hovering like a mother bird hovering over its young. Jesus compares the new creation to the action of the wind. We are born again, born from above, born of the Spirit. But the Spirit does not operate in any prescribed channels nor does He bring the new birth by some sort of ritual. Like the wind, the Holy Spirit comes in most unexpected, wonderful, and mysterious ways.

Actually, there was no wind. Rather there was a sound from heaven that was like a mighty, rushing wind. This suggests power. It was more than the breathing Jesus gave on the Resurrection Day (John 20:22). It let them know they were about to receive a mighty baptism that would give them power for service.

B. Rivers

In the Old Testament the Spirit came upon people and even filled some of them (Exodus 31:2, 3; 35:31-34; Numbers 27:18).

But on that last great day of the Feast of Tabernacles, Jesus promised something more than an inner filling. Not only would God pour out His Spirit as Joel prophesied, but rivers would flow out of our innermost being. Thus Pentecost brought a pouring forth as well as a pouring out. These rivers are available as long as we keep believing and keep receiving.

C. Fire

Isaiah first mentions the Spirit as a Spirit of judgment and a Spirit of burning. Some writers want to make this merely a burning, cleansing wind. But God is doing the work. His Spirit becomes a fire that purges away evil in order to bring in the glory of the Messianic kingdom.

When Jesus talks about fire, it is also the fire of judgment. John the Baptist also speaks of fire as judgment (Matthew 3:7, 10, 11). So John predicted Jesus would bring two baptisms, one in the Holy Spirit (which occurred on the Day of Pentecost and is still available to us) and one in fire (which will take place when Jesus comes again "in flaming fire taking vengeance on them that know not God" [2 Thessalonians 1:8]).

Then on the Day of Pentecost a tongue of flame sat on the head of each of the 120 to show God had accepted their bodies as temples into which He could pour His Spirit.

Fire also speaks of light and blessing, as do the seven lamps of fire which represent the sevenfold Spirit in Revelation 4.

D. Dove

After Jesus was baptized in the Jordan God proclaimed Him as His Son by sending the Spirit upon Him in the form of a dove. It also indicated the Father's approval on the ministry Jesus was about to begin. Thus John 1:36 draws attention to the fact that Jesus came to be the Lamb of God who takes away the sin of the world. The dove to the Jews was more than a symbol of peace and gentleness. The poor offered doves for a sin offering in place of a lamb. The dove pointed out Jesus as the poor man's Lamb, the God-given sacrifice for the sins of a poor, needy, sinful world.

TEACHING TIP 5

Note that during Israel's exodus from Egypt, they were led by a pillar of cloud by day and a pillar of fire by night. Ask: "What may be the significance of these symbols in relation to the person and work of the Holy Spirit?"

Draw attention toward the leadership and guidance given by the Spirit in the Christian's daily walk.

Guideline for Living 3

It has been noted that the dove is a gentle, peaceable bird, yet one that is easily frightened and timid in nature. This characteristic was clearly underscored in an unusual way to a missions pastor one Sunday night.

Following an anointed sermon by the pastor, a message in tongues was delivered by a member of the congregation. Silence followed as the people waited for an interpretation. At that point the pastor was impressed that the Holy Spirit wanted to use other members of the congregation in the gift of interpretation. He encouraged his people to be open to the Spirit's leading. Then an unusual thing happened. As the pastor looked over his praying congregation, the Holy Spirit allowed him to see His presence in the form of a dove hovering over the people. The dove would fly above their heads and then light upon one of them. Immediately the individual would become tense and hesitant as the Holy Spirit dealt with him or her about the interpretation. This caused the dove to fly and light upon another person, who exhibited the same

Ask one or two students or an outside guest to give brief testimonies regarding the comforting presence of the Holy Spirit. This may be in relation to His presence during times of tragedy or crisis.

There may be some who have experienced the Holy Spirit's intercession on their behalf as someone was moved to pray for them in a time of need. Or they may have felt impressed to pray for another person who was facing a crisis. Permit time for a few brief testimonies regarding these experiences.

Clarification

Comforter—Helper, Intercessor, Consoler.

Question.

Why did Jesus call Him another Comforter?

TEACHING TIP 7

The various names of the Holy Spirit may be listed as follows:

The Comforter
The Holy Spirit
The Holy Spirit of Promise
The Spirit of Truth
The Spirit of Grace
The Spirit of Life
The Spirit of Adoption

Daily Devotional Guide

M. The Spirit's Wisdom. Exodus 35:30-35
T. The Spirit's Goodness. Psalm 143:7-11
W. The Spirit's Grief. Isaiah 63:7-10
T. The Spirit's Holiness. Romans 1:1-6
F. The Spirit's Love. Romans 15:26-33
S. The Spirit's Fruit. Galatians 5:16-25

reaction. The peoples' hesitancy "frightened" the dove, who continued to search for someone willing to interpret the message in tongues.

How important it is to be open and sensitive to the moving of the Holy Spirit. He is eager to develop His gifts in our lives if we are willing to be used by Him.

IV. Names Of The Holy Spirit

John 14:16, 17; Romans 1:4; 8:2; Ephesians 1:13; Hebrews 10:29.

John 14:16. I will pray the Father, and he shall give you another Comforter, that he may abide with you forever.

A. Comforter

We can learn a great deal about the Holy Spirit from the names given Him in the Bible. (See Teaching Tip 6.)

Jesus himself was the Comforter, Helper, Intercessor, and Consoler for His disciples while He was on earth. When there were questions the disciples couldn't answer or demons they couldn't cast out, Jesus was right there with the power to help. He quieted the storms, fed the multitudes, met every need. The Latin meaning of *Comforter* gives the idea of "One who comes alongside with strength." The Greek basically means a Helper but with the added idea of encouragement, compassion, comfort, and consolation. He is indeed our Helper in a troubled world, the Helper we all need.

B. Other Names

He is called the Spirit of holiness, The Spirit of life in Christ Jesus, the Holy Spirit of promise, and the Spirit of grace. Above all, He is the *Holy* Spirit. Truly, we need Him!

LIVING THE TRUTH

Again we must come back to the basic fact that the Holy Spirit is not a thing or an experience—He is a Person. He is a living Person who is able to abide with us and within us to give comfort, guidance, and direction. He is God with us in a real, personal sense.

Our concern must always be to allow God the Holy Spirit to have free rein in our lives. Let us allow Him to do His work within us and thereby develop in us the image of Jesus Christ.

EVANGELISM OUTREACH

To know the Person of the Holy Spirit, one must have a saving knowledge of Jesus Christ. If there are some who have not accepted Christ as Saviour, encourage them to come to Him so that they too may experience the joy of the Spirit's presence in their lives.

THE WORKS OF THE HOLY SPIRIT

6

SEEING THE SCRIPTURES

Genesis 1:2

2. And the earth was without form, and void; and darkness was upon the face of the deep. And the Spirit of God moved upon the face of the waters.

John 15:26, 27; 16:7-15

26. But when the Comforter is come, whom I will send unto you from the Father, even the Spirit of truth, which proceedeth from the Father, he shall testify of me:

27. And ye also shall bear witness, because ye have been with me from the beginning.

16:7. Nevertheless I tell you the truth; It is expedient for you that I go away: for if I go not away, the Comforter will not come unto you; but if I depart, I will send him unto you.

8. And when he is come, he will reprove the world of sin, and of righteousness, and of judgment:

9. Of sin, because they believe not on me:

10. Of righteousness, because I go to my Father, and ye see me no more;

11. Of judgment, because the prince of this world is judged.

12. I have yet many things to say unto you, but ye cannot bear them now.

13. Howbeit when he, the Spirit of truth, is come, he will guide you into all truth: for he shall not speak of himself; but whatsoever he shall hear, that shall he speak: and he will show you things to come.

14. He shall glorify me: for he shall receive of mine, and shall show it unto you.

15. All things that the Father hath are mine: therefore said I, that he shall take of mine, and shall show it unto you.

Acts 2:1-4

1. And when the day of Pentecost was fully come, they were all with one accord in one place.

2. And suddenly there came a sound from heaven as of a rushing mighty wind, and it filled all the house where they were sitting.

3. And there appeared unto them cloven tongues like as of fire, and it sat upon each of them.

4. And they were all filled with the Holy Ghost, and began to speak with other tongues, as the Spirit gave them utterance.

2 Peter 1:21

21. For the prophecy came not in old time by the will of man: but holy men of God spake as they were moved by the Holy Ghost.

PREPARING TO TEACH

Study Text
Genesis 1:2; 41:38-40; Numbers 27:15-21; 2 Samuel 23:1, 2; 2 Chronicles 20:14; Ezekiel 8:1-3; 11:1-5; Micah 3:8; John 15:26, 27; 16:7-15; Acts 1:8; 2:1-4, 37; 4:31; 13:2-12; Ephesians 1:13, 14; 2 Peter 1:21; Jude 20; Revelation 1:10, 11

Outline
I. Active in the Old Testament
  A. The Creator Spirit
  B. Empowering Leaders
  C. Inspiring Prophets
II. Inspired the Scriptures
  A. Inspiring Words
  B. Inspiring To Write
III. Convicts Sinners
  A. Convincing of Sin
  B. Convincing of Righteousness
  C. Convincing of Judgment
IV. Empowers Believers

Golden Text:
When the Comforter is come, whom I will send unto you from the Father, even the Spirit of truth, which proceedeth from the Father, he shall testify of me. John 15:26

Central Truth:
The Holy Spirit, who has always been active in the world, is calling people out of sin and empowering them for service.

Learning Goals
1. To examine the work of the Holy Spirit in the past and present.
2. To recognize the importance of the Holy Spirit to our daily Christian experience.
3. To seek to be filled, led, and guided by the Holy Spirit.

GETTING STARTED

Distribute index cards or slips of paper and pencils to the students. On the chalkboard write the completion statement: "The purpose or work of the Holy Spirit in our world today is. . . ." Ask the students to finish the statement according to their own understanding.

When all have completed the statement, call for volunteers to read their responses. You may wish to jot some of the main ideas on the chalkboard. Note especially whether the statements pertain more to the emotional aspects of the Holy Spirit's work or if there is a broader understanding of the overall work of the Spirit.

Clarification

And the earth was without form, and void—now the earth (at the time of the beginning) was without landmarks and empty of inhabitants. In other words, God did not create the earth with continents and people already on it.

Moved upon—hovered over. The same word was used of a mother bird hovering over the young in her nest.

Came the Spirit—was the Spirit.

The spirit lifted—the Spirit lifted. The Holy Spirit is meant. (The Hebrew did not distinguish between capital and small letters).

Question.

Was Joshua the only Old Testament person who was indwelt by the Holy Spirit?

SETTING THE SCENE

The Holy Spirit has been active and powerful in every age. In Old Testament times no judge or prophet would have said, "I think the Holy Spirit has come upon me," or "I hope He has." They knew Him in a definite, personal, powerful way. The Hebrew of Judges 6:34 shows that the Holy Spirit clothed himself with Gideon, and Gideon blew a trumpet. The Spirit rushed mightily on Samson and he tore a lion apart (Judges 14:6).

New Testament believers did not have to guess about the reality or power of the Spirit either. The Spirit came upon Jesus in the visible form of a dove. Other manifestations, though not visible, were just as definite. The believers spoke in tongues (Acts 2:4; 10:46; 19:6). Once the place was shaken (Acts 4:31). Again and again we see that the comfort, help, and encouragement of the Holy Spirit was both powerful and real (Acts 9:31, for example). The Holy Spirit still wants to provide His help, comfort, warmth, and joy to promote the spread of the gospel and the growth of the Church.

BIBLE COMMENTARY

I. Active in the Old Testament

Genesis 1:2; Numbers 27:15-21; 2 Chronicles 20:14; Ezekiel 8:1-3

Genesis 1:2. The earth was without form, and void; and darkness was upon the face of the deep. And the Spirit of God moved upon the face of the waters. Numbers 27:18. The Lord said unto Moses, Take thee Joshua the son of Nun, a man in whom is the spirit, and lay thine hand upon him. 2 Chronicles 20:14. Then upon Jahaziel the son of Zechariah, the son of Benaiah, the son of Jeiel, the son of Mattaniah, a Levite of the sons of Asaph, came the Spirit of the Lord in the midst of the congregation. Ezekiel 8:3. He put forth the form of a hand, and took me by a lock of mine head; and the spirit lifted me up between the earth and the heaven, and brought me in the visions of God to Jerusalem, to the door of the inner gate that looketh toward the north; where was the seat of the image of jealousy, which provoketh to jealousy.

A. The Creator Spirit

In Genesis 1:2 we see the Spirit of God hovering continuously over the face of the waters that covered the earth. Evidently this was in preparation for the order and purpose that God brought forth in the six creation days that followed. The earth did not yet have its final form and was uninhabited. But the Spirit of God was there! However the Holy Spirit did more than work in darkness. Job saw him garnishing, that is, brightening the heavens (Job 26:13).

B. Empowering Leaders

(See Teaching Tip 1.)

In the building of the tabernacle God filled Bezaleel and Aholiab

TEACHING TIP 1

The story of Samson provides a dramatic and graphic illustration of a life empowered by the Holy Spirit. Yet, there came a serious decline in that empowerment when Samson yielded to temptation. This was followed by a brief "comeback" just before Samson's death.

Divide the class into study groups of three or more. Provide sheets of paper and pencils. List the following Scripture references from Judges on the chalkboard or overhead transparency. With these verses in focus, ask the groups to design a line curve graph illustrating the rise-decline-rise of Samson's experience. You may wish to have a volunteer from a study group reproduce his group's graph on the chalkboard for general discussion. 14:5, 6, 19; 15:14, 15; 16:6, 7, 11, 13, 17, 21, 22, 28.

The graph may be designed as follows:
14:5, 6 14:19 15:14, 15 16:6, 7 16:11 16:13 16:17 16:21,22 16:28

Discuss the following questions in light of Samson's story:

1. What are some events or influences that result in special spiritual empowerment in our lives?

2. What are some influences that may cause a decline in our spiritual power?

3. Would you be able to design a similar rise-decline-rise spiritual profile for your own life?

with the Spirit to sharpen their skills and enable them to teach others also (Exodus 31:2-5; 35:30-34). The Holy Spirit clothed himself with Gideon (Judges 6:34, Hebrew), which is a beautiful way of saying the Spirit was on the inside doing the work. When Samuel anointed David, the Spirit of the Lord came into him from that day "upward," that is, in a rising, growing experience (1 Samuel 16:13, Hebrew). Micah was "full of power even the Spirit of the Lord" (Micah 3:8, Hebrew).

On others the Spirit of God came sometimes suddenly and briefly, sometimes for a lifetime, always to help God's people.

Guideline for Living 1

Does God the Holy Spirit work to sharpen our talents and abilities?

It seems apparent from Biblical examples that God the Holy Spirit does sharpen our natural talents to bring glory to Christ. There are clear examples of special help in areas of craftsmanship, exhortation, and administration. These may pertain to the various spiritual gifts outlined in 1 Corinthians 12:8-10 or the offices and ministries listed in Ephesians 4:11, 12; 1 Corinthians 12:28-30, and Romans 12:4-8.

In short, God the Holy Spirit can and will provide a special measure of assistance as we willingly yield ourselves and our abilities to His control. What a delight and privilege it is to daily give ourselves to the enablement of the Holy Spirit.

C. Inspiring Prophets

Clearly, the chief work of the Holy Spirit in the Old Testament was prophecy. The word *prophet* means a speaker, and the true prophets were speakers for God.

Sometimes they gave God's guidance and encouragement to kings and rulers. Jahaziel is a good example as he encouraged King Jehoshaphat to stand still and let the Lord give them the victory (2 Chronicles 20:14-17). Azariah (2 Chronicles 15:1-8) and Elisha are other good examples.

The major portion of the prophets' work and messages was taken up with giving God's Word for the immediate needs of the people. The Spirit took Ezekiel up in vision to Jerusalem to let him see the idolatry that was causing God to withdraw the Shekinah glory and allow the destruction of the temple and city. In most cases the prophets were given visions of the future in order to reinforce God's will for the present.

Guideline for Living 2

Is prophecy a bona fide work of the Spirit today?

Prophecy is a gift of the Holy Spirit as shown in 1 Corinthians 12:10. Simply defined, prophecy is the utterance of a divine truth in a person's own language, as prompted by the Holy Spirit" (*We Hold These Truths*, Zenas J. Bicket).

Prophecy is generally the result of a spontaneous inspiration of the Holy Spirit. We must be careful, however, to realize that prophecy is not intended to supplant preaching or teaching but to supplement it. Nor is prophecy to be regarded on a par with Scripture. Such cautions are important safeguards against giving undue authority to prophetic utterances.

The purpose of prophecy in the Church today is outlined in 1 Corinthians 14:3. The prophet edifies, exhorts, and comforts believers. Through this gift, the Holy Spirit assures us of His presence in our lives and in our circumstances. What blessing and encouragement this brings to us all.

II. Inspired the Scriptures

2 Samuel 23:1, 2; Ezekiel 11:1-5; Micah 3:8; 2 Peter 1:21; Revelation 1:10, 11

2 Samuel 23:1. Now these be the last words of David. David the son of Jesse said, and the man who was raised up on high, the anointed of the God of Jacob, and the sweet psalmist of Israel, said, 2. The Spirit of the Lord spake by me, and his word was in my tongue. Ezekiel 11:5. The Spirit of the Lord fell upon me, and said unto me, Speak; Thus saith the Lord; Thus have ye said, O house of Israel: for I know the things that come into your mind, every one of them. Micah 3:8. Truly I am full of power by the Spirit of the Lord, and of judgment, and of might, to declare unto Jacob his transgression, and to Israel his sin. 2 Peter 1:21. The prophecy came not in old time by the will of man: but holy men of God spake as they were moved by the Holy Ghost. Revelation 1:10. I was in the Spirit on the Lord's day, and heard behind me a great voice, as of a trumpet, 11. saying, I am Alpha and Omega, the first and the last: and, What thou seest, write in a book, and send it unto the seven churches which are in Asia.

A. Inspiring Words

David was anointed by the Spirit, and the Spirit was in his tongue. He sang many of the psalms that are included in the Book of Psalms and made provision for them to be used in the temple worship. We have already seen that the prophets were speakers for God. God spoke to them and through them. Again and again they say, "Thus saith the Lord."

In the New Testament, we read that the Holy Spirit spoke to Philip (Acts 8:29). Paul also indicates that the Holy Spirit was active in giving him truth. (In 1 Corinthians 7:40 he may mean, however, that he does not have a saying of Jesus to back this up but he is sure that what he says comes from the Spirit.)

B. Inspiring To Write

Sometimes they did. Sometimes they saw a vision before them. Sometimes God gave them dreams. With others, God spoke to them through an inner voice. God had Jeremiah dictate his prophecies to a scribe, Baruch (Jeremiah 36:1-4, 32). We read that God specifically told Ezekiel and John to write also. Hebrews 1:1 indicates there were various ways that God spoke at various times through the words, lives, and writings of the prophets. We see also that God did not give His Word the way a businessman might take a secretary out of a secretarial pool and dictate something to her.

Clarification

By the Spirit of the Lord—even the Spirit of the Lord. The reason he was full of power was because he was full of the Spirit.

Moved—led along.

The Lord's day—probably Sunday, though some early writers indicate Easter may have been meant.

Alpha and Omega—the first and last letters of the Greek alphabet.

Book—scroll, probably a papyrus roll.

Question.

Who were some of the people to whom or through whom the Holy Spirit spoke?

Question.

Did the writers of Scripture always hear an audible voice telling them to write?

TEACHING TIP 2

Before class give a copy of the PATH information sheet entitled "Theories of Biblical Inspiration" to a student. It would be best if he could have this a week before so the information can be presented in report form at this time. This would also enable the student to do additional research if desired. Encourage the student to use the chalkboard or overhead projector in giving his report. This would be more interesting than just reading the information.

Follow the report by briefly discussing the various proofs of Biblical inspiration given below.

1. *Jesus' testimony.* Jesus himself testified to the Bible's authority and truth (Matthew 5:18; 26:54; Luke 18:31-33; 24:25; John 10:35.)

2. *Apostles' testimony.* (Luke 3:4; Acts 1:16; 3:18; Romans 3:2; 1 Corinthians 2:9-16; 2 Timothy 3:16; Hebrews 1:1; 2 Peter 1:21; 3:2)

3. *Unity of message.* God's Word presents the same theme although written by 35-40 authors over 1,600 years of time.

4. *Circulation.* No other book has been so widely circulated as the Bible.

5. *Timelessness.* God's Word is relevant to every age and generation.

6. *Preservation.* All attempts to totally destroy God's Word have failed.

7. *Fulfillment of Prophecy.* Many Old Testament and New Testament prophecies have come to pass.

Clarification

Reprove—convince (in such a way as to cause conviction).

Righteousness — includes an uprightness that is always honest, fair, and just, and is also right before God.

Judgment—including the fact that a judgment day is coming.

Pricked in their heart—pierced, stabbed, cut to the heart. Indicates sharp pain from anxiety, sorrow, remorse.

Question.

What does the Bible show is the real problem with sin?

God told Jeremiah He began to prepare him before he was born (Jeremiah 1:5). God prepared Moses through his parents' teaching, through the universities of Egypt, and then for 40 more years in the wilderness. All the writers were prepared in such a way that God could take their vocabularies and their experiences and bring out the truth in just the way He wanted it expressed.

God says in Hosea 8:12, "I have written to him [Israel] the great [the ten thousand] things of my law [torah, teaching, Scriptures]." This is what we see in 2 Timothy 3:16, 17 that all Scripture is inspired of God, literally, *God-breathed.* As Peter also says, these writers were moved or led along by the Spirit of God. Remember too that Jesus called the Holy Spirit "the Spirit of Truth." He promised that the Spirit would guide into all truth, teach them, and bring things to their remembrance (John 14:17, 26; 15:26; 16:13-15).

Guideline for Living 3

What is the greatest proof of the Holy Spirit's inspiration of God's Word?

Among the many undeniable proofs of the Bible's divine inspiration is *changed lives.* God's Word is a powerful, life-changing force. This was clearly shown following Peter's sermon on the Day of Pentecost. After hearing the Word of God the people were "pricked in their heart" (Acts 2:37) and asked what they must do. On that day 3,000 were brought into the Church.

Stories abound of lives transformed by the simple reading of God's Word. Indeed, God's Word is a powerful, two-edged sword that penetrates our very being with the light of His truth. With this in mind, we should be more confident and fervent in sharing this powerful Word with those around us.

III. Convicts Sinners
John 16:7-11; Acts 2:37

John 16:8. When he is come, he will reprove the world of sin, and of righteousness, and of judgment: 9. of sin, because they believe not on me; 10. of righteousness, because I go to my Father, and ye see me no more; 11. of judgment, because the prince of this world is judged. Acts 2:37. When they heard this, they were pricked in their heart, and said unto Peter and to the rest of the apostles, Men and brethren, what shall we do?

A. Convincing of Sin

Some worldings exalt sin. Others ignore or deny it. Some make everything a matter of personal preference. Others will condemn those things that are harmful to health or society or contrary to the ideas of a certain culture or a certain place. They are not usually willing to admit that the sins the Bible condemns are always wrong.

Sin in its essence is unbelief. Most unbelievers do not realize the seriousness of the unbelief. But when Eve listened to the old serpent in the Garden, she sinned because she no longer believed what God had said (Genesis 3:1, 3). Israel's unbelief kept a whole generation out of the Promised Land (Numbers 14:20-35). Moses' unbelief caused him to take to himself honor that was due God and this kept him out of the Promised Land too (Numbers 20:10, 12).

TEACHING TIP 3
Focus on the practical, everyday aspects of the Holy Spirit's conviction by discusing the following questions:
1. How do you feel when you have knowingly sinned against God?
2. How do you relate that feeling to the work of the Holy Spirit?
3. How would you differentiate between the conviction of the Holy Spirit and conscience?
4. Is it possible to become insensitive to the conviction of the Holy Spirit?

Question.
How does the Spirit convince of judgment?

When Jesus came He did not need to condemn anyone. By their unbelief in Him they were condemned already (John 3:18). Because people loved their sins they did not come to the light of Christ, but their real sin was still unbelief (John 3:19, 20). Through the Cross forgiveness is now available to all who believe. So if people hear the gospel and die in their sins, they do so because of unbelief.

He points us to Jesus and to His death on the cross. He makes us see how serious sin is because of the price that had to be paid for our salvation. He makes us realize that unbelief in Jesus is indeed sin. Then when unbelief is out of the way, the blood of Jesus cleanses us from all of our other sins.

B. Convincing of Righteousness

The Spirit convinces with respect to righteousness by pointing, not to our own righteousness or lack of it, but to the righteousness of Christ. In Jesus we see what righteousness really is. We see it in His life that was always upright, honest, fair, and just. He always did His Father's will. We see Him now as the Righteous One who is the propitiation, the sin offering for the sins of the whole world (1 John 2:1, 2). We see also that death could not find any sin in Him, so death could not hold Him. He rose from the grave and ascended to the Father's right hand where He is interceding for us (Romans 1:4, 16; Hebrews 7:25).

C. Convincing of Judgment

In the present age there is a continuing conflict between belief and unbelief. But it will not go on forever. There is a judgment day coming that will bring an end to this present world system and all its unbelief.

He makes us recognize who the prince of this world is and that Satan's judgment was never meant for man (Matthew 25:41). The Spirit wants to emphasize that Christ's victory at Calvary and the empty tomb sealed Satan's doom (Hebrews 2:14). The world that is under Satan's domination will share his doom if they do not cease their unbelief and accept the forgiveness and salvation we have in Jesus.

On the Day of Pentecost the Spirit spoke through Peter in prophetic utterance and convinced 3,000 of what their sin of unbelief did to Jesus. He showed them the righteousness of God's Holy One whom God did not allow to see corruption. He exhorted them to save themselves from that crooked generation. The result was surrender and glad acceptance of the truth. The same results came with the further preaching of Peter, Paul, and others down through the history of the Church.

IV. Empowers Believers

John 15:26, 27; 16:12-15; Acts 1:8; 2:1-4; 4:31; 13:2-13; Jude 20

John 15:26. When the Comforter is come, whom I will send unto you from the Father, even the Spirit of truth, which proceedeth from the Father, he shall testify of me: 16:13. When he, the Spirit of truth, is come, he will guide you into all truth: for he shall not speak of himself; but whatsoever he shall hear, that shall

Clarification
Spirit of truth—Spirit of the Truth.

Speak of himself—speak from himself (as a source).

Question.

Why is it so important that we let the Holy Spirit guide us into all the truth of Christ?

Question.

What other works of the Holy Spirit do we see?

TEACHING TIP 4

Outline the following gifts of the Spirit. Discuss each one briefly or arrange to have a student present a brief report.
1. Word of Wisdom
2. Word of Knowledge
3. Faith
4. Healing
5. Miracles
6. Prophecy
7. Discerning of Spirits
8. Diverse Tongues
9. Interpretation of Tongues

Knowing the Doctrines of the Bible by Myer Pearlman or *We Hold These Truths* by Zenas J. Bicket will provide good background material for a report.

he speak: and he will show you things to come. 14. He shall glorify me: for he shall receive of mine, and shall show it unto you. Acts 1:8. Ye shall receive power, after that the Holy Ghost is come upon you: and ye shall be witnesses unto me both in Jerusalem, and in all Judea, and in Samaria, and unto the uttermost part of the earth. 2:4. They were all filled with the Holy Ghost, and began to speak with other tongues, as the Spirit gave them utterance. 4:31. When they had prayed, the place was shaken where they were assembled together; and they were all filled with the Holy Ghost, and they spake the word of God with boldness. 13:2. As they ministered to the Lord, and fasted, the Holy Ghost said, Separate me Barnabas and Saul for the work whereunto I have called them. Jude 20. Ye, beloved, building up yourselves on your most holy faith, praying in the Holy Ghost.

The truth has power. Paul recognized that we can't really do anything against the truth (2 Corinthians 13:8). Truth can be covered up but it cannot be destroyed. Of course, the truth the Holy Spirit emphasizes is the truth that is in Jesus and from Jesus, for He is the truth.

We see also that the Spirit's great purpose is to empower us as Spirit-baptized believers to witness for Christ. But in order to witness we must know the truth about Him. The Holy Spirit makes it His business to teach us the truth that is in Jesus. He makes it possible for us to know in our own experience that Jesus is the Revealer of the Father, our Saviour, the Forgiver of our sins, our risen Lord, and our coming King.

Guideline for Living 4

The baptism in the Holy Spirit is for a purpose. It is not a Pentecostal ID certificate making us bona fide "card-carrying" charismatics. The baptism in the Holy Spirit is essentially intended to give us power to witness to those around us—by word and deed. Those who have received this wonderful infilling ought to evidence a new dimension of spiritual fervor and maturity. Is this true in your life?

He still sends forth workers as He did Paul and Barnabas. He gives gifts and performs miracles.

LIVING THE TRUTH

When Jesus called the Holy Spirit the Comforter it was an indication that the Spirit's relationship with believers would be very intimate and personal. Jesus was a constant Companion to His disciples. His teaching about the Holy Spirit emphasized that the companionship of the Spirit would be just as close and vital. We cannot have fellowship with an influence, a force, or a concept. The Holy Spirit is none of these. He is a Person and He has come to fellowship with us in just as real a sense as Jesus did with His followers, even though we cannot see the Spirit with our physical eyes.

EVANGELISM OUTREACH

Be especially sensitive to the convicting work of the Holy Spirit as this week's study is presented. Take time to counsel or pray with any who are openly seeking a new life in Christ.

7 | THE TRIUNE GOD

PREPARING TO TEACH

Study Text
Genesis 1:27; Deuteronomy 6:4; Isaiah 6:8; Matthew 3:16, 17; 28:19; Mark 12:19-32; John 3:1-8, 16-18; 14:18-26; 2 Corinthians 13:14; 1 Timothy 2:5; James 2:19

Outline
I. One God
   A. He Alone Is God
   B. One Way of Salvation
II. Three Persons
   A. A New Testament Revelation
   B. Three Distinct Persons
III. Perfect in Unity
   A. Still One
   B. Our Unity
IV. Active in Salvation
   A. God Sent His Son
   B. Jesus Fulfilled Redemption's Plan
   C. The Holy Spirit Brings New Life

Golden Text: The grace of the Lord Jesus Christ, and the love of God, and the communion of the Holy Ghost, be with you all. Amen. 2 Corinthians 13:14

Central Truth: The Bible reveals one God who exists in three persons: the Father, Son, and Holy Spirit.

Learning Goals
1. To examine the unique interrelationships of the three Persons of the Holy Trinity.
2. To recognize the unity, yet individuality of the Father, Son, and Holy Spirit.
3. To appreciate the work of the Trinity in effecting our salvation.

SEEING THE SCRIPTURES

Genesis 1:27

27. So God created man in his own image, in the image of God created he him; male and female created he them.

John 3:16, 17; 14:18-26

16. For God so loved the world, that he gave his only begotten Son, that whosoever believeth in him should not perish, but have everlasting life.

17. For God sent not his Son into the world to condemn the world; but that the world through him might be saved.

14:18. I will not leave you comfortless: I will come to you.

19. Yet a little while, and the world seeth me no more; but ye see me: because I live, ye shall live also.

20. At that day ye shall know that I am in my Father, and ye in me, and I in you.

21. He that hath my commandments, and keepeth them, he it is that loveth me: and he that loveth me shall be loved of my Father, and I will love him, and will manifest myself to him.

22. Judas saith unto him, not Iscariot, Lord, how is it that thou wilt manifest thyself unto us, and not unto the world?

23. Jesus answered and said unto him, If a man love me, he will keep my words: and my Father will love him, and we will come unto him, and make our abode with him.

24. He that loveth me not keepeth not my sayings: and the word which ye hear is not mine, but the Father's which sent me.

25. These things have I spoken unto you, being yet present with you.

26. But the Comforter, which is the Holy Ghost, whom the Father will send in my name, he shall teach you all things, and bring all things to your remembrance, whatsoever I have said unto you.

James 2:19

19. Thou believest that there is one God; thou doest well: the devils also believe, and tremble.

SETTING THE SCENE

Our last few studies have dealt with God the Father, Christ, and the Holy Spirit. We have seen that each of them are distinct, divine Persons. We have discussed the person and work of each. Now we need to bring all this together and discuss the Trinity in a little more detail.

What is usually called the Trinity is really a Triunity: one God

GETTING STARTED

This week's study deals with one of the greatest theological mysteries presented in God's Word. Initiate discussion of the Trinity by having the students review the divine characteristics shared by the Persons of the Trinity. Divide the class into pairs and give each pair a copy of the "Trinity Review" worksheet from PATH. Note that the Scripture texts refer alternately to God the Father, Son, and Holy Spirit. See the answer key provided in the PATH instruction folder.

When the students have completed the review form, take a few moments to discuss their responses.

Clarification

Is one Lord—is one Yahweh; or, Yahweh is One. The word "one" does not rule out a compound unity. (Compare Exodus 36:13.)

Men—human beings.

The man—the human being. Jesus remains the God-Man in heaven.

Devils—demons, evil spirits.

Tremble—shudder (from fear).

TEACHING TIP 1

After discussing "Guideline for Living 1" list the following items on the chalkboard. Ask the students to consider personally in what order of priority they would arrange the items.

Personal Priority Profile
Church
Money
Recreation
Job
Bible Reading
Clothes
Witnessing
Car
Family
Prayer
Tithing

Emphasize that there is a tendency in our lives to separate worldly and spiritual prior-

with one Being yet existent eternally in three Persons. Trinitarians are sometimes accused of believing in three Gods. This is not true at all. We believe in one God. But we recognize that on the human level there is only one person to one being. On the divine level there are three Persons to one Being. God has three "places" where He can say "I." We should expect God to be greater than man. Those who deny the Triunity oversimplify the facts we see in the Bible. They do God an injustice and drag Him down to the human level. The Bible honors all three, the Father, the Son, and the Holy Spirit, and does not mix them up.

BIBLE COMMENTARY

I. One God

> Deuteronomy 6:4; 1 Timothy 2:5; James 2:19

Deuteronomy 6:4. Hear, O Israel: the Lord our God is one Lord. 1 Timothy 2:5. For there is one God, and one mediator between God and men, the man Christ Jesus. James 2:19. Thou believest that there is one God; thou doest well: the devils also believe, and tremble.

A. He Alone Is God

The world once knew the true God. But they took God off the throne, put self on the throne, and then began to look for gods they could manipulate. They conceived of gods in their own image, in the likeness of fallen man. They also made gods of nature, its creatures, and its forces, or they were tricked into worshiping demons (Romans 1:20-23; 1 Corinthians 10:20).

By the time of Abraham practically the whole world had turned to the worship of idols and images of these false gods. Israel became a little island of monotheism surrounded by idolatry. It was necessary therefore to put the greatest emphasis on the fact the Lord alone is God. God is what the Bible teaches He is: eternal, self-existent, uncreated, all-powerful, all-wise, all-knowing, everywhere present, the Creator of all things. Since He is personally concerned about His creation, there is neither room nor need for any other God. Moreover, since God is one, we must not split up our love with other gods or with things less than God. As Deuteronomy 6:5 goes on to say, we are to love God with all our heart (including all our mind), with all our soul (including our feelings and emotions), and with all our might (including the strength of our will)—that is, with our whole being.

Guideline for Living 1

Is there a problem with serving other gods in our society today?

Although we may not encounter the problem of serving other gods or deities in the religious sense, there are a number of "gods" that can hinder our relationship with the one true God.

Consider the powerful influences of materialism and humanism that cause many to place self on the throne and seek after personal

ities. Yet we cannot do so realistically. It is important to consider carefully how all areas of vocation and interest affect our relationship to God.

wealth, fame, or power. How subtle is the desire to get ahead, to "keep up with the Joneses," to attain a position of esteem in the eyes of others.

Jesus exhorted His disciples, "Ye cannot serve God and mammon." By "mammon" Jesus meant the acquisition or building up of wealth. Such is perhaps the most common of all gods that stand between God and man.

In short, anything that comes between us and God violates the ancient admonition to the Children of Israel: "Thou shalt have no other gods before me" (Exodus 20:3). Let us be ever on the alert for even the most subtle influences that might hinder our relationship with God.

Question.
Is it enough to subscribe to the truth of the one God in three Persons?

B. One Way of Salvation

Demons tremble or shudder in fear, for they know who God is and who Jesus is, but they refuse to submit even though they know their judgment is sure.

We must not only believe in the one true God, we must enter into right relation with Him. Since there is only one Mediator between God and human beings, we must come to God through Him. Nor need we be afraid or tremble like the evil spirits. Jesus is at the right hand of His Father's throne interceding for us (1 John 1:9; 2:1, 2).

Guideline for Living 2

Mental assent to the fact of God's existence does not bring salvation. This is the error of some who are "professing" Christians only. They are quick to acknowledge that God exists but do not possess the new life which comes only through an active faith in the saving power of Jesus Christ.

II. Three Persons

Matthew 3:16, 17; 28:19; John 14:18-26; 2 Corinthians 13:14

Matthew 3:16. Jesus, when he was baptized, went up straightway out of the water: and, lo, the heavens were opened unto him, and he saw the Spirit of God descending like a dove, and lighting upon him: 17. and lo a voice from heaven, saying, This is my beloved Son, in whom I am well pleased. 28:19. Go ye therefore, and teach all nations, baptizing them in the name of the Father, and of the Son, and of the Holy Ghost. John 14:23. Jesus answered and said unto him, If a man love me, he will keep my words: and my Father will love him, and we will come unto him, and make our abode with him. 24. He that loveth me not keepeth not my sayings: and the word which ye hear is not mine, but the Father's which sent me. 25. These things have I spoken unto you, being yet present with you. 26. But the Comforter, which is the Holy Ghost, whom the Father will send in my name, he shall teach you all things, and bring all things to your remembrance, whatsoever I have said unto you. 2 Corinthians 13:14. The grace of the Lord Jesus Christ, and the love of God, and the communion of the Holy Ghost, be with you all. Amen.

Clarification

I am well pleased—or, I take delight.

In the name—into the Name, that is, into the worship and service of. "Name" is in the singular because it is used distributively and there is only one name or title each. Compare Ruth 1:2, "the name of his two sons, Mahlon and Chilion." A common Bible usage.

Abode—dwelling place. The same word is used of heavenly dwelling places in John 14:2.

Communion — fellowship, partnership, sharing.

Question.
Why does Acts speak of baptizing people in the name of Jesus?

Question.
Whom does the Father send?

Question.
Whose word did Jesus give?

A. A New Testament Revelation

The Old Testament gives us hints, indications, and reflections of the Trinity. We can see this especially in the revelation of the Messianic Servant of the Lord in Isaiah 42:1, 6; 52:13 through 53:12; 61:1, 2. In Isaiah 48:16 the Messiah says literally, "God has sent me and has sent His Spirit." This is about as close to a full revelation of the three divine Persons as you will find in the Old Testament.

But in the New Testament we find a full revelation, a clear revelation. At the very beginning of the public ministry of Jesus He identified himself with mankind by allowing John the Baptist to baptize Him in the Jordan River. Then as soon as Jesus came up out of the river and stood on the bank, the heavens opened and two things took place. First the Holy Spirit came down upon Him and literally into Him, appearing in the form of a dove. Then the voice of the Heavenly Father came from heaven identifying Jesus as His beloved Son. Here we have the Father, Son, and Holy Spirit clearly distinguished from each other. (See Teaching Tip 2.)

At the end of His ministry on earth Jesus gave His disciples the Great Commission, sending them out to make disciples and commanding them to baptize believers into the name, that is, into the worship and service of the Father, Son, and Holy Spirit. Thus Jesus again proclaimed the three Persons of the Triune God.

In Acts 2:38, the Greek is literally, "upon the name of Jesus," a phrase which really means "upon the authority of Jesus," that is, in obedience to Jesus' command. We have to go to Matthew 28:19 to see what that command is. Luke, the writer of Acts, often condenses things that are made clear elsewhere. So we can be sure that on the Day of Pentecost the 3,000 saved were baptized "into the name," that is, into the worship and service of the Father, Son, and Holy Spirit.

> *Guideline for Living 3*
> When we recognize that we are baptized *into* the worship and service of the Father, Son, and Holy Spirit, it lends a new meaning to the significance of water baptism. Sometimes we tend to regard this ordinance of the Church as little more than a formality. Yet when we identify with Christ at our baptism, we are totally committing ourselves to giving Him due praise and to serving Him with all our abilities. With this in view, we must continually ask ourselves if we are exhibiting such a commitment.

B. Three Distinct Persons

Many other passages show us that the Father, Son, and Holy Spirit are distinct Persons. Our study text gives us some from John 14 and 2 Corinthians 13.

Jesus said the Father had sent Him and He would send the Comforter, the Holy Spirit. Obviously, the One who sends is distinct from the One sent. It is clear also that the two whom the Father sends are distinct from each other.

Not His own, but the Father's. If Jesus and the Father were the same Person, as some teach, this would be contradictory dou-

Question.

What does 2 Corinthians 13:14 show about the three Persons in the Godhead?

ble-talk. Jesus would be saying, "These are not my words, these are my words." Clearly, Jesus ministered in behalf of the Father, and the Spirit ministers in behalf of Jesus.

The grace of our Lord Jesus Christ, the love of God, and the communion, fellowship, or sharing of the Holy Spirit are continually available to us. We do not have One part of the time and another part of the time. Notice in John 14:23 that the Father and the Son will both come and make their dwelling place with us. Then the Spirit will also teach us.

Clarification

First—most important.
Well—fine! true! well said!
Master—Teacher.
There is one God—God is one.
Thou hast sent me—the word "thou" is emphatic, "Thou and no other!"

Question.

Does the New Testament do away with the unity of the one true God?

Question.

Why do some people have such a hard time understanding the Trinity?

TEACHING TIP 3

A variety of object lessons can be used to help illustrate the Trinity. Use one or more of the following as you discuss the individuality/unity of the Godhead. It would be best to involve students by asking them beforehand to present the illustration.

1. *Triangle:* Refer again to the PATH transparency or draw a simple triangle on the chalkboard. Explain that in order for the triangle to remain a triangle, all three sides must be present. If one is removed, it ceases to be a triangle.

2. *Water, Ice, Steam:* Water is present in three forms: liquid, solid, and vapor. Each form is different in nature yet continues to be water in essence.

3. *Box or cube:* Ask: What three dimensions are present in a box? (Height, width, and length). If any of the three dimensions are removed, the box would become a flat plane.

III. Perfect in Unity

Mark 12:29-32; Genesis 1:27; Isaiah 6:8; John 17:21

Mark 12:32. The scribe said unto him, Well, Master, thou hast said the truth: for there is one God; and there is none other but he. Genesis 1:27. God created man in his own image, in the image of God created he him; male and female created he them. Isaiah 6:8. I heard the voice of the Lord, saying, Whom shall I send, and who will go for us? John 17:21. That they all may be one; as thou, Father, art in me, and I in thee, that they also may be one in us.

A. Still One

Not at all. Jesus drew attention to the fact that God is one when He pointed the scribe back to Deuteronomy 6:4-6.

On the human level we have only one person to one being. It does not matter which part of me does something, I am still the one doing it. But we should expect God to be greater than man. Thus, the Bible shows us that on the divine level there are three Persons to the one being of God.

One of our difficulties is the fact that there is only one Trinity, so we have nothing else in our experience to give us a comparison that will illustrate the One in Three, the compound unity of God. Isaiah 40:18 asks, "To whom then will ye liken God?" There is no way we can liken Him to anything else. To really understand the being of God in every respect we would have to be God.

One illustration might be helpful. Dr. Nathan Wood, a former president of Gordon College claimed that we ought to see at least a reflection of the triunity of God in His creation. He pointed out that space has three dimensions. But you do not add the dimensions to get the amount of space; you multiply. If the units are equal you would multiply one times one times one, which would still be one. Then, as each dimension goes through the whole of a particular unit of space, so the Father fills the whole being of God. So does the Son. So does the Holy Spirit. Yet each is distinct in His person and function, just as each dimension is distinct.

How does the Old Testament indicate this compound unity? (See Teaching Tip 4.) We see it reflected in Genesis 1:26 where God says, "Let us," then the next verse goes back to the singular form. We see it in Isaiah 6:8 where God says, "Whom shall I send, and who will go for us." Some try to say the "us" refers to an inclusion of the seraphim. But this is not likely due to their covered faces and their whole attitude. Rather, it is a reflection of the Trinity.

4. *Egg:* An egg consists of three elements—shell, white, and yolk. Each element is required in order for it to be an egg. Each part has a different function, but all are necessary to constitute the egg.

TEACHING TIP 4
Further illustrate the unity and diversity of the Trinity by outlining the following:

TRINITY/GODHEAD

One { God the Father, God the Son, God the Holy Spirit } God

TEACHING TIP 5
Unity among those of the family of God is a significant theme in God's Word. Ask volunteers to read some or all of the following Scripture passages that deal with unity. Ask the students to determine the various aspects of Christian unity outlined by the verses.

Psalm 133:1
Acts 4:32
Romans 12:16; 15:5, 6
2 Corinthians 13:11
Philippians 1:27; 2:2; 3:16; 1 Peter 3:8

Clarification

Born of water—some interpret this to mean water baptism. Others believe it refers to natural birth in contrast to spiritual birth. But Jesus did not mean literal water in John 4:10, 13, 14; 7:37-39; and it does not seem likely that He did here. Note that the emphasis of the passage is on the effectual working of the Holy Spirit. Since the Greek word for *and* also means "even," the meaning is most probably "water, even the Spirit." Others take the water to signify spiritual cleansing that comes by the work of the Spirit through the Word, not by outward forms (John 15:3; 17:17; Ephesians 5:26; Titus 3:5; 1 Peter 1:23).

Enter into—or, share in and enjoy.

Only begotten—unique, one of a kind. The same word is used of Isaac (Hebrews 11:17; Genesis 22:2).

B. Our Unity

(See Teaching Tip 5.)

The members of the Triunity are one in purpose, will, and desire. They work in perfect harmony. We can be one as the Father and Son are one. You do not become the same person as your brother or sister in Christ. But you can be one in purpose to obey God, to share the fellowship, gifts, and graces of the Holy Spirit, and to exalt our Lord Jesus. The Son loves the Father and does the Father's will. The Father and the Son send the Spirit. The Spirit glorifies Jesus and reveals the Father. We do not have to understand the Trinity. All we need to do is accept the love, the blessing, and the promise that is ours. Then we can join in worship, service, and praise to the one true God who is manifest in three wonderful Persons.

Guideline for Living 4

With regard to the special unity that exists among Christ's followers, R. V. G. Tasker makes the following comment: "This unity, like the love which produces it, is supernatural; it is fundamentally the same as the unity that exists between the Father and the Son. This is why the world, when it sees such unity among believers, will be led to recognize the divine mission of Jesus" (*The Gospel According to John,* Tyndale New Testament Commentaries).

IV. Active in Salvation
John 3:1-8, 16, 17

John 3:5. Jesus answered, Verily, verily, I say unto thee, Except a man be born of water and of the Spirit, he cannot enter into the kingdom of God. 16. For God so loved the world, that he gave his only begotten Son, that whosoever believeth in him should not perish, but have everlasting life. 17. For God sent not his Son into the world to condemn the world; but that the world through him might be saved.

A. God Sent His Son

There is no greater love than the love of God the Father as He gave His Son to die a horrible, shameful, cruel death on the cross.

"Only begotten" is one word in the Greek. In New Testament times it had lost the meaning of "begotten," and came to mean "only" in the sense of unique, special, one of a kind. It is closely related to God's own words where He said, "This is my beloved Son." It also connects with the typology where God asked Abraham to offer his only son whom he loved (Genesis 22:2; Hebrews 11:17). Isaac was thus called Abraham's "only begotten" son in the same sense. That is, Isaac was the son of promise. He was therefore Abraham's "only" son in a unique, special relationship that Ishmael could not share. So Jesus is the Son of God in a special sense that He alone can claim and that no one else can ever share. God loved Him. Yet God loved the world and gave Him for our salvation.

B. Jesus Fulfilled Redemption's Plan

God's purpose of blessing for all the families of the earth was revealed to Abraham (Genesis 12:3). God also revealed His plan of redemption in many types and shadows in the Old Testament.

But as the Book of Hebrews especially points out, all of these types were fulfilled in Jesus. By believing in Him, trusting continually in Him, committing ourselves fully, totally, daily to Him, we shall never perish. That is, we shall escape from the eternal death of the lake of fire which would otherwise be inevitable. More than that, we shall be saved, which means we shall enter into the full inheritance God has prepared for us.

C. The Holy Spirit Brings New Life

It means to be born from above. In our physical birth we receive physical life from our parents. But the one who is born again has new life from heaven because he is born of the Spirit. The Holy Spirit ministers the life of the risen Christ to us, and as we remain in Christ by continuing in faith, that life continues to flow (John 15:5).

Guideline for Living 5

Each Person of the Holy Trinity works for essentially one purpose—to bring man to God. How awesome it is to realize that we are the focus of the attention of God the Father, God the Son, and God the Holy Spirit. How thankful we ought to be each day for love and grace that is beyond our human comprehension. It is that love and grace emanating from the presence of God that draws us, saves us, keeps us, and sustains us now and throughout eternity. Glory to the Father, Son, and Holy Spirit!

LIVING THE TRUTH

We do not have to understand the mystery of the Trinity to experience and enjoy fellowship with God. In fact, we sometimes do not fully appreciate things we can explain from a natural point of view. We have all heard illustrations that were an attempt to help portray the three-in-one aspect of the Trinity, but they always fall short of really throwing light on such a tremendous truth. The Bible teaches the Trinity and if we are believers we have experienced the quickening, comforting presence of the Godhead many times. We walk by faith, not by sight. Thank God for holy mysteries!

EVANGELISM OUTREACH

This week's session has placed a good deal of emphasis upon salvation. Have a moment of silent prayer, asking each class member to carefully evaluate his or her spiritual condition. Invite any who will to pray with you and other committed Christians so that they might find new life in Christ.

Question.

What does it mean to be born again?

TEACHING TIP 6

Overview the working together of the Trinity in effecting the plan of salvation by using the following symbolic illustration:

God the
Father
sent His
Son
who
gave
His
life for
our sins
so that
He might
send His Holy
Spirit who
dwells within.

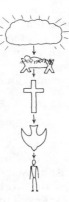

Daily Devotional Guide

M. The Father's Providence. Nehemiah 9:6-15

T. The Father's Call to Repentance. Ezekiel 18:30-32

W. The Son Speaks. Matthew 5:13-16

T. The Son's Love. John 15:1-11

F. The Holy Spirit Speaks. Acts 13:1-5

S. The Holy Spirit Indwells. 1 Corinthians 3:10-17

SATAN'S NATURE

8

SEEING THE SCRIPTURES

Job 1:12

12. And the Lord said unto Satan, Behold, all that he hath is in thy power; only upon himself put not forth thine hand.

Ephesians 6:10-16

10. Finally, my brethren, be strong in the Lord, and in the power of his might.

11. Put on the whole armor of God, that ye may be able to stand against the wiles of the devil.

12. For we wrestle not against flesh and blood, but against principalities, against powers, against the rulers of the darkness of this world, against spiritual wickedness in high places.

13. Wherefore take unto you the whole armor of God, that ye may be able to withstand in the evil day, and having done all, to stand.

14. Stand therefore, having your loins girt about with truth, and having on the breastplate of righteousness;

15. And your feet shod with the preparation of the gospel of peace;

16. Above all, taking the shield of faith, wherewith ye shall be able to quench all the fiery darts of the wicked.

Revelation 20:7-10

7. And when the thousand years are expired, Satan shall be loosed out of his prison,

8. And shall go out to deceive the nations which are in the four quarters of the earth, Gog and Magog, to gather them together to battle: the number of whom is as the sand of the sea.

9. And they went up on the breadth of the earth, and compassed the camp of the saints about, and the beloved city: and fire came down from God out of heaven, and devoured them.

10. And the devil that deceived them was cast into the lake of fire and brimstone, where the beast and the false prophet are, and shall be tormented day and night for ever and ever.

SETTING THE SCENE

This is God's world. He made it. But there is a usurper who has invaded the world and tries to claim it and everyone on it. He is introduced in the third chapter of the first Book of the Bible. The twelfth and twentieth chapters of the last Book of the Bible refer to him as that old serpent, the devil, and Satan.

PREPARING TO TEACH

Study Text

Job 1:6-12; Luke 11:18; John 8:44; 14:30; 2 Corinthians 4:4; Ephesians 2:2; 6:10-18; 1 John 2:13, 14; 3:8; Revelation 20:1-3; 7-10

Outline

I. His Character
   A. The Wicked One
   B. The Ruler of Darkness
II. His Power and Limitations
   A. The Accuser
   B. Limited to What God Permits
III. His Destiny
   A. The Bottomless Pit
   B. The Lake of Fire

Golden Text: Put on the whole armor of God, that ye may be able to stand against the wiles of the devil. Ephesians 6:11

Central Truth: The power of Christ within us gives victory over every evil force.

Learning Goals

1. To understand the character and nature of Satan.
2. To recognize Satan's power and limitations.
3. To determine to be prepared to ward off Satan's ruthless attacks.

GETTING STARTED

Military leaders know that one of the most important factors in winning a battle is to know your enemy. You must know your enemy. You must know his strengths, capabilities, and weaknesses. Otherwise you may be overwhelmed at a time when you least expect it.

As Christians we are continually engaged in a fierce battle. We must know our enemy Satan. We cannot afford to ignore him.

Initiate this week's focus on the nature of Satan by asking the students to write the letters of the alphabet (excluding X) vertically on a sheet of paper. Then ask that they list as many adjectives describing Satan as they can think of, using the alphabet letters. Take a few moments afterward to share responses.

Clarification

Ye have overcome the wicked one—you have conquered and continue to be victorious over the evil one.

Wiles—crafty schemes, deceitful strategy.

Principalities—rulers, demonic powers.

Powers—authorities, powerful demons.

Rulers of the darkness of this world—world rulers of this darkness, that is, of this sinful world.

Spiritual wickedness in high places—the spirit forces of evil in the heavenlies (probably meaning the first heaven, the atmospheric heavens where the birds fly and the clouds are).

Fiery darts of the wicked—flaming arrows of the evil one.

Question.

What does Paul warn against in Ephesians 6:11?

Some today deny the existence of a personal devil. They suppose that sin and evil are merely the absence of good, just as darkness is the absence of light. Turn the light on and the darkness disappears. So just give us more education and more science and evil will disappear.

Does it really work that way? The world has never had any more education and science than today. Yet there is more violence and corruption than ever. The world is still in the power of the evil one (1 John 5:19). He is the prince of the power of the air (Ephesians 2:2). He is the god of this world (2 Corinthians 4:4), the chief of the powers of darkness (Ephesians 6:12).

BIBLE COMMENTARY

I. His Character

1 John 2:13, 14; Ephesians 6:10-16

1 John 2:13. I write unto you, fathers, because ye have known him that is from the beginning. I write unto you, young men, because ye have overcome the wicked one. I write unto you, little children, because ye have known the Father. Ephesians 6:11. Put on the whole armor of God, that ye may be able to stand against the wiles of the devil. 12. For we wrestle not against flesh and blood, but against principalities, against powers, against the rulers of the darkness of this world, against spiritual wickedness in high places. 16. above all, taking the shield of faith, wherewith ye shall be able to quench all the fiery darts of the wicked.

A. The Wicked One

(See Teaching Tip 1.)

Someone has said that God is a good God and the devil is a bad devil. Both John and Paul refer to Satan as the wicked one because his nature is evil, bad, wicked. The same word is used of evil, base, worthless, vicious, degenerate persons. It is used of wicked, vile sins. It is used of evil, unclean spirits. But Satan is the evil one above all other evil ones. He is the most evil, the most wicked of all the beings in the universe.

Even young people can win and keep the victory over Satan. We need only use the power we have in Christ and keep full of the Word of God. (See 1 John 2:14.)

B. The Ruler of Darkness

We must not become complacent, however. Even though we have the assurance we are on the winning side, we must not treat the battle against Satan lightly. Those who deny the reality of the devil, demons, and evil spirits usually treat sin lightly as well. They are blinded by the darkness, the sin of this world. They themselves are the slaves of Satan, unwitting promoters of his schemes.

He warns against the wiles, the crafty schemes, the deceitful strategy of the devil. Whether we realize it or not, we are in a

TEACHING TIP 1

Divide the class into study groups of three or more, or have the students work in pairs. Provide the following questions, statements, and Scripture verses on the chalkboard, chart, or overhead transparency. These will help establish the origin and nature of Satan.

1. What is another name for Satan? (Isaiah 14:12) What does the name mean?

2. Describe Satan's first estate? (Ezekiel 28:12-19)

3. What was the root cause of Satan's downfall? (Isaiah 14:13, 14; Ezekiel 28:15, 17)

4. What characteristics of Satan are listed in the following verses?

2 Corinthians 4:4
Ephesians 2:2
1 Peter 5:8

An alternative to having groups discuss the statement and questions would be to provide this information for the basis of a student report.

TEACHING TIP 2

Use the overhead transparency from PATH as you overview the full armor of God.

Question.

What protection is available to us?

Question.

Does this mean we must display to others how good and righteous we are?

battle. Satan, the enemy of our souls, is very clever. He is not on the defensive. He is subtle as he plans his attack.

In a similar vein, 2 Corinthians 2:11 speaks of the devices, the evil designs, the evil plots of Satan. In the context we see that the church at Corinth was slow to forgive a repentant brother. This created a danger that Satan might get an advantage to outwit the believers and rob them of this brother. But Paul says this need not happen, for we are not ignorant of Satan's evil designs.

Ephesians 6:12 shows that our real enemies are not the people the devil uses but a well-organized army of evil spirit forces. The devil is the chief ruler of the darkness of this sinful world. Under him are other world rulers of this darkness, this atmosphere of sin and unbelief. One example might be the prince of Persia mentioned in Daniel 10:13. In addition, Satan has massed under him other demonic power and other spirit forces of evil. Because they are spirits we cannot see them with our physical eyes. But we can see all around us the tragic results of their activities. It is no accident that so many of the rulers of this world are evil. It is no accident that so many boys and girls with good upbringing are trapped by the drug culture. It is no accident that the major part of automobile-caused fatalities are the result of drunken driving. It is no accident when jealousy, greed, or sin split churches. These are all part of the wiles, the evil designs of the devil.

Guideline for Living 1

A quick scan of daily news headlines, news magazine articles, and other media reports clearly reveals the presence of a supernatural evil influence in our world. Even many who profess no particular religious faith are inclined to admit there are evil powers at work that are beyond the realm of our understanding. Crime is rampant, the family is disintegrating, wars abound, drugs and alcohol are consumed by people of all ages. Satan's influence is widespread; it cannot be denied.

Concern is warranted. Yet what an opportunity for the believer to share the hope and security that is in Jesus Christ. Those who fear the cataclysmic events of our world today can find true peace through the Prince of Peace who has overcome the prince of this world.

Only God is infinite. Only God is everywhere present. Satan is a finite, created being who fell from his original estate. So he cannot be everywhere at the same time. He depends on the evil spirits or demons who are marshaled to do his will. (See Teaching Tip 2.)

The Bible uses the armor of the Roman soldier of that day to give us a picture of the full armor, the full protection God has provided for us.

First, take your stand after you have girded your waists with truth. Like a soldier's belt, the truth of the gospel keeps everything together and allows us to move freely and confidently against the enemy. We know where we stand and we know where we are going.

Then we put on the breastplate of righteousness.

Paul makes it clear we do not stand in any righteousness of our

The nature of demon possession is clearly revealed in various New Testament passages. Arrange for a student to give a brief report on this matter based upon Scripture texts such as the following:

Matthew 4:24; 8:16; 9:32; 12:22; 17:15-18; Mark 5:1-8

How wonderful it is to know that Satan's demonic spirits do not have access to the believer's life.

Question.

All this armor is for our protection. Is it enough to keep on the defensive against Satan?

Question.

What else is necessary if we are to use the sword of the Spirit effectively?

Clarification

The sons of God—supernatural beings, as the context indicates.

Satan—the Satan; not a proper name but a title mean-

own. We stand in Christ's righteousness. He provides a cleansing, a righteousness through His blood that protects our hearts from both the temptations and accusations of the enemy.

Next we put on the shoes, sandals, or boots of readiness to spread the good news of peace. When ancient soldiers put their boots on they were ready to move out. Christians win victories against Satan by always being ready to tell others about Jesus who is our peace.

Most important is the shield of faith. The shield here was long and oblong, big enough to protect the complete body from a whole volley of flaming arrows. This lets us know too that neither Satan nor any of his demons or evil spirits can get near us as long as we keep our faith in Jesus. Notice, too, that all the fiery darts or flaming arrows come from the outside. This is another assurance that though Satan and his demons may attack the believer, they cannot enter in or take possession of any part of him—body, soul, or spirit. Faith is the victory that overcomes both the world and the evil that dominates it. That conquering faith is an obedient faith that involves total commitment to and complete trust in our Lord.

As we continue in faith, salvation is our helmet. The fact that our sins are forgiven and we have an inheritance as children and heirs of God protects our minds from the attacks of Satan.

We must also take the sword of the Spirit and learn to let the Spirit use the Word through us to attack the enemy and win victories for Christ and the gospel.

Ephesians 6:18 shows that prayer, watchfulness, and perseverance must back up the Word. Without prayer and a determination to persevere it is easy to let down our guard. Satan is watching for just such an opportunity. Let us never forget that we are in a battle.

Guideline for Living 2

It has been observed that the full armor of God makes no provision for protecting the back; only a frontal armor is described. Is it any wonder that this should be? An elementary rule of combat is that you must face your enemy. To turn your back would be fatal.

In our combat with Satan we must face him squarely with our armament in place. To turn our back as if to ignore Satan's presence would quickly bring spiritual disaster.

We can be confident in our warfare that the full armor of God will be more than sufficient to ward off Satan's attack. Our concern must always be whether we are so equipped. We cannot afford to take our adversary lightly. He is more powerful than the best of human wisdom can withstand. Let us daily clothe ourselves spiritually with the invincible armor of God.

II. His Power and Limitations

Job 1:6-12

Job 1:6. Now there was a day when the sons of God came to present themselves before the Lord, and Satan came also among them. 8. And the Lord said unto Satan, Hast thou considered my servant Job, that there is none like him in the earth, a perfect and

ing the adversary, the accuser. A related verb means to bear a grudge against or harbor animosity toward.

From going to and fro— implies going over it carefully first in one direction and then in another to be sure he did not overlook anything he could use to accuse men.

Perfect—complete, whole, well-rounded, well-adjusted spiritually and morally. Implies balance and integrity rather than absolute perfection or sinlessness.

Escheweth—avoids, keeps far from.

Touch—harm, hurt.

In thy power—in your hand.

Question.

What did Satan make his chief business?

TEACHING TIP 4

Take a few moments to discuss the following questions.

1. Has Satan ever accused you of something you have done or not done? (Perhaps there are some who would be willing to share instances when they felt accused of Satan.)

2. What are some common accusations Satan may bring against us?

3. What effect may Satan's accusations have on us spiritually and emotionally?

4. How can we best overcome Satan's accusations?

an upright man, one that feareth God, and escheweth evil? 9. Then Satan answered the Lord, and said, Doth Job fear God for nought? 11. But put forth thine hand now, and touch all that he hath, and he will curse thee to thy face. 12. And the Lord said unto Satan, Behold, all that he hath is in thy power; only upon himself put not forth thine hand.

A. The Accuser

The Book of Job shows us something Job was never allowed to see. It reveals a scene in heaven where sons of God, probably angels, present themselves before the Lord. Among them comes an intruder, the Satan, the accuser, the adversary. Some commentators suppose that all these sons of God were adversaries and that Satan comes among them as their chief. But the phrase "among them" does not imply in any way that they were a part of his company. Nor do they take part in any of the activities of Satan that follow.

Others suppose that Satan was the official "attorney general" appointed by God to bring men to judgment. But there is no indication that Satan belongs here in God's court. Even though he has access to heaven, he is an intruder.

His very title, "the satan," implies that he brings his accusations against mankind because of animosity. This hatred of man that Satan cherishes may go back to the beginning. God created man in His own image with the capability of becoming not only a son but an heir of God. Jealousy and pride not only caused Satan's fall, but made him "the accuser of our brethren" (Revelation 12:10). The Greek word *diabolos* translated "devil" confirms his evil purpose and nature. It means a slanderer, one who makes malicious accusations. (See Teaching Tip 4.)

He searched back and forth over the earth, looking for things to use against men.

Guideline for Living 3

Depression is almost epidemic in our society today. It is too prevalent even within the Christian community. Depression is characterized by despondency, a feeling of worthlessness and failure. Those suffering depression are often lethargic and continually negative in their attitude toward other people, their jobs, themselves, and the world in general.

Certainly Satan has his hand in this dread emotional state. It is his task to constantly bombard our minds with accusations, uncertainties, anxieties, and fears. He delights in bringing us to a point of complete despair over life's problems and perplexities. Even the most minor difficulties can be blown completely out of proportion. If given free reign with our emotions, Satan can cause us to move into a deep depression that may take months or years to overcome.

What is the answer? We must daily rely on the counsel of God's Word, spend time in prayer, and regularly fellowship with other believers in God's house and on other occasions. As we commit ourselves to serving God with all our heart, mind, and soul, no opening is left for Satan to gain access against us. We can be completely victorious.

Question.
What was at stake here?

Question.
What further encouragement do we have that Job did not have?

TEACHING TIP 5
It is important for each of us occasionally to evaluate our motives for serving Jesus Christ. Suggest the following acrostic of the word *motive* in relation to Job and to every believer.

More
Of
Thee, O Lord
In
View of
Eternity

Our motive for service ought to be one of knowing our Lord in a more personal way with eternal values constantly in view.

Clarification
The bottomless pit—the abyss, translated "the deep" in Luke 8:31 and Romans 10:7. (See also Revelation 9:1, 2, 11; 11:7; 17:8.) It is considered here as the abode of demons and Satan's headquarters.

Dragon—serpent.

That old serpent—the ancient snake. (See Genesis 3:1, 15; 2 Corinthians 11:3, 14.)

Shut him up—locked him up.

Deceive—lead astray, cause to wander from the right way, as well as deceive.

The breadth of the earth—rather, the broad plateau of the land (of Israel).

The beloved city—Jerusalem.

Brimstone—sulfur.

B. Limited to What God Permits
The evil, vindictive nature of Satan is also seen in the fact that he refused to admit that Job was the true servant of God he seemed to be. His claim that Job's motives were not pure implied that no man ever serves God except out of selfish desires for gain and prosperity. Satan was claiming all mankind for himself. (See Teaching Tip 5.)

God's own integrity as well as His purpose for man was being challenged. Would anyone serve God out of real love and faith? Thus God allowed Job to become a test case. But Satan could only go as far as God permitted and no farther. This is a great encouragement to us. Satan does have power. But he is not all-powerful. God is still on the throne and He knows what Satan is doing.

We have the Bible. We also have the assurance that we have an Advocate with the Father, Jesus Christ the righteous (1 John 2:1). He is at the right hand of the Father, interceding for us. As long as we keep our trust in Him we are on the winning side in this battle against Satan.

III. His Destiny
Revelation 20:1-3, 7-10
Revelation 20:1. I saw an angel come from heaven, having the key of the bottomless pit and a great chain in his hand. 2. And he laid hold on the dragon, that old serpent, which is the Devil, and Satan, and bound him a thousand years, 3. and cast him into the bottomless pit, and shut him up, and set a seal upon him, that he should deceive the nations no more, till the thousand years should be fulfilled: and after that he must be loosed a little season. 10. And the devil that deceived them was cast into the lake of fire and brimstone, where the beast and the false prophet are, and shall be tormented day and night for ever and ever.

A. The Bottomless Pit
(See Teaching Tip 6.)

The time is coming when Satan will no longer have access to either heaven or the earth. During the thousand years of Christ's reign on earth, Satan will be locked up and sealed in the pit, the abyss, that is, in the very depths of what we might call hell.

We learn more about Satan's nature and character in this passage. He is the same old serpent who tempted Eve in the Garden of Eden. But the earth will be free of his temptations, his accusations, his slander against God for the duration of the Millennium.

Most important, he will no longer deceive the nations, the peoples, during this period. Jesus called Satan a liar and the father or author of lies. Jesus also pointed out that Satan was a follower of his own desires and was a murderer from the beginning (John 8:44, 45). He is the one who has turned the peoples of the earth from the truth of God.

B. The Lake of Fire
For a thousand years after Satan is bound, the entire world will enjoy the wonderful, glorious reign of our Lord Jesus Christ. Then Satan will be loosed for a short time.

He comes out as still the deceiver and makes one last campaign

Tormented—a word used in other places sometimes of physical torture, sometimes of mental torture.

TEACHING TIP 6

Reproduce the following outline on the chalkboard or overhead transparency to put Satan's final defeat into perspective in relation to the order of end-time events.

I. The Second Coming (Rapture)
   A. Saints caught up to be with Christ
   B. Beginning of Great Tribulation on earth
   C. Judgment Seat of Christ
   D. Marriage Supper of the Lamb

II. The Second Coming (Revelation)
   A. Occurs at end of the Great Tribulation
   B. Christ returns with His saints
   C. Battle of Armageddon
   D. Satan bound for 1,000 years

III. The Millenium
   A. One-thousand-year reign of Christ on earth
   B. Satan loosed for a short season
   C. Battle of Gog and Magog—final defeat of Satan (cast into lake of fire)
   D. White Throne Judgment

IV. New Heavens and New Earth

Daily Devotional Guide

M. Prayer for Protection. Psalm 5:1-12

T. God Is Our Refuge. Psalm 46:1-7

W. A Safe Dwelling Place. Psalm 91:1-16

T. Power Over the Tempter. Matthew 4:1-11

F. Overcoming the World. 1 John 5:1-5

S. Kept From Falling. Jude 17-25

against the people of God. But God is still on the throne. Fire from heaven comes and devours those Satan has deceived. Then the devil himself is thrown into the lake of fire.

It is everlasting. (Matthew 25:41.) Other passages show it can never be quenched or extinguished. (See Matthew 3:12; Mark 9:43-48; Luke 3:17.)

We see also that it was not prepared for man but for the devil and his angels. People go there only because they allow the devil to deceive them. The sad thing is that even after the world sees how wonderful Christ's rule can be, many will follow Satan and end up with him in final separation from God in the lake of fire.

LIVING THE TRUTH

Clearly Satan is the author of all that is evil. It is he who by nature can bring nothing good to our lives. His supreme desire is that we be brought low and defeated spiritually. Yet, as God's children we need not live in subjection to Satan's evil devices. If we will give ourselves daily to God's Word and to prayer, we can live above Satan's influence. Our God is far more powerful than all the forces of evil. His overcoming power is available to all who will trust in Him.

EVANGELISM OUTREACH

Perhaps there are some who are experienceing Satan's fiery darts of accusation, fear, and anxiety. It may be that they have not committed themselves to Christ as their Lord and Saviour. Help these students to realize that through Christ they can receive victory over Satan and live in peace and security.

9 | SATAN'S WORKS

PREPARING TO TEACH

Study Text
Genesis 3:1-7; Matthew 13:36-43; 2 Corinthians 11:4; Colossians 2:13-15; James 4:6-10; 1 Peter 5:8, 9; 1 John 3:4-8

Outline
I. Enemy of God
   A. The Wicked One
   B. The Plot Fails
II. Enemy of Man
   A. A Clever Question
   B. A Denial and an Accusation
III. Defeated by Christ
   A. Defeated at the Cross
   B. Satan's Works Destroyed
IV. The Believer's Victory
   A. Resist the Devil
   B. Humble Yourselves

Golden Text: For this purpose the Son of God was manifested, that he might destroy the works of the devil. 1 John 3:8

Central Truth: Christ came to destroy the works of Satan.

Learning Goals
1. To examine the works of Satan in the world and in the lives of men.
2. To recognize that Satan is a powerful foe.
3. To appreciate the fact that Christ has defeated Satan.
4. To determine to resist Satan's devices through diligent spiritual living.

SEEING THE SCRIPTURE

Genesis 3:1-7

1. Now the serpent was more subtile than any beast of the field which the Lord God had made. And he said unto the woman, Yea, hath God said, Ye shall not eat of every tree of the garden?

2. And the woman said unto the serpent, We may eat of the fruit of the trees of the garden:

3. But of the fruit of the tree which is in the midst of the garden, God hath said, Ye shall not eat of it, neither shall ye touch it, lest ye die.

4. And the serpent said unto the woman, Ye shall not surely die:

5. For God doth know that in the day ye eat thereof, then your eyes shall be opened, and ye shall be as gods, knowing good and evil.

6. And when the woman saw that the tree was good for food, and that it was pleasant to the eyes, and a tree to be desired to make one wise, she took of the fruit thereof, and did eat, and gave also unto her husband with her; and he did eat.

7. And the eyes of them both were opened, and they knew that they were naked; and they sewed fig leaves together, and made themselves aprons.

Matthew 13:36-39

36. Then Jesus sent the multitude away, and went into the house: and his disciples came unto him, saying, Declare unto us the parable of the tares of the field.

37. He answered and said unto them, He that soweth the good seed is the Son of man;

38. The field is the world; the good seed are the children of the kingdom; but the tares are the children of the wicked one;

39. The enemy that sowed them is the devil; the harvest is the end of the world; and the reapers are the angels.

Colossians 2:15

15. And having spoiled principalities and powers, he made a show of them openly, triumphing over them in it.

James 4:7

7. Submit yourselves therefore to God. Resist the devil, and he will flee from you.

SETTING THE SCENE

We cannot blame everything on the devil. But everyone who steps out in faith to serve the Lord and spread the gospel soon finds that the enemy of our souls is active and diligent. We find

GETTING STARTED

During the week prior to this study, ask several students to bring from newspapers or magazines headlines or clippings that reflect Satan's work in our world. Encourage them to find examples of his influence in various sectors of society—in politics, the home, the environment, in our physical bodies and minds, and perhaps in or against religious institutions.

In class call for a brief review of the students' findings. You may wish to categorize some of the instances according to their realm of influence. Emphasize that Satan is indeed at work in our world today.

Clarification

Children of—sons of; used as in the Hebrew to mean all those who share the qualities of or all who belong to.

Tares—the bearded darnel; a rye-like grass *(Lolium temulentum)* still found frequently as a weed in fields of grain. In the early stages of its growth it resembles wheat, but is easily distinguished when ripe. Sometimes it becomes infected with the mold, ergot, and then it is poisonous. Perhaps for this reason it was always burned in ancient times.

The end of the world—the conclusion, consummation, or end of this present age. The Greek word for "world" in verses 39 and 40 is *aion,* used here to mean a great era or period of time. In verse 38 a different Greek word, *kosmos,* was translated "world," meaning the world as a whole or the mass of mankind.

TEACHING TIP 1

Distribute copies of the "Parable Comparatives" work sheet from PATH. Ask the students to examine Matthew 13:36-39 and fill in the "Is Compared to" side of the chart. This will help clarify the significance of Jesus' Parable of the

also that no matter where we go in this world we cannot escape contending with those who are under Satan's influence.

Some have tried to withdraw from the evils of human society by going into the wilderness or joining a monastery. But we do not win victories for Christ that way. Jesus taught His disciples they were to be in the world even though they were not of it (John 15:19; 17:14-18). We are not to partake of the world's sins. On the other hand, we must not turn our backs on the needs of those who are bound by Satan.

As we consider this study, let us be encouraged. Though Satan is at work all around us, he is already a defeated foe. Our Lord Jesus, the Son of God, won the decisive victory at Calvary. His purpose is to destroy all the works of the devil.

BIBLE COMMENTARY

I. Enemy of God

Matthew 13:36-43

Matthew 13:38. The field is the world; the good seed are the children of the kingdom; but the tares are the children of the wicked one; 39. the enemy that sowed them is the devil; the harvest is the end of the world; and the reapers are the angels. 40. As therefore the tares are gathered and burned in the fire; so shall it be in the end of this world.

A. The Wicked One

(See Teaching Tip 1.)

In the first part of Matthew 13 Jesus gave the Parable of the Sower who scattered the seed everywhere. The disciples needed to know that the response to the gospel would sometimes be disappointing, but this must not discourage them. There would be good ground. There would be people who would hear, understand, and bring forth fruit.

Then Jesus followed this with another parable where a man sowed good seed, but his servants found weeds in the field.

There were too many for these to be just a few weeds such as might appear normally in a wheat field. The Greek word in Matthew 13:25 indicates that the field was covered thoroughly and sown thickly with the seeds of the tares, the darnel, a most troublesome weed. This was the work of an enemy, an organized plot to spoil the work of the sower who was so careful to sow good seed.

Jesus wanted His disciples to know they were in a battle. The comparison of a farmer sowing seed did not give the full picture. There was an enemy at work, and they could expect some active countersowing.

Just as the tares were sown in an attempt to crowd out the wheat, so Satan, God's enemy, has his active agents everywhere attempting to discourage God's children. Jesus knew what this meant from personal experience. After He was tempted by the devil we read that the devil "departed from him for a season" (Luke 4:13). But Satan's agents were still active. Scattered through the crowds who came to hear Jesus were some whose only purpose was to try to get Him to do or say something they could use to accuse him before the authorities. (See, for example, Luke 6:7.) They thought they were pursuing their own interests. But they were really doing the work of the one who is "the accuser of the brethren." With divine insight, Jesus knew what was in their hearts. (Compare John 2:25.) Finally, He had to tell some of them, "Ye are of your father the devil, and the lusts [desires] of your father ye will do" (John 8:44). Thus, in this parable Jesus identified the tares with the children of the wicked one. They are people who are dominated by sin and unbelief. They are doing Satan's work and carrying out his desires even when they think they are carrying out their own plans.

In the parable, the servants of the owner wanted to pull the tares up by the roots. But the master refused.

For the sake of the wheat. This is a hard thing for most of us to understand. It is easy for us to ask why God puts us out in a field to grow and mature spiritually when that field is so full of people who want to do nothing but hinder us.

For one thing, God never made any spiritual giants out of hot-house plants. But the reason Jesus gave was that we may harm some of God's choice saints if we start weeding, tearing up, and pulling out. All of us can make mistakes. Luther shut out the Anabaptists. The Puritans shut out the Baptists and the Quakers. Some churches today shut out the Pentecostals.

Guideline for Living 1

A chunk of black carbon becomes a diamond only after it has been subjected to intense heat and pressure for many centuries. Even then the gem must undergo careful grinding and polishing before it achieves its true brilliance.

A cutting edge of an axhead can be sharpened only by the roughness of a grindstone or file.

These illustrations relate closely to the presence of "tares" in the world where the Christian must live. The presence of ungodliness all around serves to sharpen and more clearly define our Christian life and witness. Our Christianity is "polished" by the abrasiveness of those who do not believe and would detract us from the faith. We are made to seek God's wisdom and guidance through prayer and Bible study.

Although the influence of Satan's tares may destroy some of the wheat, there are many who are strengthened in their faith because of a determination to resist evil and maintain a strong Christian character. May it be so with every believer.

B. The Plot Fails

God knows those who are His. Romans 5:8-10 shows us that the God who loved us enough to send His Son to die for us surely loves us enough to make available everything we need to see us all the way to heaven.

We also see that God will make the separation in the end of the age. He will send His angels and we can be sure that they will make no mistakes. In the meantime, let us not carry the analogy too far. By the power of the gospel tares can be changed into wheat. Or, as Colossians 1:12, 13 puts it, we have a wonderful Father who has delivered us from the power of darkness and has translated us into the kingdom of His dear Son.

Guideline for Living 2

What should be our attitude as Christians toward the tares that exist around us?

Sin and evil can never be completely uprooted and destroyed in this present age. Such an attempt would be as fruitless as trying to drain the ocean with a bucket. Satan's forces and influence are everywhere.

The writer of the *Adult Teacher* states, "By the power of the gospel tares can be changed into wheat." In light of this, our attitude toward the ungodly should be one of concern and compassion, not eradication. We ought to do all we can through the power and prompting of the Holy Spirit to change tares into wheat. That should be our greatest retaliation against the forces of evil.

II. Enemy of Man

Genesis 3:1-7

Genesis 3:1. Now the serpent was more subtile than any beast of the field which the Lord God had made. And he said unto the woman, Yea, hath God said, Ye shall not eat of every tree in the garden? 4. And the serpent said unto the woman, Ye shall not surely die: 5. for God doth know that in the day ye eat thereof, then your eyes shall be opened, and ye shall be as gods, knowing good and evil.

A. A Clever Question

Satan appears as man's enemy shortly after man was created.

It does not. But Revelation 12:9 and 20:2 make it very clear who that old serpent was. God permitted him in the Garden of Eden just as He permitted him to test Jesus and just as He still permits him to test us. (See Teaching Tip 2.)

1. Satan chose an agent Eve did not mistrust. Satan usually works through agents. Even Peter, when Jesus talked of His coming death and resurrection, tried to turn his Master from the path of duty. Then Jesus looked beyond Peter and said, "Get thee behind me, Satan" (Matthew 16:22, 23).

2. Though Satan is a liar, he did not start with an obvious or outright lie. He is too clever for that. Instead, he introduced a question intended to throw a doubt on whether God really wanted Adam and Eve to be like Him. This is still Satan's usual method. He begins by questions that stir doubt. He makes insidious innuendos with the purpose of breaking down our faith and trust in God.

Guideline for Living 3

Subtlety is Satan's favorite and most deadly tactic. Seldom if

---

Clarification

Subtile—shrewd, clever, crafty—thus considered by Satan to be a suitable means or guise.

Yea—indeed, really; suggests surprise, astonishment.

Be as gods—that is, be like gods or like God (the Hebrew can mean either) and live on a higher level of existence.

Question.

Does Genesis call this serpent Satan or the devil?

Question.

What can we learn from the way Satan approached Eve?

TEACHING TIP 2

In relation to Satan's choosing agents to mislead us, discuss the following:

1. Who or what are some agents today that may cause us to stray from the truth?

2. How does this relate to Ephesians 4:14 and 1 John 4:1?

3. What is our best defense against being sidetracked by Satan's crafty devices?

Perhaps there is someone in your class or church who

would be willing to share an experience regarding Satan's subtle influences. If so, ask that person to share a brief testimony at this time. This may be helpful to those who can identify with such a problem and it may help someone who is presently under the subtle attack of Satan.

TEACHING TIP 3

Eve's temptation and fall is characteristic of many who are deceived by Satan. Review the progression of Eve's downfall as follows. This may be done on the chalkboard or overhead transparency.

EVE	BACKSLIDER
Looked: Saw the tree was good	Sees world and its attractions
Lusted: Desired to become wise	Begins to long after worldly pleasures
Accepted: Took the fruit	Fails to see the harm in earthly pleasures
Partook: Ate the fruit	Actively partakes of the world's pleasures
Shared: Gave fruit to Adam	Others influenced by our sins

Encourage the students to carefully examine their own lives to see if there may be this kind of progression at work. It may be appropriate to have a time of prayer to permit a time of introspection and commitment to serve Christ.

Clarification

Sins—transgressions, acts of sin.

Uncircumcision—that is, outside the covenants and promises of God and full of the sins and vices of a pagan world.

Quickened—made alive.

Trespasses—transgressions, acts of sin.

Handwriting—bond, certificate showing what was owed.

Spoiled—disarmed.

Made a show of them—exposed them to public disgrace.

Committeth—practices.

The transgression of the law—lawlessness.

ever does a Christian fall from his faith in one sudden step. It is a long, often unnoticed process.

Satan has a vast array of plans whereby he may erode our Christian experience. He may work through those with whom we work or play. He influences us through what we read or watch on TV. Satan knows our areas of weakness even better than we know them. It may be sex, wealth, or a desire for power and recognition. If Satan is allowed access to any area, he will take full advantage.

How needful it is that we immerse ourselves in the things of God. Only then can our hearts, minds, and actions remain pure.

B. A Denial and an Accusation

When Satan saw his suggestions were taking effect, he took advantage of Eve's wavering and attempted to lead her into unbelief. Boldly and emphatically he contradicted God's Word and denied God's truthfulness. Satan loves to pose as an angel of light, pretending to emancipate people from "outdated" ideas (2 Corinthians 11:14)! But underneath he is still a roaring lion, seeking whom he may devour (1 Peter 5:8).

In verse 5 Satan accused God of impure motives and unfairness. He made it appear that God was witholding something which was really good for man. At the same time he focused Eve's attention on the thing God said she could not have.

Satan did not need to force Eve to eat. Once Eve let her attention dwell on the forbidden fruit she used her own reason to justify the desire that arose in her. Then she made her own choice. No sinner can ever put all the blame on Satan.

III. Defeated by Christ
Colossians 2:13-15; 1 John 3:4-8

Colossians 2:13. And you, being dead in your sins and the uncircumcision of your flesh, hath he quickened together with him, having forgiven you all trespasses; 14. blotting out the handwriting of ordinances that was against us, which was contrary to us, and took it out of the way, nailing it to his cross; 15. and having spoiled principalities and powers, he made a show of them openly, triumphing over them in it. 1 John 3:4. Whosoever committeth sin transgresseth also the law: for sin is the transgression of the law. 5. And ye know that he was manifested to take away our sins; and in him is no sin. 6. Whosoever abideth in him sinneth not: whosoever sinneth hath not seen him, neither known him. 8. He that committeth sin is of the devil; for the devil sinneth from the beginning. For this purpose the Son of God was manifested, that he might destroy the works of the devil.

A. Defeated at the Cross

Those of whom Jesus said they were of their father the devil eventually did their worst and handed our Lord over to be crucified. (See Teaching Tip 4.)

Though the world did not know it, He was fulfilling His Father's plan. He who knew no sin was made sin for us (2 Corinthians 5:21). All the sin and guilt of sinning mankind was nailed with Him on that cross. Thus all that is written in God's books against us was

Sinneth not—does not practice sin, does not make sin his life-style.

Sinneth—practices sin.

Question.

How does this put the principalities and powers of Satan and his armies to public disgrace?

Question.

Should sin ever be treated lightly?

TEACHING TIP 4

Sketch the following cartoon figures to help illustrate the victory we have over sin and death through Jesus' sacrifice on Calvary.

Explain that had it not been for the sacrifice of Jesus, mankind would have been doomed to sin and subsequent death. However, as we believe in the sacrifice of Jesus for our sins, there is a bridge formed that allows us to move from death unto life. In this way Satan is defeated.

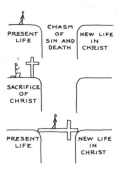

Question.

What does the believer have within him that helps him in the battle against sin?

Clarification

The proud—those who with haughty arrogance claim to be superior.

Submit—take a humble position, recognizing that God is worthy of our respect and love; then obey Him.

Resist the devil—set yourself against, take your stand against.

nailed there and was thus taken away. Praise God, when we confess our sins, not only are we cleansed (1 John 1:9) but God's books are cleansed and not one thing stands against us.

The cross was meant to bring public disgrace. But it brought glory to Christ. By it God showed that all the power of Satan and all his demon powers have done cannot stand in the presence of one drop of the blood of Jesus. The Resurrection removed all the shame of the Cross for Jesus. Now the disgrace falls on Satan and all his hierarchy, for in the Cross Jesus triumphed over Satan and left him a defeated foe.

B. Satan's Works Destroyed

John says in our "Study Text" that Jesus was manifested to take away our sins. He was also manifested, revealed, appeared on earth to destroy the works of the devil. The very price He paid in giving His own life should let us know that sin is never to be treated lightly.

Guideline for Living 4

Sin is like the low flame of a candle that attracts a butterfly. The beautiful, winged insect flies around the candle, first at a safe distance, then moving closer and closer. Suddenly a wing touches the flame and is ignited, bringing death to the butterfly.

Sin is deadly. It is a poison. We dare not take it lightly even for a moment. Satan and his evil forces are ever ready to ensnare us further until we are consumed and destroyed.

First Thessalonians 5:22 instructs us to avoid even the appearance of evil. In this way we will avoid the snares of Satan and enjoy lives that are in peace and harmony with Jesus Christ.

It is true that we may sin, and if we confess our sins He is still our Advocate with the Father. He will still cleanse us of all unrighteousness. But if we belong to Jesus we cannot practice sin. We cannot make sin our life-style, our habit. Those who do so belong to the devil, not to Jesus, no matter what the profession of their lips may be. Actually, the sinner is promoting the works of the devil that Jesus came to destroy. Thus the persistent sinner is like the devil, an enemy of both God and man.

As 1 John 3:9 goes on to say, we have that seed, that life of Christ ministered by the Holy Spirit. We cannot be happy sinning. We cannot practice sin, for the fruit of that life is seen in deeds of righteousness and love.

IV. The Believer's Victory

James 4:6-10

James 4:6. He giveth more grace. Wherefore he saith, God resisteth the proud, but giveth grace unto the humble. 7. Submit yourselves therefore to God. Resist the devil, and he will flee from you. 8. Draw nigh to God, and he will draw nigh to you. Cleanse your hands, ye sinners; and purify your hearts, ye doubleminded. 9. Be afflicted, and mourn, and weep: let your laughter be turned to mourning, and your joy to heaviness. 10. Humble yourselves in the sight of the Lord, and he shall lift you up.

Doubleminded—implies doubt, hesitation.

Be afflicted—lament your wretched condition.

Heaviness—gloominess, dejection.

Lift you up—exalt you.

Question.

Why do some people fail when they try to set themselves against the devil?

Question.

To whom does God give grace and help?

Question.

What has God promised to do if we humble ourselves as we draw near to Him?

TEACHING TIP 5

Duplicate the following items on the chalkboard or overhead transparency. Write the heading, "Resistance Profile." Encourage the students to evaluate their resistance to Satan in view of the items listed.

Yes No

____ ____ I read my Bible daily
____ ____ I pray daily
____ ____ I regularly attend church
____ ____ I frequently share my faith with others
____ ____ I control what I watch on TV
____ ____ I am careful about what I read
____ ____ I control my thoughts and desires

Daily Devotional Guide

M. God Is Our Shield. Psalm 84:1-9

T. Give Thanks for Victory. Psalm 107:1-9

W. Strength Renewed. Isaiah 40:27-31

T. Assurance of Victory. 1 Corinthians 10:1-13

F. Jesus Is Victor. Hebrews 2:10-15

S. Greater Is He That Is in You. 1 John 4:1-6

A. Resist the Devil

(See Teaching Tip 5.)

The devil knows very well he is a defeated foe. His demons also believe and tremble (James 2:19). But he still tries to deceive us. If he can put us under fear, doubt, or condemnation, he will keep on taking advantage of us. But if we take our stand against him, he knows what our resources are and who our Helper is. He will flee from us.

They may be trusting in their own strength, thinking they are better than others. But God opposes the proud.

B. Humble Yourselves

To the humble who submit to Him, honoring Him for who He is and drawing near to Him. It means quitting our sin. It means coming before Him without doubt or hesitation. The Bible is quite emphatic here. There is a place for joy and laughter. But when sin, especially the sin of pride or self-exaltation, sets God against us, it is time for real repentance. This will mean real tears, real sorrow as we let the Spirit of God do His work of conviction of sin.

He will draw near to us. What fellowship, what sharing of joy we shall have then! He will lift us so close to Him. He will exalt us and we shall share His victory.

LIVING THE TRUTH

Satan is subtle and clever. His power must never be underestimated. Yet as Christians we are given the promise that if we will resist the devil, he will flee from us. We must remember, however, that our resistance must be a daily one. We can never afford to relax our guard. Let us daily seek counsel from God's holy Word and allow His Holy Spirit to guide us into all truth. Thus we will overcome the wiles of the devil.

EVANGELISM OUTREACH

Encourage any who may not know Christ to realize that they can live in victory over Satan's influence through a right relationship with God. Be prepared to pray and counsel with anyone who wishes to find new life and hope in Christ.

ANGELS

SEEING THE SCRIPTURES

Nehemiah 9:6

6. Thou, even thou, art Lord alone; thou hast made heaven, the heaven of heavens, with all their host, the earth, and all things that are therein, the seas, and all that is therein, and thou preservest them all; and the host of heaven worshippeth thee.

Psalm 91:11, 12

11. For he shall give his angels charge over thee, to keep thee in all thy ways.

12. They shall bear thee up in their hands, lest thou dash thy foot against a stone.

Daniel 6:22

22. My God hath sent his angel, and hath shut the lions' mouths, that they have not hurt me: forasmuch as before him innocency was found in me; and also before thee, O king, have I done no hurt.

Luke 1:11-16

11. And there appeared unto him an angel of the Lord standing on the right side of the altar of incense.

12. And when Zechariah saw him, he was troubled, and fear fell upon him.

13. But the angel said unto him, Fear not, Zechariah: for thy prayer is heard; and thy wife Elisabeth shall bear thee a son, and thou shalt call his name John.

14. And thou shalt have joy and gladness; and many shall rejoice at his birth.

15. For he shall be great in the sight of the Lord, and shall drink neither wine nor strong drink; and he shall be filled with the Holy Ghost, even from his mother's womb.

16. And many of the children of Israel shall he turn to the Lord their God.

Acts 10:3-6

3. He saw in a vision evidently, about the ninth hour of the day, an angel of God coming in to him, and saying unto him, Cornelius.

4. And when he looked on him, he was afraid, and said, What is it, Lord? And he said unto him, Thy prayers and thine alms are come up for a memorial before God.

5. And now send men to Joppa, and call for one Simon, whose surname is Peter:

6. He lodgeth with one Simon a tanner, whose house is by the sea side: he shall tell thee what thou oughtest to do.

Hebrews 1:7, 13, 14

7. And of the angels he saith, Who maketh his angels spirits,

PREPARING TO TEACH

Study Text

Genesis 16:7; 19:1-25; Judges 2:1-5; 6:11-24; 1 Kings 19:5; 2 Kings 19:35; Nehemiah 9:6; Psalm 91:11, 12; Daniel 6:22; Matthew 1:18-24; 2:13, 19, 20; 13:41, 42; 28:2-7; Luke 1:5-20, 26-38; Acts 1:10, 11; 5:19; 10:3-6; 12:7, 23; 27:23, 24; Colossians 1:16; 2 Thessalonians 1:7, 8; Hebrews 1:7, 13, 14; 12:22; Revelation 7:1-3; 9:15; 15:1

Outline

I. Origin and Characteristics
  A. Created by God
  B. Powerful Spirit Beings
II. Servants of God
III. Agents of Judgment
  A. Past Judgments
  B. Future Judgments
IV. Ministers to Believers

Golden Text: He shall give his angels charge over thee, to keep thee in all thy ways. Psalm 91:11

Central Truth: God's angels serve Him, minister to believers, and carry out acts of judgment.

Learning Goals

1. To understand the origin, nature, and work of angels.
2. To appreciate God's provision of supernatural beings who work for our good and welfare.
3. To recognize that angels are instrumental in effecting the purposes of God in our world.

GETTING STARTED

Angels have been the subject of much speculation and controversy in recent years. Yet angels are a reality and are at work in our world today. Perhaps the increased interest in accounts of angelic visitation is an indicator that we are truly living in the last days. God is making every effort to prepare His people for His coming.

Set the stage for this week's discussion by asking two students to share the brief accounts of angelic visitation provided in PATH. Encourage an attitude of openmindedness toward this important aspect of the supernatural intervention of God.

Clarification

Host—the word is sometimes used of angels, sometimes of stars.

Thrones, or dominions, or principalities, or powers—enthroned angels, or bearers of ruling power, or angelic ruling powers, or angelic authorities. All these words were used of angels to whom false teachers paid worship as if they were superior to Christ.

An innumerable company—myriads. A myriad was ten thousand, the largest number commonly used in New Testament Greek.

Question.

Who is the Creator of all things?

Question.

Why does the Bible emphasize this?

and his ministers a flame of fire.

13. But to which of the angels said he at any time, Sit on my right hand, until I make thine enemies thy footstool?

14. Are they not all ministering spirits, sent forth to minister for them who shall be heirs of salvation?

SETTING THE SCENE

How many have seen an angel? Though angels are mentioned nearly three hundred times in the Bible, actually not very many people saw them in Bible times. At least, angels did not appear in visible form every day or even every year. Yet it is clear that angels are active in heaven as well as all around us on earth. The Book of Revelation pictures ten thousand times ten thousand plus thousands of thousands more, all gathered around the throne in heaven. There they sing loud praises to Jesus, God's Lamb.

The word *angel* in both the Hebrew and the Greek is the ordinary word for a messenger. The Old Testament word is translated "messenger" about 98 times, the New Testament word seven times. But in practically all the cases where these words are translated "angel," the context shows that a supernatural messenger of God is meant.

It was a great encouragement to God's people in Bible times to know angels were surrounding them. We too can be encouraged, for we know they are with us too.

BIBLE COMMENTARY
I. Origin and Characteristics

Nehemiah 9:6; Colossians 1:16; Hebrews 12:22

Nehemiah 9:6. Thou, even thou, art Lord alone; thou hast made heaven, the heaven of heavens, with all their host, the earth, and all things that are therein, the seas, and all that is therein, and thou preservest them all; and the host of heaven worshippeth thee. Colossians 1:16. By him were all things created, that are in heaven, and that are in earth, visible and invisible, whether they be thrones, or dominions, or principalities, or powers: all things were created by him, and for him. Hebrews 12:22. Ye are come unto mount Zion, and unto the city of the living God, the heavenly Jerusalem, and to an innumerable company of angels.

A. Created by God

The Bible is clear. God alone is the Creator. As we have seen in previous studies the entire Triune Being, the Father, Son, and Holy Spirit all cooperated in the work of creation. But most passages which speak of creation speak of the material world and visible created beings. Nehemiah 9:6 and Colossians 1:16 are careful to include the invisible spirit world with its countless angels as well. God created them all.

False teachers ascribed to angels powers they do not have. Some imagined they took part in the work of creation. But the Hebrew never uses the verb *create* with any other subject than God. Some even put angels higher in authority and power than our Lord Jesus. But God through Jesus made them, just as He made everything else (John 1:3).

On the chalkboard or over-head transparency write the following headings:

ANGELS

| Characteristics | Powers |
| Appearance | Abilities |

Draw a vertical line as indicated. Then instruct various students to read aloud the following Bible passages. Fill in the information regarding angels under the appropriate heading on the chart.

Daniel 10:5,6
Matthew 28:2, 3
Luke 2:9
John 20:12
Acts 12:7-10
Revelation 10:1

TEACHING TIP 2

It is important to recognize the difference between angels and man. Although these created beings have great powers and abilities, these are some significant reasons why the redeemed man has an even greater position in the economy of God.

Billy Graham, author of *Angels: God's Secret Agents,* outlines the following distinctions. List these on an overhead transparency or on the chalkboard as you discuss them.

1. *Angels are not heirs of God.* These beings must stand aside when believers attain the riches and glory of their eternal abode.

2. *Angels cannot testify of salvation by grace through faith.*

3. *Angels have no experiential knowledge of the indwelling God.*

Being saved through Christ is not necessary for angels, since holy angels have not fallen from grace and are in no need of salvation. Angels already possess the needed power from God to perform their tasks.

Guideline for Living 1

Within the realm of the supernatural, caution must always be exercised against attributing too much authority to any power other than the Persons of the Triune Godhead. Only God is worthy of our worship and praise. This truth is borne out by the angel's response to John's attempt to worship him (Revelation 22:9). The angel rebuked John by saying, "See thou do it not: for I am thy fellow servant, and of thy brethren the prophets, and of them which keep the sayings of this book: worship God."

Heightened interest in angelic visitations can cause some to place these beings on a higher plane than intended by God. It is important to recognize that angelic intervention is the outworking of God's purposes for His people. Thus our praise, honor, and service must always be directed to God and Him alone.

B. Powerful Spirit Beings

(See Teaching Tip 1.)

Old Testament Israelites recognized that angels were good (1 Samuel 29:9), wise (2 Samuel 14:17, 20), and powerful (Zechariah 12:8). They recognized that angels worshiped God, giving Him praise and thanks (Psalms 103:20, 21; 148:2). When angels did appear to them, God usually gave them the form of young men. The same was usually true in New Testament times. On occasion, however, they appeared in dazzling light or enveloped in the glory of the Lord (Luke 2:9). They also appeared clothed all in white (John 20:12).

These appearances are, however, temporary. By their nature they do not have a physical body, but are spirits (Hebrews 1:7, 14). Probably, God creates a temporary body for them since angels themselves cannot create. (See Teaching Tip 2.)

Colossians 1:16 also shows us angels are arranged or organized into hosts or armies, probably with archangels or an archangel at their head. The Bible names only one archangel, Michael (Jude 9). There he is called the archangel, that is, the chief angel. Thus it may be that he is the archangel whose voice is heard when Jesus comes back to earth again (1 Thessalonians 4:16). Jewish tradition spoke of seven archangels: Uriel, Raphael, Raguel, Michael, Sariel, Gabriel, and Jeremiel. Later Church tradition said Satan was also an archangel before he fell. But there is no specific mention in the Bible of any archangel other than Michael. Luke 1:26, Gabriel is said to be simply an angel, not an archangel.

II. Servants of God

Judges 2:1-15; 6:11-24; Matthew 28:2-7; Luke 1:5-20, 26-38; Acts 1:10, 11; 10:3-6; Hebrews 1:7

Judges 2:4. It came to pass, when the angel of the Lord spake these words unto all the children of Israel, that the people lifted up their voice, and wept. 6:12. The angel of the Lord appeared unto him, and said unto him, The Lord is with thee, thou mighty man of valor. 22. And when Gideon perceived he was an angel of the Lord, Gideon said, Alas, O Lord God: for because I have seen

4. *Angels do not marry or procreate.* Angels are sexless beings, neither married nor given in marriage as indicated in Matthew 22:30.

Clarification

In a vision evidently—in a real appearance, clearly and distinctly. He actually saw the angel. It was no dream, no figment of the imagination.

Ministers—servants.

Question.

What do the Scripture passages in our "Study Text" show about the ways angels serve God?

TEACHING TIP 3

As servants of God, angels perform a variety of tasks to effect the outworking of God's will in the affairs of men. As the various Scriptural incidents of angelic ministry and intervention are shared from the commentary, ask the students to suggest the kinds of ministry performed by angels. These may be developed as follows:

Judges 2:1-5—Warning of God's judgment

Judges 6:11-24—Natural intervention; commissioning for ministry

Luke 1:5-20—Affirmation of answered prayer; judgment upon faithlessness

Acts 1:10, 11—Prophecy

Acts 10:3-6—Commendation; direction

Question.

What other passages can you think of that show angels are God's servants, doing His will, carrying His messages?

an angel of the Lord face to face. 23. And the Lord said unto him, Peace be unto thee; fear not: thou shalt not die. Matthew 28:2. Behold, there was a great earthquake: for the angel of the Lord descended from heaven, and came and rolled back the stone from the door, and sat upon it. 3. His countenance was like lightning, and his raiment white as snow. Luke 1:11. There appeared unto him an angel of the Lord standing on the right side of the altar of incense. 12. And when Zechariah saw him, he was troubled, and fear fell upon him. 26. And in the sixth month the angel Gabriel was sent from God unto a city of Galilee, named Nazareth. 30. And the angel said unto her, Fear not, Mary: for thou hast found favor with God. Acts 1:10. While they looked steadfastly toward heaven, as he went up, behold, two men stood by them in white apparel. 10:3. He saw in a vision evidently, about the ninth hour of the day, an angel of God coming in to him, and saying unto him, Cornelius. Hebrews 1:7. Of the angels he saith, Who maketh his angels spirits, and his ministers a flame of fire.

As messengers of God, the angels are so totally consecrated and dedicated to the service of God that Jesus called them "holy angels" (Matthew 25:31). They stand in strong contrast to the devil and his angels, his messengers (Matthew 25:41). (See Teaching Tip 3.)

In Judges 2:1-5 an angel brought a warning that caused the people to weep and turn back to worship God.

In Judges 6:11-24, an angel brought the Lord's commission to Gideon to deliver Israel from the Midianites. The angel also gave him encouragement and confirmed the commission with the sign of fire consuming Gideon's sacrifice.

Matthew 28:2-7 shows how an angel came down from heaven and rolled away the great stone from the entrance of the tomb after Jesus rose from the dead. Then the angel told the woman Jesus had risen and commissioned them to be the first evangelists, the first to carry the good news.

Luke 1:5-20 tells how an angel told the father of John the Baptist that God had heard his (priestly) prayers (for the redemption of Israel) and would give him a son. This son would be filled with the Spirit from his mother's womb and would turn many to the Lord. The angel also gave Zechariah a sign. Because he was not quick to believe the angel's message, he would be unable to speak until the child was born.

A little later, in Luke 1:26-38, the angel Gabriel appeared to Mary and told her the good news that she was to be the mother of her Lord. Gabriel also explained that the Holy Spirit would overshadow her and the Holy Child would be the Son of God.

In Acts 1:10, 11, angels give God's promise that the very same Jesus who was then ascending into heaven would return from heaven in the very same manner He went away.

Acts 10:3-6 tells how an angel commended the Roman centurion Cornelius and directed him to send for Peter.

Hebrews 1:7 takes a quotation from Psalm 104:4 to show that angels are God's servants in contrast to Jesus who is God's Son.

There are many of them. Genesis 28:12, the ladder from heaven; 2 Kings 1:3, 15, angels gave directions to Elijah; Daniel 9:21, Gabriel's message of the 70 weeks; Zechariah 1:19, the angel who explained God-given visions; Acts 8:26, the angel who directed Philip to leave the great revival in Samaria and go down to the deserted road to Gaza are a few examples.

Guideline for Living 2

When we review the activity of God's holy angels in the affairs of men, we quickly realize that their sole purpose is to do the will of the Father. They are totally committed to that task. Angels are continually working to help bring about God's plan for mankind.

It is important to recognize, however, that angels do not proclaim the gospel to others. They are not commissioned to present the plan of salvation. That remains our task as believers. Angels may help effect the right conditions by removing hindering forces, but we must then proclaim the salvation message through the enablement of the Holy Spirit.

III. Agents of Judgment

Genesis 19:1-25; 2 Kings 19:35; Matthew 13:41, 42; Acts 12:23; 2 Thessalonians 1:7, 8; Revelation 7:1-3; 9:15; 15:1

Genesis 19:1. There came two angels to Sodom at even; and Lot sat in the gate of Sodom: and Lot seeing them rose up to meet them; and he bowed himself with his face toward the ground. 11. And they smote the men that were at the door of the house with blindness, both small and great: so that they wearied themselves to find the door. 13. We will destroy this place, because the cry of them is waxen great before the face of the Lord; and the Lord hath sent us to destroy it. 2 Kings 19:35. It came to pass that night, that the angel of the Lord went out and smote in the camp of the Assyrians a hundred fourscore and five thousand: and when they arose early in the morning, behold, they were all dead corpses. Matthew 13:41. The Son of man shall send forth his angels, and they shall gather out of his kingdom all things that offend, and them which do iniquity; 42. and shall cast them into a furnace of fire; there shall be wailing and gnashing of teeth. Acts 12:23. Immediately the angel of the Lord smote him, because he gave not God the glory: and he was eaten of worms, and gave up the ghost. 2 Thessalonians 1:7. To you who are troubled rest with us, when the Lord Jesus shall be revealed from heaven with his mighty angels, 8. in flaming fire taking vengeance on them that know not God, and that obey not the gospel of our Lord Jesus Christ. Revelation 7:2. I saw another angel ascending from the east, having the seal of the living God: and he cried with a loud voice to the four angels, to whom it was given to hurt the earth and the sea. 9:15. The four angels were loosed, which were prepared for an hour, and a day, and a month, and a year, for to slay the third part of men. 15:1. I saw another sign in heaven, great and marvelous, seven angels having the seven last plagues; for in them is filled up the wrath of God.

Clarification

All things that offend—or, all those who tempt or entice others to sin.

Do iniquity—practice lawlessness.

Taking vengeance—inflicting punishment.

Hurt—harm.

A. Past Judgments

Since God is a holy God, He brings judgment on sin. The Bible gives a number of examples where God used angels as agents of

Question.

Whom did Jesus mention first in Matthew 13:41?

His righteous judgment in the past. Angels brought judgment on the wicked city of Sodom. They were able to protect Lot in the city. Then they led him and his family out of the city and destroyed it. An angel destroyed 185,000 of the troops of Sennacherib in fulfilment of Isaiah's prophecy. An angel struck down King Herod Agrippa I when he failed to give God the glory. All these things were warnings to the world and encouraged God's people to worship and serve Him.

B. Future Judgments

(See Teaching Tip 4.)

God is still a holy God and He will carry out the judgments prophesied for the end of the age. Most of these will be carried out by angels as God's agents.

Those who offend God by tempting or enticing others to sin. Before the Flood the whole world had come to that condition. People were not satisfied to sin themselves. They had to try to drag others down with them. It was like this in the last days of Israel before God sent them into exile. Today also, as the New Testament foretold, evil men and seducers are growing worse and worse (2 Timothy 3:13). But the same judgment will fall on those who live lawless, careless lives that are indifferent to God and His Word.

Guideline for Living 3

How foolhardy for anyone to disregard the moral and spiritual principles of godliness! The consequences of such folly are evident on every hand. Rampant crime, economic upheavals, epidemics, drug abuse, alcoholism, and the disintegration of the home are but a few of the telltale signs of moral decay. Even the earth and universe seem to be "groaning and travailing."

Whether angelic forces are bringing about some of the current world conditions as acts of divine judgment is speculative. Yet the underlying principle of all that is happening is clear—God cannot and will not tolerate continued transgression of His laws. Judgment must come. How careful we ought to be to maintain a life of holiness. We should be equally concerned with reaching out to those who will soon know the wrath of a righteous God unless they repent and turn from their wicked ways.

The Book of Revelation also shows that special angels will be designated to bring about the judgments of the Tribulation period before Jesus comes with the multitude of angels and destroys the armies of the Antichrist.

IV. Ministers to Believers

Genesis 16:7; 1 Kings 19:5; Psalm 91:11, 12; Daniel 6:22; Matthew 1:18-24; 2:13, 19, 20; Acts 5:19; 12:7; 27:23, 24; Hebrews 1:13, 14

Genesis 16:7. The angel of the Lord found her by a fountain of water in the wilderness, by the fountain in the way to Shur. 1 Kings 19:5. As he lay and slept under a juniper tree, behold, then an angel touched him, and said unto him, Arise and eat. Psalm 91:11. He shall give his angels charge over thee, to keep thee in

Clarification

Ministering spirits—spirits in holy service.

Refer again to the incidents of angelic visitations given in PATH. Perhaps there are some in your class who have experienced angelic intervention, or you may know of someone within the church who can testify of such an experience. If so, allow time for sharing.

Question.

What kind of help did angels bring people in Bible times?

Question.

Are angels available to give us the same kind of help, direction, and deliverance today?

all thy ways. Daniel 6:22. My God hath sent his angel, and hath shut the lions' mouths, that they have not hurt me. Matthew 1:24. Joseph being raised from sleep did as the angel of the Lord had bidden him, and took unto him his wife. 2:13. when they were departed, behold, the angel of the Lord appeareth to Joseph in a dream, saying, Arise, and take the young child and his mother, and flee into Egypt. Acts 5:19. The angel of the Lord by night opened the prison doors, and brought them forth. 27:23. There stood by me this night the angel of God, whose I am, and whom I serve. Hebrews 1:14. Are they not all ministering spirits, sent forth to minister for them who shall be heirs of salvation?

(See Teaching Tip 5.)

Twice an angel gave direction and encouragement to Hagar—once when she fled from Sarah; once when Abraham sent her away (Genesis 16:7-11; 21:17, 18).

When Elijah was under the juniper tree an angel brought him two supernatural meals. He was able to go for forty days in the strength of that food.

When Daniel was thrown into the lions' den an angel closed the lions' mouths and thus spoiled the plot of Daniel's enemies and brought glory to God.

Three times angels appeared to Joseph, once to explain why he should take the virgin Mary as his wife, once to tell him to take the mother and Child to Egypt to escape King Herod's plot, and once to return from Egypt.

Twice in the Book of Acts an angel opened prison doors, once for the 12 apostles, once for Peter (Acts 5:17-19; 12:7-11).

Then when Paul was about to be shipwrecked on the Island of Malta, an angel gave him assurance that God would not only protect his life, but give him the lives of all the 276 people on board the ship.

The Old Testament sets no time limits on the promises of Psalms 34:7 and 91:11. The New Testament promise of Hebrews 1:14 shows God still sends out angels to minister to us. Usually, they appear only under unusual circumstances. But even when we cannot see them, they are present to minister to us.

Daily Devotional Guide

M. Angels Lead God's People. Exodus 23:2-27
T. Angels Are Innumerable. Psalm 68:7-17
W. Angels Stand Before God. Daniel 7:9-12
T. Angels Carry Believers to Heaven. Luke 16:19-31
F. Angels Comfort the Sorrowing. John 20:1-16
S. Angels Serve God. Revelation 8:1-4

LIVING THE TRUTH

When we consider the marvelous intervention of a mighty angelic host on our behalf we cannot help but be thankful for such providence. Let us daily praise God for His care. And let us walk circumspectly, for we may "entertain angels unawares."

EVANGELISM OUTREACH

Angelic intervention on our behalf is but one of the many benefits of salvation. How wonderful it is to know that God goes to such an extent to keep, protect, and guide us throughout our daily lives.

If there are those who do not know this assurance, encourage them to accept Jesus Christ as their personal Saviour.

11 | DEMONS

PREPARING TO TEACH

Study Text
Leviticus 20:27; 2 Chronicles 18:18-22; Matthew 8:28-34; 9:32, 33; 10:1; 12:43-45; 15:22-28; 25:41; Mark 1:23-26; 6:7; 9:17-27; Luke 4:40, 41; 10:17-19; 13:11-13; Acts 5:14-16; 8:5-7; 16:16-18; 19:11, 12; 1 Timothy 4:1; James 2:19; 2 Peter 2:4; Jude 6; Revelation 12:7-17

Outline
I. Workers of Evil
  A. Deceivers
  B. Wicked and Unclean
II. Subject to Christ
  A. Demons Recognized His Power
  B. Deliverance for All
III. Overcome by Faith
  A. Christ's Authority
  B. Special Miracles
IV. Demons' Final Punishment
  A. Cast Out of Heaven
  B. Final Judgment

Golden Text: I give unto you power to tread on serpents and scorpions, and over all the power of the enemy; and nothing shall by any means hurt you. Luke 10:19

Central Truth: Although demons have power, God limits their power and through Christ believers are victorious over them.

Learning Goals
1. To understand the nature and work of demonic spirits.
2. To recognize that demons are a reality not to be taken lightly.
3. To appreciate the fact that demons are subject to Christ's power and authority.
4. To stand upon the authority of the Word in fighting demon influence.

SEEING THE SCRIPTURES

Matthew 12:43-45

43. When the unclean spirit is gone out of a man, he walketh through dry places seeking rest, and findeth none.

44. Then he saith, I will return into my house from whence I came out; and when he is come, he findeth it empty, swept, and garnished.

45. Then goeth he, and taketh with himself seven other spirits more wicked than himself, and they enter in and dwell there: and the last state of that man is worse than the first. Even so shall it be also unto this wicked generation.

Luke 13:11-13

11. And, behold, there was a woman which had a spirit of infirmity eighteen years, and was bowed together, and could in no wise lift up herself.

12. And when Jesus saw her, he called her to him, and said unto her, Woman, thou art loosed from thine infirmity.

13. And he laid his hands on her: and immediately she was made straight, and glorified God.

James 2:19

19. Thou believest that there is one God; thou doest well: the devils also believe, and tremble.

Jude 6

6. And the angels which kept not their first estate, but left their own habitation, he hath reserved in everlasting chains under darkness unto the judgment of the great day.

SETTING THE SCENE

The word *demon* does not occur in the King James Version of the Bible. Actually, the word *demon* comes from the Greek word *daimon*, which is translated "devil" five times in the KJV. A closely related word, *daimonion*, is translated "devil" 59 times and "gods" once. These words are not related to the Greek *diabolos* ("slanderer") which is applied to Satan and is also translated "devil" 35 times.

Originally the ancient Greeks used both *daimon* and *daimonion* of the heathen gods, divinities, or spirits they worshiped. Thus the Greek philosophers in Athens mocked Paul as a preacher of "foreign divinities," using the word *daimonion* (Acts 17:18). But the Jews knew these words were used in heathen worship that was inspired by Satan and his demons, so they borrowed the words to describe demon spirits subject to Satan.

The Bible also refers to demons as evil spirits and as unclean spirits with the connotation that they are impure, vicious, and defiling. Let us not treat them lightly!

GETTING STARTED

On the chalkboard or overhead transparency, list the following:

Ouija boards
Seances
The Exorcist
Satan worship
Black magic

Ask: "What do these depict regarding the present age?"

The wave of "new morality" that swept our world in the late 60s and 70s brought about a tragic decline in the moral stability of our society. The loss of moral guidelines bred an increased interest in the occult and the supernatural. Satanism, demon possession, and demon oppression are realities which cannot be denied. Yet, for the believer there is hope and security in Christ.

Clarification

A familiar spirit—a spirit that pretends to be a spirit of the dead. That is, a man or woman who is a spiritist medium.

Wizard—one who claims to give prophecies by a spirit of the dead; a soothsayer.

Garnished—put in order and beautifully decorated.

Seducing—deceitful. Implies they are in deceivers and impostors whose purpose is to lead people astray.

Doctrines of devils—teachings inspired by demons.

TEACHING TIP 1

Provide a quick overview of the demon world by having the students look up the following Bible passages.

Existence—James 2:19; Revelation 9:20

Nature—Luke 4:33; 6:18

Activity—1 Timothy 4:1; Revelation 16:14

Opposition to the believer—Ephesians 6:10-20

Abode—Revelation 9:11

Ephesians 6:12 sheds further light on the world of demons by describing them as:

BIBLE COMMENTARY

I. Workers of Evil

Leviticus 20:27; 2 Chronicles 18:18-22; Matthew 12:43-45; 1 Timothy 4:1

Leviticus 20:27. A man also or woman that hath a familiar spirit, or that is a wizard, shall surely be put to death: they shall stone them with stones; their blood shall be upon them. 2 Chronicles 18:22. Now therefore, behold, the Lord hath put a lying spirit in the mouth of these thy prophets, and the Lord hath spoken against thee. Matthew 12:43. When the unclean spirit is gone out of a man, he walketh through dry places, seeking rest, and findeth none. 44. Then he saith, I will return into my house from whence I came out; and when he is come, he findeth it empty, swept, and garnished. 45. Then goeth he, and taketh with himself seven other spirits more wicked than himself, and they enter in and dwell there: and the last state of that man is worse than the first. 1 Timothy 4:1. Now the Spirit speaketh expressly, that in the latter times some shall depart from the faith, giving heed to seducing spirits, and doctrines of devils.

A. Deceivers

(See Teaching Tip 1.)

Demons are mentioned only a few times in the Old Testament. In his final song Moses equates them with foreign gods worshiped by the Israelites when they backslid (Deuteronomy 32:17). So does the Psalmist in Psalm 105: 37. Paul points out the same thing in 1 Corinthians 10:20. By this we can understand that demons take advantage of the heathen and whatever response their sacrifices bring is really from demons. The Bible also shows that the idols are nothing and that the heathen gods are no gods at all and have no real existence.

(See Teaching Tip 2 and 3.)

Demons were also involved in the occult practices of the heathen. Because of this the law of Moses warned the Israelites not to have anything to do with astrology, fortune-telling, or spiritist mediums. Such things are defiling and would make them unclean before God (Leviticus 19:26, 31). Any contact with the dead through spiritist mediums or the "wizards" was not only forbidden but would bring the judgment of God. The mediums themselves and the wizards were to be put to death. Even King Saul put to death all he could find. Only when he was at the end of his life and could get no word from God did he seek out a woman who claimed to be under the control of a spirit. When she knew who he was, she thought the king was setting a trap for her. It is clear also that when Samuel did appear, she was almost knocked out of her senses with surprise. This was something far more than the demon deceptions she was used to passing on to others (1 Samuel 28:3, 7, 9, 12).

Guideline for Living 1

What is wrong with astrology and horoscopes?

At the outset, it must be understood that astrology is a pseu-

1. Principalities
2. Powers
3. World rulers of darkness
4. Spirits of wickedness in the heavenly realm

TEACHING TIP 2

As a point of general information regarding the work and influence of demon powers, ask one or more individuals to present a brief report on some of the following areas of demonic activity:

black magic
psychic phenomena
palmistry
cartomancy
fortune-telling
astrology
psychometry

An investigation of these topics clearly underscores the widespread influence and activity of demon powers.

TEACHING TIP 3

Deception is the name of Satan's game. It is his objective to mislead and deceive mankind into believing that what he has to offer is as good if not better than what God has to offer. In so doing, Satan has devised a clever and subtle counterfeit of the influence of the Holy Spirit. Focus on this by presenting the "Satanic Counterfeits" overhead transparency from PATH. Use a sheet of paper and uncover subsequent points of comparison as you discuss them.

TEACHING TIP 4

Present the following questions for class discussion:

1. Although Christians cannot be demon possessed, can they be subject to demon oppression or influence?

2. What may be some characteristics of demon oppression?

3. How can we best battle against demon influence? (See Matthew 4:1-11; Ephesians 6:16; James 4:7; 1 Peter 5:8, 9.)

doscience. It is not based upon concrete, scientific fact. There is no evidence that planetary or stellar configurations have an effect on our behavior or future.

Astrology causes individuals to become dependent upon horoscopes rather than God's Word for daily direction. This places an individual on dangerous ground. It opens his mind to all kinds of satanic suggestions.

Interest in astrology characteristically parallels a nation's moral decline. This was true of the Roman empire and is becoming more and more evident in the world today.

God's Word and will must constantly be our source of direction. There is no other substitute. Astrology is a clever satanic device to counterfeit the leading of the Holy Spirit. It must have no place in the life of the believer.

It is evident also that mediums and heathen prophets actively sought to be possessed and thus were willing agents of the demons who possessed them. It is also apparent that men who claimed to be prophets of the Lord but actually prophesied for the money or to please the king instead of the Lord could be possessed by a lying spirit.

Paul warned Timothy that false teachers in the last days would be possessed by lying spirits. John also warned that we must try the spirits or put them to the test (1 John 4:1-6).

B. Wicked and Unclean

Both terms (demons and unclean spirits) are used in the account of the Gadarene demoniac (Luke 8:27-39). There also Jesus not only healed the man, but the man sat at the feet of Jesus (learning from Him) and then became a witness for Jesus.

In Matthew 12, the demon left looking for another resting place. Because the influence of the demon was no longer there, the man cleaned up his life, reformed, decorated everything nicely so that he seemed to be a wonderful person. But he had not replaced that old influence by the power and presence of Christ and the Holy Spirit. Thus, the demon returned with seven others more wicked than himself. (See Teaching Tip 4.)

Demons may leave a person, but that does not mean he is free from their power. Demons can actually do more of their wickedness through a man who is externally cleaned up and wealthy than when he had the appearance of a drunken bum. Those who are demon possessed need to be delivered, healed, and filled with God and His Word. Otherwise, like the Pharisees Jesus was talking to, they may be filled with more demons without knowing it.

II. Subject to Christ

Matthew 8:28-34; 9:32, 33; 15:22-28; Mark 1:23-26; 9:17-27; Luke 4:40, 41; 13:11-13; James 2:19

Matthew 8:29. Behold, they cried out, saying, What have we to do with thee, Jesus, thou Son of God? art thou come hither to torment us before the time? 9:33. When the devil was cast out, the dumb spake: and the multitudes marveled, saying, It was never

Clarification

What have we to do with thee—a phrase expressing rejection.

Grievously vexed with a devil—badly demonized, severely tormented by a demon.

Teareth him—dashes him down in a convulsion or spasm.

A spirit of infirmity—a spirit causing weakness.

Tremble—shudder from fear.

Question.

Why do the four Gospels have more to say about demons than any other part of the Bible?

Question.

Why was there a time when the disciples could not cast them out?

Question.

How did the demons respond to Jesus?

Question.

Does the New Testament blame all sickness on demon possession?

TEACHING TIP 5

Examine the response of demon powers to the person and presence of Jesus Christ by having the students read aloud or scan the following Bible passages:

Matthew 8:29
Mark 1:23, 24; 3:11; 5:7
Luke 8:28
Acts 19:15

Ask: "What assurance does this give us in our warfare against demonic forces?"

Question.

Did Jesus ever refuse to cast out a demon?

so seen in Israel. 15:22. Behold, a woman of Canaan came out of the same coasts, and cried unto him, saying, Have mercy on me, O Lord, thou Son of David; my daughter is grievously vexed with a devil. Mark 1:27. They were all amazed, insomuch that they questioned among themselves, saying, What thing is this? what new doctrine is this? for with authority commandeth he even the unclean spirits, and they do obey him. 9:18. Wheresoever he taketh him, he teareth him; and he foameth, and gnasheth with his teeth, and pineth away: and I spake to thy disciples that they should cast him out; and they could not. Luke 13:11. There was a woman which had a spirit of infirmity eighteen years, and was bowed together, and could in no wise lift up herself. 13. And he laid his hands on her: and immediately she was made straight, and glorified God. James 2:19. Thou believest that there is one God; thou doest well: the devils also believe, and tremble.

A. Demons Recognized His Power

Some believe Satan marshaled his armies of demons to bring special opposition to Jesus during His earthly ministry. More important, the Gospels show us the power of Jesus in every realm, both physical and spiritual. For the first time there was One on earth who could not only cast out demons, but could give the same power and authority to His disciples.

The record shows they were arguing instead of fasting and praying. (See Teaching Tip 5.)

They recognized Him for who He is, the Son of God, the promised Messiah and Saviour.

We see also that the demons tried to resist the command of Jesus and would tear or convulse people before coming out, sometimes even leaving them "as one dead." But they could not stay when Jesus said, "Go!" Neither could they stop Jesus from healing and restoring those they had afflicted.

Matthew 4:24 clearly distinguishes demon possession from sickness, disease, (physical) torments or pains, mental illness, and palsy or paralysis. Other passages show that various illnesses may be accompanied or induced by demon possession. But it is clear that this was not by any means always true.

Some skeptics today say that demon possession was just a way the ancients had of describing such things as mental illness and epilepsy. But the Bible never links demon possession with either. The descriptions of the way demons tore and convulsed their victims show clearly that they were not epileptic seizures. Demons did affect the mind and personality of those they possessed. But the Bible makes it clear that demon possession was by a personal demon, and was not caused by the pressures that bring on mental illness. These demons believed in God and Jesus and trembled.

B. Deliverance for All

He did test the woman of Canaan. He also permitted the legion of demons to enter a herd of pigs. But His compassion always reached out to those who were attacked by Satan or possessed by his demons. They always had to obey His command.

Guideline for Living 2

Can a born-again Christian be demon possessed?

Considerable controversy has arisen over this issue. Some have argued that it is possible for Christians to be demon possessed, while others take a firm stand against such a position.

Unfortunately, there are those who major on the subject of demon possession. Their teaching tends to become morbid and at times the experiences they relate are bizarre. One thing is always noticeable—they base their doctrine on experience, not Scripture. Nevertheless, Christians who tend to be fearful and apprehensive often fall into worse bondage when exposed to this type of teaching.

First of all, Jesus came to destroy the works of the devil (1 John 3:8). While on earth He healed all that were oppressed of the devil (Acts 10:38). We must not confuse Satan's attacks, such as temptation, with demon possession. Satan was allowed to test Job severely, even bringing terrible physical affliction upon him, but in no sense was Job demon possessed. As we study the effects of demon possession in the New Testament we see it is an extreme situation. The demon actually controls the individual, even speaking through his lips (Mark 5:9). A demon cannot possess a person who is at the same time filled with the presence of the Holy Spirit.

Through Christ God has "delivered us from the power of darkness" (Colossians 1:13). There is no Biblical basis for teaching that a child of God, washed in Jesus' blood and indwelt by His Spirit, can be possessed by a demon. God has not given us the spirit of fear (2 Timothy 1:7), and a spirit of fear is inevitably produced by the teaching that a Christian can be demon possessed.

III. Overcome by Faith

Matthew 10:1; Mark 6:7; Luke 10:17-19; Acts 5:14-16; 8:5-7; 16:16-18; 19:11, 12

Matthew 10:1. When he had called unto him his twelve disciples, he gave them power against unclean spirits, to cast them out, and to heal all manner of sickness and all manner of disease. Luke 10:17. The seventy returned again with joy, saying, Lord, even the devils are subject unto us through thy name. 19. Behold, I give unto you power to tread on serpents and scorpions, and over all the power of the enemy; and nothing shall by any means hurt you. Acts 5:16. There came also a multitude out of the cities round about Jerusalem, bringing sick folks, and them which were vexed with unclean spirits: and they were healed every one. 19:11. God wrought special miracles by the hands of Paul: 12. so that from his body were brought unto the sick handkerchiefs or aprons, and the diseases departed from them, and the evil spirits left them.

A. Christ's Authority

When Jesus sent out the Twelve and again when He sent out the Seventy, He gave them authority over demons to cast them out. After His resurrection He recommissioned His disciples and included the same thing among the signs which would follow those who believe (Mark 16:17).

Question.

What did the disciples mean when they said the demons were subject to them through the name of Jesus?

Question.

How can we avoid the presumption of these seven sons of Sceva?

TEACHING TIP 6

Demonology is a subject of which Christians should be aware without being preoccupied. We cannot afford to ignore the work of demons, but a balance must be maintained in our perspective. First of all, we must not go beyond the Bible's teaching no matter what kind of spectacular experiences we may hear about. Our thinking should be concentrated mainly on the Bible's great themes that relate to our redemption in Christ. Our faith should be positive. We must not spend our time cringing in fear of demonic powers. Having committed our lives to the Lord Jesus Christ, we should let His peace reign in our hearts.

We would do well to begin every day by reading the Scripture, "Ye are of God, little children, and have overcome them: because greater is he that is in you, than he that is in the world" (1 John 4:4). Write this Scripture on the blackboard. Encourage your students to memorize it and repeat it every day, claiming the victory of its promise.

Clarification

Everlasting fire—that is, the lake of fire, the second death (Revelation 20:10, 15).

Hell—Tartarus (not the usual word for hell); a place of punishment lower than Hades.

Chains of darkness—chains of the darkest hell.

It meant more than repeating the name, "Jesus." It meant more than saying words. To do something in or through the name of Jesus meant to act as His representative using His delegated authority. Acts 19:13-17 gives us an incident where the seven sons of Sceva tried to use the name of Jesus without knowing Him and without His giving them the assurance that they had His authority. The demon spoke through the demon-possessed man and said literally, "Jesus I recognize, and Paul I know about, but who are you?" Then the demon-possessed man jumped all over them and they ran out of the house naked and wounded.

Let us be sure we know Jesus in a personal, living relationship. In this age, too, we must remember that Jesus works in the Church through the Holy Spirit. Revelation 5 pictures Jesus at the Throne having seven horns and seven eyes which are the seven Spirits (or seven-fold Spirit) of God sent out into all the earth. The horns represent power. The eyes represent wisdom. Thus, we must by faith receive through the Holy Spirit the perfection of power and wisdom that will enable us to exercise the name, that is, the authority of Jesus against demons.

Guideline for Living 3

When we review the response of demons to the authority of Jesus Christ, we are reminded that there is indeed power in the name of Jesus. A simple whisper of His name in faith brings power beyond our comprehension. It is greater than all of Satan's forces. How wonderful it is to serve a Lord who is able to deliver us from evil!

B. Special Miracles

(See Teaching Tip 6.)

Paul was ministering in a great center of heathen worship. We can be sure there was an unusual concentration of demonic powers in that place. So God gave miracles there that were beyond the ordinary. Undoubtedly, we can still expect special, extraordinary miracles when opening up new areas where demon powers have been rampant.

IV. Demons' Final Punishment
Matthew 25:41; 2 Peter 2:4; Jude 6; Revelation 12:7-19

Matthew 25:41. Then shall he say also to them on the left hand, Depart from me, ye cursed, into everlasting fire, prepared for the devil and his angels. 2 Peter 2:4. If God spared not the angels that sinned, but cast them down to hell, and delivered them into chains of darkness, to be reserved unto judgment. . . . Revelation 12:9. The great dragon was cast out, that old serpent, called the Devil, and Satan, which deceiveth the whole world: he was cast out into the earth, and his angels were cast out with him. 12. Therefore rejoice, ye heavens, and ye that dwell in them. Woe to the inhabiters of the earth and of the sea! for the devil is come down unto you, having great wrath, because he knoweth he hath but a short time.

Some ancient manuscripts read, "the deepest pit of the darkest hell."

Question.

Is there a difference between Satan's angels and demons?

Question.

For whom was the lake of fire prepared?

A. Cast Out of Heaven

Jesus foresaw (and so did John) Satan cast out of heaven. Revelation 12:9 adds that his angels were also cast out. Thus the world at the end of the age will be subject to both the wrath of Satan and the wrath of God.

The Bible does not give us a clear answer and Bible students disagree. Perhaps we should keep in mind that angels are spirit beings, *angel* means "messenger," and demons act in behalf of Satan and therefore might be considered his messengers. But we must remember also that just as there are different classes of angels, there are different classes of demons. This may explain some of the difference of opinions.

B. Final Judgment

The Bible is clear about this. It was prepared for the devil and his angels. Since all who follow Satan will also be cast into the same lake of fire, it seems clear that all his angels and/or demons will be cast into it also. This lake of fire is outside the entire new creation. Thus it separates them forever and makes it impossible for them to spoil the new heaven and the new earth.

LIVING THE TRUTH

Warding off Satan's forces requires more than casual lip service. We must be continually filled with the Word of God and the power of the Holy Spirit. Only then can we be assured of a position of peace and security against the powers of darkness.

EVANGELISM OUTREACH

Demon oppression and possession are grim realities for many who are unsaved. Assure the students Christ gives deliverance and peace. Encourage any who may be suffering from Satan's devices to place their trust in Jesus and give their lives to His sovereign control.

Daily Devotional Guide
M. God Is With Us. Deuteronomy 31:3-8
T. The Lord Our Strength. Psalm 27:1-6
W. The Power of Jesus' Name. Mark 16:15-20
T. More Than Conquerors. Romans 8:35-39
F. Victory Through Faith. Hebrews 11:32-40
S. Overcomers Rewarded. Revelation 3:7-13

VISIONS AND DREAMS

SEEING THE SCRIPTURES

Genesis 37:5-11

5. And Joseph dreamed a dream, and he told it his brethren: and they hated him yet the more.

6. And he said unto them, Hear, I pray you, this dream which I have dreamed:

7. For, behold, we were binding sheaves in the field, and, lo, my sheaf arose, and also stood upright; and, behold, your sheaves stood round about, and made obeisance to my sheaf.

8. And his brethren said to him, Shalt thou indeed reign over us? or shalt thou indeed have dominion over us? And they hated him yet the more for his dreams, and for his words.

9. And he dreamed yet another dream, and told it his brethren, and said, Behold, I have dreamed a dream more; and, behold, the sun and the moon and the eleven stars made obeisance to me.

10. And he told it to his father, and to his brethren: and his father rebuked him, and said unto him, What is this dream that thou hast dreamed? Shall I and thy mother and thy brethren indeed come to bow down ourselves to thee to the earth?

11. And his brethren envied him; but his father observed the saying.

Acts 2:16, 17; 26:19

16. But this is that which was spoken by the prophet Joel;

17. And it shall come to pass in the last days, saith God, I will pour out of my Spirit upon all flesh: and your sons and your daughters shall prophesy, and your young men shall see visions, and your old men shall dream dreams.

26:19. Whereupon, O king Agrippa, I was not disobedient unto the heavenly vision.

SETTING THE SCENE

Throughout history mankind has had a great curiosity about dreams and their meaning. Many books have been written on the subject in both ancient and modern times. Most of this literature is pure speculation and of no real value. Some in modern times have theorized that the brain is always active and that we are dreaming all the time. However, studies dealing with brain waves seem to show this is not true. There is still much that we do not know about why we dream.

The Bible does show that God sometimes uses dreams as a means of revealing His will to individuals. Yet during most of Bible history, dreams and visions were not the primary means God used. Sometimes they were more prominent than at other times. Gen-

PREPARING TO TEACH

Study Text
Genesis 15:1; 20:3; 28:12; 31:11-13, 24; 37:5-11; 46:2; Deuteronomy 13:1-5; Ecclesiastes 5:3; Isaiah 6:1-8; Jeremiah 23:32; Daniel 2:1-45; 4:4-28; 7:1-28; Joel 2:28, 29; Matthew 1:20-23; 2:12, 13, 19, 20, 22; 27:19; Acts 2:16-19; 10:1-33; 16:9, 10; 23:11; 26:19

Outline
I. The Purpose of Visions and Dreams
II. Interpreting Visions and Dreams
  A. Meaningless Dreams
  B. False Dreamers
  C. God-Given and Clear
  D. God-Given and Needing Interpretation
III. Accompanying the Spirit's Outpouring

Golden Text:
It shall come to pass in the last days, saith God, I will pour out of my Spirit upon all flesh: and your sons and your daughters shall prophesy, and your young men shall see visions, and your old men shall dream dreams. Acts 2:17

Central Truth:
Although the Bible is our primary source of guidance there are occasions when God may give special direction to His people through visions and dreams.

Learning Goals
1. To gain insight into the realm of dreams and visions.
2. To recognize that God does use dreams and visions to speak to us.
3. To avoid attaching significance to every dream, premonition, or intuition.

Write the following question on the chalkboard or on an overhead transparency: "What did you dream about last night?" Follow through by asking the students to share with their neighbor what they dreamed. Some may not feel comfortable sharing their most recent dream, so let the students share any particular dream that was especially memorable.

Another approach may be to have two or three volunteers share dreams or visions that had a particular impact on their lives.

Do not put anyone on the spot with this activity. It is important to realize that, as a rule, we prefer to discuss matters which pertain to the observable, physical, rational world around us. Some may feel uncomfortable sharing experiences outside this realm.

Clarification

Vision—supernatural vision, Hebrew *mahazeh*. This word is used of visions of God only here (Genesis 15:1) and of the last vision of Balaam (Numbers 24:4, 16) and of the claims of false prophets who had really seen nothing (Ezekiel 13:3, 7).

Visions of the night—Hebrews, *mar'ot* used elsewhere only of God's word to the boy Samuel.

The year that king Uzziah died—739 B.C. (recent scholars).

I saw also the Lord—"saw" is the ordinary word for seeing with your eyes. The Bible does not explain how Isaiah saw the Lord. It seems he was in the court of the temple when suddenly he saw beyond the earthly temple to the heavenly temple.

In a vision evidently—in a supernatural vision clearly. In this case Cornelius was awake. The same word is also used of

esis mentions dreams about 38 times and visions twice. Daniel mentions dreams about 29 times and visions 31. Jeremiah mentions dreams about six times. Most of the other Old Testament Books do not mention them more than two or three times if at all. In the New Testament they are seldom mentioned outside of Matthew and Acts. Yet those which are mentioned are important.

BIBLE COMMENTARY

I. The Purpose of Visions and Dreams

Genesis 15:1; 46:2; Isaiah 6:1-8; Daniel 4:4-28; Acts 2:17; 10:1-33; 16:9, 10; 23:11; 26:19.

Genesis 15:1. After these things the word of the Lord came unto Abram in a vision, saying, Fear not, Abram: I am thy shield, and thy exceeding great reward. 46:2. God spake unto Israel in the visions of the night, and said, Jacob, Jacob. And he said, Here am I. Isaiah 6:1. In the year king Uzziah died I saw the Lord sitting upon a throne, high and lifted up, and his train filled the temple. 8. Also I heard the voice of the Lord, saying, Whom shall I send, and who will go for us? Then said I, Here am I; send me. Daniel 4:18. This dream I king Nebuchadnezzar have seen. Now thou, O Belteshazzar, declare the interpretation thereof, forasmuch as all the wise men of my kingdom are not able to make known unto me the interpretation: but thou are able; for the spirit of the holy gods is in thee. Acts 10:3. He saw in a vision evidently, about the ninth hour of the day, an angel of God coming in to him, and saying unto him, Cornelius. 5. Send men to Joppa, and call for one Simon, whose surname is Peter. 19. While Peter thought on the vision, the Spirit said unto him, Behold, three men seek thee. 16:9. A vision appeared to Paul in the night; There stood a man of Macedonia, and prayed him, saying, Come over into Macedonia, and help us. 26:19. Whereupon, O king Agrippa, I was not disobedient unto the heavenly vision.

What is the difference between dreams and visions? Some passages seem to use the words *dream* and *vision* interchangeably. But in the passages we are considering in this portion of our study the visions were genuine appearances which a person could see with his eyes open. Dreams in these passages are the same thing that the ordinary sleeper has when he sees things in his mind while asleep.

Let us take a look at these passages now and try to determine the purpose of the vision or dream in each case. (See Teaching Tip 1.)

1. In Genesis 15:1 we find Abram alone in his tent. He had just come back from rescuing Lot from the armies of four kings. Then he had had fellowship with Melchizedek and had refused to take the spoils from the king of Sodom. In all this he gave a great testimony to his faith in the Lord. Now in the darkness it seems he remembers how these kings had come back against Sodom.

supernatural visions given when a person is asleep. In either case they are very real and are not figments of the imagination. In other words, an angel actually came to him. The same word *horama* is used in Acts 10:19.

The heavenly vision—*horama* the supernatural vision from heaven. "Vision" here is the Greek *optasia* and is used of very special visions.

TEACHING TIP 1

Divide the class into study groups of three or more. Give each group or individual a copy of the work sheet from PATH. Ask the students to examine the passages listed and fill in the appropriate information.

If time does not allow each group to look up all the passages, assign one or two per group.

Another alternative would be to have the students complete the information as the commentary is presented.

TEACHING TIP 2

Inject the following thought questions as you discuss the Biblical examples of dreams in the commentary. These may not be answerable in a definitive sense but may heighten interest in the realm of dreams and visions. Follow through by presenting the "Guideline for Living"

1. Does it seem that there is little teaching today on God's speaking to us through dreams and visions? If so, why may this be the case?

2. May a de-emphasis on this area of divine communication be in conflict with Acts 2:17?

3. Are there dangers in giving a high degree of importance to dreams and visions? If so, what may they be?

4. Should we pay more attention to our dreams?

5. If dreams and visions are a way God communicates with man, are we missing a lot by not being more open to what

What would happen if they came back against him? Then he remembered all the spoil he had refused. What if he needed some of that some day? Suddenly, in a supernatural vision or appearance that must have made him conscious of the presence of God, a voice came giving him the assurance he needed. If the kings came back, God himself was there as his shield, his protection. If he would remain faithful, God himself would be His exceeding great reward. In other words, the purpose of the vision was to get Abram's attention on the Lord. God, in effect, is saying, "Be concerned with Me, and I will take care of everything else." Then, as we go on in the passage we see God challenging Abram's faith in Him with respect to His promise. After that God confirmed the promise by giving a covenant and sealing it with the sign of fire. This, we can be sure, brought a further strengthening of Abram's faith.

(See Teaching Tip 2.)

2. In Genesis 46:2 God spoke to Jacob to give him assurance that it was His will for him to go down to Egypt to be with Joseph. Then God confirmed to him the promise given to Abraham.

3. In Isaiah 6 God let Isaiah see a vision of His glory that humbled him and made him feel his need of cleansing. Then God provided the cleansing and Isaiah was able to see the need and respond to God's call.

4. Daniel 4 tells how a dream terrified King Nebuchadnezzar and prepared him for a humbling experience that made him glorify God.

5. Acts 2:17 shows dreams and visions will further the ministry of the Spirit.

6. Acts 10 shows how God sent an angel in an objective vision or appearance to reassure Cornelius and give him directions to send for Peter. Then as Peter was resting on the flat roof of the house of Simon the tanner, a feeling of amazement came over him and he saw a vision. This vision showed him his prejudice against Gentiles was wrong and prepared him to obey the voice of the Holy Spirit. The result was salvation and the baptism in the Holy Spirit for the Roman centurion Cornelius and all those friends gathered in his house.

7. Acts 16:9, 10 shows how a vision directed Paul west after the Spirit had checked him from going east. Thus Paul was impelled to bring the gospel to Europe.

8. In Acts 23:11 Jesus stood by Paul in the night and gave him assurance that God was going to use his imprisonment to give him an opportunity to testify for Christ in Rome.

9. Then in Acts 26:19 Paul declared that he had not been disobedient to the heavenly vision on the Damascus Road. There Jesus personally appeared to Paul, stopped him, changed him, and commissioned him to carry the gospel to the nations.

Some dreams and visions brought warnings. Some brought promises. Most brought direction and encouragement. All of them made the recipients very conscious of the reality of the presence of God.

Guideline for Living 1

Are dreams really important to us spiritually? Should a Christian consider every dream carefully? Does God regularly communicate with us through dreams?

God may be trying to say to us?

Biblical and experiential evidence clearly indicates that dreams can be of great significance. Yet, as with any supernatural experience, there is danger in overstressing the importance or unimportance of dreams. Maturity and understanding are needed.

God can and does speak to us through dreams. Most of us are not accustomed to thinking of our dreams as important, even though some may affect our thinking for some time. The problem largely lies in the fact that we usually think of God as speaking to us only through the "usual" means—prayer, Bible reading, preaching, counseling, etc. Yet in the stillness of the night, God has the unique opportunity of capturing our consciousness or subconsciousness at this deepest level. He may so strongly impress our mind with a truth or directive that we will make necessary adjustments or take appropriate action in certain areas of our lives.

Caution must be exercised, however, in attaching importance to every dream. Scriptural examples point to a very selective use of divine communication through dreams. When it is God, we will have a strong sense of His direction and counsel.

II. Interpreting Visions and Dreams

Deuteronomy 13:1-5; Ecclesiastes 5:3; Jeremiah 23:32; Genesis 20:3; 28:12; 31:11, 13, 24; 37:5-11; Daniel 2:1-45; Matthew 1:20-23; 2:12, 13, 19, 20, 22; 27:19

Deuteronomy 13:1. If there arise among you a prophet, or a dreamer of dreams, and giveth thee a sign or a wonder, 2. and the sign or the wonder come to pass, whereof he spake unto thee, saying, Let us go after other gods, which thou hast not known, and let us serve them; 3. thou shalt not hearken unto the words of that prophet, or that dreamer of dreams: for the Lord your God proveth you, to know whether ye love the Lord your God with all your heart and with all your soul. Ecclesiastes 5:3. A dream cometh through the multitude of business; and a fool's voice is known by multitude of words. Jeremiah 23:32. Behold, I am against them that prophesy false dreams, saith the Lord, and do tell them, and cause my people to err by their lies, and by their lightness; yet I sent them not, nor commanded them: therefore they shall not profit this people at all, saith the Lord. Genesis 20:3. God came to Abimelech in a dream by night, and said to him, Behold, thou art but a dead man, for the woman which thou hast taken; for she is a man's wife. 28:12. He dreamed, and behold a ladder set up on the earth, and the top of it reached to heaven: and behold the angels of God ascending and descending on it. 31:11. The angel of God spake unto me in a dream, saying, Jacob: and I said, Here am I. 24. God came to Laban the Syrian in a dream by night, and said unto him, Take heed that thou speak not to Jacob either good or bad. 37:5. Joseph dreamed a dream, and he told it to his brethren: and they hated him yet the more. Daniel 2:28. There is a God in heaven that revealeth secrets, and maketh known to the king Nebuchadnezzar what shall be in the latter days. Thy dream, and the visions of thy head upon thy bed, are these. Matthew

Clarification
Proveth you—is putting you to the test.

Lightness—loose talk, boastful stories.

Ladder—a great wide staircase.

2:22. When he heard that Archelaus did reign in Judea in the room of his father Herod, he was afraid to go thither: notwithstanding, being warned of God in a dream, he turned aside into the parts of Galilee. **27:19.** When he was set down on the judgment seat, his wife sent unto him, saying, Have thou nothing to do with that just man: for I have suffered many things this day in a dream because of him.

A. Meaningless Dreams

(See Teaching Tip 3.)

The various dream books on the market cater to people who believe all dreams have some sort of meaning. Most of us have considerable curiosity about the meaning of our dreams. The Bible does show that some dreams are significant because they come from God. Yet, when we look at the Bible as a whole, we see that there are fewer dreams mentioned than one might expect. After all, the Bible deals with a large number of people who lived over a period of thousands of years. Only a comparatively small number had dreams that came from God.

Solomon indicated that most dreams come from the pressure of the business and cares of the day. They are no more inspired of God than are the many words of a godless fool. Ecclesiastes 5:7 goes on to indicate that much of our dreaming is meaningless, just as the many words rattled off by a godless fool are meaningless. Neither show any connection with God's will. Therefore we should give our attention to the Lord. If He has given a dream or vision, he will make it clear to us.

Guideline for Living 2

A preoccupation with dreams and their interpretation or significance can be damaging to our emotional, mental, and even physical well-being. There are those who take too much stock in what they dream, always wondering what possible doom or destruction might befall themselves or a loved one in the near future.

God does move in mysterious ways. He may even speak to us in mysterious ways. Yet, when it is indeed God speaking and our hearts are attuned to His voice, we will have an inner witness that it is His message.

Jesus is our Shepherd; we are His sheep. As His sheep, we know His voice (John 10:4). As we remain within the fold and heed Jesus' Word, we will not be drawn away by strange voices, whether they come through dreams or visions. We will know when it is the voice of the Good Shepherd.

B. False Dreamers

Some dreams or visions seem to have meaning, but false teachers use them to lead people astray.

Deuteronomy 13 shows that God permits this in order to test our faith and love for Him. God always tests our faith, not to destroy it, but to direct it and help it to grow. From this passage also we see that any dream or vision that does not cause us to give glory to God or that does not encourage us to worship and serve Him is false and will deceive and mislead us.

Jeremiah records God's judgment on those who prophesy false

Question.

Do all dreams have meaning?

TEACHING TIP 3

As a point of interest regarding the "mechanics" of sleeping and dreaming, present the following information.

Research of brainwave readings indicates that the process of sleep takes place in four distinct stages. These can be graphically described by the diagram below.

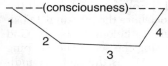

At first we drift into an almost hypnotic state in a half-awake, half-asleep phase. This moves deeper and deeper through stages 2 and 3 and then progresses toward consciousness in stage 4.

Stage 4 is the period of vivid dreaming. Dreams are extremely realistic. It is also described as the REM (rapid eye movement) period when the mind is actively engaged in the dreaming process.

Generally speaking our dreams do not last long. Time lengthens with depth of sleep. Five to seven dream patterns may occur on a typical night.

Question.

Why does God allow this?

dreams, that is, who use dreams to back up their lies and try to make gullible people believe they are giving God's message. If you listen closely to them, you will find their words have no depth of scriptural truth. Instead, such false prophets are superficial in what they say and they tell a great many boastful stories about their own exploits.

C. God-Given and Clear

Question.
Why did some dreams and visions need interpretation?

Many, perhaps the majority, of the dreams and visions recorded in the Bible had a simple, clear meaning that brought direction, warning, or encouragement to those who received them. King Abimelech did not need anyone to interpret the dream God gave him about Abraham and Sarah, and he was quick to do something about it. Neither did Joseph need anyone to interpret the dreams in which God gave him directions concerning Mary and Baby Jesus.

D. God-Given and Needing Interpretation

Question.
Do all dreams and visions need interpretation?

Some of them use symbols or illustrations from the natural realm to teach spiritual truth.

Question.
Does the Bible give interpretation for all such dreams and visions?

Sometimes the illustrations are obvious. Jacob saw a vision of a ladder or staircase to heaven with the Lord standing above it. This made it clear that heaven was open, God was concerned about him, and God had provided access to His throne.

In many cases God gave the interpretation, either directly to the dreamer or through a man of God. Jacob dreamed that all the males mating with the females of the flock bore the markings Laban said the young must have if they were to belong to Jacob. God explained that this was his way of evening the score and keeping Laban from cheating Jacob any further. So, as the Hebrew indicates, Jacob used peeled rods to fence in all the strong females and allowed in only the males that had the markings he wanted. God knew the laws of heredity and used them for Jacob's benefit long before men figured them out.

Then Nebuchadnezzar's dreams were so strange that the wisest of men could not interpret them. But God himself gave the interpretations to Daniel.

Question.
What should we do with visions or dreams that God impresses us are from Him?

We need to search the Scripture. God will never tell us to do anything that is contrary to His Word or contrary to His nature as revealed in the Word. Neither will He ask us to do anything that will hurt the faith of others or divide the Church. We must also seek the help of the Holy Spirit to obey in a way that will show our love and faith.

Guideline for Living 3

What should be done if it is felt that God is definitely speaking through a dream?

It may be that if God is attempting to communicate through the dream process, it will be repeated. If so, care should be taken to focus on details in the dream. Writing them down may be helpful, since the details are usually soon forgotten.

A dream should always be carefully evaluated in light of God's Word. Is it consistent with His nature? Does it align with Scripture?

Talk over the details of the dream with your pastor or someone else who has mature judgment and understanding. A sounding

Clarification

The last days—the last age before the Millennium; that is, the age between Calvary and the Second Coming.

Visions—Greek, *horaseis,* which may mean eyes, sights, appearances, dreams, or supernatural visions. Here, the mention of prophecy shows that Joel and Peter meant supernatural dreams and visions including supernatural insight.

Dream dreams—have visions in dreams.

Question.

Does the Bible mean that young men and old men will have different kinds of visions and dreams?

TEACHING TIP 4

Focus on the last part of Joel 2:28 by outlining the verse as follows:

1. Your daughters shall prophesy
2. Your young men shall see visions
3. Your old men shall dream dreams

Ask: "Is this taking place in our church world today? Is there an increasing frequency of God speaking through dreams and visions? What may this mode of divine communication indicate regarding God's relationship to man in the end-time? Is He needing to speak with us on a different level?"

board is often helpful. Then pray that God will confirm His direction. This should clarify the import of a dream and show what direction must be taken.

III. Accompanying the Spirit's Outpouring
Joel 2:28, 29; Acts 2:17

Acts 2:17. It shall come to pass in the last days, saith God, I will pour out of my Spirit upon all flesh: and your sons and your daughters shall prophesy, and your young men shall see visions, and your old men shall dream dreams.

(See Teaching Tip 4.)

Joel foresaw and Peter confirmed that the outpouring of the Holy Spirit would be followed by supernatural visions and dreams. The New Testament confirms that this did take place. Church history also records many dreams and visions that brought great blessing to the Church. The dream of John Bunyan that led him to write *Pilgrim's Progress* is an example.

These words are often used interchangeably in the Greek. The fact that young men will see visions or dreams and old men will have visions in dreams simply emphasizes the truth that God will give dreams and visions to both young and old. The Holy Spirit will work through believers regardless of race, sex, or national origin.

LIVING THE TRUTH

Dreams are as common as sleep. Yet God can and does speak to us through this means. We should never ignore such divine communication. However, caution must always be exercised to avoid undue concern, anxiety, or fear over the details of dreams we may have. Again, the important thing is to know the voice of the Shepherd and seek His leading. He will never lead us astray.

EVANGELISM OUTREACH

Be prepared to pray or counsel with any who may sense their need to know the voice of the Shepherd. Help them find the needed guidance for their daily lives.

13 | LIFE AFTER DEATH

PREPARING TO TEACH

Study Text
Luke 16:19-31; John 5:24-29; 1 Corinthians 15:21-26, 42-44, 51-58; Revelation 20:4-6, 12-15

Outline
I. Understanding Death
   A. Death Through Adam
   B. Death an Enemy
II. Resurrection of the Body
   A. Resurrection to Life
   B. Resurrection to Judgment
III. Eternal Destiny
   A. The Intermediate State
   B. Final Judgment

Golden Text: The wages of sin is death; but the gift of God is eternal life through Jesus Christ our Lord. Romans 6:23

Central Truth: At death the Christian enters eternal happiness, while the sinner goes to eternal torment.

Learning Goals
1. To gain an understanding of the Biblical teaching on life after death.
2. To recognize the importance of living today with eternal values in view.
3. To appreciate the hope of the resurrection given to all believers.
4. To determine to be prepared for eternity.

SEEING THE SCRIPTURES
1 Corinthians 15:21-26, 42-44, 51-58

21. For since by man came death, by man came also the resurrection of the dead.

22. For as in Adam all die, even so in Christ shall all be made alive.

23. But every man in his own order: Christ the firstfruits; afterward they that are Christ's at his coming.

24. Then cometh the end, when he shall have delivered up the kingdom to God, even the Father; when he shall have put down all rule, and all authority and power.

25. For he must reign, till he hath put all enemies under his feet.

26. The last enemy that shall be destroyed is death.

42. So also is the resurrection of the dead. It is sown in corruption, it is raised in incorruption:

43. It is sown in dishonor, it is raised in glory: it is sown in weakness, it is raised in power:

44. It is sown a natural body, it is raised a spiritual body. There is a natural body, and there is a spiritual body.

51. Behold, I show you a mystery; We shall not all sleep, but we shall all be changed,

52. In a moment, in the twinkling of an eye, at the last trump: for the trumpet shall sound, and the dead shall be raised incorruptible, and we shall be changed.

53. For this corruptible must put on incorruption, and this mortal must put on immortality.

54. So when this corruptible shall have put on incorruption, and this mortal shall have put on immortality, then shall be brought to pass the saying that is written, Death is swallowed up in victory.

55. O death, where is thy sting? O grave, where is thy victory?

56. The sting of death is sin; and the strength of sin is the law.

57. But thanks be to God, which giveth us the victory through our Lord Jesus Christ.

58. Therefore, my beloved brethren, be ye steadfast, unmovable, always abounding in the work of the Lord, forasmuch as ye know that your labor is not in vain in the Lord.

SETTING THE SCENE
"If a man die, shall he live again?" This is the cry, not only of Job, but of many today (Job 14:14). Job later came to the place of faith when he declared, "I know that my Redeemer liveth" (Job 19:25).

Bankruptcy
Crime
War
Death
Injury
Illness
Divorce
Natural calamity

Ask: "How would you rank these in the order of least favorite subjects for thought or discussion? How would the world rank them?"

Allow a few moments for response. It is likely that death will rank number 1 or very high in both cases. Keep this list in perspective throughout the class session.

Clarification

By man—through a man.
Destroyed—brought to an end. The same word is translated "put down" in verse 24.

Question.

Did all the Jews in New Testament times believe in a resurrection?

TEACHING TIP 1

Focus on the vital significance of the Resurrection by developing the following argument outlined by Paul in 1 Corinthians 15:13-19. You may wish to reproduce this beforehand on an overhead transparency or on a sheet of newsprint.

IF
there is no resurrection of the body,
THEN:
Christ (who took on human form) did not rise from the dead.
IF
Christ did not rise from the dead,
THEN:
Paul's preaching is empty

How sad that so many today have not yet come to that same assurance!

As we turn to the New Testament we find the greatest assurance of our resurrection is the fact that Jesus rose from the dead and is ascended to the right hand of the Father where He is now interceding for us. The Holy Spirit also gives believers assurance that we are sons and heirs of God, fellow heirs with Jesus Christ. We have the assurance also that to be absent from the body is to be present with the Lord (2 Corinthians 5:6-8).

Even Old Testament saints caught a glimpse of what God has prepared for us after death. David knew he would dwell in the house of the Lord forever (Psalm 23:6). Solomon saw (as the Hebrew indicates) that for the wise there is a way of life to the place above that he may avoid hell (Sheol) beneath (Proverbs 15:24).

BIBLE COMMENTARY

I. Understanding Death

1 Corinthians 15:21-26

1 Corinthians 15:21. Since by man came death, by man came also the resurrection of the dead. 22. For as in Adam all die, even so in Christ shall all be made alive. 23. But every man in his own order: Christ the firstfruits; afterward they that are Christ's at his coming. 25. For he must reign, till he hath put all enemies under his feet. 26. The last enemy that shall be destroyed is death.

A. Death Through Adam

One of the central truths of the gospel is that Jesus rose from the dead, and His resurrection guarantees ours.

The Pharisees did, but the Sadducees did not. The Sadducees also denied any kind of life after death and thought their only immortality was through their children. The Greeks who lived in Corinth were probably divided in their view of life after death. Some Greeks believed the soul lived on in a shadowy existence in Hades. Others thought death ended it all. Thus the Christian believers in Corinth were surrounded by people who denied the possibility of a bodily resurrection. Apparently false teachers arose who denied the literal resurrection of Jesus. Others supposed His resurrection was a special event that showed His deity but gave no hope for us since we are not gods. (See Teaching Tip 1.)

Paul countered the false teachers by reminding the Corinthians of the many witnesses who saw Jesus after He arose. Most of these were still alive and their testimony still available. Then Paul declared that if Christ did not rise, the gospel is false, our Christian hope meaningless, and the forgiveness of our sins nonexistent. Worse, to build our hope on a lie would be a most miserable sort of thing.

But the fact is, Christ has risen from the dead. Paul then compared the first resurrection, the resurrection to life (John 5:29) to a harvest. Christ is the firstfruits of that harvest, the guarantee of

talk, false and misleading.

IF

Paul's preaching is in vain
THEN:

The faith and hope of all who accept it is also in vain.

IF

Christ did not rise from the dead
THEN:

There is no salvation for sin without Christ's resurrection.

IF

Jesus did not rise from the dead,
THEN:

What hope is there for those who trust in Him?

IF

All this is true
THEN:

Sacrifice, self-denial, and suffering for the sake of Christ have been in vain.

(Drawn from *Knowing the Doctrines of the Bible* by Myer Pearlman)

Question.
How is this changed when we take Jesus as our Saviour?

Question.
Does the statement that "in Christ shall all be made alive" suggest a universal salvation for all mankind whether they are believers in Christ or not?

Question.
Does death ever come as a friend?

Question.
What keeps the believer from being dominated by the fear of death?

a great harvest to follow. Then the main body of the harvest will be the resurrection of the believers at Christ's coming (verse 23).

Guideline for Living 1
If it can be said that salvation is at the heart of our new life in Christ, perhaps it can also be stated that the Resurrection is at the heart of our hope for eternal life with Christ. Jesus' resurrection is a historical fact. It is well documented by the many who saw Him afterward.

Jesus' resurrection makes it certain that every believer will live beyond the grave. This event eliminated the sting and victory of death for all who trust Christ. It is a great source of hope for the living. How wonderful it is to be able to say with Job of old: "I know that my redeemer liveth, and that he shall stand at the latter day upon the earth: and though after my skin worms destroy this body, yet in my flesh shall I see God" (Job 19:25, 26)

Paul made a contrast between Adam whose disobedience brought sin and its wages into the human race, and Christ whose resurrection brought the assurance of eternal life to all believers.

As human beings we share the attitudes of Adam and we sin as he did. He chose deliberately to go against a holy God who placed him in an ideal environment, supplied every need, and wanted only good for him. Since then every individual has made wrong choices that go against God and are contrary even to what they believe is right. (See Romans 3:23.)

We have a new desire to please God and a new power from the Holy Spirit to help us. We also have spiritual life, the life of Christ, in us through the agency of the Holy Spirit. On the other hand, we still have mortal bodies that can die, but which will be made alive again at the time of the Rapture and resurrection. (See Romans 8:10,11.) We are saved from eternal death, but as long as we are still in this body our outward man is perishing, gradually dying, even though the inward man is being renewed day by day (2 Corinthians 4:16).

The next verse (23) makes it clear. Only those who are Christ's partake of His resurrection at His coming. That is, all who are in Adam (as human beings) die. All who are in Christ (as believers) will be made alive.

B. Death an Enemy
Some have referred to death as a friend bringing relief from suffering. But the Bible still looks at physical death as an enemy, an enemy that in the final consummation of God's plan will be brought to an end.

We can face the threat of death without fear because we know we shall rise again. We are coming back. The unbeliever loses everything he has worked for when he dies. But if our aim is to glorify Christ and live for Him, He will resurrect us to live and reign with Him. Death cannot rob us of anything we are really working for. At the same time we recognize that all our hope and inheritance is a gift of God's free grace.

Bertrand Russell, the English philosopher, before his death penned the words, "There is darkness without, and when I die there will be darkness within. There is no splendour, no vastness anywhere; only triviality for a moment, and then nothing." Such is the conception of many who are without the hope of eternal life. Death is an empty void with no purpose or meaning.

Such a view causes many to regard death as an enemy. For them it brings a life full of dreams, wishes, and ambitions to an end. It brings separation from family and friends. It thrusts man into the unknown realm beyond life.

For many, death brings terror. Images of the "grim reaper" and the vast, dark abyss of the "other side" loom in their minds.

"Death haunts our days and nights," states David Winter in his book *Hereafter*, "when in fact he is a crippled and disabled foe whose days are numbered." The latter statement must be the Christian's perspective, for death is a defeated foe—thanks to Calvary and the glorious resurrection of Jesus Christ.

Clarification

Corruption—a perishable or deteriorated condition: subject to decay.

Incorruption— incorruptibility and immortality; indestructibility; not subject to decay or death.

Dishonor—humiliation.

Glory—radiant glory.

Weakness—including sickness, disease.

Natural—physical, material.

The dead—that is, the rest of the dead; those who had no life from Christ. (See Revelation 20:5.)

Hell—Hades; in the New Testament always a place of punishment.

Question.

Why does the Bible speak of the body as being sown?

Question.

What will our new bodies be like?

Question.

Does this mean our new bodies will be ghostly, filmy, or lacking in substance?

II. Resurrection of the Body

1 Corinthians 15:42-44; Revelation 20:12, 13

1 Corinthians 15:42. So also is the resurrection of the dead. It is sown in corruption, it is raised in incorruption: 43. it is sown in dishonor, it is raised in glory: it is sown in weakness, it is raised in power: 44. it is sown a natural body, it is raised a spiritual body. There is a natural body, and there is a spiritual body. Revelation 20:12. I saw the dead, small and great, stand before God; and the books were opened: and another book was opened, which is the book of life: and the dead were judged out of those things which were written in the books, according to their works. 13. And the sea gave up the dead which were in it; and death and hell delivered up the dead which were in them: and they were judged every man according to their works.

A. Resurrection to Life

Just as the bare grain is sown and the hull decays in the ground but the life within it springs forth as a wheat plant, so the body is buried and decays, but God brings it forth as a brand-new body. We see also that the new resurrection body will be as different from our present body as a whole wheat plant is from a bare grain.

(See Teaching Tip 2.)

They will present a strong contrast to the mortal body that dies. At death our bodies show the results of a deterioration and decay that began as soon as we were born. At death the body is humiliated in that all its strength is gone and it is reduced to total weakness. It may also show the signs of sickness and disease. But the new bodies of the believers will be immortal and incorruptible, not subject to death or decay. They will be full of glory and mighty, supernatural power as God causes us to rise to meet Jesus in the air and share His glory forever. They will also be spiritual, supernatural bodies, very different from the present physical, material body.

The Bible goes on to show that our new bodies will be like

TEACHING TIP 2

A great deal of attention has been given in recent years to what are called "paranormal" experiences at the cessation or near cessation of life. This pertains most often to out-of-body experiences that enable the individual to view his own body and all activities going on around him. Discuss the following questions with the class in light of this phenomenon.

1. What may the out-of-body phenomenon suggest regarding the relationship of the body, mind, and spirit (or soul)?

2. What may be suggested regarding the nature of our immortal bodies by the ability of those who have had this paranormal experience to see, hear, understand, rise, move through solid barriers, etc? How does this relate to Christ's resurrected body?

Note that paranormal experiences cannot be documented scientifically and are subject to speculation. However, this phenomenon does present some interesting insights into the possible nature of the immortal state.

Question.

Do Jesus or Paul show the time difference between the first resurrection to life and the second resurrection to judgment?

Question.

What is meant by "the dead" in Revelation 20:12, 13?

Christ's glorious resurrection body. The body of the resurrected Jesus was in some ways like and in many ways different from our present body. It was real and substantial, not ghostly. He could eat. He could be touched. The woman could grab Him by the feet. He had flesh and bones just as the bodies of Adam and Eve had (Genesis 2:23).

Yet the resurrection body of Jesus was different. He could enter locked rooms. Some suggest that if there is a true fourth dimension He may have come in and out through that fourth dimension without His disciples being aware of it. Others point out that with only a slight change in the structure of our bodies we could walk through walls as easily as we now walk through air. The Bible simply lets us know that our new bodies will no longer be subject to all the limits of our present bodies. They will belong to a new supernatural order. They will be a new creation. (See 2 Corinthians 4:17; 5:1-4.)

> *Guideline for Living 3*
>
> Some of our most beautiful Christian songs carry the message of victory over death through Christ. Any comfort that people find apart from the gospel in times of grief is only temporary. The resurrection of Jesus is a truth that stands through every storm. Through our tears, our physical suffering, our anxieties, and fears, we can lift up our heads and sing the victors' song. Because Jesus lives, we too shall live.

B. Resurrection to Judgment

Jesus does show there will be two distinct resurrections (John 5:29) but the Bible gives us a step-by-step revelation. The Old Testament does not show the time difference between the first and second comings of Christ. The New Testament makes it clear that the Church Age comes between them. The Gospels and Epistles do not make the time difference between the first and second resurrections clear. But Revelation 20 makes it clear that the thousand years of Christ's millennial reign come between them.

Revelation 20:4 makes it clear that the first resurrection includes two groups. The first group includes faithful believers who are the overcomers of the Church Age. They are those who stayed true by keeping the hand of faith in the hand of Jesus and will be given thrones and judgment or rulership. (See 1 John 5:4; Revelation 3:20-22; 5:10.) This is the main body of the harvest and includes all who are resurrected and given new bodies at the time of the Rapture. The second group includes those who have been martyred because they refused to take the mark of the beast. These might be compared to the gleanings after the main harvest. They complete the harvest. That is, with them the first resurrection, the resurrection to life, will come to an end. The rest of the dead will not live (will not be resurrected) until after the Millennium is over.

Thus the dead who will be brought before the Great White Throne include only those who will have no part in the first resurrection because they did not know and serve the resurrected Saviour.

Question.

What kind of bodies will they have in this second resurrection, the resurrection to final judgment?

Clarification

Hell—hades.

Torments—continual torture or pain.

In his bosom—in a place of honor and fellowship on the couch at Abraham's right at the banquet table in paradise. A person reclining at table would literally put his head back into the bosom (against the breast) of the person on his left in order to talk to him. (Matthew 8:11. See John 13:23.)

Tormented—suffering pain, anguish, insatiable desires, and remorse.

Son—child. Abraham spoke tenderly.

Receivedst—received in full. He had all he wanted and had denied himself nothing. But he failed to consider the future and laid up no treasures in heaven.

Gulf—chasm; literally, a yawning; an unbridgeable space. This teaching was contrary to the Jewish rabbis of that day who taught there were two divisions of the place of the afterlife separated only by a finger breadth or at most a handbreadth. Jesus knew better.

Heareth my word, and believeth—keeps on hearing (and obeying) My Word, and keeps on believing (or continues to be a believer).

Hath everlasting life—keeps on having eternal life; that is, Christ's life in him.

Condemnation—judgment; or punishment (the punishment of the second death, the lake of fire).

Life in himself—that is, by His nature and as a source.

The hour—the time.

Good—the good things, including what is right, honest, useful, kind, generous.

Done evil—made a practice

We are not told. But resurrection here can only mean the resurrection of the body. God will give them some kind of body. These bodies will also in some sense be eternal, for the lake of fire will bring suffering but not an end to these bodies.

III. Eternal Destiny
Luke 16:19-31; John 5:24-29

Luke 16:23. In hell he lifted up his eyes, being in torments, and seeth Abraham afar off, and Lazarus in his bosom. 24. And he cried and said, Father Abraham, have mercy on me, and send Lazarus, that he may dip the tip of his finger in water, and cool my tongue; for I am tormented in this flame. 25. But Abraham said, Son, remember that thou in thy lifetime receivedst thy good things, and likewise Lazarus evil things: but now he is comforted, and thou art tormented. 26. And beside all this, between us and you there is a great gulf fixed: so that they which would pass from hence to you cannot; neither can they pass to us, that would come from thence. John 5:24. Verily, verily, I say unto you, He that heareth my word, and believeth on him that sent me, hath everlasting life, and shall not come into condemnation; but is passed from death unto life. 26. As the Father hath life in himself; so hath he given to the Son to have life in himself; 27. and hath given him authority to execute judgment also, because he is the Son of man. 28. Marvel not at this: for the hour is coming, in which all that are in the graves shall hear his voice, 29. and shall come forth; they that have done good, unto the resurrection of life; and they that have done evil, unto the resurrection of damnation.

A. The Intermediate State

(See Teaching Tip 3.)

Some take the story of the rich man and Lazarus to be a parable. However, it is not called a parable, and even if it were it would not go against truth and reality. (See Teaching Tip 4.)

Angels carry believers to a place of blessing and comfort. Second Corinthians 5:8 gives us the further revelation that for the Christian this means we are brought into the presence of our Lord Jesus.

Those who live for self instead of God go to a place of torment, pain, anguish, and remorse. They have no second chance to repent, for a great gulf, an unbridgeable chasm separates them from the place of the blessed.

B. Final Judgment

Those who take part in the first resurrection will reign with Christ throughout eternity. After the final judgment of the wicked they will enjoy the glories and blessings of the New Jerusalem and the new heavens and earth. The wicked will be cast into the lake of fire prepared for the devil and his angels. They will be eternally separated from God.

of doing worthless, bad, evil, or base deeds.

Damnation—judgment; or punishment (the punishment of the second death).

TEACHING TIP 3

Ask three volunteers to share the three erroneous views of the intermediate state as given in PATH. Suggest that the reporting students call on others to read the Scripture verses given with each report. The references could be written on the chalkboard. Also write the name of each view on the board.

TEACHING TIP 4

Ask the students to write a cinquain on the subject of death or eternity. This will help them express their thoughts and feelings regarding their subjects.

A cinquain is a five-lined stanza form of poetry that is developed as follows:

Line 1: Title (a noun, one word) In this case the title will be either "Death" or "Eternity."
Line 2: Describe the title (2 words)
Line 3: Action words or phrase about the title (3 words)
Line 4: Describes a feeling about the title (4 words)
Line 5: Refers to the title (1 word)

The following is an example:

Eternity
Endless existence
Life with Christ
Joy for the believer
Forever

Allow volunteers to share what they have written.

Daily Devotional Guide

M. Rest for the Weary. Job 3:11-19
T. Eternal Dwelling Place. Psalm 23:1-6
W. Brevity of Life. Psalm 103:15-22
T. Heavenly Home. John 14:1-3
F. Eternal Life. Romans 6:15-23
S. Words of Comfort. 1 Thessalonians 4:13-18

Guideline for Living 4

Life after death is a reality, not a theory. God's Word clearly proclaims, "It is appointed unto men once to die, but after this the judgment" (Hebrews 9:27). With this fact in mind, it is imperative that we live with eternity in view. Life here must become a preparation for life forever. May God grant every believer a special urgency to be prepared for life everlasting with Him.

LIVING THE TRUTH

Eternal values are the only ones that really matter. Life is not meat or drink, or what we will do today or tomorrow. It is doing the will of the Father. When this is our guiding principle of life, we need not fear death. Instead, we can look death squarely in the face with a smile, knowing we are secure in the Father's love.

EVANGELISM OUTREACH

The prospect of death can be very unsettling to those who have no hope beyond this life. Perhaps this week's discussion will bring someone to a point of recognizing his or her need of a life-giving Saviour. Pray that the Holy Spirit will so direct and give you the wisdom to guide that individual to the hope of eternal life.

Recommended Resources

The Winter 84/85 theme is 1 and 2 Timothy, Titus, and 1, 2, and 3 John. The teacher will find the following books very helpful in advance preparation and in classroom use.

GENERAL REFERENCE WORKS

The New Bible Commentary: Revised by D. Guthrie, J. A. Motyer, A. M. Stibbs, and D. J. Wiseman. This distinctly evangelical one-volume commentary on the entire Bible is a completely revised edition. Order # 03 WX 0888, $24.95.

The New International Commentary on the Epistles of John by I. Howard Marshall. Use with studies 10-13. Order # 03 WX 0204, $12.95.

Cruden's Concordance by Alexander Cruden. Inexpensive paperback which references great topics of the Bible alphabetically. Order # 03 WX 1328, $3.95.

Jensen's Survey of the New Testament by Irving L. Jensen. Each study includes background information on each book, a summary of content, key words, verses, and survey charts. Use with each study. Order #38 WX 0254, $18.95.

Baker's Dictionary of Theology by Everett F. Harrison, editor. Biblical terms of theology simply defined and alphabetically referenced. Order # 03 WX 0909, $17.95.

SELECTED STUDY HELPS

The Christian's Secret of a Happy Life by Hannah Smith. A classic best-seller for more than 80 years. Order # 03 WX 1271, $2.50.

The Measure of a Man by Gene Getz. This book speaks to women as well as men in outlining 20 characteristics of leadership from Paul's letters to Timothy and Titus. Use with studies 1-9. Order # 03 WX 1999, $3.50.

Women and Church Leadership by Dr. Margaret E. Howe: Grand Rapids, Zondervan Publishing House, 1982. Thorough study of the church's interpretation of the place of women in leadership compared with New Testament teaching on the place of women in leadership. Order # 38-0252, $6.95 paperback.

The Letters of Paul by P. C. Nelson. An analysis of each of Paul's 14 epistles. Use with studies 1-9. Order # 02 WX 0546, $2.00.

Live up to Your Faith: Studies in Titus by James T. Draper. An easy reading commentary on the book of Titus. Use with studies 8 and 9. Order # 03 1935, $3.95.

Letters to Timothy by Gary Leggett. A pleasantly flowing commentary dealing with Christian living today. Use with studies 1-7. Order # 02 WX 0877, $1.95.

Leadership by Hudson T. Armerding. Places emplasis on individual's own personal growth as the necessary foundation for his leadership. Use with study 2. Order # 03 WX 1879, $4.95.

Yes Yes Living in a No No World by Neil Eskelin. Positive living at its fullest. It offers a never-ending source of personal energy and motivation. Order # 03 WX 2568, $2.95.

How To Use Your Adult Teacher

It is imperative that you read the Adult Student quarterly during your advance study. Pay particular attention to the questions under "Applying the Word." Be ready to discuss any one of these questions during class time if a student brings it up. You may wish to integrate specific questions into your presentation for a given Sunday.

Wide and Narrow Columns

Instead of the two equal columns used in the past, your *Adult Teacher* now uses the format of a wide and narrow column. Each study contains the same information as before, but it has been rearranged.

The wide column contains the following: SEEING THE SCRIPTURES, SETTING THE SCENE, BIBLE COMMENTARY (including Scripture blocks), Guidelines for Living, LIVING THE TRUTH, and EVANGELISM OUTREACH.

On the first page of each study, the narrow column contains an overview of the study under the heading, PREPARING TO TEACH. This column shows the Study Text, Outline, Golden Text, Central Truth, and Learning Goals.

On the remaining pages, the narrow column includes: GETTING STARTED, Clarification, Teaching Tips, questions from the commentary, and the daily devotional guide.

Helps Where You Need Them

The commentary, application, and methodology sections are totally integrated so the teacher has what he needs at the point of use. The section headed, GETTING STARTED, is at the beginning—where it would be used. It contains suggestions for getting the students' immediate attention and providing a bridge to the Bible study that follows.

The "Clarification" section, which explains words or expressions in the study text that might be difficult to understand, is placed opposite the Scripture block to which it applies.

Each Teaching Tip is placed or referred to at the point where it would be used to help students get a better grasp of that part of the Bible Commentary. If a Teaching Tip calls for the use of PATH (Packet of Adult Teaching Helps), that information will be given. When you see the heading, "Question," in the narrow column, it is a question answered in the Bible Commentary at that point.

The guidelines for living are considered a part of the application, but are so closely related to the commentary that this section is inserted in the commentary. It is set off by a long, narrow bracket and by the heading, "Guideline for Living," followed by the number. This section should not be considered an interruption of the commentary. It is for the purpose of helping the teacher apply to daily life the Bible truth being studied.

The daily devotional guide is for the teacher's personal benefit. It is to help you get into the Word throughout the week, and hopefully you will find in the daily devotionals truths you will use in the lesson.

At the end of the study, "Living the Truth" is a summary of all the guidelines for living. "Evangelism Outreach" is actually a sub-head under "Living the Truth." It is a reminder to use the class not only as a time to nurture Christians but also to bring the unsaved to a decision for Christ.

Use It as a Tool

You will find more material in the *Adult Teacher* than you can use in any one session. Your own advance study will show you what to include and what to omit. You may sometimes develop activities of your own that will seem more suitable. The *Adult Teacher* is a tool, not a substitute for the Bible or personal preparation. Use this quarterly for the purpose for which it has been designed and your efforts will be rewarded.

One-on-One

We may think evangelism means preaching to great crowds. However, a crowd is simply a gathering of individuals. Each one has a unique set of needs that God knows about. The Holy Spirit works with them as individuals. If they are born again it will not be a mass experience, but an individual one.

Some of the greatest evangelizing has been a one-on-one effort. Jesus did not preach a sermon on the new birth to multitudes on the hillside. He talked about this great truth to an individual in the quiet of the night. Where did His beautiful teaching on the water of life take place? It happened while He sat on Jacob's well and spoke to a woman with a turbulent past but an open heart. The tax collector Zaccheus was in a crowd when he was converted, but Jesus' message to him was very personal: "Come down out of the tree. I'm going home with you for dinner."

We must never pass up the individual because we think we need a large audience for witnessing. Philip surely was happy over the crowds who accepted Christ in Samaria. Yet when the Lord said, "It's time to leave," Philip responded without hesitation. From a surging revival to a desert road was quite a change, but the Holy Spirit had other work for His servant to do.

What the Spirit saw that Philip did not see at first was a hungry-hearted man down there in the desert, reading the Scriptures. He was not just anybody. This was Ethiopia's secretary of the treasury and he was headed home from Jerusalem. He must have gone there because he was reaching out for spiritual peace, but you can't help sensing from the record that his soul was still empty.

Philip's experience in Acts 8 shows why we must always be sensitive to the Lord's leading in our soulwinning efforts. The Holy Spirit is ever reaching out to touch lives. He knows whose spirits are beginning to stir. It would be tragic to miss an opportunity to present Christ's claims to a heart that is already opening.

Philip was the kind of man to whom the Lord did not have to speak twice. When he got his orders from heaven to catch up with the government official's chariot, he ran to it quickly. Seeing the scroll in the man's hand must have made Philip's heart beat faster. When he got close enough to hear, he realized the man was reading what we know as Isaiah 53. Philip was beginning to understand why the Lord had led him that way.

Philip was full of the Spirit and full of the Word. He took the Scripture and pointed to Jesus in Isaiah's prophecy. The Spirit was working. He always honors the Word and exalts Christ. He was blessing Philip's witness to the Saviour. The seeker was listening as the chariot rolled along. Something wonderful was about to happen. It would be just as thrilling as the conversion of multitudes in Samaria.

As the two men traveled on, a soul was born into the Kingdom. Philip had omitted nothing—apparently covering even the subject of water baptism. There was not much water in that area, so when they came to the first pool the secretary of Ethiopia's treasury declared himself a candidate for baptism.

Philip wanted to be certain the man understood what he was doing. Before they headed for the water Philip stated the single requirement: "If thou believest with all thine heart, thou mayest." The Ethiopian's reply shows where Philip's conversation had been focused: "I believe that Jesus Christ is the Son of God."

We are thrilled at seeing large numbers of converts follow the Lord in water baptism. But heaven surely rejoiced over this baptismal service where only one candidate and a preacher participated.

Philip's departure from the spot was unusual. He was needed somewhere else. The Spirit of the Lord caught him away and gave him new territory for his evangelistic assignment. We never hear again of this convert, but the last report assures us his encounter with Christ was real: "He went on his way rejoicing." One man had met one man and told him how to be delivered from his sins. A new name had been written in the Lamb's Book of Life.

As a teacher you have the advantage of knowing your students personally. If it becomes apparent that some are not Christians, let this become a challenge. Begin your one-on-one evangelism without delay.

A teacher whose class was growing by leaps and bounds was asked how it was happening. The reply was short and simple: "I just single them out and pray them in." There is nothing complicated about that kind of strategy. It was working in that class. It will work in every class because it is Biblical.

Unsaved people sometimes have unanswered questions that stand between them and Christ. Be the kind of friend who will make it easy for them to open up and bring their questions to you. Through prayer and the study of the Word, stay prepared for such opportunities. Be a good listener. Avoid controversy. Some questions have no easy, cut-and-dried answers, but the questioner may receive an answer while he talks. Perhaps he only needs to get the problem out in the open and face it. When he does, it may not seem so insurmountable. But the individual needs someone to whom he can unburden his heart, and you can fill that role as part of your ministry of evangelism.

Opportunities do not usually hit us in the face. We find most of them because we are looking for them. This is true of soulwinning. We should not excuse ourselves from witnessing because the Lord has not flung someone across our path unexpectedly. Witnessing should be such a part of our Christian life-style that we find ourselves concerned about it even in the midst of busy days.

Of course, as a teacher you are not supposed to do it all. Every Christian is responsible for carrying out the Great Commission. But those in positions of leadership (including Sunday school teachers) are in the forefront and must point the way for others. Challenge your class continually. Pray they will become uneasy if they aren't witnessing. In fact, pray that the Lord will make *you* uneasy if you slacken your efforts!

The Bible frequently compares soulwinning to a harvest. Everyone knows the days for any harvest are limited. We may not have much more time to win the lost before eternal night falls. May we labor so faithfully that when our work is over we will know we have done our best.

Because of the importance of soulwinning we have included an "Evangelism Outreach" section at the end of each study. We hope it will be a help to you and every teacher in using your class time as a means of reaching out to the unsaved and bringing them to Christ.

1 and 2 TIMOTHY, TITUS, 1, 2, and 3 JOHN

1

SOUND DOCTRINE

SEEING THE SCRIPTURES
1 Timothy 1:3-7, 12-20

3. As I besought thee to abide still at Ephesus, when I went into Macedonia, that thou mightest charge some that they teach no other doctrine,

4. Neither give heed to fables and endless genealogies, which minister questions, rather than godly edifying which is in faith: so do.

5. Now the end of the commandment is charity out of a pure heart, and of a good conscience, and of faith unfeigned:

6. From which some having swerved have turned aside unto vain jangling;

7. Desiring to be teachers of the law; understanding neither what they say, nor whereof they affirm.

12. And I thank Christ Jesus our Lord, who hath enabled me, for that he counted me faithful, putting me into the ministry;

13. Who was before a blasphemer, and a persecutor, and injurious: but I obtained mercy, because I did it ignorantly in unbelief.

14. And the grace of our Lord was exceeding abundant with faith and love which is in Christ Jesus.

15. This is a faithful saying, and worthy of all acceptation, that Christ Jesus came into the world to save sinners; of whom I am chief.

16. Howbeit for this cause I obtained mercy, that in me first Jesus Christ might show forth all long-suffering, for a pattern to them which should hereafter believe on him to life everlasting.

17. Now unto the King eternal, immortal, invisible, the only wise God, be honor and glory for ever and ever. Amen.

18. This charge I commit unto thee, son Timothy, according to the prophecies which went before on thee, that thou by them mightest war a good warfare;

19. Holding faith, and a good conscience; which some having put away, concerning faith have made shipwreck:

20. Of whom is Hymeneus and Alexander; whom I have delivered unto Satan, that they may learn not to blaspheme.

SETTING THE SCENE
This quarter of studies provides an opportunity to examine 1 and 2 Timothy, Titus, and 1, 2, and 3 John. Scholars generally refer to the first three of these as the pastoral epistles. Paul wrote two of his letters to young ministers, Timothy and Titus, between his first and second Roman imprisonments. He penned the words of 2 Timothy after his second arrest and not long before his execution. (See Teaching Tip 1.)

Refer to the material in "Setting the Scene" in introducing this new quarter of studies. Explain that the first three books under study comprise the pastoral epistles. Distribute copies of the outline of the Book of 1 Timothy from the Packet of Adult Teaching Helps. If you do not have the PATH materials available, briefly review the topics that will be covered in the first five studies.

Clarification

Besought—urged, entreated.

Charge—give orders, command, a military term.

Other doctrine—heretical, twisted teaching.

Unfeigned—genuine, sincere, without hypocrisy.

Vain jangling—fruitless discussion.

Profane—unhallowed, irreligious, godless.

Them that defile themselves—homosexuals.

Sound doctrine—healthy teaching.

Question.

Why did Paul need to entreat Timothy to remain with the church at Ephesus?

TEACHING TIP 1

Write the following questions on the chalkboard, overhead transparency, or sketchpad.

Imagine for a moment that you are Timothy. Paul has left you in the large city of Ephesus to organize the church he planted there. How do you feel about being left in Ephesus? What questions would you like to ask Paul after having been there for some time? How would you have received Paul's first letter?

If you have a large class (15 or more students), instruct them to discuss their response to these questions with those sitting near them. If you have a smaller class, lead them in a general discussion based on these questions.

BIBLE COMMENTARY

I. Rejecting False Doctrine

1 Timothy 1:3-11

1 Timothy 1:3. I besought thee to abide still at Ephesus, when I went into Macedonia, that thou mightest charge some that they teach no other doctrine, 4. neither give heed to fables and endless genealogies, which minister questions, rather than godly edifying which is in faith: so do. 9. Knowing this, that the law is not made for a righteous man, but for the lawless and disobedient, for the ungodly and for sinners, for unholy and profane, for murderers of fathers and murderers of mothers, for manslayers. (See Teaching Tip 2.)

A. A Difficult Assignment

Paul's first epistle to Timothy has the usual opening salutation of the letters of the day. It identifies the writer as well as the addressee and then presents a formal greeting. In this case the word "mercy" is added to the more common prayer for grace and peace as a benediction on the recipient.

Following the salutation the apostle immediately addresses some issues at hand. He has previously given Timothy a difficult assignment. Upon departing for Macedonia, Paul urged the young preacher to remain at Ephesus in ministry to the church there. (See Teaching Tip 3.)

Apparently Timothy was somewhat reluctant to do Paul's bidding at the time. The apostle found it necessary to exhort, entreat, or urge him to stay at Ephesus. After all, it was a big city for a small-town young man. It was full of pagan influences dominated by the great temple of Diana or Artemas. Besides, Timothy was not anxious to give up his close association with Paul in the life of an itinerant missionary to preach to the same people week after week.

But more than any of this, the job the apostle asked the younger minister to do was not an easy one. Timothy was to order certain teachers at Ephesus to cease preaching a doctrine different from what Paul had shared there. The Greek indicates it was not another of the same kind. No such thing exists. Its religious myths and endless Jewish genealogies gave rise to mere speculations and promoted controversies. The new teaching failed to minister adequately the treasures of God contained in the gospel. It was a crooked rather than a straight message.

B. Misguided Teachers

Paul was as concerned about keeping territory he had gained for Christ as he was in conquering new areas. The misguided teachers must be dealt with. They rejected the fact that the purpose of God's law is to promote love in a pure heart and to provide a good conscience based on a genuine rather than a hypocritical faith.

Further, the new doctrine at Ephesus caused both preacher and audience to turn aside and miss the mark. The shooting aim of its

TEACHING TIP 3

Ask a student to prepare a brief (2-3 minutes) report on the city of Ephesus. Direct him to the material on the subject in the student curriculum. Also encourage him to use other resources such as a Bible dictionary or handbook. Call for the report at this time.

Question.

What attitude does Paul take toward using the Law in the preaching of the gospel?

TEACHING TIP 4

Display or develop the following visual to illustrate the difference between the Law and the Cross.

THE LAW— A THERMOMETER

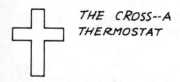

THE CROSS--A THERMOSTAT

Like a thermometer, the Law can make us aware of our present condition. But only the Cross, like a thermostat, can do something to change our condition.

promoters was a careless one. Its pathway led only to fruitless discussion of religious and philosophical speculations that get people nowhere. Proudly proclaiming they were true to the law of Moses, these teachers understood little of what they attempted to explain to others.

Guideline for Living 1

We all know people who like to argue about doctrine and other religious subjects. Some are unbelievers who use this tactic to keep from having to face the truth about their own spiritual condition. But others are Christians who engage in these discussions merely for the sake of argument.

Sometimes we are uncertain how to respond to these people. Should we become engaged with them in endless, fruitless talk in hopes that we can help them? Or should we refuse to even get started with them? We can take some direction from the Lord in this matter. He never turned away a sincere seeker. Notice the time He took to explain the new birth to Nicodemus. But He did not waste a great deal of time debating with the scribes and Pharisees.

It will help if we can determine the motive behind the question. If the person honestly wants to learn more about spiritual things, we may be able to help him. But if his motives are less honorable, we need not feel obligated to engage him in conversation.

C. Misuse of the Law

In resisting the Judaizers the apostle is not opposed to including elements of the Law, as long as it is done correctly, in preaching the gospel. Of course he cannot condone the use of animal sacrifices for sins any longer. The slaying of God's Son as the spotless Lamb took away the sins of the world once for all. That act forever abolished the ritual of the Law, including circumcision. However, Paul recognizes that certain of the Law's moral aspects still serve a useful purpose. (See Teaching Tip 4.)

The apostle says the Ten Commandments show man his sinfulness and thus his need of a Saviour. In a sense then the Law is the thermometer which indicates the patient has a fever, and the gospel is the medicine which provides the cure. Paul's list of sins here is intended to illustrate that fact.

The apostle's list includes various names for the wicked. They are the lawless and disobedient, the ungodly and sinners, as well as the unholy and profane, or irreligious. Paul also names specifically several sins here. Among those still prevalent in today's world are child and parental abuse and homosexuality.

Guideline for Living 2

A growing problem in American society today is physical abuse among family members. In some states, often those with high unemployment, reported incidents of child abuse are up 50% in a single year.

Many times we assume that these problems are among unchurched families, but that is not necessarily so. Children from supposedly Christian homes are sometimes abused. Some Christian couples are also guilty of beating one another.

As a Church, we have a responsibility to speak out against the sin of physical abuse. We must teach and preach about the damage, both physical and emotional, that parents inflict on each other and on their children when they vent their frustration in violence. As individuals we can learn to be more alert to telltale signs of physical abuse. If we suspect someone is being abused, we must pray earnestly about what we can do. The victims of abuse are often helpless or do not know where to turn for help.

Further, the apostle says fornication, kidnapping, lying, and perjury are sin. However, he makes no attempt to present an exhaustive list of evils. He concludes by declaring that "any other thing that is contrary to sound doctrine" is wrong. Paul's purpose here, as elsewhere, is to list not all but some examples of sinful activity. In Galatians his list of sins ends with "and such like" (5:19-21).

Paul explains that the moral aspects of the Law are meant to proclaim to the wicked that their ways lead to death. They cannot sin and get by. However, he protests that the Judaizers are wrong in preaching that the ritual of the Law saves from sin.

II. A Faithful Example
1 Timothy 1:12-17

Clarification
Injurious—violent.
Pattern—example, model.
Immortal—imperishable, not subject to death.

1 Timothy 1:12. And I thank Christ Jesus our Lord, who hath enabled me, for that he counted me faithful, putting me into the ministry; 13. who was before a blasphemer, and a persecutor, and injurious: but I obtained mercy, because I did it ignorantly in unbelief. 16. Howbeit for this cause I obtained mercy, that in me first Jesus Christ might show forth all long-suffering, for a pattern to them which should hereafter believe on him to life everlasting.

A. Paul's Present Position

As he contrasts the counterfeit message of the false prophets at Ephesus with the glorious gospel of grace, Paul is grateful for the teaching which has been committed to his trust. He thanks God for counting him faithful or trustworthy enough to put him in the ministry. With his background (which he is about to share) this was an amazing thing. A pardon may return a prisoner to society, but it takes a long time before anyone really trusts him.

The apostle did not choose to preach the gospel as one might select any lifetime profession. His was a divine call that required divine enablement. None is ever good enough, able enough, or experienced enough in himself to successfully occupy the high office of the minister.

B. Paul's Past Conduct

In his worship Paul remembers what his conduct was like before his conversion. He was a blasphemer, speaking injurious words against both God and man. He was a persecutor of the Church. He cast its members whether male or female into prison for their testimony of Christ (Acts 9:1, 2). When they were on trial for their lives he voted against them. With memory of such deeds, the apostle characterizes himself as having been a violent man. Though God freely forgave all, Paul never forgot what he had done.

Question.
What reasons does Paul list for
having been forgiven his sins?

C. Reasons for the Change

Through the years Paul has seriously pondered the reasons behind the change from his past to his present position. He lists first the fact that he originally opposed the gospel of Christ out of ignorance. As he explains elsewhere, "I verily thought with myself, that I ought to do many things contrary to the name of Jesus of Nazareth" (Acts 26:9).

The Law afforded sacrifices for sins of ignorance while making no allowances for those of a willful, presumptuous nature. Thank God, the gospel provides pardon for all sin.

However, the Lord did not simply forgive Paul because he did not fully realize his wrong in violently opposing the gospel. The apostle also says the love, mercy, and grace of God were involved along with his faith. He recognizes it was an exceeding abundant grace which saved him.

Further, the Lord delivered Paul from sin specifically to use him as an example of His power to save. He became a model to encourage others who afterward considered believing on Jesus. He ranked number one among the sinners of the world. The unconverted looked at him and said, "If the Lord can change a man as mean as Paul, He can save anyone." His conversion demonstrated more than that of any other the fact that "Christ Jesus came into the world to save sinners." That truth is the core of the gospel.

D. Gratitude for Grace

Contemplating all this as he writes, the apostle bursts forth into praise. His doxology is among the most beautiful of the Bible. Quickened by the Spirit, he exclaims, "Now unto the King eternal, immortal, invisible, the only wise God, be honor and glory for ever and ever."

Clarification
Having put away—having rejected, repudiated, pushed aside.
Delivered unto Satan—turned over to the custody of Satan.
Learn—by being disciplined with punishment inflicted by Satan.

III. Keeping the Faith
1 Timothy 1:18-20

1 Timothy 1:18. This charge I commit unto thee, son Timothy, according to the prophecies which went before on thee, that thou by them mightest war a good warfare; 19. holding faith, and a good conscience; which some having put away, concerning faith have made shipwreck: 20. of whom is Hymeneus and Alexander; whom I have delivered unto Satan, that they may learn not to blaspheme.

A. Present Responsibility

Returning more to the issue at hand, Paul once more speaks of Timothy's responsibility at Ephesus in dealing with the false teachers in the church there. The apostle gives him a charge. He is as one under military orders. Therefore, he dares not take his assignment lightly. Timothy must war a good warfare. As if he were an army officer, he is expected to conduct a successful campaign.

Frequently Paul's writings indicate it takes strong language to depict the life of a minister of the gospel. As with the military commander, his responsibilities concern literally matters of life and death. Standing in such a position, the pastor needs the prayer support of the people.

Timothy's present responsibility is also a matter of trust. In referring to what has been committed to the young preacher, Paul

Ask: "What are some assurances we are given from time to time that we are in the will of God? Why do we occasionally need these reassurances?" Refer to "Guideline for Living 3" in discussing these questions.

TEACHING TIP 6

Develop or display the following visual to illustrate the downward spiral of those who accept false doctrine.

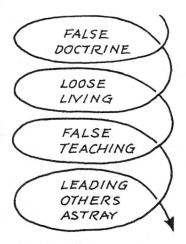

TEACHING TIP 7

Lead the class in discussing some of the following questions: 1) What are some things that can lead to false doctrine? 2) What can we do to combat false doctrines? 3) In what areas is it easiest to fall into false doctrines? 4) How can we remain on guard in these areas of vulnerability? Refer to the information in "Living the Truth" in discussing where wrong doctrines sometimes come from—namely, our attempts to justify wrong practices or as a result of a slow erosion of principles.

Distribute 3 by 5 cards or

uses an economic analogy. In ancient times men used temples as banks. They gave their valuables to the priests for safekeeping. Chests and vaults for that purpose have been uncovered by archaeologists. As a priest in the temple of God, Timothy has had the most precious treasure of eternity, the gospel, committed to his trust. He must guard it with his life.

Timothy's responsibility included that of defending the faith. At the same time, though, he must maintain a clear conscience as far as his own conduct is concerned. Correct doctrine and right living go hand in hand for the Christian. Faith and morals are inseparable.

B. Underlying Assurances

To hold him steady in the fierce fight against the foes of the gospel, the youthful minister had wonderful underlying assurances. They indicated that what he was doing was in the perfect will of God for his life. (See Teaching Tip 5.)

Guideline for Living 3

Serving as he was in a difficult place, Timothy needed Paul to reassure him that he was still in the will of God. We occasionally need that same affirmation.

There are several ways we can be assured. One is the Word of God. Often verses come to mind that give us just the word we need. Another is the encouragement of a trusting friend, someone who knows our circumstances and assures us of God's love and care. A third way is through spiritual manifestations. Often a word of prophecy or the interpretation of a message in tongues in a service will remind us that God knows and understands our struggles and is with us always.

The apostle reminds Timothy of these assurances by referring to "the prophecies which went before" on him. Apparently they came at his ordination. Later in this letter Paul recalls gifts the young preacher received through prophecy given "with the laying on of the hands of the presbytery" (4:14).

No doubt this all happened when the apostle asked Timothy to join him in missionary ministry (Acts 16:1-3). The Spirit indicated such a work was the will of God for his life as He had done earlier for Paul (Acts 13:1, 2). For Timothy and for us there is no greater stabilizing force in the face of difficulty than to know we are doing the express will of God.

C. Negative Examples

To further encourage the young minister to be true to his calling, Paul mentions two who failed in theirs. Let Timothy take note that Hymeneus and Alexander have not kept the faith nor guarded their conduct to maintain a good conscience.

Perhaps they went wrong first in thinking correct doctrine is of little importance. Paul reveals later that one of them was preaching the resurrection was past already (2 Timothy 2:17, 18). You can almost hear these men saying what one believes about the debatable subject of prophecy is of little consequence. However, the apostle declares that by such false teaching they had overthrown the faith of some. (See Teaching Tip 6.)

Of course, their doctrinal errors had affected their own lives first. Soon after slipping in what they believed about the resurrection of the dead, the two false teachers began to live loose lives.

slips of paper of that size. Ask
each student to write down one
area in which he/she is sometimes tempted to accept false
doctrine. Also instruct them to
write down one thing that will
most help them to develop
sound doctrine. If you feel the
class members know each
other well enough, you may ask
them to share what they wrote
with one other person and then
pray together regarding their
stated areas of need.

Question.
In what way did Paul deliver
Hymeneus and Alexander over
to Satan?

Question.
What was Paul's reason for
turning the two false teachers
over to Satan?

Daily Devotional Guide
M. Testing False Teachers.
Deuteronomy 18:15-22
T. Defending the Faith.
1 Kings 18:30-39
W. Delighting in the Word.
Psalm 1:1-6
T. Guarding Against False
Doctrine. Revelation 2:1-
7
F. Hating False Doctrine.
Revelation 2:12-17
S. Judgment Upon False
Doctrine.
Revelation 2:18-29

They no longer had the incentive of the Second Coming to keep
themselves pure (1 John 3:3).

In this way Paul says Hymeneus and Alexander put away the
faith from them. They repudiated it, rejected it, and thrust it away
from themselves. Theirs was a deliberate and forceful action. It
was no mere drift in the wrong direction.

The apostle describes the consequence of the conduct of the two
false preachers in graphic terms. He pictures them as having made
shipwreck of their lives. Timothy can mentally stand on the seashore and view the debris of the catastrophe as it washes ashore.
He is sobered by the thought of the horrible way those on board
drowned.

Figuratively, the two suffered shipwreck. However, they actually occupied positions of leadership in the Church. For that
reason Paul found it necessary to take action against them. He
turned them over to Satan.

The apostle's remarks here are similar to what he said to the
church at Corinth on the subject of discipline. Concerning a sinning
member, he instructed the congregation "to deliver such a one
unto Satan" (1 Corinthians 5:5). Further, to do this the apostle
told them to "put away from among yourselves that wicked person"
(verse 13). They were to dismiss him from their fellowship. The
people of Corinth must know he belonged to the camp of Satan.

With regard to the two false teachers—as with the sinning member at Corinth—Paul's purpose in discipline was corrective rather
than punitive. Some suffering was involved, but punishment was
not the intent behind the action. He wanted the guilty ones to
learn not to blaspheme. To accomplish this he thought it necessary
to surrender them to Satan for a time. Even Satan, through inflicting punishment, unintentionally may serve the will of God.

LIVING THE TRUTH

Sound doctrine. Is it only a problem for those who are in gross
error? Or can we who hold firmly to the truth also slip into error?
Often wrong doctrine comes from our attempts to justify some
wrong practice. When how we act doesn't align with what we
believe, we are tempted to change our beliefs rather than our
behavior.

Have you adjusted your beliefs lately? Are there things you
believe differently now than you did 5, 10 years ago? Were you
wrong then or are you wrong now? Often defections from sound
doctrine are not sudden or sweeping. Rather it is a process of
gradual erosion. Is that true of you? Are there some areas in which
you are slipping? Now is the time to return to the solid foundation
of sound doctrine. (See Teaching Tip 7.)

EVANGELISM OUTREACH

Some people say it doesn't really matter what you believe just
as long as you are sincere in your beliefs. Some even go so far as
to say that all roads of faith lead to the same destination. Paul
wouldn't agree with this philosophy at all. He would say it certainly
does make a difference what you believe. If you believe wrong,
you will live wrong. If you live wrong, you will die wrong. The
only way to believe right, live right, and die right is to accept
Jesus Christ as your Saviour.

SPIRITUAL LEADERSHIP

SEEING THE SCRIPTURES

1 Timothy 2:1, 2; 3:1-15

1. I exhort therefore, that, first of all, supplications, prayers, intercessions, and giving of thanks, be made for all men;

2. For kings, and for all that are in authority; that we may lead a quiet and peaceable life in all godliness and honesty.

3:1. This is a true saying, If a man desire the office of a bishop, he desireth a good work.

2. A bishop then must be blameless, the husband of one wife, vigilant, sober, of good behavior, given to hospitality, apt to teach:

3. Not given to wine, no striker, not greedy of filthy lucre; but patient, not a brawler, not covetous;

4. One that ruleth well his own house, having his children in subjection with all gravity;

5. (For if a man know not how to rule his own house, how shall he take care of the church of God?)

6. Not a novice, lest being lifted up with pride he fall into the condemnation of the devil.

7. Moreover he must have a good report of them which are without; lest he fall into reproach and the snare of the devil.

8. Likewise must the deacons be grave, not double-tongued, not given to much wine, not greedy of filthy lucre;

9. Holding the mystery of the faith in a pure conscience.

10. And let these also first be proved; then let them use the office of a deacon, being found blameless.

11. Even so must their wives be grave, not slanderers, sober, faithful in all things.

12. Let the deacons be the husbands of one wife, ruling their children and their own houses well.

13. For they that have used the office of a deacon well purchase to themselves a good degree, and great boldness in the faith which is in Christ Jesus.

14. These things write I unto thee, hoping to come unto thee shortly:

15. But if I tarry long, that thou mayest know how thou oughtest to behave thyself in the house of God, which is the church of the living God, the pillar and ground of the truth.

SETTING THE SCENE

Being a leader in the Church carries with it heavy responsibilities. In speaking to the elders of the church at Ephesus Paul stressed the seriousness of their duties (Acts 20:28-31). The Holy Spirit had put them in the position of overseers of the church. They must guard its members from teachers who would come in

Outline

I. The Ministry of Prayer
   A. Nature of Prayer
   B. Purpose of Prayer
   C. Manner of Prayer
II. Qualifications for Church Leaders
   A. Bishops
   B. Deacons
   C. Deacons' Wives
III. Godly Conduct
   A. Conduct of the Minister
   B. Character of the Church
   C. Content of the Gospel

Golden Text: These things write I unto thee, . . . that thou mayest know how thou oughtest to behave thyself in the house of God, which is the church of the living God, the pillar and ground of the truth. 1 Timothy 3:14, 15

Central Truth: A godly character and reputation are essential for effective spiritual leaders in the body of Christ.

Learning Goals
1. To determine to develop a deeper prayer life.
2. To desire to become a qualified spiritual leader.
3. To examine our daily Christian conduct.

GETTING STARTED

Distribute paper and pencil. Ask the students to write down whether they agree or disagree with each of the following statements as you read them.

1. We should pray for the success of government leaders even if they are seemingly in opposition to the Church and the work of the gospel.

2. Every Christian should aspire to a position of leadership in the church.

3. The most important aspect of our Christian life is our daily conduct.

As you reread each statement, ask the students to indicate with a raised hand whether they agreed or disagreed. Call on several to explain their response to each statement. Explain that further answers will be shared as the study develops.

Clarification

Supplications—earnest entreaties.

Intercessions—a general word for "prayer" here. Paul uses the specific Greek word for "intercession" in Romans 8:26.

Honesty—dignity, respectfulness, seriousness.

Preacher—herald.

Verity—truth.

Doubting—dispute, argument.

TEACHING TIP 1

Develop a chart defining the four different elements of prayer mentioned in this passage. Refer to the material in the wide column. Invite students with different translations or paraphrases to share other meanings for these terms.

SUPPLICATION	
PRAYERS	
INTERCESSION	
THANKSGIVING	

like wolves among the sheep, not sparing the flock. They must also watch those who rise up from among the membership, preaching error and drawing away disciples to themselves.

Some time later, as we studied last week, the apostle spoke to the pastor at Ephesus again of unpleasant duties in dealing with false teachers. Today he speaks of other ministerial duties concerning worship and personnel for church leadership.

BIBLE COMMENTARY

I. The Ministry of Prayer

1 Timothy 2:1-8

1 Timothy 2:1. I exhort therefore, that, first of all, supplications, prayers, intercessions, and giving of thanks, be made for all men; 2. for kings, and for all that are in authority; that we may lead a quiet and peaceable life in all godliness and honesty. 3. For this is good and acceptable in the sight of God our Saviour; 4. who will have all men to be saved, and to come unto the knowledge of the truth. 8. I will therefore that men pray every where, lifting up holy hands, without wrath and doubting.

A. Nature of Prayer

The responsibilities of Pastor Timothy at Ephesus were not as unpleasant as those of dealing with the false teachers of last week's study. There were the more delightful duties of directing worship. These included giving guidance in public prayers at the church. (See Teaching Tip 1.)

In this passage Paul indicates the basic elements of petitioning the Lord are supplications, prayers, intercessions and thanksgiving. Though these words are somewhat synonymous, each does have its own shade of meaning. Prayer is the simple matter of presenting petitions to God in sacred communion. Supplication adds earnest entreaty to one's request. A good example of such fervency in prayer is that of Daniel in 9:17-19. While waiting for the Holy Spirit baptism the 120 also prayed with great earnestness (Acts 1:14).

The common meaning of intercession is prayer for others. Though in the Greek Paul uses a rather general word for prayer here (rather than the specific word for intercession as in Romans 8:26), petitioning for others is a part of the context. Christians are to plead especially for the salvation of the lost of the world.

Finally Paul says we should always include the element of thanksgiving in our prayers. In Philippians 4:6 he also encourages us to make our requests known to God with thanksgiving. If we teach our children it is rude to ask, then receive and not say, "Thank you," can we afford to be less courteous in relating to the Lord?

Guideline for Living 1

The way we pray most often is to simply express our thoughts, desires, and needs to God spontaneously. We pray from our hearts. But sometimes our prayer life can become a bit routine. Using

Develop the following acrostic to illustrate the balance we should strive for in our prayers.

A—doration
C—onfession
T—hanksgiving
S—upplication

Question.
What is the purpose of prayer as outlined in this passage?

TEACHING TIP 2
Develop the following visual to illustrate the fact that Christ is the only mediator between God and man.

GOD

some of the following prayer forms can help to add variety and new interest to our prayer life:

Written prayers. Try writing out your prayers. It may help you to think through your requests more clearly.

Read prayers. Reading the prayers of others can be a meaningful experience. Prayers from the Psalms can become our own prayers as we read them aloud to God.

Prayer log. Keep a log or diary of your prayer requests. Record the nature of the request, the date you first began to pray for it, and the time and way in which it was answered.

Prayer sentences. If you pray with another person or two, try having each person express a one-sentence prayer. Then the other may pray a single sentence on the same thought.

B. Purpose of Prayer

Paul tells Pastor Timothy to instruct the people to pray for government leaders. Rather than hate the hostile administration of Nero, they were to seek God for him. They prayed he might allow them to live quiet and peaceable lives in godliness and dignity.

But Christians are to include all men in their prayers, whether of high or low estate. They must seek the Lord earnestly for their salvation. Such petitions are specifically according to the will of God. He would have all men, not just a certain elected few, to be saved. H. A. Ironside said the "whosoever wills" constitute the elect while the "whosoever won'ts" are the non-elect. (See Teaching Tip 2.)

Here Paul explains at length that the Church holds in its hands the only hope for the recovery of dying sinners. There is only one God, not many. He has provided only one (not several) Mediator between himself and man. That Person himself is a Man, Christ Jesus. As honored as she should be, His mother Mary is not a mediatrix, nor are any other revered believers.

For a moment the apostle thinks of his own responsibility in getting the message of Christ to the lost of the world. He has been ordained by God as a preacher, an apostle, and a teacher to the nations. With Paul, Christians today must not only pray for sinners but also go with the gospel to them.

C. Manner of Prayer

Paul urges that public prayer be offered constantly by all men. It is not restricted to elders in the Church. In the process, an acceptable physical posture is that of standing with upraised hands. However, men must take care to lift up only holy hands. David says only those with clean hands should ascend the hill of the Lord (Psalm 24:4, 5). Further, he declares "If I regard iniquity in my heart, the Lord will not hear me" (Psalm 66:18).

In public prayers Christians should maintain peace among themselves. Their petitions to God must be free of anger. No disputing or arguing should be going on in the background.

Guideline for Living 2
Praying in public—We do it in almost every church service, yet we never talk or teach much about it. In this study Paul writes about both the manner and motive of public prayer.

Manner. Those who pray in public are addressing God as representatives of the rest of the people. As such they should speak loudly and clearly enough to be heard by the group. They should also pray about those needs that are relevant to the interests and desires of the group.

Motive. Being called on to pray in public should not be seen as reason for spiritual pride. Prayertime is not the time to preach. And of course it is not the time to reveal all the "juicy" details of the "unspoken prayer request." The purpose of public prayer is to bear one another's burdens, to uplift and encourage.

II. Qualifications for Church Leaders
1 Timothy 3:1-13

1 Timothy 3:2. A bishop then must be blameless, the husband of one wife, vigilant, sober, of good behavior, given to hospitality, apt to teach; 3. not given to wine, no striker, not greedy of filthy lucre; but patient, not a brawler, not covetous; 4. one that ruleth well his own house, having his children in subjection with all gravity; 6. not a novice, lest being lifted up with pride he fall into the condemnation of the devil. 8. Likewise must the deacons be grave, not double-tongued, not given to much wine, not greedy of filthy lucre; 9. holding the mystery of the faith in a pure conscience.

A. Bishops

After discussing public worship, Paul turns next to Timothy's duties in approving personnel for church leadership. He lists requirements for the offices of bishop and deacon. In New Testament times the bishop was an overseer in the local church. Unlike today, he was not a clergyman over ministers in several churches. The bishop was also known as an elder.

The apostle commends those who aspire to serve in positions of church leadership. They desire a good work. For the bishop the duties include both teaching and administration. The ministry is still earth's highest calling. The Church today as in Paul's day, should exalt the ministry before its youth.

In order to qualify for Church leadership a person must meet certain qualifications. Some of them concern his family life. The Church is to set before mankind both by precept and example God's ideal for the home, the first institution the Lord provided to maintain order in society. (See Teaching Tip 3.)

The bishop must be the husband of one wife. He is not to be a divorced and remarried person whose former companion still lives. Though Paul's words certainly prohibit a polygamist from the ministry, his concern here is something else. Polygamy was not practiced in the first century by Romans, Greeks, or Jews. It was against the law anywhere in the borders of Imperial Rome. The apostle says by example the preacher is to counter divorce, a thing which God hates (Malachi 2:14-16).

At home the bishop was also to manage the affairs of his household well, financially and otherwise. If he is a poor administrator

Bishop—overseer.

Vigilant—temperate, self-controlled.

Of good behavior—respectable, honorable.

No striker—not violent, not given to blows.

Not a brawler—peaceable, not quarrelsome.

Purchase . . . a good degree—obtain a good standing.

Question.

Why is correct conduct in the home so important for Church leaders?

TEACHING TIP 3

Develop the following chart in defining what a bishop must be and not be:

BISHOP MUST	
BE . . .	NOT BE . . .
Blameless	Given to wine
Husband of one wife	Striker
Vigilant	Greedy
Sober	Brawler
Of good behavior	Covetous
Hospitable	Novice
Children in subjection	
Apt to teach	
Rule house well	
Patient	

there he will not do well in overseeing things at church. Paul says let him also lead his children with dignity. If their subjection to him is from fear of his ruthless conduct, he will likely demand the same at church.

As to the more personal requirements for the bishop, the apostle declares he is not to be addicted to wine nor greedy of money. He must be self-controlled, wise, respectable, not given to violence, gentle, not quarrelsome, and above reproach in his conduct.

Further, the bishop must be a mature believer. He is not to be a newly converted person. The temptation to be proud in a leadership position in the Church can be damaging to the young Christian. His pride may lead to his downfall as Satan's did in the beginning.

Finally, to qualify for the position of overseer one must have a good report of men outside the Church. If his conduct raises questions about propriety in the minds of sinners, he is not likely to succeed in leading the Church in evangelizing the community. (See Teaching Tips 4 and 5.)

B. Deacons

The other office in the local church for which Paul lists qualifications is that of the deacon. Deacons were servants who attended to routine Church matters such as administering the welfare program for widows as at Jerusalem (Acts 6:1-7). They were assistants to ministers of the Word much as the Levites helped the priests in Old Testament times.

As with the bishop, the deacon must be a man of dignity, not given to wine, not greedy of dishonest gain, and irreproachable in his conduct. He too was to be the husband of one wife and a man who managed his household well. He also must have been a believer long enough to demonstrate the permanence of his faith and the sterling quality of his character.

In addition to what was said of the bishop, the deacon must not be double-tongued. He must be sincere and consistent in what he says. With conviction he is to hold correct doctrine. His behavior is to be such that his is always a clear conscience. In Scripture faith and morals are inseparable.

Guideline for Living 3

Many churches today use a committee to nominate prospective deacons or board members for consideration by the congregation. Maybe we should include some of these persons on that committee:

A local banker or credit manager: No one should be elected to manage the financial affairs of the church who cannot take care of his personal finances.

A neighbor or friend: Unfortunately the conduct of some people in church is sharply contrasted by the way they behave outside of church.

A spouse or child: How we relate to those closest to us will reveal how we can get along with others in leadership.

Now we are not really suggesting that these people be placed on the nominating committee. But it is important that we consider all areas of a person's life before we place him or her in an important position of leadership in the church.

C. Deacons' Wives

Paul gives specific attention to the wives of deacons. Since the Greek word here is the common one for women, some conclude the apostle has the office of the deaconess in view. Phoebe was such a servant of the church at Cenchrea (Romans 16:1, 2). Rather than being an administrative position, the deaconess likely worked with the deacon in such things as caring for the needy as Dorcas did (Acts 9:36-41). Indeed the deacons' wives may have acted in the capacity of deaconesses. In that case the import is the same whether the Greek is rendered wives or women.

Then wives of deacons are to be worthy of respect. They are not to be given to malicious gossip. Since the very word "devil" means "slanderer," they must not join him in one of his chief works. They are also to be self-controlled and trustworthy in everything.

Some wonder why Paul says nothing specifically about the bishop's wife. No doubt, however, what is said here concerning the wife of the deacon applies in both cases. What is true of the lesser office of the deacon would certainly hold true for the one of even greater responsibility.

Question.
What rewards does Paul promise for faithful service in local church leadership?

Paul promises two rewards. First, by this service one obtains a good standing both in the sight of God and man. Second, he gains confidence or assurance in his approach to God. His boldness in the faith is also demonstrated in his witness for Christ.

III. Godly Conduct
1 Timothy 3:14-16

1 Timothy 3:14. These things write I unto thee, hoping to come unto thee shortly: 15. but if I tarry long, that thou mayest know how thou oughtest to behave thyself in the house of God, which is the church of the living God, the pillar and ground of the truth. 16. And without controversy great is the mystery of godliness: God was manifest in the flesh, justified in the Spirit, seen of angels, preached unto the Gentiles, believed on in the world, received up into glory.

Clarification
House—household.
Church—literally, assembly.
Pillar—column, upright support.
Ground—foundation.
Mystery—truth previously hidden but now revealed.
Gentiles—nations.

A. Conduct of the Minister

To conclude his comments on spiritual leadership Paul turns to the matter of the conduct of the minister. We learn here specifically Paul's reason for writing this letter to Timothy. He hopes to come to Ephesus to provide counsel for the pastor without delay. However, if for some reason that is not possible, he wants to assist all he can with his pen. He desires that Timothy know how to conduct himself in the house of God.

A lot could be said about conducting oneself in a becoming manner in the house of worship. Here reverence, dignity, and orderliness are much to be desired. Distracting talk and boisterous behavior seem entirely out of place. However, in this passage Paul is concerned with the administrative conduct of the pastor. His attention is not on how to act in a church building.

Question.
What kind of conduct in church does Paul speak of here?

B. Character of the Church

To reinforce his emphasis on correct administrative procedure the apostle speaks briefly of the character of the Church. It is like a family as the household of God. It is also similar to an assembly of citizens in transacting business for God. Further, the Church

TEACHING TIP 6

Use the overhead transparency from the Packet of Adult Teaching Helps to illustrate the different pictures Paul uses to describe the character of the Church.

Question.

What elements of the gospel message does Paul list here?

TEACHING TIP 7

What doctrines of Christ are found in Paul's song (verse 16)? 1) the Incarnation, 2) the Resurrection, 3) the Ascension, 4) salvation, 5) worship.

TEACHING TIP 8

Read the last paragraph in the "Living the Truth" section. Conclude the study by leading the students in discussing the following questions: 1) What are the *desires* (motives) of spiritual leadership? 2) What is the *development* of spiritual leadership?

You may want to assign one of these questions to two different discussion groups. Allow them several minutes to prepare their summary. Give each group a large sheet of paper or blank transparency to record their comments. Then call for a report from each.

Daily Devotional Guide

M. Call to Leadership.
Exodus 3:1-12
T. Successful Leadership.
Joshua 1:2-9
W. Leadership in Prayer.
1 Samuel 12:16-25
T. Leadership's Reward.
Matthew 25:14-30
F. Servant Leadership.
Mark 9:33-37
S. Co-Workers With God.
1 Corinthians 3:5-23

is the divinely instituted support of the truth. Using an architectural analogy Paul says the Church supports the truth as its very foundation. It is also like the basic column, pillar, or upright support of the truth. The Church is not the source of the truth; it merely supports what God reveals. It is God, not the institutional church, who gives us Scripture.

C. Content of the Gospel

All this leads Paul to think on the content of the gospel. What he says here is arranged poetically. There are three sets of two lines each. In every case the second line contains a contrasting truth to the first. Some think Paul quotes an early Church hymn in this paragraph. (See Teaching Tip 7.)

The apostle speaks of the gospel as the mystery of godliness. It contains truth once hidden but now revealed. In it is the good news of the Incarnation—that God was manifested in the flesh. Coming in flesh as Jesus He was crucified like a criminal by men, but Paul says He was vindicated by the Spirit at the Resurrection. He deserves worship, another element of the gospel, as indicated by the song of the angels on seeing His birth in Bethlehem.

Such good news should be preached among the nations, Paul's song suggests. Evangelism is an essential part of the gospel. This will lead to Jesus' being believed on in the world. Implied here is the central truth that we are saved by faith.

The final element of the gospel on which the apostle focuses is the Ascension when Christ was received again in glory. All this is included in the truth the Church supports.

If these lines are from an early Church hymn, song writers of today should note the nature of the lyrics. They have a doctrinal message as inspiring as you will ever hear. Words like these in a song not only promote worship, but they teach truth as well. Regrettably, the lyrics of some Christian songs of our times don't compare well with these. Their message seems light compared to the one the song of Paul gives us.

LIVING THE TRUTH

Leadership is more a position of servanthood than lordship. It is desirable, and yet it should not be sought after for selfish means. It has its rewards, but it also has its requirements.

The best way to train to be a good leader is to learn to be a good follower. It begins with a consistent prayer life. It includes developing leadership qualifications, and it must be backed with godly conduct.

Do you desire to be a spiritual leader? Why? What are you doing now to develop leadership traits? Are you willing to be a good follower first? Are you ready to meet the demands of leadership? (See Teaching Tip 8.)

EVANGELISM OUTREACH

Have you ever been disappointed by someone in a position of spiritual leadership? Many people use that as an excuse to reject the message of the gospel. But it is an excuse that won't stand up before God. You will be judged solely on the basis of your acceptance or rejection of Jesus Christ.

3

RELATIONSHIPS IN THE CHURCH

Study Text
1 Timothy 4:1 through 5:25

Outline
I. Example for Believers
  A. In Daily Conduct
  B. In Christian Service
  C. In Spiritual Growth
II. Caring for People
  A. Age Groups
  B. Older Widows
  C. Younger Widows
III. Honoring Leaders
  A. Paying Preachers
  B. Disciplining Ministers

Golden Text: As we have therefore opportunity, let us do good unto all men, especially unto them who are of the household of faith. Galatians 6:10

Central Truth: The Church is a fellowship of light and love in a world of darkness and hate.

Learning Goals
1. To understand the importance of right relationships in the Church.
2. To evaluate our relationships with others.
3. To begin to work to improve problem relationships.

SEEING THE SCRIPTURES
1 Timothy 4:12-16; 5:17-22

12. Let no man despise thy youth; but be thou an example of the believers, in word, in conversation, in charity, in spirit, in faith, in purity.

13. Till I come, give attendance to reading, to exhortation, to doctrine.

14. Neglect not the gift that is in thee, which was given thee by prophecy, with the laying on of the hands of the presbytery.

15. Meditate upon these things; give thyself wholly to them; that thy profiting may appear to all.

16. Take heed unto thyself, and unto the doctrine; continue in them: for in doing this thou shalt both save thyself, and them that hear thee.

5:17. Let the elders that rule well be counted worthy of double honor, especially they who labor in the word and doctrine.

18. For the Scripture saith, Thou shalt not muzzle the ox that treadeth out the corn. And, The laborer is worthy of his reward.

19. Against an elder receive not an accusation, but before two or three witnesses.

20. Them that sin rebuke before all, that others also may fear.

21. I charge thee before God, and the Lord Jesus Christ, and the elect angels, that thou observe these things without preferring one before another, doing nothing by partiality.

22. Lay hands suddenly on no man, neither be partaker of other men's sins: keep thyself pure.

SETTING THE SCENE
There is a sense in which one might say all the world's problems are human in origin. Difficulties at the factory more often center around personnel than machinery. Major conflicts on the college campus are not due as much to lack of adequate facilities as to misunderstandings in the area of human relations. The defeat of armies may happen through the low morale of men rather than outdated weapons.

It is little different in the Church. For that reason Paul now addresses the subject of relationships in his letter to Timothy as pastor at Ephesus. To be effective he must set a good example before them and relate to the various groups in the church as a genuine Christian gentleman.

GETTING STARTED

Have the following phrases written on the chalkboard, overhead transparency, or sketchpad: Relationships with: spouse, family, God, self, friends, church members, business acquaintances, relatives.

As the students arrive, have them work in small groups of 4 or 5 to rank the above list of relationships by indicating which should be of first importance, second importance, third importance, etc. After 4-5 minutes, call for reports from each group. Rearrange the list of priorities above according to the order of priorities suggested by the work groups. Seek to arrive at a consensus regarding the first three or four priorities as follows:

#1—Our relationship with God.

#2—Our relationship with self. A positive self-respect is a basic requirement for successful interpersonal relationships.

#3—Relationship with spouse. Our most beneficial, supportive, and intimate relationship is with our spouse.

#4—Relationship with family. Secondary to marriage, the family relationship is the most fulfilling.

Clarification

Youth—used of men up to age 40.

Conversation—way of life, conduct, behavior.

Reading—public reading.

Presbytery—elders.

Profiting—progress.

TEACHING TIP 1

Ask several students to read 1 Timothy 4:12 from different versions or paraphrases of the Scripture. Develop definitions for the terms used in this verse. Record these definitions on a chart.

BIBLE COMMENTARY

I. Example for Believers

1 Timothy 4:12-16

1 Timothy 4:12. Let no man despise thy youth; but be thou an example of the believers, in word, in conversation, in charity, in spirit, in faith, in purity. 13. Till I come, give attendance to reading, to exhortation, to doctrine. 14. Neglect not the gift that is in thee, which was given thee by prophecy, with the laying on of the hands of the presbytery. 15. Meditate upon these things; give thyself wholly to them; that thy profiting may appear to all.

A. In Daily Conduct

If the minister is to succeed as a church administrator he must take care in his relationship to the membership. He will gain the respect of the people more by correct conduct than by lordly command. This is more true than ever with the younger pastor.

Paul told Timothy to give no one any occasion to despise his youth. He was by no means a teenager at the time, but in comparison to the aging apostle he was young. The Greek term for youth here was used of men up to age 40. If Timothy was no more than 16 when he first joined Paul in about A. D. 50 (since it was now around A. D. 63) he was at least approaching age 30.

Many in the church at Ephesus would be much older than Timothy. The elders he worked with probably were. Some of his critics and the false teachers he must discipline were too. Sometimes people fail to understand that gifts from God for ministry are as important as experience; therefore, they tend to give the younger preacher less respect than they should.

In his daily conduct Timothy must counter this tendency. He needs to be a model for believers in speech, overall behavior, love, spirituality, faith, and purity of life. The present tense of the Greek indicates he must do this with consistently correct conduct. He will gain the respect of some over a period rather than in a moment's time.

Guideline for Living 1

Like a family, the Church is made up of people of all ages. As with a family, there can sometimes be some "generation gaps" in the Church. The Bible makes it clear that the young are to give proper honor and respect to their elders. (And we like to remind them of this whenever we can!) But we are not always as quick to remember that we are also to give proper respect to the young. When Paul encourages Timothy not to let anyone despise his youthfulness, there is also an implied message to the older Christians that they are, therefore, not to disdain anyone just because he or she is young.

B. In Christian Service

Timothy's example for believers needs to extend to the area of Christian service. Paul says he is to make good use of the time in three ways while the apostle makes his way to Ephesus: public

Clarification

Honor—in the sense of giving financial support.

Nephews—descendants, specifically grandchildren.

Requite—repay a debt.

Desolate—alone.

Infidel—unbeliever.

Be taken into the number—be formally enrolled.

Wax wanton against Christ—when natural desires cause dedication to Christ to wane.

Having damnation—subject to condemnation.

Cast off their first faith—break their first pledge.

Busybodies—curious, meddlesome.

Question.

What guidelines does Paul offer for wholesome relationships in the Church?

reading of Scripture, exhortation of believers, and teaching of converts. All of this was a part of early meetings of the Church as in the synagogue (Acts 13:15).

Further, Timothy was to use well his gifts for ministry as indicated through prophetic utterance at his ordination. He must not neglect his call to preach the gospel. With the call came special spiritual abilities. The Lord called and equipped him for pastoral ministry.

C. In Spiritual Growth

Finally, the young pastor was to set the pattern for the membership in spiritual growth. He was to give himself fully to meditation or serious study. He must take heed first to himself and then to his teaching ministry. This is always the correct order.

Careful, personal attention to the preacher's own spiritual advancement is necessary first for his salvation. However, by being a prayerful student who faithfully communicates God's Word, he will also contribute greatly to the salvation of others who hear him. Paul desired Timothy to live so that his progress in the faith would be evident to all.

II. Caring for People

1 Timothy 5:1-16

1 Timothy 5:1. Rebuke not an elder, but entreat him as a father; and the younger men as brethren; 2. the elder women as mothers; the younger as sisters, with all purity. 3. Honor widows that are widows indeed. 4. But if any widow have children or nephews, let them learn first to show piety at home, and to requite their parents: for that is good and acceptable before God. 5. Now she that is a widow indeed, and desolate, trusteth in God, and continueth in supplications and prayers night and day. 6. But she that liveth in pleasure is dead while she liveth.

A. Age Groups

(See Teaching Tip 2.)

Not only should the young pastor Timothy be an example to believers, but he must also use wisdom in relating to various age groups in the Church. First, he is never to rebuke an elder. Since he speaks specifically later in this chapter of disciplining those in the office of elder, Paul refers now simply to older men in the congregation.

It is never pleasant to correct a fellow believer. When necessary in the case of an older gentleman Pastor Timothy is to entreat him as a father. Where it involves a younger man, the minister must treat him as a brother. In discipline and in all other matters relating to older women, Timothy is to respect them as mothers. He must regard younger women as sisters in associating with them in the purest of motives.

Guideline for Living 2

Working closely together in the Church with members of the opposite sex has sometimes led to immoral involvement that has

TEACHING TIP 3

Ask: "What financial needs may the widowed have? How could the Church help to provide some of these needs without giving money directly to them?" Possible replies: 1) Provide transportation, 2) assist with home maintenance, 3) offer financial and legal counsel.

Question.
What are Paul's rules for listing a widow's name on the welfare roll of the Church?

TEACHING TIP 4

Compile a list of deserving widows as discussed in this section. 1) Devout Christians; 2) 60-year-old or older; 3) wife of one husband; 4) having well-trained children; 5) doers of good works; 6) hospitable.

ruined lives and ministries and brought shame to the name of Christ. Paul has some words of instruction to the Church that will help guard against this problem. He says we are to treat others in the Church as if they are members of our family. We will not be tempted to get involved with a young man or young woman if we look on them as our brother or sister. We will not take advantage of older men or women if we consider them our father or mother. This attitude allows us to have warm, loving relationships and yet prohibits our getting too close.

What is true for the minister-member relationship is also correct between member and member. Treating each other with all due respect is the best way to avoid problems. The proper conduct of the lady and gentleman is always in order in the Church. Being overly familiar still breeds contempt. A degree of dignity safeguards wholesome associations among Christians.

B. Older Widows

Paul has special instructions for Timothy in showing his care for older widows in the congregation. He is to honor them with the common courtesies due them. However, his respect must be demonstrated in seeing that their financial and other needs are supplied. Even in the modern welfare state the Church must still consider carefully Paul's words here. (See Teaching Tip 3.)

Interestingly, Paul says family members have the first responsibility in supporting widows. Children, grandchildren, or other descendants have the duty before the Church. Christian relatives need to first act reverently at home in this matter. Any who fail to provide for their own, conduct themselves worse toward loved ones than most unbelievers do. They should take care of their aging parents and thereby repay a debt they have owed since infancy. (See Teaching Tip 4.)

Only where the widow is desolate or without living relatives is the Church responsible. Even so, she must meet specific requirements to qualify for aid. First, she is to be a devout Christian who trusts in God with prayers night and day. The pleasure-loving person, though a professed believer, did not qualify for full-time support from the Church. The main ministry of the Church to such widows is to remind them that the one who lives in pleasure is dead spiritually though alive physically. The pastor must challenge such persons to live blameless lives.

Further, to qualify for permanent assistance a widow must be no less than 60 years old. She must have a flawless marital history, having been the wife of only one husband. She could not have been divorced and married again. Children born to her must have been trained in the ways of the Lord.

The worthy widow was to have diligently followed every good work. In the days when she could afford it, she must have herself aided needy people. She was to have been hospitable in entertaining strangers, a thing so necessary in the ancient world. In most cases inns were few and far between. They often served as houses of prostitution and were otherwise dens of iniquity. When traveling believers stayed at the widow's house, she must have seen to it that the courtesy of washing their feet was extended to them.

C. Younger Widows

Paul's rules say widows under 60 were not to be enrolled for full-time financial assistance from the Church. Indeed, the congregation might well offer temporary relief for such needy persons in its membership. The Body might even do that for destitute persons outside its ranks, as Jesus indicated His followers would (Matthew 25:34-40).

However, the apostle advised Timothy that younger widows not be listed for permanent church welfare aid. Such is not wise though they rashly vow to never marry again. In time their natural desires will likely lead to a change of mind. Then they will feel condemned for having gone back on their first pledge to remain single.

Besides, with nothing constructive to do, Paul says the energies of the young widows will likely be spent in wandering from house to house meddling in the affairs of others. Gossip will be the order of the day for them. H. A. Ironside suggests that when people are short on something worthwhile to do with their hands, they usually work their tongues overtime. (See Teaching Tip 5.)

For these reasons the apostle recommends that younger widows remarry. It is wholesome for them to have the challenge of motherhood to walk the right pathway in life. They do well to engage in the creative business of managing a household. This is a noble calling. A Christian lady once proudly introduced herself as a household executive.

Little if any gainful employment outside the home was open to the young widow of the first century. Prostitution was a notable exception. Remarriage removed this temptation and eliminated questionable activities the Christian widow might fall into. Paul is concerned she do nothing to bring reproach on the gospel. He has seen some turn aside because they failed to follow a wise course of action after the crisis of losing a husband.

TEACHING TIP 5

Ask: "What are some ways the widowed can be involved in the work of the church?" Possible replies: Assist in providing child care; provide secretarial or clerical assistance; conduct telephone or letter writing campaigns; assist in preparing meals.

III. Honoring Leaders
1 Timothy 5:17-22

1 Timothy 5:17. Let the elders that rule well be counted worthy of double honor, especially they who labor in the word and doctrine. 18. For the Scripture saith, Thou shalt not muzzle the ox that treadeth out the corn. And, The laborer is worthy of his reward. 19. Against an elder receive not an accusation, but before two or three witnesses. 20. Them that sin rebuke before all, that others also may fear.

Clarification

Rule—manage, superintend.

Double honor—especially in financial support.

Labor—work hard.

Treadeth out the corn—threshing grain.

A. Paying Preachers

Another area of concern for Timothy in promoting harmonious relationships in the Church has to do with honoring leaders. Matters of importance here include selecting, disciplining, and giving adequate remuneration.

First, Paul says all Church leaders should be given due respect, even those who serve on a part-time basis without salary. Apparently there were elders at Ephesus who assisted in managing the affairs of the church without pay. No doubt their support came from regular jobs outside the church. No church today can do its work without the help of such persons. When they do well in their assignments, the pastor must see they are properly honored.

However, we see here again that to honor a person sometimes includes financial assistance. Some elders at Ephesus worked for the church full time. They devoted their days entirely to study, prayer, preaching, and teaching. Paul's remarks show they worked hard at the task. These were to receive double honor. In short, the apostle says the Church should pay its preachers well. (See Teaching Tip 6.)

Guideline for Living 3

How much should a church pay its pastor? What factors need to be considered in setting salaries that are fair and adequate? Here are some things to keep in mind:

1. *Age and Experience.* A pastor who has spent many years in effective ministry should be rewarded for those years of faithful service. Those gray hairs should be worth something!

2. *Family Needs.* Often a young man with a growing family will have greater needs than an older man whose family is already grown and gone. These two elements of experience and need must be balanced against each other.

3. *Living Costs.* The cost of living varies greatly from one part of the country to another. As a professional with church and community obligations, the pastor's living costs may be considerably higher than the average lay person in the church.

4. *Financial Resources of the Church.* Of course, churches cannot pay beyond what they are financially able to do. But sometimes it may be necessary for church leaders to take a step of faith and set a salary above what they may think they are able to do and trust the Lord to help them meet their obligation. This is better than always expecting the minister to be the one to "live by faith." God will bless the church that pays its pastor as much as possible rather than as much as they have to.

Question.
In what way does Paul support with Scripture his policy on paying preachers?

Paul's words are more than just good advice. What he says is supported by Scripture. The Old Testament prohibited a farmer from working an animal without feeding him. Surely the Church would not do less for an able minister. What is more, Jesus taught that the Christian worker is worthy of receiving adequate wages. (The apostle here classifies Luke's gospel with Deuteronomy in equating them both as Scripture.)

Question.
What steps should the Church take in the discipline of leaders?

B. Disciplining Ministers

A much less pleasant task of Pastor Timothy was that of sometimes having to discipline church leaders at Ephesus. Paul says this should always be done with due process to ensure justice. For guilt to be established, any accusation against an elder must be supported by two or three witnesses. Moses required the same in legal proceedings against anyone (Deuteronomy 17:6). Jesus set up similar safeguards for the accused church member (Matthew 18:16). Since Church leaders sometimes have enemies without just cause, the safeguard is especially needed for elders.

When guilt is well established, Paul says the sinning elder is to be censured publicly. This will serve as a warning to others who might be tempted to go astray. The Lord gave similar reasons

Be sure to allow enough time for the students to work through this concluding activity. Include time for individual or group prayer. Distribute paper and pencils and ask the students to complete the following sentence completion evaluation:

1. A relationship I am struggling with right now is . . .
2. The basic problem is . . .
3. One way I could help to improve the situation would be to . . .
4. To do this I would need to . . .
5. I will need the Lord to help me . . .

After the students have completed writing their responses to the above statements, encourage them to spend the remainder of the time in prayer regarding their problem relationship. If the students know each other well enough, you may want to ask them to pray with one or two other persons about their need.

Daily Devotional Guide

M. Example of Selflessness.
Genesis 13:1-12
T. Example of Forgiveness.
Genesis 50:15-21
W. Discipline in the Church.
Matthew 18:15-20
T. Christian Benevolence.
Acts 9:36-42
F. Unity of Believers.
1 Corinthians 12:12-26
S. Bearing Burdens.
Galatians 6:1-6

concerning the discipline of the juvenile delinquent in ancient Israel (Deuteronomy 21:18-21).

Once more Paul tells Timothy discipline is to be administered with due respect for all involved. He was to do nothing in partiality never preferring one before another. He must avoid the tendency to treat some as though they could do no wrong while concluding others can do no right.

Finally, the apostle says Timothy should examine carefully all candidates for ministerial service before laying hands on them to ordain them. To approve too quickly only to later learn a leader is living in sin is to share a degree of his guilt. John gives a similar warning against befriending unworthy ministers (3 John 10, 11).

Paul's last word to Timothy is that he must keep himself pure. He must not be so taken up with the discipline of others that he neglects his own soul.

LIVING THE TRUTH

The principles for good relationships outlined in this study apply in all areas of life. They affect how we get along with our spouse, our family, and our relatives. They regulate our relationships with neighbors and friends, fellow workers, and those with whom we do business. And, of course, they determine how we relate to one another in the Church.

The only way we can hope to maintain good relationships with all these people is to maintain a good relationship with the Lord. Our vertical relationship with Him will affect our horizontal relationships with all others. (See Teaching Tip 7.)

EVANGELISM OUTREACH

Are you struggling in your relationships with others? Have you ever considered that the problem may lie with you and not with them? Maybe you are all too aware of that fact, but don't know what to do about it. The solution is to turn your life over to Jesus. The secret to living in right relationship with others is to have a right relationship with Jesus Christ.

THE INCARNATION

4

SEEING THE SCRIPTURES

Matthew 20:28

28. The Son of man came not to be ministered unto, but to minister, and to give his life a ransom for many.

John 10:10

10. The thief cometh not, but for to steal, and to kill, and to destroy: I am come that they might have life, and that they might have it more abundantly.

Galatians 4:4-7

4. When the fulness of the time was come, God sent forth his Son, made of a woman, made under the law,

5. To redeem them that were under the law, that we might receive the adoption of sons.

6. And because ye are sons, God hath sent forth the Spirit of his Son into your hearts, crying, Abba, Father.

7. Wherefore thou art no more a servant, but a son; and if a son, then an heir of God through Christ.

1 Timothy 1:15

15. This is a faithful saying, and worthy of all acceptation, that Christ Jesus came into the world to save sinners; of whom I am chief.

1 Peter 1:18

18. Ye know that ye were not redeemed with corruptible things, as silver and gold, from your vain conversation received by tradition from your fathers.

SETTING THE SCENE

A systematic schedule for a study of Scripture should always ensure the coverage of the whole Bible. This should include a major emphasis on the life of Christ. Members of the Evangelical Curriculum Commission do both. This publisher follows its guidelines in the production of this quarterly.

The current schedule of the Commission covers the Bible in a seven-year period. Two full years of the seven concentrate on Jesus, with one focusing on His life while the other considers His teachings.

Further, it is fitting to look at the birth of Christ annually. However, instead of studying the birth story, this time we view topically the doctrine of the Incarnation.

PREPARING TO TEACH

Study Text

Genesis 3:15; 49:10; Daniel 9:24-26; Matthew 20:28; John 1:14; 10:10; Romans 1:3; Galatians 4:4-7; 1 Timothy 1:15; Hebrews 2:14; 1 Peter 1:18; 1 John 4:1-10

Outline

I. In God's Time
  A. The Promise Made
  B. The Time Set
  C. The Prophecy Fulfilled
II. In God's Way
  A. A Plan for Victory
  B. A Place Among Men
  C. A Son of David
  D. A Child of the Law
  E. A Common Sufferer
III. For God's Purpose
  A. To Be a Servant
  B. To Bring Life
  C. To Provide for Spiritual Adoption
  D. To Save Sinners
  E. To Redeem Men

Golden Text: When the fulness of the time was come, God sent forth his Son, made of a woman, made under the law. Galatians 4:4

Central Truth: Through the Incarnation God made possible His plan of redemption.

Learning Goals

1. To understand how the birth of Christ fulfilled Old Testament prophecies.
2. To appreciate the fact that Jesus experienced life as we experience it.
3. To determine to celebrate Christmas in its true meaning.

If you have a smaller class (15 or less students), invite each one to share a personal or family Christmas tradition. If you have a larger class, invite the students to share with a person sitting next to them. Or invite four or five students to share their Christmas tradition with the entire class.

Christmas is a holiday with many family traditions and personal memories rooted in the past. The first Christmas was also firmly rooted in the past. Old Testament writers from Moses to Malachi foretold the coming of the Messiah. This Christmas study begins with a look at the Old Testament prophecies regarding the coming of Christ.

Clarification

Lawgiver—ruler's staff.
Shiloh—perhaps, "he whose it is," or "that which belongs to him."
Gathering of the people—obedience of the nations.
Seventy weeks—literally, seventy sevens or periods of seven.
Make an end of—restrain.

TEACHING TIP 1

Ask the students to turn in their Bibles to Matthew 1:2-16 and Luke 3:23-38. Point out in these verses how the lineage of Christ can be traced back to David, Judah, Abraham, and Adam.

Question.

How did Daniel predict the time of Messiah's coming?

BIBLE COMMENTARY

I. In God's Time

Genesis 49:10; Daniel 9:24-26; Galatians 4:4

Genesis 49:10. The sceptre shall not depart from Judah, nor a lawgiver from between his feet, until Shiloh come; and unto him shall the gathering of the people be. Daniel 9:24. Seventy weeks are determined upon thy people and upon thy holy city, to finish the transgression, and to make an end of sins, and to make reconciliation for iniquity, and to bring in everlasting righteousness, and to seal up the vision and prophecy, and to anoint the Most Holy. 25. Know therefore and understand, that from the going forth of the commandment to restore and to build Jerusalem, unto the Messiah the Prince, shall be seven weeks, and threescore and two weeks: the street shall be built again, and the wall, even in troublous times.

A. The Promise Made

One of the early promises of the coming of Christ to earth appears in Jacob's final blessing on his sons. The patriarch sat up on the edge of his deathbed and spoke prophetically of the future of each of his twelve sons and their descendants. (See Teaching Tip 1.)

From Judah and his tribe, Jacob said, time would bring a kingly line. The dynasty would continue indefinitely. The throne would not pass from the house of Judah by violent overthrow or otherwise.

In fact, the patriarch promised the royal scepter would not depart from Judah nor the ruler's staff from between his feet until a notable King appeared. Here He is called Shiloh. The name may refer to "that which belongs to him." It speaks of Him whose right the throne is. Once He is here, the tribe of Judah, all the tribes of Israel, and in fact the nations of the world will gather to Him in obedience.

B. The Time Set

Centuries later another prophet spoke of the coming of the same King. Daniel calls this Prince the "Messiah" or "Anointed One." He indicates rather specifically the time of the Messiah's arrival.

In response to his prayer concerning the end of the 70-year Babylonian captivity, the Lord speaks to the prophet Daniel about an important 70-week segment of Israel's future (Daniel 9:24-27). It is obvious these are weeks of years rather than days. The Hebrew word for "weeks" simply means "sevens."

Daniel separates one week from the other 69. The 69 weeks run "from the going forth of the commandment to restore and to build Jerusalem, unto the Messiah" (verse 25). Various Medo-Persian rulers issued different decrees to end the Babylonian captivity of the Jews. However, only one of these specifically legalized the rebuilding of the holy city. This decree came from Artaxerxes in 445 B.C.

Since the 69 weeks spoken of in Daniel are weeks of years, the amount of time involved would total 483 years. However, Bible

TEACHING TIP 3

Have the following references from the Gospel of Matthew written out on individual slips of paper: 1:22; 2:4, 5; 2:15, 17; 2:23. Distribute the slips of paper to the students and ask them to read these verses as you call for them. Point out that all of these verses refer to ways in which the birth of Christ fulfilled Old Testament prophecies.

TEACHING TIP 4

Ask: "In what way was the world prepared for the first coming of Christ? In what way is the world today prepared for the second coming of Christ? What similarities are there between conditions surrounding His first coming and His second coming?"

Question.

In what way was the first century the "fulness of the time?"

Clarification

Bruise—grind, crush, destroy.

Dwelt among us—pitched his tent or lived temporarily among us.

Destroy—render powerless.

Devil—accuser, slanderer.

years consisted of twelve 30-day months. So, when the 69 weeks are calculated using months of today's length, they total 476 years. Of course, mathematical exactness is impossible because of differences in calendar calculations during the course of history. But 476 years from 445 B.C. takes one to about the time of the crucifixion of Jesus, around A.D. 30.

Daniel also tells of the great work the Anointed One will do when He comes. He will finish transgression, restrain sin, make reconciliation for iniquity, and bring in everlasting righteousness. (See Teaching Tip 2.)

Guideline for Living 1

Jesus said we would not know the day nor the hour of His return (Mark 13:32), but we can know the times and seasons. Devout Old Testament saints earnestly sought the Scriptures to learn what they could about their coming Messiah. Believers today are also told to watch for His return. Endless speculation and arguments about prophetic events serve no useful purpose. But an honest desire to be watching and waiting for our Lord's return can help us to be ready when He comes.

C. The Prophecy Fulfilled

New Testament writers also note these prophecies were fulfilled according to God's timetable. When Jesus began His main Galilean ministry Mark says He announced, "The time is fulfilled, and the kingdom of God is at hand" (1:15). Paul also declares the prophecy of the Messiah's coming was fulfilled in God's time. He explains, "When the fulness of the time was come, God sent forth his Son" (Galatians 4:4). (See Teaching Tips 3 and 4.)

The world was uniquely prepared for the spread of the gospel exactly at the time Jesus came. Under Rome there was worldwide peace. A system of roads made travel far and near the easiest of history. Roman citizens need not even stop at any national borders. The common language of Greek lessened the difficulty of communication. History indicates how in the wisdom of God this was the "fulness of time."

II. In God's Way

Genesis 3:15; John 1:14; Romans 1:3; Galatians 4:4; Hebrews 2:14

Genesis 3:15. I will put enmity between thee and the woman, and between thy seed and her seed; it shall bruise thy head, and thou shalt bruise his heel. John 1:14. The Word was made flesh, and dwelt among us, (and we beheld his glory, the glory as of the only begotten of the Father,) full of grace and truth. Romans 1:3. Concerning his Son Jesus Christ our Lord, which was made of the seed of David according to the flesh. Hebrews 2:14. Forasmuch then as the children are partakers of flesh and blood, he also himself likewise took part of the same; that through death he might destroy him that had the power of death, that is, the devil.

THE CRIB

THE CROSS

THE CROWN

A. A Plan for Victory

Jesus came into the world not only in God's time but also in God's way. This included a plan for Him to be born of a virgin. Evidence for the Virgin Birth in the Bible begins with the first promise of man's Redeemer (Genesis 3:15). To the devil while yet in the Garden of Eden, God said the Redeemer was "her seed," with strong implications that a male would play no part in His birth.

After a miraculous birth, God's plan calls for a vicious struggle. According to this first prophecy this would involve war between the seed of woman and the seed of the serpent who had tempted Eve to sin. The climax of the conflict would come at the Cross. True to the Word of the Lord, Satan bruised the heel of the Christ. But that would heal. In the struggle Jesus bruised or crushed the serpent's head. That was a mortal wound.

Then God's way included a plan for victory. In seed thought at least, the first promise of man's Redeemer included prophecies of the Virgin Birth, the Crucifixion, and great victory at the Resurrection. (See Teaching Tip 5.)

B. A Place Among Men

John spoke of Christ's coming after it was an accomplished fact. His powerful words are, "The Word was made flesh" (John 1:14). Becoming flesh speaks of something more than ordinary human birth. What parent uses such an expression to talk of a newborn babe? John's words refer to the miracle of the Incarnation.

The eternal Word took His place among men in becoming flesh. This made it possible, as John says, for Him to dwell among us. The Greek indicates He merely "pitched His tent" or lived temporarily on earth. But it was long enough for those near Him to behold His glory as the Father's only Son, full of grace and truth. (See Teaching Tip 6.)

Guideline for Living 2

One of radio commentator Paul Harvey's famous stories has become a modern-day Christmas parable. It is the account of a man who did not believe the message of the Incarnation. He couldn't understand why God would have come to earth in the form of a man. Because he did not want to be a hypocrite, he stayed home while his wife attended the annual Christmas Eve service at church. Shortly after she left, it began to snow. As he sat in his chair reading, he heard a thudding sound outside the large picture window. It sounded like someone throwing snowballs against the window. When he went to investigate, he saw a flock of birds floundering in the snow. They had been caught in the storm and in a desperate search for shelter were trying to fly through his window. As he ran out to try to help them, he thought of the barn as a place of shelter for the birds. So he opened the doors and turned on the lights, but the birds would not come in. He sprinkled bread crumbs in the doorway, but still they flew into the window or huddled in the snow. He tried to chase them into the barn, but they only became more confused.

If only I could become one of them, he thought, *maybe I could direct them into the shelter of the barn.* Just then the church bells began to ring above the sound of the storm. And in that moment the Incarnation became real to him. Suddenly he knew why God had come into the world in the form of a Man: to become one of them so He could lead them to safety and salvation.

Years later in his old age John again declares, "That which was from the beginning, which we have heard, which we have seen with our eyes, which we have looked upon, and our hands have handled, of the Word of life; (for the life was manifested, and we have seen it, and bear witness . . .)" (1 John 1:1, 2). The Incarnation is a reality despite those who have denounced and ridiculed it.

C. A Son of David

Indeed God's plan was that Jesus be born "according to the flesh," as Paul expresses it (Romans 1:3). Further, he was to become a man as the "seed of David." The Lord promised to bless the world through the "seed" of Abraham. David was among his descendants, but he was not that seed. The "seed" was one, not many, as Paul makes clear (Galatians 3:16). That "seed" was Christ.

The promise to David was that he would always have a descendant on the throne of Judah (1 Kings 2:4). Jewish people knew this word well. Repeatedly Jesus was addressed as the Son of David while on earth. He will yet occupy David's throne during the Millennium.

D. A Child of the Law

Yes, God's plan was that His Son be born of a woman and of the seed of David. Perhaps with the Virgin Birth in mind Paul states he was "made of a woman" (Galatians 4:4). It is fitting that since sin came into the world by woman, so should the Saviour.

Paul declares Jesus was born a child of the Law. He learned of its burden and purpose through personal experience. As a son of the Law He was circumcised the eighth day to symbolize the cutting away of the flesh. He submitted to this though He knew no sin in the flesh. In the same way He insisted John baptize Him though He had no sin to repent of.

E. A Common Sufferer

The writer of Hebrews explains in all this God's plan was that Jesus be a common sufferer with fellowmen (2:14). He suffered so He may better help them, knowing by experience how they feel (verse 18). However, there was a greater reason. He lived in the same body of flesh and blood as all men so He might die and be raised again. In being raised He rendered powerless the one who for the moment has the power of death—the devil. Thereby He freed those who would otherwise all their lifetime be subject to the fear of death (verse 15). (See Teaching Tip 7.)

III. For God's Purpose

Matthew 20:28; John 10:10; Galatians 4:5-7; 1 Timothy 1:15; 1 Peter 1:18

(See Teaching Tip 8.)

Matthew 20:28. The Son of man came not to be ministered unto, but to minister, and to give his life a ransom for many. John 10:10. The thief cometh not, but for to steal, and to kill, and to destroy:

Question.
In what sense was Jesus made "under the Law"?

TEACHING TIP 7
From the Packet of Adult Teaching Helps use the chart of the three appearances of Christ to summarize the discussion of this section of the study and to explain how each of Christ's appearings is different from the others.

TEACHING TIP 8
Make the following listening assignment before reading these verses of Scripture: "Listen for the things mentioned in these verses that Christ came to do." On the chalkboard list their responses, which should include the following: to minister, to give His life, to give life, to redeem us, to make us sons, to make us heirs of God, to save sinners.

Clarification

Ransom—price of release.

Kill—slaughter.

More abundantly—in its fullness.

Servant—slave.

Vain conversation—futile way of life.

Question.

In what way is the Bible's servanthood principle a radical one?

TEACHING TIP 9

Ask: "How is the life that Christ brings different from life in this world?" Possible responses: 1) brings lasting satisfaction, 2) is eternal, 3) brings wholeness and fullness.

TEACHING TIP 10

How does the Bible compare our spiritual relationships with God and others with that of a family? 1) God our Father; 2) Christ our Elder Brother; 3) other Christians, our brothers and sisters; 4) the Church our family, the bride of Christ.

Question.

What are some of the benefits of being adopted into the family of God?

I am come that they might have life, and that they might have it more abundantly. Galatians 4:5. To redeem them that were under the law, that we might receive the adoption of sons. 6. And because ye are sons, God hath sent forth the Spirit of his Son into your hearts, crying, Abba, Father. 7. Wherefore thou art no more a servant, but a son; and if a son, then an heir of God through Christ. 1 Timothy 1:15. This is a faithful saying, and worthy of all acceptation, that Christ Jesus came into the world to save sinners; of whom I am chief. 1 Peter 1:18. Ye know that ye were not redeemed with corruptible things, as silver and gold, from your vain conversation received by tradition from your fathers.

A. To Be a Servant

On one occasion Jesus took note that men the world considers great lord it over their fellows (Matthew 20:25). They consider it their privilege. However, God sees things differently. Jesus said in the Church the great serve rather than rule. He uses himself as the prime example. God's purpose in His coming to earth was that He give of himself to others rather than having them wait on Him hand and foot.

Our Lord demonstrated the serving principle graphically when He washed His own students' feet (John 13:1-17). However, His giving of self for others included the ultimate at the Cross. There He gave His life as the price of release for all who are slaves to sin.

Guideline for Living 3

The servant style of leadership advocated and demonstrated by Jesus was in sharp contrast to that practiced by many leaders then and now. Even some leaders in the Church see their position as one of privilege and power rather than a place of servanthood. As Charles Swindoll has pointed out in his book, *Improving Your Serve*, leadership is an opportunity to minister, not to be ministered to; to give, not hoard; to obey, not be obeyed; to serve, not to be served; to be humbled, not exalted; to be reachable, not out of reach.

B. To Bring Life

The purpose of God in the Incarnation was also to bring life to men. As Jesus himself said, false religious leaders bring death (John 10:10). They come only to steal, slaughter, and destroy. They are selfishly concerned for the fleece but care nothing for the sheep. In contrast, Jesus as the true Shepherd wants His flock to enjoy life—real life in its fullness. (See Teaching Tip 9.)

C. To Provide for Spiritual Adoption

Another purpose in God's sending Jesus to earth was to provide for spiritual adoption. The practice of adoption was little known among Jewish peoples but was prevalent among Gentiles. Paul uses this well-known custom to illustrate what Christ does for men at salvation (Galatians 4:5-7). (See Teaching Tip 10.)

At the moment of conversion former sinners receive adoption as sons into the family of God. The reality of the transaction becomes clear as the Lord pours His Spirit into the heart of the believer. As a newborn babe he cries, "Abba, Father."

Further, he is no more a servant to sin, but is now a son of God.

As a son he is, through union with Christ the Son, an heir of God the Father.

D. To Save Sinners

Still another purpose of the Incarnation is to save sinners. In fact, Paul states the gospel in just nine words saying, "Christ Jesus came into the world to save sinners" (1 Timothy 1:15). Luke says simply, "The Son of man is come to seek and to save that which was lost" (19:10). Paul declares these truths worthy of all trust. As chief of sinners he speaks from experience.

E. To Redeem Men

Finally, let us note with Peter that all these purposes in the Incarnation were accomplished at a great price (1 Peter 1:18). Our release from slavery to sin was not purchased with decaying things like silver or gold. It was the priceless blood of Christ who was slain as a Lamb without blemish or spot that set us free.

Peter reminds us of the hopelessness of man apart from the Incarnation. The need of redemption from slavery to sin is apparent to all. In refusing to accept God's provisions for release, men devise their own ways to seek freedom. The apostle refers to these as encouraging futile ways of life. From such traditions Christ freed us.

LIVING THE TRUTH

With all the trappings of the holiday season focusing our attention on Christmas, it is hard to even think about another holiday still 4 months away—Easter. And yet if it were not for Easter, Christmas would have no meaning. The Cross is what gives significance to the crib. As Christians our celebration of Christmas should be vastly different from that of the world around us. We know not only that He came, but also why He came. How have you been celebrating this season? Are you caught up in the excitement of His birth? Or do you also think of His death? Remember, He was born to die. (See Teaching Tip 11.)

EVANGELISM OUTREACH

Do you know the real meaning of Christmas? Do you know that Jesus came to die for your sins? This could be the best Christmas of your life. It will be if you accept Jesus Christ as your personal Saviour. You could receive the most wonderful gift this year—the gift of eternal life.

5 | CONSISTENT CHRISTIAN LIVING

Golden Text: Follow after righteousness, godliness, faith, love, patience, meekness. 1 Timothy 6:11

Central Truth: Those who live godly avoid evil, seek good, and delight in sharing with others.

Learning Goals
1. To become aware of the dangers of covetousness.
2. To accept the challenge to live a consistent Christian life.
3. To be willing to share our resources with others.

SEEING THE SCRIPTURES
1 Timothy 6:3-17

3. If any man teach otherwise, and consent not to wholesome words, even the words of our Lord Jesus Christ, and to the doctrine which is according to godliness;

4. He is proud, knowing nothing, but doting about questions and strifes of words, whereof cometh envy, strife, railings, evil surmisings,

5. Perverse disputings of men of corrupt minds, and destitute of the truth, supposing that gain is godliness: from such withdraw thyself.

6. But godliness with contentment is great gain.

7. For we brought nothing into this world, and it is certain we can carry nothing out.

8. And having food and raiment, let us be therewith content.

9. But they that will be rich fall into temptation and a snare, and into many foolish and hurtful lusts, which drown men in destruction and perdition.

10. For the love of money is the root of all evil: which while some coveted after, they have erred from the faith, and pierced themselves through with many sorrows.

11. But thou, O man of God, flee these things; and follow after righteousness, godliness, faith, love, patience, meekness.

12. Fight the good fight of faith, lay hold on eternal life, whereunto thou art also called, and hast professed a good profession before many witnesses.

13. I give thee charge in the sight of God, who quickeneth all things, and before Christ Jesus, who before Pontius Pilate witnessed a good confession;

14. That thou keep this commandment without spot, unrebukable, until the appearing of our Lord Jesus Christ:

15. Which in his times he shall show, who is the blessed and only Potentate, the King of kings, and Lord of lords;

16. Who only hath immortality, dwelling in the light which no man can approach unto; whom no man hath seen, nor can see: to whom be honor and power everlasting. Amen.

17. Charge them that are rich in this world, that they be not high-minded, nor trust in uncertain riches, but in the living God, who giveth us richly all things to enjoy.

SETTING THE SCENE
Following the passage in last week's study Paul spoke of the relationship of two other groups in the Church. They are masters and slaves. He said slaves of unbelieving masters must give them

GETTING STARTED

Have the following sentence completion statement written on the chalkboard, overhead transparency, or sketchpad: "The best Christmas gift I got this past week was . . ." As the students arrive, instruct them to write down or share and explain their response to this statement with two or three other people. Ask: "Why do you feel this gift will be of value? How will it bring you happiness or contentment? How would you have felt if you had not received this item?"

TEACHING TIP 1

Before reading the following passage, give the students this assignment. "Listen for the things Paul says result from 'doting about questions and strifes of words.'" After the verses are read, call for responses from the students.

Clarification

Wholesome—healthy, sound.

Proud—puffed up, blinded, foolish.

Doting—being sick over, having a morbid craving for.

Railings—abusive speech.

Perverse disputings—constant wranglings.

Destitute—having been robbed, deprived.

Perdition—utter destruction.

all due respect. Their conduct at work was to be such that the name of God and His teaching be not blasphemed.

Christian slaves with believing masters were not to envy them. Nor were they to expect special favors from them just because they were brothers in Christ. Rather, they should render faithful service from a heart of brotherly love. Pastors can apply the principles of the passage to employees on the church staff.

In closing his letter to Timothy, Paul once again writes of problems with false teachers.

BIBLE COMMENTARY

I. Be Content

1 Timothy 6:3-10

(See Teaching Tip 1.)

1 Timothy 6:3. If any man teach otherwise, and consent not to wholesome words, even the words of our Lord Jesus Christ, and to the doctrine which is according to godliness; 4. he is proud, knowing nothing, but doting about questions and strifes of words, whereof cometh envy, strife, railings, evil surmisings, 5. perverse disputings of men of corrupt minds, and destitute of the truth, supposing that gain is godliness: from such withdraw thyself. 6. But godliness with contentment is great gain. 9. But they that will be rich fall into temptation and a snare, and into many foolish and hurtful lusts, which drown men in destruction and perdition.

A. The Source of Discontent

Paul's final words to Timothy concerning his relationship to false teachers at Ephesus center on consistent Christian living. This leads to a discussion of the source of discontent in the hearts of believers.

From the beginning of his first letter to the young pastor the apostle has addressed problems false teachers caused in the city where Diana was worshiped. They refused to embrace the healthy teachings of Jesus and His doctrine which promoted upright living. They had another, a twisted message.

In turning to the subject one last time near the end of his correspondence, Paul says pride and ignorance are behind the position these teachers have taken. Their warped minds have left them with a morbid craving for endless arguments about controversial questions. They love wars over words. Rejecting sound or healthy doctrine, they have been made sick by their own teachings.

The results of the erroneous instructions at Ephesus were far from desirable. Paul lists them as envy, fighting, abusive speech, and false speculations. Involved also are constant wranglings of men of corrupt minds. They were men who had been robbed of the truth they once possessed.

But more, these false teachers suppose that godliness is a means of gain. Their doctrine becomes the source of discontent among believers. With its implications that God's chief aim for His children on earth is that they become rich, it serves as a cloak for covetousness. Paul tells Timothy he is to withdraw fellowship from those who preach such a doctrine.

Write out or display the following formula for happiness:
GODLINESS
+
CONTENTMENT
=
GREAT GAIN

Question.
What is the nature of the sin of covetousness?

Question.
What effect does covetousness have on one's life?

TEACHING TIP 3
You may want to assign a student to bring a brief (3-5 minutes) report on the sin of covetousness. Instruct him to give a definition of covetousness, its effects on people, and its end result. Refer the researcher to the material in the *Adult Teacher* as well as to other resources.

TEACHING TIP 4
Ask: "How rich do you have to be before your money can begin to get in the way of your relationship to God? How do riches hinder our relationship to God?" Refer to "Guideline for Living 2" in discussing these questions.

Guideline for Living 1

History records that while the Russian Orthodox Church was in a conference hotly debating some minor issue of church doctrine, the Bolsheviks were overthrowing the government of Russia and setting up a Communist regime. What a tragedy it is when Christians become embroiled in pointless argument while the world around them is perishing in revolution! We must continually guard against the danger of majoring in minors. To paraphrase the prayer of Reinhold Niebuhr, "May God grant us the courage to stand firmly for those issues that are truly essential to the truth of the gospel, the grace to humbly accept the viewpoints of others who may differ with us in those nonessential areas, and the wisdom to know the difference between the two."

B. The Curse of Covetousness

(See Teaching Tips 2 and 3.)

His reference to the use of religion as a means for personal financial gain leads the apostle to discuss at length the curse of covetousness. It is possibly the most subtle of all sins. The Greek word refers to "the wish to have more." One is guilty of covetousness when the desire for material gain becomes the driving force in his life. He lives and labors with that one purpose in mind. It is so much at the center of his life it becomes his religion. Thus it is idolatry (Ephesians 5:5).

Covetousness is not only subtle; it is deadly. For one thing, Paul implies it robs a person of his contentment. Godliness should never be viewed as a means of material gain. To be sure, the Lord abundantly supplies the needs of His children. However, the real gain of godliness is in the spiritual realm. Trust in God leads to the priceless possession of contentment. With food, clothing, and shelter the Christian should be content (Philippians 4:11).

Paul also declares covetousness ignores the facts of life. As is often said, "You can't take it with you when you die." Job, among the world's richest, exclaimed, "Naked came I out of my mother's womb, and naked shall I return" (1:21).

Further, the apostle declares this subtle sin is at the root of many others. This is so much the case that Paul says, "The love of money is the root of all evil." Some people will commit all kinds of crime for money. It is even listed as a basic cause of divorce today.

But more than anything else, the apostle declares covetousness robs a man of his soul. It leads him into temptation and a trap. It fosters foolish and harmful lusts. It ends in destruction and utter ruin. (See Teaching Tip 4.)

Guideline for Living 2

The great industrialist and financier John D. Rockefeller was once asked how much money it takes to make people happy. He replied, "A little more than they have." For many people it is not that they are unhappy with what they have, but with what they don't have. Greed is unsatiable; it can never be satisfied!

Unfortunately, unbelievers are not the only ones who have problems with greed and covetousness. And it certainly is not limited to those Christians who are more wealthy. Poor people can be stingy too.

Before reading the following passage, give the students the following assignment: "Listen for the things Paul said Timothy should flee and follow, and areas involving a fight." After the verses have been read, call for a response from the students to this listening assignment: Possible replies:

Flee: false doctrine, covetousness, perverse disputings.

Follow: righteousness, godliness, faith, love, patience, meekness.

Fight: the good fight of faith, lay hold on eternal life, keep the charge, keep the commandment.

Clarification

Patience—remaining steadfast under trial, perseverance, endurance.

Meekness—gentleness.

Unrebukable—without reproach.

Power everlasting—eternal dominion.

Question.

What truth does Paul share here concerning motives for ministry?

Paul uses two forceful figures to drive home his point. Covetousness "drowns" men's souls—among the most feared of all deaths. In another sense it leads men to commit spiritual suicide. By it, men have pierced themselves through with many sorrows. The mental anguish of covetousness stabs them in the heart spiritually.

In all of this Paul addresses those who have their heart set on becoming rich (verse 9). Contrary to the thinking of some, covetousness is a temptation to the poor and not just the rich.

In today's world, for example, those who have little of this world's goods are tempted to envy those who have much. Envy is really hatred of another for having something you wish you had. As Paul makes clear, those without worldly possessions are tempted to do almost anything to get them. Sometimes they have their heart so set on material things they are willing to sell their souls to gain them.

The wife may work away from home at nights and the husband during the day, not of necessity but simply to have an ever higher standard of living. The husband may even seek a second job, working evenings and weekends just to afford more luxuries. As a result there is little time left for self, family, or God.

II. Fight the Good Fight
1 Timothy 6:11-16

(See Teaching Tip 5.)

1 Timothy 6:11. Thou, O man of God, flee these things; and follow after righteousness, godliness, faith, love, patience, meekness. 12. Fight the good fight of faith, lay hold on eternal life, whereunto thou art also called, and hast professed a good profession before many witnesses. 13. I give thee charge in the sight of God, who quickeneth all things, and before Christ Jesus, who before Pontius Pilate witnessed a good confession; 14. that thou keep this commandment without spot, unrebukable, until the appearing of our Lord Jesus Christ.

A. Flee False Doctrine

To practice consistent Christian living, the apostle exhorts young Timothy to flee the things he has been discussing. This includes the false doctrine of the troublesome teachers at Ephesus. It also involves their life-style. Like Simon of Samaria, they were in the ministry for the money it brought them (Acts 8:18-24).

Rather than using religion for personal gain, Timothy was to conduct himself as the man of God he was. Paul honored the young minister by conferring on him this title. It was used of some of God's greatest in Old Testament times. The highest compliment yet is to say a preacher is a man of God.

While fleeing these things, Timothy was also to follow hard after the true riches of life. The tense of the Greek verbs suggests he was to continuously run from the one while continuously pursuing the other. He was to set his heart on righteousness, godliness, faith, and love. He must seek to remain steadfast under trial. He should always strive to manifest gentleness of temper in relating to men.

B. Fight a Good Battle

The life of the minister of the gospel is at times demanding. Paul challenges Timothy to fight a good battle against sin and Satan. His is like the duty of the soldier in front-line combat. While he fights off sin for a good cause, he must also lay hold on or stoutly defend eternal life for his own sake. It is for this purpose he was selected as a soldier.

C. Keep the Commandment

Question.
What important event in the past life of Timothy does Paul recall here?

Paul follows his military challenge to the young preacher with a solemn charge. It is one frequently given even yet to ministers in ordination services. Paul issues the call to Timothy in the sight of God who gives life to all. Also present is Jesus who set before Timothy a good example. Though He knew it meant His death, Christ gave true testimony before Pilate. Timothy made a good start with a similar public confession, perhaps at his ordination. Now the apostle charges him to continue courageously in the cause.

Specifically, Paul's charge is that the pastor at Ephesus keep the commandment. He must do so with a spotless life which leaves him above reproach.

D. Remember the Second Coming

Question.
What major incentive for consistent Christian living does Paul remind Timothy of in this passage?

To inspire consistency in Christian living Paul suggests Timothy keep ever before him the hope of the coming of Christ. No one knows the day nor the hour of His return. Paul simply says, "Which in his times he shall show" (verse 15).

God the Father alone knows the time of His Son's appearing (Mark 13:32). With this truth in mind the apostle breaks forth in worship. Jehovah is the blessed and only Sovereign. He is King of kings and Lord of lords. He alone is immortal by nature. He lives in a light no man can approach to. No one has ever seen Him in the fullness of His glory. To Him rightly belongs honor and everlasting dominion. (See Teaching Tip 6.)

TEACHING TIP 6

A charge often hurled at Christianity is that our doctrine of the Second Coming is a religious form of escapism. Ask: "In what way is the doctrine of the return of Christ a practical doctrine? How does it help us live for Christ on a daily basis?"

III. Share With Others

1 Timothy 6:17-21

(See Teaching Tip 7.)

1 Timothy 6:17. Charge them that are rich in this world, that they be not high-minded, nor trust in uncertain riches, but in the living God, who giveth us richly all things to enjoy; 18. that they do good, that they be rich in good works, ready to distribute, willing to communicate. 20. O Timothy, keep that which is committed to thy trust, avoiding profane and vain babblings, and oppositions of science falsely so called.

A. Material Goods

Clarification

Ready to distribute—generous.

Willing to communicate—liberal in sharing one's goods with others.

Eternal life—life indeed.

Keep—guard the deposit.

Profane . . . babblings—godless chatter.

Science—literally, "knowledge."

Erred—missed the mark.

One other aspect of consistent Christian living at Ephesus needs attention. Paul now returns to the other side of the coin of covetousness. He considers here how it affects the rich. It seems clear the church at Ephesus had some wealthy members. In short, Paul says to them they should share their material goods with others to keep down the subtle sin in their lives. Covetousness can involve selfishness and can tempt the rich as well as the poor.

The rich may sometimes be tempted to look down on the poor.

Question.
In what way are wealthy Christians to resist the temptation to covetousness?

TEACHING TIP 7

Before reading this passage, give the students the following assignment: "Listen for the seven things Timothy was to mention as a charge to the rich regarding their riches." Following the reading of the passage, call for a response from the students to this listening assignment. Their responses should include the following: The rich 1) are not to be highminded, 2) are not to trust in riches, 3) should trust in the living God, 4) should do good, 5) should be rich in good works, 6) should be ready to distribute or give to others, 7) should be willing to communicate or fellowship with others.

TEACHING TIP 8

How can we share material resources with others in such a way that they will not be offended?

Paul says they should guard against the tendency to feel superior. Those who acquire riches on their own may be inclined to despise those they consider less shrewd in business matters. Or if they inherit their wealth, they may feel unduly proud of their family background.

Further, Paul instructs Timothy to warn the wealthy not to trust in "uncertain" riches. To do so is foolish. They may lose it overnight to robbery or a stock market crash. The possibility of political change or spiraling inflation makes wealth equally uncertain.

It is also irreverent to trust in riches. It is God who gives them. The wealthy should worship Him for what they have. He gave it for their enjoyment. (See Teaching Tip 8.)

Coming more to the point, the apostle instructs the rich to make good use of their money. They are to do good, yes, and even be rich in good works. They must be generous in sharing their goods with others.

The apostle indicates that using money in this way is among the best investments. By sharing, the rich lay "in store for themselves a good foundation against the time to come" (verse 19). Thereby they also come to know what real life is.

Guideline for Living 3

So many Christian families today are caught in the trap of materialism. They are looking to things to bring them fulfillment and happiness. Things, however, are a very unreliable means of achieving true family happiness. The item that was so earnestly desired by all soon loses its appeal, and then something else must be acquired to take its place. Jesus expressed it best when He said, "A man's life consisteth not in the abundance of the things which he possesseth" (Luke 12:15). To underscore this point He told His listeners the parable of the fool who was rich in the things of this world but a pauper toward God.

Author James Dobson put the matter of wealth and fame in proper perspective in this statement: "I have concluded that the accumulation of wealth, even if I could achieve it, is an insufficient reason for living. When I reach the end of my days, a moment or two from now, I must look backward on something more meaningful than the pursuit of houses and land and machines and stocks and bonds. Nor is fame of any lasting benefit. I will consider my earthly existence to have been wasted unless I can recall a loving family, a consistent investment in the lives of people, and an earnest attempt to serve the God who made me. Nothing else makes much sense" (from: *What Wives Wish Their Husbands Knew About Women,* by Dr. James Dobson. Published by Tyndale House Publishers, Inc., © 1975. Used by permission).

B. Spiritual Riches

Indirectly Paul also reminds Pastor Timothy he has things to share with others. His are spiritual treasures. They have been entrusted to him as the true riches.

To be a good steward, Timothy must guard carefully the treasure which has been committed to his trust. This includes seeing it is not mixed with counterfeit items. He must avoid the godless and empty chatter of the false religious leaders at Ephesus. Their message stands in opposition to that of the gospel. Those who serve

Question.
What is the "science" Paul tells Timothy to avoid?

TEACHING TIP 9

Paul makes it clear that just as covetousness is not limited to the rich, neither is generosity. Ask: "What are some things we can all give to others regardless of our financial status?" Include some of the following: 1) time, 2) kindness, 3) courtesy, 4) friendly smile, 5) respect. You may want to encourage the students to write a New Year's resolution regarding their willingness to share some of these things with people in the coming year. They may want to word their resolution as follows: "With the Lord's help I will resolve to be more generous in giving of my _____to others in the coming year."

As an alternative closing activity you may want to use the "Self-evaluation" from the Packet of Adult Teaching Helps.

Daily Devotional Guide
M. Resisting Temptation. Genesis 39:7-9
T. Confidence in Conflict. 2 Chronicles 14:9-15
W. A Holy Life. Psalm 15:1-5
T. Cure for Anxiety. Matthew 6:25-34
F. Trusting God. Philippians 4:10-19
S. Christian Graces. Colossians 3:12-17

the flesh and Satan do not merely stand neutral on doctrinal matters. They openly oppose the true man of God.

Timothy is not to be persuaded by the claims of the opposition. They declare they have the real "knowledge rather than specifically to modern science. These religious philosophers claim to have deep insights into real truth. Some may have testified it was revealed to them through mystical experiences.

The apostle correctly labels what the false prophets proclaim as knowledge falsely so called. It is mere philosophical speculation. It is human theory. It may sound intellectually appealing, but it is a deadly poison. Therefore, Timothy was to avoid being attracted to it.

Indeed, Paul says those who had embraced this wisdom of man had erred concerning the faith. They had missed the mark in aiming for what brings peace with God. Salvation comes through the gospel rather than human wisdom.

Finally, with one of the shortest of all Paul's benedictions he closes his first letter to Timothy. He simply prays, "Grace be with thee." The final pronoun in the Greek is plural. Since the epistle was to be read publicly, Paul pronounces a blessing on all who hear and not just on Timothy.

LIVING THE TRUTH

As we come to the end of another year, it is a good time to reflect back on God's goodness to us. Like Timothy we have been the recipients of many spiritual treasures. What are some of these treasures? What daily blessings have you received from the Lord? What special needs has He met in your life this year? What prayers has He answered for you? How has He helped you to grow in Him this year? Have you been as thankful and appreciative as you should? What kind of steward have you been of these resources? (See Teaching Tip 9.)

EVANGELISM OUTREACH

What are you trusting in to give you peace of mind? Your good deeds? Your material resources? Your grasp of human knowledge? None of these things can ever bring satisfaction. Peace with God comes only through faith in the saving work of His Son Jesus Christ. Don't begin another year without Him.

LOYAL SERVANTS

6

SEEING THE SCRIPTURES

2 Timothy 1:8-14; 2:1-7, 15

8. Be not thou therefore ashamed of the testimony of our Lord, nor of me his prisoner: but be thou partaker of the afflictions of the gospel according to the power of God;

9. Who hath saved us, and called us with a holy calling, not according to our works, but according to his own purpose and grace, which was given us in Christ Jesus before the world began;

10. But is now made manifest by the appearing of our Saviour Jesus Christ, who hath abolished death, and hath brought life and immortality to light through the gospel:

11. Whereunto I am appointed a preacher, and an apostle, and a teacher of the Gentiles.

12. For the which cause I also suffer these things: nevertheless I am not ashamed; for I know whom I have believed, and am persuaded that he is able to keep that which I have committed unto him against that day.

13. Hold fast the form of sound words, which thou hast heard of me, in faith and love which is in Christ Jesus.

14. That good thing which was committed unto thee keep by the Holy Ghost which dwelleth in us.

2:1. Thou therefore, my son, be strong in the grace that is in Christ Jesus.

2. And the things that thou hast heard of me among many witnesses, the same commit thou to faithful men, who shall be able to teach others also.

3. Thou therefore endure hardness, as a good soldier of Jesus Christ.

4. No man that warreth entangleth himself with the affairs of this life; that he may please him who hath chosen him to be a soldier.

5. And if a man also strive for masteries, yet is he not crowned, except he strive lawfully.

6. The husbandman that laboreth must be first partaker of the fruits.

7. Consider what I say; and the Lord give thee understanding in all things.

15. Study to show thyself approved unto God, a workman that needeth not to be ashamed, rightly dividing the word of truth.

SETTING THE SCENE

At the end of his Third Missionary Journey, Paul returned to Jerusalem. There he met with violent opposition and was arrested. Leaders in Judaism accused him of criminal activity. To save him

PREPARING TO TEACH

Study Text
2 Timothy 1:1 through 2:26

Outline
I. Godly Heritage
  A. Salutation
  B. Thanksgiving
  C. Exhortation
II. Unashamed Witness
  A. Paul
  B. Asian Associates
  C. Onesiphorus
III. Faithful Service
  A. Teaching Others
  B. Singleness of Purpose
  C. Following Paul
  D. True to God
IV. Approved Workers
  A. Focusing on the Truth
  B. Used of God
  C. Gentleness With Men

Golden Text: Study to show thyself approved unto God, a workman that needeth not to be ashamed, rightly dividing the word of truth. 2 Timothy 2:15

Central Truth: The Christian seeks to glorify God through a life of faithful service.

Learning Goals
1. To recognize the characteristics of a faithful servant.
2. To evaluate myself by the Biblical pattern for servanthood.
3. To identify and begin working on areas in my life needing change and improvement.

"When you hear the word 'servant,' what do you think of? What is your mental image of a servant? Is it a positive or a negative image?" Call for responses to these questions from the students. You may want to have them discuss these questions with the person sitting next to them and share their ideas with the rest of the class.

Ask: "How does our concept of a servant compare with the Biblical concept? According to the Bible, what does it mean to be a servant?" Discuss these questions for several minutes. Explain that this session deals with the subject of loyal servanthood. Review the "Central Truth" for this session.

Clarification

Prayers—supplications.

Unfeigned—genuine, sincere, without hypocrisy.

Stir up—continuously rekindle.

Fear—cowardice.

Sound mind—good judgment, moderation, self-discipline.

Question.

In what way did Paul serve God with a pure conscience from childhood?

from a plot against his life, the Roman government took the apostle to Caesarea and finally to Rome. The Book of Acts ends by saying he was in the imperial city two years under house arrest (28:30).

All indications are that Paul was released from this first Roman imprisonment. Several ancient writers say so. Among them are Clement of Rome, Chrysostom, Jerome, and Eusebius. In this week's study Paul has been arrested again. His second stay in Rome's prison ends in death.

BIBLE COMMENTARY

I. Godly Heritage

2 Timothy 1:1-7

2 Timothy 1:3. I thank God, whom I serve from my forefathers with pure conscience, that without ceasing I have remembrance of thee in my prayers night and day. 5. When I call to remembrance the unfeigned faith that is in thee, which dwelt first in thy grandmother Lois, and thy mother Eunice; and I am persuaded that in thee also. 6. Wherefore I put thee in remembrance that thou stir up the gift of God, which is in thee by the putting on of my hands. 7. For God hath not given us the spirit of fear; but of power, and of love, and of a sound mind.

A. Salutation

Paul is now in a Roman jail for the second time. He has none of the liberties he enjoyed during his two-year house arrest earlier. Now he is chained to a soldier of the royal guard. However, he makes good use of his time in writing another letter to Timothy.

The letter opens with the usual salutation. It identifies Paul as the author. He is an apostle by the will of God sent to proclaim the promise of life which is in Christ Jesus. He addresses Timothy his dearly beloved son in the faith. The apostle prays that grace, mercy, and peace from the Father and the Son will abide with Timothy.

B. Thanksgiving

Following the general form of epistles of the first century, Paul's letter next includes thanksgiving and commendation for the addressee. His praise comes from remembering Timothy's godly heritage.

The apostle's thanksgiving is more than mere commendation for admirable human qualities. It is true worship. His praise goes to God whom he has served sincerely from his forefathers. Of course, until he was converted to Christ on the road to Damascus Paul was sincerely wrong in the way he served God. Even in persecuting the Church he thought he pleased the Lord (John 16:2). Sincerity in religious activity does not justify every action. Only faith in Jesus saves.

Paul's thanksgiving to God for Timothy is a part of his prayers for him. Night and day the apostle earnestly entreats God that he might see Timothy's face again. How beautiful it is to see such a

Question.
Why does Paul recall Timothy's godly heritage at this time?

TEACHING TIP 1

Display or develop the following visual of 2 Timothy 1:7.

GOD GIVES US:	
Not a spirit of	{ FEAR
But of	{ POWER { LOVE { SOUND MIND

Clarification

Be not . . . ashamed—Greek, "Don't start being ashamed."

Abolished death—rendered it ineffective.

Preacher—herald.

Keep—guard.

Form—standard.

strong bond of love between an aged apostle and a young preacher. Paul remembers the tears shed at their last parting.

The apostle recalls the godly heritage of Timothy centered in a genuine, non-hypocritical faith passed on from his grandmother to his mother and then to him. No doubt there is a challenge here that Timothy be true to the faith in view of the trying times.

Guideline for Living 1

While it is true that God has no spiritual "grandchildren," the value of a Christian heritage cannot be overestimated. Children from a Christian home tend to receive Christ at an earlier age. Supplemental spiritual training in the home helps the child grow in his relationship with Christ. Firm but fair discipline helps him to be more obedient to God and submissive to His will. Faithful attendance at church helps him learn to put God first in his life and support the work of the church. Seeing his parents work to bring others to Christ helps him understand his part in winning the lost.

C. Exhortation

Paul follows his thanksgiving with an exhortation to faithfulness. Timothy is to keep rekindling the fires of ministerial gifts and graces which prophecy indicated he had at his ordination. With Paul's second arrest and coming execution it was a sobering time for all gospel ministers. No matter—the apostle reminds the young preacher that God does not give a spirit of cowardice, but of authority, love, and self-control. (See Teaching Tip 1.)

II. Unashamed Witnesses
2 Timothy 1:8-18

2 Timothy 1:8. Be not thou therefore ashamed of the testimony of our Lord, nor of me his prisoner: but be thou partaker of the afflictions of the gospel according to the power of God. 12. For the which cause I also suffer these things: nevertheless I am not ashamed; for I know whom I have believed, and am persuaded that he is able to keep that which I have committed unto him against that day. 16. The Lord give mercy unto the house of Onesiphorus; for he oft refreshed me, and was not ashamed of my chain: 17. but, when he was in Rome, he sought me out very diligently, and found me.

A. Paul

To further support his exhortation that Timothy not act cowardly in the face of persecution, Paul sets before him the example of unashamed witnesses for Christ. The first is the apostle himself.

During this time of suffering for the saints under Nero it was dangerous to be a Christian. For that reason the apostle encourages the young minister not to start being ashamed of the gospel. Further, he should not hesitate to identify himself with Paul the prisoner in spite of the threat involved. Rather, by the power of God he should boldly suffer the present adversities with the apostle.

Paul explains in several verses that theirs is a just cause. It involves a call to preach the gospel of grace. God designed the plan of salvation before the world began. However, only with the coming of Jesus was it made clear to men. He brought to light the life the plan brings. In so doing He made death—man's age-old-enemy—ineffective.

Paul is proud to have been appointed an apostle, a preacher, and a teacher of this glorious gospel. Seeing he attached these three titles to himself in one breath, perhaps God never intended for us to be too taken up with titled positions in the Church. These and other designations in Scripture generally speak synonymously of the varying responsibilities of the one office of the ministry.

As Timothy knows, the apostle suffers imprisonment just because he is a preacher of the gospel. Still he is not ashamed. His physical life he commits to God. His very soul he entrusts to the Saviour for safekeeping until His return.

Timothy should take Paul for an example of courage in the face of persecution. He must hold fast to the standard of healthy teaching he received from the apostle. He must guard as a faithful sentry what was committed to his keeping. He has the Holy Spirit within to help him in his duty. (See Teaching Tip 2.)

B. Asian Associates

Obviously, not everyone was courageous in those difficult times. In fact, Paul says Timothy already knows his Asian associates have deserted him. In fear of their lives they have stopped going to see him in prison. The two he names, Phygellus and Hermogenes, may have done more. They may have all but denied the Lord in acting as if they were no longer friends of Paul.

C. Onesiphorus

One notable exception to the others who have turned away from Paul the prisoner is Onesiphorus. He was not ashamed of Paul's chains. In fact, he frequently brought the apostle food and clothing. No doubt his very presence was a source of encouragement while visiting the apostle in jail.

In these ways Onesiphorus had refreshed Paul during a recent stay in Rome. On his arrival he had difficulty in finding the apostle. Courageously he sought diligently until he discovered him in his cell. Souls of less stature would gladly have avoided the risks involved in identifying themselves as a friend to such a prisoner. After a weak effort to find where he was, they would have soothed their conscience by saying they could not locate him. (See Teaching Tip 3.)

TEACHING TIP 3

Ask: "What are some excuses we often give for not getting more involved in helping others?" 1) Assume someone else will do it. 2) Fear we will be misunderstood or unappreciated. 3) Put personal needs and wants first. 4) Lack the motivation or initiative to get started.

Guideline for Living 2

Onesiphorus is a good example of one who did not grow weary in well doing (Galatians 6:9). It certainly would have been easy for him to give up. At times it is easy for us to give up in our efforts to do good. There are so many seemingly good reasons. Often we assume someone else will do it, so we don't. If we are careful, we can become like the "Body Brothers":

There was Brother Somebody, Brother Everybody, Brother Anybody, and Brother Nobody. All four belonged to the same church, but you would not have enjoyed worshiping with them. Everybody went fishing on Sunday. Somebody was always staying home to visit with friends. Anybody wanted to go but was afraid

Display or develop the following diagram of 2 Timothy 2:2.

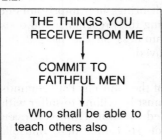

```
THE THINGS YOU
RECEIVE FROM ME
        ↓
   COMMIT TO
  FAITHFUL MEN
        ↓
Who shall be able to
teach others also
```

Clarification

My son—literally, my child.
Affairs of this life—civilian life.
Strive for masteries—compete in a contest in the arena.
Husbandman—farmer.
Trouble—imprisonment.
Evildoer—criminal.

Question.

What vocational examples requiring singleness of purpose does Paul list for Timothy?

TEACHING TIP 5

Quickly divide the class into three groups. It will not be necessary for them to change seating. Assign one part of the following question to each group: "How is being a Christian like . . . [group 1] . . . a soldier? [group 2] . . . an athlete? [group 3] . . . a farmer?" Direct the groups to one of the following three paragraphs in their quarterlies.

Somebody wouldn't speak to him. So, who went to church? Right—Nobody.

Really, Nobody was the only decent one of the four. Nobody did the visitation. Nobody worked on the church building. Once they needed a Sunday school teacher. Everybody thought Anybody would do it, and Anybody thought Somebody would do it. And you know who did it? Right again—Nobody.

It happened that a fifth neighbor (an unbeliever) moved into the area. Everybody thought Somebody should try to win him for Christ. Anybody could have made an effort. You probably know who finally won him—Nobody.

III. Faithful Service
2 Timothy 2:1-13

2 Timothy 2:1. Thou therefore, my son, be strong in the grace that is in Christ Jesus. 2. And the things that thou hast heard of me among many witnesses, the same commit thou to faithful men, who shall be able to teach others also. 3. Thou therefore endure hardness, as a good soldier of Jesus Christ. 4. No man that warreth entangleth himself with the affairs of this life; that he may please him who hath chosen him to be a soldier.

A. Teaching Others

Timothy has before him the challenge to avoid cowardly conduct though persecution threatened. As the spiritual child of Paul he receives an exhortation to remain strong in the grace of Jesus. (See Teaching Tip 4.)

This includes being faithful in service to the Lord. Though the apostle's ministry is limited by his imprisonment, Timothy must persistently teach others the doctrine he received from Paul. If he commits the teaching to faithful men they will in turn pass it on to another generation. These words serve as a basis for Christian education in the local church as well as ministerial training schools.

B. Singleness of Purpose

(See Teaching Tip 5.)

To be faithful requires singleness of purpose for the young preacher. He must be like a soldier who shuns any offers to get involved in civilian affairs. No sideline business must claim a soldier's attention. He must remain unattached so he can follow orders to go anywhere his commander directs on a moment's notice. Besides, his government will support him financially so he needs no other source of income.

Further, as the athlete, Timothy must think of only one thing in life and that is to win the contest in the arena. To do so requires total devotion to the task during a period of training as well as on the day of the event. Strict rules apply to the training period. Should the athlete break any of them, he would be disqualified even if he won.

Somewhat like the soldier, the farmer is supported by the fields he cultivates. Like him, Timothy should not be distracted by some other business. He can do his best only if he devotes all his energies to his ministry. Of course Paul of necessity worked to support himself in pioneering churches. This, however, should be the exception and not the general rule.

TEACHING TIP 6

Display or develop the following chart of 2 Timothy 2:11-13 to show God's response to us.

IF WE . . .	WE/HE SHALL . . .
Be dead with Him	Live with Him
Suffer	Reign with Him
Deny Him	Deny us
Believe not	Abides faithful

TEACHING TIP 7

Use the work sheet from the Packet of Adult Teaching Helps to develop a personal paraphrase of 2 Timothy 2:15.

Clarification

Subverting—ruining, bringing catastrophe.

Study—make every effort, take pains, be zealous or eager.

Rightly dividing—guiding along a straight path.

Vain babblings—empty talk.

Canker—gangrene, cancer.

Seal—mark, inscription.

Repentance—change of mind.

Question.

Why does Paul advise Timothy to avoid teachings of a philosophical and religious nature other than the gospel?

C. Following Paul

Again the apostle offers himself as an example for Timothy to follow in faithfully serving the Lord. He is to preach the same gospel, telling people the Man Christ Jesus was crucified but rose again. Timothy must do this even if it brings him imprisonment as a common criminal like Paul. Putting the preacher in jail does not bind the gospel. However, faithfulness on the part of the minister is necessary for men to be saved.

D. True to God

Perhaps quoting an ancient hymn of the Church, Paul reminds Timothy that to reign with Christ he must be willing to suffer with Him. To deny the Lord is to be denied by Him. However, even if the preacher is unfaithful, God is not. He cannot deny himself. (See Teaching Tip 6.)

IV. Approved Workers
2 Timothy 2:14-26

2 Timothy 2:15. Study to show thyself approved unto God, a workman that needeth not to be ashamed, rightly dividing the word of truth. 16. But shun profane and vain babblings: for they will increase unto more ungodliness. 17. And their word will eat as doth a canker: of whom is Hymeneus and Philetus; 18. who concerning the truth have erred, saying that the resurrection is past already; and overthrow the faith of some. 20. But in a great house there are not only vessels of gold and of silver, but also of wood and of earth; and some to honor, and some to dishonor. 21. If a man therefore purge himself from these, he shall be a vessel unto honor, sanctified, and meet for the master's use, and prepared unto every good work.

A. Focusing on the Truth

Paul's concern is more than simply having Timothy courageously remain his friend in a time of trouble. He wants his son in the faith to be approved of God as an able worker in the Kingdom.

The young minister must keep his focus on gospel truth. Other philosophical and religious teachings will attract his attention. However, there is no profit in them. In fact, they lead to catastrophe. They are as deadly as gangrene. Such godless and empty chatter Timothy must go out of his way to avoid. (See Teaching Tip 7.)

Timothy is to concentrate on the Word of truth. In ministry he must cut it carefully in fitting its various parts together as Paul did the pieces of leather he shaped for sewing tents. This he does with a view of the great Inspector approving his work. He must tell people attracted to error that the foundation of God is sure. It is marked by a double inscription: "The Lord knoweth them that are his," and, "Let every one that nameth the name of Christ depart from iniquity."

B. Used of God

Further, to be an approved worker Timothy must purge himself of youthful lusts. He must seek to be a clean and useful utensil. As in a large mansion with vessels for stately and common use, he

Review the marks of a loyal servant from the "Living the Truth" section. Feel free to add other qualities which you or the students may want to suggest. Compile a list of these marks of servanthood.

Distribute small pieces of paper or 3 by 5 cards and pencils. Instruct each student to write down one characteristic of servanthood that they most need to develop. Explain that they will be asked to share their response with one other person. Have them turn to the person sitting next to them and share what they have written. Instruct them to discuss with each other ways to improve in these needed areas. Have them suggest to each other two or three things each could do in the coming week to begin to develop the needed qualities of servanthood. Instruct them to take the paper or card home and place it where they will see it during the coming week. This will remind them of what they said they would be willing to do to change.

Close the class session with prayer in groups of two. Have the students pray for each other, asking God to help the other person develop the needed characteristic of servanthood. Ask the students to remember to pray for each other during the coming week.

Daily Devotional Guide

M. Consecrated Abilities.
Exodus 35:30-35
T. Parental Influence.
1 Samuel 1:9-28
W. Commitment To Serve.
Isaiah 6:1-13
T. Bold Witnessing.
Acts 4:5-22
F. Commissioned To Serve.
Acts 9:10-19
S. Good Stewards.
1 Peter 4:10, 11

should seek to be used by the Owner of the estate for the most honorable purposes. If he follows faith, love, peace, and a pure heart he will be.

Guideline for Living 3

At times today it is difficult to flee youthful lusts. Sin and sensuality seem to be everywhere—on TV—including cable, in magazines, on billboards, in the conversations of ungodly associates.

While we cannot always avoid exposure to sensual temptation, we can keep our minds from dwelling on these impurities. Like the old adage says, "We can't keep the birds from flying over our heads, but we can keep them from building their nests in our hair." The way to cultivate good thoughts is to feed our minds on good material. Counteract evil by memorizing Scripture, singing gospel songs, recalling last Sunday's sermon, breathing up a silent prayer for needs on your heart.

C. Gentleness With Men

Finally, Paul tells Timothy approved workers for God must relate gently to all men. They avoid philosophical debating which the apostle views as stemming from foolish speculations. To engage in such discussions does nothing but breed quarrels.

The servant of the Lord does not spend all his time in combat with the opposition. Rather, with kindness and patience he instructs those who will hear him. Believing unto salvation is more than a mental activity. The preacher does not argue men into the Kingdom. The Holy Spirit must help them change their minds. Only then will they acknowledge the truth. Only then will they be delivered from the devil who has blinded their minds and kept them captive.

LIVING THE TRUTH

What are the marks of a loyal servant? According to Paul, he exhibits these qualities:

1. He remembers to pray and be thankful for others.
2. He demonstrates spiritual authority, love, and self-control.
3. He is not ashamed of his relationship with Christ and His servants.
4. He seeks to teach and train those who follow Him.
5. He is able to endure hard times and testings.
6. He is a careful student of God's Word.
7. He follows God with a pure heart.

As you compare yourself to this profile of a loyal servant, how do you rate? Where do you need to make improvements? What will you do to change these areas? What help will you need from God and others? (See Teaching Tip 8.)

EVANGELISM OUTREACH

To be sure, salvation is a reasonable doctrine, but you cannot reason your way to God. We must come to God by faith. Salvation, while it involves the mind, is more an experience of the heart and will. Only the Holy Spirit can bring us to God, give us faith to trust in Him, and impart to us new life in Christ.

7

STEADFAST IN THE WORD

PREPARING TO TEACH

Study Text
2 Timothy 3:1 through 4:22

Outline
I. Perilous Times
   A. Specific Evils
   B. False Religious Leaders
   C. Persecution
II. Continuing in the Word
   A. A Trustworthy Book
   B. A Faithful Minister
III. Certain Reward
   A. Victorious Announcement
   B. Personal Requests
   C. Timely Warning
   D. God's Faithfulness
   E. Final Greetings

Golden Text: All Scripture is given by inspiration of God, and is profitable for doctrine, for reproof, for correction, for instruction in righteousness. 2 Timothy 3:16

Central Truth: Those who mature in the Word remain victorious even during perilous times.

Learning Goals
1. To desire to remain faithful to God even in perilous times.
2. To recognize the power of God's Word to correct and instruct.

SEEING THE SCRIPTURES
2 Timothy 3:1, 14 through 4:8, 16, 17

1. This know also, that in the last days perilous times shall come.

14. But continue thou in the things which thou hast learned and hast been assured of, knowing of whom thou hast learned them;

15. And that from a child thou hast known the holy Scriptures, which are able to make thee wise unto salvation through faith which is in Christ Jesus.

16. All Scripture is given by inspiration of God, and is profitable for doctrine, for reproof, for correction, for instruction in righteousness:

17. That the man of God may be perfect, thoroughly furnished unto all good works.

4:1. I charge thee therefore before God, and the Lord Jesus Christ, who shall judge the quick and the dead at his appearing and his kingdom;

2. Preach the word; be instant in season, out of season; reprove, rebuke, exhort with all longsuffering and doctrine.

3. For the time will come when they will not endure sound doctrine; but after their own lusts shall they heap to themselves teachers, having itching ears;

4. And they shall turn away their ears from the truth, and shall be turned unto fables.

5. But watch thou in all things, endure afflictions, do the work of an evangelist, make full proof of thy ministry.

6. For I am now ready to be offered, and the time of my departure is at hand.

7. I have fought a good fight, I have finished my course, I have kept the faith:

8. Henceforth there is laid up for me a crown of righteousness, which the Lord, the righteous judge, shall give me at that day: And not to me only, but unto all them also that love his appearing.

16. At my first answer no man stood with me, but all forsook me: I pray God that it may not be laid to their charge.

17. Notwithstanding the Lord stood with me, and strengthened me; that by me the preaching might be fully known, and that all the Gentiles might hear: and I was delivered out of the mouth of the lion.

SETTING THE SCENE
Certainly every word, sentence, paragraph, chapter, and book of the Bible is the Word of God. All of it is important. No part is to be neglected in favor of another. Even red letter editions of Scripture are not to be read as if some parts of the Bible are more truly the Word of God than others.

Ask: "Why is it that some-one's last words are often more meaningful than other things he may have said? What famous last words do you remember?" Invite the students to recount some last words of famous people such as the patriot Nathan Hale: "I only regret that I have but one life to give for my country." Or Douglas MacArthur when he left the Philippines: "I shall return." Some of the students may recall the last words of their loved ones. Have them explain their meaning or importance to them.

Clarification

Perilous—hard, difficult, stressful.

Without natural affection—without parental love.

Trucebreakers—irreconcilable.

Incontinent—without self-control.

Fierce—savage, brutal.

Heady—rash, reckless.

Reprobate—not standing the test.

Seducers—swindlers, impostors.

Question.

How does Paul's list of last-day sins compare with those of early men in Romans 1:26-31?

TEACHING TIP 1

Prepare on an overhead transparency or large sheet of paper a list in the left-hand column of the actions and attitudes Paul said would characterize people during the last days. In the right column ask the students to help you list examples of present-day behavior or conditions that fulfill these predictions. Point out that these fulfillments of prophecy are further evidence that we are indeed living in the end-times.

However, some portions of Scripture may at times hold more interest than others. Second Timothy may be the latter since it contains our last recorded words of Paul. Generally we listen to the final whispers of a dying person in a way we cling to no other words he has ever uttered. The end of the apostle's last letter speaks of certain reward for faithfulness to God in dangerous times.

BIBLE COMMENTARY

I. Perilous Times

2 Timothy 3:1-13

2 Timothy 3:1. This know also, that in the last days perilous times shall come. 2. For men shall be lovers of their own selves, covetous, boasters, proud, blasphemers, disobedient to parents, unthankful, unholy. 10. But thou hast fully known my doctrine, manner of life, purpose, faith, longsuffering, charity, patience, 11. persecutions, afflictions, which came unto me at Antioch, at Iconium, at Lystra; what persecutions I endured: but out of them all the Lord delivered me. 12. Yea, and all that will live godly in Christ Jesus shall suffer persecution.

A. Specific Evils

As he prepares to bring his last letter to Timothy to a close, Paul speaks of perilous, hard, difficult times ahead. Times of great stress demand much of the preacher. The apostle predicts what will come in the last days. In a sense the Church has lived in the last days since Pentecost (1 John 2:18), but how much closer we are now to the end.

(See Teaching Tip 1.)

Paul lists specific evils that will mark the last days. Men will be lovers of themselves, lovers of money, and lovers of pleasures more than lovers of God. At the same time they will be void of natural family love. Couples will not love each other nor will parents love children as they ought. Children will be disobedient to parents as they were in the early days of backsliding man (Romans 1:30).

Further, in these difficult days ahead the apostle says men will be boasters, proud, blasphemers, unthankful, and unholy. They will be irreconcilable, either refusing to make peace or failing to keep a trace once it is made. In the last days men will also be false accusers, slandering fellowmen. They will not practice self-control. In much of their conduct they will be brutal and savage. They will despise those that are good. They will be quick to betray so you dare not trust them. Paul's picture of reckless and conceited men is not a very pretty one.

What is worse, many such people will claim to be religious. They will have a form of godliness, but deny its reality by their conduct. No wonder Paul tells Timothy to turn away from them.

B. False Religious Leaders

Of course, these religious men with an empty profession are not without their leaders. Their prophets know how to worm their way into the homes and lives of the simple. Among them, Paul

Ask: "How do we suffer persecution today? What kinds of persecution do we encounter? What other forms of persecution are Christians suffering around the world? How is the persecution we encounter in America different from that experienced in other parts of the world?

Question.
In what sense do all Christians suffer persecution?

Clarification
From a child—from infancy.
Given by inspiration—God breathed.
Reproof—correction, refutation.
For correction—for setting up straight again those who have fallen.
Perfect—complete.
Quick—living.
Be instant—be ready, be on hand.
In season—when it is convenient.
Their own lusts—their desires.
Watch thou—be self-possessed.
Make full proof—fully accomplish.

Question.
Where did Timothy get his religious education?

says, are silly women loaded down with sin and driven by various lusts. They are curious to know religious teachings but lack the ability to arrive at truth and stay with it. These, along with men much like themselves, make up the congregations of the false prophets of the last days. They readily submit to be captives of hypocritical teachers.

Paul says the false religious leaders of the difficult times ahead resist the truth much as men of the past. His example is two magicians who withstood Moses. They were named Jannes and Jambres, as the apostle knew from Jewish tradition. They imitated the truth in opposing Moses, but only to a point. They could turn sticks into snakes too, but the snake of the man of God swallowed theirs (Exodus 7:12).

The prophecy of Paul is that false teachers of the last days will likewise have their limits. Many will see through them soon enough. They will come to appear as what they are, men of corrupt minds and rejects concerning the faith.

C. Persecution

The apostle also says persecution will come in the last days. Timothy was to endure it patiently as Paul had. The young preacher knew well the integrity Paul maintained in the face of opposition. He saw him suffer before he joined him in missionary work. In fact, as a youth Timothy may have watched as those of Lystra, his home town, stoned Paul and left him for dead (Acts 14:19, 20).

The young preacher knew, though, how God raised the apostle up that day. He also understood Paul's statement that all the godly suffer persecution in one form or another. Always there is a stigma attached to genuine Christianity. Timothy realized too that counterfeit Christianity would increase. With confidence in God and encouragement from Paul, he would remain true whatever came. (See Teaching Tip 2.)

II. Continuing in the Word
2 Timothy 3:14 through 4:5

2 Timothy 3:14. Continue thou in the things which thou hast learned and hast been assured of, knowing of whom thou hast learned them. 16. All Scripture is given by inspiration of God, and is profitable for doctrine, for reproof, for correction, for instruction in righteousness. 4:2. Preach the word; be instant in season, out of season; reprove, rebuke, exhort with all longsuffering and doctrine. 3. For the time will come when they will not endure sound doctrine; but after their own lusts shall they heap to themselves teachers, having itching ears.

A. A Trustworthy Book

With the revelation that evil men and impostors will increase in the land, deceiving and being deceived, Paul tells Timothy to stay true to the Word. He had been taught the Holy Scripture and had been assured of its trustworthiness. He could trust his teachers, including his grandmother, his mother, and Paul.

From his infancy Timothy's mother had taught him the Bible. Today's parents might well follow the example. What others taught him from the Book was the source of Timothy's salvation. Though

TEACHING TIP 3

Display or develop the following visual, listing the ways in which Scripture is profitable.

Refer to the "Clarification" section above as well as other versions and paraphrases of the Scripture in developing a definition of the four key words in 2 Timothy 3:16. List these definitions on the suggested visual above.

SCRIPTURE IS
PROFITABLE FOR . . .

DOCTRINE
REPROOF
CORRECTION
INSTRUCTION

TEACHING TIP 4

Ask one of the students to read the article entitled "Instructions" from the Packet of Adult Teaching Helps.

TEACHING TIP 5

Develop a list of the three aspects of ministry with which Paul charged Timothy in verse 2 regarding his preaching ministry: 1) reprove 2) rebuke 3) exhort. Ask several students to read this verse from different translations and paraphrases to develop a more complete definition of these three terms.

Question.

What specific aspects of the preacher's work does Paul name here?

---

his early teachers were Jewish, they prepared him to accept Jesus as Messiah upon hearing the gospel.

Guideline for Living 1

Timothy was the product of teaching and training in a godly home. Someone has compared the training of children to that of building bridges. A bridge is an extension to new territory in the same way that new experiences are an extension of the growing process. Some bridges we need to help our children build are:

1. *A bridge to salvation.* What a thrill it is to bring a new life into this world. But for Christian parents it is even more important that we help our children experience eternal life. We must accept our personal responsibility to bring our children to Christ.

2. *A bridge of self-worth.* One of the greatest emotional gifts we can give our children is a healthy sense of self-worth. There seems little need to worry about our children's developing a proud spirit. They live in a harsh, even cruel world. They need to be built up and encouraged at home. And the home is the most influential force in developing self-image. Children see their reflection of self in the mirror of the family.

3. *A bridge to self-discipline.* Children are naturally self-centered and self-willed. So when God commands them to be obedient to their parents, it is implied that their parents will take action to bring them into obedience. Discipline is an expression of parental love and concern. Proverbs 13:24 says, "He that spareth his rod hateth his son: but he that loveth him chasteneth him betimes." The purpose of parental discipline is to develop self-discipline and submission to the will of God. As our children grow older, we gradually release them to their own self-control and the control of the Holy Spirit.

Paul declares Scripture is God-breathed. Its source is the very mouth of the Lord. He inspired the writing of all its truths, whether historical, theological, or moral. All the Bible contains is profitable for teaching, for refutation of error, for correction of those who have fallen, and for instruction in righteousness. (See Teaching Tip 3.)

Writing to Timothy as a man of God, Paul says Scripture is sufficient to outfit him completely for his work. The pages of the Bible will furnish him fully with the tools necessary for every good work as a minister.

B. A Faithful Minister

(See Teaching Tip 4.)

One final charge comes from the pen of Paul to Timothy. The apostle presents it by calling God the Father and the Lord Jesus Christ to witness. No doubt the young preacher is sobered by Paul's reminder that Christ will judge all men including preachers, both living and dead, at His appearing and in His kingdom. He will judge the quality of everyone's ministry.

With such accountability in view, the apostle charges Timothy to preach the Word faithfully. He is to proclaim the truth, not philosophize nor argue. This he must do in season or out, literally, "in good season" and "in no season." Whether it is convenient or not he is to preach the gospel. (See Teaching Tip 5.)

Timothy's ministry will include reproof in efforts to convince. In doing so he will appeal to reason. At times he will also rebuke or correct with authority. The appeal here is more to conscience. Further, he will exhort or challenge his audience in an effort to affect their will. All of this, Paul instructs, must be done with long-suffering and through careful teaching.

The apostle tells Timothy the day will come when men will no longer desire to hear healthy teaching. Following their own desires they will seek out preachers willing to scratch their itching ears with what they prefer to listen to. They will turn their ears from truth to lies.

In the midst of such difficulties Pastor Timothy must "watch" or practice self-control under all circumstances. He must not be so taken up with problems of false teaching that he forgets to spread the good news as an evangelist. Winning the lost is a standing assignment for all ministers. Finally, Paul says Timothy must fully accomplish his ministry with most careful attention to every detail.

III. Certain Reward

2 Timothy 4:6-22

2 Timothy 4:6. I am now ready to be offered, and the time of my departure is at hand. 7. I have fought a good fight, I have finished my course, I have kept the faith: 8. henceforth there is laid up for me a crown of righteousness, which the Lord, the righteous judge, shall give me at that day: and not to me only, but unto all them also that love his appearing. 16. At my first answer no man stood with me, but all men forsook me: I pray God that it may not be laid to their charge. 17. Notwithstanding the Lord stood with me, and strengthened me; that by me the preaching might be fully known, and that all the Gentiles might hear: and I was delivered out of the mouth of the lion.

A. Victorious Announcement

Only now does Paul tell Timothy of his approaching execution. In fact it is so near at hand he says his life's blood is already being poured out as a drink offering before the Lord. Such libations were frequently presented to God in Old Testament times (2 Samuel 23:16).

However, his announcement is a victorious one. Paul views his death as a departure or release. The word is used in Scripture to speak of loosing a vessel from its moorings, of unyoking an animal, and of loosing the fetters of the prisoner. (See Teaching Tips 6 and 7.)

Facing execution, the apostle looks back on his life with satisfaction rather than regret. He has fought a good fight as a soldier. He has finished his race like an athlete. He has been true to the faith as a Christian.

Looking forward, Paul sees his sure reward. It is a crown of righteousness. The righteous Judge will give it. At the moment he may think of his unjust sentence before the wicked Nero. The apostle adds that reward is just as certain for others who have looked forward to Christ's return.

Clarification

To be offered—his blood was being poured out as a drink offering.

Departure—literally, loosing.

Books—scrolls.

Parchments—writings on leather, probably Scripture.

Be thou ware—be on your guard.

TEACHING TIP 6

Ask three or four students to serve on a brief discussion panel. Address the following questions to the panel members:

1. How is the death of the saints different from the death of sinners?

2. In what way is the death of God's saints precious in His sight?

3. How is our sorrow different from those who have no hope?

4. How can we best help those who are sorrowing over the loss of a loved one?

TEACHING TIP 7

According to verse 7, what three things did Paul say he had done?

Question.
What personal requests does Paul make of Timothy as he closes this letter?

B. Personal Requests

For whatever time remains of his life on earth, Paul needs Timothy's help. Therefore, the end of his letter presents some personal requests. He wants the younger preacher to come to him as quickly as possible. He also urges that Mark be brought to him. It is inspiring to learn that he who once turned back from a preaching mission and was therefore rejected by Paul as a partner is now viewed as a useful assistant (Acts 15:36-41).

The apostle is anxious for his friends to come. Those who have worked closely with him are all gone now except Luke. Demas left because he loved the world more than the Lord. Paul found it necessary to send others away on various missions.

The condemned prisoner also asks his young associate to bring his cloak, an outer garment worn as a coat. He had left it behind with Carpus, a friend. Next to clothing in importance, was reading material. Therefore he requests Timothy to bring his books. The parchments he refers to were likely Scriptures written on leather material. Though death is near Paul will remain a student of the Word to the end.

Guideline for Living 2

Paul valued his books. We should too. Good Christian books can make a valuable contribution to our lives. But most of us are frustrated with not having enough time to read. One way to read more is to take advantage of brief moments of time. A person reading at average speed for only 15 minutes a day will read 18 books in a year. Put out books at several places around the house. Keep a copy in your pocket or purse. Read while waiting for an appointment or while riding in a car or bus. Invest the lost minutes of the day in worthwhile reading. You will be surprised how much reading you get done in a year.

C. Timely Warning

For a moment Paul turns from his pressing situation to think of Timothy's welfare. He remembers Alexander the coppersmith had done him much evil. He may have opposed the apostle much as Demetrius had done (Acts 19:23-29). Paul prays the Lord of vengeance to repay him. He then gives a timely warning for Timothy to be on guard against this enemy of the gospel. No doubt he lives in the area of Ephesus where the young pastor presently ministers.

D. God's Faithfulness

Concerning himself again, the apostle tells Timothy all his friends deserted him during his first trial in Rome. He learned by experience how Jesus felt under the same circumstances (Mark 14:50). But like the Master, Paul asks that their sin not be held against them.

Question.
What happened at Paul's first trial in Rome?

More important is the fact that the Lord stood by the apostle in the hostile courtroom. He provided the strength needed for the trying hour. In His faithfulness He even providentially arranged Paul's acquittal. The Lord had plans for him to preach the gospel to other Gentiles. For that reason he was released from his first Roman imprisonment.

Further, the apostle has confidence God will yet deliver him, though he thinks no more of being physically freed from prison.

TEACHING TIP 8

Refer to the "Living the Truth" section in explaining that in 2 Timothy Paul was actually writing his personal epitaph. Ask the class to reread 2 Timothy 4:6-8. Lead them in compiling a list of phrases from these verses which could have served as Paul's epitaph. Their suggestions may include: "I am ready." "I have fought a good fight." "I have finished my course."

Ask: "If your life were to end soon, what would your epitaph be? What would you like it to be? What can we do now to write or rewrite our epitaph?"

You may want to give each student a piece of paper and pencil and ask them to write out what they would like the epitaph of their life to be.

The assurance of the preservation of his soul unto the heavenly kingdom is what brings praise here.

E. Final Greetings

In the last words of his letter, Paul asks Timothy to greet his old friends Prisca and Aquila as well as Onesiphorus. He explains that Erastus is no longer with him. He stayed behind at Corinth. Trophimus could not continue with Paul in his final journey on earth because he became too sick at Miletum to travel.

Once more the apostle urges the young preacher to hurry to him. He is anxious that he arrive before winter, perhaps due particularly to his need of the coat.

Some specifically named ones near Paul send greetings to Timothy. In fact, all the brethren in the area of Rome do.

The last recorded words of Paul on earth contain a prayer for Timothy and all who read his letter. It is, "The Lord Jesus Christ be with thy spirit. Grace be with you. Amen."

LIVING THE TRUTH

Author James Dobson is a collector of epitaphs. His favorite is one suggested by his mother. When asked what she would like inscribed on her tombstone, she thought a moment, then said: "I *told* you I was sick!"

In his Second Epistle to Timothy Paul was, in effect, writing his epitaph. He was summarizing the results of his life and ministry and passing along a few final words of instruction to his beloved son Timothy.

There are certainly a number of appropriate epitaphs that could be suggested for the apostle Paul, such as: "I am ready," or "I have fought a good fight."

But what about you? If your life were to end soon, what phrase or statement would summarize its impact and purpose? What epitaph would your family suggest? your friends? your work associates? What epitaph would God write for your life?

If you are not satisfied with the direction of your life, now is the time to do something about it. You will likely have time to write another epitaph. (See Teaching Tip 8.)

Daily Devotional Guide

M. Resisting the Truth.
Exodus 7:10-25

T. Prospered by the Word.
2 Chronicles 20:14-20

W. Delight in the Word.
Psalm 119:33-40

T. False Teachers.
2 Peter 2:1-22

F. Contend for the Faith.
Jude 1-7

S. Future Glory.
Revelation 21:1-21

EVANGELISM OUTREACH

Paul was ready to die as he had lived—for Jesus. Would the same be true of you? Or would you have to make a drastic change in order to be assured of a life in heaven? Now is the time to make that change, to accept Christ as your Saviour. You have no assurance of tomorrow. Today is the day of salvation.

KNOWLEDGE OF TRUTH

8

SEEING THE SCRIPTURES

Titus 1:1-16

1. Paul, a servant of God, and an apostle of Jesus Christ, according to the faith of God's elect, and the acknowledging of the truth which is after godliness;

2. In hope of eternal life, which God, that cannot lie, promised before the world began;

3. But hath in due times manifested his word through preaching, which is committed unto me according to the commandment of God our Saviour;

4. To Titus, mine own son after the common faith: Grace, mercy, and peace, from God the Father and the Lord Jesus Christ our Saviour.

5. For this cause left I thee in Crete, that thou shouldest set in order the things that are wanting, and ordain elders in every city, as I had appointed thee:

6. If any be blameless, the husband of one wife, having faithful children not accused of riot or unruly.

7. For a bishop must be blameless, as the steward of God; not self-willed, not soon angry, not given to wine, no striker, not given to filthy lucre;

8. But a lover of hospitality, a lover of good men, sober, just, holy, temperate;

9. Holding fast the faithful word as he hath been taught, that he may be able by sound doctrine both to exhort and to convince the gainsayers.

10. For there are many unruly and vain talkers and deceivers, specially they of the circumcision:

11. Whose mouths must be stopped, who subvert whole houses, teaching things which they ought not, for filthy lucre's sake.

12. One of themselves, even a prophet of their own, said, The Cretians are always liars, evil beasts, slow bellies.

13. This witness is true. Wherefore rebuke them sharply, that they may be sound in the faith;

14. Not giving heed to Jewish fables, and commandments of men, that turn from the truth.

15. Unto the pure all things are pure: but unto them that are defiled and unbelieving is nothing pure; but even their mind and conscience is defiled.

16. They profess that they know God; but in works they deny him, being abominable, and disobedient, and unto every good work reprobate.

PREPARING TO TEACH

Study Text
Titus 1:1-16

Outline
I. Revelation of God's Word
  A. A High Calling
  B. A Divine Mission
II. Responsibilities of Leaders
  A. Church Order
  B. Qualified Leadership
III. Sound in the Faith
  A. Perverting the Truth
  B. Combating Heresy

Golden Text: God hath from the beginning chosen you to salvation through sanctification of the Spirit and belief of the truth. 2 Thessalonians 2:13

Central Truth: God has revealed in His Word the knowledge of truth which produces godliness in the lives of believers.

Learning Goals
1. To understand the structure and purpose of Paul's epistle to Titus.
2. To review the qualifications for spiritual leaders.
3. To examine our beliefs and our behavior.

GETTING STARTED

Have the following questions written on the chalkboard, overhead transparency, or sketchpad when the students arrive: 1) What are some areas in which people are searching for truth? 2) For what problems are people searching for answers? 3) Where are they turning for truth? for answers?

Leave space after each question to list the responses from the students. Explain that this study deals with the ultimate source of truth—the Word of God.

Clarification

A servant of God—literally, "a bond slave."

God's elect—all saved people.

The acknowledging of the truth—the full truth, i.e., Christianity.

After godliness—according to godliness, literally "Godlikeness."

Before the world began—before eternal times, ages ago.

In due times—in His own seasons, or "at the proper time."

My own son—literally, "my true child." Titus was Paul's spiritual son as was Timothy (1 Timothy 1:2).

Question

Explain the meaning of "a servant of God, and an apostle of Jesus Christ."

TEACHING TIP 1

Divide the students into three study groups. Provide each group with copies of the following instructions:

SETTING THE SCENE

Titus contains one of the most practical messages of all the epistles. This pastoral letter deals with the worship and divine order of the Church. In the two letters to Timothy, Paul stresses the importance of sound doctrine. In Titus he dwells on sound behavior—"the truth which is after godliness" (verse 1).

Bishops and pastors are enjoined to set good examples before their people, teach true doctrine, and emphasize the maintaining of good works. We are not saved by good works, but because of God's grace and mercy (3:5, 7) we are under obligation to be "zealous of good works" (2:14). The indictment of false teachers was that they were "unto every good work reprobate" (1:16). Their lives were anything but consistent with their profession. (See Teaching Tip 1.)

BIBLE COMMENTARY

I. Revelation of God's Word

Titus 1:1-4

Titus 1:1. Paul, a servant of God, and an apostle of Jesus Christ, according to the faith of God's elect, and the acknowledging of the truth which is after godliness; 2. in hope of eternal life, which God, that cannot lie, promised before the world begin; 3. but hath in due times manifested his word through preaching, which is committed unto me according unto the commandment of God our Saviour; 4. to Titus, mine own son after the common faith: Grace, mercy, and peace, from God the Father and the Lord Jesus Christ our Saviour.

A. A High Calling

Like Timothy, Titus was an early convert of Paul. Although his name does not appear in the Book of Acts which records the history of the Early Church, we do know a good deal about him. He was a Greek, a beloved friend and co-worker of the apostle. He is pictured as a trustworthy and godly man, capable and unselfish. See 2 Corinthians 2:13; 7:6, 13; 8:23; Galatians 2:1-3; 2 Timothy 4:10. (See Teaching Tip 2.)

Paul had given Titus the responsibility of superintending the churches on the island of Crete, a most difficult field. When Judaizers began teaching Cretans that Law keeping was essential to salvation, the churches were in an uproar. Paul's letter gives Titus instructions on how to reestablish order.

Before dealing with the problems in the Cretan churches, Paul focuses attention on his credentials as "a servant of God, and an apostle of Jesus Christ." His salutation reveals the very heart of the Christian faith. The word "servant" literally means "bond slave." In the Old Testament a bond slave was one who chose to remain a slave of his master for life. To follow Jesus Christ means we become a slave to Him. We are totally committed to serving Him.

Group 1: Read Titus 1:1-4. Prepare a list of the main teachings in these verses. Summarize the emphasis in one sentence. Discuss the following questions:
1. How could Paul be both a servant and an apostle with authority?
2. Who are God's elect?
3. How has God chosen to make known His Word?

Group 2: Study Titus 1:5-9. Prepare a list of the main teachings in these verses. Summarize the main emphasis in one sentence. Discuss the following questions:
1. Why was Titus left at Crete?
2. What should a bishop be and not be?
3. Why is it important that a bishop be able to exhort and convince?

Group 3—Study Titus 1:10-16. Prepare a list of the main teachings in these verses. Summarize the emphasis in one sentence. Discuss the following questions:
1. What motivates the unruly and vain talkers?
2. Does the fact that "to the pure all things are pure" mean that as Christians we can do anything we want?
3. What three condemnations does Paul level against the deceitful as defined in verse 16?

TEACHING TIP 2

Distribute slips of paper with one of the following verses written on each: 2 Corinthians 2:13; 7:6, 13; 8:23; Galatians 2:1-3; 1 Timothy 4:10. As these verses are read, instruct the students to listen for personal information regarding Titus. From this information develop a personal profile of Titus.

Question

Was Paul authorized to set standards of faith and conduct for the churches of Crete? If so, by whom?

"What! know ye not that . . . ye are not your own? For ye are bought with a price" (1 Corinthians 6:19, 20).

The word *apostle* means literally "one sent forth." Since Paul will give instruction to the churches he asserts his apostleship—but as "an apostle of Jesus Christ." In joining together "servant" and "apostle" Paul tells us that the chiefest offices in the Church are for service. Jesus, though Head of the Church, came not into the world to be served but to minister and to serve (Matthew 20:28; Mark 10:44, 45). As Christians we are to be servants of God and representatives of Jesus Christ.

Guideline for Living 1

One requirement of church growth is willingness on the part of the people to follow pastoral leadership. The pastor must be given enough room to lead if the church is to grow. When he has sought and received direction from the Lord for his church and ministry, his people must give him their full support in implementing his vision.

B. A Divine Mission

The work of an apostle of Jesus Christ is to further the faith of God's people and their knowledge of the truth. Paul is stating the missionary purpose of the Church in his opening words to Titus. He affirms that his calling is consistent with the faith that operates in the lives of God's people.

The answer to doubt, discouragement, and despair is the faith and confidence that comes through the knowledge of the Word of God. The word translated "acknowledging" in verse 1 is a noun meaning "full knowledge." The only way one can cope with the vexing problems of life is by a full and complete knowledge of the truth of God's Word.

It matters eternally what one believes. The phrase "according to the faith" refers to the standard of faith which is set for God's people. Salvation *does* rest on what a person believes about Jesus Christ, His death and resurrection, and God's Word. It is "according to the faith of God's elect." Paul is speaking of saved people here. He is not discussing the doctrine of election. "The faith of God's elect" is the truth God's children have cherished through the ages. "Truth" speaks of God's faithful revelation. Jesus could say, "I am . . . the truth" (John 14:6; see also John 1:14; 18:37). The "hope of eternal life" is promised by God who "cannot lie." If God is not a God of honesty and integrity who keeps His word, we have no hope. Paul wrote, "God forbid: yea let God be true, but every man a liar" (Romans 3:4; see also Deuteronomy 32:4; 2 Samuel 7:28; Psalm 146:6; Hebrews 6:18).

By the "commandment of God" Paul was given the right to preach the doctrine of faith and to be an instrument in bringing men to the obedience of faith (Romans 1:5; 10:17). As an "apostle of Jesus Christ" he had been given the right to set standards of faith and order for the Church (verse 3). God wants us to know the truth. He wants to fellowship with us. He wants to live His life through us. He wants to use us as instruments to reach a lost world. This is the eternal truth God wants His people to know.

Clarification

Set in order—properly organize.

Wanting—lacking, falling below a standard.

As I had appointed thee—rather, "as I ordered you."

Blameless—above reproach. It does not mean perfect or without sin.

Having faithful children—having children who believe.

Bishop—elder, a spiritual overseer.

A lover of good men—properly, "a lover of all that is good."

Question

Explain the meaning of the phrase, "set in order"?

TEACHING TIP 3

Assign a student to bring a brief (3-5 minutes) report on the Island of Crete. Refer the researcher to a Bible dictionary or Bible handbook. Also refer him to the following paragraphs in the *Adult Teacher*. Call for the research report at this time.

TEACHING TIP 4

Ask: "What are some of the ways in which God wants His church to conduct itself in good order?" Possible replies: 1) order of organization, 2) order of leadership, 3) order of worship.

II. Responsibilities of Leaders
Titus 1:5-9

Titus 1:5. For this cause left I thee in Crete, that thou shouldest set in order the things that are wanting, and ordain elders in every city, as I had appointed thee: 6. if any be blameless, the husband of one wife, having faithful children not accused of riot or unruly. 7. For a bishop must be blameless, as the steward of God; not self-willed, not soon angry, not given to wine, no striker, not given to filthy lucre; 8. but a lover of hospitality, a lover of good men, sober, just, holy, temperate; 9. holding fast the faithful word as he hath been taught, that he may be able by sound doctrine both to exhort and to convince the gainsayers.

A. Church Order
(See Teaching Tip 3.)

Crete, one of the largest islands in the Mediterranean Sea, lies almost equal distance from Europe, Asia, and Africa. We identify it with Caphtor of the Old Testament (Deuteronomy 2:23; Jeremiah 47:4; Amos 9:7). This Greek island was annexed to the Roman Empire about 67 B.C. It abounded with Jews of wealth and influence. It was evidently a luxurious and corrupt place, as heathenism affected the total life. The reputation of the people was anything but good. Paul himself said they were liars, and this is what they were noted for in that day. To cretize *(Kretizein)* or to play the part of a Cretan is synonymous with deceiving or lying.

We do not know how the gospel was first brought to Crete. It probably occurred soon after the first Pentecost, for we are expressly told there were Cretans present when the Holy Spirit was outpoured (Acts 2:11). Paul seems to have had a very effective ministry in Crete. There is no record of it in the Scriptures, but his writings to Titus lead us to believe he was there. "For this cause left I thee in Crete" (verse 5). The work prospered and expanded, for elders were required "in every city." "Every city" suggests a large number of churches. (See Teaching Tip 4.)

Titus was left in Crete to organize the churches and dispel disorder and confusion. The need of godly order in the churches is evident. In Crete, as in other places, there were members who were unruly, vain talkers, and deceivers. There were pastors who were not doctrinally sound or for other reasons were not qualified to give leadership. A critical mission was thrust upon Titus.

God does not condone division, confusion, contention, false teaching, or error. He wants godliness and true spirituality. He wants the Church to operate harmoniously. He wants unity among His children. It is not wrong to disagree, but it is wrong to be disagreeable. Anything that causes disorder hinders the Church's effectiveness and witness.

Guideline for Living 2

Many times the Holy Spirit spontaneously puts the various parts of the service—singing, special music, preaching—together in a beautiful pattern of ebb and flow. But that doesn't mean it is unspiritual for leaders to plan the service to the best of their ability.

The Bible instructs that worship be decent and orderly (1 Corinthians 14:40). We will continue to be blessed as we maintain a balance between these elements of structure and spontaneity.

Draw or develop the following outline of requirements for leadership.

BLAMELESS IN   Personal
                              Life
                              Family
                              Life
                              Doctrine

Explain that the word "blameless" means above reproach or not open to criticism.

Question

What do you consider to be the most essential qualifications of a pastor?

B. Qualified leadership

Paul did not stay in Crete long enough to organize the church completely. There were still things "wanting" (lacking), and Titus was commissioned to set things in proper order and to ordain elders. The word "elder" can be translated "bishop" or "pastor." The elders were the pastors and teachers of the congregations. They were called "bishops" because of their office as overseers of the flock (verse 7; Acts 20:17). They were ordained and solemnly set apart to their office as pastors.

It is well to keep in mind that the Church is a divine institution and God has ordained that men of God should lead it. This does not mean the membership has no voice. The Church, however, is not a pure democracy. The people are led by the one God has placed over them. The pastor has a responsibility under God that must be recognized. (See Hebrews 13:7, 17; 1 Corinthians 16:16; 1 Peter 5:5.) (See Teaching Tip 5.)

The primary concern of Paul was the character and qualifications of the church's leadership. Only people of sound moral character should be considered. The bishop (pastor) must be blameless in personal life, family life, and doctrine. The church must be able to respect him. He must be an example to the believer and his name must be spotless (1 Corinthians 1:8; Colossians 1:22). If a man's speech and conduct do not reflect a dedication to Christ, then the cause of Christ suffers.

The qualifications of elders given in Titus should be compared with what Paul gave in 1 Timothy 3:1-7—only some things have been added. The leader will be judged in part by his success in leading his own family to Christ. If he cannot communicate faith to his household, how can he lead other families to the Lord? The pastor cannot have more than one wife. The family arrangements on Crete were the result of heathenism. Polygamy prevailed and many believers had more than one wife. "The husband of one wife" in the Greek literally means "one woman man."

Guideline for Living 3

Psalm 127:3 says children are a blessing and heritage of the Lord. When children are faithful to God and obedient and respectful to their parents, the blessing is doubled. Bad children can come from good homes, but the reverse is seldom true. Nothing gladdens the hearts more than to see their children live for the Lord.

Well-behaved children are also a blessing to the church. People often judge a church by the children it produces.

By raising well-mannered, hardworking children, Christian parents can make a contribution to the quality of community life. An old adage says: "As goes the family, so goes the nation." Habits and attitudes learned at home usually determine how we live the rest of our days.

The elder must understand he is God's steward and as such is responsible to God for his deportment. He must not be self-willed, arrogant, ill-tempered, or covetous. If he cannot control himself he is not qualified to govern the church of God.

In addition to basic moral qualifications, the leaders of the Church must be well established in the faith and be able to give instruction

Clarification

Unruly—not under rule or subjection; insubordinate.

Vain talkers—empty talkers, speaking only nonsense.

Deceivers—Judaizing teachers who were contradicting Paul's teaching.

One of themselves—a Cretan. The reference is to Epimenides, a poet who lived in the sixth century B.C.

Liars—deliberate deceivers.

Slow bellies—idle gluttons, living only to satisfy their stomachs.

Jewish fables—Jewish philosophy, ritual, and tradition.

Unto the pure all things are pure—moral impurity is not in question. Those who are of sound faith need not be troubled by such things as laws of clean and unclean, nor degrees of ceremonial defilement.

Question

How would you define the word *heresy*? Why is it so dangerous?

TEACHING TIP 6

Use the overhead transparency from the Packet of Adult Teaching Helps to illustrate the two ways in which the Church is under attack.

Write the following phrase on the chalkboard or overhead projector as you discuss the subject of heresy and how to combat it: "Truth, the antidote to heresy."

in sound doctrine. They should have the ability to answer adequately those who would contradict it. Heresy must be repudiated. It is understandable why Paul exhorted Timothy to "lay hands suddenly on no man" (1 Timothy 5:22).

III. Sound in the Faith
Titus 1:10-16

Titus 1:10. There are many unruly and vain talkers and deceivers, specially they of the circumcision: 11. whose mouths must be stopped, who subvert whole houses, teaching things which they ought not, for filthy lucre's sake. 12. One of themselves, even a prophet of their own, said, The Cretians are always liars, evil beasts, slow bellies. 13. This witness is true. Wherefore rebuke them sharply, that they may be sound in the faith; 14. not giving heed to Jewish fables, and commandments of men, that turn from the truth. 15. Unto the pure all things are pure: but unto them that are defiled and unbelieving is nothing pure; but even their mind and conscience is defiled. 16. They profess that they know God; but in works they deny him, being abominable, and disobedient, and unto every good work reprobate.

A. Perverting the Truth

(See Teaching Tip 6.)

The Christian church has been attacked in many ways from its very beginning. It has suffered under the heavy hand of persecution and survived. In fact, persecution has never hindered the Church's growth. A greater danger to the Church has been false doctrine and heresy. When man's errors are mixed with God's truth we have what the Bible calls heresy.

Paul describes something of the nature of Judaistic Christianity. First, the leaders of this party within the Cretan church refused to recognize the authority of Paul as an apostle or of Titus as his representative. Second, the Judaizers sought to shackle Christianity to the observances of the old Pharisaic legalism. Titus was well acquainted with this legalism. He had become a Christian in the church at Antioch which Barnabas and Paul pastored (Acts 11:19-26; 13:1-3). A great controversy between Jewish and Gentile members had broken out over the question of requiring circumcision for all Gentile converts. Paul and Barnabas took the issue before the apostles in Jerusalem (Acts 15:1-21). Titus, a Greek, was a test case and Paul said he was not forced to be circumcised "that the truth of the gospel might continue with you" (Galatians 2:5). The Jerusalem council agreed.

The Judaizers' teaching was contrary to Paul's understanding of the gospel. Their teaching was rooted in Jewish myth and liturgical customs with the attending taboos and superstitions. In stinging language, Paul points to the confusion in the churches wrought by insubordinate men, empty talkers, and deceivers. They had upset whole families, sowed seeds of distrust, and turned people away from the truth in Christ Jesus. They were perverting the truth for personal gain (filthy lucre).

The warning is clear. We are to avoid heresy and false doctrine in any form. A pseudo-intellectualism that humanizes God and His Word and makes man's intelligence the final authority is heresy. We must also guard against taking a legalistic point of view in our

TEACHING TIP 7

Direct some of the questions from the "Living the Truth" section above to the students. Distribute paper and pencil. Ask the students to complete the following three sentence prayers:

1. Lord, I have not always reflected truth in . . .

2. To be more truthful in both belief and behavior I need to . . .

3. Help me begin to work on this by . . .

Question

How should heresy be dealt with? How may a heretic be silenced or discouraged?

personal interpretation of holiness and building a system of doctrine upon it. This is heresy also.

B. Combating Heresy

Guideline for Living 4

What a high price we pay for disputes and disagreements in the church. Often the innocent victims of a church fight are the children. They may be too young to understand all the issues involved, but they are firsthand witnesses to its effects on their parents and others.

Often their social life is disrupted when they or their young friends suddenly find themselves in another church or, worse yet, no church at all. It may take months or even years for them to settle into a satisfying routine again. The disillusionment may never go away completely.

Another group affected by disagreements among saints are sinners—those who might have come to Christ and His church were it not for the fussing and fighting among those who got there before them. They certainly cannot be expected to come to find peace with God in an atmosphere of tension and conflict.

Wherever the Word of God is sown the devil will work. In Crete whole families had been turned away from the grace of God. By deliberate deception false teachers had captured households. The churches did not have buildings as we have today. They met in homes, so it was easy for the heretic to win families.

Paul tells Titus he will have to deal with heretics firmly. They must be stopped. They must be silenced. The apostle adds, if possible, restore them to spiritual health through faith in Christ (verse 13). They needed deliverance from their sin and error.

The only way heresy can be successfully combated (literally "cut off") is by preaching the truth of the Word of God. Ceremonies and rituals cannot change the evil heart of man. Only God's Word can change the human heart. (See Jeremiah 23:29; Romans 1:16; Hebrews 4:12.)

LIVING THE TRUTH

The Christian life is not merely a matter of right beliefs. It is also a matter of right behavior. This does not mean right beliefs are unimportant, for often wrong behavior starts with wrong beliefs.

If your life was seen as a letter or essay (which, by the way, it is), would it contain any heresy or false teaching? By following you, could others find their way to God? Would they develop right beliefs and behavior by patterning themselves after your example? Where do you need to portray more clearly the truth in your life? (See Teaching Tip 7.)

EVANGELISM OUTREACH

What do you believe about Jesus Christ? that He was a good man? that He came to show us how to live? that He was a great teacher? Jesus was all of these. But He is more. He is the Son of God. He came to be our Saviour. To be saved we must believe that with our whole heart. And we must express personal trust in His saving work.

9 | GOD'S MARVEL-OUS GRACE

PREPARING TO TEACH

Study Text
Titus 2:1 through 3:15

Outline
I. Encouraging Godly Living
   A. Sound Teaching
   B. Practical Godliness
II. Responding to God's Grace
   A. Saving Grace
   B. Instructing Grace
III. Maintaining Good Works
   A. Submission to Constituted Authority
   B. Charitableness Toward Others

Golden Text: The grace of God that bringeth salvation hath appeared to all men. Titus 2:11

Central Truth: God's grace teaches us to live righteously.

Learning Goals
1. To develop a fuller understanding of God's gracious plan of salvation.
2. To develop a fresh love and appreciation of God and His grace.
3. To determine to share the message of God's grace with others.

SEEING THE SCRIPTURES
Titus 2:1-14; 3:8

1. Speak thou the things which become sound doctrine:
2. That the aged men be sober, grave, temperate, sound in faith, in charity, in patience.
3. The aged women likewise, that they be in behavior as becometh holiness, not false accusers, not given to much wine, teachers of good things;
4. That they may teach the young women to be sober, to love their husbands, to love their children,
5. To be discreet, chaste, keepers at home, good, obedient to their own husbands, that the word of God be not blasphemed.
6. Young men likewise exhort to be sober-minded.
7. In all things showing thyself a pattern of good works: in doctrine showing uncorruptness, gravity, sincerity,
8. Sound speech, that cannot be condemned; that he that is of the contrary part may be ashamed, having no evil thing to say of you.
9. Exhort servants to be obedient unto their own masters, and to please them well in all things; not answering again;
10. Not purloining, but showing all good fidelity; that they may adorn the doctrine of God our Saviour in all things.
11. For the grace of God that bringeth salvation hath appeared to all men,
12. Teaching us that, denying ungodliness and worldly lusts, we should live soberly, righteously, and godly, in this present world;
13. Looking for that blessed hope, and the glorious appearing of the great God and our Saviour Jesus Christ;
14. Who gave himself for us, that he might redeem us from all iniquity, and purify unto himself a peculiar people, zealous of good works.
3:8. This is a faithful saying, and these things I will that thou affirm constantly, that they which have believed in God might be careful to maintain good works. These things are good and profitable unto men.

SETTING THE SCENE
Dr. J. H. Jowett said, "Grace is more than mercy. It is more than tender mercy. It is more than a multitude of mercies. Grace is more than love. It is more than innocent love. Grace is holy love in spontaneous movement going out in eager quest toward the unholy and unlovely."

A poor man prayed, "Lord give me grace to feel my need of

GETTING STARTED

Begin the class session by asking one of the students to lead the class in singing one verse of the song, "Marvelous Grace" or "Amazing Grace." Ask the students to mention what they could learn about God's grace from this song.

Read the definition and statement about grace from the "Setting the Scene" section. Ask the students to work with one or two other persons sitting near them in developing a one-sentence definition of grace. Allow the groups 3 or 4 minutes to complete their definitions. Then call for responses from each. Write the key phrases from each. Write the key phrases of their definitions on the chalkboard, overhead transparency, or sketchpad.

Clarification

Sound doctrine—sound teaching, the doctrine of the gospel, truth.

Not false accusers—not slanderers or gossips.

Discreet—conducting themselves properly.

Chaste—of good character.

Good—kindly.

Obedient—responsive, subject.

Sober-minded—sensible, temperate, self-controlled.

Not purloining—not stealing.

Question

Why is it essential that sound doctrine be taught? What is meant by "sound doctrine"?

TEACHING TIP 1

Have one of the students read John 4:23, 24. Draw or display the following visual to illustrate the need for balance both in our worship to God and in our work for Him.

SPIRIT   TRUTH
            /\

grace. And give me grace to ask for grace. And give me grace to receive grace. And, O Lord, when grace is given, give me grace to use it. Amen."

Paul knew the Cretans were sinful, but he also knew the power of the grace of God—"the grace that bringeth salvation." But he says there is more in God's plan than being saved. God's grace will teach the believer how to live a good, God-fearing life.

BIBLE COMMENTARY

I. Encouraging Godly Living

Titus 2:1-10

Titus 2:1. Speak thou the things which become sound doctrine: 2. that the aged men be sober, grave, temperate, sound in faith, in charity, in patience. 3. The aged women likewise, that they be in behavior as becometh holiness, not false accusers, not given to much wine, teachers of good things; 4. that they may teach the young women to be sober, to love their husbands, to love their children, 5. to be discreet, chaste, keepers at home, good, obedient to their own husbands, that the word of God be not blasphemed. 6. Young men likewise exhort to be sober-minded. 7. In all things showing thyself a pattern of good works: in doctrine showing uncorruptness, gravity, sincerity, 8. sound speech, that cannot be condemned; that he that is of the contrary part may be ashamed, having no evil thing to say of you. 9. Exhort servants to be obedient unto their own masters, and to please them well in all things; not answering again; 10. not purloining, but showing all good fidelity; that they may adorn the doctrine of God our Saviour in all things.

A. Sound Teaching

Paul emphasizes the importance of solid, sound, and sober teaching of the gospel of Christ. This is in contrast to the vain talk of the heretical teachers who were turning the minds of many in the Cretan churches against the gospel. The "sound doctrine" in verse 1 (as in 1 Timothy 1:10 and 6:3) means "the Christian faith," or "the doctrine of the gospel." The soundness of the gospel plan of salvation differs from the teaching of the Judaizers. False doctrine corrupts; sound doctrine purifies and elevates. Jesus said, "Sanctify them through thy truth" (John 17:17).

It is the responsibility of the ministry to preach and teach sound doctrine. It should be plainly and forcefully proclaimed, since there are so many enemies of the gospel. In chapter 1, the elders Titus was instructed to ordain were to be adept at preaching the Word of God, and refuting heretics. This does not mean that we should major in negatives. God's servant should know what the Bible teaches. He must allow the Holy Spirit to reveal the truth to him, and then he must stand upon that truth. There cannot be a healthy Church without Bible truth. (See Teaching Tip 1.)

On the Day of Pentecost many were added to the Church. We are told they "continued steadfastly in the apostle's doctrine and fellowship, and in breaking of bread, and in prayers" (Acts 2:42). Being faithful to the "apostle's doctrine" was the hallmark of the

Question

What is the fruit of sound doctrine?

TEACHING TIP 3

Use the write-on poster from the Packet of Adult Teaching Helps to compile a list of requirements for the five groups of people mentioned in these verses.

Early Church. It is the message that is preached and taught which determines whether the Church is really a church. (See Teaching Tip 2.)

In *Knowing the Doctrines of the Bible* (Gospel Publishing House) Myer Pearlman commented, "There is a tendency in some quarters not only to minimize the value of doctrine but to dismiss it as outgrown and useless. However, as long as men think about the problems of existence they will feel the need of an authoritative and systematically arranged answer to these problems. Doctrine will always be necessary as long as men ask, 'Where did I come from, what am I, and whither am I going?'

"It is often said, 'It does not matter what a man believes so long as he does right.' This is one way of dismissing doctrine as having no importance in relation to life. But every person has a theology whether he knows it or not. Man's actions are influenced by what he believes . . . strong beliefs make for strong character." (Copyright, Gospel Publishing House. Used by permission).

B. Practical Godliness

Through Titus Paul was giving instruction to the entire membership of the Cretan church. His theme was the application of sound doctrine. To hold forth the Word of life is one thing; to adorn it is another. The Bible holds up a standard of living far different from man's. God has never lowered these standards. The morality and ethical behavior urged by Paul should be the behavior of all Christians everywhere. Titus was not only admonished to preach sound doctrine, but was asked to give practical counsel to five groups within the local church. They were older men (verse 2), older women (verse 3), younger women (verses 4, 5), younger men (verse 6), and slaves (verses 9, 10). A second admonition to Titus was also included (verses 7, 8).

It is imperative that the Church have godly leadership, but it must also have godly members. When practiced, the standards set forth by Paul will make for harmony within the Church and cause those on the outside to respect it. Each Christian should be a pattern for the rest of the Church. This responsibility is not incumbent on the clergy only. There is no double standard in the New Testament. (See Teaching Tip 3.)

Older men are expected to be temperate, sober, self-controlled, sound in the faith, loving, and patient. The same requirements are laid down for bishops in 1 Timothy 3:2, and for women in 1 Timothy 3:11. (See 1 Thessalonians 1:3; 1 Timothy 3:8; 6:11, 12; 2 Timothy 3:10.) Therefore the virtues listed in verses 2-5 are family virtues. Older women are urged to live as consecrated Christians ("as becometh holiness") so they will be good examples and good teachers to younger women. "Keepers at home" means they will become good housekeepers, faithful wives, and loving mothers. They will have homes where "the Word of God [is] not blasphemed."

Guideline for Living 1

The Bible has always placed high value on the role of a godly wife and mother. The modern feminist movement has caused some women to feel almost apologetic about their role as a homemaker. Yet there really is no higher calling. As one wife remarked, "Any-

Clarification

That bringeth salvation— that saves.

To all men—Grace is the only means by which salvation is possible for the human race. This does not imply that all men will eventually be saved.

Teaching us—instructing us. Grace saves, and also teaches and trains in godly living.

Soberly, righteously, and godly—True morality concerns ourselves ("soberly"), our fellowman ("righteously"), and God ("godly").

That blessed hope— Christ's coming to take His Church out of this world.

Redeem—ransom or deliver by payment of a price (1 Peter 1:18).

From all iniquity—from the curse of the Law, from all sin, guilt, and condemnation.

Let no man despise thee— be a true example of the Christian faith.

Question

What is salvation? What does it mean to be saved? Define the phrase, "the grace of God."

one can be a secretary or sales representative, but I am the only one God has called to be a wife to my husband and a mother to my children."

Some situations require a wife and mother to work outside the home. But when it is possible for her to remain at home, the entire family benefits from her presence. Young children are reassured when their mother is there to send them off to school in the morning and welcome them home in the afternoon. A husband is benefited by a wife who makes it her full-time responsibility to care for him and his children.

A wife who devotes full attention to her housekeeping responsibilities can often find better bargains for her family by being able to spend more time in comparative shopping. By careful planning and adequate time for preparation, she can often cook less expensive but more nourishing meals for her family.

Not all people mellow with age. Some become grouchy, irritable, bitter, and cynical. If we expect to be kind, loving, gentle, and gracious in old age we must begin cultivating these virtues when we are young.

The young men must also control themselves. Titus must be a model of good works. As a faithful minister of God he was to reflect in his life and teachings the doctrines of the gospel of Jesus Christ. He must show in his teachings integrity, gravity, and sound speech ("sound doctrine"). Finally, Christian servants are to obey their masters and be cooperative and honest. (See Teaching Tip 4.)

The Christian ethic is essentially the same for all—young and old, men and women, slave and free. The call is to live sober, upright, godly lives in this world. (See Leviticus 11:45; Luke 1:74, 75; 2 Corinthians 7:1; Hebrews 12:14; 1 Peter 1:16; 2 Peter 3:11.)

II. Responding to God's Grace

Titus 2:11-15

Titus 2:11. The grace of God that bringeth salvation hath appeared to all men, 12. teaching us that, denying ungodliness and worldly lusts, we should live soberly, righteously, and godly, in this present world; 13. looking for that blessed hope, and the glorious appearing of the great God and our Saviour Jesus Christ; 14. who gave himself for us, that he might redeem us from all iniquity, and purify unto himself a peculiar people, zealous of good works. 15. These things speak, and exhort, and rebuke with all authority. Let no man despise thee.

A. Saving Grace

The ultimate purpose of God's grace is that all men, Jew and Gentile alike, may receive forgiveness and enter the family of God. Paul makes it clear that the grace of God is sufficient for any circumstance. God's grace is something that is desperately needed but not deserved. It is God acting toward us in a way we do not expect and do not merit.

"The grace of God that bringeth salvation to all men hath appeared" means that all the attributes of God are flowing out in order to save men. Instead of responding in anger and judgment for our sinfulness, He offers us His grace. This is seen at Calvary in the Son of God's bleeding and dying for guilty men. We deserve wrath, but God offers forgiveness. Sin must be punished. God is holy and hates sin. Christ, by dying for our sins, met the holy demands of God's justice and He can now save us by His grace.

The clause "that bringeth salvation" is used as an adjective, so Paul is saying literally, "The salvation-bringing grace of God hath appeared." "All men" stresses the universality of the gospel. God's grace is sufficient for everyone, but the apostle is not saying that all will receive the salvation which is brought to them. "That bringeth salvation" does not describe an actuality, but a potentiality and possibility. Salvation is available to "all men." God makes no exception. He excludes none. All we have to do is believe Christ, trust Him, and receive Him.

God does not save us by His love nor by His mercy. Ephesians 2:8 reminds us: "By grace are ye saved through faith; and that not of yourselves: it is the gift of God." Love is the divine motive. God is love, but He is also justice and judgment. If a man could be saved by the mercy of God only, all mankind would be saved and it would not have been necessary for Christ to die. Salvation cannot be bestowed indiscriminately upon all people regardless of their relation to God. There must be trust in Christ and spiritual receptivity. (See John 3:18; 5:24; Romans 10:9; James 1:21; 2 Peter 3:9; Revelation 22:14.)

B. Instructing Grace

"Teaching us" (verse 12) means we are to be taught through the grace of God as revealed by Jesus Christ. Grace not only saved us but also trains us. Knowing Jesus as our personal Saviour is a wonderful experience, but there is more to God's plan for us than being saved. His grace will move us onward toward growth and maturity in our Christian faith. (See Teaching Tip 5.)

God calls the redeemed to live for Him and to avoid ungodliness and worldly lusts. Ungodliness must be denied before one can walk with God. This is the first lesson taught by grace. It is a negative lesson. Paul speaks of "denying ungodliness." He does not suggest gradually progressing from a state of ungodliness into a state of godliness. We are to deny ungodliness, turn away from it, reject it. Why? Because ungodliness is the cardinal and root sin of the world. It is the parent of all sins and the first sin in the life of each individual.

The redeemed should deny anything that is not in keeping with the Spirit of God. This includes "worldly lusts." "Worldly" is the Greek word *kosmos,* used to describe the world system. "Lusts" refers to strong passionate desires and represents the system of evil operating in the world. Paul is saying we should not allow the world to set our standards or influence our decisions. The world system is under the power and control of Satan. The Christian life is to be a resisting life. It is to be a sober life. It is to be a righteous life. It is to be a godly life. It is to be an active life—"zealous of good works." The grace of God makes it possible to live such a life "in this present world." (See Teaching Tip 6.)

The hope of the second coming of Christ should have a profound influence on the believer's daily walk. We should be "looking for that blessed hope." The word *blessed* is sometimes translated "happy." The hope of Christ's coming is a happy hope. It puts

Question
In what ways is the grace of God a teaching grace?

TEACHING TIP 5

Draw or develop the following visual to show the two sides of our salvation experience.

TWO SIDES OF THE COIN

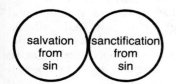

salvation from sin / sanctification from sin

TEACHING TIP 6

Develop a list of the following qualities of godly living mentioned by the author in this paragraph. The Christian life is a: 1) resisting life, 2) sober life, 3) righteous life, 4) godly life, 5) active life.

Question

How should the "blessed hope" of Christ's return influence our lives?

meaning and purpose into our lives. It means sin's dominion and power will be forever broken. When Jesus comes, our redemption will be complete. This is the next event in the program of God.

Guideline for Living 2

The thought of the coming of Christ often prompts us to ask ourselves the question, "Am I ready for His return?" Titus 2:13 and Hebrews 9:28 give us a simple way to determine our state of preparedness. These verses tell us Christ is coming for those who are expecting and anxiously looking for His appearing. They know they are ready because they are trusting in the grace of God to make them ready and keep them that way.

So maybe the question we need to ask ourselves is not, "Am I ready?" but, "Am I looking for Him? Am I excitedly and anxiously looking for Him to return? Do I look forward to His coming with dread or with hope? Will it be a glorious appearing for me or a terrible calamity?" How you answer these questions determines whether you are ready for Him to come again.

III. Maintaining Good Works
Titus 3:1-5

Titus 3:1. Put them in mind to be subject to principalities and powers, to obey magistrates, to be ready to every good work, 2. to speak evil of no man, to be no brawlers, but gentle, showing all meekness unto all men. 3. For we ourselves also were sometime foolish, disobedient, deceived, serving divers lusts and pleasures, living in malice and envy, hateful, and hating one another. 4. But after that the kindness and love of God our Saviour toward man appeared, 5. not by works of righteousness which we have done, but according to his mercy he saved us, by the washing of regeneration, and renewing of the Holy Ghost.

A. Submission To Constituted Authority

The whole spectrum of God's purpose for the Church is presented in the Book of Titus. In chapter 1 we are told God wants an orderly Church. In chapter 2 the emphasis is on sound doctrine. In chapter 3 Paul reminds us that the Church is expected to perform good works. The Christians' responsibility is to demonstrate good works before men. The grace of God is the root; the good works are the fruit.

Titus was asked to remind the Cretan believers of their obligations as Christian citizens. Once a democratic state, Crete had chafed under Roman law over 125 years. Their impatience with authority fostered a spirit of insubordination. Paul must have observed this on his visit to the island. He was convinced Christians of all people should be law-abiding citizens, subject to the principalities and powers over them. This could be a police officer, a judge, or other government official. That subjection (obedience) is not to the man, but to the office he represents. Christians should manifest a spirit of understanding and cooperation instead of unfair criticism and contention. Without the protection of the law we would be in constant danger. (See Teaching Tip 7.)

Our responsibility to be subject and obey is defined more fully by Paul in Romans 13:1-5. The Living Bible paraphrase reads: "Obey the government, for God is the one who has put it

Clarification

Put them in mind—call it to their attention.

Principalities—the chief government authorities.

Magistrates—lower government authorities.

Speak evil of no man—do not slander, malign, or repeat gossip.

Be no brawlers—don't be contentious.

Washing of regeneration—This does not refer to water baptism. It is literally the "laver of regeneration" and refers to sins being washed away.

Renewing—comes from two words meaning "new" and "again," an obvious reference to the new birth when the Holy Spirit comes to dwell in us.

Being justified—being judged righteous.

Question

What does it mean to be subject to the principalities and powers over us?

TEACHING TIP 7

The following questions can be used to guide a panel discussion or a general class discussion of the subject: What should be the Christian attitude toward civil authority? Is civil disobedience ever justified? To what extent should Christians become involved in politics? How could this help and/or hinder their influence for Christ?

TEACHING TIP 8

Refer to the "Living the Truth" section in the wide column. Distribute paper and pencil and instruct the students to list the names of five or six people they are close to such as friends, family members, neighbors, or associates who are unsaved. Ask them to bow their heads and ask the Lord to lay on their hearts one of these persons they feel He may want them to witness to in the coming week. Instruct them to circle or underline that name.

Next, have them make a list of times, places, or circumstances during which they will be with that person in the next week. Also have them write down several possible ways they could turn the conversation to spiritual matters. Close the session by asking the students to share with someone sitting next to them the name of the person they would like to witness to this week. Instruct them to pray for each other, asking God to lead and direct them and to open doors of opportunity.

Daily Devotional Guide

M. Following the Lord.
Joshua 14:1-15
T. Hating Evil.
Job 1:1-12
W. Forgiving Grace.
Psalm 32:1-5
T. Pleasing the Lord.
Colossians 1:9-13
F. Helping Others.
James 1:22-27
S. Doing Good.
Galatians 6:7-10

---

there. There is no government anywhere that God has not placed in power. So those who refuse to obey the laws of the land are refusing to obey God, and punishment will follow" (Romans 13:1-2).

We may not agree with everything the government does, but we should respect constituted authority. The Christian should be the best citizen in his community. He is to be obedient to the law, pay his taxes, and pray for those who are in positions of authority.

B. Charitableness Toward Others

Paul never forgot what he once was and it moved him to a deep compassion for the lost. He believed every Christian should be a true example of Christ. The virtues listed in verse 2 are oriented toward the unbelieving world and not just those within the Church fellowship. Christians are "to speak evil of no man." If the evil which one speaks of another is false, that is slander. If it is true, it is a sin against charity. In both cases it reveals a malignant spirit. Slander, gossip, and contentiousness are hurtful, not only to those directly involved but to the Church, the community, and the cause of Christ. Christians must beware of such practices.

Kindness and consideration should be the pattern of our lives toward others. We should be interested in those things which are a blessing to mankind. "As we have therefore opportunity, let us do good unto all men" (Galatians 6:10). (See also Psalm 34:14; 37:3; Luke 6:35; Hebrews 13:16; James 4:17.) By such behavior the Christian proves to the world he is indeed a new creation in Christ Jesus.

LIVING THE TRUTH

In this study we have learned that God's grace is not simply something we enjoy; it is also something we must obey. It is not something to be hoarded for ourselves; it is something we must share in turn with others. The Bible makes it clear that we are all to be actively involved in spreading the good news. There are some Christians who seem to be especially gifted with effectiveness in personal evangelism, but all of us are called to be witnesses (Acts 1:8). The Holy Spirit is given to empower us for this ministry.

One of the most effective ways to witness for Christ is to share Him with our friends and family—those closest to us. Often it is necessary to win a person as a friend before we can win him to the Lord. This kind of "friendship evangelism," as it is sometimes called, is a natural way to share Christ. It is also a rewarding way to win people to Christ. When those who are closest to us come to Christ, we have special cause for rejoicing. This approach to evangelism also makes it easier to bring the new convert into full fellowship and involvement in the church, since he or she may be already acquainted with others in the church. (See Teaching Tip 8.)

EVANGELISM OUTREACH

What is your view of God? Is it that of an angry taskmaster waiting to strike you down for displeasing Him? Nothing could be farther from the truth. God is a loving Father. His grace makes it possible for all to come to Him through faith in Jesus Christ. Come to Him today while you feel His Spirit drawing you.

FELLOWSHIP WITH GOD

SEEING THE SCRIPTURES

1 John 1:9 through 2:11, 15-17

9. If we confess our sins, he is faithful and just to forgive us our sins, and to cleanse us from all unrighteousness.

10. If we say that we have not sinned, we make him a liar, and his word is not in us.

2:1. My little children, these things write I unto you, that ye sin not. And if any man sin, we have an advocate with the Father, Jesus Christ the righteous:

2. And he is the propitiation for our sins: and not for ours only, but also for the sins of the whole world.

3. And hereby we do know that we know him, if we keep his commandments.

4. He that saith, I know him, and keepeth not his commandments, is a liar, and the truth is not in him.

5. But whoso keepeth his word, in him verily is the love of God perfected: hereby know we that we are in him.

6. He that saith he abideth in him ought himself also so to walk, even as he walked.

7. Brethren, I write no new commandment unto you, but an old commandment which ye had from the beginning. The old commandment is the word which ye have heard from the beginning.

8. Again, a new commandment I write unto you, which thing is true in him and in you: because the darkness is past, and the true light now shineth.

9. He that saith he is in the light, and hateth his brother, is in darkness even until now.

10. He that loveth his brother abideth in the light, and there is none occasion of stumbling in him.

11. But he that hateth his brother is in darkness, and walketh in darkness, and knoweth not whither he goeth, because that darkness hath blinded his eyes.

15. Love not the world, neither the things that are in the world. If any man love the world, the love of the Father is not in him.

16. For all that is in the world, the lust of the flesh, and the lust of the eyes, and the pride of life, is not of the Father, but is of the world.

17. And the world passeth away, and the lust thereof: but he that doeth the will of God abideth for ever.

SETTING THE SCENE

The First Epistle of John is addressed to believers. The apostle emphasizes the essentials of the gospel and warns against the er-

PREPARING TO TEACH

Study Text
1 John 1:1 through 2:17

Outline
I. Cleansing Provided
   A. A Christian Manifesto
   B. Walking in the Light
   C. Confession of Sin
II. Proofs of Fellowship
   A. A Knowledge of God
   B. Brotherly Love
   C. Spiritual Understanding
III. Call to Separation
   A. Worldliness Forbidden
   B. Reasons for Not Loving the World

Golden Text: If we walk in the light, as he is in the light, we have fellowship one with another, and the blood of Jesus Christ his Son cleanseth us from all sin. 1 John 1:7

Central Truth: We are brought into fellowship with God by the cleansing of the blood of Christ.

Learning Goals
1. To be willing to confess our sins to God.
2. To desire to let our lights shine for God.
3. To ask God to help us love those who are sometimes hard to love.

GETTING STARTED

As the students arrive, divide them into two groups. Instruct group 1 to compile a list of ways our world is getting better. They may want to include things such as medical advances, better means of communication, better educational systems, etc.

Instruct group 2 to compile a list of ways our world is getting worse. Their list may include things like moral breakdown, drug and alcohol abuse, wars and rebellion, etc.

Call for reports from each group. Explain that as Christians we have cause for both concern and rejoicing. The opening lines from Charles Dickens' historical novel, *A Tale of Two Cities,* describes our world: "It was the best of times. It was the worst of times."

Explain that this study begins a consideration of the First Epistle of John which outlines the believer's walk of light in a world of darkness.

Distribute copies of the outline of 1 John from the Packet of Adult Teaching Helps.

Clarification

God is light—God is holy; God is pure.

Darkness—signifies lack of truth and purity.

Walk in the light—walk in the likeness of God in truth, holiness, and love.

Fellowship—communion.

We deceive ourselves—lead ourselves astray, delude ourselves.

Confess—from the Greek verb *homologeo,* meaning "to say the same thing." When you confess, you are agreeing with God that the thing you did is sin.

Advocate—lawyer who appears in court on behalf of his client; a defense lawyer.

Propitiation—atoning sacrifice, a sin offering.

roneous teachings which were invading the churches of Asia Minor. An attempt was being made by false prophets to "improve" the gospel by amalgamating it with prevailing philosophies and systems of thought. Gnosticism was Christianity's deadly enemy. It has its modern counterpart in the liberal religion which has infiltrated so many denominations.

John sets before the saints those things by which they may know they are saved. The plan of salvation is presented in plain and positive statements. The incarnation of God's Son is declared to be the foundation of the Christian faith. Believers are encouraged to live lives that give evidence of their fellowship with God.

BIBLE COMMENTARY

I. Cleansing Provided

1 John 1:1 through 2:2

1 John 1:5. This then is the message which we have heard of him, and declare unto you, that God is light, and in him is no darkness at all. 6. If we say that we have fellowship with him, and walk in darkness, we lie, and do not the truth: 7. but if we walk in the light, as he is in the light, we have fellowship one with another, and the blood of Jesus Christ his Son cleanseth us from all sin. 8. If we say we have no sin, we deceive ourselves, and the truth is not in us. 9. If we confess our sins, he is faithful and just to forgive us our sins, and to cleanse us from all unrighteousness. 10. If we say that we have not sinned, we make him a liar, and his word is not in us. 2:1 My children, these things write I unto you, that ye sin not. And if any man sin, we have an advocate with the Father, Jesus Christ the righteous: 2. and he is the propitiation for our sins: and not for ours only, but also for the sins of the whole world.

A. A Christian Manifesto

(See Teaching Tip 1.)

One of the dangerous heresies that threatened the Early Church was gnosticism. According to the Gnostics the only hope of salvation is through self-knowledge and not by faith in Jesus Christ. They taught that man is fallen and lost because he is imprisoned in a material body. Since the material body is sinful, God cannot dwell in such a body. Therefore the Gnostic could not believe in the incarnation of the Son of God. Since matter was viewed as evil, one could engage in unbridled indulgence of the flesh without any ill effects upon his real self—his spirit. This false teaching had become a threat and some believers were actually turning from the faith because of the Gnostic influence.

This epistle was written by John to meet the heresy by presenting the true knowledge of God. The first four verses of the letter are often called "A Christian Manifesto." In verse 3 the apostle declares that his purpose in writing is to proclaim the reality of God as revealed in Christ. Error is best confronted by the truth it denies. The words "proclaim," "testify," and "testimony" appear

TEACHING TIP 1

You may want to assign a student to bring a brief (3-5 minutes) report on the heresy of gnosticism. Direct the researcher to report on the origin and concepts of gnosticism as well as its threat to the Early Church.

TEACHING TIP 2

Ask: "In what ways can God be likened to light?" Possible responses: He is pure. He dispels darkness. He is indispensable. He is life.

You may want to ask a student to compile a list of Scripture verses which refer to light. Include some of the references regarding light mentioned in this study.

Question.

Can a Christian live the same way he did before, after he becomes a believer? What is meant by walking in the light?

nineteen times. The proclamation of positive convictions concerning the gospel will win souls and establish them in the faith. A message must be personally believed and experienced if it is to avail. The first person is used repeatedly: "We have heard . . . We have seen . . . We have looked upon and touched with our hands." The message of the gospel of Jesus Christ cannot be comprehended apart from personal experience. Only then will Jesus become a reality.

John had seen Jesus in person, heard His voice, and touched Him. We do not have Christ's physical presence with us, but we can see Him with the eye of faith. Peter said, "Whom having not seen, ye love; in whom, though now ye see him not, yet believing, ye rejoice with joy unspeakable and full of glory" (1 Peter 5:8). Jesus can become as real to us in our walk of faith as He was to Peter, Thomas, and others during His life on earth. When we place our faith in Christ, we enter a fellowship that includes God the Father and God the Son, as well as all who have received Christ as Saviour. John states the purpose of this letter in verse 4: "that your joy may be full."

B. Walking in the Light

(See Teaching Tip 2.)

There is a standard by which fellowship with God is to be tested. Walking in the light and obeying the commandments of God are proofs of our Christian experience.

The term "light" is used metaphorically to describe the nature of God. Light speaks of the purity and holiness of God. In the Old Testament light is a figure for purity, truth, and life. Darkness represents impurity, falsehood, and death. Wishing to protect the believers from the subtle errors surrounding them, John reminds them that "God is light" and that the Christian must "walk in the light."

There is no greater blessing than light. It is indispensable to our existence. Without light all would perish. Light is life and God is life. Light speaks of the glory, radiance, beauty, and wonders of God. (See Psalm 27:1; 84:11; Isaiah 60:20; Micah 7:8; Revelation 21:23; 22:5.)

To walk in the light "as He is in the light" means that our whole life is influenced and our thoughts and acts illuminated by the transfiguring light which comes from God. John is not making an impossible demand. He is simply saying that God's children should live in accordance with the gospel. This requires honesty with God and confession of sin. As Christians we are "the children of light" (Luke 16:8; John 12:36; Ephesians 5:8) who bear "the armor of light" (Romans 13:12), and in whom are found the characteristics of light (Ephesians 5:9).

Guideline for Living 1

When confessing our sins to the Lord, we must be totally open and honest. But what about confessing our faults to one another (James 5:16)? How far should we go in admitting our failures to others? One rule to follow in some of these personal matters is that our confession should be as public as our failure. Only those directly involved should hear it.

Another question in this area is: How far should we go in con-

Draw or display the following written on the overhead transparency, chalkboard, or sketchpad.

Two ways to handle sin: 1) Cover it. 2) Confess it.

Clarification

We do know that we know him—not knowing about God, but knowing Him; an experiential knowledge.

Saith I know him, and keepeth not—profession of faith is not enough.

Whoso keepeth—whoever keeps on keeping. Obedience is the test.

Ought . . . also . . . to walk—to keep on walking, a continuous performance.

An old commandment—refers to Jesus' "new" commandment, "that ye love one another" (John 13:34, 35; 15:10, 12).

The darkness is past—man need not grope; God's Light (Jesus) has come.

Hateth—has malicious feelings toward.

Little children—means Christians in general: children, fathers, young men, etc.

Question.

How can a person know he is truly a Christian?

TEACHING TIP 4

Ask: "Why does the apostle John refer to those to whom he is writing as his "little children"?

TEACHING TIP 5

Ask: "To what commandments was John referring in verses 3 and 4?" Refer to the material below in answering this question.

fessing all to another? Here we should consider the effect on the other individual. If our admission of wrongdoing is simply transferring a burden from our heart to the heart of another, it may be better to refrain from sharing the full disclosure. This may be one place where we are each to bear our own burden (Galatians 6:5).

C. Confession of Sin

The false teachers not only lived in sin, but they denied moral responsibility. Their claim, "We have no sin," proved they did not have a right understanding of the gospel of grace. If anyone claims he has no sin and does not need cleansing, he is deceiving himself. He is ignorant of God's revealed truth. (See Genesis 6:5; 1 Kings 8:46; Psalm 53:3; Isaiah 53:6; 64:6; Romans 3:23.) (See Teaching Tip 3.)

"If we confess our sins" we find forgiveness and cleansing. There are two alternatives: we can try to cover our sins, or we can openly confess them. Proverbs 28:13 says, "He that covereth his sins shall not prosper: but whoso confesseth and forsaketh them shall have mercy." Confession of our sins parallels walking in the light. Both indicate recognition of things as they are. Forgiveness and cleansing are necessary for a person to be in fellowship with God.

II. Proofs of Fellowship

1 John 2:3-14

1 John 2:3. Hereby we do know that we know him, if we keep his commandments. 4. He that saith, I know him, and keepeth not his commandments, is a liar, and the truth is not in him. 5. But whoso keepeth his word, in him verily is the love of God perfected: hereby know we that we are in him. 6. He that saith he abideth in him ought himself also so to walk, even as he walked. 7. Brethren, I write no new commandment unto you, but an old commandment which ye had from the beginning. 10. He that loveth his brother abideth in the light, and there is none occasion of stumbling in him. 11. But he that hateth his brother is in darkness, and walketh in darkness, and knoweth not whither he goeth, because that darkness hath blinded his eyes. 12. I write unto you, little children, because your sins are forgiven you for his name's sake. (See Teaching Tip 4.)

A. A Knowledge of God.

The knowledge of God of which John writes is not theoretical or speculative as claimed by the Gnostic heretics. It is experiential and personal. It is not the trained intellect that sees God, but the pure heart. True knowledge of God is that inward and spiritual acquaintance which comes when we accept Christ as our Saviour and yield to Him as our Lord. We must trust in Him, esteem Him, and "keep his commandments." (See Teaching Tip 5.)

"If we keep his commandments" (verse 3) does not refer to the Ten Commandments given to the nation of Israel. John is talking about the commandments Jesus gave to the Church. In 1 Thessalonians 4:2 Paul said, "Ye know what commandments we gave you by the Lord Jesus." Jesus said, "He that hath my commandments, and keepeth them, he it is that loveth me" (John 14:21). The sure evidence that we know Him is that we keep His commandments.

False religions and cults today prey on credulous minds with promises of privileged knowledge and unlocked mysteries. Paul's heartcry was, "That I may know him" (Philippians 3:10). He could also testify, "I know whom I have believed" (2 Timothy 1:12).

Question.
Is there any difference between the "old" and "new" commandments? Is it possible to love all Christians?

B. Brotherly Love

The command to love, the apostle makes clear, is not a novel or strange kind of commandment. He describes it as both old and new (2:7, 8). The followers of Christ had been familiar with it "from the beginning" of their Christian experience. Jesus had declared, "A new commandment I give unto you, that ye love one another as I have loved you; that ye also love one another. By this shall all men know that ye are my disciples, if ye have love one to another" (John 13:34, 35). John was saying, "This old commandment is what I am giving to you. It is what Jesus taught us when He was here on earth."

Jesus' death on the cross gave a new meaning to the old law of love. He had demonstrated what love really is. His death gave the command to love a "new" meaning—a vicarious and redemptive meaning. The love of Calvary is a continuous, ever-flowing fountain.

The essence of the commandment, old and new, is that we are to make a practice of loving our brethren in Christ. The reference here concerns an unselfish devotion to the welfare of fellow Christians. This is the true meaning of the priesthood of believers. Opposed to love is hatred. If a person hates or even dislikes a brother or sister in Christ, he is "in darkness" and cannot claim fellowship with Christ. A love for the people of God is proof that one is abiding "in the light." There may be in some members of the family of God certain personality traits and habits you dislike, but that does not give you the right to hate them. You are to love them as children of God. (See Proverbs 10:12; 1 Corinthians 13:1; Galatians 5:13; Philippians 1:9; 1 Thessalonians 4:9; 1 Peter 4:8; 1 John 4:21.)

Guideline for Living 2

In what ways should Christian love operate in our lives? These are some dimensions it should include:

Individual. We are to love the world, but we must not lose sight of the individuals who make it up. Life is a very impersonal experience for many. We need the Lord to help us understand, appreciate, and relate to people as individuals.

Unconditional. The natural tendency is to love those who love us and dislike those who dislike us. But Jesus said we are to love our enemies, do good to those who hate us, and pray for those who misuse us (Matthew 5:44). Unconditional love requires that we love the unkempt, the unclean, the unlearned, the unlovely, whether they respond or not.

Active. True Christian love is not just expressed in words and gestures. Real love is something we do. It expresses itself in actions and deeds. We put our love into action when we are willing to inconvenience ourselves to help someone else.

C. Spiritual Understanding

"Little children" in verse 12 refers to all Christians, regardless of age or maturity as believers. Some find the classification, "little

Clarification

The world—The word for "world" here is *cosmos* and means the evil world system controlled by Satan and in opposition to God.

The lust of the flesh—the desires of the flesh, bodily appetites, propensities, and passions which draw people away from God.

Lust of the eyes—The eyes are the gate from the world to the flesh.

Pride of life—ostentatious pride in the possession of worldly goods.

The lust thereof—lust for all worldly objects that entice to sin.

Question.

How would you define "worldliness"? What is meant by the statement, "Love not the world"?

children," "fathers," and "young men," subtly significant. But all the privileges mentioned belong to all believers. John is addressing people who know Jesus Christ as Saviour. Because they are children of God John feels it is necessary to warn them against the Gnostic error which is threatening them. Then he gives the best of reasons why any compromise is unthinkable.

John writes not to inform them but to refresh their memories. We might paraphrase verses 12-14 thus: "Count your blessings! Your sins are forgiven for Christ's sake. You know God as an abiding reality. You have won the victory over Satan. You are strong because you have God's Word in your hearts."

Guideline for Living 3

Both the church and home must work together to help children, youth, and adults have the Word of God abiding in their hearts (verse 14). We need to take advantage of the many Bible teaching ministries the church provides for us. These include Sunday school, children's church, Teen Bible quiz, midweek Bible study, home Bible study groups, vacation Bible school, youth camp.

However, teaching the Bible cannot be left only to the church. The home must assume its responsibility also. Family doctrine is a must! It takes effort to make time for family devotions. Several possibilities are: Before the family leaves for work and school, after the evening meal, or before bedtime.

It also takes effort to make devotions meaningful. Parents must plan the devotional time and secure books and other resources to use. Many excellent materials are available. Of course, the Bible itself should be the focal point of devotions.

III. Call to Separation
1 John 2:15-17

1 John 2:15. Love not the world, neither the things that are in the world. If any man love the world, the love of the Father is not in him. 16. For all that is in the world, the lust of the flesh, and the lust of the eyes, and the pride of life, is not of the Father, but is of the world. 17. And the world passeth away, and the lust thereof: but he that doeth the will of God abideth for ever.

A. Worldliness Forbidden

John employs the term *world* more than twenty times in this epistle. The meaning of each usage must be carefully distinguished. Here it refers to the present world system that is in opposition to God. It does not refer to a world of people (John 3:16), nor to the created world (John 17:24), but to an evil system controlled by Satan. It is a world order that has no time for God. We should shun and even hate anything that is against God because it is satanic. Jesus said, "Hereafter I will not talk much with you: for the prince of this world cometh, and hath nothing in me" (John 14:30). Our Saviour referred to the satanic system when he said, "The prince of this world is judged" (John 16:11).

We are living in a world in open rebellion against God. It is a world filled with greed, selfish ambition, sensual pleasures, deceit, lying, and violence. John reminds us that "the whole world lieth in wickedness" (1 John 5:19). We will be obedient to one world or the other. We are going to obey the world system or we will

Helps. If you do not have the PATH materials available, compile a list of the characteristics of the two different worlds discussed in this study: The world of light, and the world of darkness.

TEACHING TIP 8

Ask: "How can we be 'in' the world but not 'of' the world?" Refer to the material in the "Living the Truth" section in the wide column in discussing this question. Ask: "How can we let our light shine for Christ in our home? on the job? at school? with friends? in our neighborhood? Who are some people that need to feel the effect of our love? How can we demonstrate true Christian love?"

Distribute paper and pencil. Ask the students to write down the one situation in which they find it most difficult to let their light shine for Christ. Also ask them to write down the name of the one person they find most difficult to love. Conclude the class session with prayer. Encourage the students to ask the Lord to help them let their light and love have its effect in these difficult situations. You may want to ask the students to pray with each other about these situations. Also encourage them to make these needs a matter of prayer during the coming week.

obey God. We must choose between the world and the Cross of Christ.

Christians have to move in the business and social world, but they do not have to become a part of it. We are "in" the world, but we are not "of" the world. (See Teaching Tip 6.)

In verse 16 the apostle warns against three specific forms of sinfulness: (1) "The lust of the flesh," which is the vain pampering of the fleshly nature. It is a passionate desire for self-satisfaction which comes from the carnal or sinful tendency in man's nature. (2) "The lust of the eyes," the desire to feast the eyes on that which is pleasant, whether good or bad. (3) "The pride of life," that proud pretension which revels in material things or causes one to feel superior to someone else. John is saying we are to reject the world and its ways.

B. Reasons for Not Loving the World

There are many reasons for not loving the world. John declares that love of the world is not compatible with loving God. We can love either God or the world, but we cannot at the same time love both. No human heart can hold two opposing affections—love for a holy God and love for an evil world. No man can serve God and mammon (1 Samuel 7:3; 2 Chronicles 15:15; Matthew 4:10; 6:24; Luke 16:13). Either of them excludes the other.

Another reason for not loving the world is that the world and worldly things are transient. "The world passeth away, and the lust thereof." The present tense of the verb indicates that even now the world is in the process of dissoution. By its very nature evil is self-destructive. When Jesus returns to establish His kingdom, He will completely destroy evil. How foolish to love the world when it is already condemned!

The believer, however, is not disturbed. He is working at something that is permanent, something with stability, something which will last for eternity. "He that doeth the will of God abideth for ever" (verse 17). (See also Luke 20:36; John 8:51; 11:26; Romans 2:7; 1 Corinthians 15:53; 2 Corinthians 5:1; 1 Thessalonians 4:17; 2 Timothy 1:10). (See Teaching Tip 7.)

LIVING THE TRUTH

We live in a world that pulls at us from many directions. We must constantly brace against those influences that would draw us away from God. But we cannot isolate ourselves from our world. We must be a *light*. Our life-style can be a guiding light for others. Our godly influence can make a difference if we will let our light shine.

And we must *love*. The only ingredient missing in many lives is love. We can meet that need as we take a personal interest in those around us. Even the most hardened heart cannot resist the power of love. (See Teaching Tip 8.)

EVANGELISM OUTREACH

Salvation begins with an honest confession of our sinfulness. You will never be saved until you are willing to admit your need of God. But you can be sure that when you confess your sins to God, He will forgive you and cleanse you from all your sins by the blood of His Son Jesus Christ.

11

GOD IS LOVE

PREPARING TO TEACH

Study Text
1 John 3:1-24; 4:7-21

Outline
I. Miracle of Love
   A. The Wonder of God's Love
   B. The Purpose of God's Love
   C. The Rewards of God's Love
II. Obligation of Love
   A. Love for Others
   B. Love in Action
III. Demonstration of Love
   A. Love Is of God
   B. Love Implies Fellowship
   C. Love Eliminates Fear

Golden Text: Hereby perceive we the love of God, because he laid down his life for us: and we ought to lay down our lives for the brethren. 1 John 3:16

Central Truth: God's love motivates us to love others.

Learning Goals
1. To be reminded of the greatness of God's love for us.
2. To accept our obligation to share God's love with others.
3. To apply God's love to our worries and fears.

SEEING THE SCRIPTURES
1 John 3:1-3, 11-14; 4:15-21

1. Behold, what manner of love the Father hath bestowed upon us, that we should be called the sons of God: therefore the world knoweth us not, because it knew him not.

2. Beloved, now are we the sons of God, and it doth not yet appear what we shall be: but we know that, when he shall appear, we shall be like him; for we shall see him as he is.

3. And every man that hath this hope in him purifieth himself, even as he is pure.

11. This is the message that ye heard from the beginning, that we should love one another.

12. Not as Cain, who was of that wicked one, and slew his brother. And wherefore slew he him? Because his own works were evil, and his brother's righteous.

13. Marvel not, my brethren, if the world hate you.

14. We know that we have passed from death unto life, because we love the brethren. He that loveth not his brother abideth in death.

4:15. Whosoever shall confess that Jesus is the Son of God, God dwelleth in him, and he in God.

16. And we have known and believed the love that God hath to us. God is love; and he that dwelleth in love dwelleth in God, and God in him.

17. Herein is our love made perfect, that we may have boldness in the day of judgment: because as he is, so are we in this world.

18. There is no fear in love; but perfect love casteth out fear: because fear hath torment. He that feareth is not made perfect in love.

19. We love him, because he first loved us.

20. If a man say, I love God, and hateth his brother, he is a liar: for he that loveth not his brother whom he hath seen, how can he love God whom he hath not seen?

21. And this commandment have we from him, That he who loveth God love his brother also.

SETTING THE SCENE
The aged apostle John is awed as he contemplates the wonder of God's love in Christ. As a young man he began to realize something of the infinite love of God when he laid his head on Jesus' bosom at the Last Supper. Later as he stood by the cross, the love of God was an even greater reality to him. When he saw the resurrection glory in the face of the risen Lord, God's love became a stronger power within him. At Pentecost the Holy Spirit inten-

Have your class assist you in compiling a list of secular songs that speak about human love. List these song titles on the chalkboard, overhead transparency, or sketchpad. Ask: "What concept of love do we get from these song titles? How are secular human concepts of love different from the Biblical concept of love?" List their comments in two columns as shown below.

HUMAN LOVE	BIBLICAL LOVE
Temporary	Permanent
Fickle	Satisfying
Selfish	Spiritual
Sensual	Practical
Sad	Uplifting

Clarification

Behold—Greek aorist imperative meaning, "Just take a look at."

What manner of love—*agape* love, a selfless outgoing love.

Sons of God—from the Greek *tekna*, "children," coming from the verb *tiktein* meaning "to bear." We have entered God's family by way of the new birth.

We shall be like him—transfigured, changed. Sonship becomes the guarantee of future likeness to our Lord.

Purifieth himself—the blessed hope is an incentive for holy living.

TEACHING TIP 1

Use the "Inductive Bible Study Questions" from the Packet of Adult Teaching Helps to guide a discussion of the three Biblical passages comprising the study verses for this study.

TEACHING TIP 2

Use the overhead transparency from the Packet of Adult Teaching Helps to illustrate the great concepts from John 3:16.

sified that love and John went forth as one of the first missonaries of the Church.

Now as eternity is drawing near for this aged saint, the revelation of God's love still amazes him. Because of God's love the redeemed are called His children and they call Him "Father." (See Teaching Tip 1.)

BIBLE COMMENTARY

I. Miracle of Love

1 John 3:1-3.

1 John 3:1. Behold, what manner of love the Father hath bestowed upon us, that we should be called the sons of God: therefore the world knoweth us not, because it knew him not. 2. Beloved, now are we the sons of God, and it doth not yet appear what we shall be: but we know that, when he shall appear, we shall be like him; for we shall see him as he is. 3. And every man that hath this hope in him purifieth himself, even as he is pure.

A. The Wonder of God's Love

Words cannot express the wonder that grips John's soul as he reflects on the infinite love of God. What a revelation of divine truth! We who were once children of darkness are now the children of light. We who were children of the wicked one are now the children of God.

Love is the keynote of this epistle. It is the apostle John's favorite theme. The love he is talking about is spontaneous. It is a kind of love to which we are not accustomed. When human love is genuine it is a beautiful thing. But God's love for His children far exceeds anything we experience on the human plane.

God loves us. His love for us is shed abroad in our hearts by the Holy Spirit. God demonstrated His love by giving His Son to die for us. (See Teaching Tip 2.)

The phrase, "love the Father hath bestowed upon us" (verse 1), is full of meaning. It is not love that God has simply felt toward us, but the love He has given to us. John expressed this same remarkable truth when he said, "God so loved the world that he gave." He *gave* "his only begotten son" (John 3:16). God's love manifested itself in the form of incarnate love, God's unspeakable gift to man. John saw divine love in the glory conferred on those who believe in Jesus Christ. (See Deuteronomy 7:8; Jeremiah 31:3; Romans 5:8; Ephesians 2:4, 5; 1 John 4:16.)

B. The Purpose of God's Love

John's words, "that we should be called the sons of God" (verse 1), mean more than the fact that God is the Father of all men. There is a fatherhood of God which is called "creative fatherhood," and all men are included. The Creator gave His love to man whom He had created in His own image. He made him capable of fellowship with himself. God loves, provides for, and cares for His creation.

The apostle, however, is not referring to man as he was created

NOW	THEN
WE ARE THE SONS OF GOD	WE SHALL BE LIKE HIM

Question.

What is meant when John says, "Therefore the world knoweth us not"?

Question.

What is meant by the expression, "a purifying hope"?

TEACHING TIP 4

Write only the capital letters of the following visual vertically down the left side of the chalkboard, overhead transparency, or sketchpad. Ask if any students can guess what these letters stand for.

P lease	N ot
B e	F inished
P atient;	W ith
G od	M e
I s	Y et

After Several have offered their suggestions, add the words to the visual as shown above.

TEACHING TIP 5

Use the following visual to list the three aspects of our salvation experience.

REDEMPTION—Saved from the penalty of sin.
SANCTIFICATION—Saved from the power of sin.
GLORIFICATION—Saved from the presence of sin.

by God, but to man as he was when he was marred by sin and alienated from the Father. There is a higher, redemptive fatherhood which includes all who have come back to the Father through Jesus Christ. Only those who have known and experienced the redemptive love of Calvary are called "the sons of God" in the New Testament.

The purpose of God's love is not only to call us His children, but to bring us into a right relationship with Him. Through faith in the Lord Jesus Christ we become a part of the family of God. "As many as received him, to them gave he power to become the sons of God, even to them that believe on his name: which were born . . . of God" (John 1:12, 13). (See also Romans 8:14; Galatians 4:7; Philippians 2:15.)

The world does not recognize us as children of God because it doesn't recognize God. The love that God bestows on His children results in such a change in their disposition and character, their principles and practices, that unbelievers cannot understand them. The divine image in a Christian is a mystery to the world. (See John 1:10; 4:10; 9:30; Acts 13:27; 17:23.)

C. The Rewards of God's Love

(See Teaching Tip 3.)

According to John, sonship is both present and future. "What we shall be" has not been fully revealed. We are already God's children, but the nature of our future condition is a mystery to us at present. We do know that our soul will continue to live when it has departed from the physical body. Jesus said to the penitent thief, "Today shalt thou be with me in paradise" (Luke 23:43). Paul wrote, "We are willing rather to be absent from the body, and to be present with the Lord" (2 Corinthians 5:8). "To me to live is Christ, and to die is gain" (Philippians 1:21). (See Teaching Tip 4.)

The believer has a wonderful prospect. God is not through with us yet. "We know that, when he shall appear, we shall be like him" (verse 2). God sees in each of us what He will make of us. We may become discouraged when we look at what we are now, but the Lord sees us as we shall be when He shall appear. We are going to be like the glorified Christ—not equal to Him, but like Him. We will still possess our own personalities. We will have our own individualities and be our own selves. We will not be identical to Him, but like Him.

The process of sanctification will reach its glorious consummation. Sin will no longer dwell in us. The body will be changed so it will never be subject to death and deterioration. Even more wonderful, we will love everybody and everybody will love us. What a "blessed hope" for the children of God! (See Romans 8:29; 2 Corinthians 3:18; 2 Peter 1:4.) (See Teaching Tip 5.)

Because he is born of God and possesses a purifying hope, the believer lives a life of righteousness as a member of God's family. Can there be a greater incentive for holy living than the coming of Christ and the prospect of being like Him?

Clarification

The message—the law of brotherly love given by Jesus (John 13:34, 35).

Marvel not—don't be surprised; don't act as if some strange thing has happened.

Hateth ... murderer—murder is hatred in action; hatred is murder in feeling.

Perceive—know.

The love of God—the absolute, the standard set before us.

If our heart condemn us—The reference is to the conscience and not to the affections.

Question.

Can one call himself a Christian and still not have a love for all fellow believers?

II. Obligation of Love

1 John 3:11-24.

1 John 3:11. This is the message that ye heard from the beginning, that we should love one another. 12. Not as Cain, who was of that wicked one, and slew his brother. And wherefore slew he him? Because his own works were evil, and his brother's righteous. 13. Marvel not, my brethren, if the world hate you. 14. We know that we have passed from death unto life, because we love the brethren. He that loveth not his brother abideth in death. 15. Whosoever hateth his brother is a murderer: and ye know that no murderer hath eternal life abiding in him. 16. Hereby perceive we the love of God, because he laid down his life for us: and we ought to lay down our lives for the brethren. 17. But whoso hath this world's good, and seeth his brother have need, and shutteth up his bowels of compassion from him, how dwelleth the love of God in him? 18. My little children, let us not love in word, neither in tongue; but in deed and in truth. 22. And whatsoever we ask, we receive of him, because we keep his commandments, and do those things that are pleasing in his sight.

A. Love for Others

In his writings John often speaks of "the beginning." By doing so he is reaffirming Christ's message, "By this shall all men know that ye are my disciples, if ye have love one to another" (John 13:35). The command to "love one another" is the message which is from "the beginning." Jesus said it and all the apostles taught it. The message is "the word of truth, the gospel of your salvation" (Ephesians 1:13).

Guideline for Living 1

Some couples today feel they have sufficient grounds for divorce when they no longer feel love for each other. The fact is, it is not so much love that supports marriage as it is marriage that supports love. The commitment to one another provides the security in which love can grow. There are times when all couples do not "feel" in love. But they remain together because they have made a vow to do so for better or worse.

Love is not an emotion over which we have no control. Otherwise, God would not have commanded us to love one another. Love is more an act of the will than an emotion or feeling. To be sure, it can be and often is a wonderful feeling. But it is more than that.

Sometimes we wait for our emotions to motivate us to action—when in fact it is more often our actions that produce the emotional feeling. If you will think back to your courting days, you will discover it was your loving actions toward one another that produced and affirmed your feeling of love.

It is possible to build love back into a relationship. We do so, however, not by waiting for the feeling to return, but by doing loving things with and for each other. The feelings will follow as we continue to act in loving ways.

Christian love is not a mere intellectual concept. It has its meaning in the attitude we hold toward other believers. It is love for the brethren. The words *brother* and *brethren* are used often by

John. "Brother" here means a fellow believer. The apostle considers the Church a fellowship of love. Efficient organization, worldly influence, and wealth cannot make up for the absence of love in the Church. Christian love is the hallmark of the true disciple of Christ. "Behold, how good and how pleasant it is for brethren to dwell together in unity!" (Psalm 133:1).

Question.
Explain the meaning of verse 15.

Hatred as the antithesis of love is expressed by the contrast of Cain with Jesus, who "laid down his life for us." Why did Cain murder his brother? "Because his own works were evil, and his brother's righteous." Jealousy and envy led to Cain's sin. These are sins of the heart. It is not that the wicked envy the righteous. They hate the righteous because their own wickedness is condemned by the presence of righteousness. The evil world system is always disturbed by the condemning presence of righteousness.

The fact that the world hates the Christian is no great mystery. See Isaiah 66:1-5; Matthew 24:9; Luke 6:22; 21:17; John 15:18, 19; 17:14. There is an offence of the Cross, but it is also possible for Christians to make themselves objectionable, offensive, and rude. May the love and tenderness of our Lord be always seen in us.

John makes a strong statement in verse 15 when he says, "Whosoever hateth his brother is a murderer: and . . . no murderer hath eternal life." Again he is quoting Jesus. In Matthew 5:21, 22 He said that if you have hatred in your heart toward a fellow believer you are a murderer. Envy and jealousy lead to hatred, and hatred is murder. John is saying that when a person is born again he will no longer live with these sins in his heart. It does not mean that a person who has taken the life of another cannot be saved and receive eternal life. Christ paid the penalty for all sin, even murder. But hatred is as brutal a sin as murder and the hater will not inherit eternal life. (See Teaching Tip 6.)

TEACHING TIP 6

What are some of the different ways Christians respond to anger? Refer to "Guideline for Living 2" in discussing this question.

Guideline for Living 2

There are many ways Christians respond to feelings of anger. Some deny or repress their anger. They feel it is wrong to be angry, so they refuse to admit they are. Often these denied or displaced feelings surface in other, more harmful ways. John Powell says, "When I repress my emotions, my stomach keeps score."

Some delay or suppress their anger. They recognize they are angry, but they wait until it is safe to express it. Delaying our response to anger may be the best course of action at times, but eventually we must deal openly with our feelings.

Others simply demonstrate or express their anger. They cut loose and speak or act out exactly what they are feeling. This may help to get things "off our chest," but the results are often not positive because others are hurt by these words or actions.

A better way to respond to anger is to declare or confess it. To admit our feelings of anger does not mean we have to act them out. The key here is to confess our anger in such a way that others can accept it and understand it. The very act of declaring our anger helps to relieve some of its destructive power. Now we can more easily control our feelings and direct them toward a more positive course of action.

B. Love in Action

Love is not just a sentiment. It expresses itself in action. It cannot be hidden. Genuine love will sacrifice for the one who is

Question.
In what ways can a Christian prove his love?

loved. It will give to the brother and sister in need. Love should be full of tender compassion. "If we see our brother in need and do not help him, how can God's love be in us?" John questions.

Love is a matter of action. Part of the meaning of verse 18 is expressed in Shakespeare's line, "They do not love that do not show their love." See Matthew 25:35-45; Luke 3:11; 10:30-35; 2 Corinthians 9:6-11; James 2:15-17.

God answers our prayers and blesses us "because we keep his commandments, and do those things that are pleasing in his sight" (verse 22). (See also John 15:7.)

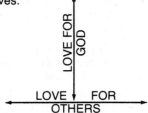
III. Demonstration of Love

1 John 4:7-21

1John 4:7. Beloved, let us love one another: for love is of God; and every one that loveth is born of God, and knoweth God. 8. He that loveth not, knoweth not God; for God is love. 9. In this was manifested the love of God toward us, because that God sent his only begotten Son into the world, that we might live through him. 10. Herein is love, not that we loved God, but that he loved us, and sent his Son to be the propitiation for our sins. 11. Beloved, if God so loved us, we ought also to love one another. 12. No man hath seen God at any time. If we love one another, God dwelleth in us, and his love is perfected in us. 18. There is no fear in love; but perfect love casteth out fear: because fear hath torment. He that feareth is not made perfect in love. 19. We love him, because he first loved us.

A. Love Is of God

In the first six verses of chapter 4, John gives a timely warning against false teachers and false prophets. He advises the churches to test the preachers to see whether they come from God or not. The first test concerns their message: Are they teaching the deity of Jesus? The other test concerns the nature of their followers: Who listens to them? the people of God or the people of the world?

In verse 7 John returns to his favorite theme, love. He makes it clear that genuine love is possible only for those who have been spiritually begotten of God, for God is love. In this epistle he gives us three great descriptions of God: (1) God is spirit (John 4:24), (2) God is light (1 John 1:5), (3) God is love (1 John 4:8). The true essence of love is found in God's love for us as sinners who did not merit His love. God's love is the pattern for human love.

B. Love Implies Fellowship

There is a tradition that when John was too old and feeble to walk he was carried by his friends to the church in Ephesus. There followed a hush among the people as John spoke words he had used often. They were, "Beloved, let us love one another." (See Teaching Tip 7.)

Love for God and love for man are inseparably linked. Any man who says he loves God while he is unconcerned about his brother in Christ "is a liar." John adds, "If he doesn't love his brother who is right there in front of him, how can he love God whom he has

be helpful in combating worry and fear. Encourage the students to share verses they have found helpful. You may want to have a list of some of the following verses ready to offer: Psalms 23:4; 41:10; 46:2; Isaiah 12:2; John 15:27; 16:33; 1 Corinthians 3:17; 2 Timothy 1:7; 1 John 4:4, 18.

Distribute small slips of paper or card stock the size of a business card (approximately 1¹/₂ x 3 inches). Distribute red, broad-tipped marking pens. Instruct the students to write the words "STOP—THINK" in large red letters on one side of the card and on the other side of the card the words of one of the verses which they feel would be most helpful to them in combating worry and fear.

Instruct the students to carry their card with them next week and to get it out every time they begin to think worrisome or fearful thoughts. Tell them to read (out loud if possible) the words "STOP—THINK," then turn the card over and read (again, out loud if possible) three times the verse written there. They are to do this every time they are plagued by worrisome thoughts. Ask them to take note of how the power of God's Word can overcome feelings of fear and anxiety. You may want to give several students opportunity next Sunday to tell how this technique has helped them.

Daily Devotional Guide
M. Love's Provision.
   Genesis 22:9-18
T. Love's Deliverance.
   Exodus 14:21-31
W. Love's Compassion.
   Hosea 2:16-23
T. Love's Cost. John 3:14-18
F. Love's Salvation.
   Romans 5:1-11
S. Love's Commitment.
   1 Corinthians 13:1-13

never seen?" (verse 20, TLB). To love another is the way to have fellowship with the invisible God (verse 12).

C. Love Eliminates Fear

Both psychology and psychiatry recognize fear as one of the most destructive of emotions. A life in which the love of God is being perfected from within by the Holy Spirit has no reason to fear the judgment. Because you love the Lord and your brethren, fear has been cast out. "Perfect love casteth out fear" (verse 18). "Perfect love" means you love God and seek to do His will.

If you are fearful and apprehensive, you cannot enjoy your salvation. The more fear there is, the less love; the more love, the less fear. (See Isaiah 43:1; 2 Timothy 1:7; Revelation 1:17, 18.)

LIVING THE TRUTH

What are some of the things you fear or worry about? Is it money or family? the future or your health? the opinions of others? Someone has determined that less than 10 percent of all the things we worry about provide real cause for concern.

Worry and anxiety really don't change anything, but they can rob us of peace of mind. That is why John said, "Fear hath torment." But mature Christian love can cast out fear. Usually we cannot reason our fears away, but we can love them away. We can come to a place where our love and trust in God are strong enough to overcome worry and fear. Knowledge of God's Word can help us defeat fear. As we know God better, we come to love Him more. And as we love Him more, we trust Him more. As we trust Him more, we have less cause to worry or fear. So the more love, the less fear. (See Teaching Tip 8.)

EVANGELISM OUTREACH

The most effective way to win people to Christ is to tell them about God's love. True, they need to be confronted with their own sinfulness and God's punishment of sin. But what will draw them to Christ is the knowledge of His love for them as demonstrated by His death on the cross for their sins. This is our obligation to the lost—to tell them of God's love for them and His provision of salvation through faith in Christ.

ETERNAL LIFE

12

SEEING THE SCRIPTURES

1 John 5:1-15

1. Whosoever believeth that Jesus is the Christ is born of God: and every one that loveth him that begat loveth him also that is begotten of him.

2. By this we know that we love the children of God, when we love God, and keep his commandments.

3. For this is the love of God, that we keep his commandments: and his commandments are not grievous.

4. For whatsoever is born of God overcometh the world: and this is the victory that overcometh the world, even our faith.

5. Who is he that overcometh the world, but he that believeth that Jesus is the Son of God?

6. This is he that came by water and blood, even Jesus Christ; not by water only, but by water and blood. And it is the Spirit that beareth witness, because the Spirit is truth.

7. For there are three that bear record in heaven, the Father, the Word, and the Holy Ghost: and these three are one.

8. And there are three that bear witness in earth, the spirit, and the water, and the blood: and these three agree in one.

9. If we receive the witness of men, the witness of God is greater: for this is the witness of God which he hath testified of his Son.

10. He that believeth on the Son of God hath the witness in himself: he that believeth not God hath made him a liar; because he believeth not the record that God gave of his Son.

11. And this is the record, that God hath given to us eternal life, and this life is in his Son.

12. He that hath the Son hath life; and he that hath not the Son of God hath not life.

13. These things have I written unto you that believe on the name of the Son of God; that ye may know that ye have eternal life, and that ye may believe on the name of the Son of God.

14. And this is the confidence that we have in him, that, if we ask any thing according to his will, he heareth us:

15. And if we know that he hear us, whatsoever we ask, we know that we have the petitions that we desired of him.

SETTING THE SCENE

One day, realizing he was not long for this world, D. L. Moody said to a friend, "Someday you will read in the papers that Moody is dead. Don't you believe a word of it! At that moment I shall be more alive than I am now. I shall have gone up higher, that is all—out of this old clay tenement into a house that is immortal, a body that sin cannot touch, that sin cannot taint, a body fashioned

PREPARING TO TEACH

Study Text
1 John 5:1-15

Outline
I. New Birth
   A. Saving Faith
   B. The Test of Love
   C. Overcoming Faith
   D. Divine Witness
II. Life in Christ
   A. Inward Assurance
   B. Eternal Life
III. Confidence in Prayer
   A. How to Pray
   B. Conditions to Be Met

Golden Text: He that hath the Son hath life; and he that hath not the Son of God hath not life. 1 John 5:12

Central Truth: The new life we have in Christ gives us victory over the world.

Learning Goals
1. To understand how our new life in Christ gives us victory over the world.
2. To desire to live in obedience to the will of God.
3. To approach God in prayer with confidence.

Use the "Agree-Disagree Statements" from the Packet of Adult Teaching Helps to begin the session.

If you do not have the PATH materials available, read the opening quotation from D. L. Moody in "Setting the Scene." Ask: "When do you think eternal life begins? In what sense do we have eternal life now? What benefits of eternal life can we enjoy now?" Refer to "Guideline for Living 1" in discussing these questions.

Clarification

Born of God—When you accept Christ you are "born again" and God becomes your Heavenly Father.

Begat—procreate as a father.

Grievous—heavy, burdensome.

Overcometh—Conquers, gets the better of.

like unto His glorious body. I was born of the flesh in 1837; I was born of the Spirit in 1856. That which is born of the flesh may die; that which is born of the Spirit will live forever."

Eternal life begins when a person is saved, and it never ends. John says "These things have I written unto you that believe . . . that ye may know that ye have eternal life" (1 John 5:13).

BIBLE COMMENTARY

I. New Birth

1 John 5:1-9

1 John 5:1. Whosoever believeth that Jesus is the Christ is born of God: and every one that loveth him that begat loveth him also that is begotten of him. 2. By this we know that we love the children of God, when we love God, and keep his commandments. 3. For this is the love of God, that we keep his commandments: and his commandments are not grievous. 4. For whatsoever is born of God overcometh the world: and this is the victory that overcometh the world, even our faith. 5. Who is he that overcometh the world, but he that believeth that Jesus is the Son of God? 6. This is he that came by water and blood. . . . And it is the Spirit that beareth witness, because the Spirit is truth. 7. For there are three that bear record in heaven, the Father, the Word, and the Holy Ghost: and these three are one. 8. And there are three that bear witness in earth, the spirit, and the water, and the blood: and these three agree in one. 9. If we receive the witness of men, the witness of God is greater: for this is the witness of God which he hath testified of his Son.

A. Saving Faith

The entire matter of becoming a Christian begins with the new birth. One is not saved by trying to improve or change himself. The apostle says, ". . . whosoever believeth that Jesus is the Christ is born of God" (5:1). This is the only way. This is how we are born again. It is a matter of simple faith in Jesus Christ. To believe "that Jesus is the Christ" is to believe Jesus is the Son of God. This means that when you accept Christ as your personal Saviour, you trust who He is as well as what He did. What He did on Calvary has no value if He is not who He said He is. Belief in the virgin birth of Christ is essential to salvation. "As many as received him, to them gave he power [the right and authority] to become the sons of God, even to them that believe on his name" (John 1:12). The new birth is not for a favored few. God says it is for "whosoever will" if they come to Him through Jesus Christ.

Guideline for Living 1

When can we begin to enjoy the benefits of eternal life? Do we have to die before we can "cash in the policy"? Certainly the greatest blessings of eternal life are yet to come, but there are many benefits we can enjoy this side of the grave.

Assurance of everlasting life gives us a different perspective on life *now*. We see our earthly existence as only a fraction of time compared to the endless ages that await us. This perspective enables us to endure unpleasant things now, knowing it will not always be that way.

Possession of eternal life now also helps us develop a right set of priorities. The things we live for are seen in the light of eternity. Serving the Lord and others takes top priority, for it is the only expression of our earthly life that will have eternal consequences. It has been said, "We can't take it with us, but we can send it on ahead."

The Gnostics made a distinction between the human Jesus and the divine Christ. They denied that Jesus of Nazareth is the Christ. John makes this truth an essential test of being born again. We are not born again by believing Jesus was a good Man, a great Teacher, or an outstanding example of ethics and morals. He is God, the Second Person of the Trinity. We must believe that.

B. The Test of Love

Question.
What are some evidences or proofs that a person is born again?

The apostle reminds us again that he who loves God loves God's children, and he who loves God's children loves God. Love for a fellow believer is a direct result of the new birth. John said, "We know that we have passed from death unto life, because we love the brethren" (1 John 3:14). Jesus said, "By this shall all men know that ye are my disciples, if ye have love one to another" (John 13:35). Christian love for one another is a foretaste of the love that will fill heaven.

The love of God requires that we obey and keep His commandments. Love and obedience go together. "Commandments" here does not refer to the Old Testament law. They are the commandments Jesus gave us during His ministry. There are many commandments in the New Testament and every child of God should want to keep them. John says, "His commandments are not grievous" (verse 3). The word "grievous" *(bareiai)* refers to a load that is excessively heavy. His commandments do not impose a burden on us that is too heavy to bear. It is possible for us to keep them, not because they are easy, but because we are given the strength and ability to meet their demands. We keep them through love. Christianity affirms that man is made for obedience to God's commandments, and that abiding peace and happiness lie in surrendering fully to God. (See Matthew 11:28-30; John 14:15, 21; 2 John 6.) The ungodly feel that God's commandments are like chains that make them miserable. This is because their lives are full of things contrary to the laws of God. When we delight in His commandments, they become a joy. We would not be happy if we did not keep them.

Guideline for Living 2

Obedience is not a natural response for most of us, but it is something we must all learn. The question is how? Like Christ, we will develop this quality in our lives through suffering (Hebrews 5:8).

There is also the question of what motivates us to obedience. There are the more negative types of motivation such as fear and the approval or disapproval of others. But what should really motivate us to obedience as Christians is our love for Christ.

TEACHING TIP 1

You may want to assign a student to compile a list of verses from the writings of John which contain different forms of the word *overcome*. Direct the researcher to an exhaustive concordance such as Strong's or Young's. You may also want to ask him to be prepared to read some of these verses at this time.

TEACHING TIP 2

Use the following chart to outline the author's comments about the way victory overcomes the world:

WE CAN OVERCOME		
Unhappiness	**W**	Joy
Loneliness		Fellowship
Deception	**I**	Honesty
Sin		Righteousness
Error	**T**	Truth
Worldly Lusts		Purity
Hatred	**H**	Love
Death		Life

TEACHING TIP 3

Draw or display the following visual illustrating the three heavenly and earthly witnesses involved in the new-birth experience.

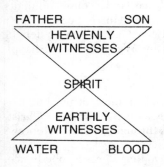

FATHER   SON

HEAVENLY
WITNESSES

SPIRIT

EARTHLY
WITNESSES

WATER   BLOOD

Point out that the Spirit is a member of both the heavenly and earthly triad of witnesses.

C. Overcoming Faith

John was addressing churches and congregations that were going through severe persecutions. Believers had been put to death because they refused to worship the Roman emperor. They were surrounded by an evil society that tolerated vices of every kind. In the church false prophets were causing problems. Yet John says, "This is the victory that overcometh the world, even our faith" (verse 4). What an amazing statement! What audacity! The faith of small, insignificant churches overcoming the world? Yes! (See Teaching Tip 1.)

John wrote of battle and victory in his epistles and in the Book of Revelation. He writes of "overcoming the wicked one," and records glorious promises to overcomers in Christ's messages to the seven churches. John had learned the secret of faith. He had confidence in the power of God. Through faith's eye he could see only victory. We are saved by faith, we walk by faith, and we overcome the world around us by faith.

Our world is much different in many ways from the world of the first century. But the fight of faith is as much ours as it was the early Christians'. (See Romans 7:23; Ephesians 6:12; 1 Timothy 1:18; 6:12; 2 Timothy 2:4; 1 John 2:15.)

Victory is won by faith. (See Teaching Tip 2.) He who is born again overcomes. The victory that overcomes matches at every point the assaults and temptations of the world. It is joy over unhappiness; fellowship over loneliness; honesty over deception; righteousness over sin; truth over error; purity over worldly lusts; love over hatred; life over death.

Some Christians seem to hold a shallow view of victory. We have heard the expression, "I've got the victory," when the individual simply means he is feeling good at the moment—"on the mountaintop." If his "victory" ebbs and flows according to his emotions, his testimony may be quite different the next time you see him. The kind of victory about which John is writing is based on Christ's death, resurrection, and ascension. That redemptive work is completed no matter what our feelings are. This is the foundation on which faith must rest. Otherwise it will not stand the strain of life's many tests.

D. Divine Witness

Verse 6 has been given numerous explanations. Some see the water as the living Word applied by the Spirit of God, and the blood referring to the death of Christ. "Except a man be born of water and of the Spirit, he cannot enter into the kingdom of God" (John 3:5).

Others believe that water refers to the baptism of Jesus, and blood speaks of His death. This emphasis by John was a refutation of the Gnostic teaching that the divine Christ came upon the human Christ at His baptism and left Him just prior to His death. The apostle is insisting not only that Jesus' baptism give witness to His incarnation, but that the cross is also a testimony. (See Teaching Tip 3.)

To the elements of the water and blood, John adds the testimony of the Holy Spirit: "It is the Spirit that beareth witness" (verse 6). Only the Spirit of God can make the death and resurrection of Christ real to us. (See Teaching Tip 4.)

Clarification

The witness in himself—a new proof of the truth: personal experience, inward assurance.

Hath made him a liar—The unbeliever makes God a liar about the plan of redemption.

Record—witness or testimony.

These things—the whole epistle.

Question.

How is a believer assured that he is a child of God?

Question.

What is meant by the term, "eternal life"? When does it begin?

The last part of verse 7 (after "For there are three that bear record") and all of verse 8 have been the subject of controversy among Bible scholars because they were not in early manuscripts. The truth they teach, however, is consistent with Scripture. The entire Godhead does witness to the person and work of the Son. On the earthly scene the Holy Spirit bears witness and so does Jesus' own work, which is summed up under the two great events—His baptism and sacrifical death.

II. Life in Christ
1 John 5:10-13

1 John 5:10. He that believeth on the Son of God hath the witness in himself: he that believeth not God hath made him a liar; because he believeth not the record that God gave of his Son. 11. And this is the record, that God hath given to us eternal life, and this life is in his Son. 12. He that hath the Son hath life; and he that hath not the Son of God hath not life. 13. These things have I written unto you that believe on the name of the Son of God; that ye may know that ye have eternal life, and that ye may believe on the name of the Son of God.

A. Inward Assurance

The witnesses of verse 6 are external witnesses to the deity of Christ. At our Lord's baptism, the Father and the Holy Spirit bore witness that He is the Son of God (Matthew 3:16, 17). Jesus said, "The Spirit of truth, which proceedeth from the Father, he shall bear witness of me" (John 15:26). The Holy Spirit bore witness to the messiahship of Jesus when He descended upon the waiting disciples at Pentecost and made the gospel they preached the power of God unto salvation (Acts 2:4-31). John writes, "It is the Spirit that beareth witness, because the Spirit is truth" (verse 6).

Now the apostle deals with the witness of God in personal experience. Verses 10-12 speaks of an internal witness which coroborates the external testimony. The believer "hath the witness in himself." This inward assurance is wrought by faith. Logic and reason will not bring to men the truth of the deity of Christ and redemption's plan. "He that believeth" has this inward witness. Such belief is not in a doctrine, but in a Person—the Son of God. The Holy Spirit bears witness to Christ in the hearts of Christians. (See Romans 8:16; Galatians 4:6; 1 John 3:24; 4:13; 5:6.)

The one who does not believe the truth of God's witness concerning His Son is guilty of making God a liar. This was John's response to the false teachers (Gnostics) who denied that Jesus is the Christ, the Son of God.

B. Eternal Life

The purpose of this letter as stated by John in verse 13 is twofold: (1) salvation, "that ye may believe on the name of the Son of God." (2) knowledge concerning life in Christ, "that ye may know that ye have eternal life" (verse 13). This life is only attainable through Jesus Christ. "He that hath the Son hath life" (verse 12).

If one is walking in the light (1:7), confessing his sins (1:9), obeying the Lord (2:3-5), loving fellow believers (2:9-11), believing in Jesus, God's Son (2:22, 23), and living righteously (2:29; 3:6-10), he is assured by "these things" that he has eternal life.

The gift of eternal life belongs to every believer in Christ. (See John 1:12; 3:16; 5:24; 6:47; Romans 6:23; 8:17, 38, 39; 1 John 2:25.)

III. Confidence in Prayer
1 John 5:14, 15

1 John 5:14. This is the confidence that we have in him, that, if we ask any thing according to his will, he heareth us: 15. and if we know that he hear us, whatsoever we ask, we know that we have the petitions that we desired of him.

A. How To Pray

It has been said that prayer is the breath of the new man, the motion of the renewed heart, and is essential to the existence of God's life in the soul. Prayer is both the duty and privilege of God's children. The child of God has assurance that God will hear his prayers. This assurance gives one confidence in prayer. The word *confidence* actually means "boldness." Bold confidence will produce freedom of speech in God's presence. "Let us therefore come boldly unto the throne of grace, that we may obtain mercy, and find grace to help in time of need" (Hebrews 4:16). (See also Ephesians 3:12; 1 Timothy 3:13; Hebrews 10:19; 1 John 4:17.)

Guideline for Living 3

God's Word invites us to come boldly into His presence to make our needs known. One reason we can do this is because we have a High Priest who is touched, not only with the *fact* of our infirmities, but also the *feeling* of them. (Hebrews 4:15). He experienced these emotions during the days of His flesh (Hebrews 5:7), especially during the final hours before and during His death on the cross. Isaiah said He was "a man of sorrows and acquainted with grief" (Isaiah 53:3). He understands the awful gamut of emotions which go along with our weaknesses and infirmities—those feelings of fear, depression, loneliness, and rejection.

Life has sometimes been called "a lonesome valley." But it is a valley we do not walk by ourselves.

Prayer is calling upon God. "Call unto me" (Jeremiah 33:3). It is the creature calling upon the Creator, the child petitioning the Father. Prayer begins with God. He takes the initiative and by the Holy Spirit makes man the channel of the petition. The Holy Spirit helps us in our praying (Romans 8:26). Whenever man responds to God's invitation to call, there is response on God's part. It is impossible to pray right and not have an answer, for He says, "Call unto me, and I will answer." His answer may be direct, different, delayed, or denied. But He will hear us when we meet His conditions.

We must never feel that prayer is an imposition on God. Jesus gave much teaching on prayer, and all of it assures us that God not only hears but wants us to call on Him. Our most insignificant need is of interest to our Heavenly Father. Jesus said He numbers the hairs of our head, sees even the sparrow that falls, and gives good gifts to His children. He does not divide our needs into small and large ones. God desires to share the total life of each child of

Clarification

Confidence—state of feeling sure, boldness.

According to his will—in harmony with God's will.

Petition—a formal request, prayer, entreaty.

Question.

How should one approach God in prayer?

TEACHING TIP 5

Before concluding your study of the Book of 1 John, lead the class in summarizing some of the main teachings of this epistle. You may want to assign five students and have each summarize one of the chapters from the book. Or you could ask three students to each give a brief review of one of the three studies from this unit.

Another approach would be to write the following Golden Text references for these three sessions on slips of paper to distribute to the students: 1 John 1:7; 1 John 3:16; 1 John 5:12. Call for the verses to be read at this time. As they are read, ask the students to listen for ways they summarize the main teachings of this book. List their comments on the chalkboard, sketchpad, or overhead transparency.

TEACHING TIP 6

Lead the class in discussing the three ways God answers your prayers. Write the words "Yes," "No," and "Wait" on the chalkboard, sketchpad, or overhead transparency. Ask: "Which of these answers is sometimes most difficult to accept? Why?" Refer to the "Living the Truth" section in discussing this question.

TEACHING TIP 7

Distribute paper and pencil to the students. Ask them to write down the one prayer request they most want God to answer. After they have written their request, read the seven statements which conclude the "Bible Commentary" section. Ask each student to answer in his own mind each question as it relates to his most desired prayer request. After the questions have been read, instruct the students to examine the reasons for any negative answer and write down several steps they could take to correct the situation.

Conclude the session by asking four or five students to volunteer to lead in sentence prayers expressing their appreciation for some truth learned in this session or some personal expression they would like to make to the Lord in response to this study.

His. This is only possible when the prayer channel is kept open and used often.

B. Conditions To Be Met

(See Teaching Tip 5.)

Our prayer must be in accord with God's will (verse 14). The certainty of answered prayer is described as "the confidence that we have in him." When our requests are in harmony with God's will, we have the assurance that He listens favorably to our petitions. If we are walking in close fellowship with God, our praying will be for God's will to be done. This guideline is essential. God's will is supreme. He cannot grant requests which are out of harmony with His will. In our ignorance we may pray to God for things that would be hurtful to us.

When our desires are in harmony with the will of God, He takes pleasure in bestowing and we are blessed in receiving. "Delight thyself also in the Lord; and he shall give thee the desires of thine heart" (Psalm 37:4).

Is it always possible to know God's will? First of all, the Word reveals the principles by which He expects us to live. We need never be in doubt about God's guidelines for our conduct. In matters not specifically mentioned in the Bible, the Holy Spirit will guide us by His checks, inward impressions, and ordering of outward circumstances.

When a good businessman discovers his business is operating at a loss he takes stock, draws up a balance sheet, and discovers why he has made no profit. Then he takes remedial steps. Shall we be less careful in our spiritual accounting? Have we honestly faced the question of unanswered prayer? Do we simply accept prayer failures fatalistically? Or do we ask ourselves honest questions?

(See Teaching Tip 6.)

LIVING THE TRUTH

To be invited to come with confidence to the Lord in prayer does not mean we come arrogantly or presumptuously. At all times we recognize He is still the sovereign God and we must always submit our will to Him.

Sometimes in His love and wisdom He grants us our full request. At other times—with the same love and wisdom—He does not. And still at other times He asks us to wait. Of these possible responses—yes, no, and wait—often the hardest to accept is "Wait."

What requests have you made of the Lord lately? How had He answered you? Have you submitted your requests to the sovereignty of His will? Can you accept His answer as an expression of His will for you at this time? (See Teaching Tip 7.)

EVANGELISM OUTREACH

Are you trying to live like a Christian without a personal relationship with Jesus Christ? Are you trying to live the spiritual life without a spiritual birth? It can't be done. The only way to have eternal life is to be born again. Then you will be a child of God. If you will receive Christ, He will give you the power to live for Him. Otherwise, your best efforts are a waste of time and strength.

13

FAITHFUL SERVICE

PREPARING TO TEACH

Study Text
Second and Third John

Outline
I. Walking in Truth
  A. Exemplary Christians
  B. The Power of Truth
  C. Mutual Love
  D. A Timely Warning
II. Helping Others
  A. Ideal Prosperity
  B. Christian Hospitality
III. Doing Good
  A. A Bad Example
  B. A Good Example

Golden Text: Follow not that which is evil, but that which is good. He that doeth good is of God: but he that doeth evil hath not seen God. 3 John 11

Central Truth: Christians should live according to the truth and manifest love to all.

Learning Goals
1. To understand how to be both loving and truthful.
2. To desire to be a good example for others to follow.
3. To review the studies of the quarter and evaluate their impact on our lives.

SEEING THE SCRIPTURES

2 John 4-6
4. I rejoiced greatly that I found of thy children walking in truth, as we have received a commandment from the Father.
5. And now I beseech thee, lady, not as though I wrote a new commandment unto thee, but that which we had from the beginning, that we love one another.
6. And this is love, that we walk after his commandments. This is the commandment, That, as ye have heard from the beginning, ye should walk in it.

3 John 2-8, 11-14
2. Beloved, I wish above all things that thou mayest prosper and be in health, even as thy soul prospereth.
3. For I rejoiced greatly, when the brethren came and testified of the truth that is in thee, even as thou walkest in the truth.
4. I have no greater joy than to hear that my children walk in truth.
5. Beloved, thou doest faithfully whatsoever thou doest to the brethren, and to strangers;
6. Which have borne witness of thy charity before the church: whom if thou bring forward on their journey after a godly sort, thou shalt do well:
7. Because that for his name's sake they went forth, taking nothing of the Gentiles.
8. We therefore ought to receive such, that we might be fellow helpers to the truth.
11. Beloved, follow not that which is evil, but that which is good. He that doeth good is of God: but he that doeth evil hath not seen God.
12. Demetrius hath good report of all men, and of the truth itself: yea, and we also bear record; and ye know that our record is true.
13. I had many things to write, but I will not with ink and pen write unto thee:
14. But I trust I shall shortly see thee, and we shall speak face to face. Peace be to thee. Our friends salute thee. Greet the friends by name.

SETTING THE SCENE

This week's study is taken from the Second and Third Epistles of John. First John is addressed to a church or to several churches. Second John is written to a Christian family, and Third John to an individual church member. Some of the great truths considered in First John are continued in Second and Third John.

GETTING STARTED

Use the responsive reading from PATH to begin this session.

If you do not have the PATH materials available to you, lead the class in developing a definition of the word "truth." Refer to the following dictionary definition of the word: "an established or verified fact."

You may want to develop your definition of truth as an acrostic as shown below:

T-rustworthy
R-eliable
U-nchanging
T-ested
H-elpful

Clarification

The elect lady—probably a well-known lady in whose home a church met.

In the truth—in Christian sincerity.

For the truth's sake—in defense of the truth.

Walking in truth—refers to the manner of life; children walking in obedience to God's commandments.

The beginning—Reference is to the beginning of Jesus' teaching ministry.

An antichrist—one who rejects the deity of Christ. The Gnostic heresy is the product of Satan himself.

Transgresseth—the Greek *proago* means "to go before" or "to go ahead"; to go further than what is right, to be extreme.

The emphasis is on love, truth, and obedience, which involve and supplement one another. Obedience without love is difficult; love without obedience is unreal. Neither can exist outside the realm of truth.

John is concerned about the family of God. In 1 John he says the mark of a child of God is love within the family. Truth is given prominence in 2 John. Christian love and service are the products of truth's dwelling in the believer. Love and truth are linked together.

BIBLE COMMENTARY

I. Walking in Truth

2 John 1-13.

2 John 4. I rejoiced greatly that I found of thy children walking in truth, as we have received a commandment from the Father. 5. And now I beseech thee, lady, not as though I wrote a new commandment unto thee, but that which we had from the beginning, that we love one another. 6. And this is love, that we walk after his commandments. This is the commandment, That, as ye have heard from the beginning, ye should walk in it. 7. For many deceivers are entered into the world, who confess not that Jesus Christ is come in the flesh. This is a deceiver and an antichrist. 8. Look to yourselves, that we lose not those things which we have wrought, but that we receive a full reward. 9. Whosoever transgresseth, and abideth not in the doctrine of Christ, hath not God. He that abideth in the doctrine of Christ, he hath both the Father and the Son. 10. If there come any unto you, and bring not this doctrine, receive him not into your house, neither bid him Godspeed: 11. for he that biddeth him God-speed is partaker of his evil deeds.

A. Exemplary Christians

Second and Third John are personal letters to friends John expected to visit soon. Possibly he wrote many letters (1 John 2:14; 3 John 9), but the Holy Spirit has preserved these brief epistles for the Church. Their message concerns the importance of knowing the truth of the gospel of Jesus Christ.

Second John is addressed to an "elect lady and her children, whom I love in the truth" (verse 1). Some hold that the phrase "elect lady" is a figurative way of designating a church or a group of churches. Nothing in this epistle suggests that John is writing to a church. The evidence for such an interpretation is weak. The phrase "elect lady and her children" is sufficient to indicate that the letter was written to a Christian family John respected and loved because of their outstanding Christian testimony. It is more natural to take John's word literally.

The word "elect" means "chose," and it may have reference to the lady's spiritual position as a leader among the believers. She

Question.

How would you describe the truth as it is in the gospel of Christ?

Question.

What is Christian love? What does it involve?

TEACHING TIP 2

Use the following brief case studies to generate a discussion on the proper way to use truth.

Case study 1: Mary prides herself on being a very truthful person, but at times she can be very blunt and untactful. She defends her actions by saying she is only telling the truth. Is this a proper way to handle truth? How can truth be spoken more lovingly and more kindly?

Case study 2: Jack wants everyone to like him. He finds it very difficult to be direct with people. He would rather tell them what they want to hear. Is this a proper use of truth? How can we be honest with people and yet maintain their friendship and respect?

You can assign each of the above case studies to a different discussion group. Or you can use them to lead a general discussion on the subject. Refer to "Guideline for Living 1" in discussing these case studies.

was undoubtedly an exemplary Christian who found a sphere of usefulness in receiving God's servants into her home. The apostle expresses appreciation and commendation to this woman because he found her children "walking in truth." This means living in obedience to the commandments "from the Father." The commandment that we "walk in the light, as he is in the light" (1 John 1:7), means that we order our lives by the Word of God.

B. The Power of Truth

(See Teaching Tip 1.)

The word "truth" is used five times in the first four verses: (1) love in truth, (2) know the truth, (3) truth dwells in us, (4) grace, mercy, and peace, in truth, (5) walking in truth. John also says that truth is the true doctrine of Christ (verse 9). It is truth that unites in love all members of the body of Christ. Fellowship in love and truth in the family of God transcends time and place, and "will be with us forever" (verse 2).

On the rocks and crags of the California coast near Monterey, one can see cedars of Lebanon growing in the very midst of the rock. In some way each seed found a place in the rock, and nature took over with its mysterious and mighty power of germination and growth. The plant drove its way straight up and through the heart of the rock until it found the sun and light. So is the power of even one single seed of divine truth.

C. Mutual Love

(See Teaching Tip 2.)

Christian love is the product of truth in the believer. John exhorts the "elect lady" to love her fellow Christians. Here, as in 1 John 2:8, he speaks of the "new commandment" that we have had "from the beginning" of our Christian experience (verses 5, 6). Because Jesus referred to it as a "new commandment," this old commandment is called "new."

Walking in truth and loving one another is needed today in both the Church and home. The Bible does not view Christian love as mere sentiment or empty profession. It is possible to be overly sentimental. Much is said about "agape love" today, but how many fully understand what it is?

Guideline for Living 1

As Christians we must be truthful, but sometimes truth can be used in a hurtful way. In the guise of being truthful some have been too blunt in their assault on others. Both John and Paul caution us to balance truth with love. In Ephesians 4:15 we are told to speak the truth in love.

To be lovingly truthful means we will not deliberately hurt someone with the truth. This is not to say that at times our truthful words will not cause hurt. But our motive should always be to bring help and healing and not hurt and harm. There are ways to soften the blow, to speak the truth in such a way that it can be accepted and acted upon.

The substance of this divine command is "that we love one another," not momentarily but habitually (Greek present tense). Love is not a matter of momentary sentiment. The affection of which John writes differs from matrimonial, parental, filial, and

friendly love. It cannot be exercised toward the wicked. This love has a higher meaning. It is a sacred and holy love which involves respect and esteem for every member of the family of God.

Love is what causes a person to do something for another. Love is a matter of walking in humble obedience to the Lord. It is walking after His commandments. Love is letting the Holy Spirit show the believer His way. Love is loving like Christ. Love loves forever.

Balance is what John advises and what is needed today. We are to walk in truth and love one another. Ordinary affection is raised to a holy level by the bond of mutual faith in the truth of the gospel. (See John 13:35; 15:12; 1 Thessalonians 3:12; 1 Peter 1:22.) (See Teaching Tip 3.)

Guideline for Living 2

There are three kinds of love needed in every marriage. They are *eros* love, *phileo* love, and *agape* love.

Eros love is romantic, physical love. It is a warm kiss, candles, and music at dinner. Many couples begin their marriage with much of this kind of love, but fail to continue developing romance in their relationship.

Phileo love is companionship love. It is sharing with your spouse something you read in a book, or feeling lonely when you are apart from each other. It is a relationship between two people who not only *"love"* each other, but "like" each other and want to be together.

Agape love is self-giving love. It is being kind and sympathetic to each other and learning to forgive and make allowances for each other. It means being sensitive, gentle, and supportive. *Agape* love means we put the well-being of our spouse before our own needs and desires.

Question.

What should be the believer's attitude toward false teachers and teachings?

D. A Timely Warning

John warns that many deceivers have gone out into the world. Gnosticism was one of the most dangerous cults of John's day. In 1 John 4:1 he mentioned that many false teachers were traveling from place to place, propagating their errors. Everywhere the gospel is preached, cults have followed.

The Corinthian Gnostics refused to believe that the divine Christ actually came in the flesh. They taught that Jesus and Christ were two different entities. The docetic Gnostics denied the reality of the physical body of Christ. There are false religions and cults today that teach the same errors. In John's day there were Jewish sects that mixed the teachings of Christ with their own legalistic viewpoints—like some false teachings today.

The apostle characterizes those who reject the truth of the gospel as deceivers and antichrists. The Gnostic heresy and their liberal counterparts today come from Satan himself and are propagated by the antichrist spirit.

The menace of deceivers is cause for alarm and warning. John says, "Look to yourselves" or in modern terms . . . "Watch yourselves!" False teachers will rob a careless believer of his spiritual gains. One cannot be a Christian and not believe in the Virgin Birth, Christ's deity, and His redemptive work on Calvary. If you are abiding in the doctrine of Christ (the truth), you have access to the Father through the Son (verse 9).

The good woman (elect lady) may have shown hospitality to false teachers in her home. John insists that such indiscriminate practices should never take place. To entertain a false teacher makes you a partner with him in his deeds. (See Matthew 5:17; 15:19; Romans 16:17; 1 Timothy 1:7; 4:1, 2; 6:3; Titus 1:11; 2 Peter 2:1.)

II. Helping Others
3 John 1-8

3 John 1. The elder unto the well-beloved Gaius, whom I love in the truth. 2. Beloved, I wish above all things that thou mayest prosper and be in health, even as thy soul prospereth. 3. For I rejoiced greatly, when the brethren came and testified of the truth that is in thee, even as thou walkest in the truth. 4. I have no greater joy than to hear that my children walk in truth. 5. Beloved, thou doest faithfully whatsoever thou doest to the brethren, and to strangers; 6. which have borne witness of they charity before the church: whom if thou bring forward on their journey after a godly sort, thou shalt do well: 7. because that for his name's sake they went forth, taking nothing of the Gentiles. 8. We therefore ought to receive such, that we might be fellow helpers to the truth.

A. Ideal Prosperity

(See Teaching Tip 4.)

The Third Epistle of John gives us an interesting glimpse into the New Testament church of the first century. The brief letter contains no significant doctrinal teachings or new revelations. It introduces us to an interesting person, the "well-beloved" Gaius. The aged John, now in his 90s, expresses his feelings and the feelings others shared about this good man.

Gaius was apparently one of John's spiritual children who gave the apostle great joy (verse 3). He had many admirable qualities. He was sound in doctrine—"whom I love in the truth." Gaius not only stood for the truth, but worked for it in love. He was what we would call a genuine Christian. Such people are a delight to the Lord and a blessing to the Church. (See Teaching Tip 5.)

"Above all things" in verse 2 means "in all respects." John has heard of the prosperity of Gaius' soul. He prays that he may enjoy the same blessing in every area of his life. The Greek word translated "prosper" is *eudoo*, meaning literally, "have a good way." It is a term often used in connection with walking or taking a trip. It appears in Romans 1:10 where Paul prays for "a prosperous journey" to see the saints in Rome. Obviously this does not mean he expected to become wealthy along the way, but would have a journey blessed by God and kept free from danger and hindrances. In 1 Corinthians 16:2 Paul tells the Corinthians that each believer should "lay by him in store, as God hath prospered him." This refers to financial offerings, but the word "prospered" does not imply the individual is rich. It simply means that his giving is to be in proportion to the amount of money he has received.

In his letter to Gaius John prays that God will give "a good way" to this Christian "in all respects" (as the NASB translates it). This includes his financial needs as well as his health, but it does not

Clarification

The elder—could refer to John's age or his position as a leader of the Church.

Walkest in truth—refers to both doctrine and conduct.

Strangers—Christian workers, traveling missionaries.

Taking nothing of the Gentiles—accepting nothing from the heathen.

Fellow helpers—fellow workers.

Question.

What was it about Gaius that made him a "well-beloved" person?

TEACHING TIP 4

Instruct the students to underline in their Bibles the word "truth" as it appears in verses 3, 4, and 12 of 3 John

Question.

Does God want all believers to prosper? What does prosperity mean to you?

TEACHING TIP 5

What order of priority is suggested in 3 John 2? Lead the class to the following conclusion regarding right priorities of prosperity: 1) spiritual prosperity, 2) physical prosperity, 3) marital prosperity.

imply that John prays for Gaius to be wealthy. Our materialistic age has become so absorbed with securing every "want" as well as actual needs that our idea of prosperity has become distorted. As it is commonly used today, the word means something different than John meant when he penned these words.

B. Christian Hospitality

Question.
How may we determine the validity of a minister and a ministry seeking our support?

The apostle commends Gaius heartily for his hospitality in opening his heart and home to those who are brethren even though they were "strangers" to him. Traveling missionaries and other Christian workers were dependent on the help of fellow believers. Gaius not only entertained them in his home but helped pay the expense of their travel (verse 6). These workers were not to receive support from the unbelievers to whom they were ministering. John believed God's people should support His work.

Guideline for Living 3

An important ministry in the Early Church is hospitality. It is much needed in the Church today. The ministry of hospitality is that special ability God gives some Christian to make people feel warm and welcome. Persons with this gift or ability have a way of meeting people easily and helping them feel at peace and welcome. They are quick to spot newcomers and seek to help them feel at home in the group. They are also good at getting people acquainted with each other.

These people make excellent greeters or social chairpersons. They like to have people in their home and would be effective in inviting people to a neighborhood Bible study or other home gathering.

As stewards of God we should be careful that the ministries we support are responsible, real, and genuine. We should not give money God has entrusted to us to religious hucksters and racketeers—and there are many today!

III. Doing Good

3 John 9-14

3 John 9. I wrote unto the Church: but Diotrephes, who loveth to have the preeminence among them, receiveth us not. 10. Wherefore, if I come, I will remember his deeds which he doeth, prating against us with malicious words: and not content therewith, neither doth he himself receive the brethren, and forbiddeth them that would, and casteth them out of the church. 11. Beloved, follow not that which is evil, but that which is good. He that doeth good is of God: but he that doeth evil hath not seen God. 12. Demetrius hath good report of all men, and of the truth itself: yea, and we also bear record; and ye know that our record is true.

A. A Bad Example

(See Teaching Tip 6.)

John has introduced us to Gaius, a choice saint of the Early Church, a man who brough joy to his heart. Now we meet a person named Diotrephes, a jealous, self-centered troublemaker in the church. John doesn't tell us much about him—whether he was a pastor, elder, deacon, or some other officeholder in the Church. Apparently Diotrephes was in a position of leadership because he

Clarification

Preeminence—superiority, prominence.

Prating—talking nonsense, chattering, idle talking.

Malicious—evil.

The truth itself—God's revelation in the gospel.

TEACHING TIP 6

Develop a character comparison chart on Gaius and Diotrephes.

GAIUS	DIOTREPHES
Sound doctrine	False teacher
Generous	Jealous
Hospitable	Trouble maker
Humble	Proud

TEACHING TIP 7

Briefly review the studies of the quarter as outlined in the "Living the Truth." Distribute paper and pencil to the students. Ask each student to write down his/her responses to the following three questions: 1) What were three new truths you discovered in this series of studies? 2) What are three new attitudes you need to develop? 3) What are three new courses of action you need to begin?

Help the students to understand it is not enough simply to become aware of spiritual truth. We must respond to it by changing our attitudes and our actions.

Invite three or four students to share with the class what they have written in response to these questions.

Allow time in the schedule to use the Course Evaluation form from the Packet of Adult Teaching Helps. If you do not have the PATH materials available, ask the students to write their personal response to the following open-ended sentences: 1) The thing I enjoyed most about this course of study was . . . 2) The thing I enjoyed least was . . . 3) This course of study will help me to . . . 4) It would have improved the sessions if we had . . . 5) In general I would say . . .

Daily Devotional Guide

M. Walking in Faith.
2 Kings 2:1-14
T. A Caring Witness.
2 Kings 5:1-5
W. Trusting God.
Psalm 25:1-7
T. Spirit of Truth.
John 14:12-17
F. Walking in Obedience.
Ephesians 5:6-16
S. Practice of Faith.
1 Peter 4:1-11

refused to receive any written communication sent from John to the Church. John had recommended that the Church receive certain men, among whom was one Demetrius, an outstanding Christian worker. But Diotrephes refused to receive any such teachers.

Why this man had resentment against John we do not know. It appears he was jealous of the apostle. He was a man who in his place of leadership enjoyed having "preeminence." Diotrephes wanted his voice to be heard, not John's or anyone else's. He was the type who would brag on being a self-made man instead of letting the Holy Spirit make him over. The desire for power and glory had become an obsession to this church boss. He was self-exalting instead of self-effacing. He used high-handed methods in defying the leadership of John.

People like Diotrephes have wrecked churches, destroyed fellowships, brought shame on themselves, and disgraced the cause of Christ. (See Proverbs 17:19; Obadiah 4; Matthew 23:12.)

B. A Good Example

Having dealt with the unpleasant matter of ecclesiastical ambition and dominance, John advised Gaius not to be influenced by the bad example of Diotrephes. His injunction to imitate good (verse 11) reminds us that a living example may be much more effective than verbal exhortations. Being a Christian involves setting an example to others. (See Matthew 5:14, 15; John 13:15, 35; 2 Thessalonians 3:5; 1 Timothy 4:12; Titus 2:7; James 5:10.) However, people need both spoken instruction and living examples to remind them there are such things as right and wrong.

Demetrius is a good example of what a Christian worker should be. He had a testimony for Christ and was sound in the faith. All who knew Demetrius spoke favorably about him. To those testimonies John adds his own witness. There is only brief mention of Demetrius in the Bible—one verse. Yet he is one of the shining lights of the Early Church, a humble and dependable man of God.

While evil may be working in churches, there is good also working. The evil is there for us to avoid, the good to imitate. We need to "discern between the righteous and the wicked, between him that serveth God and him that serveth him not" (Malachi 3:18).

LIVING THE TRUTH

Let us reflect on our studies over the past 13 weeks. In 1 Timothy we studied the importance of sound doctrine, good leadership, and right relationships in the Church. In 2 Timothy we learned that as Christians we should be loyal servants of the Lord and careful students of His Word. In Titus the emphasis was on the word of truth which reveals God's grace and produces godly living. In John's first epistle we learned why he is called the disciple of love as he urges us to live in light and love. Here in his second and third letters the emphasis again is on truth.

EVANGELISM OUTREACH

The most effective way to witness for Christ is to live a life of example before the lost. They will be turned toward or away from Christ by what they see in our lives. Are you a help or a hindrance to the spread of the gospel? a stepping stone or a stumbling block? There really is no neutral ground. You are one or the other.

Recommended Resources

The spring/85 theme is "Message of the Old Testament Prophets." The teacher will find the following books very helpful in advance preparation and classroom use:

GENERAL REFERENCE WORKS

The *Packet of Adult Teaching Helps* (PATH) contains teaching and learning aids especially designed to supplement the spring studies. Use with every study. Order #67-1375, $5.05.

The *Book of Isaiah* by Edward J. Young. The New International Commentary of the Old Testament. Volume 1 chapters 1-18, order #38-0100, $18.95; volume 2 chapters 19-39, order #38-0101, $15.95; volume 3 chapters 40-66, order #38-0102, $15.95.

SELECTED STUDY HELPS

Through the Bible Book by Book: Part 2 From Job to Malachi by Myer Pearlman. An inspirational, personal approach to many of the prophets. Use with studies 1-13. Order #02-0661, $2.50.

Thus Says the Lord by Reidar B. Bjornard. How what Isaiah said centuries ago applies to us today. Use with studies 1-3. Order #03-2688, $3.50.

The Prophets of Israel by Leon J. Wood. The prophets studied as people. Use with all studies. Order #03-2325, $14.95.

My Servant Job by Morris A. Inch. Easy-to-follow study of God's estimate of Job and Job's faith. Use with study 6. Order #38-0109, $2.95.

Jeremiah: Prophet Under Seige by James M. Efird. The author paints a flesh and blood picture to make this prophet come alive. Use with study 4. Order #03-1730, $4.95.

What You Should Know About Prophecy by C. M. Ward. The author takes a fascinating look at the prophets and their amazing prophecies. Use with all studies. Order #02-0890, $2.50.

Isaiah, Prophecies-Promises-Warnings by W. E. Vine. Concentrated moral and spiritual lessons of Isaiah. Use with studies 1-3. Order #38-0103 (paper), $5.95.

The Minor Prophets by Jack P. Lewis. Hosea, Micah, Jonah, Habakkuk, Haggai, Malachi, and others all neatly presented in summary. Use with studies 7-13. Order #38-0104, $3.95.

Jeremiah by Dr. Theo Laetsch. In-depth commentary of the prophet and his message. Use with study 4. Order #38-0106 (paper), $11.95.

Ezekiel the Prophet by H. A. Ironside. A running commentary on the Book of Ezekiel. Use with study 5. Order #38-0107, $8.75.

A New Discovery by Donald Gee. The author deals with all the basic problems in connection with receiving the baptism in the Holy Spirit. Use with study 13. Order #02-0569, $1.00.

Isaiah: the Salvation of Jehovah by Alfred Martin. A brief, elementary survey of Isaiah. Use with studies 1-3. Order #38-0108, $4.50.

They Speak With Other Tongues by John L. Sherrill. A skeptical reporter researching speaking in tongues reveals Biblical confirmation of this miracle. Use with study 13. Order #03-2698, $2.50.

Unto You Is the Promise by Robert W. Cummings. Personal account of the author's baptism in the Holy Spirit. Use with study 13. Order #02-0750, 79 cents apiece.

The above items are available from the Gospel Publishing House, 1445 Boonville Avenue, Springfield, Missouri 65802. We do not necessarily endorse the entire content of these publications. Minimum order is $1.00. Prices and availability are subject to change without notice.

How To Use Your Adult Teacher

It is imperative that you read the Adult Student quarterly during your advance study. Pay particular attention to the questions under "Applying the Word." Be ready to discuss any one of these questions during class time if a student brings it up. You may wish to integrate specific questions into your presentation for a given Sunday.

Wide and Narrow Columns

Instead of the two equal columns used in the past, your *Adult Teacher* now uses the format of a wide and narrow column. Each study contains the same information as before, but it has been rearranged.

The wide column contains the following: SEEING THE SCRIPTURES, SETTING THE SCENE, BIBLE COMMENTARY (including Scripture blocks), Guidelines for Living, LIVING THE TRUTH, and EVANGELISM OUTREACH.

On the first page of each study, the narrow column contains an overview of the study under the heading, PREPARING TO TEACH. This column shows the Study Text, Outline, Golden Text, Central Truth, and Learning Goals.

On the remaining pages, the narrow column includes: GETTING STARTED, Clarification, Teaching Tips, questions from the commentary, and the daily devotional guide.

Helps Where You Need Them

The commentary, application, and methodology sections are totally integrated so the teacher has what he needs at the point of use. The section headed, GETTING STARTED, is at the beginning—where it would be used. It contains suggestions for getting the students' immediate attention and providing a bridge to the Bible study that follows.

The "Clarification" section, which explains words or expressions in the study text that might be difficult to understand, is placed opposite the Scripture block to which it applies.

Each Teaching Tip is placed or referred to at the point where it would be used to help students get a better grasp of that part of the Bible Commentary. If a Teaching Tip calls for the use of PATH (Packet of Adult Teaching Helps), that information will be given. When you see the heading, "Question," in the narrow column, it is a question answered in the Bible Commentary at that point.

The guidelines for living are considered a part of the application, but are so closely related to the commentary that this section is inserted in the commentary. It is set off by a long, narrow bracket and by the heading, "Guideline for Living," followed by the number. This section should not be considered an interruption of the commentary. It is for the purpose of helping the teacher apply to daily life the Bible truth being studied.

The daily devotional guide is for the teacher's personal benefit. It is to help you get into the Word throughout the week, and hopefully you will find in the daily devotionals truths you will use in the lesson.

At the end of the study, "Living the Truth" is a summary of all the guidelines for living. "Evangelism Outreach" is actually a sub-head under "Living the Truth." It is a reminder to use the class not only as a time to nurture Christians but also to bring the unsaved to a decision for Christ.

Use It as a Tool

You will find more material in the *Adult Teacher* than you can use in any one session. Your own advance study will show you what to include and what to omit. You may sometimes develop activities of your own that will seem more suitable. The *Adult Teacher* is a tool, not a substitute for the Bible or personal preparation. Use this quarterly for the purpose for which it has been designed and your efforts will be rewarded.

EVALUATION
ADULT

Please respond to the questions below at the end of the quarter. Then remove, fold, tape, stamp, and return this form.

1. _____ Average Sunday school attendance.
2. _____ Average class attendance.
3. Did you find the following sections of the lesson format helpful? (Check one)

Yes	No	Didn't Use	
___	___	___	Setting the Scene
___	___	___	Learning Goals
___	___	___	Communicating Bible Truth
___	___	___	Clarification
___	___	___	Teaching Tips
___	___	___	Guidelines for Living
___	___	___	Living the Truth
___	___	___	Preparing for Next Week
___	___	___	Daily Devotional Guide

Is the general reaction of your class to the Adult Student favorable? ____YES ____No

Additional comments: (If appropriate, please indicate publication, item, and page number.)

Thank you,
The Editors

Fold

Place
stamp
here

CHURCH SCHOOL LITERATURE DEPARTMENT
Gospel Publishing House
1445 Boonville Avenue
Springfield, MO 65802

Attention: Adult Section

Fold

MESSAGE OF THE OLD TESTAMENT PROPHETS

1 | SEEING GOD'S GLORY

SEEING THE SCRIPTURES
Isaiah 6:1-13

1. In the year that king Uzziah died I saw also the Lord sitting upon a throne, high and lifted up, and his train filled the temple.

2. Above it stood the seraphim: each one had six wings; with twain he covered his face, and with twain he covered his feet, and with twain he did fly.

3. And one cried unto another, and said, Holy, holy, holy, is the Lord of hosts: the whole earth is full of his glory.

4. And the posts of the door moved at the voice of him that cried, and the house was filled with smoke.

5. Then said, I, Woe is me! for I am undone; because I am a man of unclean lips, and I dwell in the midst of a people of unclean lips: for mine eyes have seen the King, the Lord of hosts.

6. Then flew one of the seraphim unto me, having a live coal in his hand, which he had taken with the tongs from off the altar:

7. And he laid it upon my mouth, and said, Lo, this hath touched thy lips; and thine iniquity is taken away, and thy sin purged.

8. Also I heard the voice of the Lord, saying, Whom shall I send, and who will go for us? Then said I, Here am I; send me.

9. And he said, Go, and tell this people, Hear ye indeed, but understand not; and see ye indeed, but perceive not.

10. Make the heart of this people fat, and make their ears heavy, and shut their eyes; lest they see with their eyes, and hear with their ears, and understand with their heart, and convert, and be healed.

11. Then said I, Lord, how long? And he answered, Until the cities be wasted without inhabitant, and the houses without man, and the land be utterly desolate,

12. And the Lord have removed men far away, and there be a great forsaking in the midst of the land.

13. But yet in it shall be a tenth, and it shall return, and shall be eaten: as a teil tree, and as an oak, whose substance is in them, when they cast their leaves; so the holy seed shall be the substance thereof.

SETTING THE SCENE

As we study the prophets it is helpful to note what kings reigned during their ministry. By referring to the Old Testament's historical books we can discover the background of the conditions God's messengers addressed. History repeats itself. It is amazing how much those days were like our own.

We should be alert to the basic spiritual principles the Lord declared through His prophets.

By no means did prophets only foretell the future. They also comforted, rebuked, instructed, and warned the people.

GETTING STARTED

Write on the chalkboard or overhead transparency: "What can we learn from the Old Testament prophets?" Give each student one chenille wire as he arrives. Instruct each one to twist the wire into a shape that represents his answer to the question.

In groups of two or three, have students share what their wire sculpture represents. Ask for two or three volunteers to share with the entire class. Lead into this week's Bible study by singing the first verse of the hymn, "Holy, Holy, Holy."

Clarification

Uzziah—also called Azariah (2 Kings 14:21; 15:1-7; 1 Chronicles 3:12).

His train—the flowing folds of His robe.

Temple—not the earthly temple but God's dwelling place, for His throne is seen in the vision. The same Hebrew word is translated both "temple" and "palace" in various Old Testament passages.

Seraphim—burning ones. See additional explanation in the commentary.

Posts of the door—foundations of the thresholds.

TEACHING TIP 1

As you begin the study of Isaiah's vision, clearly state your learning goals to the class. These goals will help both you and your students to be aware of what should be emphasized and keep on track.

Read Isaiah 6:1-4 aloud, asking students to be thinking of adjectives that describe how Isaiah might have felt. Write responses on the chalkboard.

BIBLE COMMENTARY

I. A Holy God

Isaiah 6:1-4

Isaiah 6:1. In the year that king Uzziah died I saw also the Lord sitting upon a throne, high and lifted up, and his train filled the temple. 2. Above it stood the seraphim: each one had six wings; with twain he covered his face, and with twain he covered his feet, and with twain he did fly. 3. And one cried unto another, and said, Holy, holy, holy, is the Lord of hosts: the whole earth is full of his glory. 4. And the posts of the door moved at the voice of him that cried, and the house was filled with smoke.

A. Spiritual Deterioration

Isaiah could never forget "the year that King Uzziah died." It was the climax of an era with a bright beginning but a painful ending.

In many ways Uzziah's 52-year reign was a golden age for Israel, but the outward glory was superficial. God saw a nation grown inwardly corrupt. The beginning of Isaiah's prophecy records the Lord's stinging indictment of His people. They were rebellious children, He said. Their gratitude for His blessings was inferior to that of animals who appreciated the grain their owners fed them (Isaiah 1:2, 3). Isaiah 1:4 brands them a "sinful nation, a people laden with iniquity, a seed of evildoers, children that are corrupters."

Second Chronicles 26 details Uzziah's reign. The career that began with great promise when he was only 16 deteriorated tragically in the latter years. Verse 16 is the key: "When he was strong, his heart was lifted up to his destruction."

This arrogance led Uzziah to try to usurp the priest's office by burning incense in the temple. For his sin God struck him with leprosy. It was the end of Uzziah's public life. His disease forced him into isolation the rest of his days (2 Chronicles 26:21) without his formally abdicating the throne.

During the last years of Uzziah's life his son Jotham attempted to fill the vacuum in a role that might be described as "acting king" (2 Chronicles 26:21). But it must have been somewhat like a vice president trying to carry out the duties of an incapacitated president without being elevated to the higher office. This was a time of tension and uncertainty for the nation. Isaiah must have felt the uneasiness deeply.

B. A Life-Changing Vision

Isaiah does not say what led up to the experience. But on an unforgettable day he suddenly found himself in the presence of God. He already loved and served God but had never encountered Him in such fashion before.

Oriental thrones were usually elevated and had to be approached by climbing many steps. This emphasized the exalted position of the ruler. It was fitting that in Isaiah's vision God's throne was "high and lifted up." Kings wore long, flowing robes and the folds of God's robes seemed to fill the throne room. It was an awesome reminder that there is one Kingdom above every other and one King whose glory overshadows the combined splendor of all earthly rulers.

Furthermore, the administration of human governments is interrupted by the deaths of the Uzziahs and others who lead nations for a time. But the government of the King whom Isaiah saw never suffers interruption, for He is eternal.

This is the only place the Bible mentions seraphim. Obviously they are supernatural beings with a special place near God's throne. The Hebrew word *sarap* means "burning." It is translated "fiery" in describing fiery serpents (Numbers 21:6 and other references). Apparently the word is used for these heavenly creatures to emphasize their burning devotion to God.

Although each seraphim had six wings he used only two to fly. The other wings covered his face and feet, showing his deep humility in God's presence. It suggested the seraphim's desire to divert attention away from themselves so all eyes would be turned toward God.

Isaiah was so impressed with their antiphonal chant, "Holy, holy, holy, is the Lord of hosts," that he uses the expression over and over in his messages. The holiness of God was the never-ending theme of the seraphim. After this vision it was a vital part of Isaiah's preaching.

Even though the earth is cursed by sin, the seraphim declared it is full of God's glory. As Isaiah beheld the scene, the very thresholds of the doorposts seemed to shudder at the awful presence of One who is unspeakably holy.

In the Scriptures fire often symbolizes God's presence, but smoke seems to picture especially His anger. Deuteronomy 29:20 speaks of God's anger and jealousy smoking against the wicked. The Psalmist wrote, "Bow thy heavens, O Lord, and come down: touch the mountains, and they shall smoke" (Psalm 144:5). The Day of the Lord will be accompanied by 'blood, and fire, and pillars of smoke" (Joel 2:30).

A holy God had to feel anger at the sin engulfing the nation. While the foundations of the thresholds shook, the smoke that filled the temple declared to the stunned prophet how overpoweringly the holy nature of God was reacting against the iniquity of His people.

It is possible that God also intended for the scene to remind Isaiah of the day He gave Israel the Law from Mount Sinai. On that momentous occasion the mountain shook and was covered with smoke (Exodus 19:18). Recalling the event would make the prophet acutely conscious of his nation's continual violations of the Law.

Question.
Who were the seraphim and what part did they play in God's revelation of himself?

Question.
What is the significance of the smoke that filled the house?

TEACHING TIP 2
Use the student guide sheet in *PATH* to help students respond in worship to the holiness of God. Three short writing activities are provided to help students think creatively in expressing praise to God.

Guideline for Living 1

What does it mean to be holy?

Sinlessness, purity, righteousness, glory, perfection. These are words that come to mind as we think of God's holiness. The Ten Commandments were given as a standard of righteousness, which of course no man has ever been able to achieve. Jesus demonstrated a life of holiness which we are commanded to strive to imitate (1

Clarification

Woe is me—a cry of extreme distress; literally, "Woe to me." Our interjection "Oh!" may be a transliteration of the Hebrew word *oy* rendered "woe" in this verse.

I am undone—I am lost, ruined, cut off.

The altar—the altar of incense. See further explanation in the commentary.

Purged—removed; expiated.

Question.
Why did Isaiah confess the impurity of his lips?

TEACHING TIP 3

On the chalkboard list these references which help us see what is involved in true repentance: Leviticus 5:5 Psalms 38:18; 51:1, 2; Proverbs 28:13; James 5:15; 1 John 1:9.

Assign students to read each verse and sum up in two or three words what is needed for true repentance. (See "Guideline for Living 2".) List responses on the chalkboard opposite the Scripture reference.

Allow time for students to meditate privately on 1 John 1:9. Ask these thought questions as students bow in silent prayer:

What shortcomings do you need to confess to God?

In what area of your life do

Peter 2:21, 22). God said to be holy because He is holy (Leviticus 19:2; 1 Peter 1:16). As Isaiah worshiped God, He was aware that God's glory fills the whole earth. It surrounds everything. The holiness of God demands a response of worship.

II. Sinful Man
Isaiah 6:5-7

Isaiah 6:5. Then said I, Woe is me! for I am undone; because I am a man of unclean lips, and I dwell in the midst of a people of unclean lips: for mine eyes have seen the King, the Lord of hosts. 6. Then flew one of the seraphim unto me, having a live coal in his hand, which he had taken with the tongs from off the altar. 7. and he laid it upon my mouth, and said, Lo, this hath touched thy lips; and thine iniquity is taken away, and thy sin purged.

A. Sinfulness Recognized

There is no reason to believe Isaiah had been leading a wicked life. Yet when he was faced with the absolute purity of a holy God he was horrified at his spiritual condition. A cry of pain came from the depths of his being. He may have feared immediate death as people in the Old Testament did when they had seen God or His angel (Judges 6:22; 13:22).

Isaiah realized more profoundly than ever the sinfulness of his nation, but his confession began with an indictment of himself. The lips of the people he lived among were unclean but so were his. He could not comfort himself with the feeling that he was better than his neighbors. He was too stricken with feelings of personal guilt.

Although Isaiah mentioned only his lips, this expression involved the whole person. If lips are unclean it is because the heart is impure (Matthew 12:34, 35). Sin will express itself in words as well as deeds. Isaiah was conscious of a totally sinful condition.

The prophet heard the seraphim worshiping God but was unable to join them because he was sinful. How could defiled lips sing, "Holy, holy, holy"? (See Teaching Tip 3.)

Guideline for Living 2

What was Isaiah's response to his glimpse of the holiness of God?

God's holiness is the standard by which all men have or will become aware of their own sinfulness and unworthiness. "All have sinned and come short of the glory of God" (Romans 3:23). But we have God's promise that "if we confess our sins, he is faithful and just to forgive us our sins, and to cleanse us from all unrighteousness" (1 John 1:9). True repentance will include: confession of sin (Leviticus 5:5; James 5:15); godly sorrow (Psalm 38:18); asking forgiveness (Psalm 51:1, 2); forsaking sin (Proverbs 28:13); and receiving forgiveness (1 John 1:9).

B. Sin Cleansed

This is an Old Testament scene. Isaiah lived under the Law. Yet the grace of God burst through the darkness enveloping the

you need to be more holy?

What is Jesus' message to you as you confess your sin to Him?

What is your response to His forgiveness?

prophet. His confession brought a quick response of divine mercy.

The altar has not been previously mentioned but now it becomes prominent. One of the seraphim flew to the altar and from it lifted a hot coal with the tongs he carried.

This was not an altar where sacrifices were offered, for such an altar would be out of place in heaven. Revelation 8:3-5 describes a golden altar before God's throne where fire is burning and incense is offered. It would appear this is the altar Isaiah saw. Incense is not mentioned in his vision, but there were coals of fire on the altar, suggesting the burning of incense (Leviticus 16:11-13). The whole symbolism fits the scene in this passage.

Hebrews 9:23 indicates the furnishings and articles of ministry in the tabernacle were patterned after "things in the heavens." The golden altar of incense in heaven seems to be the model for the altar of incense before the veil in the tabernacle (Exodus 30:1-8).

In Leviticus 16:11-13 God commanded Aaron to take burning coals from the altar to the mercy seat behind the veil on the Day of Atonement. Aaron was also instructed to take incense and place it on the coals so "the cloud of the incense may cover the mercy seat that is upon the testimony, that he die not."

This shows the symbolic importance of burning incense. Clearly it illustrated the continual intercession of Jesus Christ our High Priest. We are assured this mediatorial ministry never ends (Hebrews 4:14-16; 7:25).

The seraphim could not cleanse Isaiah, but fire from God's altar could. With the glowing coal he had taken from the altar the heavenly being touched the part of Isaiah's body which expressed his impurity—the lips. The use of fire in removing impurities from metal was familiar to the Hebrews. Malachi saw it as a picture of God purging the sins of His people (Malachi 3:2, 3). Isaiah would understand the purpose of the fiery coal in the same way.

Isaiah lived centuries before Jesus came to earth, but by the Holy Spirit's revelation he saw that future day and prophesied of it (John 12:41). The prophet's cleansing is a picture of repentant sinners who trust Christ's shed blood and are pardoned because His intercession—like the cloud of incense—rises continually before the Throne.

Clarification

Fat—calloused, insensitive.

Heavy—dull.

Shut their eyes—literally, besmear their eyes. This may refer to the practice of some Oriental kings who punished individuals by sealing their eyes shut.

Convert—turn; in this case, turn to God.

Healed—made whole by turning to God.

A great forsaking—forsaken places in the land would be many.

III. Answering God's Call
Isaiah 6:8-13

Isaiah 6:8. Also I heard the voice of the Lord, saying, Whom shall I send, and who will go for us? Then said I, Here am I; send me. 9. And he said, Go, and tell this people, Hear ye indeed, but understand not; and see ye indeed, but perceive not. 10. Make the heart of this people fat, and make their ears heavy, and shut their eyes; lest they see with their eyes, and hear with their ears, and understand with their heart, and convert, and be healed. 11. Then said I, Lord, how long? And he answered, Until the cities be wasted without inhabitant, and the houses without man, and the land be utterly desolate. 12. and the Lord have removed men far away, and there be a great forsaking in the midst of the land. 13. But yet in it shall be a tenth, and it shall return, and shall be eaten: as a teil tree, and as an oak, whose substance is in them, when they cast their leaves; so the holy seed shall be the substance thereof.

A. The Mission Described

"I heard the voice of the Lord." This was the first effect of the vision. Cleansing from his impurity made Isaiah sensitive to divine communication.

God's message was a question. He was inviting a response, but not compelling it. The wording is unusual, for both "I" and "us" are in the same sentence. While the Old Testament does not specifically reveal the Trinity, it implies the doctrine in a number of passages. Genesis 1:26 and 3:22 are examples and this verse seems to be another.

"Who will go for us?" God needed a man who would go. Isaiah's response was almost military, like a soldier reporting for duty: "Here am I; send me."

The prophet's mission would be a disheartening one. The people had already made up their minds to disobey God and Isaiah's preaching would only harden them more. They would follow the same path as Pharaoh, who became more obstinate with each plague God sent on Egypt.

This spiritual principle recurs throughout the Bible. Jesus' preaching drew many people into the Kingdom, but the same message made the hearts of unbelievers harder. At the end of this age God will send "strong delusion" to unbelievers who persist in their rejection of the truth (2 Thessalonians 2:11, 12).

Each time the Israelites heard Isaiah preach their hearts would become harder, their spiritual ears more dull, and their spiritual eyes more tightly shut. (See Teaching Tip 5.)

Guideline for Living 3

God wants us to serve Him, but we must let Him cleanse us before He can work through us. From reading Isaiah 6, what do you think is the proper motive for serving God?

All believers have been called to serve the Lord: "Each one should use whatever gift he has received to serve others, . . . so that in all things God may be praised through Jesus Christ" (1 Peter 4:10, 11, *New International Version*). God did not call Isaiah to an easy ministry. He would not be appreciated, listened to, or understood. Jesus often warned His disciples that many would not believe their witness. We need to follow God's leading for our lives whether or not we receive encouragement and appreciation from those we are ministering to.

Teaching, helping or serving, encouraging, counseling, prophesying, giving generously, showing mercy, and providing leadership are all mentioned as gifts given in various degrees to members of the body of Christ. (See Romans 12:5-8.) What gift has God given you? Have you answered His call to use that gift in serving Him?

B. Judgment Mingled With Mercy

Isaiah loved his people. In his distress he cried, "How long?" Would the recurring blows of judgment wipe out the nation? God's answer reveals a grim picture. For the rebellion of Israel the divine

Question.
What was the first evidence that Isaiah was truly cleansed?

TEACHING TIP 4
Ask: "What was Isaiah's commission? What did God ask him to do?" Briefly discuss the examples given in the "Bible Commentary" of other messengers who gave God's message to hardhearted people.

TEACHING TIP 5
Divide the class into the original small groups. (If possible, the entire class session could be conducted with students seated in groups.) Give each group an instruction slip from PATH to explore some of the gifts God has given His people. As reports of group work are made, ask students to take notes on those gifts they think God may have given them.
Ask: "In what ways are you answering God's call to serve Him? In what areas of your life could you be doing more for God?" Ask students to write private, brief answers to these questions.
Write 1 Peter 4:10, 11 on the chalkboard or display an overhead transparency of these verses. Ask students to copy these verses below their personal notes. Use material from the "Bible Commentary" and "Guideline for Living 3" to comment on the need for commitment to God's call even in disheartening circumstances.

TEACHING TIP 6
On the chalkboard or overhead, list the five parts of Isaiah's worship experience. Ask students to give the references from Isaiah 6 for each aspect of worship. (See "Living the Truth.")

Summarize the goals that have been achieved in this class session in these areas: worship of God for who He is, confession of sin, and answering God's call. Challenge students to be sensitive to God's voice this week and to consciously answer His call in a specific area of life.

Daily Devotional Guide
M. Deliverance Through Prayer.
2 Chronicles 32:20-26
T. Acknowledging God's Glory.
Psalm 19:1-6
W. God's Glorious Kingdom.
Isaiah 2:1-5
T. Christ's Glory Revealed.
Matthew 17:1-9
F. Obeying Christ's Call.
Acts 26:9-19
S. Christ's Glorious Return.
Revelation 19:11-16

discipline would continue until the land was emptied of its people, cities were ruined, houses deserted, and fields became desolate because no one was left to till them. Both the Assyrian and Babylonian captivities lay ahead. This prophecy points especially to the latter.

God would not utterly destroy His people. His relationship with them was not based on their goodness but on His covenant with Abraham. Despite Israel's apostasy, God would remain faithful to the promises He had made to the father of the nation. Even the "tenth" of the population left in the land would be partially decimated ("eaten"), yet a remnant (a "holy seed") would be preserved.

God compared this remnant to the teil (terebinth) and oak trees so common in Palestine. The terebinth especially was noted for being able to renew itself from a stump.

"Substance" refers to the vitality remaining in the stump of these trees even when the trunk is cut down, enabling them to survive and grow back. God's faithful remnant would be the "stump" that would send out new shoots and renew the nation's life.

LIVING THE TRUTH

Isaiah's worship experience outlines a pattern for us to follow today. The five stages of his experience are essential to true worship: awe, confession of sin, receiving forgiveness, a challenge from God, and acceptance of God's call. Isaiah's worship experience resulted in his being sent to the hardhearted people of Judah. As the result of a worship service in Antioch, Paul and Barnabas were sent off on the First Missionary Journey. As a result of worship, we must not only ascribe praise to God and admit our need for forgiveness, but must allow God to use us to achieve His purposes in the world.

EVANGELISM OUTREACH

There is no conflict between worshiping God and winning lost souls. In Mark 16:15 Jesus gave the Great Commission, "Go ye into all the world, and preach the gospel to every creature." The first word of Isaiah's commission was also *go*. Are you and your students fulfilling the Great Commission? Perhaps some in your class have never admitted their need for cleansing from sin. Give an opportunity for them to respond to God's call to salvation.

GOD'S SUFFERING SERVANT | 2

SEEING THE SCRIPTURES

Isaiah 53:1-12

1. Who hath believed our report? and to whom is the arm of the Lord revealed?

2. For he shall grow up before him as a tender plant, and as a root out of a dry ground: he hath no form nor comeliness; and when we shall see him, there is no beauty that we should desire him.

3. He is despised and rejected of men; a man of sorrow, and acquainted with grief: and we hid as it were our faces from him; he was despised, and we esteemed him not.

4. Surely he hath borne our griefs, and carried our sorrows: yet we did esteem him stricken, smitten of God, and afflicted.

5. But he was wounded for our transgressions, he was bruised for our iniquities: the chastisement of our peace was upon him; and with his stripes we are healed.

6. All we like sheep have gone astray; we have turned every one to his own way; and the Lord hath laid on him the iniquity of us all.

7. He was oppressed, and he was afflicted, yet he opened not his mouth: he is brought as a lamb to the slaughter, and as a sheep before her shearers is dumb, so he openeth not his mouth.

8. He was taken from prison and from judgment: and who shall declare his generation? for he was cut off out of the land of the living: for the transgression of my people was he stricken.

9. And he made his grave with the wicked, and with the rich in his death; because he had done no violence, neither was any deceit in his mouth.

10. Yet it pleased the Lord to bruise him; he hath put him to grief: when thou shalt make his soul an offering for sin, he shall see his seed, he shall prolong his days, and the pleasure of the Lord shall prosper in his hand.

11. He shall see of the travail of his soul, and shall be satisfied: by his knowledge shall my righteous servant justify many; for he shall bear their iniquities.

12. Therefore will I divide him a portion with the great, and he shall divide the spoil with the strong; because he hath poured out his soul unto death: and he was numbered with the transgressors: and he bare the sin of many, and made intercession for the transgressors.

SETTING THE SCENE

The Ethiopian eunuch was reading what we know as Isaiah 53 when Philip came to his chariot. From this text Philip preached Jesus to him (Acts 8:26-35). Few Old Testament passages are referred to as frequently in the New Testament as this one.

PREPARING TO TEACH

Study Text
Isaiah 52:13 through 53:12

Outline
I. Rejected by Men
  A. God's View and Man's
  B. Tragic Unbelief
II. Suffering for Others
  A. Nature of the Suffering
  B. The Servant's Response
III. Results of His Sufferings
  A. God's Will Accomplished
  B. Sinners Redeemed

Golden Text
He was wounded for our transgressions, he was bruised for our iniquities: the chastisement of our peace was upon him; and with his stripes we are healed. Isaiah 53:5

Central Truth
Jesus died on the cross in fulfillment of God's eternal plan of redemption.

Learning Goals
1. To show an understanding of the "Suffering Servant" chapter by describing some of the details and their meanings.
2. To contrast the feelings of sinners toward Christ with our personal feelings toward Him.
3. To accept Jesus' suffering and death as the atonement for our sins.

GETTING STARTED

Begin the class by brain-storming on words which describe hateful feelings. To encourage interaction and fellowship among class members, the brainstorming may be done in pairs or small groups. After 2 minutes, ask for volunteers to call out some of their ideas. List these on the chalk-board. (i.e., violence, rejection, cruelty, mocking, ignoring others, etc.)

Point out that these are all attitudes and actions that were directed against Christ, the suffering Servant. Encourage students to be alert throughout this week's study to the ways in which Christ suffered and to keep in mind that His suffering was for us.

Clarification

A tender plant—a sapling, or perhaps a frail shoot.

A dry ground—parched, arid ground. A reference either to the condition of the nation of Israel at the time of Christ or to the lowly circumstances of His birth and early life.

No form nor comeliness—not a suggestion of physical unattractiveness. It is a reference to the lack of worldly pomp and splendor by which men are likely to be drawn to a leader.

No beauty that we should desire him—no regal trappings that would attract men to Him.

Despised—accorded little worth; disdained; held in contempt.

Rejected—forsaken; shunned.

Esteemed him not—judged Him to be of no value or importance.

Clearly the last 3 verses of chapter 52 belong to chapter 53 and make the picture complete. Verse 13 declares the Servant's wisdom and exaltation. This underscores the sharp contrast between the Father's view of His Son and the humiliation to which men subjected Him. The effect of His enemies' brutal treatment on His very physical appearance (verse 14) is a shocking commentary on the depths of their hatred for Him. Verse 15 looks beyond this scene to the redemptive effects of His suffering.

BIBLE COMMENTARY

I. Rejected by Men

Isaiah 53:1-3

Isaiah 53:1. Who hath believed our report? and to whom is the arm of the Lord revealed? 2. For he shall grow up before him as a tender plant, and as a root out of a dry ground: he hath no form nor comeliness; and when we shall see him, there is no beauty that we should desire him. 3. He is despised and rejected of men; a man of sorrows, and acquainted with grief: and we hid as it were our faces from him; he was despised, and we esteemed him not.

A. God's View and Man's

From what points of view is the Servant described? At times in this passage God is the Speaker. In other verses it is Isaiah—representing his nation. In 52:13-15 we hear the voice of God calling His Son "My servant."

Following the Father's testimony to His Servant's wisdom ("shall deal prudently") and honor ("exalted . . . extolled . . . very high") there is a brief but shocking change of thought. Verse 14 describes the Servant's physical appearance following what could only be vicious punishment. The translation in the *Good News Bible* may help us grasp the picture more clearly: "Many people were shocked when they saw him; he was so disfigured that he hardly looked human."

Some scholars feel that "sprinkle" in 52:15 should be "startle." Several Bible translations render it this way. However, the evidence supports "sprinkle." The Hebrew word is *naza*, which is constantly used in the Old Testament in connection with expiation of sin and the consecration of individuals for holy service. *Naza* describes the sprinkling of blood, oil, and water (Exodus 29:21; Numbers 8:7). The Servant's sprinkling of many nations (with His atoning blood) shows that His gospel will be carried throughout the world and accepted by multitudes.

"The kings shall shut their mouths at him." This is a blessed contrast with the preceding verse, which tells of people being shocked at the Servant's appearance after He was physically manhandled. Isaiah declares that in the future He will shock people again—even rulers of nations. It will not be due to a battered physical appearance but because of His glory, power, and mighty works.

As the Servant's sufferings begin to unfold in chapter 53 it is

On the left side of the chalk-board or overhead transparency write the heading, "God's Perspective" and the question: "What was the distant view of God's plan that Jesus was able to see even as He endured great suffering?" Write these references and have students read them aloud: Isaiah 52:13, 15; 53:11, 12; and Hebrews 12:2. In the "Suffering Servant" passage, this view of Christ's true position and destiny forms the background for the description of the sorrow and agony He endured. List summary statements in the left column.

Ask: "How can we take personal encouragement from an understanding of God's perspective of Christ's suffering?" In small groups have students read 2 Timothy 2:12; 1 Peter 2:21; 4:13; and discuss responses to this question.

Question.
Why was the arm of the Lord not revealed to the majority of Israel?

---

good to have been given this distant view which takes us past those terrible days. Jesus himself saw the joy that lay beyond the Cross (Hebrews 12:2). (See Teaching Tip 1.)

Guideline for Living 1

God's perspective is always different from man's. But as God's children, we can learn to lift our heads above present difficulties and see the ultimate goal—that Christ's life be made manifest in us. Whatever the occasion, no matter how much it hurts, we can see it as God's opportunity to manifest himself in our life.

This perspective is seen in the "Suffering Servant" passage. It is put together like a sandwich: at the beginning and end the Servant's glory and exaltation is described (52:13, 15; 53:11, 12). In between, the Servant's extreme anguish, suffering, and rejection are described. We should not expect our lives to be any different. The glory and blessing will come later, as they did for Christ. "Christ suffered for you, leaving you an example, that you should follow in his steps" (1 Peter 2:21, NIV). When we find ourselves in difficulties and trials, we should not be surprised or discouraged. We need to recall the perspective of Isaiah 53—while we are suffering, we are in the middle of the "sandwich." Our ultimate outcome, if we remain true and let Christ's life shine through, will be to share in His glory. "Rejoice that you participate in the sufferings of Christ, so that you may be overjoyed when his glory is revealed" (1 Peter 4:13, NIV). "If we suffer, we shall also reign with him" (2 Timothy 2:12).

B. Tragic Unbelief

"Who hath believed our report" is the prophet's cry of dismay at Israel's callous indifference to his messages concerning the promised Messiah. John quotes this verse in describing the unbelief of the people after Jesus had performed many miracles (John 12:38). Paul also quotes it in Romans 10:16. Jesus himself "marvelled because of their unbelief" when He faced the descendants of the people to whom Isaiah referred (Mark 6:6).

God delivered Israel from Egypt with "a stretched out arm" (Exodus 6:6). This expression occurs frequently in the Old Testament. Isaiah 52:10 speaks of the Lord baring His holy arm in the eyes of all the nations. Even in our culture the picture of a man with rolled-up sleeves and bare, muscular arms suggests a strong individual about to go into action.

The greatest display of God's power—the mightiest baring of His arm—was in the future. It would happen when His Servant came to earth to become the perfect sacrifice for sinners. Because Isaiah's contemporaries turned a deaf ear to his prophecies they could not comprehend that coming day of redemption. The arm of the Lord would never be revealed to them; but it was because of their own stubborn unbelief, not His indifference.

Verse 2 describes how the majority of Israelites would regard the Servant. A sapling growing out of parched desert earth is not awe-inspiring. There was nothing about Jesus that would arrest the attention of a nation expecting a king who would make short work of their enemies.

Verse 3 continues man's view of God's Servant. When He finally came to earth multitudes followed Him at first. But when they discovered He was not the kind of Messiah they expected they turned against Him. Unknowingly they fulfilled Isaiah's prediction, "We hid . . . our faces from him." The Hebrew could also be translated, "As one who hid his face from us," suggesting the actions of a leper who was required by the Law to cover part of his face (Leviticus 13:45). In either case the basic meaning is the same.

In the Hebrew "a man of sorrows, and acquainted with grief" means "a man of pains, and familiar with sickness." "Acquainted" comes from a Hebrew word often translated "know" and used to express many shades of knowledge. In some passages it refers to the most intimate acquaintance (Exodus 33:17; Deuteronomy 34:10; Psalm 139:2). This is the sense in which Isaiah uses it here. In the deepest way Jesus knew all through His ministry the pain, sickness, despair, and bondage the human race experiences because of sin.

"We esteemed him not" is a picture of men passing judgment on something and deciding it is too worthless to merit further attention. Centuries after Isaiah this was Israel's ultimate verdict concerning the Servant who came to offer redemption to them and the whole world. (See Teaching Tip 2.)

Guideline for Living 2

The picture of the world's response to God's Servant contrasts sharply with God's view of His Servant. When Jesus appeared, most of the Jewish leaders responded with unbelief and indifference. They thought Him weak and undesirable as a leader. Because He did not behave according to their ideas of a Messiah, they despised and rejected Him. Because he was gentle and did not retaliate, the Jews mistook Him as weak and ineffective. They did not respect or esteem Him, but instead turned away from Him.

By comparison, those who truly wanted to know God received His perspective of Christ. They recognized Jesus as having come from the Father (John 1:14); as the King of Israel (John 1:49); as the Saviour of the world (John 4:42).

II. Suffering for Others
Isaiah 53:4-9

Isaiah 53:4. Surely he hath borne our griefs, and carried our sorrows: yet we did esteem him stricken, smitten of God, and afflicted. 5. But he was wounded for our transgressions, he was bruised for our iniquities: the chastisement of our peace was upon him; and with his stripes we are healed. 6. All we like sheep have gone astray; we have turned every one to his own way; and the Lord hath laid on him the iniquity of us all. 7. He was oppressed, and he was afflicted, yet he opened not his mouth: he is brought as a lamb to the slaughter, and as a sheep before her shearers is dumb, so he openeth not his mouth. 8. He was taken from prison and from judgment: and who shall declare his generation? for he was cut off out of the land of the living: for the transgression of my people was he stricken. 9. And he made his grave with the wicked, and with the rich in his death; because he had done no violence, neither was any deceit in his mouth.

Question.
When did Jesus begin to suffer?

TEACHING TIP 2
Add to the previous material on the chalkboard by writing the heading, "Man's Perspective," on the right-hand side. Include the reference, Isaiah 53:1-3.

In small groups, have students list as many words as they can think of to describe man's view of the suffering Servant. After about 2 minutes, call for responses from each group. Instruct students not to duplicate what has already been reported, but to add further insights not yet mentioned. List these descriptions on the chalkboard.

Read John 1:14, 49; 4:42 and add the descriptions of Jesus found in these verses to the left column, "God's Perspective." Ask students to consider which column describes their view of Christ.

Clarification
Stricken, smitten—The same Hebrew word is used for both of these English words. With various shades of meaning it carries the idea of touching. In this verse it implies being struck—as with a loathsome disease.

Afflicted—dealt with harshly; browbeaten.

Chastisement—severe punishment.

Oppressed—The Hebrew word means to exert pressure. It is translated "taskmaster" in Exodus 3:7.

Question.

Why are so many different words used to describe the Servant's experience?

TEACHING TIP 3

Ask students to skim chapter 53, underlining or listing the words used to describe the Servant's sufferings. Display the PATH transparency of this passage and use a red marker to underline the words as students mention them. The various translations will enrich students' understanding of what Jesus suffered.

Use material from the Bible Commentary to discuss the purpose of Jesus' suffering.

A. Nature of the Suffering

(See Teaching Tip 3.)

Notice the words used throughout chapter 53 to describe Jesus' sufferings: "despised," "rejected," "sorrows, grief," "stricken," "smitten," "afflicted," "wounded," "bruised," "chastisement," "stripes," "oppressed," "travail." "Despised," "sorrows," "stricken," "afflicted," and "bruised" are used twice. "Grief" occurs three times.

The total picture concerns sufferings that reached deep into our Saviour's inner being. It is difficult to translate the Hebrew words into English expressions that convey their full meaning. One or two words would not be adequate. Even with this long list we can hardly grasp the price He paid for our salvation.

Verse 4 describes the attitude of the onlookers when Jesus was arrested, tried, and crucified. They assumed He was being punished by God. Their religious leaders accused Him of blasphemy and the crowds felt that divine justice was catching up with Him. Yet Isaiah declares it was our sins that brought Him this agony.

Matthew 8:17 points to Jesus' healing ministry as a fulfillment of Isaiah 53:4. Matthew quotes the verse a little differently, although this is the literal meaning of the statement: "Himself took our infirmities, and bare our sicknesses."

In what sense did Jesus bear infirmities and sicknesses before He even went to the cross? Jesus' suffering reached its terrible climax in Gethsemane and on Calvary. Only by the shedding of His blood could atonement for sin be made. Yet through Matthew the Holy Spirit indicates that all through His ministry—in a way probably incomprehensible to the human mind—He was lifting off people and taking upon himself their sicknesses, sorrows, bondage, and guilt. Of course this was happening to Him inwardly. Unlike His beating and crucifixion, it was the kind of suffering the eye could not see.

Verses 5 and 6 reveal further that it was not for His own sins but ours that the Servant was wounded, bruised (literally, crushed), and chastised. For us to have peace He must be punished. For us to be healed He must be scourged.

Through Isaiah's pen the Holy Spirit pictures the human race as a flock of straying sheep determined to travel their own path instead of following the Shepherd. Yet it is the Shepherd who suffered to bring them back to safety. "The iniquity of us all" indicts the whole human race as sinners.

TEACHING TIP 4

Ask students to write personalized versions of Isaiah 53:5, 6, using their own names and/or personal pronouns. Below their personalized verses, ask students to write a one-sentence payer of response to God.

Guideline for Living 3

What do we learn from verses 4-9 about our relationship with God?

The extent of God's love for us is hard to comprehend. In this passage we can begin to see how deep that love is and how determined God is to win back His lost sheep. God loved the world so much that He gave His only Son to suffer for us. Our response when we realize the price God has paid for us must be humble confession that we deserved Christ's punishment, and grateful acceptance of His free gift.

B. The Servant's Response

What could illustrate submission and non-retaliation better than a lamb being led to the slaughter or a sheep waiting silently to be sheared. Like the submissive lamb, Jesus refused to defend himself at His hearing before the Sanhedrin and through all the brutality associated with it. In verse 8 "prison" (arrest) and "judgment" speak of the so-called trial from which Jesus was taken to His death. "Judgment" refers to the Jewish council's "guilty" verdict.

Some other translations make the latter part of verse 8 clearer. The *New American Standard Bible* renders it, "And as for His generation, who considered that He was cut off out of the land of the living, for the transgression of my people to whom the stroke was due?" Again Isaiah emphasizes the false view of Jesus' contemporaries about His sufferings. They could not comprehend that He was bearing the punishment due others, including "my people"—Israel, the very ones who had Him put to death.

Verse 9 is an amazing prophecy of God's overruling the designs of His Servant's enemies. Since they considered Him a criminal they would assign Him a grave with the wicked. Yet His body would instead be buried in a rich man's tomb (Matthew 27:57-60). The latter part of this verse focuses again on the complete innocence of the Servant. His death was for those who were *not* innocent—you and me and every other human (Romans 3:23).

III. Results of His Sufferings
Isaiah 53:10-12

Isaiah 53:10. Yet it pleased the Lord to bruise him; he hath put him to grief; when thou shalt make his soul an offering for sin, he shall see his seed, he shall prolong his days, and the pleasure of the Lord shall prosper in his hand. 11. He shall see of the travail of his soul, and shall be satisfied: by his knowledge shall my righteous servant justify many; for he shall bear their iniquities. 12. Therefore will I divide him a portion with the great, and he shall divide the spoil with the strong; because he hath poured out his soul unto death: and he was numbered with the transgressors: and he bare the sin of many, and made intercession for the transgressors.

A. God's Will Accomplished

(See Teaching Tip 5.)

We know that "pleased" does not mean the kind of morbid delight that insensitive people take in another's suffering. God was pleased in the sense that the bruising (crushing) of His Son was the only way the plan of redemption could be accomplished. Doing His Father's will was Jesus' own pleasure throughout His life. To His last breath He did not deviate from that goal.

The Hebrew word for "soul" in verse 10 is used often in various contexts throughout the Old Testament, but the basic meaning is "life." The Servant's whole self was offered in sacrifice for sin. He held back nothing.

"His seed" refers to the multitude of spiritual children the Servant would draw to himself through His atonement. He could not see them with His natural eye during His suffering, but His vision reached into future centuries when those bearing His name would become a great host.

How could the prophet predict the Servant's death, yet still speak of His days being prolonged? This expression refers clearly to His resurrection. His enemies were permitted to cut His physical life short but He conquered death and His "days" are "prolonged" forever.

B. Sinners Redeemed

"The travail of his soul"—another insight into the deep sufferings of Jesus' spirit which far outweighed the physical pain of the Crucifixion.

"By his knowledge" means "by the knowledge of him." It refers to the knowledge of His atoning work. As the Servant imparts this knowledge to others they will be justified when they believe and repent. This statement is connected with the phrase, "for he shall bear their iniquities." This is the basis of justification—the just One's suffering for the unjust (1 Peter 3:18).

Verse 12 pictures the aftermath of battle when a victorious army seizes enemy weapons and property—the spoil. Having defeated the enemy, Jesus has great rewards for those who serve Him. First the Father divides the spoil with the Son. The Son in turn divides it with "the strong"—His followers who also wage war with the adversary. This "spoil" includes all the blessings and victories Jesus purchased by His atonement.

The Hebrew word for "poured out" means to lay bare, to make naked in the sense of emptying. Jesus did this with His very life. He exposed himself completely to God's wrath against sin. Transgressors can now be saved because He makes intercession for them. He pleads their case when they repent and trust Him as Saviour.

LIVING THE TRUTH

If God would go to such extremes to rescue us and make us right with Him, we must be faithful in pleasing Him. He provides the strength we need each day to show forth His life in us, and He has even further blessings and victories in store for us when Jesus reigns over heaven and earth.

EVANGELISM OUTREACH

You may have students who have never accepted Christ's atonement for their sins. This passage shows clearly that God greatly desires to bring men and women into right relationship with himself. "For God so loved the world that he *gave* . . . ." Give an opportunity for unsaved students to accept Christ as Saviour.

TEACHING TIP 6

In small groups, have students work together to see how much of the "Suffering Servant" passage they can reconstruct without referring to their Bibles. Write these guidelines on the chalkboard:

> God's Perspective
> Man's Perspective
> Purpose of Suffering
> Results of Suffering

Allow about 5 minutes for students to work without Bibles on a summary outline and details of the passage. Then give 2 minutes to use Bibles to supplement work already done.

Ask each group to choose a key verse and one word to describe what response they will make to the sufferings of Christ. Give each group an opportunity to share. List the one-word responses on the chalkboard.

Daily Devotional Guide

M. Saved by the Blood. Exodus 12:1-11

T. Christ's Suffering. Psalm 22:1-18

W. Christ's Compassion. Isaiah 42:1-7

T. Christ's Atonement. Matthew 27:33-50

F. Called to Repentance. Acts 2:22-31

S. Salvation Proclaimed. Acts 3:12-26

3

MESSIAH'S MISSION

PREPARING TO TEACH

Study Text
Isaiah 61:1-11

Outline
I. Great News
   A. Divine Credentials
   B. Response to the Message
   C. Two Views
II. Great Blessings to Israel
   A. Restoration
   B. Testimony
III. Great Joy for All
   A. The Song of the Redeemed
   B. The Whole World Blessed

Golden Text
I am come that they might have life, and that they might have it more abundantly. John 10:10

Central Truth
God's offer of salvation is to the whole world.

Learning Goals
1. To describe the Messiah's mission as seen in Isaiah 61.
2. To praise God for His faithfulness and blessings.
3. To choose to live a life of righteousness while waiting for the blessed hope and to select one way to improve in godly living this week.

SEEING THE SCRIPTURES
Isaiah 61:1-10

1. The Spirit of the Lord God is upon me; because the Lord hath anointed me to preach good tidings unto the meek; he hath sent me to bind up the brokenhearted, to proclaim liberty to the captives, and the opening of the prison to them that are bound;

2. To proclaim the acceptable year of the Lord, and the day of vengeance of our God; to comfort all that mourn;

3. To appoint unto them that mourn in Zion, to give unto them beauty for ashes, the oil of joy for mourning, the garment of praise for the spirit of heaviness; that they might be called Trees of righteousness, The planting of the Lord, that he might be glorified.

4. And they shall build the old wastes, they shall raise up the former desolations, and they shall repair the waste cities, the desolations of many generations.

5. And strangers shall stand and feed your flocks, and the sons of the alien shall be your plowmen and your vinedressers.

6. But ye shall be named The priests of the Lord: men shall call you The ministers of our God: ye shall eat the riches of the Gentiles, and in their glory shall ye boast yourselves.

7. For your shame ye shall have double; and for confusion they shall rejoice in their portion: therefore in their land they shall possess the double: everlasting joy shall be unto them.

8. For I the Lord love judgment, I hate robbery for burnt offering; and I will direct their work in truth, and I will make an everlasting covenant with them.

9. And their seed shall be known among the Gentiles, and their offspring among the people: all that see them shall acknowledge them, that they are the seed which the Lord hath blessed.

10. I will greatly rejoice in the Lord, my soul shall be joyful in my God; for he hath clothed me with the garments of salvation, he hath covered me with the robe of righteousness, as a bridegroom decketh himself with ornaments, and as a bride adorneth herself with her jewels.

SETTING THE SCENE
Any question about the identity of the speaker in this passage is answered by Luke 4:17-21. When Jesus was handed the scroll in the Nazareth synagogue, this is the passage to which He turned. He had just returned "in the power of the Spirit" from His temptation (Luke 4:14). The Father had publicly anointed Him as the Spirit descended on Him at His baptism (Luke 3:22). In the synagogue He read the Scripture with such authority that even before He finished the congregation sensed He was speaking of himself ("The eyes of all them that were in the synagogue were fastened

GETTING STARTED

As students arrive, give them copies of the "Scrambled Statements" sheet provided in PATH. Students may work together or separately to unscramble the sentences. Allow about 5 minutes, then call for volunteers to read each sentence correctly. Correct sentences will read:

1. Messiah's mission, as seen in Isaiah 61, was to offer abundant life to the whole world.

2. When God restores His people, both Jews and Gentiles, He clothes them with salvation and righteousness.

3. Since Christ's mission on earth will not be complete until His second coming, our task is to continue His mission to those who need His help.

Clarification

The meek—the humble, especially those whose humility is the result of affliction.

The brokenhearted—from two Hebrews words which, taken together, mean the shattering of one's inner self.

The captives—those taken prisoner by hostile forces. In most passages the Hebrew word also indicates they were exiled to foreign lands.

The opening of the prison—In most passages, the Hebrew word means the opening of the eyes. In Luke 4:18 it is translated "recovering of sight to the blind." In either case it indicates deliverance from a situation of suffering.

Acceptable—favorable.

Trees—oaks or terebinths, the large, flourishing trees common in Palestine.

Planting—In the agricultural society of Palestine, the word described all types of crops, especially vineyards.

TEACHING TIP 1

Read Luke 4:14-21. *Ask:* "What were Jesus' credentials as the Messiah? What evidence showed He was from God?" (See also Luke 3:21, 22;

on him," verse 20). He stopped reading before the words, "and the day of vengeance of our God." His first coming was for salvation, not judgment, so "he closed the book . . . and sat down."

BIBLE COMMENTARY

I. Great News

Isaiah 61:1-3

Isaiah 61:1. The Spirit of the Lord God is upon me; because the Lord hath anointed me to preach good tidings unto the meek; he hath sent me to bind up the brokenhearted, to proclaim liberty to the captives, and the opening of the prison to them that are bound; 2. to proclaim the acceptable year of the Lord, and the day of vengeance of our God; to comfort all that mourn; 3. to appoint unto them that mourn in Zion, to give unto them beauty for ashes, the oil of joy for mourning, the garment of praise for the spirit of heaviness; that they might be called Trees of righteousness, The planting of the Lord, that he might be glorified.

A. Divine Credentials.

(See Teaching Tip 1.)

The credentials an ambassador presents to a foreign nation show his authority to represent his government. On that day in the synagogue Jesus revealed His credentials as the Messiah.

First of all He declared that God had anointed Him. The Jews recognized anointing with oil as an important symbol. It signified the commissioning of men for the offices of prophet, priest, and king. Jesus was all of these. He did not need to be anointed with oil, for He was endued with the power of the Holy Spirit of whom the oil was a type. The Spirit of the Lord God was upon Him.

The Hebrew word *mashiah* and Greek word *christos* means "anointed" and refer to anyone anointed for divine service. We have anglicized these words to "Messiah" and "Christ," applying them to the one Messiah (Christ) for whom the Jews looked and whom we know has come. Usually we omit the article and simply say "Christ," but it is more proper to refer to our Saviour as "the" Christ. Technically this distinguishes Him from all others who have been anointed for a divine mission.

B. Response to the Message

Is there a relationship between Isaiah 61:1 and the Sermon on the Mount? (Matthew 5,6,7). The description of the people who will respond to the Messiah's good news reminds us of Jesus' teaching in the Sermon on the Mount. It is the meek, the brokenhearted, the captives, and the prisoners who will receive the message. Jesus spoke of the blessedness of the poor in spirit, the mourners, the meek, and the spiritually hungry and thirsty (Matthew 5:3-6).

The gospel is offered to everyone, but the proud, the self-sufficient, the self-righteous, and people who are satisfied with this present age ignore or reject it. Those who are conscious of spiritual poverty rejoice at the offer of God's riches. Individuals whose

4:1, 23.) The Spirit descending upon Jesus like a dove at His baptism showed He was anointed by God for His ministry. The work He had already been doing fulfilled the mission described in Isaiah 61:1-3.

TEACHING TIP 2

On the chalkboard or overhead make two columns. Label the left column, "THE SPIRITUALLY NEEDY." Brainstorm with the class on what types of people are most open to the gospel message. List these descriptions in the left column. (The right column will be used later.) Briefly discuss areas in which Christians today can be involved in ministries to these needy people. (i.e., rescue missions, hospital or prison visitation, giving generously to Christian hunger and disaster relief organizations, literacy classes for refugees, telephone counseling for Christian TV, etc.)

Question.

What is the relationship between God's vengeance and His mercy?

lives have been shattered by sin welcome tender hands that will bind up their wounds. The world is full of people who recognize their spiritual bondage and long for deliverance. To these multitudes Jesus' offer of salvation is "good tidings."

Guideline for Living 1

In a real sense, we who are Christians share in the Messiah's mission. We have been left on earth as representatives of Christ. Our mission, too, is to the spiritually needy. We can expect rejection from those who are blind to their spiritual needs. But this passage points out where to start in our ministry to others—with those who are conscious of their need, who desperately need help. Missionaries find such people among the poor, the starving, earthquake victims, those who are in deep sorrow. Refugees from other countries are lonely, bewildered, in need of help. Sick people, the recently bereaved, the unemployed, those in prison—all are in a state of dissatisfaction with life. They need help, and the one who offers help and comfort earns the opportunity to share the life-changing message of the gospel with someone ready to listen.

"The acceptable year of the Lord" beautifully describes the age of grace our Saviour came to introduce. It announces God's favor toward men—favor unmerited but provided freely through Jesus' blood.

C. Two Views

Like many prophetic passages, this one blends the near and distant views. It deals with Jesus' first and second comings. This is why He stopped His reading in the synagogue with "the acceptable year of the Lord." Proclaiming that news was His mission then. His second coming will be very different. The message then will be of vengeance. It is important that we understand the meaning of this word. It is not revenge. There is a sharp difference. God's vengeance must be understood in the light of His holiness and justice. He would not be true to His own nature if He did not ultimately bring to the bar of judgment those who have defiantly broken His laws. It is not a matter of "getting even" as the case is with revenge. God's vengeance is His preservation of order in the universe by enforcing the laws through which He governs.

God's vengeance must not be viewed apart from His purpose to show mercy. If He were not a God of wrath, His mercy would have little meaning. There would be no punishment from which to be spared—no reason to need mercy.

It is significant that in verse 2 the reference to "the day of vengeance of our God" is followed immediately by the Messiah's promise "to comfort all that mourn." This assurance, which continues with the description of other blessings, focuses especially on the delivered remnant of Israel following the day of vengeance. Yet the picture also illustrates the experience of every individual who receives Jesus. He provides consolation for those who mourn over their sins. The change from sorrow to joy is striking. First we see a person in mourning, symbolized by ashes heaped on his head. But he casts off the ashes in exchange for the ornamental

On the chalkboard, label the right-hand column, "SPIRITUAL BLESSINGS." Christ's mission was (and is) to bring spiritual blessings to the spiritually needy. Divide the class into small groups of four to six. Ask students to compare Matthew 5:3-6 with Isaiah 61:1-3 and to list the spiritual blessings found in each passage. After about 5 minutes call for each group to name two or three blessings. List these on the chalkboard.

headdress worn on occasions of rejoicing—the meaning of the Hebrew word translated "beauty."

Then comes the oil of joy—the perfumed ointment poured on guests at festive occasions. In seasons of mourning this ointment was not used. Next the individual puts on the garment of praise—the bright clothing worn during celebrations of joy. Forgotten is the former "heaviness"—a Hebrew word translated "dark" in several other passages. Here it indicates despair—darkness of spirit.

The picture of large, flourishing oaks and vineyards laden with grapes ("Trees of righteousness, The Planting of the Lord") suggests the stability and fruitfulness of every life that experiences Jesus' work of redemption. (See Teaching Tip 3.)

> ## Guideline for Living 2
>
> Jesus came to preach good news, to bind up broken hearts, to proclaim freedom and release, to comfort, to announce God's favor toward men, and to bring beauty, gladness, praise, and righteousness into the lives of those who accept His message.
>
> > Blessed are the poor in spirit,
> > for theirs is the kingdom of heaven.
> > Blessed are those who mourn,
> > for they will be comforted.
> > Blessed are the meek,
> > for they will inherit the earth.
> > Blessed are those who hunger and thirst for righteousness,
> > for they will be filled (Matthew 5:3-6, NIV).
>
> Which of God's blessings have you seen in your life? In what ways has Jesus ministered to your needs in the past? In what way do you need the ministry of the Messiah in your life today?

Clarification

The double—a double portion.

Judgment—justice.

I will direct their work in truth—I will faithfully reward them.

Confusion—disgrace; dishonor. The Hebrew word comes from a root meaning "to wound."

Their portion—the territory allotted to them.

II. Great Blessings to Israel

Isaiah 61:4-9

Isaiah 61:4. And they shall build the old wastes, they shall raise up the former desolations, and they shall repair the waste cities, the desolations of many generations. 5. And strangers shall stand and feed your flocks, and the sons of the alien shall be your plowmen and your vinedressers. 6. But ye shall be named The priests of the Lord: men shall call you The ministers of our God; ye shall eat the riches of the Gentiles, and in their glory shall ye boast yourselves. 7. For your shame ye shall have double; and for confusion they shall rejoice in their portion: therefore in their land they shall possess the double: everlasting joy shall be unto them. 8. For I the Lord love judgment, I hate robbery for burnt offering; and I will direct their work in truth, and I will make an everlasting covenant with them. 9. And their seed shall be known among the Gentiles, and their offspring among the people: all that see them shall acknowledge them, that they are the seed which the Lord hath blessed.

A. Restoration

God's relationship with Israel is based on His covenant with the father of their nation Abraham. From ancient times Israel has often

To help students explore verses 4-7 and understand the details of the restoration of Israel, give each small group a choice of assignments from the PATH "Group study Instructions." Allow about 7 minutes for students to work. Try to get at least one group to work on each assignment: "News Headlines," "Rebus Writing," and "Familiar Tune Rewrite." Ask each group to share its work with the entire class.

failed spiritually, especially in their rejection of Jesus Christ, but God has never abandoned them. To do so would be to break His promises.

The Messiah's mission involves the restoration and conversion of Israel (Zechariah 12:10; 13:1). This will come after terrible suffering. The Great Tribulation is called "the time of Jacob's trouble" (Jeremiah 30:7). Quoting Isaiah, Paul wrote in Romans 9:27, "Though the number of the children of Israel be as the sand of the sea, a remnant shall be saved." With this remnant God will make a new beginning. Isaiah received many revelations of that future day. In one of his prophecies he wrote, "Israel shall blossom and bud, and fill the face of the world with fruit" (Isaiah 27:6).

Throughout the centuries Palestine (now Israel) has often been ravaged by war. Battle always leaves ruins. Cities are wrecked; the land is scarred. When peace comes one of the first tasks is restoring communities as nearly as possible to their former condition. However, due to discouragement or lack of resources some wreckage remains for years as a silent testimony to the horrors of war.

Extensive rebuilding of old ruins (verse 4) has taken place in Israel since the new state was established in 1948. This will undoubtedly accelerate after the Messiah's return. Israel's territory will be expanded then to include all the land God has promised them. They will discover more "old wastes" to build in their enlarged domain. Instead of being under foreign domination, the Jews will hire citizens of other nations to do their farm work (verse 5).

In our own time we have seen the miraculous transformation of the land formerly called Palestine into the vigorous new nation of Israel. However, this is only the beginning. The Jews now occupy but a small portion of the territory God promised the nation when He commissioned Joshua to lead them into Canaan (Joshua 1:3, 4).

Isaiah 61:2 passes quickly to more pleasant subjects after a brief reference to the day of vengeance. At this point the prophet did not stop to tell of the slaughter and devastation his people will endure. Inspired by the Spirit, he looked past the days of sorrow to the time when Abraham's sons and daughters shall accept Jesus as their Messiah and live securely in the land God promised them.

B. Testimony

God commanded Abraham to leave his idolatrous homeland to become the father of a nation which would receive and teach the divine laws (Genesis 12:1-3; Romans 3:1, 2; 9:4). This is still the Jews' ultimate destiny. The greater miracle after the day of vengeance will not be the regathering of the people and the rebuilding of the ruined cities. It will be the outpouring of the Spirit upon Israel (Ezekiel 37:11-14; 39:25-29). They will finally assume their God-ordained role as spiritual leaders of the world. The nations of earth will look to them as God's special representatives. They will fulfill their destiny as His witnesses to all mankind.

Furthermore, the wealth of other lands will pour into Israel (verse 6). God will recompense His people double for their suf-

Question.
In what sense are the Israelites called to be God's priests and ministers?

fering. This reward probably includes both spiritual and material blessings (verse 7).

In verse 8 God assures Israel that He loves justice and hates the robbery and wickedness to which they have been subjected. He will faithfully compensate them for what they have lost through oppression. They will be the beneficiaries of His everlasting covenant—a covenant made first to Abraham and renewed with his descendants after the Messiah's return.

Verse 9 foretells the international effect of God's blessings on Israel. The Lord's goodness to Abraham's descendants will testify to the whole world of His intervention in behalf of those to whom He is bound by an unchangeable covenant. (See Teaching Tip 5.)

Guideline for Living 3

What does the fulfillment of God's promises to Israel mean for us personally? Verses 4-9 describe in detail how God will finally keep His covenant with Israel. He has not abandoned Israel—He will not break His promises. The *faithfulness* of God is seen in this passage. For us today this means simply that God is faithful; we can count on Him. We can build our lives on Him. "Great is Thy faithfulness, O God my Father."

Clarification

Soul—The total self with all its feelings, drives, and emotions.

Righteousness—The Hebrew word is used in many contexts, referring basically to the kind of justice and upright dealings characteristic of those who have a right relationship with God.

III. Great Joy for All

Isaiah 61:10,11

Isaiah 61:10. I will greatly rejoice in the Lord, my soul shall be joyful in my God; for he hath clothed me with the garments of salvation, he hath covered me with the robe of righteousness, as a bridegroom decketh himself with ornaments, and as a bride adorneth herself with her jewels. 11. For as the earth bringeth forth her bud, and as the garden causeth the things that are sown in it to spring forth; so the Lord God will cause righteousness and praise to spring forth before all the nations.

A. The Song of the Redeemed

There is some difference of opinion about the speaker's identity in verses 10 and 11. The context seems to favor the whole nation of Israel, speaking as one man. The symbolism of garments and adornment is similar to the language of verse 3, which clearly illustrates the restored people.

This passage is a spontaneous burst of song—an anthem of praise for God's goodness to those who previously had been scattered, tortured, and humiliated.

Scripture frequently uses clothing as a symbol of personal characteristics both good and bad: the filthy rags of self-righteousness (Isaiah 64:6); the white raiment of holiness (Revelation 3:5, 18), etc. Verse 10 illustrates salvation as beautiful clothing adorned with the kind of jewels a bridegroom and his bride would wear in celebration of their wedding.

The joy of the redeemed is all the more fervent because it celebrates deliverance that follows unbelievable suffering and humiliation.

TEACHING TIP 6

Read Isaiah 61:10, and 11. Ask students to write a definition of righteousness. Then ask them to explore in small groups the key words found in Titus 2:11-14 which describe righteous living. Each group should write one definition of righteousness to share with the entire class.

Ask students to list privately several areas where they need to improve in righteous living. Ask: "What steps will you take to begin worshiping God with your manner of life in one of these areas? Give students 1 or 2 minutes to jot down their thoughts.

TEACHING TIP 7

Guide the class in meditating on the garden imagery of Isaiah 61:11. Point out that as Christ's kingdom comes in our lives, He begins to cover us with righteousness and our lives become full of praises to God. Close the class session by repeating the Lord's Prayer.

Guideline for Living 4

When God restores us to himself He clothes us with salvation and righteousness (Isaiah 61:10). Our responsibility as redeemed people is described by Paul in Titus 2:11, 12: "The grace of God . . . teaches us to say 'No' to ungodliness and worldly passions, and to live self-controlled, upright and godly lives in this present age" (NIV). We must worship God with our manner of life as well as with words of praise.

B. The Whole World Blessed

As Paul wrote concerning Israel, "If the casting away of them be the reconciling of the world, what shall the receiving of them be, but life from the dead?" (Romans 11:15). Isaiah 61:10, 11 is a glimpse of mankind after Israel has returned to God.

Further light is shed on this passage by Paul's statement in Romans 11:25: "I would not, brethren, that ye should be ignorant of this mystery, lest ye should be wise in your own conceits, that blindness in part is happened to Israel, until the fulness of the Gentiles be come in." Every Christian is part of this fullness of the Gentiles.

The Messiah's mission will be complete when the effects of sin have been banished from the earth. Verse 11 is a millenial scene when the Jews and all other nations will worship God.

The prophet uses the imagery of a garden. Seed that had been sown but apparently lying dormant suddenly sprouts. Across the land there are flowers, fruit-laden trees, and plants bearing every kind of vegetable.

This is a view of the day when the whole world will be a spiritual garden. Praises to God will rise everywhere like bursting blooms. Righteousness will cover the earth like beautiful flowers. This will not happen because men have gradually learned to be peaceful and good. The scene of beauty will appear only after God's intervention in vengeance and the Messiah's return as Judge. The government of the world will then be in His hands.

LIVING THE TRUTH

Christ's mission on earth will not be complete until His Second Coming. But in the meantime, we can allow His mission to come to completion in our own lives. We can experience the freedom, gladness, and righteousness Jesus came to bring His people. He wants to minister to our personal needs on a daily basis. Then we must become channels for these blessings to flow out to others.

EVANGELISM OUTREACH

Jesus came to offer abundant life to the whole world. There may be students in your class who have not received that abundant life. Christ stands ready to meet them at their point of need. Ask the Holy Spirit to give you insight into the areas where your unsaved students may be hurting. Appeal to them to accept Christ's comfort and healing for life's hurts.

GOD'S MERCY

SEEING THE SCRIPTURES

Jeremiah 18:1-11

1. The word which came to Jeremiah from the Lord, saying,

2. Arise, and go down to the potter's house, and there I will cause thee to hear my words.

3. Then I went down to the potter's house, and, behold, he wrought a work on the wheels.

4. And the vessel that he made of clay was marred in the hand of the potter: so he made it again another vessel, as seemed good to the potter to make it.

5. Then the word of the Lord came to me, saying,

6. O house of Israel, cannot I do with you as this potter? saith the Lord. Behold, as the clay is in the potter's hand, so are ye in mine hand, O house of Israel.

7. At what instant I shall speak concerning a nation, and concerning a kingdom, to pluck up, and to pull down, and to destroy it;

8. If that nation, against whom I have pronounced, turn from their evil, I will repent of the evil that I thought to do unto them.

9. And at what instant I shall speak concerning a nation, and concerning a kingdom, to build and to plant it;

10. If it do evil in my sight, that it obey not my voice, then I will repent of the good, wherewith I said I would benefit them.

11. Now therefore go to, speak to the men of Judah, and to the inhabitants of Jerusalem, saying, Thus saith the Lord; Behold, I frame evil against you, and devise a device against you: return ye now every one from his evil way, and make your ways and your doings good.

SETTING THE SCENE

Parables and other types of imagery are common in the literature of the East. Some of the prophets' most powerful messages were illustrated by parables or vivid word pictures. This week's study is an example.

Unfortunately, some people associate God's mercy only with the New Testament and see nothing but His wrath in the Old. This week's passage is a striking example of God's offer of forgiveness even as He warned of coming judgment. To illustrate His message God sent Jeremiah to the potter's workshop. There he observed the reshaping of pieces of clay which had to be made into vessels different than the potter had originally planned. Jeremiah quickly saw the picture of God's mercy to His nation.

PREPARING TO TEACH

Study Text
Jeremiah 18:1-17

Outline
I. Broken Vessels
  A. The Skilled Potter
  B. The Imperfect Clay
II. God's Power To Restore
  A. Another Opportunity
  B. God's Sovereignty
  C. Mercy Still Extended
  D. Hands of Mercy
III. Call to Repentance
  A. God's Control of Nations
  B. Divine Warnings

Golden Text
The mercy of the Lord is from everlasting to everlasting upon them that fear him, and his righteousness unto children's children. Psalm 103:17

Central Truth
God seeks to mold our lives according to His plan.

Learning Goals
1. To describe the similarities between the work of a potter with his clay and God's work in our lives.
2. To compare the results of cooperating with God's plans with the results of following our own plans.
3. To respond positively to God's plan for our lives by choosing one way to let Him have more of His way in our lives this week.

GETTING STARTED

Before class begins, write this verse on the chalkboard or overhead: " 'Go down to the potter's house, and there I will give you my message' " (Jeremiah 18:2, NIV).

As students arrive, give each one a small lump of modeling clay. Instruct them to make any shape they would like, share it with someone, and make it into a second shape. When they share their second project with another person, students should tell what the first shape was.

Read aloud Jeremiah 18:1-4. Ask: "In what ways is the work of a potter similar to God's work in our lives?"

Clarification

The wheels—two stone discs joined by a vertical axle. The clay rested on the upper stone, which turned as the potter worked the lower one with his foot.

Marred—spoiled; ruined.

TEACHING TIP 1

On the chalkboard, write the word *POTTER* in vertical letters. Have students pair off to write with these letters an acrostic that describes the work of a potter with his clay and the work God does to mold our lives according to His plan. As a variation, students may put words before as well as after the acrostic letters. For example:

> P lans his work
> O ther ideas in reserve
> Wants T o fulfill clay's potential
> T ries to mold it
> E xpects a useful vessel
> R esult is pleasing

Ask two or three volunteers to share their work. Use material from "Guideline for Living 1" to help students begin thinking about what God's plan for their lives might be.

BIBLE COMMENTARY

I. Broken Vessels

Jeremiah 18:1-4a

Jeremiah 18:1. The word which came to Jeremiah from the Lord, saying, 2. Arise, and go down to the potter's house, and there I will cause thee to hear my words. 3. Then I went down to the potter's house, and, behold, he wrought a work on the wheels. 4a. And the vessel that he made of clay was marred in the hand of the potter.

A. The Skilled Potter

Pottery is one of the oldest crafts. In the beginning the task of shaping the vessels was done with no tools but the potter's hands. The wheels used in Jeremiah's time (see "Clarification") must have seemed like sophisticated machinery. The potter's "house" was his place of business, not his residence.

When the clay was dug from the ground it was brought to the "potter's field," the area near his workshop. After several weeks of drying, the clay was stirred in water until it disintegrated and became thin slime. The stones and lumps were removed by drawing the slime off into settling tanks, and the clay was then pliable and ready for the shaping process.

The potter did not put the clay on the wheel aimlessly. He had a specific plan in mind for the vessels he wanted to make. When God called Abraham to be the father of Israel he had a plan. No Scripture describes it better than Deuteronomy 7:6: "Thou art an holy people unto the Lord thy God: the Lord thy God hath chosen thee to be a special people unto himself, above all people that are upon the face of the earth."

Through the centuries the hand of God had been at work shaping His people to be what He desired. He is the most skillful Craftsman of all. (See Teaching Tip 1.)

Guideline for Living 1

"God loves you and has a wonderful plan for your life," states the first of four "Spiritual Laws" in the Campus Crusade for Christ evangelism booklet. We have been saved for the purpose of letting God's life be made manifest in our lives. At times God allows difficulties to come into our lives to see if we will overcome them through His power. He wants to work through us to bless others. As we continue to let His love show through us, even during upsetting circumstances, He continues to work all things according to His divine plan. Each of us has been gifted by God for ministry. According to our natural abilities, education, and opportunities, we must serve God and allow Him to bless our ministry with supernatural power. "Each one should use whatever gift he has received to serve others" (1 Peter 4:10, NIV). In these ways we discover and fulfill God's plan for our lives.

B. The Imperfect Clay

The Hebrew construction of this passage indicates that what

Jeremiah saw did not happen only once. Some imperfection in the clay made it impossible for the potter to make what he had originally planned for several projects. The vessels kept being "marred"—spoiled. They would not conform to the shapes the potter had in mind.

In the chapters preceding this passage Jeremiah had declared in strong language God's displeasure with Israel. "The sin of Judah is written with a pen of iron, and with the point of a diamond: it is graven upon the table of their heart, and upon the horns of your altars" (Jeremiah 17:1). What could be plainer?

A Scripture we often quote to emphasize the depravity of human nature is found in this indictment of ancient Israel: "The heart is deceitful above all things, and desperately wicked: who can know it?" (Jeremiah 17:9).

These were not heathen God was talking about. They were His covenant people—the nation for which He had designed such glory. As the skilled Potter He was working to make Israel a vessel of great beauty. But the people were like the clay Jeremiah saw on the potter's wheel—resisting again and again the craftsman's attempts to make what he had dreamed of.

Though this passage has direct application to national Israel, Christians have always seen in it a beautiful lesson for individuals. The hymn writer expressed it in words we have sung many times: "Have Thine own way, Lord! Have Thine own way! Thou art the Potter; I am the clay."

II. God's Power To Restore
Jeremiah 18:4b-6

Jeremiah 18:4b. So he made it again another vessel, as seemed good to the potter to make it. 5. Then the word of the Lord came to me, saying, 6. O house of Israel, cannot I do with you as this potter? saith the Lord. Behold, as the clay is in the potter's hand, so are ye in mine hand, O house of Israel.

A. Another Opportunity

The potter did not discard the clay and fling it aside. Though he could not carry out his first design he saw possibilities remaining in the clay. In his mind there were other plans—other vessels whose shapes would be compatible with the characteristics of the clay.

"He made it again another vessel." Do any words describe better the mercy of God? Whether He is dealing with individuals or nations He invariably grants them another opportunity if they fail to meet His expectations the first time.

If this were not true, Israel would have been cast off long before this. Their failures were multiplied. They had disappointed the Potter again and again, but still He was working patiently with them.

Clarification

Vessel—The Hebrew word is used to describe many kinds of utensils. The particular meaning depends on the context of the passage.

Mine hand—an anthropomorphism showing God's complete possession and control of Israel.

Question.

What do you see as the main lesson of the potter's making another vessel?

Guideline for Living 2

In our human weakness, we often fail to live up to the image of Christ that is being formed in us. Think about some of the tragedies or disappointments that may have caused students in your class to feel God would not consider them worthy of a place in His plan:

repeated backsliding, failure in business, divorce, uncontrolled temper, bad habits, alcoholism, lack of education, etc. To each person with one of these or similar problems, God would say, "Can I not do with you as this potter does?" (Jeremiah 18:6, NIV). God always has a plan for us if we will yield ourselves to His molding.

B. God's Sovereignty

This is an important expression: "as seemed good to the potter." The sovereignty of God is one of the great truths of Scripture and also one of the most difficult for human reasoning to comprehend. We must view it always in balance with the freedom God has granted each individual to exercise his own will. God's sovereignty should be a comfort to believers but a warning to the rebellious.

The potter Jeremiah was watching had exercised his sovereignty. He did not have to choose the particular clay he put on the wheels. It was there because he had decided to use it.

Israel had no reason to boast of its favored position. God had chosen them to be His people. He could have called someone else to be the father of His special nation, but He called Abraham.

Of course, natural illustrations break down at some point. We must not go too far in comparing the clay to human beings. Clay has no will of its own. It has no choice but to submit to whatever the potter wants to do with it. Not so with people. As hard as it may be to explain, a sovereign God will work to bring man into line with His will and plan, but the ultimate choice is made by the individual.

C. Mercy Still Extended

We must not read more into Scripture than God intended. In studying this passage we sometimes assume that the second vessel the potter made was inferior to the original design. We are not told that it was. The clay was not made into the same vessel but it would still be useful and serve a purpose. The same patient skill the potter employed as he sought to make the first vessel would be evident as he began the second.

Even as God was warning Israel they were headed for destruction because of their sin He was telling them, "You are still in My hand. I have not cast you aside. I have power to restore and pardon you. Israel can still be a vessel that will bring Me glory."

Question.
How would you apply this truth to individuals?

The clay would never be anything but an ugly lump unless the potter chose to take it in his hands and make a vessel out of it. No person can be what he ought to be if he resists the will of God. He can reach his potential only as he allows the Potter to take him and mold his life.

We are not creatures of chance. God has a purpose in every life. He will not make the same kind of vessel of all of us. Yet each life will be successful as the individual allows God to work out His purpose.

The potter shaped the clay on the stone discs. God shapes us through the circumstances of life by His discipline and providence. A sovereign God, who could destroy us for our failures if He chose, continues to work with us in mercy even if we have disappointed Him.

D. Hands of Mercy

"As the clay is in the potter's hand, so are ye in mine hand."

TEACHING TIP 2

Distribute copies of the PATH "Inductive Study." Have the class divide into small groups to discover answers to these questions based on Jeremiah 18:4-6. Allow 5 minutes for discussion, then have one group report for each question.

TEACHING TIP 3

Give each small group a hymnbook which contains the song, "Have Thine Own Way, Lord" (347, *Hymns of Glorious Praise*). Instruct the groups to read aloud one verse of the song at a time, allowing time to discuss and write down answers to the first two questions on the "Hymn Response" section of the PATH work sheet. Students should write privately their answers to the third question.

Call for reports from each group. Summarize the responses and include comments from "Guideline for Living 3."

Clarification

The virgin of Israel—better translated, "Virgin Israel," the nation betrothed to God.

Vanity—emptiness. The Hebrew word is used for anything unreal or worthless. It often refers to idols.

A way not cast up—a road not built up; a bypath rather than a highway.

A perpetual hissing—a continual expression of astonishment and derision.

What merciful words coming from One whose power is so great.

Before the potter could make another vessel he had to remove the clay from the upper stone and rework it. To the inanimate clay there was no discomfort, but this may not be true of humans. God often had to "rework" Israel by severe discipline. He allowed enemy invasions. The Jews were sometimes captured and used as slaves. But they were still in God's hands. He was working to achieve His plan for His people instead of discarding them.

It is better to feel pain now and be restored to God than to resist Him and endure suffering forever. When we have been "marred" the Potter may have to put us through uncomfortable chastening in order to make us pliable again. If this happens we must not see it as His "getting even" with us but His longing to use us for His glory.

This entire passage presents the sovereignty of God and the free will of man in balance. There is no conflict in these truths.

Guideline for Living 3

God is willing—are you? Unlike the lump of clay, we have a choice. We can choose to let God shape our lives according to His plan, or we can choose to go our own way. The paths where God leads us may not be easy. There are many Christians who feel the blessings of ease, comfort, good health, and wealth should be ours in this life at our request. However, Scripture teaches that God has far higher goals for us than these material signs of prosperity. He desires the prosperity of our souls. We know that in all things God works for the good of those who love Him. He wants to mold our lives according to His plan. We must choose to let Him.

III. Call to Repentance

Jeremiah 18:7-11

Jeremiah 18:7. At what instant I shall speak concerning a nation, and concerning a kingdom, to pluck up, and to pull down, and to destroy it; 8. if that nation, against whom I have pronounced, turn from their evil, I will repent of the evil that I thought to do unto them. 9. And at what instant I shall speak concerning a nation, and concerning a kingdom, to build and to plant it; 10. if it do evil in my sight, that it obey not my voice, then I will repent of the good, wherewith I said I would benefit them. 11. Now therefore go to, speak to the men of Judah, and to the inhabitants of Jerusalem, saying, Thus saith the Lord; Behold, I frame evil against you, and devise a device against you: return ye now every one from his evil way, and make your ways and your doings good. 12. And they said, There is no hope: but we will walk after our own devices, and we will every one do the imagination of his evil heart. 13. Therefore thus saith the Lord; Ask ye now among the heathen, who hath heard such things: the virgin of Israel hath done a very horrible thing. 14. Will a man leave the snow of Lebanon which cometh from the rock of the field? or shall the cold flowing waters that come from another place be forsaken? 15. Because my people hath forgotten me, they have burned incense to vanity, and they have caused them to stumble in their ways from the ancient paths, to walk in paths, in a way not cast up; 16. to make their land desolate, and a perpetual hissing; every one that passeth thereby shall be astonished, and wag his head. 17. I will scatter them as with an east wind before the enemy; I will show them the back, and not the face, in the day of their calamity.

A. God's Control of Nations

The destiny of nations and individuals is in the hands of God. Their indifference, hostility, or rebellion against His laws does not free them from His sovereignty. It only brings them injury and ultimate destruction. Through the centuries many governments have been "plucked up," "pulled down," and destroyed. The student of history may attribute these events to the various pressures and circumstances the nations have encountered. But the Bible shows us God's hand in such upheavals.

B. Divine Warnings

"At what instant I shall speak concerning a nation." God warns before He destroys. He does it in many ways—the preaching of His Word, the outpouring of His Spirit, natural disasters, wars, and providential circumstances of various kinds. He is not willing that any should perish. He delights to show mercy.

Question.
What does the Bible mean when it says God repents?

God never changes. His actions are determined by man's conduct. Even though He pronounces judgment on individuals or nations, if that person or nation will turn from sin, God will turn from the announced destruction.

"Turn from their evil"—that is the key. The Hebrew word translated "turn" also means "return" and is used in some passages to describe Israel's return from exile. In verse 8 it speaks of returning from spiritual exile caused by sin and coming back to God. This is the Biblical meaning of repentance.

Although the Word frequently speaks of God's repenting, obviously the meaning is not the same. In verse 8 a different Hebrew word is used for "repent" than the one translated "turn." It sometimes refers to God's repentance—the change in His dealings with man. We must remember, however, that such divine actions are a change only as viewed from man's limited perspective. The apparent change is due to man's response. God can deal with persistent evil only by exercising His justice in punishment. But His attitude toward those who repent is one of mercy. If His warnings are met with human repentance, the repentant sinner has placed himself in a position where God can show him mercy. It is the individual, not God, whose attitude has changed.

Verses 9 and 10 show that the same principle works in reverse. If God's desire to bless is met by continued sin, He will turn from blessing to punishment. Again the word "repent" is used, and again God's apparent change of stance is due to man's attitude.

TEACHING TIP 4
To compare the results of choosing God's way with following our own plans, assign each small group one of the following sets of Scripture passages: Jeremiah 13:6-10; Romans 8:31-39; Jeremiah 18:11, 12, 15-17; Hebrews 2:10, 11; Deuteronomy 30:15-20; Revelation 1:4-6.

Instruct students to work together to summarize the mes-

This was the danger facing Israel during Jeremiah's ministry. God wanted to bless them but they had turned away from Him. This meant that sending judgment was the only course God could take. Still He continued to call in mercy before unleashing the calamities of which He spoke.

Guideline for Living 4

It is shortsighted and foolish to continue with our own way of living. We cannot see the end results of our choices—God can.

sage of each passage in as few words as possible. Allow about 3 minutes, then ask each group to share their "abridged editions" with the entire class. Brainstorm with the class on key words that describe the consequences of each way of life. List these on the chalkboard under the headings, "God's Way Leads to . . ." and "Our Own Way Leads to . . . ." (Examples: life, glory, justification, death, disaster, uselessness).

TEACHING TIP 5

Changing to a metaphor from a different craft, weaving instead of pottery, read the poem quoted in "Living the Truth." Ask each one to write privately one area of life where circumstances are difficult and in which he needs to let God's character show forth more fully. If you have access to a handwoven blanket or other item, display both sides, showing the contrast between the upper and under sides. Read Ephesians 2:10: "We are God's workmanship, created in Christ Jesus to do good works, which God prepared in advance for us to do" (NIV).

Have students compare their responses to the poem with their response to the hymn, "Have Thine Own Way, Lord." Ask each one to write at least one thing he/she will do this week to let God have more of His way in his/her life.

Daily Devotional Guide

M. Choosing Life or Death. Deuteronomy 30:15-20
T. God's Enduring Mercy. Psalm 118:1-5
W. God's Everlasting Love. Jeremiah 31:1-7
T. Forgiveness Needed. Romans 3:9-18
F. Forgiveness Experienced. 1 Corinthians 6:9-11
S. God's Abundant Grace. Romans 5:15-21

Like little children who would eat candy bars and cookies for every meal if allowed, we choose for ourselves what feels good right now. Neither the child nor we can see the end result of our present choices. In the Bible we see that God greatly desires to lead us to our full potential in Him. The alternative to God's way is ultimately personal disaster.

God's warning, "I frame evil against you" is an interesting illustration based on the work of the potter. The Hebrew word *yasar* translated "frame" is also translated "potter"—one who fashions clay. "Device" means "plan." The potter at the wheel had a plan for the kind of vessel he was making. The divine Potter had a plan for the kind of punishment He would bring on the nation if they did not repent. His plan was "against" them. Only their turning from wickedness could change that plan.

God's description of Israel as a virgin is one He frequently used to describe the nation as a bride He had chosen for himself. But the bride had been unfaithful to the Bridegroom and engaged in idolatry, which produced every other form of sin. In contrast to the perpetual snow on Mount Lebanon and its gushing streams which never failed, Israel had failed God. They had forsaken the highway of His will to wander in sin's endless byways that lead nowhere. If they stayed on this course, God's judgment would leave such desolation in their land that everyone passing through would shake their heads in astonishment. They would whistle (the literal meaning of "hissing") in surprise and contempt.

God would scatter His people like a strong east wind that blows everything before it. Instead of showing His face to them in blessing He would turn His back when their troubles came. If this seems harsh, remember that the nation's response to God's overtures was the impudent reply, " 'It's no use. We will continue with our own plans; each of us will follow the stubborness of his evil heart' " (verse 12, NIV).

God's call had gone out. Israel's future depended entirely on how the people answered. The Potter was ready. How would the "clay" respond?

LIVING THE TRUTH

My life is but a weaving between my Lord and me
I cannot choose the colors, He worketh steadily.
Oftimes He weaveth sorrow, and I in foolish pride,
Forget He sees the upper, and I the underside.
Not till the loom is silent and the shuttles cease to fly
Shall God unroll the pattern and explain the reason why
The dark threads were as needful in the Weaver's skillful hand
As the threads of gold and silver in the pattern He has planned.

—Author Unknown

EVANGELISM OUTREACH

"The Lord . . . is not willing that any should perish, but that all should come to repentance" (2 Peter 3:9). There may be students in your class who have never accepted God's mercy and salvation. Because of the grace and power of God, no sinner is ever beyond hope of redemption.

5

GOD'S NEW COVENANT

Study Text
Ezekiel 36:16-38

Outline
I. Sin Brings Judgment
   A. God's Indictment
   B. The Nation's Punishment
II. God's Purpose Unchanged
   A. God's Name Profaned
   B. God's Name Sanctified
III. Cleansing and Renewal
   A. Deliverance From Captivity
   B. Guilt Removed
   C. A New Heart

Golden Text
I will put my spirit within you, and cause you to walk in my statutes, and ye shall keep my judgments, and do them. Ezekiel 36:27

Central Truth
God is faithful and will fulfill all His promises.

Learning Goals
1. To describe the purpose of the Old and New Covenants.
2. To identify behavior in our lives that may be dishonoring God's name among those around us.
3. To allow God to cleanse and renew our hearts.
4. To determine to follow God's way and make a habit of obeying Him.

SEEING THE SCRIPTURES
Ezekiel 36:16-28

16. Moreover the word of the Lord came unto me, saying,

17. Son of man, when the house of Israel dwelt in their own land, they defiled it by their own way and by their doings: their way was before me as the uncleanness of a removed woman.

18. Wherefore I poured my fury upon them for the blood that they had shed upon the land, and for their idols wherewith they had polluted it:

19. And I scattered them among the heathen, and they were dispersed through the countries: according to their way and according to their doings I judged them.

20. And when they entered unto the heathen, whither they went, they profaned my holy name, when they said to them, These are the people of the Lord, and are gone forth out of his land.

21. But I had pity for mine holy name, which the house of Israel had profaned among the heathen, whither they went.

22. Therefore say unto the house of Israel, Thus saith the Lord God; I do not this for your sakes, O house of Israel, but for mine holy name's sake, which ye have profaned among the heathen, whither ye went.

23. And I will sanctify my great name, which was profaned among the heathen, which ye have profaned in the midst of them; and the heathen shall know that I am the Lord, saith the Lord God, when I shall be sanctified in you before their eyes.

24. For I will take you from among the heathen, and gather you out of all countries, and will bring you into your own land.

25. Then will I sprinkle clean water upon you, and ye shall be clean: from all your filthiness, and from all your idols, will I cleanse you.

26. A new heart also will I give you, and a new spirit will I put within you: and I will take away the stony heart out of your flesh, and I will give you a heart of flesh.

27. And I will put my Spirit within you, and cause you to walk in my statutes, and ye shall keep my judgments, and do them.

28. And ye shall dwell in the land that I gave to your fathers; and ye shall be my people, and I will be your God.

SETTING THE SCENE
When the Israelites were taken as captives to Babylon Ezekiel was among them (Ezekiel 1:1). He was a priest who was also called to be a prophet. His messages deal extensively with the reasons God permitted Israel's captivity. They were His covenant people but had repeatedly gone into idolatry like the heathen. Their oppression by the Babylonians was part of God's discipline to bring

GETTING STARTED

Distribute copies of the PATH "Word Association" list to students as they arrive. Students should write the first word or phrase that comes to their minds as they read each word listed. Volunteers may share responses with the entire class.

These words describe how God viewed the actions of the people of Israel and the consequences of those actions. Read Ezekiel 36:16-20. Point out that today we as Christians may be at times dishonoring God's name among those around us.

Clarification

Son of man—an expression by which God constantly addresses Ezekiel throughout the book. The Hebrew word translated "man" is *adam,* used in the Old Testament for human beings. Apparently God intended to impress Ezekiel that he was only a mortal even though he was receiving divine revelations.

Defiled . . . polluted—both words are translated from the same Hebrew word. Basically it means to become unclean.

Judged—After examining their deeds (as in a judicial process) God had found them guilty and punished them.

TEACHING TIP 1

To illustrate God's standards for purity and holiness, divide the class into small groups to study some of God's laws given to His people. Write these questions on the overhead or chalkboard:

1. What are the general categories of unclean things?

2. What was the purpose of God's laws about ceremonial defilement?

Assign each group one of the following sets of passages:
Leviticus 7:19-27; 11:1-47
Leviticus 12:1 through 13:18
Leviticus 18:1 through 19:21
Leviticus 20:1-7; Deuteronomy 18:9-13

Allow about 5 minutes for

them back to himself. His purpose was accomplished. After their deliverance from this captivity the Jews never returned to idol worship even though they disobeyed God in other ways.

The dominant theme of the Book of Ezekiel is the recurring expression, "They shall know that I am God."

BIBLE COMMENTARY

I. Sin Brings Judgment

Ezekiel 36:16-20

Ezekiel 36:16. Moreover the word of the Lord came unto me, saying, 17. Son of man, when the house of Israel dwelt in their own land, they defiled it by their own way and by their doings: their way was before me as the uncleanness of a removed woman. 18. Wherefore I poured my fury upon them for the blood that they had shed upon the land, and for their idols wherewith they had polluted it: 19. and I scattered them among the heathen, and they were dispersed through the countries: according to their way and according to their doings I judged them. 20. And when they entered unto the heathen, whither they went, they profaned my holy name, when they said to them, These are the people of the Lord, and are gone forth out of his land.

A. God's Indictment

False prophets had often soothed the Israelites' consciences by assuring them all was well even when they were far from God. Ezekiel's message was a sharp contrast. Using clear, forceful language he stood as God's spokesman delivering the divine indictment of the nation.

Once Israel had lived securely in the land God gave them. But instead of demonstrating the beauty of holiness the people had constantly turned to the worship of false gods. Rather than testifying to their heathen neighbors of the one true God they had served the idols of those very heathen.

"Uncleanness"—that was God's word for Israel's condition. The Hebrew word *tame* is used frequently in the Old Testament in connection with ceremonial uncleanness. *Tuma,* translated "uncleanness" in verse 17, is a derivative of *tame.* (See Teaching Tip 1.)

The many laws God gave His people concerning ceremonial defilement were His way of picturing moral contamination. The regulations connected with uncleanness set Israel apart from other nations. In committing such sins as idolatry, the Israelites broke the laws of separation and dishonored God's name.

The Israelites could not blame their present situation on anyone else. It was "their own way and by their doings" that they had rendered unclean the land God had given them. They were not being indicted for only occasional sin. The Hebrew word *derek,* translated "way," means a path worn by constant walking. Disregarding God's laws had become a way of life with Israelites.

Sin has a terrible way of multiplying itself. Once the people

TEACHING TIP 2

On the chalkboard make two columns titled, "BAD HABITS" and "GOOD HABITS." Brainstorm with the class on one list at a time, writing responses on the chalkboard.

Present the material in "Guideline for Living 1." You may wish to ask a class member to give a brief testimony about how God helped him break a particularly bad habit and form good ones instead.

plunged into idolatry they lost all moral restraint. Verse 18 indicates that murder had also become widespread.

If any Israelites asked, "Why are we suffering this way?" they had their answer. Through His prophet God laid bare the nation's record of lawlessness and disobedience.

Guideline for Living 1

Forming the right habits can save a lot of trouble and heartache. Because the people of Israel had formed the habit of disregarding God's laws, they fell into all types of evil and had to suffer the consequences. When we are in the habit of doing good things, we not only receive God's approval, but we will have energy in reserve that can be used in deciding to do other good things. For instance, when we don't have to decide every Sunday morning whether we will attend Sunday school, we can put our energy instead into thinking of ways we can help others, or preparing our minds for worship, or getting up in plenty of time to avoid last minute hassles with the family. Other good habits that need to become second nature in our lives include regular prayer and Bible study, ministry in the local church, tithing, praising God throughout the day.

One of the most important habits to form is the habit of listening to our conscience and obeying what we know God wants us to do. This is the opposite of Israel's way of life. God wants us to be so sensitive to Him that in every circumstance we can hear the still, small voice of His Spirit and choose to obey. (See Teaching Tip 2.)

B. The Nation's Punishment

"I poured out my fury upon them." What a description of divine judgment! *Hema*, translated "fury," means intense heat. Although God had used human instruments to punish Israel, it was His own hot wrath that had gushed out on them.

The Assyrian captivity of the ten tribes in the north had taken place about 120 years earlier. The Babylonian captivity of Judah in the south proceeded in several stages. First, Nebuchadnezzar defeated King Jehoiakim and took him prisoner to Babylon. At the same time Nebuchadnezzar carried some of the vessels from the temple and placed them in his own heathen temple. A number of other captives, including Daniel, were also removed to Babylon. (See 2 Chronicles 36:5-7; Daniel 1:1-7.)

Several years later Nebuchadnezzar returned. This time he seized the rest of the temple treasures. He also carried captive King Jehoiachin and his family along with 10,000 men—the nation's most prominent and skilled—back to Babylon (2 Kings 24:8-16).

Apparently this was when Ezekiel was taken. He associates the beginning of his prophetic ministry in Babylon with the era of Jehoiachin's captivity (Ezekiel 1:2).

Finally, during the reign of Zedekiah, Nebuchadnezzar came back to burn Jerusalem, break down its walls, and take more captives. Only the poorest class of people were left in Judah. As a further act of cruelty, the Babylonians forced Zedekiah to watch while they killed his sons. Then they put out the king's eyes and bound him with chains (2 Kings 25:1-12).

Nebuchadnezzar was not through. Five years after he had burned Jerusalem he returned to take additional captives (Jeremiah 52:30).

Ezekiel declared that all this suffering was the outpouring of God's fury because His people had sinned. Nebuchadnezzar was only the human instrument God had used in disciplining Israel.

II. God's Purpose Unchanged
Ezekiel 36:21-23

Ezekiel 36:21. But I had pity for mine holy name, which the house of Israel had profaned among the heathen, whither they went. 22. Therefore say unto the house of Israel, Thus saith the Lord God; I do not this for your sakes, O house of Israel, but for mine holy name's sake, which ye have profaned among the heathen, whither ye went. 23. And I will sanctify my great name, which was profaned among the heathen, which ye have profaned in the midst of them; and the heathen shall know that I am the Lord, saith the Lord God, when I shall be sanctified in you before their eyes.

A. God's Name Profaned
(See Teaching Tip 3.)

In our society a child's name is usually based on its appeal to the parents or because a father, grandfather, grandmother, aunt, or other relative had the name. To the Hebrews, however, a name was more than just something to call a person. It was bound up with the individual's character or the parents' expectations for him. God himself sometimes gave names or commanded them to be changed, as in the cases of Abraham, Sarah, and Jacob (Genesis 17:5, 15; 35:10).

God frequently gave further revelations of himself to His people by calling himself another name they had not heard before. Each name provided a fresh insight into His character and nature. Thus the name of God could never be taken lightly, for it involved His self-disclosure. To disobey God's laws was to dishonor His name, reflecting unfavorably on His very person. (See Teaching Tip 4.)

Israel's turning from God had discredited His name among the heathen. Because he had to punish His people by allowing their enemies to conquer and capture them, the idolaters assumed that Israel's God was too weak to help them. To the heathen their victory indicated their gods were greater. Since the name of the Lord was so bound up with His people, pagans assumed that the dispersion of the Israelites indicated God could no longer protect them or had even abandoned them.

Guideline for Living 2

As Christians today, we are God's people; we are called by His name. When we disobey God's Word, we fail to show forth His character by the example of our lives and we dishonor His name. Many different statements are made in Scripture about the characteristics of God. Each name or characteristic requires a response on the part of His people. We are being continually changed into His character as we yield ourselves to Him. Consider the following characteristics of God. What response is called for from His people? GOD IS: Almighty (Genesis 17:1); Eternal (Psalm 90:2); All-knowing (Psalm 147:5); Good (Mark 10:18); Holy (John 17:11); Merciful (James 5:11); Love (1 John 4:8, 16); Truth (1 John 5:20).

Clarification
Pity—Although the Hebrew word means basically to have compassion, in this context it means concern or regard.

Profaned—defiled; desecrated.

Sanctify—make hallowed or sacred as distinguished from the common and profane.

Question.
What is the significance of God's concern for His name?

TEACHING TIP 3
As a class, consider some of the key words in Ezekiel 36:21-23. Use information from the Clarification and Bible Commentary sections to help students understand these terms. Ask: "What did it mean for God to have 'pity' for His name?" "What is the meaning of the word *profaned?*" "In what sense did God want to sanctify His name? How would He do this?"

Now that you have talked through several of the key words in this passage, ask students to see if they can write the passage in their own words so the verses are more understandable to them. Distribute paper and pencils and give students about 5 minutes to work on their paraphrases. Call for volunteers to share their work.

TEACHING TIP 4
Write this guideline on the chalkboard: "Describe God's name and the response this name calls for from His people. Distribute several containers which you have filled in advance with small slips of pa-

per each with one of the following passages written on it: Genesis 17:1; Psalm 90:2; 147:5; Jeremiah 23:23, 24; Mark 10:18; John 17:11; James 5:11; 1 John 4:8, 16; 5:20. Ask each student to take one slip of paper, read the passage, and think about his or her answer to the instructions on the chalkboard. Have students pair off to share their responses, then call for volunteers to report their findings.

B. God's Name Sanctified

God was going to deliver His people, but He wanted them to understand it was not because they deserved it. It would be due to His concern for His name. That name had been profaned in the minds of the heathen by the scattering of Israel, but it would be sanctified by their regathering.

Because we ordinarily use "sanctify" in a different context, the word may sound strange as it is employed in connection with God's name. Here the expression has the same sense as "hallowed" in the Lord's Prayer ("hallowed be thy name"). It sets God's name apart from the common, the ordinary, the secular.

By a miracle of divine deliverance Israel would be brought back to their homeland. Idol worshipers would thus see again the power of Israel's God. They might not worship Him, but they would be afraid to disdain His name anymore. They would be awestruck at His intervention against Israel's enemies. God's action would force the heathen to acknowledge they had been mistaken in their previous conclusion that He had become weak.

"The heathen shall know that I am the Lord" (verse 23). This is a recurring expression in Ezekiel's prophecy. God declared again and again that His actions were to show that He is Lord. Even if idolatrous nations did not turn to God, the demonstrations of His power would leave them without excuse. They would have to acknowledge His greatness even if they did not abandon their sin.

Again God uses the word *qadash* ("sanctified"): "I shall be sanctified in you before their eyes." Despite Israel's sin and failure God would still use them to reveal His power, authority, wisdom, and holiness. This was His original purpose for the nation. He called Abraham out of an idolatrous land to become head of a nation entrusted with the divine laws. Israel was chosen to be the channel through which God would speak to the world and ultimately bring forth the Redeemer.

That plan had not changed. Even man's unfaithfulness cannot sidetrack God's purposes. He will overrule human failure and turn it to His glory. This is what God told Ezekiel He would do for Israel, but He wanted them to understand they would have no room for boasting. The punishment the Jews had received was just. They deserved to stay in captivity. No one could have fairly accused God of injustice even if He obliterated them. But this would have been completely inconsistent with His purpose. Because the honor of His name was involved, He would deal with Israel's enemies so forcefully they would have to acknowledge once more, "Their God is the greatest." (See Teaching Tip 5.)

TEACHING TIP 5

Ask: "How can we summarize the message of verses 21-23 in one sentence?" Ask students to write a personalized version of the last half of verse 23. Point out that this was the purpose of both the Old and New Covenants—to "show myself holy through you before their eyes" (Ezekiel 36:23, NIV).

Guideline for Living 3

Israel failed in their mission to show the world what God is like. In their own strength, they could not keep their behavior in line with God's law. But under the New Covenant, we can receive God's own power to live in ways that honor His name. God wants to reveal His power, wisdom, holiness, love, and mercy through us to a world that does not know Him.

III. Cleansing and Renewal
Ezekiel 36:24-28

Ezekiel 36:24. For I will take you from among the heathen, and gather you out of all countries, and will bring you into your own land. 25. Then will I sprinkle clean water upon you, and ye shall be clean: from all your filthiness, and from all your idols, will I cleanse you. 26. A new heart also will I give you, and a new spirit will I put within you: and I will take away the stony heart out of your flesh, and I will give you a heart of flesh. 27. And I will put my Spirit within you, and cause you to walk in my statutes, and ye shall keep my judgments, and do them. 28. And ye shall dwell in the land that I gave to your fathers; and ye shall be my people, and I will be your God.

A. Deliverance From Captivity

The Jews' immediate desire was for deliverance from Babylon. God promised that. However, like so many Old Testament prophecies, this one also looks into the distant future. The Israel of Ezekiel's day would be delivered from Babylon. The Israel of the last days is being regathered from every other nation where they have been scattered. In that future age they will occupy the entire land promised by God to Abraham. This is an important part of His covenant with Abraham and his descendants.

In the Olivet Discourse Jesus foretold the destruction of Jerusalem, which happened in A. D. 70. At that time, our Lord said, the Jews "shall fall by the edge of the sword, and shall be led away captive into all nations: and Jerusalem shall be trodden down of the Gentiles, until the times of the Gentiles be fulfilled" (Luke 21:24).

In our day we have seen the State of Israel established and many Jews returning to make their homes there. However, the present boundaries are but a small part of the land God included in the covenant. To Ezekiel He reveals the time when there will be no more captivities for Israel and they will live permanently within the borders God has planned for them.

Other Scriptures also focus on this final regathering, among them Isaiah 11:11, 12; 43:5, 6; Jeremiah 29:14; Ezekiel 37:21, 22.

B. Guilt Removed

Of more concern to God than His people's physical captivity was their slavery to sin. Restoring them to their land was not enough. They must be turned away from the sin which caused their suffering.

God used the language of the Mosaic ritual to describe Israel's future spiritual restoration. Sprinkling with clean water was part of some ceremonies under the Law. Israelites understood this terminology. "Ye shall be clean"—this mattered more than their being released from Babylon or any other captivity.

"I will cleanse you." They could not cleanse themselves. Like all other sinful humans, they were powerless to remove their own guilt. But the God of grace and mercy would take the initiative to redeem them.

This passage reminds us of Zechariah 13:1: "In that day there shall be a fountain opened to the house of David and to the in-

Ask students to respond in writing to the following question and have them write their response below their personal paraphrase of Ezekiel 36:23: "What changes does God need to make in your life in order to show himself holy through you?" When you see that most students have made their response, ask them to circle one change they will work on. Ask them to keep a record of this decision in a place where they will see it every day this week to remind them to begin developing good habits that honor God in place of old ways of living.

Question.

Why did God promise to give His people a new heart?

Daily Devotional Guide

M. God's Word Is Pure.
Psalm 19:7-14

T. God's Word Cleanses.
Psalm 119:9-16

W. God's Word Directs.
Psalm 119:105-112

T. God's Word Is Eternal.
Matthew 5:17, 18

F. God's Word Is a Weapon.
Luke 4:1-13

S. God's Word Is Powerful.
Hebrews 4:12, 13

habitants of Jerusalem for sin and for uncleanness." (See Teaching Tip 6.)

Guideline for Living 4

The cleansed and renewed heart which God promised the people of Israel has been made available to us today through Jesus' death and resurrection. Because we still have a human nature, we will undoubtedly find ourselves seeking our own ways rather than God's at times. When these occasions come, we must realize we are always welcome to ask again for cleansing from sin. Then we have God's promise that He will do more than simply forgive our sins—He will help us to quit making a habit of sinning. (See Ezekiel 36:27.)

C. A New Heart

Again we are looking past the immediate scene and seeing Israel as they will be when Jesus comes to set up His kingdom. The Jews will not only be home forever, but will recognize Jesus as their Messiah and turn to Him in repentance (Zechariah 12:10).

"A new heart." Here is the miracle of grace. Under the Law the people were constantly reminded that they were unable to keep God's commandments. This applies to everyone, both Jew and Gentile. It is the inner man—the heart—that causes us to sin (Proverbs 4:23; Matthew 15:18-20). Law cannot change the heart.

The reason the Israelites continually returned to wickedness was because their nature was inclined that way. God compared their hearts to hard, unyielding stone. He promised to remove that sinful nature and in its place put one tender and sensitive to His Spirit—"an heart of flesh."

Because God will put His Spirit within the restored Israelites (verse 27), they will have His laws written on their hearts instead of stone tablets. They will live righteously because the Spirit gives them that desire. Born-again believers already enjoy this relationship with God. Under the new covenant, Israel will share the same blessing through Jesus Christ (Jeremiah 31:33, 34; Hebrews 8:7-11).

LIVING THE TRUTH

God puts His Spirit and His laws within us when we trust Christ as Saviour. We are no longer slaves to our human nature. But we have to keep listening to the Spirit and obeying His voice. Being a Christian is not a lazy way of life. It requires determination and loyalty to God, whose people we are.

EVANGELISM OUTREACH

God's offer to cleanse from sin is open to those in your class who have never accepted Christ as Saviour. God is holy and cannot tolerate sin. The only way to get right with God is to accept the cleansing of Jesus' blood. Encourage all your students to let their lives and conversation reveal God to the world.

THE LIVING HOPE

SEEING THE SCRIPTURES

Job 19:25-27

25. I know that my Redeemer liveth, and that he shall stand at the latter day upon the earth:

26. And though after my skin worms destroy this body, yet in my flesh shall I see God:

27. Whom I shall see for myself, and mine eyes shall behold, and not another; though my reins be consumed within me.

Psalm 16:8-11

8. I have set the Lord always before me: because he is at my right hand, I shall not be moved.

9. Therefore my heart is glad, and my glory rejoiceth: my flesh also shall rest in hope.

10. For thou wilt not leave my soul in hell; neither wilt thou suffer thine Holy One to see corruption.

11. Thou wilt show me the path of life: in thy presence is fulness of joy; at thy right hand there are pleasures for evermore.

Ephesians 1:15-23

15. I also, after I heard of your faith in the Lord Jesus, and love unto all the saints,

16. Cease not to give thanks for you, making mention of you in my prayers;

17. That the God of our Lord Jesus Christ, the Father of glory, may give unto you the spirit of wisdom and revelation in the knowledge of him:

18. The eyes of your understanding being enlightened; that ye may know what is the hope of his calling, and what the riches of the glory of his inheritance in the saints,

19. And what is the exceeding greatness of his power to us-ward who believe, according to the working of his mighty power,

20. Which he wrought in Christ, when he raised him from the dead, and set him at his own right hand in the heavenly places,

21. Far above all principality, and power, and might, and dominion, and every name that is named, not only in this world, but also in that which is to come:

22. And hath put all things under his feet, and gave him to be the head over all things to the church,

23. Which is his body, the fulness of him that filleth all in all.

SETTING THE SCENE

Jesus is alive! This is not just a theme for Easter. The Early Church shook the world with the message of the Resurrection. It is the foundation on which the Church is built and the living hope of every individual believer.

This week's study is taken from three passages. The first is the

PREPARING TO TEACH

Study Text
Job 19:25-27; Psalm 16:8-11; Ephesians 1:15-23

Outline
I. The Redeemer Lives.
  A. Light in the Darkness
  B. The Bright Future
II. Hope for the Future
  A. The Grave Defeated
  B. Eternal Joy
III. Resurrection Power
  A. Ultimate Manifestation of Power
  B. The Risen Christ Exalted

Golden Text
This Jesus hath God raised up, whereof we all are witnesses. Acts 2:32

Central Truth
Only the living Christ has power to change lives.

Learning Goals
1. To describe what it means to be "redeemed."
2. To contrast what life is like with and without Christ's resurrection power.
3. To identify one area of life where resurrection power is needed to work in us what is pleasing to God.

Focus the thinking of the class on the true meaning of Easter with a slogan-writing activity. Before classtime, prepare on the chalkboard or overhead transparency the following directions:

BADGE-A-MINUTE

"Take paper and felt pen and create a badge you can wear that focuses on what Easter means to you."

Have one or more tables with the following materials, or have chairs arranged in circles of 4-6 with supplies in the middle: paper, scissors, felt pens, straight pins. Wear a sample badge you have made yourself. Ask students to share their badges in groups of 4-6.

Clarification

Redeemer—vindicator; defender.

Stand—rise up.

The latter day—at the last.

The earth—the dust.

My skin—my body.

Reins—kidneys; a symbol of the innermost being. Job's longing made him feel that this part of him was wasting away, being "consumed."

TEACHING TIP 1

In small groups, have students conduct the "Scripture Search" provided in PATH. Each group will read the following passages and look for answers to one of the questions on the "Scripture Search" cards. Students will research: Leviticus 25:25-28; Ruth 4:1-10; Isaiah 41:13, 14; 43:14, 15; 44:21-23; Galatians 3:13, 14. 1 Peter 1:18,19.

classic selection from Job where we share the revelation that suddenly burst from the lips of God's suffering child. The second passage is from a Messianic Psalm quoted by Peter in his Pentecostal sermon. The third is taken from Paul's letter to Ephesus. Old Testament believers did not have a clear view of the living hope, but they embraced through faith the portion of truth God had revealed to them.

BIBLE COMMENTARY

I. The Redeemer Lives

Job 19:25-27

Job 19:25. I know that my Redeemer liveth, and that he shall stand at the latter day upon the earth: 26. And though after my skin worms destroy this body, yet in my flesh shall I see God: 27. whom I shall see for myself, and mine eyes shall behold, and not another; though my reins be consumed within me.

A. Light in the Darkness

This passage is such a contrast to the way Job had been speaking that it is like a light suddenly flashing in the dark. His words are a revelation from God, not the outcome of human reasoning. Like the prophets on many occasions, Job probably spoke more than he realized.

Verses 23, 24 are not included in our study text but they are an introduction to Job's testimony. The accusations of his "friends" made his suffering even more unbearable. He was weary with their repeated statements that his misfortunes were a sure sign he had displeased God. Job knew this was not true but felt powerless to answer.

He wished he could leave a written record of the real facts. He longed for future generations to know the truth of his innocence. In those days writing often consisted of engraving in stone. This was the kind of testimonial Job wanted—one chiseled with an iron stylus in a rock, with molten lead poured into the letters to make them stand out. (Job's desire has been granted. His words are "printed in a Book"!)

The truth seems to dawn suddenly on the beleaguered child of God. Certainty replaces confusion; Job "knows." He had previously cried for a "daysman" (9:33), a mediator, an umpire, to stand between him and God. The daysman would be an arbiter, reconciling the apparent conflict. Thus far it seemed there was no daysman. Job continued to be tormented by the endless speeches of his companions and what seemed to him the silence of God.

Now God speaks to the heart of His servant. The word translated "redeemer" is the Hebrew *goel*. Originally it referred to a kinsman who saved his relative from difficulty or danger. The *goel* paid the price to free one from slavery when he had sold his services because of his poverty (Leviticus 25:28). He also bought back property sold in time of financial need (Leviticus 25:25). The Book of Ruth provides a clear example of the *goel* in Boaz who redeemed the wid-

Brainstorm with the class on specific things people try to correct in their lives, but often fail at again and again. List these on the left side of the chalkboard. (i.e., losing weight, smoking, controlling one's temper, etc.) On the right side, list words suggested by the class that describe Christ's nature (i.e., patient, loving, kind, self-controlled, etc.) Point out that the purpose of Christ's death and resurrection is to make us like Him. Circle the descriptions of Christ's nature. Ask students to think of this as a seed that has been planted in their spirits at the time of salvation. When Christ redeems us, He puts the seed of His own nature in us. Read 1 Corinthians 15:49.

owed Naomi's parcel of land. Isaiah often describes God as a *goel*, especially in His deliverance of Israel from bondage (Isaiah 41:14; 43:14; 44:24; 48:17).

A number of Bible versions translate *goel* in Job 19:25 as "vindicator." Job was uplifted by the revelation that he had a Vindicator in heaven. Despite the harsh judgment passed on him by his self-righteous "friends," he was now certain God would defend him. No human could be Job's vindicator. What man was powerless to do, God, his *Goel*, would accomplish.

Guideline for Living 1

By His death and resurrection, Christ redeemed us from the power of sin and the penalty for sin. He paid the price to set us free from the consequences of having a sinful, human nature. We are not condemned for having the heredity of sin. The condemnation comes when a person realizes Christ came to deliver him from his sinful nature but refuses to let Him do so. Redemption means that Jesus will put in us His own nature, which is sinless and always seeks to please the Father. When we are redeemed we experience a miracle—God puts His Spirit in our spirit and we are energized by the Spirit of Christ "until Christ be formed in you."

B. The Bright Future

How thorough was the Old Testament believer's understanding of life after death? The resurrection of the dead was a subject which could not be fully comprehended until Jesus died and rose again. The most devout believer who lived before Christ could not have had the kind of knowledge given to Paul and recorded in 1 Corinthians 15. Yet from time to time in the Old Testament we see that God's servants had a partial grasp of this truth, as Job did.

Without realizing it, Job testified to the future work of Christ. He did not say his Vindicator would exist at some far-off time, but was alive at that very moment. This was New Testament truth foreshadowed by the Holy Spirit's revelation in the Old Testament. Job saw Jesus' day as Abraham did (John 8:56) even though his knowledge of the coming *Goel* was incomplete.

"At the last"—at some future day unknown to him—Job said his Vindicator would arise over his dust (the probable meaning of "stand upon the earth") and call his body out of the grave. His vindication would then be complete.

For the present Job would have to endure the slurs of the men facing him. But the sting of their remarks was eased by the knowledge that in heaven his Vindicator, his *Goel*-Redeemer, was alive and he would see Him someday.

Job knew that eventually his body would return to dust. "In my flesh" is probably better translated, "after my flesh." Though he did not possess full knowledge of the subject, we see in this verse that Job understood there would be some kind of resurrection body: "[After] my flesh shall I see God." God had revealed to him that a great change was coming, giving him new life that would be free from the sufferings and limitations of the present world.

Clarification
At my right hand—close by, ready to help and defend.

My glory—my whole being.

Hell—*sheol,* the grave, not the place of torment.

See corruption—undergo decay, as the body would experience in the grave.

II. Hope for the Future
Psalm 16:8-11

Psalm 16:8. I have set the LORD always before me: because he is at my right hand, I shall not be moved. 9. Therefore my heart is glad, and my glory rejoiceth: my flesh also shall rest in hope. 10. For thou wilt not leave my soul in hell; neither wilt thou suffer thine Holy One to see corruption. 11. Thou wilt show me the path of life: in thy presence is fulness of joy; at thy right hand there are pleasures for evermore.

A. The Grave Defeated

We must go to the New Testament for light on these verses. Without the Holy Spirit's revelation to Peter, a reader would naturally assume the Psalmist was speaking of himself (Acts 2:25-31).

Under the Spirit's inspiration Old Testament men of God frequently spoke words which appeared to refer to themselves but did not. Psalm 22:1 is an example. It is actually the Lord Jesus, not the Psalmist, crying, "My God, my God, why hast thou forsaken me?" (Matthew 37:46).

As Peter explained to the crowd at Pentecost, David could not have been referring to himself in Psalm 16 because he was still buried and his body had long ago turned to dust (Acts 2:29-31). As the apostle rose to preach, the Holy Spirit gave him this text as a scriptural foundation for his testimony that Jesus has risen from the dead.

Verse 8 is an insight into the thoughts of the Saviour as He faced the Cross. His agony in Gethsemane was real. The horror of bearing the world's sin was almost more than He could endure. He told His disciples, "My soul is exceeding sorrowful, even unto death" (Matthew 26:38). Luke's account is powerful: "Being in an agony he prayed more earnestly: and his sweat was as it were great drops of blood falling down to the ground" (Luke 22:44).

Yet during the conflict Jesus knew, "I shall not be moved" (verse 8). This means literally, "I shall not be shaken nor slip." The Hebrew word translated "moved" was often used as a figure of speech referring to great insecurity. Jesus knew that even the death He was facing would not defeat Him nor shake His eternal relationship with the Father. That fellowship would be disrupted temporarily while Jesus became sin on the cross (2 Corinthians 5:21; Matthew 27:46), but it would be renewed after the Resurrection. The Lord Jesus would never slip from His exalted position even though men would kill His body.

No wonder our Lord's whole being rejoiced (verse 9) despite the suffering awaiting Him. His very body was strengthened by the assurance of Resurrection victory ("My flesh also shall rest in hope"). This reminds us of Hebrews 12:2: ". . . Jesus the author and finisher of our faith; who for the joy that was set before him endured the cross."

In introducing these words from Psalm 16 Peter told the multitude at Pentecost concerning Jesus, "Whom God hath raised up, having loosed the pains of death: because it was not possible that he should be holden of it" (Acts 2:24). Apart from the Resurrection, death has real pain (literally, "agonies, travail"). Jesus bore the pain so He could take away death's sting (1 Corinthians 15:55). It was impossible for death to hold Him because He is the Son of God.

Jesus knew He would go to *sheol,* the grave. But His body would not stay buried long enough to decay (verse 10). By His victory over the corruption death brings to the flesh, Jesus assured the redemption of both the body and soul of every believer. Though we will die if Jesus tarries, we will receive our immortal bodies when he returns (1 Corinthians 15:51-54; 1 Thessalonians 4:13-17).

B. Eternal Joy

Question.
What is "the path of life" referred to in this passage?

"The path of life" (verse 11) is a picture of Christ's ascension and return to heaven. That path would lead back to the Father's presence. There our Saviour would know again the fullness of joy that was His in the eternities of the past. To save man He had to come to a sin-cursed earth. After the Resurrection He would be with the Father again.

The right hand of a ruler was the place of dignity and special honor. Verse 8 speaks of the Father's being at the Son's right hand to sustain Him during His terrible ordeal. Verse 11 is a different scene—the Son is now at the Father's right hand. He is again in His rightful place (Hebrews 1:3).

Psalm 16:8-11 shows the Lord Jesus facing the Cross and the grave but looking past it all to the eternal future. In this passage He sings the victory hymn even as He faced indescribable suffering and death. Every believer can sing with Him, for we share in His triumph.

TEACHING TIP 3
Ask the following questions to be answered from Psalm 16:8-11:
Why was Jesus able to face suffering and death unmoved and unshaken?
What is meant by the "pathway of life"?
What is our hope for the future?
Ask each one to think privately about these questions: "Have you received Jesus' resurrection life in you? In what ways has this made a difference in the way you live?"

Guideline for Living 2
"Ought not Christ to have suffered these things, and to enter into His glory?" (Luke 24:26). Before His death, Jesus agonized in Gethsemane, but He looked toward the cross knowing the result would be to bring "many sons unto glory." He considered this goal so important that He was willing to pay the price of terrible pain and humiliation. In His triumph over death, Jesus opened to all men the pathway to life—*His* life. His resurrection means that He can give His life to us. When we are "born again," we receive Jesus' own life. One day we will not only experience a new spiritual life, but will have a new body similar to Jesus' glorious body. But for now we can walk "in newness of life," praising God for providing the means for our redemption.

III. Resurrection Power
Ephesians 1:15-23

Clarification
Exceeding greatness—greatness that surpasses and excels.
The heavenly places—the heavenly realms.
Principality . . . power . . . might . . . dominion—rule and authority, whether in the earthly or spiritual realm.
The fulness of him—the completeness of His Being.

Ephesians 1:15. Wherefore I also, after I heard of your faith in the Lord Jesus, and love unto all the saints, 16. cease not to give thanks for you, making mention of you in my prayers; 17. that the God of our Lord Jesus Christ, the Father of glory, may give unto you the spirit of wisdom and revelation in the knowledge of him: 18. the eyes of your understanding being enlightened; that ye may know what is the hope of his calling, and what the riches of the glory of his inheritance in the saints, 19. and what is the exceeding greatness of his power to us-ward who believe, according to the working of his mighty power, 20. which he wrought in Christ, when he raised him from the dead, and set him at his own right hand in the heavenly places, 21. far above all principality, and power, and might, and dominion, and every name that is named, not only in this world, but also in that which is to come; 22. and hath put all things under his feet, and gave him to be the head over all things to the church, 23. which is his body, the fulness of him that filleth all in all.

A. Ultimate Manifestation of Power

Paul gives thanks for what he has heard of the Ephesian believers' spiritual progress. He assures them of his unceasing prayers for them (verse 16), including specific petitions. Paul continually asked God to quicken their wisdom and knowledge. He prays that "the eyes of your understanding" may be enlightened (verse 18). This means literally, "the eyes of your heart." The eyes of our intellect may be enlightened by natural means, but only the Holy Spirit can enlighten the eyes of our heart.

Such enlightenment would mean the increase of their spiritual understanding—"that ye may know" (verse 8). Paul mentions three things expecially that he wants them to know: (1) The hope to which they have been called. (2) God's view of every believer as His own inheritance—rich and glorious. (3) The surpassing greatness of God's power.

It is this divine power that accomplishes everything believers have ever experienced and will experience in the future. That power surpasses anything that can be humanly comprehended. It belongs to the realm of the supernatural. It is not passive, for in verse 19 the apostle refers to God's power "working." The Greek word translated "working" is *energia*, from which we get "energy."

The Bible records many instances of God's power's being demonstrated. But Paul declares that the ultimate manifestation is His raising of Christ from the dead. This is the greatest of all miracles. If we believe it, we have no problem accepting every other miracle in the Bible.

The power by which God raised His Son from the dead is the same power that has saved us and continues to keep us. It is the power by which He delivers us daily from the attacks of Satan. Because God has raised His Son from death, we have a firm basis for believing His power will do for us everything we need in this life and the next. (See Teaching Tip 4.)

Guideline for Living 3

Jesus' resurrection assures us that all the power we need to live a life that pleases God is available to us. If God could raise Jesus from the dead, He is able to supply all the needs we may have. "May the God of peace, who through the blood of the eternal covenant brought back from the dead our Lord Jesus, . . . equip you with everything good for doing his will, and may he work in us what is pleasing to him" (Hebrews 13:20, 21, NIV).

God not only expects us to do His will, but He is in us to do it. We must keep ourselves fit to manifest the life of Christ. This is the purpose of our salvation—to let God manifest himself in our mortal bodies. He is in charge of our lives. Paul said we are "more than conquerors in all these things." It is Jesus' resurrection power working in us that makes us triumph over circumstances and sin, just as He triumphed over death.

Question.
How does Paul apply the truth of resurrection power to our everyday lives?

TEACHING TIP 4
On the chalkboard or overhead draw the following chart. If you prefer, it can be duplicated on paper and given to students to complete:

	Characteristics of a Christian	Characteristics of a non-Christian
Eph. 2:1-10		
Phil. 3:1-11		
Col. 3:1-17		

In small groups, students should gather information to complete the chart. Assign each group one section of the chart to fill in. Allow about 5 minutes, then have groups share their work with the class. Individuals can complete their own copies of the chart as reports are made. Add a third column, "Differences between Christians and non-Christians." Work together as a class to fill in this column.

Use material from "Guideline for Living 3" to discuss the resurrection power of Jesus that makes the difference—that makes it possible to live a new kind of life.

TEACHING TIP 5

Ask each one to write privately one area of his life where he is not experiencing resurrection power and victory. Have each one also write down as many reasons as he can think of that he *should* be receiving Christ's power to show forth His nature.

Close in prayer that God's power will be at work in these areas of your students' lives this week, making them pleasing to himself.

B. The Risen Christ Exalted

The Resurrection and Ascension are part of the same miracle. The Son who humbled himself to become a man and die on the cross returned to heaven after His resurrection and took His place again at the Father's right hand. This is the place of honor, authority, and dignity. He is there now as our Intercessor, our High Priest.

The expressions, "principality, and power, and might, and dominion," emphasize Christ's universal authority. In the New Testament these words refer both to earthly rulers and the hierarchy of angels, fallen and unfallen. Jesus has been exalted above all of them.

To help us comprehend fully our Lord's exaltation, Paul adds the words, "and every name that is named." As further emphasis he says this refers to the present world and the one to come. The Name is eternally preeminent. It will never be eclipsed by any other. No name of man or angel is worthy of comparison. Jesus has died, risen, ascended, and rules from His throne. We worship Him as Lord and King.

"Under his feet" probably refers to Psalms 8:6 and 110:1. Paul uses the same terminology in 1 Corinthians 15:27. This declares Christ's universal dominion. The expression seems to recall the ancient practice of a conqueror placing his foot on the neck of defeated enemies. However, it is not only enemies who are under Christ's feet. "All things" are subject to Him, including creation itself.

In His exaltation Christ is also Head of the Church. It is His body. He fills it with His life and demonstrates through it the power by which He was raised from the dead.

LIVING THE TRUTH

Through the Holy Spirit, God fills with the life of Christ those who have been redeemed. He then begins to work out in us the nature of Christ as we obey Him. It is a miracle: we can live a totally new life! Paul said his ultimate goal in life was "that I may know him, and the power of His resurrection" (Philippians 3:10). God's ultimate purpose in us is that His Son's resurrection life shall be manifested in us.

EVANGELISM OUTREACH

The power of the Resurrection shows that sinners can be turned into saints. Twisted and unhappy lives can be put right. To the extent we have experienced God's power in our lives, we are able to realize that God can change *anyone*. Pray that the Spirit will reveal to unsaved students in your class what they are really like in God's sight. Give them the opportunity to accept Christ's redemption and to experience His resurrection power at work in their lives.

Golden Text
Come, and let us return unto the Lord: for he hath torn, and he will heal us; he hath smitten, and he will bind us up. Hosea 6:1

Central Truth
God is longsuffering and reaches out to us in love.

Learning Goals
1. To contrast the difference between God's attitude toward Israel and Israel's attitude toward God.
2. To identify areas in our lives where we need God's forgiveness.
3. To choose ways to demonstrate our faithfulness to God in response to His love.

SEEING THE SCRIPTURES
Hosea 11:1-11

1. When Israel was a child, then I loved him, and called my son out of Egypt.
2. As they called them, so they went from them: they sacrificed unto Baalim, and burned incense to graven images.
3. I taught Ephraim also to go, taking them by their arms; but they knew not that I healed them.
4. I drew them with cords of a man, with bands of love: and I was to them as they that take off the yoke on their jaws, and I laid meat unto them.
5. He shall not return into the land of Egypt, but the Assyrian shall be his king, because they refused to return.
6. And the sword shall abide on his cities, and shall consume his branches, and devour them, because of their own counsels.
7. And my people are bent to backsliding from me: though they called them to the Most High, none at all would exalt him.
8. How shall I give thee up, Ephraim? how shall I deliver thee, Israel? how shall I make thee as Admah? how shall I set thee as Zeboim? mine heart is turned within me, my repentings are kindled together.
9. I will not execute the fierceness of mine anger, I will not return to destroy Ephraim: for I am God, and not man; the Holy One in the midst of thee: and I will not enter into the city.
10. They shall walk after the Lord: he shall roar like a lion: when he shall roar, then the children shall tremble from the west.
11. They shall tremble as a bird out of Egypt, and as a dove out of the land of Assyria: and I will place them in their houses, saith the Lord.

SETTING THE SCENE
Love despite unfaithfulness—that is the theme of Hosea. God often expressed His love for Israel even in the face of their waywardness, but He did it in an unusual way through Hosea. The prophet experienced the heartbreak of loving a wife who forsook him to live an immoral life with many lovers. She fell so low that even her former paramours disdained her (2:7, 10). Yet Hosea's love for his wife never failed. Finally he went to the slave market and paid the price to recover her. As no other prophet, Hosea could understand the love of God for the nation He frequently calls His bride. Israel, like Hosea's wife, had been unfaithful. Yet God never stopped loving her and seeking to recover her.

GETTING STARTED

As students arrive, give them copies of the PATH "Lifeline" sheet. Ask them to complete their sheets privately. This will help them identify areas of their lives where they have been inconsistent in their relationship with God, just as the nation of Israel was.

Begin the class session by drawing on the chalkboard or overhead a line representing the ups and downs of Israel's relationship with God. In general, this line should gradually get farther and farther from the straight line representing God's plan for His people. Read Hosea 11:1, 2.

Clarification

Ephraim—the dominant tribe of the northern kingdom where Hosea prophesied. In this passage Ephraim is synonymous with Israel.

Cords of a man—the kind of halter a parent would use to lead a young child, as opposed to the strong ropes used in taming or breaking unmanageable animals.

Laid meat unto them—bent down to feed them.

TEACHING TIP 1

Collect magazine pictures of children and families. You could make one composite picture on notebook paper and Xerox it for each student, or else bring enough different pictures to have one for each small group.

In groups of four to six, have students look at one or more pictures and respond to these questions. List these on the chalkboard or overhead transparency:

1. What hopes might a parent have for this child?

2. What feelings does this parent have for this child?

3. What problems might

BIBLE COMMENTARY

I. God Yearns for the Wayward

Hosea 11:1-6

Hosea 11:1. When Israel was a child, then I loved him, and called my son out of Egypt. 2. As they called them, so they went from them: they sacrificed unto Baalim, and burned incense to graven images. 3. I taught Ephraim also to go, taking them by their arms; but they knew not that I healed them. 4. I drew them with cords of a man, with bands of love: and I was to them as they that take off the yoke on their jaws, and I laid meat unto them. 5. He shall not return into the land of Egypt, but the Assyrian shall be his king, because they refused to return. 6. And the sword shall abide on his cities, and shall consume his branches, and devour them, because of their own counsels.

A. The Beloved Son.

What period of Israel's national history was God referring to by the statement, "When Israel was a child"?

Yearning is a word that describes the feelings of God expressed in this passage. He reminds Israel of His past mercies, especially their deliverance from Egypt. The nation was in its infancy during that period; hence God's description of it as His child. "Then I loved him"—the tender words of a parent whose heart aches to have a son back in his arms even though he has now grown to manhood.

Matthew quotes this verse in connection with Jesus' being taken to Egypt as an infant, then brought back to His homeland after the danger to His life was past (Matthew 2:13-15). This is another example of a prophecy's merging two views and two time periods. God was referring here to His deliverance of the young nation of Israel from Egyptian slavery. But—probably unknown to Hosea— the passage blends together the experiences of the covenant people and their Messiah. God was identifying Jesus with the nation of Israel centuries before He was born in Bethlehem.

God's tone is still one of deepest love. His words are full of sorrow as He remembers how His people have spurned His affection. In verse 2, He recalls that the more He called His son Israel, the farther Israel went away from Him. Invariably such rebellion led to idolatry. The son who was called out of bondage turned from the service of his Father to worship idols of every kind.

B. The Faithful Father

Elsewhere in the Book of Hosea, God uses the figure of husband and wife to emphasize His love for Israel. In this passage He illustrates it by the father-son relationship. Both figures reveal beautifully the tender heart of God.

Those who say the Old Testament reveals a harsh God should read this passage carefully. Verse 3 shows Him as a loving parent teaching infants to walk, "taking them by their arms." What father and mother can forget the concern they felt as they helped their little ones take those first steps?

parents face in this child's future?

Use the material in the Bible Commentary to draw parallels to this discussion in the relationship between Israel and God.

How was this love treated? It was ignored, God said. His desire to heal the nation and restore them spiritually was treated with complete indifference as though the people did not even know who their Healer was (verse 3).

Guideline for Living 1

God's love for His people can be compared to a parent's love for a son or daughter. Consider the following concerns and characteristics that are true of parents and which illustrate God's love for us. A parent (and God):
—desires that the child be healthy and strong
—wants the child to grow and develop normally
—hopes to see the child enjoy happiness and success
—plans for the child's safety and well-being
—wants what is best for the child
—has compassion on a child who has been injured or offended
—provides for the child's basic needs
—disciplines and trains a child to get along well in relationships with others.
—instructs the child in the things he needs to know
—does not disown a child for disappointing behavior
—still loves a rebellious child
—desires an enjoyable relationship with the child, with love returned to the parent by the child.

Question.
Why does God use several types of imagery in this passage?

There are some subjects where a single illustration cannot give the whole picture. One symbol alone could not demonstrate to Israel the completeness of God's love. Now He describes himself in another way. He is a Farmer, kind and humane. First He refers to the cords of love by which He constantly sought to draw His people. These bands were quite different from the strong ropes used in taming animals who resisted control. Then God pictures himself loosening the straps by which the ox's yoke is fastened to its neck so He can give the animal food and water (verse 4). The Hebrew wording shows the farmer actually bending down to deliver the food to his beast. A pastoral people could understand such language, and God used it as another illustration of His love for those who returned His kindness with ingratitude.

C. Inevitable Consequences

Now God begins His warning of the inevitable consequences of Israel's apostasy (verses 5, 6). The Lord is longsuffering. He will hold back His judgment as long as possible, showing love and mercy to the fullest extent. But His law of sowing and reaping is inexorable, and eventually rebels must pay for their deeds. The Assyrian captivity was coming, and it would be worse than the bondage of Egypt. The sword—Biblical symbol of judgment—would descend on the idolatrous nation. God did not love them less, but His concern for them demanded discipline. The time of grace and mercy had been extended for a long time. Now it was ready to expire.

Clarification
Backsliding—turning away, being disloyal or faithless.

Admah, Zeboim—cities destroyed with Sodom and Go-

II. Sorrows of Backsliding

Hosea 11:7, 8

Hosea 11:7. And my people are bent to backsliding from me; though they called them to the Most High, none at all would exalt

morrah (Deuteronomy 29:23).

Mine heart is turned—an indication of a change from wrath to mercy on God's part.

My repentings are kindled—my compassion is stirred.

Question.
Why did the expression, "backsliding," fit the actions of the Israelites in Hosea's day?

TEACHING TIP 2
Ask: "In what ways do we sometimes show evidence that our minds are out of touch with God?" Distribute copies of the following checklist which is provided in PATH:

Not thinking of the needs of others

Overlooking the ways my actions and words affect others

Ignoring opportunities to help others

Neglecting to read God's Word and pray

Not trusting God

Making choices and plans based on selfish desires

Thinking or speaking unkindly of others

Unreasonable behavior

Overindulgence in certain pleasures

Being anxious and worried

Other _____

Ask students to complete the checklist privately. Then read aloud Psalm 51:1, 2, 10. Ask each one to write these verses in his own words below the checklist.

him. 8. How shall I give thee up, Ephraim? how shall I deliver thee, Israel? how shall I make thee as Admah? how shall I set thee as Zeboim? mine heart is turned within me, my repentings are kindled together.

A. Human Rebellion
The attitude of Israel was stubbornly defiant. They were not innocently trapped by sin. The nation was "bent" in the wrong direction—"hung up" on backsliding as the Hebrew wording indicates.

We sometimes use the term *backsliding* to describe Christians who have grown spiritually cold. They have become inconsistent in their church attendance, seldom pray or read the Bible, and probably are involved in worldly activities. Such a condition does betray a turning back toward this present age, but as God uses "backsliding" here it is a far more serious term. It denotes actual apostasy. The people to whom God had delivered His laws not only turned away from Him but gave themselves to idolatry. They were not merely cold in heart; they were open rebels. Their disloyalty to God was not passive; it was determined and deliberate.

"Though they called them to the Most High, none at all would exalt him." "They" seems to refer to God's prophets who called the nation to Him but met with constant indifference or hostility. Despite the repeated calling the people would not exalt God nor give Him glory.

The whole picture shows what happens to those who have had spiritual light but have turned from it. When someone closes his eyes to truth he becomes more blind and confused than those who have had no contact with God's way. Israel's disregard of the prophets' cries made their hearts harder than those who had not heard such preaching.

This was nothing new. Jeremiah frequently spoke of "backsliding Israel" (Jeremiah 3:6, 8, 11, 12). Disloyalty to the God who had brought them out of bondage and made them His covenant people had become a tragic way of live with Abraham's descendants. They often suffered greatly for it. Under pressure they invariably cried to God for help. When He gave it they would serve Him again for a time, only to return eventually to their old ways. (See Teaching Tip 2.)

Guideline for Living 2
Parents who have known the sorrow of a rebellious, wayward child, or a spouse who has been rejected and abandoned can identify with the pain God felt at Israel's habitual backsliding. On a smaller scale, God's children today may find themselves in a position similar to Israel's. Instead of trusting God, we may choose to figure things out for ourselves. Instead of turning to God in times of trouble, we may complain and worry. Instead of treating a person in need with the compassion of Christ, we may treat them heartlessly or pass them by because of our busy schedule. Instead of seeking first to let Christ's life be manifested in us, we get sidetracked in pursuing earthly interests. While we may not be openly rebellious, there are many things that can hinder our relationship with God. We have to consciously work at coming to God to let His will be done in us. This is what pleases the Father.

B. Divine Compassion

The human reaction to such treatment would be, "They deserve anything that happens to them. I'm not going to spend any more time trying to help them." But God is not a man. His mercy is so far beyond human comprehension that our minds have difficulty understanding its depths. The most amazing aspect of His love is the way He extends it repeatedly to those who spurn it. Nowhere is this demonstrated more than in His dealings with Israel.

Question.
Why did God refer to the ancient cities of Admah and Zeboim?

Verse 8 reveals the tenderness of God's heart as few other passages do. Israel deserved to be handed over to their enemies. Their sin merited the severest chastisement. God would be just if He annihilated the rebels. He reminds them that such judgment had happened before. Sodom and Gomorrah and the nearby cities, Admah and Zeboim, are reminders that even God's mercy has its limits. There is a point at which He must demonstrate that sinners cannot escape paying the price for their godless way of living.

Israel was approaching such a place. But the heart of God cries out, "How can I do it? How can I surrender my people to their enemies? How can I deliver to judgment those I love so much?"

TEACHING TIP 3
Ask a student to prepare and present a 2-minute report explaining who "Ephraim" is and what happened to the cities of Admah and Zeboim. Use a Bible dictionary and a commentary. You might also give this student a copy of the *Adult Teacher* commentary.

"Mine heart is turned within me." This exprsses God's deepest yearning that He will not have to execute the judgment Israel deserves. The depths of His nature revolts at the idea. Judgment is His strange work. He longs to show mercy. Through Hosea He pleads again with His people to change their attitude and ways so He can spare them.

God's compassion is "kindled." It is warm and intense. In the face of unending defiance of His laws, His heart burns with love for the nation He calls His son.

Again the idea of repentance on God's part does not mean any change in His nature or purpose. He is ready to turn when man turns. He can change His dealings from wrath to mercy when sinners turn toward Him instead of away from Him. This is the only way God can "repent." (See Teaching Tip 3.)

III. God Will Forgive
Hosea 11:9-11

Hosea 11:9. I will not execute the fierceness of mine anger, I will not return to destroy Ephraim: for I am God, and not man; the Holy One in the midst of thee: and I will not enter into the city. 10. They shall walk after the Lord: he shall roar like a lion: when he shall roar, then the children shall tremble from the west. 11. They shall tremble as a bird out of Egypt, and as a dove out of the land of Assyria: and I will place them in their houses, saith the Lord.

A. Mercy, Not Destruction

Clarification
Tremble—shake. In this context the shaking is not from fear but eager anticipation.
From the west—from the lands of the West, the countries in the Mediterranean region.

God has already given ample reason the Israelites deserve severe punishment. He does not minimize their sin and rebellion. They have consistently spurned His love and pleadings.

Scripture shows many results of God's executing "the fierceness of His anger." The Hebrew word translated "fierceness" means "heat," and is frequently used in Scripture to picture divine anger. The word translated "execute" is used in many passages to describe the activities of God in various areas. Here it refers to His activity

Question.

What is the significance of the statement, "I am God, and not man"?

in the fiery heat of judgment. In verse 8 God has already reminded Israel what this activity was like when He turned the cities of the plain to ashes.

But God will now act toward His people in mercy. "I will not return to destroy Ephraim" means "I will not destroy Ephraim again." There had been times in the past when these people had felt the blows of divine judgment, but God is not going to repeat them in the immediate future. This promise is in harmony with the spirit of compassion He has expressed in verse 8: "How shall I give thee up, Ephraim?" There would be a time in the future when God would have to send the judgment He is now postponing. Tragically, His people did not turn permanently from their waywardness. But for now the Lord is not going to execute His wrath as He did upon Admah, Zeboim, Sodom, and Gomorrah. He will extend the season of mercy and continue to plead with His people to repent. (See Teaching Tip 4.)

We are so accustomed to human attitudes that it is difficult for us to comprehend the contrast between God's thinking and man's. If God were man, there would be no hope for Israel. But we must not measure Him by our own standards. Man is ruthless and vindictive, eager for revenge. He enjoys punishing his enemies until he exterminates them. The carnal nature is pleased when it can return more blows than it has received.

Not so with God. He punishes so there may be eventual healing, not destruction. He exercises discipline to bring offenders back to himself, not to wipe them out.

Furthermore, man often breaks his promises. He may agree to show mercy but then change his mind. God will not do this. When He says, "I will not destroy," He will not destroy. When He says, "I will show mercy," He will show mercy.

Man is impatient. If his enemies are slow to change their ways he cannot wait. There can be no second chance; he must strike back now. But God is "slow to anger" (Psalm 103:8). When He does bring judgment it is only after repeated and prolonged warnings and entreaties to the guilty parties. A tremendous truth is bound up in this simple statement: "I am God, and not man."

Mercy is not something God decides to show on certain occasions. It is an integral part of His nature. When He contrasts His ways with man's He is speaking of two completely opposite natures.

God also refers to himself as "the Holy One." His people must never forget that side of His nature. There are two aspects to this truth. God's holiness demands that He chasten the disobedient. He cannot simply look the other way when people sin. But as the Holy One He also loves and forgives when His plea for repentance is answered positively.

Furthermore, the Holy One was not a far-off Being out of touch with the situation and only vaguely interested. He was "in the midst of thee," among His people. He constantly observed their activities and heard their conversation. He knew when they sinned; He also knew when they suffered.

There is some disagreement among Bible scholars about the meaning of the statement, "I will not enter into the city." The best explanation seems to be that God was not coming in wrath or fury to punish as He had done to other cities. This is a further expression of His long-suffering.

B. Restoration, Not Oblivion

Again we have a passage that refers to the near future but also looks past it to a distant day. The ultimate restoration of Israel will be in the last days when they return to their homeland and accept Jesus Christ as their Messiah. Though that time was far away in Hosea's day, God mentioned it frequently through His prophets.

"They shall walk after the Lord" pictures the Israelites' obedience to God's summons from the lands of their dispersion, especially in the last days. It also indicates their spiritual restoration as they turn from rebellion to obedience.

"He shall roar like a lion"—an example of the strong imagery used so much in the literature of the East. There is nothing weak or uncertain about a lion's roar. When God calls His children back to their land forever, He will do it with authority. His command will be so clear that they will respond quickly and eagerly—like birds winging their way rapidly homeward.

"The west . . . Egypt . . . Assyria." This indicates that the Children of Israel will be scattered widely—that dispersion is destined to end. God's covenant people will some day be back in their Promised Land to leave no more. When they hear God's "roar," they will hasten home.

"As a dove" is an apparent contrast to God's previous indictment of the nation as "a silly dove" (Hosea 7:11). The silly dove would not go to its own nest, but in the time of restoration it will fly straight to its home.

"I will place them in their houses"—a beautiful picture of the day when Israel's wanderings are over. The NIV translates it, "I will settle them in their homes." At last they will have the peace and security they had lost so often by their sinning. They will worship and serve the Messiah they rejected and crucified when He came the first time.

Since God is not a man He will not forget His covenant with Abraham and his descendants. Since He is not a man He seeks opportunities to demonstrate compassion, not revenge.

LIVING THE TRUTH

The appropriate response to God's tender love is a commitment to follow His way. Following the Lord requires the same willingness Abraham displayed when he left everything to follow God. God desires our complete trust and devotion. He wants us to remain faithful in times of testing, and even to be thankful for these times which give Him the opportunity to display His supernatural life in our lives. As we study God's Word each day, we need to let Him speak to us about attitudes He wants us to have and actions He wants us to take. God wants to make a difference in our lives.

EVANGELISM OUTREACH

God's call and yearning for the wayward applies to unsaved students in your class. Have they realized the price God paid to make it possible for them to have fellowship with Him? God's forgiveness is not just a lenient willingness to overlook our faults. His justice demands a price to be paid for willful disregard of His laws. That price was paid by Jesus. Ask anyone who wants to know more about salvation to stay and talk with you after class.

FAITH IN TROUBLED TIMES | 8

SEEING THE SCRIPTURES

Habakkuk 1:1-4

1. The burden which Habakkuk the prophet did see.

2. O Lord, how long shall I cry, and thou wilt not hear! even cry out unto thee of violence, and thou wilt not save!

3. Why dost thou show me iniquity, and cause me to behold grievance? for spoiling and violence are before me: and there are that raise up strife and contention.

4. Therefore the law is slacked, and judgment doth never go forth: for the wicked doth compass about the righteous; therefore wrong judgment proceedeth.

2:1-4, 20

1. I will stand upon my watch, and set me upon the tower, and will watch to see what he will say unto me, and what I shall answer when I am reproved.

2. And the Lord answered me, and said, Write the vision, and make it plain upon tables, that he may run that readeth it.

3. For the vision is yet for an appointed time, but at the end it shall speak, and not lie: though it tarry, wait for it; because it will surely come, it will not tarry.

4. Behold, his soul which is lifted up is not upright in him: but the just shall live by his faith.

20. The Lord is in his holy temple: let all the earth keep silence before him.

3:16-19

16. When I heard, my belly trembled; my lips quivered at the voice: rottenness entered into my bones, and I trembled in myself, that I might rest in the day of trouble: when he cometh up unto the people, he will invade them with his troops.

17. Although the fig tree shall not blossom, neither shall fruit be in the vines; the labor of the olive shall fail, and the fields shall yield no meat; the flock shall be cut off from the fold, and there shall be no herd in the stalls:

18. Yet I will rejoice in the Lord, I will joy in the God of my salvation.

19. The Lord God is my strength, and he will make my feet like hinds' feet, and he will make me to walk upon mine high places.

SETTING THE SCENE

We should not be misled by the term "minor" prophets. There is nothing minor about their messages. The expression is used because these books are short compared to the longer prophecies called "major." Although the Book of Habakkuk contains only three chapters, it is quoted several times in important New Testament

APRIL 21, 1985

247

PREPARING TO TEACH

Study Text
Book of Habakkuk

Outline
I. Perplexing Questions
  A. A Godly Man's Despair
  B. Ineffective Law
II. God's Answer
  A. The Waiting Watchman
  B. The Necessity of Faith
  C. God's Absolute Authority
III. Triumphant Faith
  A. A Believer's Alarm
  B. A Believer's Victory

Golden Text
The just shall live by his faith. Habakkuk 2:4

Central Truth
God's work is not defeated by the sinfulness of man.

Learning Goals
1. To compare the troubled times and perplexing questions of Habakkuk's day with today's.
2. To express both confidence in God's control of our circumstances and willingness to wait for Him to act.
3. To determine to rejoice in the Lord during a specific troubling circumstance.

GETTING STARTED

Before class, write this question on the chalkboard or overhead transparency: "What are the most troubling issues Christians face today?"

Give copies of the PATH "News Headlines" sheet to students as they arrive to help them start thinking about the perplexing questions and troubled times people face.

Begin the class session by having students form groups of three to discuss the question on the chalkboard for 3 minutes. Ask them to agree on five major issues. Call for a few of the groups to tell the rest of the class what they felt were the major troubling issues. State your learning goals and read aloud Habakkuk 1:1-4.

Clarification

Burden—from the Hebrew *massa,* frequently applied to prophetic utterances. The word basically means a load. The prophetic messages called burdens were often heavy with warnings of judgment, although there are exceptions.

Grievance—The Hebrew word refers to the kind of misery connected with unpleasant toil.

Spoiling—havoc, destruction.

Slacked—grown numb, paralyzed.

TEACHING TIP 1

Ask, "What were Habakkuk's perplexing questions and complaints to God?" Ask students to scan Habakkuk 1:1-4, looking for these questions. Call for volunteers to state these questions in their own words and write the responses on the chalkboard.

TEACHING TIP 2

Divide the class into small groups to discuss what the Christian's attitude should be in the midst of troubling circumstances and perplexing

passages: Acts 13:40, 41 (Habakkuk 1:5), Romans 1:17, Galatians 3:11, Hebrews 10:38 (Habakkuk 2:4). The prophecy is mostly a series of conversations between Habakkuk and God. The prophet cries out in perplexity over circumstances he cannot understand, and God answers. Despite his many questions, Habakkuk concludes his message with a strong testimony of faith.

BIBLE COMMENTARY

I. Perplexing Questions

Habakkuk 1:1-4

Habakkuk 1:1. The burden which Habakkuk the prophet did see. 2. O Lord, how long shall I cry, and thou wilt not hear! even cry out unto thee of violence, and thou wilt not save! 3. Why dost thou show me iniquity, and cause me to behold grievance? for spoiling and violence are before me: and there are that raise up strife and contention. 4. Therefore the law is slacked, and judgment doth never go forth: for the wicked doth compass about the righteous; therefore wrong judgment proceedeth.

(See Teaching Tip 1.)

A. A Godly Man's Despair

Little actually changes in human affairs. Few problems today trouble believers more than the question that perplexed Habakkuk: Why does God seem to be silent in the face of widespread sin and injustice?

Habakkuk saw many situations comparable to those with which we struggle in our own time. The godly were afflicted while the wicked prospered. Worse than that, the wicked were suffering no punishment. It was as though God paid no attention or was unconcerned. We know this is never true, but some conditions might make it seem that way. (See Teaching Tip 2.)

Guideline for Living 1

"Why does God allow suffering and injustice?" "Why do evil people prosper?" These are questions we ask today and they are the same Habakkuk asked of God. We see men and women of God afflicted by painful diseases, suffering for years without relief. Or a tiny baby is handicapped for life by brain damage—why does God allow it? Where is God while thousands of women kill their unborn babies each year with the permission of the law? Why does God stand by while cruel governments deprive people of justice and their leaders torture those who displease them? Why do we see so many broken homes, including Christian homes, with the sorrow and heartache that accompany these shattered relationships? Why doesn't God do something about the mess we are in?

God doesn't keep His child isolated from trouble. But He does promise, "I will be with him in trouble" (Psalm 91:15). Nothing can separate us from our relationship to God. Paul asked, "Shall trouble or hardship or persecution or famine . . .? No, in all these things we are more than conquerors through him who loved us" (Romans 8:35, 37 NIV). The important thing in life is to determine to abide in Christ in whatever circumstances we are placed.

questions. Write these Scripture references on the chalkboard or overhead:
Psalm 9:9
Psalm 46:1
Psalm 91:15
Psalm 138:7
John 14:1, 27
2 Corinthians 4:8
1 Peter 2:20, 21
1 Peter 3:14, 15

Give students about 7 minutes to write out several guidelines for a Christian attitude toward trouble. Ask each group to report one or two points they discussed.

Question.
What connection is there between the violence and injustice of Habakkuk's time and the "slacking" of the law?

Question.
Basically, what was the dilemma confronting Habakkuk?

"How long?" Many of God's people have uttered the same cry. Habakkuk had been pleading but God had not acted. The natural conclusion was that He had not heard.

In Habakkuk's case we are not listening merely to a personal grievance. The prophet spoke for all the godly people of the nation. More than anything else, he was jealous for God's glory. How could God's name be exalted when His enemies were having their way and He did not stop them? Habakkuk had cried, "Violence!" but violence was still everywhere. No matter where he looked he was forced to witness iniquity that multiplied daily.

Note the repetition of Habakkuk's reference to violence. In any age this is a deadly by-product of sin. The more men disregard the laws of God the less concern they have for the well-being of one another. Drifting farther from the God of compassion and mercy, they become more and more prone to torture, maim, and murder fellow humans. But why does God continue to permit it? This was Habakkuk's cry.

The strife and contention the prophet mentions seemed to be among God's own people. Believers are often affected by the atmosphere in which they live. Surrounded by arguing, quarreling, and dissension, they may fall into the same pattern of behavior if they do not maintain their communion with God.

B. Ineffective Law

The Israelites were supposed to be under the government of God. The commandments of the Law affected every phase of Jewish life—moral, domestic, religious, and political. But as the prophet viewed the nation's general condition it seemed the Law was paralyzed. There was a direct relation between disregard of the Law and the turmoil that prevailed. Man's fallen nature needs strict controls. It easily breaks through restraints and manifests itself in violence, immorality, and other forms of wickedness. While the Law cannot make men righteous, it did set standards of conduct which protected society when these regulations were obeyed. But when people cast off the laws of God they start living by the law of their own will.

"Judgment doth never go forth" means that justice was never done. When a nation disregards God's commandments, its own laws become increasingly lax. Undue "tolerance" prevails even toward brutal crimes.

The result is that "the wicked doth compass about the righteous." Habakkuk saw the wicked literally hemming them in. They surrounded them with hostility. Since the wicked were in the majority, the righteous man's plight had become precarious. He could not expect justice from other men because for the most part they sided with the ungodly. Even the courts of law would not provide the kind of protection the righteous needed.

"Wrong judgment proceedeth." When judicial decisions were rendered they were perverted, twisted, distorted. They were not based on God's laws but on permissive, lawless man's changing standards.

The prophet was wrestling with a complex theological problem. He knew God is holy. He is just. This is His very nature. But if that is true, how could God's apparent silence be explained? In the face of disastrous moral and spiritual conditions, why did a just, holy God fail to intervene quickly?

Clarification
Watch—guard post.
Tower—a rampart on the city wall.
When I am reproved—when I make my complaint.
The vision—a supernatural revelation.

II. God's Answer
Habakkuk 2:1-4, 20

Habakkuk 2:1. I will stand upon my watch, and set me upon the tower, and will watch to see what he will say unto me, and what I shall answer when I am reproved. 2. And the Lord answered me, and said, Write the vision, and make it plain upon tables, that he may run that readeth it. 3. For the vision is yet for an appointed time, but at the end it shall speak, and not lie: though it tarry, wait for it; because it will surely come, it will not tarry. 4. Behold, his soul which is lifted up is not upright in him: but the just shall live by his faith. 20. The Lord is in his holy temple: let all the earth keep silence before him.

A. The Waiting Watchman

In Habakkuk 1:5-11 God had answered the prophet's cry about the widespread evil in Israel. The wicked would be punished and the Lord's instrument would be the Chaldeans (Babylonians). In graphic language God describes the fierceness of the enemy He will use to chastise His erring people.

Habakkuk is disturbed at this announcement. The Babylonians themselves are wicked. They deserve punishment. How could a righteous God use heathen like this to discipline His own people (1:12-17)?

Since God had answered Habakkuk's first inquiry the prophet believed He would reply again, so he determined to make his plea. He thinks of himself as a sentinel keeping watch over a city. The language of this passage probably does not mean that Habakkuk literally climbed up to a tower on the wall. The wording seems symbolic, indicating the watchfulness and anticipation of the prophet as he prepared himself to approach God. His cry might be considered a complaint, but Habakkuk's heart was honest. He was coming to God in perplexity, not unbelief. He was sure the Lord would give him a hearing and tell him what to do next.

B. The Necessity of Faith

"And the Lord answered." He did not disappoint His servant. To make sure the divine revelation was fully understood, God commanded Habakkuk to write it upon tables. It was to be "plain"—legible and easily read. The words must be spread throughout the nation. Those who read them would run as heralds with God's message. It would bring joy to those who heard it because it foretold Israel's ultimate deliverance. It also promised that divine judgment would eventually fall on the Babylonians who would have been used as God's scourge for a time.

The prophecy would not be fulfilled immediately. Its accomplishment was in the future—"for an appointed time." The Babylonians, wicked as they were, had a place in God's plans. The divine purposes must be worked out, yet there was no question about the final outcome. "At the end it shall speak, and not lie." The NASB is clearer: "It hastens toward the goal, and it will not fail." Actually the wording pictures the "vision" of a runner literally "panting" as he races to fulfill his mission. (See Teaching Tip 3.)

"Though it tarry, wait for it." This is where faith enters the picture. God does not always act as quickly as man wishes. Habakkuk and his fellow Israelites would not see an immediate ful-

TEACHING TIP 3
On the chalkboard, sketch a runner racing toward the finish line. Read Habakkuk 2:2, 3 from a modern translation.

This goal Habakkuk looked toward is still the one we look forward to today—the time when all of God's enemies have been defeated and He reigns throughout the earth.

We can have confidence that God's goal for the earth and for us as individuals will be reached. But in the meantime, we are still running toward that goal and will encounter difficulties along the way.

On the chalkboard write this statement:

GOD'S PURPOSE: THAT WE MANIFEST CHRIST'S LIFE THROUGH OUR LIVES

Ask students to discuss in small groups what evidence in a Christian's life would show this purpose had been accomplished.

When we realize these goals are the really important things in our lives, other circumstances can be seen in their true light. Anything that happens to us can either make us more Christlike or more insistent on our own way. It all depends on the way we respond. If we respond by letting Christ work through us, we have moved a step closer to God's purpose for us. When we understand what God is after, we will not become mean, cynical, nervous, or depressed in the face of trouble.

Question.
What does it mean to "live" by faith?

fillment of the prophecy. There would be times in the future when their faith would be sorely tried. Waiting is one of the most difficult things God asks us to do. But He adds the encouraging promise, "It will surely come." The prophet and his people would need to fall back on this divine assurance many times in days to come. The Babylonian captivity was ahead, and the suffering would be great.

Verse 4 is the key to the "vision." God contrasts two different kinds of individuals. First He speaks of the proud, the one who is not upright. This describes any evil person, but in the context of the passage it applies especially to the Chaldeans. Instead of being upright (Hebrew, *yashar*—literally, "straight"), they were dishonest and deceitful.

In contrast to the proud, God speaks of the just, the righteous man. He is humble, recognizing the authority of God. His whole relationship with Him is based on faith. (See Teaching Tip 4.)

Guideline for Living 2

We need patience as we wait in faith for God's purposes to be accomplished. This is true in our private lives as well as in the public affairs of nations and people. God has a goal for our lives that we cannot fully see, but we know His plan includes obedience to the teachings of Jesus as we let Him live His life in us. To accomplish this, God will stretch us and allow circumstances to test us. These can keep us headed toward becoming the person He means for us to be.

In all troubled times, we need to trust ourselves in God's hands. When we take the view that God is in control of our circumstances, we can let Him work out in us His characteristics through the way we respond to those circumstances. Our whole relationship with God is one of living by faith.

The fact that verse 4 is quoted three times in the New Testament shows its importance. (See "Setting the Scene.") The "just" is the one who has been declared righteous by God, not by his own works but by his trust in the atoning work of Jesus Christ. Even in Old Testament times believers became just in God's eyes through faith, as we learn from Abraham's example (James 2:23).

Faith accepts as already accomplished that which is not yet seen (Hebrews 11:1). Faith is based on God's Word, not wishful thinking. Habakkuk and other just Israelites would be sustained daily by their belief in the deliverance God promised, even though they might have to wait years to witness it.

"The just shall live by faith" is the Scripture God brought to the mind of Martin Luther while he was struggling to find peace of heart through a multitude of religious works. Conversion is our first spiritual experience involving faith. But from the moment of our new birth until the end of our days we, like Habakkuk and his people, learn that our spiritual life is sustained by believing in the certainty of victories promised by God but still unseen. The "vision" given Habakkuk was for a time in the future known only to God, but the prophet and his fellow Jews must never abandon their faith that God's Word will not fail.

C. God's Absolute Authority

The rest of chapter 2 describes God's ultimate dealing with the Babylonians in judgment. It concludes with the majestic declaration, "But the LORD is in his holy temple: let all the earth keep silence before him." God's people need not fear, for He is on His throne. He is sovereign; His control over the affairs of men is absolute. "All the earth"—the whole population—must stop their mouths in reverent silence. The Lord is still ruling the universe by His unfailing laws. Nations who break those laws will be punished, but the righteous will be victorious as they maintain their faith.

The Hebrew word translated "silence" means literally "to hush." The proud Chaldeans and all others who have tried to exalt themselves against the rule of God must end their rebellious speech. Naturally the command also includes the godly, but their silence is out of reverence, not compulsion. Despite their perplexity at God's apparent delay in answering some of their prayers, the just recognize that His purposes are firm and unchanging. In His own appointed time every "vision" will be fulfilled exactly as He said.

Clarification

Like hinds' feet—The hind (gazelle) was a deer noted for its ability to escape its enemies by its swiftness and surefootedness.

High places—a description of the hilly country of Palestine.

III. Triumphant Faith

Habakkuk 3:16-19

Habakkuk 3:16. When I heard, my belly trembled; my lips quivered at the voice: rottenness entered into my bones, and I trembled in myself, that I might rest in the day of trouble: when he cometh up unto the people, he will invade them with his troops. 17. Although the fig tree shall not blossom, neither shall fruit be in the vines; the labor of the olive shall fail, and the fields shall yield no meat; the flock shall be cut off from the fold, and there shall be no herd in the stalls: 18. yet I will rejoice in the Lord, I will joy in the God of my salvation. 19. the Lord God is my strength, and he will make my feet like hinds' feet, and he will make me to walk upon mine high places.

A. A Believer's Alarm

Question.

What caused Habakkuk's feelings of dread and fear?

We need to read all of chapter 3 to understand the setting of verses 16-19. After hearing God's promises and warnings, the prophet concludes his message with prayer and praise. The recurrence of the musical term "Selah" (verses 3, 9, 13) indicates this passage was designed for public worship.

God's revelation of the Babylonians' coming attack on Judah and His subsequent punishment of the attackers has filled Habakkuk with terror. He knows his own nation will undergo great suffering before deliverance finally comes. In verse 2 he beseeches God to temper His wrath with mercy.

"My belly trembled" describes the turmoil of Habakkuk's inner being. When he tried to speak, his lips quivered. "Rottenness entered into my bones" pictures the prophet's very skeletal structure feeling weak and ready to collapse.

B. A Believer's Victory

Despite the news of coming trouble, Habakkuk's faith in the promises of God caused his strength and joy to be renewed. "That I might rest in the day of trouble" shows the prophet's realization that this posture of faith was necessary. It would not be easy to wait quietly while anticipating the Babylonian invasion, but Habakkuk knew this attitude would please God.

Ask each one to identify what response he needs to make to the truths found in the Book of Habakkuk. Read aloud Habakkuk 3:17-19. Ask students to rewrite these verses in their own words, substituting troubling circumstances in their own lives for those mentioned in verse 17.

"Though He slay me, yet will I trust in Him" said Job. We can't always understand what God is doing, but we know Him. Our faith is based on the person of Christ—we have confidence in Him.

Close in prayer, committing these troubling circumstances to the Master Planner of our lives and of the whole universe.

Guideline for Living 3

As we wait patiently in faith for God's purposes and glory to be revealed to the world, we have good reason to rejoice. By faith, we can see now what God is able to do and *will* do. So we rejoice in Him in the midst of all kinds of circumstances—in drudgery, in the commonplace, in physical distress, in financial difficulty, in danger, in uncertainty. In the face of unexplained suffering and trouble we can respond, "But the Lord is in his holy temple; let all the earth keep silence before him."

The fig trees, grape vineyards, olive groves, fields of grain, and herds of livestock represented the wealth and livelihood of the nation. When the invaders came, this would be seized or destroyed. Despite the dark picture, Habakkuk's dread turns to faith. He bursts out in a song of praise. He will trust God even if all material blessings are lost. He will find his sufficiency in God himself.

"The God of my salvation" means "The God who saves me." Instead of Habakkuk's steps being slow and faltering, God will make him like the swift gazelle he had often seen running across the high, narrow ridges and exhausting its pursuers. The prophet's communion with God has brought him, peace, joy, and courage.

LIVING THE TRUTH

The sinfulness of man does not defeat God's work. Instead, our all-powerful and-wise God actually uses the actions of sinful men to accomplish His own purposes. The end result is not always seen in this life by a Christian going through extreme hardships, but who ever said this life would contain end results? We live by faith in a Kingdom that is not of this world. Nothing can separate us from our relationship with the King. As we live by faith we are going to experience troubled times. But God is in control, shaping us into His image and accomplishing His purposes.

EVANGELISM OUTREACH

The unsaved students in your class cannot claim the certainty and hope offered to those who are living by faith. For them, life must seem at times to be out of control and purposeless. The good news you can offer them today is that God provides hope and salvation for anyone who will believe on Christ.

Daily Devotional Guide

M. Faithful in Wicked Times.
Genesis 6:1-9

T. Committed to God.
Joshua 24:14-18

W. Trusting in God.
Psalm 11:1-7

T. Promise of Protection.
Mark 16:15-20

F. Prayer for Boldness.
Acts 4:23-31

S. God Is in Control.
Revelation 19:1-6

9

REPENTANCE AVERTS JUDGMENT

PREPARING TO TEACH

Study Text
Book of Jonah

Outline
I. Grace Before Judgment
  A. Coming Destruction
  B. An Extention of Time
II. Judgment Averted
  A. The Message Believed
  B. Humiliation and Repentance
III. Faith Rewarded
  A. Divine Response
  B. An Angry Prophet
  C. A Lesson From a Vine

Golden Text
The people of Nineveh believed God, and proclaimed a fast, and put on sackcloth, from the greatest of them even to the least of them. Jonah 3:5

Central Truth
Those who repent of their sins find God's grace and forgiveness.

Learning Goals
1. To write a sentence summary of God's attitude toward the unsaved.
2. To identify groups of people within your church's influence who need to be urged to repent.
3. To describe ways class members can participate in calling others to repentance.
4. For unsaved students to repent and turn to God.

SEEING THE SCRIPTURES
Jonah 3:1-10

1. And the word of the Lord came unto Jonah the second time, saying,

2. Arise, go unto Nineveh, that great city, and preach unto it the preaching that I bid thee.

3. So Jonah arose, and went unto Nineveh, according to the word of the Lord. Now Nineveh was an exceeding great city of three days' journey.

4. And Jonah began to enter into the city a day's journey, and he cried, and said, Yet forty days, and Nineveh shall be overthrown.

5. So the people of Nineveh believed God, and proclaimed a fast, and put on sackcloth, from the greatest of them even to the least of them.

6. For word came unto the king of Nineveh, and he arose from his throne, and he laid his robe from him, and covered him with sackcloth, and sat in ashes.

7. And he caused it to be proclaimed and published through Nineveh by the decree of the king and his nobles, saying, Let neither man nor beast, herd nor flock, taste any thing: let them not feed, nor drink water:

8. But let man and beast be covered with sackcloth, and cry mightily unto God: yea, let them turn every one from his evil way, and from the violence that is in their hands.

9. Who can tell if God will turn and repent, and turn away from his fierce anger, that we perish not?

10. And God saw their works, that they turned from their evil way; and God repented of the evil, that he had said that he would do unto them; and he did it not.

4:10,11

10. Then said the Lord, Thou hast had pity on the gourd, for the which thou hast not labored, neither madest it grow; which came up in a night, and perished in a night:

11. And should not I spare Nineveh, that great city, wherein are more than sixscore thousand persons that cannot discern between their right hand and their left hand; and also much cattle?

SETTING THE SCENE
The theme emerging clearly from the Book of Jonah is God's love for all nations and races. Other prophets were sent to the Jews: Jonah was commanded to preach to a Gentile city. Furthermore, it was the capital of a fierce, warlike nation that threatened the physical safety of Israel. Preaching to these people was the last thing Jonah wanted to do. The unusual way God stopped

GETTING STARTED

Before class, write this verse on the chalkboard or overhead (without the reference): "You are a gracious and compassionate God, slow to anger and abounding in love, a God who relents from sending calamity" (Jonah 4:2, NIV).

Prepare slips of paper numbered 1 through 5, enough for all class members. As students arrive, give each one a slip of paper with one number on it. Begin the class session by asking students to find one or two other people with the same number and share together one item in their wallet that helps explain something about how they feel about God. Then have the same groups discuss one of the words or phrases on the chalkboard that describe God, listing other words that come to mind in association with that word. Allow 3-5 minutes.

Clarification

Three days' journey—That is, it took three days to go through the city on foot.

Overthrown—The same Hebrew word is used to describe God's destruction of Sodom and Gomorrah (Genesis 19:25, 29). This indicates the devastation awaiting Nineveh if the people would not repent.

TEACHING TIP 1

On the chalkboard add the reference to the verse already printed: Jonah 4:2. Also list these references: Jonah 1:1, 2; Genesis 6:5, 11-13; Genesis 19:13; Malachi 3:5; Matthew 3:11, 12.

Divide the class into small groups to read these verses and answer this question: "Based on what we know about God from Jonah 4:2, from these other passages and from personal experience with God, how would you expect God to respond to the wickedness of the people of Nineveh?"

God cannot tolerate willful

His prophet's attempted escape emphasizes His yearning over the souls of Nineveh. The Book of Jonah has been rightly called the Old Testament's greatest missionary book. Its content is largely the prophet's biography rather than his message. In this respect the book's format is different from the writings of the other prophets.

BIBLE COMMENTARY

I. Grace Before Judgment

Jonah 3:1-4

Jonah 3:1. And the word of the Lord came unto Jonah the second time, saying. 2. Arise, go unto Nineveh, that great city, and preach unto it the preaching that I bid thee. 3. So Jonah arose, and went unto Nineveh, according to the word of the Lord. Now Nineveh was an exceeding great city of three days' journey. 4. And Jonah began to enter into the city a day's journey, and he cried, and said, Yet forty days, and Nineveh shall be overthrown.

(See Teaching Tip 1.)

A. Coming Destruction

Nineveh, first mentioned in Genesis 10:11, was the ancient capital of the Assyrian Empire. God's announcement to Jonah shows the city's moral condition: "Their wickedness is come up before me" (Jonah 1:2). We find the same expression concerning mankind's condition before the Flood: "And God said unto Noah, The end of all flesh is come before me" (Genesis 6:13). The angels who visited Lot to deliver him from Sodom used similar language about evil of that place: "The cry of them is waxen great before the face of the Lord" (Genesis 19:13). Such passages emphasize that sinners cannot conceal their ways from God. All their actions are in full view of the One who is holy and just.

Now God was preparing to send upon Nineveh the same kind of judgment that obliterated Sodom and Gomorrah. This was the warning Jonah must carry to the population of that great city. (See Teaching Tip 2.)

Guideline for Living 1

What groups of people within your church's sphere of influence are in need of repentance?

Consider the following categories of people with special needs, among whom are sure to be people ignoring God and going their own way: inner city children and parents; refugees, single-parent families, high school and college graduates, the elderly, the recently bereaved, those living in poverty. Some of the "other gods" these people might be putting in God's place could include material wealth, social and service clubs, education, vocational success, a good home, false religions, etc.

Christians also fail at times to put God first in their lives. Signs of a need for repentance include not attending church regularly, spending money on self rather than giving generously for God's work, withholding help from those in need because it would cause personal inconvenience.

wickedness, but He does want people to have a chance to repent. If Nineveh had not repented, we can be sure God would have destroyed them as just punishment.

Question.
What is our best proof that the events of the Book of Jonah are an authentic record?

TEACHING TIP 2
Ask: "What are the signs that a person needs to repent?" Brainstorm with \the class on indications of the need for repentance. Point out the signs seen in the lives of Christians who are growing cold in their relationship with God. (See "Guideline for Living 1).

Ask each one to write privately the name of a person or group within his or her area of influence who needs to be given the opportunity to repent.

It is shocking to read of a prophet's rejecting God's orders. Jonah knew the Assyrians had an army capable of destroying Israel and that they had this very purpose in mind. He wanted God to wipe them out, not spare them.

Certainly Jonah knew he could not actually escape the Lord's presence, but his actions show how desperately he wanted to avoid the mission. Nineveh was east of Palestine. Jonah headed west to Tarshish, which was probably in southern Spain. His course was directly opposite from the one God had directed him to travel.

Jonah's being swallowed by the great fish while running from God is one of the best-known incidents in the Bible. Unfortunately it has been a favorite target of the skeptic's ridicule. Our best answer to unbelievers comes from the highest authority, the Lord Jesus himself. He treated the whole account as a historical fact, not a legend nor an allegory. He once shamed His critics by reminding them that Nineveh repented at the preaching of Jonah while the scribes and Pharisees were rejecting the preaching of One greater than Jonah. At the judgment, Jesus said, the men of Nineveh will condemn the generation to which He had come. Our Lord authenticated Jonah's experience of being three days and three nights in the fish's belly. Furthermore, He said this was a sign of His own burial and resurrection (Matthew 12:38-41; 16:4).

After Jonah's cry from his strange prison and God's miraculous deliverance (chapter 2), the disobedient prophet was given another opportunity. It is heartening to note how different his response was this time. In Jonah 1:3 we read that Jonah "rose up," but it was to flee to Tarshish. Jonah 3:3 tells us that the prophet "arose" again but this time it was to go to Nineveh to carry out God's commission.

B. An Extension of Time
Considering the urgency of his task, it seems reasonable to assume that Jonah would have covered 20 miles a day. This means Nineveh was about 60 miles in circumference as many scholars believe. The prophet entered the city loudly announcing God's warning that the population was marked for doom. Yet Jonah was spokesman for a God so merciful that He was going to allow 40 days for the people to abandon their wicked ways and turn to Him.

The Ninevites worshiped the fish god Dagon, but he could not save them from the wrath of the true God. Their only hope was to abandon Dagon and every other non-existent deity and worship the One who had created them. He could have destroyed them without warning. Their wickedness called for such punishment. Yet—as always—God so longed to save instead of destroying that He extended the deadline.

II. Judgment Averted
Jonah 3:5-9
Jonah 3:5. So the people of Nineveh believed God, and proclaimed a fast, and put on sackcloth, from the greatest of them even to the least of them. 6. For word came unto the king of Nineveh, and he arose from his throne, and he laid his robe from him, and covered him with sackcloth, and sat in ashes. 7. And he caused it to be proclaimed and published through Nineveh by the

Clarification

The violence that is in their hands—the violent acts their hands have committed.

TEACHING TIP 3

In the same small groups used earlier, ask students to do a "hymn search." (Try to provide at least one hymnbook for every three people.) Write these instructions on the chalkboard:

"Search for hymns and gospel songs which express the condition of the people of Nineveh and/or God's response to their repentance. Choose one song and be ready to explain your choice to the rest of the class."

As a way of selecting a spokesperson for each group, ask for the person wearing the most green to explain which song their group chose and why.

Question.

What is signified by the outward signs of the Ninevites' reaction to Jonah's preaching?

decree of the king and his nobles, saying, Let neither man nor beast, herd nor flock, taste any thing: let them not feed, nor drink water: 8. but let man and beast be covered with sackcloth, and cry mightily unto God: yea, let them turn every one from his evil way, and from the violence that is in their hands. 9. Who can tell if God will turn and repent, and turn away from his fierce anger, that we perish not?

A. The Message Believed

This is an astounding statement: "The people of Nineveh believed God." The message of judgment is never popular. The skeptical and rebellious easily find reasons to turn it aside. Yet we have the record here of a Gentile city accepting the warning of a Jewish prophet. They turned from their multitude of gods and cried to the one true God of the Hebrews. In the eyes of the Assyrians, Israel was a despised people. This makes the account of the Ninevites' belief and prayers all the more remarkable. The whole picture is a miracle. What happened can only be attributed to the work of the Holy Spirit.

The wickedness of Nineveh was not "ordinary." The prophet Nahum would later call it "the bloody city" (Nahum 3:1). Archaeological records show the unbelievable cruelty of the Assyrians, especially in their treatment of prisoners taken in war. The Hebrew word translated "violence" in verse 8 is the same one that describes the violence filling the earth in the days before the Flood (Genesis 6:11, 13).

Yet this is the city that believed the warning God sent by Jonah. No wonder Jesus commented favorably on their conduct and was distressed that Israel's rejection of Him was such a sharp contrast to the Ninevites (Matthew 12:41). (See Teaching Tip 3.)

Guideline for Living 2

The people of Nineveh would seemingly have been a "hopeless" group of people to preach to, yet they repented when they heard God's Word. Today, we may feel it would be impossible for a certain individual or group to come to know and serve Christ. And yet, when we honestly recognize what potential for evil lies within ourselves apart from God, ("I know that in me . . . dwelleth no good thing"), we can have hope for the salvation of others. What God has done in me, He can do in another.

B. Humiliation and Repentance

Bible students are familiar with many passages referring to sackcloth. Modern sackcloth is usually made of burlap or hemp, but in ancient times it was woven from the long, dark hair of the camel or the Oriental goat. The name "sackcloth" originated with its being made into sacks or bags, but the main use was as articles of clothing.

Sackcloth eventually came to have a symbolic meaning, which is the one most familiar to us. Being dark in color, sackcloth was considered fitting to wear in times of grief and sadness. It was also a mark of repentance. Tossing ashes over the sackcloth became a widespread practice that was not confined to Israel. The Scripture refers to it in connection with the people of Moab (Isaiah 15:3), Ammon (Jeremiah 49:3), Tyre (Ezekiel 27:31), and Nineveh.

The populace did not wait for orders from their ruler. Before the decree came from the king they proclaimed a fast, putting on

Still in the same small groups, have students assign summary phrases to each of the passages listed in "Guideline for Living 3". List these on the chalkboard with the following heading:

REPENTANCE IS . . .

1. Jeremiah 3:22
2. 2 Corinthians 7:9
3. Luke 19:8
4. 2 Chronicles 7:14; James 4:6, 7, 9, 10)
5. (Psalm 119:11; Ephesians 4:22-24)

Allow about 5 minutes, then call for reports from each group.

Clarification

God repented—dealt with them in mercy instead of wrath because they had turned from their sin.

Gourd—a broad-leafed vine of uncertain variety.

That cannot discern between their right hand and their left hand—a description of the very young children who were not accountable for their deeds. Yet if judgment came they would perish as innocent victims of their elders' wickedness.

Much cattle—another class of innocent victims.

---

sackcloth which they covered with ashes. No one was excepted. All ages and classes were involved—"from the greatest of them even to the least of them."

When the king heard Jonah's message, he quickly exchanged his royal robes for the somber garb being worn by everyone else. He abandoned his throne to sit in ashes.

To be sure no one failed to show humiliation and repentance, the king issued a stern order. Beasts as well as people would perish if God's judgment fell, so the ruler commanded that both animals and humans must wear sackcloth. The animals were also included in the fast. Along with their owners, they must not touch food or water. No effort was spared to show how seriously the Ninevites took God's message.

There must be more than abstinence from food and drink and the wearing of garments that symbolized penitence. The king also commanded his subjects to "cry mightily unto God." Coming from the leader of a people saturated with idolatry, this decree reveals further the mighty impact of God's Spirit on these heathen hearts.

There was also confession. The king referred to the "evil way" from which each person must turn. He admitted the violence so characteristic of the Assyrians. He was convinced of the "fierce anger" such deeds had aroused in God and made no attempt to excuse this conduct. Verse 9 indicates the king was not certain that even such measures taken by him and his people would turn God's wrath aside ("Who can tell . . . ?"). But he realized there was no other way to avoid the destruction of the entire population. (See Teaching Tip 4.)

Guideline for Living 3

What is involved in true repentance? Among the indications of true repentance should be the following:

1. Recognizing that God is in charge of our lives (Jeremiah 3:22)
2. Showing sorrow for sin (2 Corinthians 7:9)
3. Confessing the sin and turning away from it. Making restitution where possible (Luke 19:8)
4. Showing a spirit of humility (2 Chronicles 7:14; James 4:9, 10)
5. Accepting God's laws and standards as a way of life (Psalm 119:11; Ephesians 4:22-24).

III. Faith Rewarded

Jonah 3:10; 4:10, 11

Jonah 3:10. And God saw their works, that they turned from their evil way; and God repented of the evil, that he had said that he would do unto them; and he did it not. 4:10. Then said the Lord, Thou hast had pity on the gourd, for the which thou hast not labored, neither madest it grow; which came up in a night, and perished in a night: 11. and should not I spare Nineveh, that great city, wherein are more than sixscore thousand persons that cannot discern between their right hand and their left hand; and also much cattle?

A. Divine Response

"God saw their works" (verse 10). The works He had been seeing were unspeakably wicked. He had seen violence, idolatry, and cruelty of the worst sort. But God also sees men's works when they repent, confess their sin, and seek His forgiveness. The all-seeing Eye that had looked so long on a scene of moral degradation and brutality now beholds a king, his people, and even their livestock in the garments of penitence.

The word *repented* as it refers to God has no connection with evil. Most definitely it does not indicate He is fickle. His response to men depends on their response to Him. If the Ninevites had ignored Jonah's message and continued sinning, God would have destroyed them as He said. But their relationship to Him was changed by repentance and confession. There is no vacillation in God's character. He always punishes sin but shows grace to the repentant. When the people of Nineveh became numbered among the penitent, they were in a position to be recipients of this divine grace.

The Ninevites "turned from their evil way." This is the key to the outcome of God's dealing with them. Noah preached to the people of his day and they did not turn, so God destroyed them. The people of Ninevah did turn, and they were spared.

Such "turning" is the basis of repentance. Merely feeling contrition and sorrow is not enough. True repentance goes beyond feeling to a conscious decision of turning to God. This involves repudiation of sin and acceptance of God's laws and standards as the only way of life.

God's actions following the people's response is summed up in three words concerning the judgment He had said He would send: "He did it not."

Eventually Nineveh was destroyed, but it was approximately 250 years after Jonah's mission. The prophet Nahum came on the scene about 150 years later. He had one theme—the destruction of Nineveh. The Book of Nahum contains only warnings with no call to repentance. This apparently indicates that by then Nineveh's cup of iniquity had become full. Yet despite this condition the city was spared nearly 100 more years after Nahum's ministry. Nineveh's whole story underscores the mercy and long-suffering of God. The people's repentance in Jonah's day postponed the city's destruction for $2\frac{1}{2}$ centuries.

B. An Angry Prophet

If the Bible were only the product of human minds it would have omitted the record of Jonah's strange behavior after he finished his preaching. "Displeased exceedingly . . . very angry." This is a shocking description of a servant of God who had just witnessed such evidence of divine mercy (4:1). In verse 2 Jonah reveals the actual reason he had tried to flee to Tarshish. He knew God is gracious, merciful, slow to anger, of great kindness, and ready to turn from judgment. He was actually afraid that after he had predicted judgment it would not happen! At least the prophet must be given credit for realizing the true character of God. This part of his complaining prayer is really an answer to those who see only a God of wrath in the Old Testament. Even a man who carried a warning of impending judgment knew God would quickly extend grace if the changed attitude and actions of sinners made it possible.

Jonah's cry in verse 3 reminds us of a child having a tantrum. He blurted out, "It is better for me to die than to live." Apparently

Ask each one to write privately two or three different things he or she enjoys doing. Next have students write two or three ways they enjoy serving God. Then ask: "How can you use one of these activities you enjoy doing as a way to help someone see their need for repentance?"

Call your students' attention to the name or group they wrote down earlier in the class period of someone within their influence who needs to be given the opportunity to repent.

Question.

What is the timeless truth emerging from the Book of Jonah?

Daily Devotional Guide

M. Sin Brings Judgment.
   Genesis 19:24-28
T. God's Power To Deliver.
   Exodus 3:7-14
W. God Answers the Skeptics.
   Malachi 3:13-18
T. Call to Repentance.
   Luke 13:1-5
F. Returning to the Father.
   Luke 15:11-24
S. Diligence Needed.
   2 Peter 1:4-11

he was referring to the humiliation he felt because the destruction he had preached about did not take place. It is clear now that all the time he was prophesying he had not wanted the city to be spared. Verse 5 suggests Jonah entertained hope that Nineveh still might be destroyed. (See Teaching Tip 5.)

C. A Lesson From a Vine

The weather was hot and the sun intensely bright. In His mercy to the overwrought prophet God made a broad-leafed vine grow rapidly so Jonah had shade. His joy was brief, however, for the next day God prepared a worm that destroyed the vine. As the sun beat down on his head Jonah repeated his prayer to die, and God repeated His question, "Doest thou well to be angry?" (4:8, 9). Jonah's peevish answer was a pathetic attempt to justify his attitude. Impudently he declared he had every right to be angry. Now it was time for the lesson God was preparing to teach His servant.

Verses 10, 11 show why this has been called the Old Testament's missionary book. What a contrast—a vine and a city! Jonah had nothing to do with the vine's existence, yet he was grieved over its death. But what about the thousands of human beings in Nineveh? They were not Jewish like Jonah, but God had created them. Based on the number of infants God referred to (120,000), many scholars estimate Nineveh's total population at 600,000. When the vine wilted it was gone forever, but when those people died they would not cease to exist. Eternally they would be in bliss or torment. The tenderness of God is expressed in His mention of the cattle who would also have died if judgment came. They did not have souls, but they were part of God's creation and He had pity on them.

The Hebrew word translated "spare" in verse 11 is rendered "pity" in verse 10, and this is its meaning. If Jonah had pity on a short-lived plant, what kind of God would not pity eternity-bound souls? Here is the permanent lesson, the timeless truth of this book—God's love for the whole lost world.

LIVING THE TRUTH

Let's not be like Jonah! His attitude was that he didn't care if the people were punished for their sins because they deserved it anyway. God is gracious, merciful, slow to anger, and of great kindness. Does this describe your attitude toward the unsaved? What people within your influence need to be called to repentance? How can you give them God's message? (See Teaching Tip 6.)

EVANGELISM OUTREACH

Challenge unsaved students to follow the example of the people of Nineveh and to repent. Sin is rejection of Jesus and failure to live pleasing to God. Those who trust in themselves instead of God need to repent. (See Romans 8:7, 8.) God will always answer the prayer of a repentant sinner no matter how deep into sin he has gone.

KINGDOM BLESSINGS

10

SEEING THE SCRIPTURES

Micah 4:1-8

1. But in the last days it shall come to pass, that the mountain of the house of the Lord shall be established in the top of the mountains, and it shall be exalted above the hills; and people shall flow unto it.

2. And many nations shall come, and say, Come, and let us go up to the mountain of the Lord, and to the house of the God of Jacob; and he will teach us of his ways, and we will walk in his paths: for the law shall go forth of Zion, and the word of the Lord from Jerusalem.

3. And he shall judge among many people, and rebuke strong nations afar off; and they shall beat their swords into plowshares, and their spears into pruning hooks: nation shall not lift up a sword against nation, neither shall they learn war any more.

4. But they shall sit every man under his vine and under his fig tree; and none shall make them afraid: for the mouth of the Lord of hosts hath spoken it.

5. For all people will walk every one in the name of his god, and we will walk in the name of the Lord our God for ever and ever.

6. In that day, saith the Lord, will I assemble her that halteth, and I will gather her that is driven out, and her that I have afflicted;

7. And I will make her that halted a remnant, and her that was cast far off a strong nation: and the Lord shall reign over them in mount Zion from henceforth, even for ever.

8. And thou, O tower of the flock, the stronghold of the daughter of Zion, unto thee shall it come, even the first dominion; the kingdom shall come to the daughter of Jerusalem.

SETTING THE SCENE

Will there ever be an end to war, crime, hunger, immorality, and the other consequences of sin? Or is our present course destined to continue indefinitely? The Bible is our only source of reliable information. It assures us of a day when God shall break into human history supernaturally and send His Son back to earth. When this happens humanity will be brought under the government of God. Old Testament prophets, including Micah, had a revelation of that glorious era. We frequently refer to it as the Kingdom age, but more often call it the Millenium because Revelation 20:4 tells us it will be for 1000 years. Micah, like the other prophets, does not mention the length of this period, but describes its chief characteristics.

PREPARING TO TEACH

Study Text
Micah 4:1-8

Outline
I. Universal Worship
   A. God's Reign Begins
   B. The House of the Lord
II. Peace on Earth
   A. A Just Judge
   B. Worldwide Disarmament
   C. Individual Security
III. Restoration and Healing
   A. Exiles Regathered
   B. Ruled by God
   C. Former Glory Enjoyed

Golden Text
We will walk in the name of the Lord our God for ever and ever. Micah 4:5

Central Truth
God's kingdom will ultimately triumph regardless of the world's opposition:

Learning Goals
1. To describe the conditions that will prevail when God's Kingdom is established on earth.
2. To state what it means to walk in the ways of the Lord.
3. To choose specific ways to live this week according to God's Word and rule.

GETTING STARTED

Begin the class session by having students form small groups to participate in a "circle response" activity. Write this question on the chalkboard: "What is one blessing of Christ's coming kingdom that you look forward to?" Each student should respond to this question, with no one speaking a second time until all have spoken once. After all have responded, call for a few volunteers to share some of the blessings mentioned in their group. Lead into this week's Bible study by stating the "Central Truth": "God's kingdom will ultimately triumph regardless of the world's opposition." Read aloud Micah 4:1, 2.

Clarification

The last days—a frequent expression in prophetic writings, referring to the events surrounding the ushering in of Messiah's kingdom.

The house of the Lord—the millenial temple.

The mountain of the house of the Lord—the mountain or hill on which the temple will be built.

Zion—originally a fortress in an elevated place captured by David. Afterward it was called the city of David (2 Samuel 5:6-9). In Old Testament writings "Zion" eventually came to be used as the equivalent of Jerusalem.

Question.

Why does this prophecy speak of worship before describing the other effects of Messiah's reign?

BIBLE COMMENTARY

I. Universal Worship

Micah 4:1, 2

Micah 4:1. But in the last days it shall come to pass, that the mountain of the house of the Lord shall be established in the top of the mountains, and it shall be exalted above the hills; and people shall flow unto it. 2. And many nations shall come, and say, Come, and let us go up to the mountain of the Lord, and to the house of the God of Jacob; and he will teach us of his ways, and we will walk in his paths: for the law shall go forth of Zion, and the word of the Lord from Jerusalem.

A. God's Reign Begins

God's covenant with David included His promise that there would be a permanent kingdom with a descendant of David always on the throne (2 Samuel 7:12-17). "Thy throne shall be established for ever" summed up the promise to the king God called "a man after his own heart" (1 Samuel 13:14; Acts 13:22).

The Jewish people referred to Messiah as the Son of David (Mark 12:35) because they knew the eternal kingdom would be ruled by one of David's descendants. In the beginning of his Gospel, Matthew makes it clear that Jesus is from the line of David as far as His humanity is concerned (Matthew 1:1). This established Jesus' right to the throne promised to David's descendants. The angel Gabriel assured Mary her Child would receive from God "the throne of his father David" (Luke 1:32).

Events through the centuries following David's reign seemed to make the fulfillment of God's promise unrealistic. Much of the time wicked kings sat on the throne. Again and again Israel turned from God to idols. They were sometimes captured and ruled by enemies. When Jesus was born the world was being governed by one of the Caesars of Rome, not a descendant of David. Instead of accepting the true Messiah as their king, Israel rejected Him and had Him crucified.

But God's promise had been made and the dark events of history could not obliterate it. The first three chapters of Micah's prophecy contain God's indictment of His covenant people for their sin and apostasy. Then suddenly He breaks into the message of denunciation with a revelation of Israel's glorious future when the Davidic kingdom is restored. "In the last days it shall come to pass"—the outworking of God's plan for the ages will be fulfilled at the time He has ordained. The whole world will become a theocracy. David's great Son will take His throne and nothing can overthrow His kingdom. (See Teaching Tip 1.)

B. The House of the Lord

A government cannot remain permanently stable if it follows policies contrary to God's law. Those laws are based on complete submission to the supreme Ruler. Man was created to be a worshiper. When something becomes a substitute for God as the object of worship, increasing trouble and chaos will follow. To enjoy the blessings of a world without war, crime, and hunger, men must bow their knees, their wills, and their hearts to God.

This passage teaches that a house of worship in Jerusalem will be the center of the coming kingdom. It will be built on one of Jerusalem's many hills. The expressions, "in the top of the mountains," and, "exalted above the hills," seem to suggest the temple mount will tower above the other hills of the city. However, this picture probably implies more than the physical elevation of the house of worship. Devotion to God will be the highest goal of all people. God's name will be exalted above every other. Worshiping Him will be the population's top priority. In a spiritual and moral sense God's kingdom will be lifted up above everything else.

Although Jerusalem will be the capital city of the Kingdom, the whole earth will come under God's rule and turn to Him in worship. "People shall flow unto it" is a beautiful way to describe multitudes converging on the temple like a great river surging irresistibly on its course.

It is significant that these continual pilgrimages to Jerusalem are not the result of a stern command from the King. The movement originates spontaneously with the people. Verse 2 describes the citizens of "many nations" inviting one another to come and go to the temple. Past rebellion will be replaced by a desire to be taught by God so everyone will know how to walk in "his ways" and travel "his paths."

The rule of man, so often unjust and even cruel, will be replaced by divine justice and order. A new and firm basis of government will be established—"the word of the Lord." This is the law that will be proclaimed from Jerusalem. Those who come there to worship will carry back to their homelands the teaching they have received concerning the laws by which God intends them to live. (See Teaching Tip 2.)

Guideline for Living 1

What is involved in walking in the name and paths of the Lord? Micah testified, "Truly I am full of power by the Spirit of the Lord" (3:8). His contemporary Isaiah recorded the beginning of his walk with God: "I heard the voice of the Lord, saying, Whom shall I send, and who will go for us? Then said I, Here am I; send me. And he said, Go . . ." (Isaiah 6:8, 9). The lives of these prophets indicate two generalizations about walking in the name of the Lord: (1) God chooses our ministry for us and sends us out. (2) God gives us the power through His Spirit to fulfill His call.

God's Word gives us the guidelines we need to walk or live the way He wants us to. Psalm 119 is built on the themes of obeying God's Word and walking in His ways. The First Epistle of John tells us that if we walk in the light of Christ we show we have been cleansed from sin. "He that saith he abideth in him ought himself also to walk, even as he walked" (1 John 2:6).

II. Peace on Earth

Micah 4:3-5

Micah 4:3. And he shall judge among many people, and rebuke strong nations afar off; and they shall beat their swords into plowshares, and their spears into pruninghooks: nation shall not lift up

TEACHING TIP 1
On the chalkboard write these references: Isaiah 11:1-16; 65:18-25; Revelation 21:1-6. Give each small group a large sheet of paper and a felt pen. Ask students to read these passages and make a list of the characteristics of Christ's reign on the earth as seen in Scripture. Allow about 5 minutes, then call for reports from each group. Students may be interested in comparing their personal hopes for what Christ's kingdom will be like with what the Bible says it will be like.

TEACHING TIP 2
Distribute copies of the PATH "Crossword Puzzle" to help students get right to the heart of what it means to walk in God's paths. Have them work individually or in pairs for about 10 minutes to solve the puzzle. Then discuss as a class what each word should be and the meanings of those words. Ask: "What thematic title would you give this puzzle?"

Judge—The Hebrew word means to exercise all the functions of government.

Rebuke—bring a charge against, as in a lawsuit; expose wrongdoing in order to correct it.

Sit—dwell securely.

TEACHING TIP 3

Ask the class to list each of the promises given in Micah 4:3-5. Write these on the chalkboard. Ask: "What is the significance of beating swords into plowshares and spears into pruning hooks?" Use the material in the Bible Commentary to supplement student responses.

Question.

What is the significance of God's rebuking "strong nations"?

Question.

Why is there reference to plowshares and pruninghooks?

a sword against nation, neither shall they learn war any more. 4. But they shall sit every man under his vine and under his fig tree; and none shall make them afraid: for the mouth of the Lord of hosts hath spoken it. 5. For all people will walk every one in the name of his god, and we will walk in the name of the Lord our God for ever and ever.

A. A Just Judge

One of the main causes of war is injustice. The strong know how to achieve positions of power. When they do they often crush the weak. Powerful nations bring smaller ones to their knees and rule them by constant fear of attack. Many well-meaning statesmen have tried to bring such conditions to an end through peace conferences, treaties, and negotiations. But the basic cause of war is sin. When men continually violate God's laws they will have difficulty living peacefully with each other.

When Messiah returns the whole world will be under one completely just Ruler. His law will be the standard on which international decisions are based. He will exercise all the processes of government—legislative, judicial, and executive. His unchangeable holiness will be the guarantee that every verdict He renders will be just and fair to all.

It is the law of the jungle that only the strong survive. Unfortunately, this rule often manifests itself among nations. When Christ returns He will not hesitate to indict "strong nations" for their oppression of the weak. He will be the Arbiter of all international disputes even if they are among distant nations ("afar off"). By His administration of justice He will eliminate the causes of war. (See Teaching Tip 3.)

B. Worldwide Disarmament

Plowshares and pruninghooks are agricultural implements. They are involved in the production of food. One of the greatest problems of our time is hunger. What if the unbelievable sums of money spent on weapons and armies were used instead to feed the starving? Even nations in the free world grapple with the dilemma of maintaining necessary social programs while budgeting enough for defense to discourage an emeny's attack.

When the Prince of Peace rules, these gigantic problems will disappear. There will be no defense budgets because nations will not have to defend themselves. They will be free to use their financial resources for peaceful purposes.

Swords and spears were the weapons of Micah's day, so he used this terminology. Nations may literally melt down their tanks, missiles, planes, and guns to manufacture tractors, plows, combines, and other farm machinery from the steel. However, the reference to beating swords into plowshares and spears into pruninghooks means particularly that the world's wealth will be channeled into beneficial enterprises instead of preparations for battle.

There are many training institutions around the world where men go to "learn war." This is a necessity in the present order even though it drains money and manpower from other projects. But the need to study military tactics and develop battle plans will disappear when Jesus takes His throne.

C. Individual Security

The world is not a great formless mass; it is made up of individuals. Micah turns from speaking of nations to describing the happy lot of "every man" when the King reigns.

Question.
What do the vine and fig tree symbolize?

The vine and fig tree were an important part of life in Palestine. As universal crops they supplied much of the country's food and money. Micah's picture of individuals sitting in their vineyards and fig groves describes the security of that coming day. It symbolizes the safety people will enjoy even apart from the customary dwelling places. They will be as secure in the open fields as in their houses. They will not have to fear that a greedy enemy will seize their property. No matter how vast their holdings, they will never be compelled to post guards.

No announcement could be more welcome to a fear-ridden world than this: "None shall make them afraid." As men have become increasingly godless they have had less respect for one another. Greed and selfishness have often replaced concern and compassion. Consequently we live behind locked doors and shun city streets at night.

But the climate of fear will disappear during the Kingdom Age. There will be no reason to fear being murdered, robbed, or assaulted. The peace that prevails among nations will extend to every household. As if to emphasize the authority behind this proclamation, Micah writes, "For the mouth of the Lord of hosts hath spoken it." This is not wishful thinking; it is a divine promise.

Verse 5 is a testimony of the faithful Jewish remnant who enter the Millenium. They want to go on record with their renunciation of idolatry. This was the sin that often brought judgment on their nation, but then it will be permanently eradicated. These believers are saying that even if all other nations serve other gods, they pledge eternal allegiance to the Lord alone.

TEACHING TIP 4

Ask: "If we are walking in the name of the Lord, in what ways might His peace be seen in our lives?" Brainstorm with the class on ways Christians can display peace—part of the fruit of the Spirit and one of the signs of God's kingdom. Ask students to write privately one area of life where they need to experience God's peace.

Guideline for Living 2

We cannot see this promised worldwide peace today because people still walk in the name of their false gods. For many, the "god" they are following is money or power. These people are hard and ruthless. God wants His people to follow the Lord, seeking to be like Jesus in every area of their lives. (See Micah 6:8; 1 John 1:7.) It is God's will in our present age for all men to seek His Word and His ways. We can have the privilege now that someday all nations will seek. We need to take advantage of our opportunity.

III. Restoration and Healing

Micah 4:6-8

Clarification
Halteth—was lame.
Driven out—exiled.
Afflicted—literally, broken, shattered.
Tower of the flock—a high wooden platform from which the shepherd could watch the sheep.
Stronghold—fortress.
Daughter of Zion—a poetic description of Jerusalem.

Micah 4:6. In that day, saith the Lord, will I assemble her that halteth, and I will gather her that is driven out, and her that I have afflicted; 7. and I will make her that halted a remnant, and her that was cast far off a strong nation: and the Lord shall reign over them in mount Zion from henceforth, even for ever. 8. And thou, O tower of the flock, the stronghold of the daughter of Zion, unto thee shall it come, even the first dominion; the kingdom shall come to the daughter of Jerusalem.

Prepare a brief lecture summarizing the historical background of Micah 4:6-8. Use material from the Bible Commentary. Before presenting this information, divide the class into listening teams. Assign each team to listen for the explanation of one of these key words or phrases (which you can list on the chalkboard): those who halt; remnant; tower of the flock; first dominion.

Ask each group to report back to the class on the meaning and significance of their assigned phrase.

A. Exiles Regathered

"I will assemble her that halteth." Here God describes the nation of Israel as a flock of sheep exhausted and lame from much wandering. It is a picture of people weary of exile in foreign lands. They had been driven from the home God had promised them. God himself allowed it to discipline His covenant people for their sinful ways. Now He gives Micah a view of the day when the discipline has ended. The great Shepherd will bring His weary, limping flock back to the fold of the Promised Land. He will heal their lameness and lead them in the way of righteousness.

At times Israel has been so afflicted for her waywardness that it seemed impossible she could ever be restored. But God made a promise to Abraham He will not forget even when Abraham's descendants turn their backs on Him. The day of total restoration will come.

Note the progression: First "a remnant," then "a strong nation." The battered flock will be preserved by God during the time of "Jacob's trouble" (Jeremiah 30:5-7). They are but a remnant, hardly representative of the vast number of descendants God promised Abraham in Genesis 13:16 ("as the dust of the earth") and Genesis 15:5 (like "the stars"). But God will protect the remnant through the horrors of the Great Tribulation. They will become the "strong nation" God assured Abraham would descend from him. (See Teaching Tip 5.)

B. Ruled by God

Best of all, Israel will at last be ruled by God alone. His government of the nation will not be temporary as it often was in the past. There will be no more turning back to wickedness. The once-exiled flock will be safely in the fold from which they will never depart. God's rule over them will be "from henceforth, even for ever." This was His original plan for Israel. Their trouble started when they demanded a human king so they could be like the other nations (1 Samuel 8:5). God's indictment of His people was, "They have rejected me, that I should not reign over them" (1 Samuel 8:7). This scorning of the theocracy brought endless chaos and suffering to the nation. During the Kingdom Age that will be past. The afflicted but divinely guarded remnant will become a strong nation with God as its Sovereign.

C. Former Glory Enjoyed

The reign of David was the high point in the nation's history. His son Solomon enjoyed prosperity and success for a time but later forsook the ways of the Lord. After that, Israel never regained the strength and power it had under David.

But during the Millenium when David's great Son the Lord Jesus rules Israel and the world, the glory of past days will return and, in fact, be surpassed. (See Teaching Tip 6.)

Question.

What is the significance of God's reference to the "first dominion"?

TEACHING TIP 6

To help students realize God's kingdom is meant to be established *now* in the lives of His people, give the following word association quiz. Ask students to write down the first word or phrase that comes to mind while you read each of

Guideline for Living 3

When God's kingdom is established, then the prayer Jesus taught His disciples to pray will be fulfilled: "Thy kingdom come. Thy will be done in earth, as it is in heaven" (Matthew 6:10). However, we don't have to wait for the Millenium to experience God's rule in our lives. We can be sure of abiding in Christ no matter where we are and no matter what is going on. God puts His kingdom in

these words and phrases aloud:

Thy kingdom
Millenium
Now
Personal relationship
I delight
Circumstances
Abiding
God's rule
Yielding
Thy will

Use these words and phrases as an outline for presenting the material in "Guideline for Living 3."

TEACHING TIP 7

Ask students to look again at their completed crossword puzzles. Ask each one to circle one word on the puzzle which indicates a way he would like to let God's Word make him a better example of God's kingdom and rule. Ask students to share the word they have chosen with one other student and explain why they chose it. Have them conclude with prayer for one another.

Daily Devotional Guide

M. Triumph of the Kingdom.
Psalm 2:1-12

T. Characteristics of the King.
Isaiah 11:1-5

W. Blessings of the Kingdom.
Isaiah 35:1-10

T. Mysteries of the Kingdom.
Matthew 13:1-23

F. The King's Return.
Matthew 24:29-31

S. The Kingdom on Earth.
Revelation 20:1-6

our hearts and rules there. Our individual lives are meant to be miniature examples of what God's kingdom will be like one day when it covers the whole earth.

In verse 8 the language returns to the picture of a flock of sheep. They are guarded by Messiah like a shepherd standing on the raised platform or tower built in the pasture for that purpose.

The Hebrew word translated "stronghold" is *ophel*, meaning a mound or hill. The name "Ophel" was given to a location on Mount Moriah which was fortified by Jotham and Manasseh (2 Chronicles 27:3; 33:14). This location typified the strength of the nation because Ophel was virtually impregnable against attacking enemies.

The reference to Ophel here indicates that during the Kingdom Age the prestige and might which belonged to Israel in ancient times will be theirs again. God himself will be their stronghold. Like a fair daughter of the King, Jerusalem will be capital of the millenial earth.

Those coming days will be reminiscent of the time when Solomon was on the throne. In many ways the early years of his reign symbolize the Millenium. "King Solomon exceeded all the kings of the earth for riches and for wisdom. And all the earth sought to Solomon, to hear his wisdom, which God had put in his heart" (1 Kings 10:23, 24). Jerusalem then was like a magnet that drew the great of earth to behold Israel's glory. Remember the Queen of Sheba's visit recorded in 1 Kings 10:1-13? Tragically those wonderful days did not last. Solomon's backsliding brought God's judgment and an eventual split in the once powerful kingdom. But when Jesus comes back to earth the "first dominion" will be restored. In its glory, power, and influence the reign of our Lord will, of course, far exceed anything Israel ever knew even under David's leadership.

LIVING THE TRUTH

God's kingdom is characterized by those qualities seen in Christ—the One who will some day rule over all. Isaiah described this Ruler as having a spirit of wisdom and understanding, of counsel and power. He will judge with righteousness and justice (Isaiah 11:1-5).

A hunger for the Word of the Lord is characteristic of those who make up God's kingdom. The Bible gives us guidelines for living, encouragement, a right perspective on life, a reason for existence, and instruction in righteousness.

"Come, and let us go . . . to the house of the God of Jacob; and he will teach us of his ways, and we will walk in his paths . . . we will walk in the name of the Lord our God for ever and ever" (Micah 4:2, 5). (See Teaching Tip 7.)

EVANGELISM OUTREACH

Wouldn't you like to be part of God's kingdom? God wants people who will walk in His ways and seek to be like Him. People sometimes assume mistakenly that God's blessings will be with them even when they ignore the commands and conditions of His Word. But those who deliberately ignore God's Word will suffer the consequences of all God's enemies. Give unsaved students an opportunity to become part of God's kingdom by accepting Christ's death as the atonement for their sin.

PREPARING TO TEACH

Study Text
Book of Haggai

Outline
I. Distorted Priorities
  A. Spiritual Indifference
  B. Divine Rebuke
II. Chastised by God
  A. Called to Self-Examination
  B. Consequences of Disobedience
III. Blessed Through Obedience
  A. Immediate Response
  B. God's Unfailing Promise

Golden Text
Thus saith the Lord of hosts; Consider your ways. Haggai 1:7

Central Truth
When people become indifferent to the things of God, misfortune follows.

Learning Goals
1. To compare the indifference of the people in Haggai's day with the indifference sometimes found in Christians today.
2. To differientiate between our own priorities and God's.
3. To identify one priority God has for our lives and to work on it during the coming week.

SEEING THE SCRIPTURES

Haggai 1:2-13

2. Thus speaketh the Lord of hosts, saying, This people say, The time is not come, the time that the Lord's house should be built.

3. Then came the word of the Lord by Haggai the prophet saying,

4. Is it time for you, O ye, to dwell in your ceiled houses, and this house lie waste?

5. Now therefore thus saith the Lord of hosts; Consider your ways.

6. Ye have sown much, and bring in little; ye eat, but ye have not enough; ye drink, but ye are not filled with drink; ye clothe you, but there is none warm; and he that earneth wages, earneth wages to put it into a bag with holes.

7. Thus saith the Lord of hosts; Consider your ways.

8. Go up to the mountain, and bring wood, and build the house; and I will take pleasure in it, and I will be glorified, saith the Lord.

9. Ye looked for much, and, lo, it came to little; and when ye brought it home, I did blow upon it. Why? saith the Lord of hosts. Because of mine house that is waste, and ye run every man unto his own house.

10. Therefore the heaven over you is stayed from dew, and the earth is stayed from her fruit.

11. And I called for a drought upon the land, and upon the mountains, and upon the corn, and upon the new wine, and upon the oil, and upon that which the ground bringeth forth, and upon men, and upon cattle, and upon all the labor of the hands.

12. Then Zerubbabel the son of Shealtiel, and Joshua the son of Josedech, the high priest, with all the remnant of the people, obeyed the voice of the Lord their God, and the words of Haggai the prophet, as the Lord their God had sent him, and the people did fear before the Lord.

13. Then spake Haggai the Lord's messenger in the Lord's message unto the people, saying, I am with you, saith the Lord.

SETTING THE SCENE

Haggai was the first prophet who ministered to the Jewish remnant returning from Babylonian captivity. It is helpful to read the Book of Ezra in connection with the study of Haggai. Ezra 5:1 and 6:14 mention the prophesying of Haggai and Zechariah during the trying time of rebuilding. Haggai dates all his messages carefully. They were delivered during the second year of Darius' reign and the prophet names the month and day when the word of the Lord came to him. Haggai's chief concern was the rebuilding of the

GETTING STARTED

Before class, write the word, *PRIORITIES* in large letters on the chalkboard. Begin the class session by asking students to list individually the things they want to do this coming week. Then ask each one to assign the following code letters to each item:

A—Must Do
B—Should Do
C—Would like to do

Point out that this exercise has just helped students set priorities for their week's plans. On the chalkboard write the second "Learning Goal": "To differentiate between our own priorities and God's."

Clarification

You, O ye—you yourselves.
Ceiled—paneled.
Waste—desolate; ruined.

TEACHING TIP 1

On the chalkboard list these references (or use the half sheet transparency provided in PATH):
Ezra 1:2-5; 3:1-3, 10, 11
Ezra 4:4, 5, 23, 24
Haggai 1:1-4
Ezra 6:13-16

Also write the question, "What was the attitude of God's people toward rebuilding the temple?" Divide the class into small groups and assign one set of references to each group. After 5 minutes, call for reports from each group.

TEACHING TIP 2

On the chalkboard list the following everyday experiences of life: jobs; friendships; recreation; TV; caring for family, home, yard, car, other possessions; shopping for more possessions.

Ask students to talk with one other person for 2 minutes about one of these categories, discussing the following question: "In what ways can the 'cares of this world' cause us

BIBLE COMMENTARY

I. Distorted Priorities

Haggai 1:2-4

Haggai 1:2. Thus speaketh the Lord of hosts, saying, This people say, The time is not come, the time that the Lord's house should be built. 3. Then came the word of the Lord by Haggai the prophet, saying, 4. Is it time for you, O ye, to dwell in your ceiled houses, and this house lie waste?

A. Spiritual Indifference

During his reign, the Persian Cyrus ordered the Jews repatriated and their temple rebuilt (2 Chronicles 36:22, 23; Ezra 1:1-4). Remarkably, God had revealed this to Isaiah nearly 200 years before, even calling Cyrus by name (Isaiah 44:28; 45:1-4).

Less than 50,000 Jews went back to Jerusalem during the first stage of the restoration. They were led by Zerubbabel the civil leader, or governor, and the religious leader Joshua the high priest, also called Jeshua (Ezra 2:2; 3:2; Haggai 1:1). Rebuilding the temple was the burning passion of the returning people (Ezra 1:5). The temple's destruction by Nebuchadnezzar had been one of the Jews' great national tragedies (2 Kings 25:8, 9).

When the first group reached Jerusalem they set up an altar and began the Mosaic ritual of burnt offerings. They observed the Feast of Tabernacles and laid the foundations of the new temple (Ezra 3:1-13).

Unfortunately, the non-Jews of the land were hostile to the rebuilding of the temple and persuaded King Artaxerxes to order the work stopped (Ezra 4:1-24). For approximately 15 years nothing more was done. Then God brought Haggai on the scene—and Zechariah shortly thereafter. (See Teaching Tip 1.)

If the opposition of enemies had stopped construction of the temple at first, the people's indifference was the main hindrance now. As the years went by, they had lost their first vision, settling into a comfortable routine that centered mostly in their own interests.

Guideline for Living 1

It is easy to lose sight of the supernatural nature of our relationship with God. As we surround ourselves with the natural things of our environment, the things of God begin to seem ordinary too. Consider some of the experiences which can occupy most of our time if we let them: jobs, friendships, recreation, TV, taking care of family, home, yard, car, and various possessions, shopping for *more* possessions, etc. Of course, there is nothing basically wrong with any of these—in fact many of them are necessary. But when our attitude and use of time are determined by these natural aspects of life, we begin to forget and lose interest

to become indifferent to God?"
Ask three or four volunteers to
share their thoughts with the
rest of the class.

in what God wants to be doing in our lives in supernatural ways.

Jesus told us to seek first the kingdom of God and His righteousness and all these things will be added to us. If we are filling our minds with thoughts about God, other things fall into place as time allows. A regular devotional life, church attendance, and ministry to others should be considered as both evidence of, and necessity for, maintaining a close relationship with God.

B. Divine Rebuke

Haggai made it clear he was God's spokesman: "Thus speaketh the Lord of hosts." His messages were short and to the point. Calling the Jews "this people" instead of "My people" was a sharp reproof by God, implying that they were not behaving like His people.

Haggai addressed the leaders, Zerubbabel and Joshua (verse 1). They were held accountable for the people's actions, but the prophet's rebuke was for the whole nation. He reinforces his simple style of speaking by frequent questions. Verse 4 is an example.

When the people left Babylon to return home, their minds were full of one thing—rebuilding God's house and restoring worship. Now lethargy had taken its toll. Each day they procrastinated, their vision grew dimmer. Enemy hostility may have stopped the work originally, but there was no excuse now. Darius had succeeded to the Persian throne. After discovering Cyrus' decree in the government records he had ordered resumption of the work on the temple (Ezra 6:1-11).

The Jews did not say they would never complete the temple. They simply kept repeating, "It isn't time yet," but God pointed out that they seemed to find time to build their own homes. Furthermore, they spared no expense in furnishing them. They were paneled and luxuriously fitted. While the people enjoyed their comfort, the empty foundations where the temple was supposed to be built were a source of constant displeasure to God.

Question.
Is this passage intended to condemn the building of expensive houses by believers?

The essence of God's rebuke was not that nice homes are sinful. His displeasure stemmed from the emphasis the people were placing on their personal needs while neglecting His work. Haggai's picture of the desolate temple site is sharpened by its contrast with the well-constructed and expensively furnished houses nearby.

Note how God answers the people's excuse, "The time is not come," with a question also involving time: "Is it time for you . . .?" Why did they find time so easily for one project but not for another? The prophet does not give the answer. He leaves that for the people's consciences to resolve. (See Teaching Tip 3.)

TEACHING TIP 3
Point out the real issue between God and His people. What should be their first priority?
Display the transparency provided in PATH, "PURPOSES AND GOALS." Ask: "Remembering that God's priority for us is living a Christlike life, what would we need to do or say as evidence that this purpose is being accomplished?" List responses on the transparency under the "GOALS" column.

Guideline for Living 2
God's priority for us is that we have His nature living in us and shining forth to the world. When we are letting God's priority be *our* priority we will look at everything in relation to God. The consciousness of God will push its way to the front in all circumstances. If those circumstances are disagreeable, it gives God all the more opportunity to manifest His life through us as we obey Him. Jesus taught that we must put our relationship to God first and everything else second.

II. Chastised by God

Haggai 1:5-11

Haggai 1:5. Now therefore thus saith the Lord of hosts; Consider your ways. 6. Ye have sown much, and bring in little; ye eat, but ye have not enough; ye drink, but ye are not filled with drink; ye clothe you, but there is none warm; and he that earneth wages, earneth wages to put it into a bag with holes. 7. Thus said the Lord of hosts; Consider your ways. 8. Go up to the mountain, and bring wood, and build the house; and I will take pleasure in it, and I will be glorified, saith the Lord. 9. Ye looked for much, and, lo, it came to little; and when ye brought it home, I did blow upon it. Why? saith the Lord of hosts. Because of mine house that is waste, and ye run every man unto his own house. 10. Therefore the heaven over you is stayed from dew, and the earth is stayed from her fruit. 11. And I called for a drought upon the land, and upon the mountains, and upon the corn, and upon the new wine, and upon the oil, and upon that which the ground bringeth forth, and upon men, and upon cattle, and upon all the labor of the hands.

A. Called to Self-Examination

Twice in this passage God tells His people to give careful thought to their experiences ("consider their ways"). He challenged them to determine if their hardships were a coincidence or if they conveyed a divine message. The people should take a careful look at the interruption of the temple's rebuilding in light of the personal comforts which seemed so important to them. Were they measuring up to the standards God had set for His chosen nation? Were they enjoying the spiritual and material blessings He intended for them?

Question.

What "ways" was God calling the people to consider?

In summary, the Israelites were admonished to examine the consequences of the priorities they had chosen. They had decided to put their own interests ahead of God's. Had it paid off well? Or did it bring them disappointment and frustration? "Face it honestly," God was saying.

There is no contradiction between God's reference to their "ceiled houses" and the conditions described in verse 6. Like other nations, Israel had both its poor and rich. Of course drought and crop failures affect everyone, even the wealthy. Undoubtedly the poor were the majority and suffered most. Yet they were not blameless, for poverty is not synonymous with godliness. The temptation of the poor is to try to acquire as much as the rich, to live in the same kind of "ceiled houses."

TEACHING TIP 4

In small groups, ask students to read Haggai 1:5-11 from more than one translation and make a list of the consequences of the priorities the Israelites had chosen.

If the Jews had seen no relation between their spiritual apathy and their economic troubles, they had no excuse after God spoke through Haggai. No matter how much seed they sowed, their harvests were meager. Their diet seemed to leave them physically unsatisfied and their clothing was not warm enough in winter.

The statement, "He that earneth wages, earneth wages to put it into a bag with holes," reminds us of our own struggles with inflation and economic difficulty. No matter how much they earned it was not enough to keep up with the demands of life. It was as though their purses had holes in the bottom through which the money kept falling out. When they reached in to get more for their financial needs, the purses were empty.

After describing the situation with which the people were quite familiar, God repeats His command: "Consider your ways" (verse 7). He is saying, "There is a reason for all this and I will tell you what it is." (See Teaching Tip 5.)

Guideline for Living 3

It is much easier to consider the ways of others than our own ways. We see the mote in our brother's eye immediately but do not realize there is a beam in our eye. No matter how long we have served the Lord, we never outgrow the need for self-examination from time to time. This does not mean we should develop a morbid spirit nor condemn ourselves unnecessarily. But each time we read the Word, each time we pray, each time we are in God's house, it is spiritually healthy for us to ask the Holy Spirit to keep us lined up with His will. He can see what we cannot see. A small correction in the direction of our life now may help us avoid the need for a major correction later.

Prosperous times present a special danger as well as a blessing. It is not easy to discipline ourselves when we see others surrounding themselves with luxuries we want but can't really afford. Sometimes Christians get themselves so heavily in debt they feel they cannot pay God His tithe. The results of this are spiritually disastrous.

There may be times when God lets unpleasant things happen to wake us up. This does not mean that every bad circumstance is punishment from the Lord, for even the most godly go through times of suffering. But testing times are occasions when we should stop and ask ourselves, "Is God trying to tell me something by all of this?" If we are sincere in such a prayer, God will enable us to see clearly the purpose of the pressure we are undergoing.

B. Consequences of Disobedience

In verse 8 God breaks into His denunciation with a promise. The hill country around Jerusalem was full of timber. If the people would start cutting it and making it into boards for the new temple, God would be pleased ("take pleasure"). Such actions would glorify Him and make it possible for Him to bless His people again.

But the Lord was not through calling attention to the results of their twisted priorities. He turns back to this subject in verse 9. Every expectation the people had cherished constantly failed to materialize—they "looked for much, and, lo, it came to little." The picture of God blowing their crops away may have meant He sent strong winds that leveled their granaries. It may also have been simply an illustration of the way He made their blessings dissipate—like the wind blowing chaff in every direction. Whether the language is literal or figurative, the consequences God described were the same. He wanted them to know their misfortunes were not simply strange quirks of nature. They were part of God's discipline, aimed at bringing His children to a place of repentance and obedience.

"Mine house" represented the spiritual interests of the nation. Their "own house" typified selfish, personal concerns. They had allowed God's house to lie in ruins, but it was a different story when their own activities were concerned. They pursued them with great zeal, running to accomplish their projects. They did not even seem to notice the desolate temple site—or did not want to. But they could hardly wait to get to the security of their homes to start new plans that would benefit them.

During the dry summer months the crops were ordinarily sustained by heavy dews. By God's command these had been absent. One crop failure after another had resulted. The drought was widespread, blighting both the valleys and mountains. All crops were affected: grain, grapes, and the olives which produced the oil so important to them. Both men and beasts were suffering. All the hard work expended to plant, harvest, and prosper had come to naught. There was barely enough food for the people and undoubtedly a shortage for their animals.

The Hebrew words translated "waste" in verses 4, 9 and "drought" in verse 11 are closely related: *hareb* and *horeb*. It seems God is playing on words, implying that since they had left His house in ruins He was doing the same to everything they tried to accomplish.

III. Blessed Through Obedience
Haggai 1:12 through 2:9

Haggai 1:12. Then Zerubbabel the son of Shealtiel, and Joshua the son of Josedech, the high priest, with all the remnant of the people, obeyed the voice of the Lord their God, and the words of Haggai the prophet, as the Lord their God had sent him, and the people did fear before the Lord. 13. Then spake Haggai the Lord's messenger in the Lord's message unto the people, saying, I am with you, saith the Lord. 14. And the Lord stirred up the spirit of Zerubbabel the son of Shealtiel, governor of Judah, and the spirit of Joshua the son of Josedech, the high priest, and the spirit of all the remnant of the people; and they came and did work in the house of the Lord of hosts, their God. 2:9. The glory of this latter house shall be greater than of the former, saith the Lord of hosts: and in this place will I give peace, saith the Lord of hosts.

A. Immediate Response

With no dissension or division, Zerubbabel, Joshua, and the people immediately obeyed. "The people did fear before the Lord." This shows humility and a recognition of their wrong attitude. Three weeks after Haggai started preaching, workmen were at the temple site to make a new beginning (verses 1, 15). The statement linking "the voice of the Lord their God" with "the words of Haggai the prophet" and the recognition that "the Lord their God had sent him" shows the new spiritual sensitivity of the Jewish remnant.

It is clear from the continued account that after the resumption of work some of the Jews needed encouragement. It came quickly in the words, "I am with you, saith the Lord." In turning from apathy to obedience and diligent effort, the people had placed themselves in a position for God to bless them again. In Haggai 2:15, 18, they are told to remember the exact day they began to lay the temple's new foundations: "Consider from this day and upward." This was so they could compare the future days of blessing with their past troubles and understand it was no coincidence. The difference lay in their obedience to God's command and their attention to His work. (See Teaching Tip 6.)

Clarification

Stirred up—aroused, awakened, incited.

Shake—cause to tremble or quake.

The Desire of all nations—although some recent interpretations have led to the translation of "Desire" as "desirable things" (the wealth of nations), Christian scholars from earliest times believed the word referred to the Messiah. Jewish tradition held the same view. Who but the Messiah can fulfill the longings and desires of the nations?

TEACHING TIP 6

In the same small groups used earlier in the class session, ask students to survey Haggai 1:12 through 2:9, looking for answers to this question: "What promises and encouragement does God give His people who obey Him and follow His priorities?" After about 5 minutes, ask each group to report one finding. List these on the chalkboard.

Question.

What is the significance of God's stirring up the spirits of the people?

TEACHING TIP 7

Ask students to look over their responses to the "SELF EVALUATION." Ask each one to circle one area in which he would like to improve in his relationship with God. Using the "PURPOSES AND GOALS" format from the PATH transparency, have students work privately for 3-5 minutes on listing the specific things they would be doing or saying if the circled area (their "Purpose") was being accomplished.

Example:

Purpose	Goals
To have a regular devotional life	1. Find and use a systematic Bible reading outline. 2. Get up 10 minutes earlier. 3. Keep a list of prayer requests and answers.

Question.

Does Haggai 2:9 look past Haggai's day to a future time?

The Hebrew word translated "stirred up" is a strong, active one. It is translated "raised" in Jeremiah 6:22; 50:41 to describe military movements. In Daniel 11:2, 25 it pictures the king of the north stirring up armies against the king of the south.

The statement that God himself aroused the spirits of the leaders and people shows that He is not a passive observer of history. He does not stand by and simply let events take care of themselves. The Scripture also records that He stirred up the spirit of Cyrus to order the return of the Jews to rebuild their temple (2 Chronicles 36:22). God is not a mere spectator.

The prophet is careful to date the resumption of work on the temple (1:15) because it would mark a turning point in the history of Israel.

B. God's Unfailing Promise

Haggai 2:1-3 shows another reason the people needed encouragement. Some of them remembered Solomon's temple (Ezra 3:12). The new building would never compare with the glory of that one.

God's response was, "Be strong." The same God who led His people when they built the first temple was still with them. The promises He made when He delivered them from Egypt had never failed.

Haggai 2:6, 7 may have had an initial reference to political upheavals following this time, but the ultimate fulfillment is clearly future. This passage is quoted in Hebrews 12:26, 27 in a reference to end-time events.

"This latter house" is the millenial temple which will be built after the shaking of the nations. The people of Haggai's day must not be discouraged because the temple they were building was not as glorious as the former one. Their faith must focus on the nation's future under Messiah's reign. The very city where they lived would be the center of the peace that will pervade the world during the Kingdom Age. The present duty of the people was to be strong in faith and serve their own generation by doing God's work.

LIVING THE TRUTH

When we are living according to God's priorities, we will see His blessing on our lives. It will be obvious to others that we are God's people. The righteousness, peace, and joy of the Holy Spirit will shine forth out of our lives, glorifying God and making others hungry to know Him. (See Teaching Tip 7.)

EVANGELISM OUTREACH

The first priority of life is a right relationship with God. Until a person admits his sinful condition and accepts God's provision for cleansing from sin, he cannot experience God's blessing on his life. Challenge unsaved students to choose God as their first priority in life.

FAITHFUL STEWARDSHIP

SEEING THE SCRIPTURES

Malachi 3:7-18

7. Even from the days of your fathers ye are gone away from mine ordinances, and have not kept them. Return unto me, and I will return unto you, saith the Lord of hosts. But ye said, Wherein shall we return?

8. Will a man rob God? Yet ye have robbed me. But ye say, Wherein have we robbed thee? In tithes and offerings.

9. Ye are cursed with a curse: for ye have robbed me, even this whole nation.

10. Bring ye all the tithes into the storehouse, that there may be meat in mine house, and prove me now herewith, saith the Lord of hosts, if I will not open you the windows of heaven, and pour you out a blessing, that there shall not be room enough to receive it.

11. And I will rebuke the devourer for your sakes, and he shall not destroy the fruits of your ground; neither shall your vine cast her fruit before the time in the field, saith the Lord of hosts.

12. And all nations shall call you blessed: for ye shall be a delightsome land, saith the Lord of hosts.

13. Your words have been stout against me, saith the Lord. Yet ye say, What have we spoken so much against thee?

14. Ye have said, It is vain to serve God: and what profit is it that we have kept his ordinance, and that we have walked mournfully before the Lord of hosts?

15. And now we call the proud happy; yea, they that work wickedness are set up; yea, they that tempt God are even delivered.

16. Then they that feared the Lord spake often one to another: and the Lord hearkened, and heard it, and a book of remembrance was written before him for them that feared the Lord, and that thought upon his name.

17. And they shall be mine, saith the Lord of hosts, in that day when I make up my jewels; and I will spare them, as a man spareth his own son that serveth him.

18. Then shall ye return, and discern between the righteous and the wicked, between him that serveth God and him that serveth him not.

SETTING THE SCENE

Malachi prophesied about 100 years after Haggai and Zechariah. Most of his messages are full of condemnation and rebuke. The spiritual awakening attending the rebuilding of the temple had faded. The nation's spiritual leaders had defiled their priesthood. Often the animals the people brought to the altar were not fit to

PREPARING TO TEACH

Study Text
Malachi 3:7-18

Outline
I. Stewardship Required
   A. God's Call To Return
   B. Indicted for Robbery
II. Blessings of Stewardship
   A. Promised Abundance
   B. Evidence of God's Favor
III. Wrong Attitudes
   A. Harsh Words
   B. False Conclusions
IV. Faithfulness Rewarded
   A. The Righteous Observed
   B. The Righteous Evaluated

Golden Text: Bring ye all the tithes into the storehouse, that there may be meat in mine house, and prove me now herewith, saith the Lord of hosts, if I will not open you the windows of heaven, and pour you out a blessing, that there shall not be room enough to receive it. Malachi 3:10

Central Truth: God requires faithful stewardship in all things.

Learning Goals
1. To contrast God's attitude toward those who serve Him and those who do not.
2. To identify areas of life in which stewardship is required.
3. To describe attitudes and actions we can work on that will please God.

GETTING STARTED

As students arrive, give them copies of the "Acrostic Puzzle" provided in PATH. Students may work individually or in pairs to fill in the word for each clue. When all words are written in correctly, the first letters of each word vertically will spell the study theme, *STEWARDS*.

On the chalkboard write the study outline:

I. Stewardship Required
II. Blessings of Stewardship
III. Wrong Attitudes
IV. Faithfulness Rewarded

Clarification

Ordinances—the decrees and regulations by which God governed His people.

Robbed—defrauded. The same Hebrew word is translated "spoiled" in Proverbs 22:23.

Cursed with a curse—bound under a curse, declared detestable.

TEACHING TIP 1

Have students pair off to write an "abridged edition" of Malachi 3:7-9. Ask one person to read the passage aloud, then give the following instructions: "Write an abridged edition of these verses by condensing them into one statement which expresses their essential meaning."

Allow 3 minutes, then call for volunteers to share their work. These abridged editions help us see more clearly the contrast between God's expectations and the Israelites' performance.

TEACHING TIP 2

Relate the incident mentioned in "Guideline for Living 1." Ask: "What was lacking in both the Israelites' and the liberal church's experience that would make God call them to return to Him?"

be offered, for they were blind, lame, or sick. The religious state of Israel was so deplorable that God declared He was weary of their forms and ceremonies. In a time of such spiritual declension it is not surprising that the people had neglected the tithe and offerings, which is the focus of this week's study. Yet Malachi closes his prophecy with a message of hope for the faithful.

BIBLE COMMENTARY

I. Stewardship Required

Malachi 3:7-9

Malachi 3:7. Even from the days of your fathers ye are gone away from mine ordinances, and have not kept them. Return unto me, and I will return unto you, saith the Lord of hosts. But ye said, Wherein shall we return? 8. Will a man rob God? Yet ye have robbed me. But ye say, Wherein have we robbed thee? In tithes and offerings. 9. Ye are cursed with a curse: for ye have robbed me, even this whole nation.

A. God's Call To Return

The nation's appalling spiritual condition was nothing new. The Jews of Malachi's day were following a pattern set long ago by many of their ancestors. Their disobedience was not passive. They had actively "gone away" from God's laws. The Hebrew word indicates a defection, a rebellion, a turning aside as one would leave a path to travel another. (See Teaching Tip 1.)

Even with this stern indictment, it is a merciful God addressing His people. He loves them and wants nothing so much as to enjoy their fellowship and devotion. But there are two sides to the matter—they must return to Him.

The Jews answered God's charges with questions that were supposed to show how puzzled they were. But, like the questions in verses 8, 13, there is impudence in the retort, "Wherein shall we return?" (verse 7). It was a pretense of injured innocence: "What have we done that is so bad?"

Guideline for Living 1

The prophet's depiction of the Israelites sounds like a description of some of the mainline liberal churches of today. One young woman who turned to the evangelical tradition in her college days described her liberal home church's and her family's attitude toward her as "amazed and worried." They simply could not understand why she would be so "fanatical" in her beliefs and devotion to God. In their church, the young people had a special room set up for disco dancing, and wine was served at church functions. When she expressed her convictions against drinking alcoholic beverages, her family told her that was just "works righteousness." Regarding her association with a church that believes in speaking in tongues, they accused her of belonging to a "sect." One can easily imagine God's saying to such people, "Wake up! Strengthen what remains and is about to die, for I have not found your deeds complete in the sight of my God" (Revelation 3:2, NIV). And the people might easily answer, "What have we done that is so bad?"

B. Indicted for Robbery

What they had done makes a long list. The priesthood was corrupt, and the people were mocking God with their dead religious forms. Many had divorced their wives to marry heathen women. God's accusation shows the inevitable outcome of spiritual deterioration. Anyone involved in God's work soon observes that financial giving seems to rise or fall with the spiritual tide. Of course, people can give mechanically without their hearts really being in it. But generally speaking, faithful stewardship and consistent Christian living are closely connected. The carnal nature grasps material things tightly. When an individual does not walk close to God there is a tendency to use for selfish purposes the money that is rightfully His.

God's charge is serious. He uses a strong word: "robbed." The people had defrauded God by neglecting their financial obligations to Him. They were as guilty as the unscrupulous individual who cheats another in a business transaction.

The Hebrew word translated "tithe" means a tenth. There were several kinds of tithes in Israel. The tithe supported the tribe of Levi, including the priests, and all the needs of the tabernacle and temple (Leviticus 27:30, 31; Numbers 18:20; Deuteronomy 14:22, 23). Every third year another tithe was given for the poor (Deuteronomy 14:28, 29). The word for "offerings" is used in several ways, referring to the half-shekel tax for the sanctuary, firstfruits (the first part of the harvest), and the portions of the sacrifices reserved for the priests.

Underlying the system of tithes and offerings was this truth: everything we have belongs to God. He has put it in our hands as His stewards. The tithe system was one of God's great teaching tools, helping men keep material things in proper perspective.

Guideline for Living 2

Sometimes God uses strong words to get our attention. "Robbed" might seem extreme in describing the withholding of tithes, but this is only because the natural mind has difficulty comprehending the seriousness of disobeying God's commands. When His people do not pay the tithe they are saying by their actions, "What I have is all mine to do with as I shall decide." The Bible teaches that everything is God's. What we have is merely entrusted to us to be used properly with our responsibility to the Lord always in mind. Through tithes and offerings we share the financial responsibility of spreading the gospel. When we are not true to our responsibility, God's work suffers. This was happening in Malachi's day and—sad to say—it has often been repeated. It is disconcerting to think of God's finger being pointed at us and hear Him saying, "You have robbed Me!"

God is not mocked (Galatians 6:7). His law of sowing and reaping is inexorable. If the people thought they could rob God and not suffer for it, they had deceived themselves. They had withheld the tithe and offerings from Him, and He had withheld His blessings from them. One of the most noticeable effects of His curse was the scarcity of crops.

Question.
What basic lesson was God teaching when He instituted the system of tithes and offerings?

TEACHING TIP 3

Ask students to respond to the "Agree-Disagree" statements on the lower half of the PATH work sheet. (These are purposely worded to stimulate discussion.) Call for a show of hands for those who agree and disagree with each statement. Ask one or two volunteers to explain their position in each case.

Write these references on the chalkboard: Malachi 3:10; Matthew 6:33; Luke 14:33; 1 Corinthians 4:1, 2; 2 Corinthians 9:6-8, 13. Ask students to discuss in small groups what insight these verses give in the matter of stewardship of time, money, and talent.

Clarification

The storehouse—the rooms in the temple reserved for the tithes.

Meat—food for the priests and Levites. Nehemiah 13:10

Prove—examine; test.

The windows of heaven—a figure of speech describing the abundance of the blessing God promised.

The devourer—anything that could injure their crops, but the reference applies particularly to the best known devourer, the locust.

A delightsome land—a land in which God finds delight.

Question.

In what sense can God be "proved"?

TEACHING TIP 4

On the chalkboard draw a chart showing "The People's Responsibility" and "God's Blessings" as you discuss the content of Malachi 3:10-12. Responsibilities include: bringing in tithes, testing God's promises by obeying Him. Blessings include: floodgates of heaven open with blessings; pests prevented; fields will be fruitful; nations will recognize their prosperity; their land will be delightful.

Question.

How does this passage emphasize God's control of what we call "nature"?

TEACHING TIP 5

Divide the class into small groups to study some of the responsibilities and blessings of the Christian. List these passages on the chalkboard: Psalm 19:9, 11; Malachi 3:16, 17; 1 Corinthians 2:9; Philippians 3:10, 11, 14; 2 Timothy 4:8; Hebrews 11:6; James 1:12. Instruct students to read these passages and to continue the format used on the chalkboard for listing "Responsibilities" and "Blessings." Allow 5-10 minutes, then

II. Blessings of Stewardship

Malachi 3:10-12

Malachi 3:10. Bring ye all the tithes into the storehouse, that there may be meat in mine house, and prove me now herewith, saith the Lord of hosts, if I will not open you the windows of heaven, and pour you out a blessing, that there shall not be room enough to receive it. 11. And I will rebuke the devourer for your sakes, and he shall not destroy the fruits of your ground; neither shall your vine cast her fruit before the time in the field, saith the Lord of hosts. 12. And all nations shall call you blessed: for ye shall be a delightsome land, saith the Lord of hosts.

A. Promised Abundance

The people must bring "all" the tithes, not neglecting any portion. The rooms in the temple provided for the storing of the tithes were empty as they had been in the days of Nehemiah (Nehemiah 13:4-12). The people are now commanded to fill these storehouses with the tithes of their crops.

God does not need proving. His word is absolutely trustworthy. When He makes a promise, it does not have to be backed with a special guarantee. If He challenges man to test Him, it is for man's benefit, not God's. We tend to think of God in human terms. Our "proving" of Him is to help us understand His true character and realize He is not like fallible humans. (See Teaching Tip 4.)

B. Evidence of God's Favor

If the people obeyed, God would respond quickly. He is never sparing with His blessings. The opening of the windows of heaven is probably a picture of the skies opening to pour out the rain that had been lacking. The downpour would produce such harvests that the people would run out of storage space. God would hold back the locusts which were often the destroyer of Israel's crops (Deuteronomy 28:38; 2 Chronicles 6:28; 7:13). The vines which had been barren so long would be loaded with grapes.

Unbelievers might consider drought and insect invasions as part of nature's unpredictable behavior. But nature is under God's control. He can send the rain or withhold it. Stopping the movement of ravaging insects is no problem for the One who brought the whole universe into existence with only a word.

The promised blessings would be so widespread that other nations would notice and recognize God's favor on Israel. The fields of bumper crops and the fruit-laden vineyards would testify of God's delight in the land He had given His people.

Guideline for Living 3

What reward can the faithful Christian look forward to? The Psalmist said, "The judgments of the Lord are true and righteous altogether. And in keeping of them there is great reward" (Psalm 19:9, 11). Those who do the will of God, who love Him and serve Him will receive a reward (1 Corinthians 2:9; 2 Timothy 4:8; Hebrews 11:6; James 1:12). These verses speak of crowns of life and righteousness which will be given at the last day. Paul said he made it his goal to win the "prize of the high calling of God in Christ Jesus" (Philippians 3:14). Jesus said that even small seemingly insignificant deeds done in His name would not go unrecall for reports from each group. List responses on the chalkboard.

Clarification

Stout—The same Hebrew word is translated "hardened" in Exodus 7:22: "Pharaoh's heart was hardened." It means strong, obstinate, arrogant.

Vain—empty, worthless, futile.

Walked mournfully—gone about in mourning garb, i.e., sackcloth and ashes.

Proud—arrogant, presumptuous.

They that tempt God—they that have tested, challenged, and dared God to punish them by continually beaking His laws.

Set up—an architectural term meaning "to build." In this verse it describes people who are "built up" despite their disregard of God's laws.

TEACHING TIP 6

Brainstorm with the class on words which describe the attitude of the Israelites toward God in Malachi 3:13-15. List these on the chalkboard. Then brainstorm and list words which describe how God must have felt about His people.

Question.

What was the basic mistake in the conclusions the people had reached about the wicked's being better off than the righteous?

warded (Matthew 10:42). God himself is our greatest reward. In His presence there is "fulness of joy . . . for evermore." (See Teaching Tip 5.)

III. Wrong Attitudes

Malachi 3:13-15

Malachi 3:13. Your words have been stout against me, saith the Lord. Yet ye say, What have we spoken so much against thee? 14. Ye have said, it is vain to serve God: and what profit is it that we have kept his ordinance, and that we have walked mournfully before the Lord of hosts? 15. And now we call the proud happy; yea, they that work wickedness are set up; yea, they that tempt God are even delivered.

A. Harsh Words

What does this passage indicate about the motives behind the people's religious activities?

Skepticism had infected the whole nation. When God accused the people of speaking harshly against Him, they showed the same impudence with which they had answered His previous accusations. "Your words have been stout against me" brought the defensive question, "What have we spoken so much against thee?"

God replied quickly. They had maintained an outward show of religion. Yet His judgments had fallen on the land, so they complained that it really didn't do any good to serve Him.

The people insisted they had kept God's laws, including the fasts when they wore sackcloth and ashes. The motives behind their outward acts are clearly seen in their response to His charges. Their religion had become mechanical. It was actually a mockery of God because in their hearts they had departed from Him. They were going through the motions, engaging in empty forms. (See Teaching Tip 6.)

B. False Conclusions

Economically they were suffering. Unfortunately, they had not been willing to face the truth that their condition was the result of turning their backs on God. Their complaint about the happier circumstances of people who did not serve God shows their materialistic view. They had assumed their religious acts would automatically bring them prosperity. When this did not happen, they grew bitter and cynical. Their words are full of self-pity but lacking in any recognition that they had contributed to their own plight.

They were mistaken about material prosperity's being an accurate indicator of God's blessings. Poverty and trials do not necessarily mean that God is displeased. Good fortune is no certain indication of His favor.

What the people said about the wicked's being built up and prospering was probably true. But they had forgotten that such material blessing will come to naught if individuals persist in their godless ways.

In their time of financial struggle they were lashing out at God instead of examining themselves. They actually accused Him of making favorites of the ungodly. The arrogant were the happy ones, they declared. God not only built up the wicked, but "delivered" them, i.e., caused them to escape the misfortunes that had fallen on others.

Clarification
Thought upon his name— The Hebrew word translated "thought" refers to thoughts running through the mind in meditation.

When I make up my jewels—when I prepare my treasured possession.

Discern between—distinguish between after looking upon and inspecting.

IV. Faithfulness Rewarded
Malachi 3:16-18

Malachi 3:16. Then they that feared the Lord spake often one to another: and the Lord hearkened, and heard it, and a book of remembrance was written before him for them that feared the Lord, and that thought upon his name. 17. And they shall be mine, saith the Lord of hosts, in that day when I make up my jewels; and I will spare them, as a man spareth his own son that serveth him. 18. Then shall ye return, and discern between the righteous and the wicked, between him that serveth God and him that serveth him not.

A. The Righteous Observed

In the worst of times God has always had His faithful people. It was so in Malachi's day. The prophet spared no words about God's displeasure with those who considered the wicked better off than the righteous. But besides the cynics in Israel there were also God's faithful ones who reverenced and served Him.

These godly people maintained close fellowship, for they constantly conversed among themselves. The word "often" is not in the Hebrew text, but in the original the grammatical construction indicates frequent and continuing action.

Did this faithful remnant attract heaven's attention? Indeed. The Lord "hearkened, and heard." Two different Hebrew words are used here. The one translated "hearkened" means literally "to prick up the ears." It describes not only hearing but attentiveness. The word translated "heard" means to hear intelligently, indicating not only hearing words but understanding their meaning. God wanted His people to know their conversations had His complete attention. He was pleased with this activity.

Obviously God does not need a book to help Him remember, but He uses language humans can understand. In Malachi's day the "book" was a scroll which was unrolled as it was read. Psalm 56:8 and Daniel 12:1 are two examples of references to books kept in heaven. The Psalmist spoke of tears being recorded, and Daniel referred to God's book as a register where the names of the redeemed are written.

The word translated "remembrance" is rendered "memorial" in Exodus 12:14 which calls the Passover a memorial. When the Israelites kept the Passover, it brought a fresh recollection of God's deliverance from Egypt. Again God is accommodating His message to our understanding. He needs no special reminders; He is simply assuring His children they are never out of His thinking.

B. The Righteous Evaluated

How much do believers mean to the Lord? "Mine . . . my jewels." This is the language He used in His revelation through Malachi. The godly may be in the minority, but in the eyes of God they are a treasure of great value.

This passage looks at both the present and future. It focuses on Malachi's day, then leaps through the centuries to another faithful

Question.
What is the significance of the reference to "a book of remembrance"?

Question.
What future time is in view when God speaks of sparing His children?

Call attention to the list on the chalkboard labeled, "The People's Responsibility." Point out that these describe attitudes and actions that please God and which are part of our stewardship of the life and possessions He has given us. Ask each student to choose one attitude or action he would like to work on this week to become a more faithful steward of God. Have each one write privately an answer to this question: "What do I need to do differently to put this into practice in my life?"

Close in prayer that God will help each class member become a more faithful steward.

remnant in the hour of God's final reckoning with the nations. Terrible things are ahead for mankind in the Day of the Lord, but God will shelter His own. His care of them will be as tender and vigilant as that of an earthly father guarding his son from danger.

If anyone has difficulty in distinguishing between the righteous and the wicked, he can easily do it in the time of final judgment. While God's wrath is being poured out on the rebellious, the ones who have feared Him and spoken often to one another about His goodness and thought upon His name will be delivered. Those whose religion has been superficial will have their hypocrisy exposed.

Many have served God in obscurity. The world has not noticed them. Perhaps some fellow believers have not even been aware of their devotion, but God has known and will reward them.

This passage is another example of teaching by contrasts. Through Malachi, God denounces those who have forsaken His laws, turned religion into a mockery, and robbed Him by withholding the tithe and offerings. But, as always, the Lord extends His hand of mercy to all who will separate themselves from the wicked. God's pleasure in them is in sharp distinction from His anger at rebels. What a difference there is in the destinies of "him that serveth God" and "him that serveth him not."

LIVING THE TRUTH

To be the object of God's wrath or the object of His pleasure—these are the choices each person must ultimately face. In His mercy, God extends the deadline for judgment for many individuals and nations. Today we have the advantage over the people in Old Testament times of having the life of God himself dwelling in us, giving us the desire and ability to put Him first in all areas of life, including time, money, and talent. (See Teaching Tip 7.)

EVANGELISM OUTREACH

Faithfulness to God begins with committing one's whole life to Him. Unsaved students in your class need to come to a decision about what they will do with God's claims on their lives. Will they choose to go their own way, merely paying lip service to God as the Israelites did, or will they choose to serve God according to His conditions?

Daily Devotional Guide

M. Obeying God.
Joshua 1:7-9
T. Serving God.
1 Samuel 3:1-10
W. Honoring God.
Proverbs 3:1-10
T. Loving God.
John 14:21-24
F. Believing God.
Romans 4:19-25
S. Approaching God.
Hebrews 4:14-16

13 | GIFT OF THE HOLY SPIRIT

PREPARING TO TEACH

Study Text
Joel 2:28-32; Acts 2:1-39

Outline
I. The Holy Spirit Promised
   A. Everyone Included
   B. Deliverance Promised
II. The Holy Spirit Given
   A. The Day of Pentecost
   B. Heavenly Visitation
   C. Supernatural Utterance
III. The Holy Spirit for Today
   A. An Answer Sought
   B. Conditions Explained
   C. The Promise Assured

Golden Text
The promise is unto you, and to your children, and to all that are afar off, even as many as the Lord our God shall call. Acts 2:39

Central Truth
The gift of the Holy Spirit is promised to every believer.

Learning Goals
1. To describe the evidences of the Holy Spirit's outpouring.
2. To identify the characteristics of those to whom the Holy Spirit is given.
3. To contrast what life is like before and after the outpouring of the Spirit.

SEEING THE SCRIPTURES

Joel 2:28-32

28. And it shall come to pass afterward, that I will pour out my Spirit upon all flesh; and your sons and your daughters shall prophesy, your old men shall dream dreams, your young men shall see visions:

29. And also upon the servants and upon the handmaids in those days will I pour out my Spirit.

30. And I will show wonders in the heavens and in the earth, blood, and fire, and pillars of smoke.

31. The sun shall be turned into darkness, and the moon into blood, before the great and the terrible day of the Lord come.

32. And it shall come to pass, that whosoever shall call on the name of the Lord shall be delivered: for in mount Zion and in Jerusalem shall be deliverance, as the Lord hath said, and in the remnant whom the Lord shall call.

Acts 2:1-4, 38, 39

1. And when the day of Pentecost was fully come, they were all with one accord in one place.

2. And suddenly there came a sound from heaven as of a rushing mighty wind, and it filled all the house where they were sitting.

3. And there appeared unto them cloven tongues like as of fire, and it sat upon each of them.

4. And they were all filled with the Holy Ghost, and began to speak with other tongues, as the Spirit gave them utterance.

38. Then Peter said unto them, Repent, and be baptized every one of you in the name of Jesus Christ for the remission of sins, and ye shall receive the gift of the Holy Ghost.

39. For the promise is unto you, and to your children, and to all that are afar off, even as many as the Lord our God shall call.

SETTING THE SCENE

When we begin reading the Book of Joel, it seems an unlikely prophecy to contain the promise of the Holy Spirit's outpouring. It commences with the description of a locust invasion which had come as divine judgment. This ravaging of the land becomes a picture of the future Day of the Lord, which Joel describes in unforgettable language. Then he brings God's message of hope to those who will repent, moving finally past the Great Tribulation into the days of the Millenium. In the midst of such a message God introduces His promise of the time when He will pour out His Spirit on all flesh. On the Day of Pentecost the Spirit revealed to Peter that the fulfillment of Joel's prophecy had begun and he declared this to the multitude.

Begin the class session by writing on the chalkboard the words *BEFORE* and *AFTER.* Brainstorm with the class on words that could describe a person's relationship or attitude toward God before the coming of the Holy Spirit. List these in the "Before" column. (i.e., distant, impersonal, uncaring, unaware.) Then brainstorm on words that described the disciples' attitude toward God and their relationship to Him on the Day of Pentecost. List these in the "After" column. (i.e., excited, loyal, joyful, close, etc.) Read Joel 2:28 and Acts 2:38, 39.

Clarification

Wonders—signs, portents. The Hebrew word is used in Exodus 4:21 to describe the supernatural signs Moses would do before Pharaoh. In Exodus 7:3 it refers to the ten plagues God was going to send on Egypt.

Pillars—columns, clouds.

Terrible—causing fear.

TEACHING TIP 1

Bring to class a pitcher of water, an empty jar, a tray to hold these, a towel (for spills)

BIBLE COMMENTARY

I. The Holy Spirit Promised

Joel 2:28-32

Joel 2:28. And it shall come to pass afterward, that I will pour out my Spirit upon all flesh; and your sons and your daughters shall prophesy, your old men shall dream dreams, your young men shall see visions: 29. and also upon the servants and upon the handmaids in those days will I pour out my Spirit. 30. And I will show wonders in the heavens and in the earth, blood, and fire, and pillars of smoke. 31. The sun shall be turned into darkness, and the moon into blood, before the great and the terrible day of the Lord come. 32. And it shall come to pass, that whosoever shall call on the name of the Lord shall be delivered: for in mount Zion and in Jerusalem shall be deliverance, as the Lord hath said, and in the remnant whom the Lord shall call.

A. Everyone Included

We have a better understanding of many Old Testament passages when New Testament light is thrown on them. Peter's commentary on Joel provides clearer insights into some of the prophet's language.

In the Hebrew, Joel's word "afterward" means essentially what our English translation indicates, i.e., following another event— as in Genesis 15:14 (describing Israel's Egyptian bondage): "afterward shall they come out with great substance." However, the Holy Spirit revealed through Peter at Pentecost that in this context "afterward" means "in the last days."

To Old Testament believers the last days are the time when the Messiah's kingdom will be established. This will indeed be the eventual outcome of God's plan, but in the light of New Testament teaching we know the last days began with Jesus' ascension.

Other Old Testament passages speak of a new relationship between God's Spirit and believers at some future time, but the terminology is usually different. For example, in Ezekiel 11:19 God looks to a day of restoration for Israel when He will "put a new spirit within you." But through Joel God promises to "pour out" His Spirit.

There was no such general outpouring in the Old Testament. Of course, the Spirit was constantly active, coming upon certain individuals to equip them for specific tasks. He inspired prophets and the writers of Scripture. But there was not this widespread gushing out of the Spirit which God revealed to Joel. That blessing was still future.

The Hebrew word translated "pour out" is used in many passages and in various ways. It means basically an emptying. In Exodus 29:12 it describes the pouring out of sacrificial blood on the altar. The Psalmist uses the word to symbolize the pouring out of his "complaint" before the Lord (Psalm 142:2). It sometimes pictures the outpouring of God's wrath on the wicked, as in Ezekiel 20:8.

In Ezekiel 39:29 and Zechariah 12:10 this word describes the outpouring of God's Spirit on His people, and of course this is also

and a dry sponge. Use these to illustrate graphically the "pouring out" spoken of in Joel 2:28, 29.

Jesus' own words further explain the nature of the outpouring of the Holy Spirit. On the last day of the Feast of Tabernacles when traditionally water was poured from a pitcher, Jesus stood up and invited thirsty people to come to Him and drink, and out of them would flow rivers of living water. Read John 7:37-39.

The object lesson helps us understand this truth. When we become full of the Spirit to the point of saturation, then the Spirit overflows from our lives into the lives of those around us.

Question.

What is the significance of this list: sons, daughters, old men, young men, servants, and handmaids?

TEACHING TIP 2

Ask students to "neighbor nudge" for 2 minutes on the question, "What are the characteristics and qualifications of those who receive the Holy Spirit?" (Write this question on the chalkboard.) Call for several volunteers to share their responses.

Question.

Why are the Spirit's outpouring and the Day of the Lord so closely connected in Joel's prophecy?

true in Joel 2:28. It is as though God overturns a vessel full of blessing and causes its contents to gush out on all who will receive it. (See Teaching Tip 1.)

Guideline for Living 1

After Christ's work on the cross had been finished, the Holy Spirit could be outpoured on those with repentant hearts. It makes no difference what the age, sex, or social position of a person is. When any of God's people consecrate themselves and are transformed in their desires and priorities, they can be brought to the place where God can empower them with His spirit to carry out His will and plan. God accomplishes this as He pours out His Spirit in a saturating experience that fills, surrounds, and overflows. This can be illustrated by a dry sponge placed in a jar. When water is poured into the jar it first saturates and fills up the sponge. Then the water surrounds the sponge, and finally overflows the jar. In our lives, the Spirit is meant to fill and overflow us in the same way. "He that believeth on me, as the Scripture hath said, out of his belly shall flow rivers of living water. (But this spake he of the Spirit, which they that believe on him should receive)" (John 7:38, 39).

The outpouring of the Spirit is not for a religious elite. It recognizes no distinctions because of sex, age, or social status. Servants and handmaids were male and female slaves. In the Old Testament we never read of a slave prophesying. In Numbers 12:6 God speaks of prophetic revelations through dreams and visions. Joel said such knowledge would be given to both young and old during the time of the Spirit's outpouring.

Moses once prayed, "Would God that all the Lord's people were prophets, and that the Lord would put his spirit upon them!" (Numbers 11:29). In the Old Testament only a few were prophets, but through Joel, God promised that the Spirit will make prophets of all who receive His fullness. Moses' prayer has been at least partially answered! (See Teaching Tip 2.)

B. Deliverance Promised

In the Hebrew Bible the Book of Joel has four chapters. Chapter 3 is short—only five verses. In our English Bible they are the last five of chapter 2. This arrangement probably conveys the Pentecostal message more forcefully than the chapter divisions to which we are accustomed.

After the promise of the Spirit's outpouring, Joel turns to the spectacle of blood, fire, pillars of smoke, the darkening of the sun, and the moon's becoming like blood. This is end-time terminology. The prophet associates these signs with "the great and the terrible day of the Lord." The passage reminds us of the language of Revelation.

Verse 32 seems to focus especially on the Jewish remnant who turn to the Lord during the Great Tribulation. There will be divine mercy during the time of wrath, for anyone who calls on the name of the Lord shall be delivered.

Joel did not see the time gap between the outpouring of the Holy Spirit and the final judgments. God has not yet revealed this truth. But when Peter stood before the multitude on the Day of Pentecost the Spirit showed him the larger picture. Peter saw the intervening period between the time of the Spirit's outpouring and the Day of the Lord. This merciful interim is our present dispensation—the Church age.

Peter's words in Acts 2:21 show that God's promise to save "whosoever" calls on Him is not restricted to Jews who will accept Jesus during the Great Tribulation. The deliverance of which Joel spoke extends far beyond Mount Zion and Jerusalem, even though he did not realize it. Such mercy is offered during the present age to everyone who will accept God's Son as Lord and Saviour. The intervening centuries of the Spirit's outpouring have been like a dam restraining the flood of wrath that will in God's time burst over the human race.

II. The Holy Spirit Given
Acts 2:1-4

Acts 2:1. And when the day of Pentecost was fully come, they were all with one accord in one place. 2. And suddenly there came a sound from heaven as of a rushing mighty wind, and it filled all the house where they were sitting. 3. And there appeared unto them cloven tongues like as of fire, and it sat upon each of them. 4. And they were all filled with the Holy Ghost, and began to speak with other tongues, as the Spirit gave them utterance.

A. The Day of Pentecost

By God's command the calendar of Israel included feasts observed at set times throughout the year. From a New Testament viewpoint, they picture His whole plan of salvation.

Leviticus 23 lists the feasts and the activities included in their observation, although reference is made to them in many other passages. Passover, Tabernacles, and Pentecost are often called pilgrim festivals because all Jewish males were required to go to Jerusalem for their celebration.

Pentecost comes from a Greek word meaning "fiftieth" and does not appear in the Old Testament. Leviticus 23 does not give a name to this feast, but it was generally called the Feast of Weeks (Exodus 34:10; Deuteronomy 16:10, 16; 2 Chronicles 8:13). This was because it came seven weeks (a "week of weeks") after the Sabbath following Passover. Unlike the Passover and the Feast of Tabernacles, which lasted seven days each, Pentecost was a one-day feast, coming at the end of harvest.

Along with sacrifices, offerings, and other ritual, a distinctive feature of this feast was the priest's waving of two loaves of bread before the Lord (Leviticus 23:17-20). Baked with flour made from the newly harvested grain, the bread was a symbol of the whole crop. The waving of the loaves was a gesture of thanksgiving. Most New Testament scholars consider these two loaves a picture of the Church, composed of both Jew and Gentile.

B. Heavenly Visitation

God had introduced the dispensation of the Law with awesome signs. Now, on the day that had been celebrated for centuries as a harvest festival, He begins the age of grace. He did it with signs that startled a city and caused thousands to cry, "What meaneth this?" (See Teaching Tip 3.)

Clarification

Was fully come—was in the course of being completed. The day had arrived but was not ended.

Rushing—literally, borne along.

Mighty—violent.

Cloven—dividing; parting asunder.

TEACHING TIP 3

On the chalkboard write the question, "To the Jewish believers in the Upper Room, what would wind and fire symbolize?" Divide the class into small groups and give each group one instruction card from the "Scripture Search" activity provided in PATH. Ask students to discuss the first question. After 5 minutes call for reports from each group.

The wind is one of nature's most powerful forces, yet God controls it and frequently uses it to accomplish His purposes (Genesis 8:1; Exodus 10:13; 14:21; 15:10; Numbers 11:31). He took Elijah to heaven in a whirlwind (2 Kings 2:11). Isaiah spoke of "his mighty wind" (Isaiah 11:15).

In the Old Testament God often used fire to symbolize His presence. When He confirmed His covenant with Abraham, "a smoking furnace, and a burning lamp" passed between the pieces of the sacrifice (Genesis 15:17). He arrested Moses' attention by causing a bush to burn without being destroyed (Exodus 3:1-5). When God gave the Law, "Mount Sinai was altogether on a smoke, because the Lord descended upon it in fire" (Exodus 19:18). God guided His people through the wilderness by a pillar of cloud that became a pillar of fire at night (Exodus 13:21).

So when the 120 heard a sound like a violent blast of wind that moved along until the sound filled every corner of the house, they knew it was supernatural. Their familiarity with the Old Testament record made them realize immediately that God was at work.

When tongues suddenly appeared in the room and began to part and settle over each head, everyone saw that the tongues looked like fire. There was no doubt then that the God of Abraham, Moses, Elijah, and all the prophets was visiting His people again.

C. Supernatural Utterance

A new sign appeared to inaugurate the new age. Each of the 120 opened his mouth and began to speak, but it was not in his own language. Prophets had often spoken as God gave them utterance, but it was in their own tongue. Never before had believers declared His praises in languages they had not learned.

"The Spirit gave them utterance" is an important statement. Each believer's ability to speak in another tongue was given to him by the Spirit. "They were all filled . . . and began to speak." The speaking was the result of the filling and was the first physical evidence it had happened.

This was not the last time the miracle of speaking in tongues occurred. Each time an outward sign of the Spirit's infilling is named in Acts, it is tongues.

Guideline for Living 2

How is the outpouring of the Holy Spirit demonstrated in the lives of believers today?

Although the initial evidence of the baptism in the Holy Spirit is speaking in other tongues, this cannot be the *only* evidence of the Spirit's infilling. Another evidence is the life of Christ being manifest through us. The fruit of the Spirit (Galatians 5:22, 23) is a description of the characteristics of Christ's life in us: love, joy, peace, patience, kindness, goodness, faithfulness, gentleness, self-control.

In Joel 2:28 an evidence of God's Spirit's being poured out is that His people will have dreams and visions. The operation of the supernatural gifts of the Spirit further indicates the Spirit's fullness. (See Romans 12:3-8; 1 Corinthians 12:4-11.) Additional evidences include: unselfish ministry to others, joyful witness about Christ, power to overcome sins, willingness to follow God's leading.

III. The Holy Spirit for Today
Acts 2:38, 39

Acts 2:38. Then Peter said unto them, Repent, and be baptized every one of you in the name of Jesus Christ for the remission of sins, and ye shall receive the gift of the Holy Ghost. 39. For the promise is unto you, and to your children, and to all that are afar off, even as many as the Lord our God shall call.

A. An Answer Sought

Verse 6 speaks of the multitude being "confounded." The reason was "that every man heard them speak in his own language." Many of the Jews in the large crowd were of the Dispersion (verses 8-11). They lived in other lands but had come to Jerusalem for the feast days. To hear fellow Jews who obviously had not been outside their native land speaking in these many languages was too much for their natural reasoning. They cried out for an answer.

The flippant remark by some that the 120 were full of new wine is typical of the reaction of the natural mind when it encounters the supernatural. Peter dismissed it quickly as unreasonable because it was only 9 o'clock in the morning—not the hour when a large crowd would be found drunk.

But Peter had an answer. The Holy Spirit gave it to him. The ancient prophecy of Joel was finally being fulfilled. Then the apostle turned to the subject of Jesus of Nazareth—the One the Spirit came to exalt.

Their wicked hands had crucified Jesus, Peter declared, but God had allowed it because it was His plan to offer His Son as the sacrifice for sin. The unanswerable proof that Jesus is the Son of God is His resurrection from the dead. "It was not possible" for death to hold Jesus (verse 24).

Peter was speaking to Jews who knew the Old Testament. After quoting Joel he turned to the words of David (verses 25-31). Through the Spirit's revelation Peter knew that this passage from Psalm 16 concerns Jesus, not David.

If the multitude needed proof that Jesus had risen from the dead and returned to heaven, the miracle they were witnessing was all they needed. The outpouring of the Spirit testified to Jesus' victory and exaltation. "He hath shed forth this, which ye now see and hear," Peter testified (verse 33).

B. Conditions Explained

The Spirit's work in the hearts of the multitude is demonstrated by the cry, "What shall we do?" Peter's first word was, "Repent." He presented repentance as an absolute necessity, not an option.

As an outward sign of the inward work of repentance, they must be baptized. "In the name of Jesus Christ" is not a baptismal formula any more than "in the name of the Lord" is in Acts 10:48. "In the name of Jesus Christ" distinguishes Christian baptism from that of John the Baptist.

"For the remission of sins" should be translated, "unto the remission of sins." Water baptism does not wash away sins. It is part of a repentant believer's obedience which leads to the forgiveness of his sins.

week ahead of time.) Have each student give a brief report on what they have discovered from the Scriptures about the importance of the subject. Lead a brief discussion on the questions, "Do you think repentance is under-emphasized today?" and, "Do you think water baptism is under-emphasized today?"

TEACHING TIP 6

As a concluding activity, ask students to write an acrostic on the word *Pentecost*. This acrostic will be on the theme of evidences of a Spirit-filled life, using each of the letters of "Pentecost" to start a word or phrase. If your class is working well in groups, ask each group to write one acrostic. Provide a large sheet of construction paper and felt pens. (Or you may choose to have students work individually.) More than one word for each letter can be used. After all groups have finished, ask each to share one or two lines of their acrostic. Here is an example:

P atience; power
E nter into the joy of the Lord
N ever forget God's presence
T ell others about Jesus
E vidences of love, joy, kindness
C ounting everything unimportant for the sake of Christ
O peration of gifts of the Spirit
S elf-control
T ongues; temperance

Daily Devotional Guide

M. Invitation to Life.
Isaiah 55:1-3
T. A New Beginning Promised.
Ezekiel 36:26-31
W. Spiritual Thirst Quenched.
John 7:32-39
T. Promise of the Comforter.
John 14:16-26
F. Ministry of the Holy Spirit.
John 16:1-15
S. Day of Pentecost.
Acts. 2:1-13

Guideline for Living 3

Deliverance from sin follows the outpouring of God's Spirit. (See John 8:36; Galatians 5:1.) Anything that hinders our openness with God or with His children is a form of bondage from which we need to be delivered. All sin hinders communication with God. Poor relationships with family and close friends can become a form of bondage, keeping us from fulfilling the law of love, Personality and emotional disturbances can hinder us from freely enjoying healthy relationships with others. Bad habits such as the use of drugs, alcohol, and tobacco bind our personal freedom to control our lives. Which of these categories represent needs of yourself or your class members? What steps will you take to begin to allow the Spirit to bring deliverance and freedom?

C. The Promise Assured

The time was past when the Holy Spirit would come only on certain people for a specific work. God would now freely give His Spirit to all who meet His conditions.

"The promise" includes the forgiveness of sins and the gift of the Holy Spirit. "Unto you" covers all who stood before Peter. "Your children" refers to their descendants.

"All that are afar off" means the Gentiles. Paul referred to them as "you which were afar off" and Jews as "them that were nigh" (Ephesians 2:17). The Jews were "nigh" because they had received God's covenants and were acquainted with His commandments. The Gentiles were "afar off" because they were outside the nation to which God had committed the teaching of His laws. But the outpouring of the Spirit throughout this age erases all differences and opens the door of the Kingdom to every nation and race.

"Even as many as the Lord our God shall call" extends the promise in distance to the remotest place humans will ever be found. It extends it in time to the last moment of this age of grace.

LIVING THE TRUTH

The Holy Spirit is being outpoured today on people from all countries, cultures, and religions. The common factor in Spirit-filled Christians is a repentant heart and a desire to know Christ fully. The Spirit is given to us to enable us to live out His life in this world. We must choose daily to draw on this source of power and allow Christ to live through us. (See Teaching Tip 6.)

EVANGELISM OUTREACH

As Christians allow the Holy Spirit to live through them, the unsaved will be attracted to Christ. Jesus promised to satisfy the spiritual thirst of all those who call upon Him. Give unsaved students in your class an opportunity to begin a new life today. "Come, all you who are thirsty, come to the waters" (Isaiah 55:1, NIV). Jesus is the Water of Life.

Recommended Resources

The summer/85 theme is "Things To Come." The teacher will find the following books very helpful in advance preparation and classroom use.

GENERAL REFERENCE WORKS

The Packet of Adult Teaching Helps (PATH) contains teaching and learning aids especially designed to supplement these studies. Use with every lesson. Order # 67 1475, $5.05.

Systematic Theology by E. S. Williams (3 vols.) A Pentecostal theology that provides insights in all the areas of doctrine. Three-volume set: cloth. Order # 02–0650 $18.00.

Knowing the Doctrines of the Bible by Myer Pearlman. A basic theological work that will aid the teacher to understand and effectively teach most of the doctrinal truths. Order # 02–0534 $6.95.

Great Doctrines of the Bible by William Evans and S. Maxwell Coder. A well-organized handbook of fundamental doctrines. Order # 03–1611 $9.95.

SELECTED STUDY HELPS

Countdown by Dan Betzer. A look at the Rapture through the eyes of a former newsman. You'll see here the return of Jesus Christ a reality calling for immediate preparation. Use with study 5. Order # 02–0481 $1.95

Prophecy Marches On! Vol 2, Revelation by J. G. Hall. This book covers the entire Book of Revelation along with Ezekiel 38 and 39. Use with studies 8-13. Order # 03–3503 $5.95.

New Money or None? by Willard Cantelon. This book shows how to find protection in the coming financial crash and how a family can survive the economic disasters of the next decades. Use with study 2. Order # 03–3449 $2.95.

The Day The Dollar Dies by Willard Cantelon. World prophecy and world finance are two fascinating topics. Use with study 6. Order # 03–1238 $2.95.

The Book of Revelation by Clarence Larkin. With much ability he draws numerous illustrations to clarify this difficult subject. Use with studies 9-13. Order # 03–2963 $9.80.

The Coming World Dictator by John Wesley White. Is the world's desperate fear of nuclear holocaust setting the stage for a takeover by a universal dictator? This author looks at this and other mind-boggling questions about the future. Use with study 7. Order # 03–1205 $2.95.

The 1980's: Countdown to Armageddon by Hal Lindsey. A bestselling author looks at the signs of the Second Coming—religious deception, famine, plagues, war, and others. What is our only Hope? Use with studies 10 and 11. Order # 03–2140 $6.95.

The Late Great Planet Earth by Hal Lindsey. In this book the author gives the prophets of God a chance to speak, and in their speech will be found God's program for the future. Simple, easy to follow. Use with studies 6-12. Order # 03–1933 $2.95.

There's a New World Coming by Hal Lindsey. The Book of Revelation. Use with studies 8-13. Order # 03–2705 $2.95.

It's Getting Late by Stanley Horton. Do we know how soon Christ will return? Will the Church be raptured before the Tribulation? These are just a few of the questions answered in this commentary on the epistles of Thessalonians. Use with studies 5-7. Order # 02–0570 $1.25.

Israel in Prophecy by Louis H. Hauff. Use with studies 1-4. Order # 02–0532 $1.00.

What's Ahead by Charles Harris. Use with studies 1-6. Order # 02–0897 $2.50.

The above items are available from the Gospel Publishing House, 1445 Boonville Avenue, Springfield, Missouri 65802. We do not necessarily endorse the entire content of these publications. Prices and availability are subject to change without notice.

How To Use Your Adult Teacher

It is imperative that you read the Adult Student quarterly during your advance study. Pay particular attention to the questions under "Applying the Word." Be ready to discuss any one of these questions during class time if a student brings it up. You may wish to integrate specific questions into your presentation for a given Sunday.

Wide and Narrow Columns

Instead of the two equal columns used in the past, your *Adult Teacher* now uses the format of a wide and narrow column. Each study contains the same information as before, but it has been rearranged.

The wide column contains the following: SEEING THE SCRIPTURES, SETTING THE SCENE, BIBLE COMMENTARY (including Scripture blocks), Guidelines for Living, LIVING THE TRUTH, and EVANGELISM OUTREACH.

On the first page of each study, the narrow column contains an overview of the study under the heading, PREPARING TO TEACH. This column shows the Study Text, Outline, Golden Text, Central Truth, and Learning Goals.

On the remaining pages, the narrow column includes: GETTING STARTED, Clarification, Teaching Tips, questions from the commentary, and the daily devotional guide.

Helps Where You Need Them

The commentary, application, and methodology sections are totally integrated so the teacher has what he needs at the point of use. The section headed, GETTING STARTED, is at the beginning—where it would be used. It contains suggestions for getting the students' immediate attention and providing a bridge to the Bible study that follows.

The "Clarification" section, which explains words or expressions in the study text that might be difficult to understand, is placed opposite the Scripture block to which it applies.

Each Teaching Tip is placed or referred to at the point where it would be used to help students get a better grasp of that part of the Bible Commentary. If a Teaching Tip calls for the use of PATH (Packet of Adult Teaching Helps), that information will be given. When you see the heading, "Question," in the narrow column, it is a question answered in the Bible Commentary at that point.

The guidelines for living are considered a part of the application, but are so closely related to the commentary that this section is inserted in the commentary. It is set off by a long, narrow bracket and by the heading, "Guideline for Living," followed by the number. This section should not be considered an interruption of the commentary. It is for the purpose of helping the teacher apply to daily life the Bible truth being studied.

The daily devotional guide is for the teacher's personal benefit. It is to help you get into the Word throughout the week, and hopefully you will find in the daily devotionals truths you will use in the lesson.

At the end of the study, "Living the Truth" is a summary of all the guidelines for living. "Evangelism Outreach" is actually a sub-head under "Living the Truth." It is a reminder to use the class not only as a time to nurture Christians but also to bring the unsaved to a decision for Christ.

Use It as a Tool

You will find more material in the *Adult Teacher* than you can use in any one session. Your own advance study will show you what to include and what to omit. You may sometimes develop activities of your own that will seem more suitable. The *Adult Teacher* is a tool, not a substitute for the Bible or personal preparation. Use this quarterly for the purpose for which it has been designed and your efforts will be rewarded.

EVANGELISM
In the class room

What do you want to happen in your class this coming Sunday? In what direction will your teaching be pointed? Will you be only teaching the lesson or are you going to be reaching for souls? At the close of that precious hour, do you plan to leave with a sense of accomplishment or leave in defeat because you were sidetracked?

There are many things you can accomplish in the class. Keep in mind that nearly anyone can read the teacher's quarterly to a class of students, but real teaching for decision is much more than such an exercise in futility. Again, what do you plan to have happen in your class? You may think you want great things to happen, but you only have a limited time span. To make the best use of those few minutes will take an effort in planning—to make them count for eternity.

Set a Goal for This Week

You could teach with the goal of increasing Biblical knowledge. This is an excellent and worthy goal. Knowledge is knowing; recognizing, and communicating facts. It's one of the requirements for the successful Christian life. It should be an ongoing goal. It takes more than one class session to teach the major spiritual truths, much less the entire gamut of God's Word.

Or, you can teach with the goal of changing an attitude. It's a worthy goal for any lesson. Attitudes are based on emotions, feelings, understanding, and value judgments. These are built on the foundation of knowledge.

Have you taught with the goal of effecting a behavioral change? Behavior is what one does, how one solves the problem, how one treats people, and how one acts in the light of basic knowledge.

Knowing what God says about all believers being brothers and sisters in the family is a fact that can be learned because it can be taught. The ultimate learning of this truth happens when your pupils not only think in these terms, but also begin to act to serve others in this kind of relationship. Knowledge is only that until it is translated into a life-changing action.

When you teach for a goal, everything you do is geared in that direction. Too much of our classroom teaching can best be described as being like the man who flung himself on his horse and rode off in all directions at the same time!

Evangelism Is Your Highest Goal

In the light of our subject at hand, evangelism in the classroom would be the highest goal you could set! At this point you will be effecting life changes for time as well as eternity. You will be turning people from the ways of sin to a new direction to follow God. That's the definition of true repentance, "a complete turning around of direction and returning in the opposite way." As the little girl said, "It's being sorry enough for your sins to quit doing them."

Evangelism is a goal that comes directly out of the heartthrob of God: "The Lord is . . . not willing that any should perish, but that all should come to repentance" (2 Peter 3:9). This was the singular goal of Jesus Christ:

"For this cause came I unto this hour" (John 12:27). The cause was Calvary, which in turn became the vehicle of salvation for the entire world.

Evangelism is not the by-product of classroom efforts. It should be the goal, the very purpose for being. It is the reason for the entire Church to exist. Therefore, the first and most important decision you, as a teacher, will make is the classroom objective, your teaching/learning goal. My challenge to you is to make evangelism the primary goal this week and in the weeks to come.

The Teacher

God has always used people in carrying out His purpose in reaching the lost and will continue to do so. There are no "Plan B's" on the drawing board; no alternative plans to use angels or any kind of being other than mankind.

The most vital factor we will look at in this chapter is the wonderful creature called the teacher! The call of today is not for better methods, but better people! So our quest is to delve into the innermost being of that beautiful person who is a teacher. Surveys confirm the classroom teacher as the most important element in each situation. He/she is the most critical element to make all the chemistry jell for the right results.

Meaningful teaching is more than using the latest methods, the finest materials, the most sophisticated approaches, or the most dramatics. To be a teacher is to be growing in understanding and insight, because the teacher is first and foremost a learner too.

Teaching Is a Trust

Teaching takes on meaning with the realization that it is a trust from God. It is more than teacher's work. Paul informs the church at Thessalonica: "We were allowed of God to be put in trust with the gospel, even so we speak; not as pleasing men, but God" (1 Thessalonians 2:4). It's important that each teacher work from this divine motivation. Your response to God will be evident in your teaching. The teaching experience will invariably reveal to your class the most meaningful relationship in your life. If the teacher has responded to God in faithfulness, love, and consistency, then this is what will be revealed before the class. In fact, you can't hide this. Out of that life-changing experience with God

will come a teaching style that has the same kind of impact on others.

Reach for Souls Every Week

Can you think of a better setting for evangelism than in your classroom? Evangelistic teaching comes out of that vital, exciting experience each teacher must have with Jesus Christ. Teaching is the process of reproducing the life of Christ in others. The teacher, to be effective, will be prepared and relevant. The gospel is a message without change, but the methods must be contemporary in order to have a hearing. All of life's experiences can contribute to the contemporary class. Making disciples in today's world means helping the student find solutions to life. And the ultimate solution to a confusing, senseless life is Jesus! Teacher, what a fantastic privilege you have! What an exciting opportunity you have each Sunday. The privilege of inviting people to make heaven their eternal home is waiting for you in your class this coming week!

The Student

Adults are concerned about the business of living life in a real world. Many of the illusions of youth have been placed aside or knocked down by the nitty-gritty give-and-take of their world. It's not an easy place in which to live and feel productive.

We are faced with ever-growing personal problems in today's adult. Some of these difficulties have arisen as an aftermath of broken homes. Broken homes have left broken people.

Another segment that is growing in size is the senior citizen population. Loneliness, fear, worry about tomorrow, and rejection are all things with which these adults are trying to cope. The population of our nation, as a whole, is getting older each passing year, and these adults need Jesus Christ. There is an urgency because of the shortness of their remaining life.

There is a great adventure ahead for you as your turn your class into an evangelistic outreach. God has promised you His power, which will be unleashed through your life and ministry.

Evangelism . . . the Unfinished Task by Robert J. Strand. © 1981 by the Gospel Publishing House, Springfield, Missouri 65802. Used by permission.

THINGS TO COME

THE REVELATION OF JESUS CHRIST

Study Text
Revelation 1:1-20

Outline

I. The Eternal Christ
  A. Eternal Glory and Power
  B. Almighty and Eternal
II. The Majestic Christ
  A. Dazzling Splendor
  B. The Revelation of the Father
III. The Sovereign Christ
  A. Sovereign Over Life and Death
  B. Revelation for our Benefit

Golden Text
I am he that liveth, and was dead; and, behold, I am alive for evermore, Amen; and have the keys of hell and of death. Revelation 1:18

Central Truth
Every believer needs a personal revelation of the living Christ.

Learning Goals
1. To renew our vision of Christ as the triumphant Lamb of God.
2. To strengthen our grasp of God's eternal viewpoint in our lives.
3. To heighten our appreciation of the Book of Revelation as a source of blessing.

SEEING THE SCRIPTURES
Revelation 1:7-18

7. Behold, he cometh with clouds; and every eye shall see him, and they also which pierced him: and all kindreds of the earth shall wail because of him. Even so, Amen.

8. I am Alpha and Omega, the beginning and the ending, saith the Lord, which is, and which was, and which is to come, the Almighty.

9. I John, who also am your brother, and companion in tribulation, and in the kingdom and patience of Jesus Christ, was in the isle that is called Patmos, for the word of God, and for the testimony of Jesus Christ.

10. I was in the Spirit on the Lord's day, and heard behind me a great voice, as of a trumpet,

11. Saying, I am Alpha and Omega, the first and the last: and, What thou seest, write in a book, and send it unto the seven churches which are in Asia; unto Ephesus, and unto Smyrna, and unto Pergamos, and unto Thyatira, and unto Sardis, and unto Philadelphia, and unto Laodicea.

12. And I turned to see the voice that spake with me. And being turned, I saw seven golden candlesticks;

13. And in the midst of the seven candlesticks one like unto the Son of man, clothed with a garment down to the foot, and girt about the paps with a golden girdle.

14. His head and his hairs were white like wool, as white as snow; and his eyes were as a flame of fire;

15. And his feet like unto fine brass, as if they burned in a furnace; and his voice as the sound of many waters.

16. And he had in his right hand seven stars: and out of his mouth went a sharp two-edged sword: and his countenance was as the sun shineth in his strength.

17. And when I saw him, I fell at his feet as dead. And he laid his right hand upon me, saying unto me, Fear not; I am the first and the last:

18. I am he that liveth, and was dead; and, behold, I am alive for evermore, Amen; and have the keys of hell and of death.

SETTING THE SCENE
Through the centuries of church history the Book of Revelation has been a source of hope and comfort to the Christian. In times of crisis and difficulty, it has always been a special blessing. Today, when the world as a whole seems to have lost its way, this book points us ahead to the triumph of Christ.

The real title of the book is found in its first phrase, "The Revelation of Jesus Christ." Matthew presents Jesus as the promised

GETTING STARTED

Use the following agree-disagree statements to stimulate student thinking on the Book of Revelation as well as this week's study.

Write the statements on the chalkboard and ask students to raise their hands in either agreement or disagreement as you read each statement. Take little time to discuss the statements now, explaining that you will cover them more fully in the course of your study:

1. The Book of Revelation offers special blessing to those who read it.
2. Jesus as the Lamb of God is a picture of our Lord unique for our day.
3. Revelation offered comfort to early Christians who were persecuted, but isn't especially relevant for our day.
4. Revelation is the Holy Spirit's guidebook for the last days.

Clarification

The seven Spirits—that is, the sevenfold manifestation of the Holy Spirit. (See Isaiah 11:2, 3.)

First-begotten — firstborn; used here as a technical term for the Messiah who is first, special, and beloved because His resurrection guarantees ours and assures us that we shall share in His glory.

Prince—ruler.

Wail—beat their breasts in mourning because of His death. (See Zechariah 12:10.)

Alpha and Omega—the first and last letters of the Greek alphabet. We say, "A to Z."

The Lord—the Lord God, the divine Lord.

Question.

Who is the coming One in verses 7 and 8, and how does this compare with verse 4?

King. Mark shows Him as the ideal Servant. Luke pictures Him as the perfect and compassionate Son of Man. John reveals Him as the powerful Son of God. But Revelation gives us a new picture of Jesus as the Lamb of God who triumphs gloriously. We need this revelation of Jesus today.

BIBLE COMMENTARY

I. The Eternal Christ

Revelation 1:4-8

Revelation 1:4. John to the seven churches which are in Asia: Grace be unto you, and peace, from him which is, and which was, and which is to come; and from the seven Spirits which are before his throne; 5. and from Jesus Christ, who is the faithful witness, and the first-begotten of the dead, and the prince of the kings of the earth. Unto him that loved us, and washed us from our sins in his own blood, 6. and hath made us kings and priests unto God and his Father; to him be glory and dominion for ever and ever. Amen. 7. Behold, he cometh with clouds; and every eye shall see him, and they also which pierced him: and all kindreds of the earth shall wail because of him. Even so, Amen. 8. I am Alpha and Omega, the beginning and the ending, saith the Lord, which is, and which was, and which is to come, the Almighty.

A. Eternal Glory and Power

After John introduces this book as a revelation of Jesus Christ, he promises blessing for all who read the book aloud and for all who hear and obey. Then John proceeds to greet the readers with the customary first-century Christian greeting of grace and peace.

This grace and peace are ours through the full cooperative working of God the Father; God the Holy Spirit in His sevenfold manifestation as the Spirit of the Lord and the Spirit of wisdom, understanding, counsel, might, knowledge, and the fear of the Lord; and God the Son, our Lord Jesus Christ.

More specifically, this grace and peace are made available to us through the work of Jesus. He is the faithful Witness who has declared (or unfolded) the Father and His grace and truth to us (John 1:14, 18). He ministers the fullness of divine love to us (Romans 5:5). As firstborn from the dead, He takes the place of leadership which, according to the ancient custom, belonged to the heir. Thus, He is able to make us joint heirs with Him (Romans 8:17) and sharers of His triumph, for He is King of kings and Lord of lords (1 Timothy 6:15; Revelation 17:14; 19:16). In His love Christ also cleanses us from our sins by means of His own blood and makes us what God has always wanted His people to be: kings and priests unto God (Exodus 19:6; 1 Peter 2:5, 9). This is our position now, and we have the promise that we shall reign with Him when He comes (2 Timothy 2:12). No wonder He deserves the glory and dominion or power forever and ever:

B. Almighty and Eternal

In verse 4 God the Father is the coming One. Here in verses 7 and 8, Jesus is the coming One.

The Old Testament often speaks of God's coming to "visit" His people. He came sometimes to bless, sometimes to bring judgment. In the New Testament Jesus came to bring salvation. He remains the Mediator between God and man (1 Timothy 2:5). Thus He still comes to us whenever even two or three gather in His name (Matthew 18:20). But our blessed hope is that He will soon come back to earth in the same manner His disciples saw Him go (Acts 1:11). They saw a cloud bear Him out of their sight. We shall see Him return on clouds of glory (Daniel 7:13, 14; Matthew 26:64).

Before the wrath and judgments of the Great Tribulation, "the dead in Christ shall rise first: then we which are alive and remain shall be caught up together with them in the clouds, to meet the Lord in the air" (1 Thessalonians 4:16, 17). "God hath not appointed us to wrath," that is, to the wrath which will fall on those left behind (1 Thessalonians 5:9).

Then, at the close of the Tribulation, "the Lord Jesus shall be revealed from heaven with his mighty angels, in flaming fire taking vengeance on them that know not God, and that obey not the gospel of our Lord Jesus Christ" (2 Thessalonians 1:7, 8). At this time every eye shall see Him.

Those who pierced Christ include the Jews who are to be restored (Zechariah 12:10; 13:1). But the Bible here gives us a new revelation that extends the mourning of Zechariah 12:10 to include Gentiles from all tribes and nations as well. (Compare Matthew 24:30.)

Verse 8 concludes the salutation of the Book. In verse 4 God the Father is named as the eternal One. Here, Jesus shares in the Father's eternal nature and being. Jesus is the Alpha and Omega, the beginning and the ending. Thus, He himself is without beginning and without end. He who is coming again is the Almighty, a term applied in the Old Testament to the *El Shaddai* and to the Lord of hosts. He is the all-powerful, omnipotent One. In other words, all that God revealed himself to be in the Old Testament we see revealed even more fully in Jesus in the New Testament.

Question.
What are the two phases of Christ's coming at the end of the age?

Question.
Who are those who pierced Him?

TEACHING TIP 1
Write "ALPHA AND OMEGA" on the chalkboard along with the references, Revelation 1:8; 21:6; 22:13. These are the only places in Scripture where this phrase is used. Ask: "What does this phrase mean? What does it tell us about Jesus?"

As you discuss this phrase, help the students see how it reveals Jesus as: (1) the purpose of all things, and (2) the source or supplier of all needs. You might ask students to read the verses aloud to the class. See also Colossians 1:16, 17.

Guideline for Living 1

Frustration with the cares and pace of living has given rise to the term "rat race" for our 20th century life-style. Too many times Christians feel the same sense of despair as the world about the "rat race."

But God wants us to know much more joy in living. How, then, can we bring His blessings into play in such a way that we cannot only cope with life's trials, but even rise above them?

To escape the "rat race," we need to look down on life from a higher vantage point. We need to practice living each day with eternity's values in mind. That is, we must allow the Spirit—through our prayers and study of the Word—to give us God's eternal viewpoint. As we enjoy the presence of "him which is, and which was, and which is to come" (Revelation 1:4) we rise above despair.

II. The Majestic Christ
Revelation 1:9-16

Revelation 1:13. And in the midst of the seven candlesticks one

Clarification

Candlesticks—lampstands for lamps which burned olive oil.

Garment—tunic, like those worn by kings or priests.

Girdle—belt, band. This band of pure gold around the chest was a mark of triumphant royalty, in contrast to the worker or servant who wore a belt (girdle) around the waist.

Fine brass—burnished bronze. Some believe it was an alloy of gold and copper.

Question.

What is meant by the Lord's Day?

Question.

What did John see first in this great revelation?

TEACHING TIP 2

Ask: "Does it matter what day we choose to worship God? Is there need for controversy over the choice of Sunday or Saturday?"

Incorporate the "Bible Commentary" material about the Lord's Day as you discuss this question. Many believers are alternately confused or bound in spirit over this matter of which day we "must" worship the Lord. Being free from bondage to the Old Testament ritual law in Christ (Romans 8:1-4), we are free to worship God "in spirit and in truth" (John 4:23, 24).

TEACHING TIP 3

Direct the students to a map of New Testament times (map charts, a Bible atlas, or back-

like unto the Son of man, clothed with a garment down to the foot, and girt about the paps with a golden girdle. 14. His head and his hairs were white like wool, as white as snow; and his eyes were as a flame of fire; 15. and his feet like unto fine brass, as if they burned in a furnace; and his voice as the sound of many waters. 16. And he had in his right hand seven stars: and out of his mouth went a sharp two-edged sword: and his countenance was as the sun shineth in his strength.

A. Dazzling Splendor

About A.D. 95 many true believers suffered great persecution and distress under the cruel Roman emperor Domitian. Many were killed. Some, like the apostle John, were sent into exile. It would have been easy for them to compromise and escape suffering. But they remained steadfast in Jesus. He helped them bear up in the midst of all the pressures.

Out on the rocky, treeless, little island of Patmos, John may have seemed forsaken. But the Lord was with him. On the Lord's Day he was in the Spirit. Then a glorious revelation, a marvelous unveiling of God's plan, was given to him.

Since "The Lord's Day" was the common name for Sunday in second-century Christian writings, many believe it was used this way in the first century also. Others point out that the New Testament elsewhere always calls Sunday simply, "the first day of the week." Since the Book of Revelation is full of Old Testament language, it may well be that the Day of the Lord, that is, the future day of judgment, is meant. Thus, it is possible to infer that John, by the Holy Spirit, was projected into the future Day of the Lord at the end of the age. (See Teaching Tip 2.)

The Spirit focused his attention first on a new revelation of Jesus as our compassionate High Priest and conquering King. He is the Son of Man, the One who fulfills Daniel's prophecy of Him who is to come with clouds of heaven to receive "dominion, and glory, and a kingdom, that all people, nations, and languages, should serve him" (Daniel 7:14). He wears clothing that identifies Him as Priest and King, the fulfillment of the prophecies of Isaiah and Zechariah. (See Teaching Tip 3.)

He stands in the midst of seven golden candlesticks or lampstands, representing the seven churches of Asia. The gold speaks of Christ in all His deity and glory, for the Church is the body of Christ. The oil of the lamps typifies the Holy Spirit within the believers and moving in the churches. Even though persecuted, the Holy Spirit's power is still using them in enabling them to bring the light of Christ to the world.

Guideline for Living 2

The Bible contains many warnings that God's people will suffer at the hands of the ungodly. Jesus told His disciples that the same world which hated Him would hate His followers too. Paul said that all who live godly in following Christ will be persecuted. Church history is full of accounts of the persecution of Christians, and often their martyrdom.

Stangely enough, some believers have a misconception that unless they *provoke* persecution, they aren't really living for Jesus!

of-the Bible maps, etc.) and locate the seven churches of
Asia to which John sent the
messages of Revelation 1-3.

There are well-meaning Christians who are suffering more for their own unwise behavior than for the gospel.

We must ask ourselves: How do we react to persecution? What role does persecution play in our lives? Are we undergoing persecution for our own foolishness or genuinely for the cause of Christ? His glorious power is able to deliver us, or if it suits His need for our lives, to sustain us through every persecution.

B. The Revelation of the Father

The Old Testament applies these descriptions to God the Father, especially as the mighty Judge and Ruler of the universe. But, as John 5:22 shows, the Father has now given all judgment to the Son. Thus, in verses 14 and 15 the Bible shows that all the attributes ascribed to the Father in the Old Testament are also attributes of the Son.

Question.
To whom does the Old Testament apply the language used in verses 14 and 15?

Many Bible scholars recognize here that the whiteness of His hair represents absolute purity as well as the dazzling splendor of His holiness. Eyes like a flame of fire speak of His penetrating wisdom and His righteous judgment. Feet of the finest burnished bronze speak both of strength and of the brazen altar. Thus, they remind us of the sacrifice of Christ by which He triumphed over Satan and purchased our redemption. Finally, the voice of many waters pictures God's Word coming loud and clear from the One who is the Living Word. Taken together, all this pictures Jesus both as the one Mediator between God and man and the One in whom dwells the fullness of the Godhead bodily (Colossians 2:9). (See Teaching Tip 4.)

The seven stars, most probably representing the leaders or pastors of the seven churches, are in Christ's hand. This means more than protection. They are in the right hand, the hand of action, ready for Him to use them. No persecutor, no enemy of the Church, can stop them from helping the churches to do God's will and win victories for Him. The sharp sword coming from the mouth of Jesus is also their sword. The sword may also speak of reproof for the churches, since judgment must begin in the house of God (1 Peter 4:17). Later the sword brings judgment on the nations (Revelation 19:15).

Question.
What encouragement does verse 16 give?

TEACHING TIP 4

Ask three students to read these Scripture verses and explain them in their own words:
Student One: John 14:8, 9
Student Two: Colossians 2:3, 9, 10
Student Three: Hebrews 1:2, 3.
As the student explains his passage, write key words or ideas from each passage on the chalkboard. When the three have finished, use their explanations to develop a mini-lecture on the relationship of Jesus and the Father.

Notice also that the full glory of Jesus is no longer veiled as it was in the resurrection appearances in the Gospels (compare John 17:5). Now His glory is like that of the sun in its full summertime, noonday brilliance. This is the glory we all shall see when we are changed at His coming (1 John 3:2; 1 Corinthians 15:51, 52).

III. The Sovereign Christ
Revelation 1:17-20

Clarification

Fear not—stop being afraid.
He that liveth—the Living One; a title of God (Joshua 3:10; Psalms 42:2; 84:2; John 5:26).
Hell—Greek, *hades;* in the New Testament this usually

Revelation 1:17. And when I saw him, I fell at his feet as dead. And he laid his right hand upon me, saying unto me, Fear not; I am the first and the last: 18. I am he that liveth, and was dead; and, behold, I am alive for evermore, Amen; and have the keys of hell and of death. 19. Write the things which thou hast seen, and the things which are, and the things which shall be hereafter.

refers to the place of punishment.

Mystery—secret meaning (of a symbol or metaphor).

Angels—or messengers; the Greek word can mean either. These may be the pastors of the churches, since John is writing the message to them.

Question.
What assurance did Jesus give?

TEACHING TIP 5
Write the three-point outline of Revelation suggested in the "Bible Commentary" section on the chalkboard or overhead projector as you discuss the above question. You may wish to provide this basic outline on paper for more permanent reference as you work through this quarter's studies. It serves as an easy summary division of the Book of Revelation.

Question.
How does verse 19 apply to the Book of Revelation as a whole?

A. Sovereign Over Life and Death

On the Mount of Transfiguration John saw a glimpse of Christ's glory. There the face of Jesus shone like the sun and His clothes glistened and flashed like lightning from the outshining of the inner glory (Matthew 17:2). That was only a foretaste. The glory of the Transfiguration awed the disciples but did not strike them down. John on Patmos saw much more and he was not able to stand the full impact of this new revelation of Christ's glory, a glory so great that it knocked him unconscious. But the gentle touch of Jesus revived him. Then once again he heard the same "Fear not" that had so often encouraged the disciples while Jesus ministered to them during His life on earth.

1. He has not changed. He is the first and the last; the eternal, unchanging Christ; the same yesterday, and today, and forever (Hebrews 13:8).

2. He is the same living Christ who rose from the dead and inspired new faith and hope in His followers after the terrible ordeal of the Cross.

3. He lives forever and the future is in His hands. He who is our Good Shepherd, the Rock of Ages, the Prince of Life, the Author of Eternity, guarantees that because He lives we shall live also. By the same Holy Spirit who raised Him from the dead, we shall share in the coming resurrection of believers. He can guarantee this also because the keys of death and of hades are in His hands. They shall never prevail against His Church (Matthew 16:18).

B. Revelation for Our Benefit

Jesus touched John not just to revive him, but to commission him to write the revelation he had just received and the revelation he was about to receive.

Many Bible scholars see verse 19 as indicating a threefold division of the Book. (See Teaching Tip 5.)

1. The introductory revelation in chapter 1.

2. The messages to the seven churches of Asia and to all the churches of the present age, chapters 2 and 3.

3. The events of the end-times, beginning with chapter 4 and extending through the remainder of the book.

It is clear from this that God meant this book to be a means of blessing, encouragement, and revival for all churches, including ours today.

Guideline for Living 3

"Ah, the Book of Revelation isn't for us. Why, it's just somebody's bad dream from the first century and has nothing to do with the real world!"

"I'd love to understand Revelation better. I suppose it has some real answers for today. But it's so confusing. I just can't find any value in it."

How often have you heard reactions like those? But according to the Bible, "all Scripture is given by inspiration of God, and is profitable" (2 Timothy 3:16). That includes the Book of Revelation. In fact, the Holy Spirit pronounces a special blessing on us for making the effort to read and apply Revelation to our lives (Revelation 1:3).

The Holy Spirit will bless us as we meditate on this part of God's

Word. He will guide us. There are many good study guides and reliable teachers of the Word who are able to help us as God uses them and guides our minds to receive His truth.

(See Teaching Tip 6.)

1. Some interpret Revelation's symbols as a vague picture of the struggle between good and evil that is always going on. They fail to see that the symbols are given to reveal truth. Behind every symbol is a tangible reality. For example, the Antichrist is called a beast, not because he will look like one, but because of his nature. Picturing him as a beast is symbolic, but the Antichrist will be a real person. All the symbols in this book deal with realities which will actually take place.

2. Some take a "preterist" view which says the book does little more than picture the sufferings of the Church in the first century. They fail to see the relationship of the book to the other prophecies of the Bible which look ahead to a future age and a future kingdom.

3. Others take a "historical" view—really, a historicist view, since this view is not more historical than any other. They spread the events of chapters 4 through 19 over the whole of church history. For example, they try to tie some of them to the rise of the papacy and the conquests of Islam. Edward Irving, in the early 1800s for example, thought that the son of Napoleon would be the second beast in the Book of Revelation. Irving was greatly disappointed when Napoleon's son died. All such identifications are unsatisfactory.

4. The simplest and most satisfactory view is the "futurist" view which considers everything or practically everything after chapter 4 as future, occurring at the end of the age. This is the view held by most premillennialists today. It is the view we shall follow in these studies as we continue on through the Book of Revelation.

Question.
What are some of the ways Christians have interpreted the revelation of the future in this book?

TEACHING TIP 6
As you discuss the "Bible Commentary" question, "What are some of the ways Christians have interpreted the revelation of the future in this book?" display the overhead transparency, "Understanding Revelation," from PATH. Instructions in PATH suggest ways you can use the sheet for maximum effectiveness in your class setting.

TEACHING TIP 7
To conclude your class session today, sing a hymn together. The study has centered on Jesus and His glory, so select something to reinforce the glory and comfort of Christ in our lives. " 'Tis So Sweet To Trust in Jesus" would be appropriate.

Daily Devotional Guide
M. Majestic Visitation.
Judges 6:11-18
T. Transforming Vision.
Isaiah 6:1-8
W. Promised Encounter.
Luke 2:25-38
T. Unrecognized Deity.
Luke 24:13-24
F. Emphatic Revelation.
Acts 9:1-9
S. Restricted Understanding.
1 Corinthians 2:9-16

LIVING THE TRUTH

Jesus is the central theme of Revelation. We must never forget that it is the "revelation of *Jesus Christ*" (Revelation 1:1, emphasis ours), not just a set of disconnected mystery visions of the future.

In this book the Holy Spirit gives us a glimpse of the glory of the One who died for our sins and now is exalted above everything in heaven and earth. We will do well to linger in our reading of John's desciption of our glorified Lord. It will strengthen our faith to realize that this is the One who has complete control of human affairs as well as the universe itself.

As we keep Christ at the center of our study, His Word comes alive and works in our lives. (See Teaching Tip 7.)

EVANGELISM OUTREACH
Phrases such as "eternal viewpoint," "revelation of Jesus Christ," etc., have little or no meaning until you have met the One they refer to. Have you asked Jesus to reveal himself in a personal way to you? You can do so right now. He does not stand aloof, but is ready to draw near to everyone who draws near to Him.

SEEING THE SCRIPTURES

Revelation 3:14-22

14. Unto the angel of the church of the Laodiceans write; These things saith the Amen, the faithful and true witness, the beginning of the creation of God.

15. I know thy works, that thou art neither cold nor hot: I would thou wert cold or hot.

16. So then because thou art lukewarm, and neither cold nor hot, I will spew thee out of my mouth.

17. Because thou sayest, I am rich, and increased with goods, and have need of nothing; and knowest not that thou art wretched, and miserable, and poor, and blind, and naked:

18. I counsel thee to buy of me gold tried in the fire, that thou mayest be rich; and white raiment, that thou mayest be clothed, and that the shame of thy nakedness do not appear; and anoint thine eyes with eyesalve, that thou mayest see.

19. As many as I love, I rebuke and chasten: be zealous therefore, and repent.

20. Behold, I stand at the door, and knock: if any man hear my voice, and open the door, I will come in to him, and will sup with him, and he with me.

21. To him that overcometh will I grant to sit with me in my throne, even as I also overcame, and am set down with my Father in his throne.

22. He that hath an ear, let him hear what the Spirit saith unto the churches.

SETTING THE SCENE

Revelation 1 shows Jesus moving among the seven golden lampstands, representing the seven churches of the Roman province of Asia. His purpose was to encourage and challenge them. Thus, He subjects them to rigid inspection, commending their virtues and warning them of their faults.

There were more than seven churches in Asia. Probably these were chosen because they were representative. They show the variety of needs present in their day. They also provide lessons for the entire Church Age. Notice that each of the letters to these seven churches ends with a message to all the churches: "He that hath an ear, let him hear what the Spirit saith unto the churches." That includes our churches today.

PREPARING TO TEACH

Study Text
Revelation 3:14-22

Outline
I. Need for Renewal
  A. Lukewarm
  B. Self-Deceived
II. Steps to Renewal
  A. The Source for True Riches
  B. Call to Repentance
III. Promise of Renewal
  A. Present Fellowship
  B. Future Glory

Golden Text
Behold, I stand at the door, and knock: if any man hear my voice, and open the door, I will come in to him, and will sup with him, and he with me. Revelation 3:20

Central Truth
All believers should examine their motives and actions to see that they please the Lord.

Learning Goals
1. To explore and increase the depth of our commitment to Christ.
2. To open our lives to the Holy Spirit's power to help us turn from sin and spiritual lukewarmness.

GETTING STARTED

Write the words "HOT" and "COLD" on the chalkboard. Begin your class session by asking students to name various foods and beverages that are best when eaten either hot or cold.

After a brief discussion of this subject, ask how the students would enjoy the various items if they were neither hot nor cold but only lukewarm. Use this to move into a discussion of the Laodicean church.

Clarification

Laodiceans—the fertile Lycus valley and the commerce brought by important Roman roads helped make them wealthy and prosperous.

Amen—Truly. He puts the "amen" to the promises of God (2 Corinthians 1:20).

Beginning—origin, first cause, ruler. Christ as God the Son was not created. He always was, is, and will be (John 1:3, 10).

Miserable—or pitiable.

Poor—or beggarly, powerless.

TEACHING TIP 1

Bring a map to class and use it to locate Laodicea. Ask one or two students to summarize what we know about the city and the church from the Bible Commentary sections I.A, B; II., Clarification, A.1-4; and Guideline for Living 3.

Question.

How did Jesus feel about this?

BIBLE COMMENTARY

I. Need for Renewal

Revelation 3:14-17

Revelation 3:14. Unto the angel of the church of the Laodiceans write; These things saith the Amen, the faithful and true witness, the beginning of the creation of God. 16. So then because thou art lukewarm, and neither cold nor hot, I will spew thee out of my mouth. 17. . . . Thou sayest, I am rich, and increased with goods, and have need of nothing; and knowest not that thou art wretched, and miserable, and poor, and blind, and naked.

A. Lukewarm

(See Teaching Tip 1.)

The letters to the seven churches of Asia are given to us in an order which follows a geographical sequence. Ephesus was the nearest church to the Isle of Patmos. The other churches follow in order along the old Roman roads, north to Pergamum and then southeast to Laodicea, about 100 miles from Ephesus. Many Bible scholars see a historical sequence also. In a remarkable way, the church at Ephesus fits the conditions of the Church as a whole at the end of the first century. The rest of the churches then follow in sequence, ending with the Laodicean church which fits all too well the general conditions of the nominal churches today.

In these letters Jesus has some good things to say about most of the churches. But He gives the Laodiceans no commendation whatsoever. They were drifting along in a lukewarm condition that brought them a very sharp rebuke.

Before the Laodiceans were converted they were, of course, very cold spiritually. When they accepted Christ and were filled with the Holy Spirit, we can be sure they became very zealous followers of their Lord and Saviour. Unfortunately, they relapsed into a lukewarm condition. If they had been a little colder they might have realized their need. If they had been a little hotter, they might have responded to the Holy Spirit's moving and stepped out to accomplish something for God. But in their lukewarm condition they were indifferent and unresponsive.

Our Lord is disturbed when He is dealing with a people He can neither use nor bless. He was ready to spew them out of His mouth. That is, He was ready to reject them, just as one would reject a glass of lukewarm water on a hot day.

Guideline for Living 1

Fervor counts in our relationship with God. Jesus condemned the Laodicean believers because they showed no real devotion toward Him at all—they simply remained indifferent. If we do not love Him fervently, we must be honest enough with ourselves to admit it. We cannot "coast" spiritually, trusting in form or past experience.

The Lord explains the terrible danger we face if we let spiritual indifference lead us away from Jesus: "It had been better for them not to have known the way of righteousness, than, after they have known it, to turn from the holy commandment delivered unto them" (2 Peter 2:21).

Question.
Did Jesus really want to reject the Laodicean Christians?

Not at all. Notice how He presented himself to them. He wrote to them as the *Amen* (a Hebrew word meaning "truly"; a great word of assent). As the *Amen*. He guarantees the truth of God's promises. Thus, He wanted them to see all the promises of God were still available even in Laodicea. He is also the faithful and true Witness. That is, the Word, the promises He brings from the Father are reliable. He will never go back on His Word.

We know we can depend on Him also because He was with the Father in the beginning (John 1:1). In fact, He is the Beginner. John 1:3 makes it clear that all things came into being through Jesus as the living Word, and apart from Him nothing was made, created, or came into being. That is, Jesus is the living Word through whom God spoke the universe into being. He is the living Word who took the moist dust of the earth and formed a man and breathed into him the breath of life. He was the Mediator between God and man at the beginning. He is the Mediator who brings us God's redemption and forgiveness. He is the Mediator who will bring God's plan to its final consummation. How can we be lukewarm about that!

B. Self-deceived

Question.
What caused the lukewarmness of the Laodicean believers?

Listen to what they said about themselves. They took pride in their riches. In this they shared the attitude of their non-Christian neighbors. In A.D. 60 an earthquake practically leveled the city. Rome offered to help them rebuild. But the Laodiceans proudly rejected any aid, saying they could well afford to do it all by themselves.

They also took pride in their material possessions. This church, unlike most of the others, suffered no persecution. They were not even troubled with false doctrine or false teachers. The Greek might indicate they took pride in spiritual riches as well. But still they allowed themselves to be so taken up with the things money can buy that they lost their desire for the things of the Spirit. They had not learned "how to abound" as the apostle Paul had (Philippians 4:12). Thus, they become self-satisfied in their enjoyment of riches and thought they had need of nothing. Because self was central they did not see the need of others either. All they thought of was, "I am rich; I have need of nothing."

Guideline for Living 2

Self-reliance. What picture comes to your mind? Americans remember their hardy pioneer heritage, filled with brave men and women who tamed mountains and prairies. But even these pioneers learned to depend on one another and weren't totally self-reliant.

Neither are we self-sufficient as spiritual "pioneers" and pilgrims in this world. We're to be God-reliant, living Christ-centered lives built upon the Word and dependent upon the Spirit. The Laodiceans lost sight of that. As a result, Jesus had to use stern words to remind them of their need of Him (Revelation 3:17).

God saw the Laodiceans as wretched, not knowing what a miserable spiritual condition they had fallen into. He looked at them as most pitiable specimens of Christianity. He saw them as poor in spite of their big bank accounts on earth. They had no treasures laid up in the bank of heaven. They were blind to the reality of true riches. They were blind to the needs of others, blind also to the need of giving themselves for the spread of the gospel. Their rich clothing may have impressed the people around them, but they were naked in the eyes of God. They were rich and religious in the eyes of the world. They were more pitiable in the eyes of God than the most pitiable of wretched, starving, ragged beggars. How sad that they could deceive themselves so badly and not realize it!

Clarification
Buy of me—acquire from me. Compare Isaiah 55:1.
Tried—tested and refined.
Eyesalve—Laodicean physicians were famous for the powders they prepared for the treatment of eye inflammation.
Rebuke—show them their faults and correct them.
Chasten—discipline by giving both guidance and punishment.
Zealous—eager, earnest; implies deep concern and active steps of obedience.

Question.
What was Jesus' attitude toward these people?

TEACHING TIP 2
At least a week (perhaps two) ahead of time, give the reprinted article in PATH, "Some Rich People Have Money," to a student. Ask him or her to read it and be prepared to give a short oral summary of it in class. Take time for a few minutes of class interaction, then use the discussion as a transition into Guideline for Living 3 about self-reliance.

TEACHING TIP 3
Ask: "When trials or suffering come into our lives, does this mean God is chastening us for sin?"

Use these discussion points to help your students understand some truths about the

II. Steps to Renewal
Revelation 3:18, 19
Revelation 3:18. I counsel thee to buy of me gold tried in the fire, that thou mayest be rich; and white raiment, that thou mayest be clothed, and that the shame of thy nakedness do not appear; and anoint thine eyes with eyesalve, that thou mayest see. 19. As many as I love, I rebuke and chasten: be zealous therefore, and repent.

A. The Source of True Riches
What a rebuke Jesus gave Laodicea! Can you imagine how the people in this church must have felt? Imagine too how Jesus must have felt when He had to give such a rebuke. (See Teaching Tip 2.)

Jesus was grieved we can be sure. Many Bible passages show that when we sin, God is hurt more than we know. But He is grieved because He loves us so. This rebuke, though it was severe, came out of the great heart of Jesus' love. Just as the Heavenly Father chastens, disciplines, "child-trains" those He loves, so does Jesus (Proverbs 3:11,12; Psalm 94:12; Hebrews 12:5-11).

This kind of rebuking, chastening, and training may not always be so pleasant while we are going through it. But God's purposes are always good. He wants to bring us out into a place where we can enjoy the fullness of His blessings. His purpose for the Laodicean believers was restoration and renewal. (See Teaching Tip 3.)

1. The Laodiceans must look to Jesus as their source. They had been giving too much attention to material things. Now that He had made it clear to them they were poor, blind, and naked, they must turn to Him as their only hope of restoration and healing.

2. These merchants and citizens of this wealthy commercial city needed a better gold, a purer gold than the gold gained through their business ventures. Because they had taken their eyes off Jesus they were poor with respect to the gold, the fire-tested, fire-approved gold that Jesus gives. Turning to 1 Peter 1:7 we find that our faith is more precious, more valuable than gold. The faith we acquire from Christ will stand the test and will endure. It will bring praise, honor, and glory at the appearing, that is, at the revelation (Greek, *apokalupsei)* of Jesus Christ. From this also we see that our faith is not merely our attitude of faith, but it includes

reality and role of suffering in the Christian life. Cover those points you feel are most helpful:

1. Believers are not exempt from suffering (Philippians 1:29; 1 Peter 3:17).

2. Suffering and hardship aren't always a rebuke from God or a result of sin (John 9:1-3).

3. Suffering and trials are tools God may choose to use to mold and strengthen our faith (1 Peter 1:7; 3:14).

As you lead this discussion, make an effort to avoid arguments. Instead, help the students arrive at a Biblical balance between the extremes of those who see suffering and hardship for the Christian as either (1) God's punishment for sin or (2) never related to our walk with Christ.

TEACHING TIP 4

Take time out from your regular class routine to ask for special prayer requests related to specific student needs. Too often, Sunday school class becomes a time of lecture and discussion and fails to include the opportunity for class members to help each other through prayer and fellowship.

You might wish to ask one or two students to divide the requests after they have been given. Or another approach would be to ask someone to pray for each need as it is mentioned.

the content of our faith, the full gospel as it is centered in Jesus. No one is richer than the believer who is rich in faith and rich in *the* faith—both the gift of the Spirit.

3. The wools of Laodicea were famous. But Jesus has clothing of dazzling white far better than their looms could weave. His gift to His bride the Church is clothing of fine linen signifying righteousness, clean and white signifying that we are freed from sin and triumphant in Him. These robes of righteousness are Christ's righteousness given us through His grace and made real in our lives through the work of the Holy Spirit. (See Romans 4:3, 6, 11, 22-25; Philippians 3:9.)

4. The things of this world had clouded their vision so they could no longer see the value, joy, and excitment of spiritual things. Jesus has a better ointment for the eyes, for He can restore our spiritual sight. By the help of the Holy Spirit they could see their true need. Then as the Holy Spirit continued to illuminate the Word, they could come to see and understand the truths of Christ, of God's plan, of heaven, and of the gifts and blessings of the Spirit. Nothing is more thrilling than the discoveries that bless us as the Holy Spirit continues to guide us into all the truth (John 16:13, where the Greek has the article, "the truth.").

Guideline for Living 3

Jesus' call to the Laodiceans focused on the good things the people of that city thought they had to boast about. According to commentaries on Revelation, the city was noted for: (1) big banking, (2) a famous trade in black wool, and (3) a renowned medical school. So Jesus pinpointed their complacency by telling them to seek Him for gold, white raiment, and eyesalve.

In the same way today, Jesus knows how to lead each of us to trust Him as our source for all that we need most. As the Holy Spirit draws us together around individual needs, we unite as Christ's body to build up one another. (See Teaching Tip 4.)

B. Call to Repentance

At first glance it may have seemed that the situation in Laodicea was hopeless. But there is always hope for those who will repent.

Jesus loved them all. He was calling for a total repentance on the part of all the members of the church in Laodicea. "To repent" means to change the mind in the sense of changing basic attitudes and values. This change of mind and heart cannot help but be shown by a change in one's actions, manner of speech, and total life-style.

This repentance must also be shown by an earnestness that takes immediate steps to respond to the rebuke and counsel of Jesus. We can be sure that if they put this off they would become hardened in their self-satisfaction and self-deception. Surely they were in danger of becoming like the worldly rich men whom James 5:1 says will someday "weep and howl." When Jesus and the Holy Spirit gives us a call to repentance, nothing is more important or has a higher priority. Remember, too, that when we do repent we have the promise of seasons of refreshing from on high (Acts 3:19, where the Greek indicates we can continue to have these times of refreshing until Jesus comes again).

Clarification

I stand—I have been standing and still stand.

Knock—I keep knocking.

Sup—dine, eat a meal; implies fellowship.

Him that overcometh—the victor, the winner, the conqueror.

Saith—keeps on saying. The Holy Spirit wants all churches of all ages to hear this message. It is for us today.

TEACHING TIP 5

Revelation 3:20 may be one of the Bible verses best known to Christians. To gain a fresh feeling for the message of this verse, ask several students to read it from versions other than the King James. (If your students don't normally bring other versions to class, make sure you have two or three on hand.)

The beginning of the verse in the *New International Version* is especially striking as it shows Jesus' effort to gain the Laodiceans' attention: "Here I am!"

Question.

How can this be applied today?

III. Promise of Renewal

Revelation 3:20-22

Revelation 3:20. Behold, I stand at the door, and knock: if any man hear my voice, and open the door, I will come in to him, and will sup with him, and he with me. 21. To him that overcometh will I grant to sit with me in my throne, even as I also overcame, and am set down with my Father in his throne. 22. He that hath an ear, let him hear what the Spirit saith unto the churches.

A. Present Fellowship

Christ's final words to the church at Laodicea are in reality addressed to all the churches right down to the end of the Church Age. Because of His love He rebukes and disciplines every church that becomes worldly, careless, or materialistic. But He does more. He takes His stand outside the church and keeps knocking and knocking, waiting for someone to open the door. Though He has given severe warnings, His real desire is not to spew them out of His mouth but to have fellowship with them. (See Teaching Tip 5.)

Guideline for Living 4

In the end, we are accountable to Christ as *individuals.* Even if a brother or sister chooses to remain lukewarm, Jesus still invites ME to himself: "If any man hear my voice, and open the door, I will come in to him, and will sup with him, and he with me" (Revelation 3:20)!

1. It can be applied to churches where the fires of revival have died out and worldly, materialistic attitudes prevail. If someone, even one person, will open the door and enter into renewed fellowship with Jesus, this may be the key to revival for the whole church. Jesus wants to manifest His presence, His power, and His glory in our midst. He wants to make the local body of believers a holy temple, a sanctuary where He dwells to bring light, comfort, and blessing to all.

2. It can be applied to individuals whose hearts have grown cold or who have become so busy with the things of this life that they have ceased to give much time to seeking the Lord and meditating on His Word. Our Lord does not force himself upon us, but if we will just open the door of our hearts to Him, He will come in. He, the King of Glory, wants to make each one of us the place of His dwelling, to live, abide, and act in us, revealing His presence and doing His work through us. As someone has said, He will be in us "a fountain of amazing joy."

3. It can be applied to the sinner. Though this passage is specifically directed to churches, Jesus died for all the world (John 3:16) and the call to open the heart's door to Jesus is certainly to "whosoever will."

4. There is a great supper coming, the Marriage Supper of the Lamb (Revelation 19:9). Only those who sup with Him now will sup with Him then. For this reason Jesus makes the call to repentance and renewal so very urgent. No one can afford to delay.

The final challenge in Christ's letters to the churches is to us all. The challenge is to overcome, to conquer, to win, in order that we may share the results of Calvary and the triumph of Christ as we reign with Him during the thousand years of the Millennium. (See Teaching Tip 6.)

"This is the victory that overcometh the world, even our faith" (1 John 5:4). Actually, we must see this in the light of 1 John 5:1-5. Everyone who believes that Jesus is the Christ (God's anointed Messiah and Saviour; God's anointed Prophet, Priest, and King) is born of God. That is, the Holy Spirit takes this truth and uses it to bring us Christ's life within us. The evidence of this will be a love for God and for other born-again believers. In this we will be keeping the God-given, Christ-confirmed commandments that we love God with all our heart, soul, mind, and strength, and that we love one another with the same selfless, self-giving, impartial love that Jesus demonstrated on Calvary. But this is all the result of our faith, the result of our belief that Jesus truly is the Son of God.

This final challenge is thus in line with the other challenges given to all the churches. If we are winners, we shall eat of the tree of life in the midst of the paradise of God (Revelation 2:7). If we are losers, we won't. Winners will not be hurt by the second death. Losers will end up in the second death, the lake of fire. There is no middle ground, no overcomers who are better than other believers. We either keep our hand in the hand of Jesus by faith or we lose out altogether. This is the message to the churches.

Question.
How do we overcome?

TEACHING TIP 6
Be sure to direct class attention to the excellent discussion of "overcomers" in the Bible Commentary. Read or have a student read the last paragraph aloud.

TEACHING TIP 7
Conclude class today with a song celebrating the victory we have in Jesus. "Victory in Jesus" or "Redeemed by the Blood of the Lamb" would be good choices.

Daily Devotional Guide

M. Basis for Renewal.
2 Chronicles 7:12-18
T. Plea for Renewal.
2 Chronicles 29:3-11
W. Need for Renewal.
Luke 17:26-37
T. Resistance to Renewal.
John 8:30-39
F. Hindrances to Renewal.
2 Timothy 3:1-9
S. Preparations for Renewal.
James 4:1-10

LIVING THE TRUTH

Jesus demands that we abandon a life straddling the fence between the Spirit and the lure of the world.

We cannot really be "nominal" Christians. He threatened to spit out the Laodiceans for their self-confident indifference to His will. He warns us of the same danger today.

But Jesus gives us the same call to repentance and renewal which He offered these early believers. As we turn back to Him and trust Him to rekindle the passion of love He wants from us, we are given "everything we need for life and godliness through our knowledge of him who called us by his own glory and goodness" (2 Peter 1:3, *New International Version*).

EVANGELISM OUTREACH

Repentance—answering Jesus' call to turn from sin—isn't a magical or mysterious experience only a select few can achieve.

In its simplest sense repentance is turning away from sin to move toward Jesus. It means coming honestly to Christ and admitting our sins and spiritual coldness or indifference so He can stir our lives with His love. If you have never felt this love before, there's no better time than now. (See Teaching Tip 7.)

PREPARING TO TEACH

Study Text
Romans 9:1 through 11:36; Revelation 7:1-8

Outline
I. God's Instrument
   A. A Heart of Love
   B. The Word of Faith
II. Set Aside Through Unbelief
   A. Not a Permanent Rejection
   B. Not a Cause for Boasting
III. Restored to Divine Favor
   A. Our Covenant-Keeping God
   B. Sealed Servants of God

Golden Text
There shall come out of Zion the Deliverer, and shall turn away ungodliness from Jacob. Romans 11:26

Central Truth
Through Christ, God's chosen people will ultimately be triumphant.

Learning Goals
1. To explore Israel's place in God's plan.
2. To understand the role of Israel and the distinct role of the Church in God's dealings today.
3. To sharpen our sense of gratitude and worship based on God's great love for us.

SEEING THE SCRIPTURES

Romans 10:1, 2; 11:22-25

1. Brethren, my heart's desire and prayer to God for Israel is, that they might be saved.

2. For I bear them record that they have a zeal of God, but not according to knowledge.

11:22. Behold therefore the goodness and severity of God: on them which fell, severity; but toward thee, goodness, if thou continue in his goodness: otherwide thou also shalt be cut off.

23. And they also, if they abide not still in unbelief, shall be graffed in: for God is able to graff them in again.

24. For if thou wert cut out of the olive tree which is wild by nature, and wert graffed contrary to nature into a good olive tree; how much more shall these, which be the natural branches, be graffed into their own olive tree?

25. For I would not, brethren, that ye should be ignorant of this mystery, lest ye should be wise in your own conceits, that blindness in part is happened to Israel, until the fulness of the Gentiles be come in.

Revelation 7:4-8

4. And I heard the number of them which were sealed: and there were sealed a hundred and forty and four thousand of all the tribes of the children of Israel.

5. Of the tribe of Judah were sealed twelve thousand. Of the tribe of Reuben were sealed twelve thousand. Of the tribe of Gad were sealed twelve thousand.

6. Of the tribe of Asher were sealed twelve thousand. Of the tribe of Naphtali were sealed twelve thousand. Of the tribe of Manasseh were sealed twelve thousand.

7. Of the tribe of Simeon were sealed twelve thousand. Of the tribe of Levi were sealed twelve thousand. Of the tribe of Issachar were sealed twelve thousand.

8. Of the tribe of Zebulun were zealed twelve thousand. Of the tribe of Joseph were sealed twelve thousand. Of the tribe of Benjamin were sealed twelve thousand.

SETTING THE SCENE

One important question that faces us when we think of the future is: "How does Israel fit into God's plan?" The first Christians were all Jews. The first evangelists who spread the gospel to both Israel and the Gentiles were Jews. Thus, this question was something the New Testament was careful to deal with. Since salvation is only through Christ, it is obvious that Jews who rejected Jesus were not saved. Some of these Jews answered that since God had

Use the chalkboard to write down student responses. You might list one or two to get the students started: Jesus and the apostles were Jews; the Old Testament; one day in seven set aside for worship.

If you spend much time on this, you should end up with a fairly extensive list. Use this to focus on today's theme: God's use of Israel for special purposes in the past and His role for this nation in days ahead.

Clarification

A zeal of God—a zeal for God; a jealous eagerness to uphold what they thought was God's glory.

The end of the law—the termination of law. Christ has superseded all law (Jewish or Gentile) as a means of attaining righteousness.

Live by them—live in it; that is, live in the righteousness of the Law (by doing what the Law requires).

Which is of faith—that is which has faith as its source.

To bring Christ down—that is, to be born of a virgin, to identify himself with us, and to die in our place on Calvary.

The deep—the abyss, underworld.

What saith it—that is, what does the righteousness which is of faith speak? It says that the word [the message] of faith [the faith, the gospel] is near you.

Believeth—keeps believing and obeying.

Confession is made—one keeps on publicly declaring.

TEACHING TIP 1

Distribute copies of the PATH agree-disagree sheet on the nature of Israel and the Church. The PATH instruc-

made promises to them, He would have to save them even if they did reject our Lord.

Romans 9:1-29 deals with this objection on the basis of God's sovereignty. God has always had the sovereign right to make His promises available only to those who respond in faith.

BIBLE COMMENTARY

I. God's Instrument

Romans 10:1-10

Romans 10:1. Brethren, my heart's desire and prayer to God for Israel is, that they might be saved. 2. For I bear them record that they have a zeal of God, but not according to knowledge. 6. But the righteousness which is of faith speaketh on this wise, Say not in thine heart, Who shall ascend into heaven? (that is, to bring Christ down from above:) 7. or, Who shall descend into the deep? (that is, to bring up Christ again from the dead.) 8. But what saith it? The word is nigh thee, even in thy mouth, and in thy heart: that is, the word of faith, which we preach; 9. that if thou shalt confess with thy mouth the Lord Jesus, and shalt believe in thine heart that God hath raised him from the dead, thou shalt be saved.

A. A Heart of Love

Acts 21:20 shows that thousands (literally, myriads, tens of thousands) of Jews had already believed in Jesus, accepting Him as their Messiah, Lord, and Saviour. Nevertheless, Paul's heart was burdened for the many Jews who were rejecting Christ. He was called to be an apostle to the Gentiles. But everywhere he went the Spirit led him to go to the Jew first. When God brought Israel out of Egypt, He brought them to himself (Exodus 19:4). This was a wonderful expression of His great love (Deuteronomy 7:7, 8). Thus, God chose an apostle for the Gentiles who also had a great love for Israel.

Paul loved his people so much (See Romans 9:1-4.) that he was willing to give up his own salvation and spend eternity in hell if that would have guaranteed their salvation. He knew this was impossible, but that is how much he loved them. (See Teaching Tip 1.)

Paul also recognized that ever since man fell salvation has always been by grace through faith. (Compare Hebrews 11.) Esau, for example, showed a lack of faith when he despised his birthright. Later, he sought to get his father Isaac to change his mind and give him the blessing anyway. But Esau did not repent toward God, nor did he ever give God any glory.

In the same way the Jews who rejected Christ were trying to dictate to God the conditions for receiving the promises. But God had a right to set up the condition of simple faith in Jesus, just as the master potter knows what is best for the clay. His real purpose was not to reject Israel but to show them the same mercy and grace He was making available to the Gentiles.

tions suggest ways the sheet can be adapted to your class needs.

TEACHING TIP 2

Divide the class into groups for a Scripture search on the topics *faith* and *obedience.* If you have a large group, split into several groups (2 or 4) for each topic.

Give each group one of the appropriate Scripture lists:

FAITH: Hebrews 11:1-6; Romans 5:1; 10:17; Ephesians 3:16-19.

OBEDIENCE: James 1:22; 2:14-18; John 14:21; 15:10, 11.

Ask the groups to answer these questions as they search the Scriptures on their topic:

FAITH: 1. What is faith? 2. How do we get more faith? 3. What do we do with faith—that is, what are the results of faith?

OBEDIENCE: 1. What is obedience? 2. Why should we be obedient? 3. What are the results of obedience?

Appoint or let each group select a leader and a "scribe" to guide and summarize group discussion on the Scripture passages and questions.

Allow 10-15 minutes for the groups to work.

Question.

What two great works of God actually were necessary for our salvation?

Question.

What is our part?

Guideline for Living 1

It is said that the strictest Jews have through the centuries developed a system of over 600 explicit rules and applications of the Law as a fence or hedge around it. They want to be absolutely certain to cover every area where God's will might be misinterpreted and cover it fully. Better to be completely safe than sorry!

Yet Jesus condemned the traditions of men which the Jews had built around the Law. He said they were too burdensome for the path of life truly based on God's Word (Mark 7:6-13).

How many of our "sacred cows" of religious behavior and expectations are based on a tradition of man rather than God's Word?

Do we take care to find God's will for our lives—or do we rationalize ourselves into going our own way and expecting God to give our will His divine stamp of approval?

Paul also appreciated the zeal these Jews had for God, even though it was a misdirected zeal—misdirected because they rejected the knowledge available to them in and through Christ. Thus, those Jews rebelled against God's righteousness, the righteousness that is ours through Christ, the only kind of righteousness that can really please God.

Now the Law showed God wanted righteousness, and since Christ brought that righteousness, the purpose of the Law found its fulfillment in Christ. Without realizing it, the Jews who were rejecting Christ were rejecting the very thing they hoped the works of the Law would bring them. They forgot also that though the Law said, "Do this and live," it put love and faith in first place (Deuteronomy 6:5, 6).

B. The Word of Faith

Many of the Jews tried to make salvation very difficult. They added many fastings, washings, and other religious ceremonies, taking pride in the things they did. They put salvation on a distant pinnacle to be reached only by extreme effort. They wanted to be able to boast that they worked the works of God.

1. The Incarnation. Christ had to come down from heaven, be born of a virgin, live a sinless life, minister the grace and power of God to human need, identify with us as truly man, and die in our place on the cross.

2. The Resurrection. Christ had to be raised from the dead to assure us of our justification and of our own future resurrection. (See 1 Corinthians 15:20, 57.)

Could we go up to heaven to bring Christ down? Could we go down to the place of the dead to resurrect Him? Of course not! So God did it all. (See Teaching Tip 2.)

We need only respond in faith to the Word which is the gospel proclaimed by Jesus and the apostles and is recorded in the Bible for us. This faith has a two-fold expression. Inwardly it is a heart belief that God raised Jesus from the dead and that Christ's death was therefore effective for the redemption of soul and body (Romans 8:18-23). Outwardly it is expressed by a public declaration that Jesus is the Lord, our divine Master, the King of our lives, the Ruler and Guide of our destiny.

By this heart belief and public confession we enter into a new relation with the Lord. Then, as verse 10 indicates, we must keep on believing and we must keep on declaring our faith and showing it by our obedience if we want to keep on having salvation. As Chapters 4 and 7 of Romans teach, we can only continue in right relation with God by continuing in faith and obedience. We have been saved, we are being saved, and we shall be saved when Jesus comes again—all by grace through a faith that trusts God and obeys His Word.

Guideline for Living 2

"Trust and obey, for there's no other way To be happy in Jesus, but to trust and obey." The old hymn goes far toward putting the Christian life into perspective. It is impossible to have faith in God and live a life of disobedience. If we really trust Him, we will demonstrate it by taking Him at His word and living accordingly.

This means we will follow through on the commands of Christ as well as anticipating the fulfillment of His promises to us: " 'If anyone loves me, he will obey my teaching. My Father will love him, and we will come to him and make our home with him. He who does not love me will not obey my teaching' " (John 14:23, 24, *New International Version*).

II. Set Aside Through Unbelief
Romans 11:1, 13-22

Romans 11:1. I say then, Hath God cast away his people? God forbid. For I also am an Israelite, of the seed of Abraham, of the tribe of Benjamin. 13. For I speak to you Gentiles, inasmuch as I am the apostle of the Gentiles, I magnify mine office: 14. if by any means I may provoke to emulation them which are my flesh, and might save some of them. 17. And if some of the branches be broken off, and thou, being a wild olive tree, wert grafted in among them, and with them partakest of the root and fatness of the olive tree; 18. Boast not against the branches. But if thou boast, thou bearest not the root, but the root thee. 20. Well; because of unbelief they were broken off, and thou standest by faith. Be not highminded, but fear.

A. Not a Permanent Rejection

It was becoming obvious that far more Gentiles than Jews were accepting Christ and obeying the gospel. It is true that 3,000 were saved on the Day of Pentecost. But that was a small percentage of the two million Jews who crowded the temple courts on that day. Five thousand were added a little later. Then multitudes more. By the time Paul returned to Jerusalem shortly after writing this epistle, there were still more thousands, literally myriads, tens of thousands of Jews who were following Christ in Jerusalem and Judea (Acts 21:20). But even this was a comparatively small number. In the cities of the Roman Empire, many Jews accepted Christ, but there were others who became jealous of the multitudes of Gentiles who came in, and these Jews turned away.

Not at all. If God were rejecting Israel, He would have had to reject the apostle Paul. Actually, Paul knew God loved both Jews and Gentiles. Thus, though Paul was called to a special ministry to the Gentiles, he was just as concerned over the salvation of

Clarification

I say then—that is, in view of God's warnings to Israel and promises to the Gentiles.

Cast away—repudiated, rejected.

God forbid—May it not be!
Mine office—my ministry.
Emulation—jealousy.
The firstfruit—the first of the dough. See Numbers 15:20, 21.

Graffed—grafted.
The root and fatness—the rich root.

Well—well said! True!
Highminded—proud, haughty, self-exalted.

Question.

What is the problem Paul is dealing with in Romans 11?

Question.

Did this mean that God was in any way rejecting Israel or repudiating them as His people?

Duplicate copies of the PATH work sheet, "God's Plan for Israel," and distribute it for student use. You may wish to split the class into the same groups you used to do the Scripture search earlier in the class session if you choose to use the buzz group option for this worksheet. (See PATH instructions.) Also, check the PATH instructions in advance of class and/or work through the sheet for yourself in order to suggest ways to help the students answer the work sheet.

Question.

What should be the attitude of these Gentiles toward unbelieving Jews?

Question.

What warning does Paul give the Gentiles here?

Clarification

Mystery—something that was not fully revealed in Old Testament times but is now made clear.

In your own conceits—in your own estimation; that is,

Israel. In his own experience he went to the Jew first. Only when some of the Jews rose up in opposition to the gospel did he leave the synagogue and concentrate on his ministry to the Gentiles. Even then it was his hope that when the Jews saw the blessing of God on these Gentile converts, they would be stirred to jealousy and turn to the Lord.

Then the restoration of these Jews who had rejected Jesus would be like life from the dead, like a resurrection. Not only so, but God still wanted them to be a holy people dedicated to carrying out His great purposes of blessing for the entire world. Thus their restoration will mean even greater and richer blessing for us all. Thank God, He is faithful and they will be restored. Even now there is a remnant who are accepting Jesus as their Messiah, Lord, and Saviour.

B. Not a Cause for Boasting

It is clear then that God still has a place for Israel in His plan. He will be faithful to the promises given them in the Old Testament. But it is also clear that some of them have been rejected because of their unbelief. To illustrate this, Paul uses the comparison of an olive tree to reveal God's continuing plan including its promises and blessings. Unbelieving Jews (who should have received the life and blessing promised) were broken off through unbelief. Gentiles who were saved by grace through faith were grafted in. Now Gentiles were receiving the rich blessings of the Lord.

Paul warns the Gentiles against boasting. They must be careful not to think they are more special to God than the Jews. No, God is not a respecter of persons. Neither Jews nor Gentiles can be channels of the blessing of God because of their own nature. God's blessings are so rich, not because we are so good but because He is so good.

We stand by faith. Pride and self-exaltation can lead to a lack of faith and trust in God. Unbelief can cause us to be broken off too. We can only continue to enjoy the goodness of God as we continue in that goodness by grace through faith.

Guideline for Living 3

How can we tell if we are living by faith? Do we have to experience certain feelings or states of mind to be sure we are truly walking with Christ?

Assurance of salvation is independent of how we feel about the experience of conversion. It is based upon a simple, unassailable fact: "He that hath the Son hath life; and he that hath not the Son of God hath not life" (1 John 5:12). Jew and Gentile alike, we are measured in relation to what we have done with Jesus Christ. If we have Him, we are saved no matter how our feelings may fluctuate. Without Him, the strictest observance of a set of rules or regulations will mean nothing.

III. Restored to Divine Favor
Romans 11:23-27; Revelation 7:4-8

Romans 11:23. And they also, if they abide not still in unbelief, shall be grafted in: for God is able to graff them in again. 25. For

relying on your own wisdom.

Blindness—dullness, insensibility.

Fulness—full number.

Sealed—marked with a seal as a means of identification and as an enduement of power from on high. Compare Ephesians 1:13; 4:30; 2 Corinthians 1:22; John 6:27.

Question.
Does Paul agree with this?

Question.
What does Paul mean by saying all Israel will be saved?

TEACHING TIP 4
The "Bible Commentary" discusses the concept of covenant or promissory agreement. Several references are made to the old and new covenants God made with Israel and with the believer in Christ.

If possible, arrange with one of your students during the week before class to look up *covenant* in a good Bible dictionary or Bible encyclopedia to prepare a short oral report to share with the students at this time.

If you are unable to arrange this report during the week before class, (1) prepare such a report as a mini-lecture to share with the class or (2) bring a Bible dictionary or encyclopedia to class and ask someone to look up *covenant* and read or summarize the information for the class.

I would not, brethren, that ye should be ignorant of this mystery, lest ye should be wise in your own conceits, that blindness in part is happened to Israel, until the fulness of the Gentiles be come in. 26. And so all Israel shall be saved: as it is written, There shall come out of Zion the Deliverer, and shall turn away ungodliness from Jacob. 27. For this is my covenant unto them, when I shall take away their sins. Revelation 7:4. And I heard the number of them which were sealed: and there were sealed a hundred and forty and four thousand of all the tribes of the children of Israel.

A. Our Covenant-Keeping God
Some today, especially among the amillennialists and postmillennialists, teach that God has cut the Jews out of His plan forever. They say that all the promises of restoration for Israel must be spiritualized and applied to the Church.

Paul declares that God has the power to graft the Jews back into the olive tree of His promises and blessings. Not only so, this olive tree is really their own olive tree. If God has grafted wild branches into the cultivated olive tree, how much more will He graft the natural branches back in!

Gentiles who say God has no more place for Israel in His plan are following what seems logical in their own estimation. They are following the reasonings of human wisdom. But God's ways and God's thoughts are above man's. The blindness or insensibility of Israel is only temporary and will last only until the full number of the Gentiles come into the body of Christ. Then God will again bring salvation to Israel.

Paul has already made it clear that not all who are called Israel are truly Israel (Romans 9:6). Those who share in the faith of Abraham are the only ones who will share in the promise given to Abraham. Thus it is clear that when the time comes there will be a mighty revival, and overwhelming wave of repentance among the Jews. Zechariah prophesies that they will mourn when they look on Him whom they have pierced (Zechariah 12:10, 11). Jeremiah promises that God will turn their mourning into joy (Jeremiah 31:10-13). (See Teaching Tip 4.)

We see also that God will bring them under the new covenant (Jeremiah 31:31-34). This will be different from the old covenant of the Law given at Sinai. It will be written on the hearts of believers instead of on tables of stone. This new covenant prophesied by Jeremiah is clearly identified in Hebrews 8:7 to 9:22. It is the one and only new covenant put into effect at Calvary by the death of Christ and by the shedding of His precious blood. As Hebrews points out, this covenant had to be put into effect through the death of the Testator, the One making the covenant or testament. Christ died once for all. There can be no further sacrificial death for any other new covenant. Thus, Israel will repent (they will change their minds from unbelief to faith) and will be saved by grace through faith, just as we have been.

The guarantee of this is the fact that God is the Covenant-Keeper. As Ezekiel prophesied, God will restore Israel for His holy name's sake. His name speaks of His nature and character. God's own faithfulness will make sure that Israel will be restored to the land and to the Lord. Not only so, He will put His Spirit within them (Ezekiel 36:27; 37:14).

Those who try to spiritualize these prophecies and apply them to the Church forget they are tied to the restoration of Israel to the land. Again it must be emphasized that they first return to the land in unbelief. Then later, by a further powerful fulfillment of the prophetic Word, there will be a spiritual restoration (Ezekiel 36:25-27; 37:8-10, 13, 14).

B. Sealed Servants of God

On the island of Patmos John was caught away in the Spirit into heaven. There he saw a new revelation of Jesus in the midst of the heavenly throne, still bearing the marks of having been slain. As God's Lamb, Jesus is worthy to open the seals down the edge of the roll which proclaims the wrath of God. But before the seventh seal is opened so the wrath can be poured out on the earth, there is an interlude for the sealing of 144,000 from the tribes of Israel. An angel appears with the seal or signet to stamp an impression on the foreheads of God's servants from the tribes of Israel. Isaiah's prophecies show that God called Israel to be His servant. The nation as a whole failed in Old Testament times. But now these from the tribes of Israel will be sealed, not for protection, but to designate them as true servants of the Lord.

Question.
What else will be involved in the sealing?

Even in Old Testament times God did not give the outward sign without the inward reality. Since Calvary the sealing has been by the Holy Spirit (Ephesians 1:13). Thus we can be sure that these 144,000 will also experience the fulfillment of Ezekiel's prophecy that God will put His Spirit within them.

Question.
What happens to these 144,000 who are sealed?

Since the 144,000 are called servants, some believe they will serve by spreading the gospel during the first part of the Tribulation.

Others believe they will serve by joining the white-robed throng from all nations who will worship and praise God and the Lamb before the heavenly throne. (See Teaching Tip 5.)

TEACHING TIP 5
Close your class period with a hymn or chorus of worship and praise. "O for a Thousand Tongues To Sing" would be appropriate.

Daily Devotional Guide

M. A Chosen People.
Deuteronomy 14:1, 2
T. A Rebellious People.
Jeremiah 4:8-18
W. A Persecuted People.
Revelation 12:1-6, 13-17
T. A Rejected People.
Hosea 4:1-6
F. A Scattered People.
Zechariah 7:8-14
S. A Restored People.
2 Corinthians 3:6-16

LIVING THE TRUTH

God gave the people of Israel a special role in history: to prepare the world for salvation and be a witness of that salvation through their Messiah Jesus. Because of their unbelief, God had to set the Jews aside as His instruments.

But the door to God has been opened wide by the Messiah Jesus. Through faith in His finished work, we live and walk with God, secure in our salvation—whether believing Gentile or believing Jew.

God's Word prophesies there is coming a time when all the world will be blessed by Israel's turning to Christ. In a miraculous way, "Jewish evangelists" will be raised up by God to spread the gospel.

EVANGELISM OUTREACH

You need not wait in uncertainty for a time when God will bring about a special restoration of the Jews. The time for you as an individual to come to Christ is right now. You can experience by faith the life He has for every believer. Why not ask Him into your heart right now?

NATIONS IN PROPHECY

SEEING THE SCRIPTURES

Daniel 2:36-45

36. This is the dream; and we will tell the interpretation thereof before the king.

37. Thou, O king, art a king of kings: for the God of heaven hath given thee a kingdom, power, and strength, and glory.

38. And wheresoever the children of men dwell, the beasts of the field and the fowls of the heaven hath he given into thine hand, and hath made thee ruler over them all. Thou art this head of gold.

39. And after thee shall arise another kingdom inferior to thee, and another third kingdom of brass, which shall bear rule over all the earth.

40. And the fourth kingdom shall be strong as iron: forasmuch as iron breaketh in pieces and subdueth all things: and as iron that breaketh all these, shall it break in pieces and bruise.

41. And whereas thou sawest the feet and toes, part of potters' clay, and part of iron, the kingdom shall be divided; but there shall be in it of the strength of the iron, forasmuch as thou sawest the iron mixed with miry clay.

42. And as the toes of the feet were part of iron, and part of clay, so the kingdom shall be partly strong, and partly broken.

43. And whereas thou sawest iron mixed with miry clay, they shall mingle themselves with the seed of men: but they shall not cleave one to another, even as iron is not mixed with clay.

44. And in the days of these kings shall the God of heaven set up a kingdom, which shall never be destroyed: and the kingdom shall not be left to other people, but it shall break in pieces and consume all these kingdoms, and it shall stand for ever.

45. Forasmuch as thou sawest that the stone was cut out of the mountain without hands, and that it brake in pieces the iron, the brass, the clay, the silver, and the gold; the great God hath made known to the king what shall come to pass hereafter: and the dream is certain, and the interpretation thereof sure.

SETTING THE SCENE

All through history some people have dreamed of setting up a Utopia, an ideal government of some sort. From time to time some have actually tried to form a community that would be filled with love and free from sin and crime. But the prophecies of the Bible all agree that human efforts in this direction will never succeed. Sin and evil will persist and will rob the world of peace until Jesus the Prince of Peace returns in glory.

The Bible also makes it clear again and again that this present evil world deserves the wrath of God. Thus, a gospel of social

PREPARING TO TEACH

Study Text
Daniel 2:1-49

Outline
I. An Unusual Dream
   A. An Unusual Test
   B. God's Gracious Revelation
II. World Empires
   A. A Sequence of Empires
   B. A Disunited World
III. The Coming Kingdom
   A. The Kingdom of Christ
   B. A Brand-New World Order

Golden Text
He changeth the times and the seasons: he removeth kings, and setteth up kings. Daniel 2:21

Central Truth
God has revealed through prophecy the rise and fall of nations.

Learning Goals
1. To investigate God's plan for the nations.
2. To examine our present status in that plan.
3. To gain a better historical perspective to aid us in living for Christ.

During the week before class, clip from a newspaper or news magazine three or four short articles that are current news-worthy events your students would find interesting. Bring these clippings to class.

Read them—or ask some of the students to read them—as you begin. After you have read them (and taken 2-3 minutes to discuss them), ask: "What does today's news tell you about God's timetable for our world?"

After you have stimulated the students' thinking on current events and God's plan for the nations, proceed into this week's "Bible Commentary" on Daniel 2.

Clarification

Magicians—those skilled in magical sayings written in the ancient hieroglyphics.

Astrologers — conjurers who used arrows and other means for reading signs and making incantations and enchantments.

Sorcerers—users of witchcraft to cast spells.

Chaldeans — probably heathen priests who dealt in the occult.

Syriac—Aramaic, a Semitic language closely related to Hebrew. Aramaic was the language of trade and commerce in the Middle East from about 2,000 B.C. to about 300 B.C.

The thing is gone from me—the decree promulgated by me has been published. (Note, the king had not forgotten the dream.)

Rare—difficult.

Counsel and wisdom—discretion and tactful good sense.

Hasty—harsh, severe, as well as urgent.

Blessed—praised.

Soothsayers—those who consult livers to make predictions; or exorcists.

Excellent—extraordinary.

Terrible—awesome.

improvement will never meet the world's need. The kingdom of Christ is what we need. But that kingdom, as Daniel shows in chapter 2, can only be brought in through Judgment.

BIBLE COMMENTARY

I. An Unusual Dream

Daniel 2:1-36

Daniel 2:2. The king commanded to call the magicians, and the astrologers, and the sorcerers, and the Chaldeans, for to show the king his dreams. So they came and stood before the king. 8. The king answered and said, I know of certainty that ye would gain the time, because ye see the thing is gone from me. 9. But if ye will not make known unto me the dream, there is but one decree for you: for ye have prepared lying and corrupt words to speak before me, till the time be changed: therefore tell me the dream, and I shall know that ye can show me the interpretation thereof. 11. It is a rare thing that the king requireth, and there is none other that can show it before the king, except the gods, whose dwelling is not with flesh. 12. For this cause the king was angry and very furious, and commanded to destroy all the wise men of Babylon. 17. Then Daniel went to his house, and made the thing known to Hananiah, Mishael, and Azariah, his companions: 18. that they would desire mercies of the God of heaven concerning this secret; that Daniel and his fellows should not perish with the rest of the wise men of Babylon. 19. Then was the secret revealed unto Daniel in a night vision. Then Daniel blessed the God of heaven. 27. Daniel answered in the presence of the king, and said, The secret which the king hath demanded cannot the wise men, the astrologers, the magicians, the soothsayers, show unto the king; 28. but there is a God in heaven that revealeth secrets, and maketh known to the king Nebuchadnezzar what shall be in the latter days. Thy dream, and the visions of thy head upon thy bed, are these. 30. But as for me, this secret is not revealed to me for any wisdom that I have more than any living, but for their sakes that shall make known the interpretation to the king, and that thou mightest know the thoughts of thy heart. 31. Thou, O king, sawest, and behold a great image. This great image, whose brightness was excellent, stood before thee; and the form thereof was terrible.

A. An Unusual Test

Not all dreams are significant. But this dream of King Nebuchadnezzar so disturbed him that he felt he had to know its meaning. Like most ancient heathen kings he kept quite a retinue of men who dealt in the occult. They all used various means and tricks to predict the future and to give the king the advice they thought he wanted to hear. (See Teaching Tip 1.)

As in the case of those who deal in the occult today, people usually forget their predictions that do not come true and remember those that appear to do so. But this time King Nebuchadnezzar did not want to take any chances. This dream impressed him as too important. So he proposed a test of the powers of all these

Seat the class in a circle; include yourself.

Ask the person beside you: "How important are dreams? Does God speak to us in dreams?" When he has given his response, proceed around the circle student by student. Keep the comments moving as quickly as possible.

Write down key points on the chalkboard or overhead projector as you feel them significant.

As you go around the circle, make sure everyone understands that he is to be non-critical of each opinion. Your purpose is not to get "right" or "wrong" answers, but to stimulate thinking.

Use this activity to help the class see that: (1) God may guide us by dreams and visions, but (2) He will not guide us in any fashion contradictory to or in disagreement with His Word.

Lead into a discussion of "Guideline for Living 1" on the occult.

Question.
How did Daniel respond when God gave him the answer?

men who claimed supernatural wisdom. Let them tell him the dream first. Then he would know whether they had the power to reveal the correct interpretation.

Guideline for Living 1

Many men have exposed the fraud and trickery of magicians, fortune-tellers, mediums, etc. There are legitimate scientists who are critical of the studies of ESP or the "para-normal" events researchers have supposedly documented.

If this is so, does the Christian have any reason to be either involved in or fearful of the occult? Is it all merely faked?

The Christian must not be involved in the occult. The entire realm of the occult is of the devil. He uses fortune-tellers, horoscopes, ESP, and other similar practices to turn mankind away from Christ to rely on false gods and false powers that only produce despair, fear, and enslavement. For this reason a Christian should be very careful to avoid the occult. We have no business trying to serve Christ and opening our minds and homes to devilish influences.

Instead, we should be wary of our real enemy and combat him in the Spirit at every turn (Ephesians 6:10-18).

The wise men kept demanding that the king tell them the dream. Then they would give him the interpretation. But the king made it clear that he was not going to change the decree. They must tell him both the dream and the interpretation. If he told them the dream they could put their heads together and make up any old interpretation and he would not know whether they were right or not. But if they told him the dream, then he would know for sure that their interpretation was right. He also tried to hurry them up. They were just stalling to gain time and make the king change his mind.

Then these wise men told the king that no king had ever asked anything like that of any dealer in the occult. Only the gods could give that kind of answer, and they didn't live here on earth. What a confession this was! These dealers in the occult were confessing they didn't have any real contact with the supernatural nor of the divine wisdom they claimed to have.

They were also saying the king's request was unreasonable. But no one tells absolute monarchs or dictators they are unreasonable! Their answer sent the king into a rage of fury, and he decreed the death of all the wise men of Babylon. Soon Arioch the king's bodyguard and chief executioner notified Daniel that he and his friends were included.

B. God's Gracious Revelation

With courtesy and tact Daniel inquired into the cause of the death penalty and asked for a set time during which he could seek the Lord for the dream and the interpretation. This was granted and Daniel and his friends sought God.

Daniel gave God praise. Then he went to Arioch who brought him before the king. But before he told the king the dream and its interpretation, he gave God the praise. The God of heaven whom Daniel served was different from anything the king's dealers in the occult were familiar with. Nor did Daniel pretend to have any wisdom of his own. He gave all the credit, all the glory, to

Give each student a piece of paper and pen or pencil. Ask different ones to read Daniel 2:21, 22 from at least four translations if possible. Then tell the students to write in their own words what these two verses mean.

Allow 5-10 minutes for the reading and writing. Circulate around the room to answer questions and/or offer suggestions if your class members are unfamiliar with Scripture paraphrasing.

Ask several to read their paraphrases. Use this activity to help the students develop a greater appreciation for the sovereignty of God in history. (See "Guideline for Living 2" on historical perspectives.)

Clarification

Brass—copper. The alloy we call brass today was not known in Bible times.

Subdueth—crushes.

Miry clay—earthenware.

Partly broken—partly fragile.

Cleave—hold, stick.

Question.

Was the description of Nebuchadnezzar's power and rule mere flattery?

TEACHING TIP 3

Display the PATH overhead transparency, "God's Plan for the Ages," as you discuss Daniel's interpretation of the dream. PATH instructions suggest ways for using it.

the Lord. It was by His wisdom and by His grace that the king's secret was revealed to Daniel. (See Teaching Tip 2.)

II. World Empires
Daniel 2:37-43

Daniel 2:37. Thou, O king, art a king of kings: for the God of heaven hath given thee a kingdom, power, and strength, and glory. 38. And wheresoever the children of men dwell, the beasts of the field and the fowls of the heaven hath he given into thine hand, and hath made thee ruler over them all. Thou art this head of gold. 39. And after thee shall arise another kingdom inferior to thee, and another third kingdom of brass, which shall bear rule over all the earth. 40. And the fourth kingdom shall be strong as iron: forasmuch as iron breaketh in pieces and subdueth all things: and as iron that breaketh all these, shall it break in pieces and bruise. 41. And whereas thou sawest the feet and toes, part of potters' clay, and part of iron, the kingdom shall be divided; but there shall be in it of the strength of the iron, forasmuch as thou sawest the iron mixed with miry clay. 42. And as the toes of the feet were part of iron, and part of clay, so the kingdom shall be partly strong, and partly broken. 43. And whereas thou sawest iron mixed with miry clay, they shall mingle themselves with the seed of men: but they shall not cleave one to another, even as iron is not mixed with clay.

A. A Sequence of Empires
(See Teaching Tip 3.)

In his dream the king saw a giant image or statue with a head of gold, breast and arms of silver, belly and thighs of copper, lower legs of iron, and feet of iron and clay.

Then God revealed to Daniel that Nebuchadnezzar was the head of gold, and after him would come a sequence of empires represented by metals that decreased in value but not in strength.

The new Babylonian Empire was largely the result of his conquests. He made Babylon the largest and most splendid city of his time. Its great outer walls were about 344 feet high and 86 feet wide. Four-horse chariots could pass and turn on top of the ramparts. It enclosed an area of nearly 200 square miles and included famous palaces, orchards, gardens, and temples. But great as Nebuchadnezzar's empire was, it would give way to another empire, and that to another, and another.

To us today, the rise and fall of empires in past history is a well-recognized phenomenon. But in Daniel's day it was a new idea. The ancient kings and emperors hoped their kingdoms would go on forever. Thus, this dream was a God-given revelation of the future. God gave it, not for Nebuchadnezzar alone, but for all His people. He is Lord over history.

Guideline for Living 2

Secular historians are very reluctant to accept God or any sort of guiding, unifying force behind history.

But apart from God's overriding plan for mankind, historians are at a loss to see or explain any sense of unity from one civilization to another. And they have nothing left but a sense of despair. In fact, some atheistic historians have become so cynical that they have seen history as a dream or game of looking at the past and making it mean anything one wants it to mean.

The Bible makes it clear that history is truly HIS-story: "By him were all things created, that are in heaven, and that are in earth, visible and invisible, . . . all things were created by him, and for him: and he is before all things, and by him all things consist" (Colossians 1:16, 17)

Question.
What kingdoms do the silver, copper, and iron represent?

This chapter does not name them. But Daniel 8:20, 21 make it clear that Babylon would be followed first by Medo-Persia and then by Greece. Daniel himself lived to see Cyrus take over Babylon, and he took part in the silver of Medo-Persian rule there. Alexander the Great was the first king of the Greek Empire foretold in Daniel 8:21. Then the iron with its great strength was the Roman Empire. But the Roman Empire for all its power and might did not last forever. It too came to an end. However, unlike the preceding kingdoms, it was not replaced by another world empire. (See Teaching Tip 4.)

B. A Disunited World

1. They would be partly strong and partly broken or brittle, fragile, easily broken. That is, the Roman Empire gave way to nationalistic states, some strong and lasting a long time, others weak and always breaking up. A look at a historical atlas giving a series of maps identifying changes in national boundaries since Roman times shows this prophecy has certainly been fulfilled. The world is still iron and clay.

Question.
What two things are said about the feet of iron and clay?

TEACHING TIP 4

During the week before class, locate a historical Bible atlas. A flip chart set of maps would be even better.

Using these maps, help the students visually appreciate the unity of the Roman world and the extent it covered. Contrast this with the disunity and shifting boundaries of the Western world from the fall of Rome right down to the present.

(Look over the maps before class and prepare to highlight those which are especially relevant to your class needs.)

2. Iron and clay do not stick together. So also, the nations since Roman times have not stuck together. Many have dreamed of starting a new world empire. Charlemagne tried it. Napoleon tried it. Hitler and Mussolini tried it. The communist philosophers have world conquest as part of their goal. But even behind the iron and bamboo curtains, it is still iron and clay.

Every other attempt at world unity has failed. The World Court did not make it. The League of Nations did not make it. And it is hard to think of anything less united than the United Nations. The nationalistic states of today are still iron and clay. In spite of all the treaties and every attempt at diplomacy, they do not stick together. It is foolish to imagine they ever will.

Question.
Is the mention of the toes of the feet significant?

The repetition here draws attention to the toes. It seems probable that they represent the same 10 nations that are pictured by the 10 horns of the fourth beast in Daniel 7. Chapter 7 indicates that these kingdoms will come under the dominion of a little horn which represents the Antichrist. These 10 nations come out of the fourth beast which is the Roman beast. Thus, they will no doubt be parts of the territory once held by the old Roman Empire.

Clarification

Break in pieces—pulverize; grind to powder, so that the wind will blow them away. See verse 35.

Stand forever—it will also fill the whole earth, in contrast to all the kingdoms preceding it. See verse 35.

Without hands—that is, of supernatural origin, in contrast to the man-made image.

III. The Coming Kingdom
Daniel 2:44, 45

Daniel 2:44. In the days of these kings shall the God of heaven set up a kingdom, which shall never be destroyed: and the kingdom shall not be left to other people, but it shall break in pieces and

Display the second over-
head transparency from PATH
for this week, "God's Coming
Kingdom." PATH instructions
have suggestions for its use.

Question.

What does the stone represent?

Question.

What will be the extent of His
rule?

Question.

How does this fit in with the
Millennium prophesied in Revelation 20?

consume all these kingdoms, and it shall stand for ever. 45. Forasmuch as thou sawest that the stone was cut out of the mountain
without hands, and that it brake in pieces the iron, the brass, the
clay, the silver, and the gold; the great God hath made known to
the king what shall come to pass hereafter: and the dream is certain,
and the interpretation thereof sure.

A. The Kingdom of Christ

(See Teaching Tip 5.)

The climax of the king's dream came when he saw a stone cut
from the mountain without hands. This stone smashed the whole
image and brought the sequence of the kingdoms and rule of men
to a final end.

The stone represents the kingdom of Christ which He will personally establish when He comes back to earth. This is the kingdom
of peace foreseen by the prophets of the Old Testament. Isaiah
saw it as a time when "the wolf also shall dwell with the lamb,
and the leopard shall lie down with the kid; and the calf and the
young lion and the fatling together; and a little child shall lead
them." It will be a time when "they shall not hurt nor destroy in
all my holy mountain: for the earth shall be full of the knowledge
of the Lord, as the waters cover the sea" (Isaiah 11:6, 9). As the
Prince of Peace, Jesus will bring peace, justice, and righteousness
to the earth.

Two things are emphasized in Daniel 2:35-47. Great as the ancient empires were, none of them ever controlled the entire planet.
But the rule of Christ will fill the whole earth. This is more than
was ever promised even to Abraham and his descendants. God
promised them dominion from the River Euphrates to the river
of Egypt (Genesis 15:18). But with this promise in mind, Zechariah
saw the rule of the Messianic king would be "from sea even to
sea, and from the river [the Euphrates] even to the ends of the
earth" (Zechariah 9:10).

Guideline for Living 3

If Christ's kingdom over all the earth is inevitable, what is our
responsibility and role in its coming?

We have been given a very singular purpose: to share the gospel
with everyone in our generation: "Go ye into all the world, and
preach the gospel to every creature" (Mark 16:15). As we do this,
Jesus works out all the details of salvation, Christian growth, fulfillment of Bible prophecy, etc. If we let anything—even study of
the most fascinating "deeper" truths of the Scripture—distract us
from sharing His good news with our friends, family, and neighbors, we miss His mark for our lives.

Daniel also emphasizes that no longer will the earth see one
kingdom or realm give way to another. The kingdom of Christ will
last forever.

It is true that Satan must be released for a little time after the
thousand years are finished. But Christ is still on the throne. He
is still King, still in control. Satan will be defeated and cast into
the lake of fire. Then the kingdom, the rule of Christ, will continue
on forever in the new heavens and the new earth.

Why is the total destruction of the present world system necessary?

B. A Brand-New World Order

When Babylon gave way to Medo-Persia, there was a new empire, but it was still the same old world system. Medo-Persia borrowed much from Babylon and even made Babylon one of its capitals. The same sort of thing happened with each of the kingdoms that followed. Rome conquered Greece. But Greek culture and even the Greek language continued to dominate Rome and most of the Roman Empire. In our present iron-and-clay condition we still have Roman ideas such as "might makes right," Babylonian astrology, Medo-Persian ethics, and Greek philosophy imbedded in modern Western culture. Even the best of modern culture, both in East and West, is tinged with corruption that is the result of the Fall. Actually, the world has never seen a really new world order. One age has given way to another. But it is still the same old world system.

The prophets, as well as the Book of Revelation, show that the Kingdom must be brought in through judgment. Even the good things of the present world system must be destroyed to bring in the better things of the coming Kingdom.

Question.
Where does the stone hit the great image?

The stone hits the image in the feet, that is, in the present iron and clay condition. Then, with the destruction of the present world system will go the destruction of all it has inherited from the man-made kingdoms, empires, philosophies, religions, and cultures of the past. The kingdom of Christ will not be a matter of penetrating, changing, and renewing the present world order. It will be something brand new, with the world and its very atmosphere changed, cleansed by the power of the Holy Spirit. (See Teaching Tip 6.)

The fact the great image is hit in the feet also shows us that we do not need to look for any revival of previous empires as such before the Lord comes. He will come to a world like the one we have today. Let us look with joy for His appearing!

TEACHING TIP 6

As you near the close of your class session, direct the students to the beautiful picture of God's kingdom described in Revelation 22:1-7. Ask one or two of the students to read these verses.

Let the Holy Spirit turn the remainder of your classtime into a praise and worship session.

Close with an appropriate hymn or chorus. "He's Coming Soon" would be good.

LIVING THE TRUTH

In a real sense, we are the Daniels of our world. It is up to us to show the world we are in touch with the God of the Bible. Those who know we are Christians expect us to have something more than the defeated, perplexed outlook that pervades our troubled world scene.

We have the promises of God that He is in control of history—the world's history and *our* history. We can trust Him to work His will. In so doing, we can know that peace "which passeth all understanding" as He keeps our hearts and minds secure in Christ (Philippians 4:7).

EVANGELISM OUTREACH

To watch God work out His plan in history can be exciting if you know Christ as Saviour. Without Him, world events can lead to fear and cynicism as we see how out-of-control things seem to be.

Why not ask Christ into your life today. Allow Him to give you His perspective on history and life right now.

Daily Devotional Guide

M. Supernatural Revelation.
Genesis 41:1-8, 25-32
T. Divine Appointment.
1 Samuel 9:15-17
W. Divine Judgment.
Jeremiah 25:9-14
T. The Pattern Explained.
Habakkuk 1:5-11
F. The Final Kingdom.
Matthew 21:42-44
S. The City of God.
Revelation 21:1-7

5 | THE RAPTURE

PREPARING TO TEACH

Study Text
John 14:1-3; Acts 1:1-11; 1 Thessalonians 4:1-18

Outline
I. Promised by Christ
  A. Preparing a Place
  B. Coming Back Again
II. Confirmed by Angels
  A. The Ascension
  B. The Promised Return
III. Explained by Paul
  A. The Dead in Christ Rise First
  B. A Sudden Snatching Away
  C. Comfort and Encourage one Another

Golden Text
Watch therefore; for ye know neither the day nor the hour wherein the Son of man cometh. Matthew 25:13

Central Truth
The Rapture is a key doctrine of the Church and is a powerful incentive for godly living.

Learning Goals
1. To explore the nature and purpose of the Biblical event we call the Rapture.
2. To understand better the importance and perspective God places on the Rapture.
3. To use our increased understanding of the Rapture as a basis for worship and encouragement.

SEEING THE SCRIPTURES

John 14:1-3

1. Let not your heart be troubled: ye believe in God, believe also in me.

2. In my Father's house are many mansions: if it were not so, I would have told you. I go to prepare a place for you.

3. And if I go and prepare a place for you, I will come again, and receive you unto myself; that where I am, there ye may be also.

Acts 1:9-11

9. When he had spoken these things, while they beheld, he was taken up; and a cloud received him out of their sight.

10. And while they looked steadfastly toward heaven as he went up, behold, two men stood by them in white apparel;

11. Which also said, Ye men of Galilee, why stand ye gazing up into heaven? this same Jesus, which is taken up from you into heaven, shall so come in like manner as ye have seen him go into heaven.

1 Thessalonians 4:13-18

13. I would not have you to be ignorant, brethren, concerning them which are asleep, that ye sorrow not, even as others which have no hope.

14. For if we believe that Jesus died and rose again, even so them also which sleep in Jesus will God bring with him.

15. For this we say unto you by the word of the Lord, that we which are alive and remain unto the coming of the Lord shall not prevent them which are asleep.

16. For the Lord himself shall descend from heaven with a shout, with the voice of the archangel, and with the trump of God: and the dead in Christ shall rise first:

17. Then we which are alive and remain shall be caught up together with them in the clouds, to meet the Lord in the air: and so shall we ever be with the Lord.

18. Wherefore comfort one another with these words.

SETTING THE SCENE

A great many of the warnings and promises of Jesus center around the fact of His return to earth. Again and again Jesus warned believers to watch, to be alert, on guard, "for ye know neither the day nor the hour wherein the Son of man cometh" (Matthew 25:13). At the same time we rejoice, for when He comes we shall be changed into His likeness, and we shall rule and reign with Him through eternity.

We speak of His coming for believers as the Rapture. It will be a time of rapturous, overwhelming joy and ecstasy. But we use the

GETTING STARTED

Write the word *RAPTURE* on the chalkboard or overhead projector before class starts. As you begin, point to the word and ask the students to take a few minutes to find at least one Scripture passage which contains the word *Rapture*.

Allow a couple of minutes for the students to search their minds and Bibles for such a passage. Then explain or let a student explain that, although the concept the word deals with has a strong Biblical basis, the word is never used in the Bible. Use the "Bible Commentary" to explain the source of the word *Rapture*, then move into the discussion of John 14:1-3.

Clarification

Troubled—or agitated, frightened, thrown into confusion.

Ye believe in God, believe also in me—keep on believing in God, and keep on believing in Me; a double command.

Mansions—abodes, as translated in verse 23; dwelling places, rooms.

If I go—or, when I go.

Receive you—take you along, that is, in the Rapture.

Question.

Does the *if* in verse 3 imply any doubt?

Question.

What is the most important part of this promise?

TEACHING TIP 1

Use the first case study from PATH. The PATH instructions suggest ways of using it.

---

term with a meaning closer to its Latin root, which is to seize, to snatch away, to lift up and carry away. Thus, in the Rapture we shall be caught up to meet Him in the air.

BIBLE COMMENTARY

I. Promised by Christ

John 14:1-3

John 14:1. Let not your heart be troubled: ye believe in God, believe also in me. 2. In my Father's house are many mansions: if it were not so, I would have told you. I go to prepare a place for you. 3. And if I go and prepare a place for you, I will come again, and receive you unto myself; that where I am, there ye may be also.

A. Preparing a Place

The disciples were upset because they were expecting Jesus to set up His kingdom at once. But now Jesus was talking about going away to a place where they could not now come (John 13:33, 36, 37). Jesus encouraged them by challenging them to quit their fears and just keep on believing in God and in Him. Simple faith and trust would quiet their confusion and give them new assurance.

Actually, it was for their sakes He was going away. In His Father's house there is plenty of room for all. He would go and prepare a place for them. The same word is used of preparing a meal. In view of the parables of Jesus and the prophecy of Matthew 8:11 where many shall come and recline at table, preparations for the Marriage Supper of the Lamb will surely be included. (See Revelation 19:9.)

B. Coming Back Again

The *if* in verse 3 gives greater assurance. The promise is very emphatic. Has He gone away? Then just as surely He will return and take us along in the Rapture for that promised meeting in the air. This has always been the great and precious hope of the Church. (See Teaching Tip 1.)

Jesus will take us unto himself. We shall be thrilled to see our loved ones, to see the apostles and prophets, to see Moses, Abraham, and David. But the greatest thrill of all will be to see Jesus and to be united with Him forever. Jesus himself is the focus and center of the Christian hope.

Guideline for Living 1

How would you feel if you invited friends to dinner and they spent most of their time complimenting the great meal while ignoring your presence and your efforts to fellowship with them?

As we study the glorious theme of the Rapture, we must ask ourselves whether we are guilty of the same discourtesy toward our Lord. Are we guilty of spending so much time exploring, defining, and proclaiming the nature, events, and timing of the Rapture that we lost sight of the central truth: Jesus will take us to be with Him for eternity!

Clarification

A cloud—a cloud that was a token of God's presence, like the Shekinah cloud in the temple (1 Kings 8:10, 11; see Psalm 104:3; Daniel 7:13; Mark 14:62; Luke 9:34).

Received him—took Him up.

Two men—that is, two angels who had taken human form. (Compare Mark 16:5.)

Stood—standing. At first their appearance was unnoticed. Then the people suddenly saw them standing beside them.

Question.

What is the significance of the cloud?

Question.

What is the importance of Christ's ascension?

TEACHING TIP 2

Distribute paper and a pen or pencil to each student. Write the reference Acts 1:11 on the chalkboard or overhead projector.

Ask the students to read the verse 3 or 4 times in more than one Bible version if possible and then write out their responses to the following questions on the paper. (Write the questions on the chalkboard):

1. What does this verse tell you about Christ's return?

2. What does the question the angels asked have to do with our stewardship of time?

3. Why was the ascension of Christ necessary?

4. If I am to take this verse of Scripture seriously in my life each day this week, I will need to . . .

The final question is more of an open-ended statement de-

II. Confirmed by Angels
Acts 1:9-11

Acts 1:9. When he had spoken these things, while they beheld, he was taken up; and a cloud received him out of their sight. 10. And while they looked steadfastly toward heaven as he went up, behold, two men stood by them in white apparel; 11. which also said, Ye men of Galilee, why stand ye gazing up into heaven? this same Jesus, which is taken up from you into heaven, shall so come in like manner as ye have seen him go into heaven.

A. The Ascension

During the 40 days after His resurrection, Jesus ate with His disciples, walked with them, and made it clear He was no ghost, but a real person with a real body. He also taught them, opening their minds so they could understand the Scriptures concerning himself. Then, as they were assembled on the Mount of Olives, He gave them a final word emphasizing once more the Father's promise to give them the Spirit in order to empower them to be His witnesses to the end of the earth.

Then Jesus lifted His hands to bless them (Luke 24:50, 51), and in full view of the disciples, He began to ascend into the heavens. Soon a cloud appeared and, as the Greek indicates, swept under Him and lifted Him rapidly out of their sight.

A cloud often accompanied the manifestation of the divine glory and presence of God in Old Testament times. The glory cloud or clouds will also mark our Lord's second coming (Matthew 24:30; 26:64; Revelation 1:7; 14:14).

Most of the blessings which are ours through Christ's resurrection are dependent on His ascension as well. His ascension was necessary before the Spirit could be outpoured at Pentecost (John 16:7). As we have just seen, it was necessary for Him to prepare a place for us. By the Ascension also He entered into the heavenly temple to present His blood on our behalf (Hebrews 9:24; 10:12). Now He is at the right hand of the Father's throne interceding for us as the one Mediator between God and man (1 Timothy 2:5; Hebrews 4:14-16; 7:25, 26; 8:6; 9:15; 12:24). It seems probable also that the disciples could not have stood the full impact of Christ's glory, so they did not see Him as He now is. (Compare 1 John 3:2.) In other words, the transformation of His resurrection body was not complete until He ascended back to the Father's throne. Thus we can surely take it that His ascension was the firstfruits of ours, just as His resurrection is the firstfruits of our resurrection. (Compare 1 Corinthians 15:51-54.)

B. The Promised Return

While the disciples were straining their eyes trying to catch a last glimpse of Jesus as He rose out of their sight, suddenly they realized they were not alone. Two men in white stood beside them. Some believe these were the same two angels who appeared at the empty tomb when Jesus rose. Others believe they were Moses and Elijah who had appeared at the Transfiguration and talked of Christ's departure (literally, His exodus).

The angels turned the attention of the disciples away from the departing of Jesus to His return. The disciples, no doubt, were

signed to make the verse personal.

Allow 5-8 minutes for the students to work through this Bible personalization activity.

Question.
What else did the angels' question imply?

TEACHING TIP 3
The Jehovah's Witnesses have some very subtle, perverted concepts about the return of Christ. Some of them are built around Acts 1:9-11. Use the second case study from PATH to deal with questions their teaching may raise. If any of your students have discussed the Rapture with Jehovah's Witnesses, ask them to share the experience as you discuss this case study. PATH instructions suggest ways to use it.

Clarification
Asleep—that is, in death.

Sorrow—includes anguish, distress, hurt feelings (as if God were unfair to let them die).

If we believe—since we believe, as surely as we believe.

In Jesus will God bring—through Jesus (by the agency of Jesus) will God bring back (from death).

By the word of the Lord—that is, Paul had an actual saying of Jesus to back this up. (See Galatians 1:11, 12.)

Not prevent—by no means precede, get ahead of, or have the advantage over.

Caught up—snatched away, seized and carried up; that is, raptured.

To meet—for a meeting with.

Comfort—also means exhort, encourage.

Question.
How did Paul encourage them?

thinking sadly of their loss. The angels gave them assurance that Jesus would come back in bodily form in the clouds of heaven, just as they had seen Him go. Note how specific the promise is. It would hardly be possible to state the reality of His return more clearly or more emphatically. This implies also that we shall know Him when He comes. He is still the God-Man in glory. He will return with the nailprints still in His hands. (See Teaching Tip 2.)

The angels asked why the disciples were still looking into the heavens. In other words, they needed to look around them. They had obligations here on earth, obligations that would not cease until Jesus' return. This gospel must be preached unto all nations (Matthew 24:14). They must be witnesses, not only to the ends of the world, but to the end of the age. (See Matthew 28:20 where the word *world* is the Greek *aion,* meaning "age.") The assurance of the Lord's coming is one of the Bible's greatest incentives to serve the Lord and live godly lives for His glory. The closer we get to the end, the more earnestly we need to spread the gospel, the more sacrificially we need to pray and give and go. It will soon be too late. (See Teaching Tip 3.)

III. Explained by Paul
1 Thessalonians 4:13-18

1 Thessalonians 4:13. I would not have you to be ignorant, brethren, concerning them which are asleep, that ye sorrow not, even as others which have no hope. 14. For if we believe that Jesus died and rose again, even so them also which sleep in Jesus will God bring with him. 15. For this we say unto you by the word of the Lord, that we which are alive and remain unto the coming of the Lord shall not prevent them which are asleep. 16. For the Lord himself shall descend from heaven with a shout, with the voice of the archangel, and with the trump of God: and the dead in Christ shall rise first: 17. then we which are alive and remain shall be caught up together with them in the clouds, to meet the Lord in the air: and so shall we ever be with the Lord. 18. Wherefore comfort one another with these words.

A. The Dead in Christ Rise First
Paul often found it necessary to deal with problems or false teachings which arose in the churches he founded.

The Thessalonian converts were from a Greek background. From childhood they were taught that the dead went down into a dark underworld from which there was no return. Now false teachers had arisen who apparently taught them that Christians who died would miss all the glory and joy of the Rapture. They seem to have suggested also that something was wrong with a person's faith if he died before the Rapture. He might even miss the blessings of the Kingdom to come. As a result of this false teaching, many believers were full of sorrow, even anguish, because of believers who had died. (See Teaching Tip 4.)

As surely as Jesus died and rose again, so surely will dead believers be joined with Jesus when He returns. He will do it because we by faith identify ourselves with Him in His death and resurrection. Thus, His resurrection is the guarantee of ours. When He comes, the dead in Christ will be raised.

Question.
How did Paul know this?

TEACHING TIP 4

Contact a student during the week before class to prepare a brief Scripture study and a short oral report on the use of "sleep" as a reference to death in the Bible.

Some teach the heresy of "soul sleep" or the idea that the dead—saved or lost—are in an unconscious state until the resurrection. The Bible, however, says that the dead in Christ are present with Him (Philippians 1:21-23).

As sources, suggest the student try commentaries on 1 Thessalonians 4, a Bible encyclopedia, a concordance, and a Bible dictionary. You might also suggest Bible theology books and/or an interview with the pastor as sources on the Bible's teaching about death and the figure of it as sleep.

Ask the student to keep his report to 3-5 minutes.

Allow time for student questions and a discussion of the report if your classtime and interest allow. Tie this report in with the "Bible Commentary" section on the false teachings Paul was seeking to combat when he wrote 1 Thessalonians 4.

Question.
How does this fit with the warnings and prophecies Jesus gave?

TEACHING TIP 5

Many sincere believers try to comfort brothers or sisters in the Lord who have lost a loved one, but only add to their sorrow because they are not as sensitive to the loss as they could be. Use the final PATH case study to address this problem.

When Jesus revealed the gospel to Paul, probably during those 3 years in Arabia (Galatians 1:17), Jesus gave Paul a clear teaching about the Rapture. Jesus himself told Paul that not only would the dead rise, they would rise first. Then we who are still alive, that is, whatever believers are alive at the time, will be snatched away, raptured, caught up together with them. Thus, in one great body both the dead in Christ and the living believers will rise into the skies for that great meeting with Jesus in the air. In other words, the dead in Christ will not miss a thing, nor will those who are still alive have the slightest advantage over them. (See Teaching Tip 5.)

Only one thing is required of the dead: that they have died in Christ, that is, in fellowship with Christ, with Christ as the source and the sphere of their life. It follows then that for us who are still alive, the one requirement for going up in the Rapture is to be in Christ. This means we keep our faith in Jesus, and thus we stay on the winning side. As 1 John 5:4 tells us, "This is the victory that overcometh the world, even our faith." All the born-again believer needs to do in order to overcome, win, and conquer is to keep on believing with an obedient faith in Jesus the risen Son of God.

Paul's hope became brighter and more certain. A few years later he wrote, "We shall not all sleep, but we shall all be changed" (1 Corinthians 15:51). From his first imprisonment in Rome he wrote, "Let your moderation [your gentle, kind, gracious, yielding, forbearing spirit] be known unto all men. The Lord is at hand [His second coming is near]" (Philippians 4:5). From the Roman prison when he knew he was about to be martyred, he said, "Henceforth there is laid up for me a crown of righteousness, which the Lord, the righteous judge, shall give me at that day: and not to me only, but unto all them also that love his appearing" (2 Timothy 4:8). How wonderful to know that we have nothing to fear and nothing to lose by dying. Death is still an enemy. It will be the last enemy for Christ to destroy (1 Corinthians 15:26). But it is not the end. To be absent from the body is to be present with the Lord in heaven, in paradise (2 Corinthians 5:6-8; 12:2, 4). Then when Jesus comes, what a thrill it will be to rise for that meeting in the air!

B. A Sudden Snatching Away

The Greek also indicates that the Rapture will be sudden and unexpected.

Jesus reminded His listeners that when the Flood came the people had no warning other than the preaching of Noah. The day of the Flood, people were enjoying banquets. Others were in the midst of wedding celebrations, expecting to settle down and raise a family. Nothing made that day seem any different from any other day. But that day the Flood came and swept them all away in its destruction (Matthew 24:37-39).

Jesus further emphasizes that everything will be "business as usual" right up to the time of the Rapture. Men and women will be about their usual daily tasks. Then suddenly, some will be snatched away and carried up to the meeting in the air. Others will be left behind to suffer the outpouring of God's wrath described in the Book of Revelation.

> ## Guideline for Living 2
>
> "Business as usual" describes the attitudes of the world at the time the Church is raptured. In light of that, is it profitable to seek to determine God's timetable and even assign dates to the likely time of the Rapture?
>
> Perhaps a better way to ask that question would be: Do such activities add to or detract from the importance of Biblical teaching about the Rapture and the building up of the saints? The answer is obviously, "No." Any preoccupation with dates distracts us from the reality of Christ's task for us. That task is to get the gospel message to our world, not spend our time on misguided and overblown "spiritual fantasy" stories.
>
> Our business is to live so we are ready to welcome Jesus today and at the same time occupy ourselves in His work so we will be found faithful no matter how long He delays His return.

Question.
What is meant by the shout of command, the voice of the archangel, and the trump or trumpet of God?

Some try to connect these with the seventh trumpet of Revelation 10:7. But the events of the seven trumpets do not fit the time of the Rapture. In fact, we are told that the rest of mankind who were not killed by the plagues of the first six trumpets did not repent (Revelation 9:20, 21). In other words, everyone on earth at that time was totally unrepentant and full of sins. That does not leave any room for the Church to be on the earth at that time. First Corinthians 15:52 does connect our resurrection with the "last trump." But this probably means the trumpet introducing the last events of this age, and does not rule out the seven trumpets of Revelation 9 and 10 as coming later.

The Bible does not specify who the archangel is. Later Jewish tradition imagined seven archangels including Gabriel. But the Bible simply calls Gabriel an angel, while Jude 9 calls Michael the (one and only) archangel or chief angel.

On the other hand, it is possible to take "a voice of an archangel" to mean "a voice like that of an archangel." Revelation 1:10 says the voice of the glorified Christ is like the sound of a trumpet. Zechariah 9:14 pictures God as blowing a trumpet. It seems quite probable therefore that the shout, the voice, and the trumpet are just three different ways of describing and emphasizing the same thing—God's shout of command for Christ to descend back to earth again. Jesus now sits at the Father's right hand waiting for that day (Romans 8:34; Ephesians 1:20; Colossians 3:1; Hebrews 1:3, 13). This would also mean that the shout, the voice, the trumpet would be heard in heaven, not on earth. Thus the coming of Christ for His saints would be, as both Jesus and Paul teach, without prior warning that anyone can see or hear on earth. This means too there will be no time for last-minute conversions or last-minute preparations (Matthew 25:6, 10).

C. Comfort and Encourage One Another

Paul ends this explanation of the Rapture by saying we shall ever be with the Lord. In all the events that follow, we shall always be with Him.

Question.
What are some of these events?

They include the Marriage Supper of the Lamb, the judgment seat of Christ where we shall receive our rewards, His return to destroy the armies of the Antichrist, the millennial kingdom, the release of Satan and the final judgment, the new heaven and the new earth, and the New Jerusalem.

Guideline for Living 3

Is it wrong for a believer to feel sorrow over the death of saved loved ones? We know they will be raised to meet the Lord. In the light of Paul's exhortation to "comfort one another with these words" (1 Thessalonians 4:18), shouldn't we learn to put aside such grief?

To refuse to feel sorrow when a family member or close friend dies is to reject our humanity. Until that day when we are reunited with them and with the Lord in glory, we will naturally feel the loss and an empty space in our lives brought about by such a death. If we strive to deny this, we risk alienating the unsaved. They want knowledge of a Christ who is there in the midst of death's sorrow. They aren't looking for a Christ who requires His people to pretend grief doesn't exist.

Paul teaches that the truth of salvation and the glorious hope of the Rapture are able to comfort our sorrowing hearts and heal such wounds in a way the unsaved world cannot know.

We shall rule and reign with Jesus. But still the most important thing is that always, at every future time, we shall be with Him. It was an encouragement to the Thessalonians to know that the dead in Christ would rise first. But it is even more encouraging to us all to realize that the time is soon coming when we shall forever be with the Lord. (See Teaching Tip 6.)

TEACHING TIP 6

Make a special effort to encourage any unsaved class members or visitors to accept Christ in your closing prayer-time today. You may wish to read the "Evangelism Outreach" for this purpose.

Daily Devotional Guide

M. Deliverance Promised. Hebrews 10:31-39

T. Suddenness Assured. Matthew 24:42-44

W. Watchfulness Required. Matthew 24:36-39

T. Resurrection Described. Revelation 20:4-6

F. Be Ready. Matthew 24:36-44

S. Glorified Bodies. 1 Corinthians 15:42-44, 51-53

LIVING THE TRUTH

We have a specific hope in Christ which we call the Rapture. Such a hope tells us two important truths. First, we can anticipate a glorious eternity with Christ after He has caught us up to be with Him. Second, this prospect of His return for us should motivate us to live expectantly and wisely as we walk with Him each day. The Fact that the Bible forbids us to set dates makes it important for us to stay ready all the time. While we pay close attention to our personal readiness, we must never forget our task of winning the lost. The Great Commission affects every Christian, and our responsibility to spread the gospel will not end until we stand in Christ's presence.

EVANGELISM OUTREACH

If you have never given your life to Jesus, you have no share in the joy of His promises to catch up His people to be with Him. Why not ask Christ to come into your life right now? No one knows the day nor the hour He will catch His people away. It could be today.

TRIBULATION BEGINS

SEEING THE SCRIPTURES

Revelation 4:8-11; 5:11-14; 6:14-17

4:8. The four beasts had each of them six wings about him; and they were full of eyes within: and they rest not day and night, saying, Holy, holy, holy, Lord God Almighty, which was, and is, and is to come.

9. And when those beasts give glory and honor and thanks to him that sat on the throne, who liveth for ever and ever,

10. The four and twenty elders fall down before him that sat on the throne, and worship him that liveth for ever and ever, and cast their crowns before the throne, saying,

11. Thou art worthy, O Lord, to receive glory and honor and power: for thou hast created all things, and for thy pleasure they are and were created.

5:11. I beheld, and I heard the voice of many angels round about the throne, and the beasts, and the elders: and the number of them was ten thousand times ten thousand, and thousands of thousands;

12. Saying with a loud voice, Worthy is the Lamb that was slain to receive power, and riches, and wisdom, and strength, and honor, and glory, and blessing.

13. And every creature which is in heaven, and on the earth, and under the earth, and such as are in the sea, and all that are in them, heard I saying, Blessing, and honor, and glory, and power, be unto him that sitteth upon the throne, and unto the Lamb for ever and ever.

14. And the four beasts said, Amen. And the four and twenty elders fell down and worshipped him that liveth for ever and ever.

6:14. The heaven departed as a scroll when it is rolled together; and every mountain and island were moved out of their places.

15. And the kings of the earth, and the great men, and the rich men, and the chief captains, and the mighty men, and every bondman, and every free man, hid themselves in the dens and in the rocks of the mountains;

16. And said to the mountains and rocks, Fall on us, and hide us from the face of him that sitteth on the throne, and from the wrath of the Lamb:

17. For the great day of his wrath is come; and who shall be able to stand?

SETTING THE SCENE

Turning again to the Book of Revelation we see John still on the island of Patmos as far as his body was concerned, but in the Spirit he was caught away to the throne in heaven and saw things that "must be hereafter." Chapters 4, 5, and 6 deal with events and

PREPARING TO TEACH

Study Text
Revelation 4:1 through 6:17

Outline
I. Worship in Heaven
   A. God's Glorious Throne
   B. Continuous Worship
II. The Worthy Lamb
   A. Worthy To Open the Book
   B. A New Son
III. Judgment on the World
   A. Four Horsemen
   B. The Wrath of the Lamb

Golden Text
The great day of his wrath is come; and who shall be able to stand? Revelation 6:17

Central Truth
Although God is love, He is also just and certain to inflict judgment on those who persist in their evil ways.

Learning Goals
1. To visualize the glory of God John was permitted to see and describe.
2. To strengthen our sense of God's power toward us.
3. To let the reality to God's coming judgment increase our desire to spread the gospel.

GETTING STARTED

Before class begins, write the word *TRIBULATION* in large letters across the top of your chalkboard or overhead projector.

Call the class' attention to the word. Ask the students to explain what they understand about tribulation from the Bible. Record key word summaries of several of the responses underneath the word.

Use this activity to direct the class to a major portion of today's study concerning God's wrath and judgment set for the world. (See Revelation 6.)

(Important: Avoid the tendency to spend a lot of time on the subject at this point. Your purpose here is simply to introduce the theme—not to get into the fine points of Biblical eschatology.)

Clarification

Was set—was standing. John did not see the throne being set up. It was already there.

Jasper—probably diamond. It was crystal clear. (Modern jasper is opaque.)

Sardine—carnelian (orange).

Rainbow—halo, radiance (all of one color).

Emerald—a transparent green gem.

Seats—thrones.

Crowns—victors' crowns or wreaths.

A sea of glass—something like a sea of glass (or ice).

Beasts—living beings. The language used here is similar to that used by Ezekiel to describe the cherubim. The cherubim, however, were all alike. Each of these living beings is distinct and different from the others. They are not wild beasts.

Calf—young bull or ox.

Rest—cease.

When—whenever. That is, the actions of verse 9 are at the same time as those of verse 10.

visions seen at the throne. These are introductory to the rest of the Book of Revelation.

In the Spirit is a key phrase. In 1:10 it introduces the first section of the book. In 4:2 it introduces the central section of the book with Christ on the throne, breaking the seven seals, then administering the seven trumpets and the seven vials (bowls). In 17:3 it introduces another change of scene showing the final judgments and the eternal state.

BIBLE COMMENTARY

I. Worship in Heaven

Revelation 4:1-11

Revelation 4:2. Immediately I was in the Spirit: and, behold, a throne was set in heaven, and one sat on the throne. 4. And round about the throne were four and twenty seats: and upon the seats I saw four and twenty elders sitting, clothed in white raiment; and they had on their heads crowns of gold. 6. And before the throne there was a sea of glass like unto crystal. And in the midst of the throne, and round about the throne, were four beasts full of eyes before and behind. 9. And when those beasts give glory and honor and thanks to him that sat on the throne, who liveth for ever and ever, 10. the four and twenty elders fall down before him that sat on the throne, and worship him that liveth for ever and ever, and cast their crowns before the throne, saying, 11. Thou art worthy, O Lord, to receive glory and honor and power: for thou hast created all things, and for thy pleasure they are and were created.

A. God's Glorious Throne

(See Teaching Tip 1.)

Some time after John received the letters to the seven churches, he saw another vision. A door stood open in heaven, and the voice of Jesus (1:10) called him to come up. In the Spirit, he was immediately caught away into the presence of God. (See Teaching Tip 2.)

John was aware that God is on the throne. But he does not attempt to describe Him. All he can describe is the diamond brilliance and the fiery red glow of the glory. God often manifested himself in fire in the Old Testament. But this was far more glorious than anything seen before. Then around the throne was a brilliant one-color rainbow or halo of red's complementary color, a shining emerald green.

Guideline for Living 1

How do you explain God to your unsaved friends and family? How would you describe God if someone asked you about Him?

Many pagan religions don't hesitate to make images, statues, and other visual representations of their gods. Other religions scoff at visual images, saying their god or "god force" can't be expressed in any human terms.

The Bible teaches us that we can "see" and "know" everything mankind can possibly know about God and we do not need special

For thy pleasure—by Thy will.

TEACHING TIP 1

This week's study deals with some of the most awe-inspiring visions of God's glory in the entire Bible. But these scenes are complex and full of imagery. To help your students appreciate the glory of Revelation 4-6, take time during the week before class to go over the "Clarification" section of the "Bible Commentary" and sketch these scenes.

Bring your sketches of the throne room (on poster paper or an overhead transparency) to display as you discuss Revelation 4.

(Note: If you do not have the time or feel artistic enough to do the drawings, try at least a simple chalkboard drawing of general figures and relationships within the throne-room scene. It will serve to focus your students' attention and keep their interest.)

TEACHING TIP 2

Ask two of the students to read the "Guideline for Living 1" (passages from John 14 and Hebrews 1) as you discuss the Bible Commentary question, "What is God like?" Use a modern Bible translation if possible.

TEACHING TIP 3

Divide the class into groups of 2 or more.

Give each group a piece of paper and a pencil. Write this question on the chalkboard and ask each group to discuss: "What are three steps we can take to praise God more effectively?"

Explain that you are asking for practical aspects of praise which can be incorporated into our private and group worship starting today.

Allow 5-8 minutes for the couples to discuss and write their suggestions. Then call on several to share their responses, summarizing them on the chalkboard or overhead projector.

dreams, visions, or images to do so. We can know God intimately and in a very special way through Jesus: "Jesus saith unto him, . . . he that hath seen me hath seen the Father" (John 14:9); "[God] hath in these last days spoken unto us by his Son, . . . who [is] the brightness of his glory, and the express image of his person, . . ." (Hebrews 1:2, 3).

In a circle around the throne were 24 thrones for 24 elders. The Bible does not explain who the elders are. Some modern writers insist they are angels, saying Revelation 5:11 does not distinguish them from angels.

Some things do distinguish the elders from angels, however. The wreaths of gold the elders wore are victor's crowns. These are promised to believers, not to angels. The white robes are also the same as those promised to believers. All in all, it seems preferable to take the elders as in some way representing the Church.

Lightnings, thunderings, and voices add to the awe and majesty of the throne, and are indicative of judgments to come. Seven lamps of fire before the throne represent the sevenfold Spirit of God (Isaiah 11:2, 3) and let John know the Holy Spirit was present. Then, between John and the throne was a great "sea" of glass sparkling and beautiful as it reflected the glory. The "sea" in Old Testament language would correspond to the molten "sea" in the temple (1 Kings 7:23). Here it represents the cleansing, the sanctification, necessary if one is to come into the presence of God. Finally, four living beings representing all of God's creatures complete the picture.

B. Continuous Worship

Together the living creatures and the 24 elders give continuous praise and worship to God. (See Teaching Tip 3.)

Guideline for Living 2

How do we praise God? Every aspect of our walk with the Lord calls on us to praise and worship Him. But what are some practical steps we can take to praise God?

1. We can make it a *habit* to praise God. As we make the effort to praise Him always in everything, it becomes a part of our behavior (1 Thessalonians 5:16-18). Just because something is a habit doesn't mean it is empty or false. We can praise God as a natural part of our lives, and make it real.

2. We can begin and end every session or private prayer and worship concentrating on a time of praising God (Psalm 100:4).

Such concentrated praise nourishes our worship and prayertime and is a natural overflow of that time with Christ.

3. We can set aside an extra 5 minutes at the beginning or end of every day to meditate on some of the great psalms of praise (100 and 103, for example) as "fuel" for a lifetime of praise.

Like the seraphim, these living beings praise God for His Supreme holiness. Holiness in the Bible is always twofold. Its basic idea is separation, but it includes both a separation *from* and a separation *to*. It involves both difference and dedication. God is totally separated from sin. He is completely different from the fallen world order that has been marred by sin. He is also com-

Clarification

Book—roll, papyrus scroll.

Within and on the back-side—that is, on both sides of the papyrus sheets. Ordinarily only one side was used, but this book was full to overflowing and its message was very important.

Sealed—sealed up. The seals were along the outer edge of the roll. It was necessary to break all seven seals before the book could be unrolled and read.

Under the earth—or below the land; that is, in the sea.

Root—shoot or branch growing from the root. (See Isaiah 11:1, 10; 53:2; Ezekiel 19:11, 12, 14; Romans 15:12).

Prevailed— conquered, triumphed, won a great victory (John 16:33).

To open—so as to open. His victory at Calvary gave Him the right to open the book.

Slain—slaughtered. He still bears the marks of His violent death on Calvary's cross.

Harps—lyres. The Greek word used here is the root of *guitar*.

Vials—bowls.

Odors—incense. The word is the same as that used of the incense on the golden altar in the temple.

Redeemed—purchased.

Kings—a kingdom (as in Exodus 19:6; compare 1 Peter 2:5, 9).

Blessing—praise.

In the sea—on the sea.

TEACHING TIP 4

Distribute the "Lamb of God" work sheet from PATH. The PATH instructions suggest ways to use the sheet as an individual or group activity. Select the method most suitable for your class.

The PATH instructions suggest possible answers to each

pletely dedicated to the carrying out of His great plan of redemption and restoration. The heathen considered their gods fickle, changeable. But our God is faithful. We can afford to put our lives in His hands.

Then the living beings praise God for His mighty power. He is omnipotent. Not only is He dedicated to carrying out His promise to bring blessing to all the nations of the earth, He has the power to do it. No king, no dictator, no demon nor devil can withstand Him or prevent Christ's final triumph.

They praise God also for His eternality. By His very nature God cannot die or be destroyed. Atheists, communists, and rebels of all kinds may turn against Him. They will pass. He remains forever.

Because this threefold praise is no more form, the living beings from time to time overflow in a great outpouring of glory, honor, and thanks. Every time they do, the 24 elders rise from their thrones and prostrate themselves before the throne of God, casting down their crowns as they do so. At the same time they speak (or rather, sing) of His worthiness to receive glory, honor, and mighty power. He is Lord, which in Old Testament language would refer to His covenant-keeping name (*Yahweh,* Jehovah). He is also the Creator, and thus the Giver of all the good things we enjoy. His will from the beginning has been for our good.

II. The Worthy Lamb
Revelation 5:1-14

Revelation 5:1. And I saw in the right hand of him that sat on the throne a book written within and on the back side, sealed with seven seals. 4. And I wept much, because no man was found worthy to open and to read the book, neither to look thereon. 5. And one of the elders saith unto me, Weep not: behold, the Lion of the tribe of Judah, the Root of David, hath prevailed to open the book, and to loose the seven seals thereof. 6. And I beheld, and, lo, in the midst of the throne and of the four beasts, and in the midst of the elders, stood a Lamb as it had been slain, having seven horns and seven eyes, which are the seven Spirits of God sent forth into all the earth. 8. And when he had taken the book, the four beasts and four and twenty elders fell down before the Lamb, having every one of them harps, and golden vials full of odors, which are the prayers of saints. 9. And they sung a new song, saying, Thou art worthy to take the book, and to open the seals thereof: for thou wast slain, and hast redeemed us to God by thy blood out of every kindred, and tongue, and people, and nation; 10. and hast made us unto our God kings and priests: and we shall reign on the earth. 11. And I beheld, and I heard the voice of many angels round about the throne, and the beasts, and the elders: and the number of them was ten thousand times ten thousand, and thousands of thousands; 12. saying with a loud voice, Worthy is the Lamb that was slain to receive power, and riches, and wisdom, and strength, and honor, and glory, and blessing. 13. And every creature which is in heaven, and on the earth, and under the earth, and such as are in the sea, and all that are in them, heard I saying, Blessing, and honor, and glory, and power, be unto him that sitteth upon the throne, and unto the Lamb for ever and ever.

of the questions on the work sheet. Emphasize that there are no exact, absolutely correct answers. This is a study guide, not a quiz.

Question.
Why did John weep?

TEACHING TIP 5
Develop and display a drawing of the sealed scroll spoken of in Revelation 5. Follow suggestions given above in the first "Teaching Tip." The "Clarification" information on the arrangement of the seals on the outside of the scroll will be of special help with this drawing.

Question.
Why does John see a Lamb when the elder told him the Lion had conquered?

Question.
What is the significance of the sevenfold Spirit of God as seven horns and seven eyes?

Question.
How can the living beings join in praising for redemption?

Question.
Why are the golden bowls of incense mentioned here?

A. Worthy To Open the Book
(See Teaching Tip 4.)

As John looked again, he saw in the hand of the Holy One on the throne a rolled-up papyrus roll with the leading edge sealed down with seven seals. The seals indicated the authority of the message. (Ancient wills under Roman law were sealed with seven seals.) A mighty angel loudly challenged anyone to open the book. (See Teaching Tip 5.)

John recognized that the book must be connected with the promise to show him things to come (Revelation 4:1). Now it seemed no one was worthy to open the book. We can be sure John himself was also conscious of his own unworthiness. He felt disappointed, thinking the revelation would not be given.

This sets this book or roll apart from other books of prophecy. Even in the Old Testament God made it His practice to reveal His will and plan to the prophets. (See Jeremiah 7:25; Amos 3:7; 2 Peter 1:21.) These men could receive God's message, not because they were worthy, but because they were open to the Holy Spirit. Spiritual things cannot be received by the ungodly, for their hearts are not open and their minds are blinded (1 Corinthians 2:14, 15). But John was in the Spirit and still was not worthy to open this book.

As John continued weeping, one of the elders came and told him to stop. His tears were unnecessary. By a mighty victory the Lion of the Tribe of Judah had conquered and was worthy to open the roll by loosing its seals.

As the Lion, Jesus fulfills promises made to God's ancient people. As the root of David, He will make David's throne eternal (Isaiah 11:1, 10). But it was as God's Lamb He won an overwhelming victory. Calvary demonstrated that He is worthy.

Previous studies have emphasized that the Kingdom must be brought in through terrible judgments. The Opener of the book thus becomes the Administrator of the judgment. The judgments written in the book (at the blowing of the trumpets and the pouring out of the vials or bowls) would purge the earth in preparation for Christ's sovereign rule in the millennial kingdom.

Now we can see why no one else is worthy. Those who fall under these judgments cannot say to God's spotless Lamb, "You deserve this judgment too." Neither can they say, "You did not do enough to save us from this judgment." He still bears the marks of having been slain. He gave His life!

In chapter 4, the sevenfold Spirit is represented by seven lamps of fire bringing illumination. Now there are seven horns and seven eyes, indicating active power and wisdom carrying out the will of God not merely in heaven but in all the earth. Things will begin to happen when the Lamb opens the book.

B. A New Son
Up to this point all worship and praise was given to God on the throne. Now all fall in worship before the Lamb.

Paul shows that all creation groans for the day when the curse will be lifted and our redemption bodies received at Christ's appearing (Romans 8:21-23). So the living beings rejoice when they see these things about to begin.

As saints or "dedicated ones," we "love his appearing" (2 Timothy 4:8). Our prayers are for the coming of the Kingdom when we shall reign on the earth. The bowls of incense show God sees our desire. The book will be opened. The judgments of the Great Tribulation will take place. Then the prayers of the saints will be answered.

With this an outer ring of myriads of angels join in the chorus.

The angels cannot sing the song of the redeemed. But they do join in giving praise to the Lamb because He is worthy.

III. Judgment on the World
Revelation 6:1-17

Revelation 6:2. And I saw, and behold a white horse: and he that sat on him had a bow; and a crown was given unto him: and he went forth conquering, and to conquer. 8. And I looked, and behold a pale horse: and his name that sat on him was Death, and Hell followed with him. And power was given unto them over the fourth part of the earth, to kill with sword, and with hunger, and with death, and with the beasts of the earth. 9. And when he had opened the fifth seal, I saw under the altar the souls of them that were slain for the word of God, and for the testimony which they held. 11. And white robes were given unto every one of them; and it was said unto them, that they should rest yet for a little season, until their fellow servants also and their brethren, that should be killed as they were, should be fulfilled. 12. And I beheld when he had opened the sixth seal, and, lo, there was a great earthquake; and the sun became black as sackcloth of hair, and the moon became as blood. 17. For the great day of his wrath is come; and who shall be able to stand?

(See Teaching Tip 6.)

A. Four Horsemen

Each time the Lamb opens a seal, one of the living beings calls John to come and see. This seems to mean that these were a series of separate visions, each needing a new call for John's attention.

The first rider is not named. But it is clear that the next three represent war, famine, and death. Thus, it must be that the rider on the white horse personifies conquest or the lust for conquest.

John sees these visions while he is in heaven. Thus, they are anticipatory of the kind of judgments that will bring the wrath of the Lamb. In other words, there will not be conquest for a while, then war for a while, than famine, then death. All these will be part of the judgment once the book is opened.

B. The Wrath of the Lamb

The opening of the fifth seal brings another vision that anticipates what will happen when the book is opened. Others will be killed and added to the number of those who gave their lives for their faith in Christ during past ages. In the meantime, white robes, symbolizing righteousness, are given to them. They can be sure they will be with Christ in His glorious coming and they will share that glory.

The vision of the sixth seal pictured all the catastrophic signs of the end of the age, prophesied in both the Old and New Testaments. (See for example, Isaiah 34:4; Joel 2:31; Mark 13:24, 25.)

Question.
Do they sing the same song?

Clarification
A measure—about a quart.
Penny—denarius; a silver coin of o.11 ounces Troy. It was the average day's wages for a soldier or laborer at that time.
Hell—hades.
Beasts—wild animals.
Hair—from black goats.
The heaven departed—the sky split or was separated.

TEACHING TIP 6
You may wish to prepare a drawing of the four horsemen as you did of the throne room and the sealed scroll.

This vision thus anticipates the whole of the judgments which will follow after the book is opened.

Some take this picture as symbolic of the political, moral, and spiritual breakup which accompanies the end of the age. (See 2 Timothy 3:1-5.) However, the Bible presents these things as actual judgments that occur in a very literal way.

Guideline for Living 3

Our hope of the Rapture must not dull our compassion for those who are left behind to endure the horrible judgments that are to be poured out on the world. Our hope should motivate us to share Christ with those who face that danger.

Magnetized lodestones (natural magnets) indicate that the region of Hawaii was once over the north magnetic pole, and the crust of the earth once slipped around until Hawaii came to rest where it is now. Such an earthquake, if it occurred again, would open up multitudes of volcanoes throwing gas, ash, and dust into the air. The initial result would be to black out the sun. Dust remaining in the atmosphere would cause the moon to appear red for a long time. Mountains would move and islands disappear. Cosmic disturbances could bring meteor showers. The sky splitting could refer to disturbances among the clouds (called the first heavens by the ancient Jews).

The world will know it is the wrath of the Lamb. Notice too that the seven classes mentioned in verse 15 include all the leaders as well as all the common people of the earth. No one is left out. This is another indication that the Rapture will have already taken place. The true Church will be already with the Lord, for we are not appointed unto wrath (see 1 Thessalonians 5:9, where the wrath is contrasted with the salvation or inheritance we receive at the Rapture).

The day of wrath will thus bring fear on those left behind. Then will come despair as they realize they cannot hide. May we be counted worthy to escape! (Luke 21:36).

Question.

Will the world know who is bringing this judgment?

TEACHING TIP 7

Close your session today with a special group prayer and praise time. You may be able to incorporate some of the suggestions given for praise under "Teaching Tip 3."

Daily Devotional Guide

M. Suffering Foreseen.
Isaiah 26:20, 21

T. Duration Defined.
Daniel 9:20-27

W. Trouble Predicted.
Matthew 24:15-21

T. Apostates Described.
Revelation 17:1-5

F. A Remnant Sealed.
Revelation 7:4-8

S. A Multitude Saved.
Revelation 7:9-17

LIVING THE TRUTH

John's beautiful vision of heaven's throne room should excite us. It should encourage us and increase our desire to worship. As we see the awfulness of God's wrath that is coming on sinners, we must rekindle our efforts to share Christ in our world each day. Judgment is not a popular subject, but it is Biblical. We must warn sinners that a holy God will keep His Word and part of that Word involves a time of judgment. God is love and He is long-suffering, but He is also just and He cannot allow rebellion against His laws to go unpunished. He has made a way of escape through Christ, and we must spread this good news everywhere.

EVANGELISM OUTREACH

If you have never prepared yourself for the Rapture, do it today. Jesus said He will come in an hour when the world is not expecting Him. There will be no time to repent and believe then. Now is the time when God's mercy in Christ is being extended to every lost person. None of us has the guarantee of another day of life. The Spirit of God calls us to respond to the gospel *now!*

Golden Text
I heard as it were the voice of a great multitude, and as the voice of many waters, and as the voice of mighty thunderings, saying, Alleluia: for the Lord God omnipotent reigneth. Revelation 19:6

Central Truth
Even the power of Antichrist cannot prevent the triumph of Christ.

Learning Goals
1. To see what the Bible says about the coming world leader we call the Antichrist.
2. To understand the nature and limits of his power in the world.

SEEING THE SCRIPTURES

Revelation 13:1-5, 15-18; 19:20, 21

13:1. I stood upon the sand of the sea, and saw a beast rise up out of the sea, having seven heads and ten horns, and upon his horns ten crowns, and upon his heads the name of blasphemy.

2. And the beast which I saw was like unto a leopard, and his feet were as the feet of a bear, and his mouth as the mouth of a lion: and the dragon gave him his power, and his seat, and great authority.

3. And I saw one of his heads as it were wounded to death; and his deadly wound was healed: and all the world wondered after the beast.

4. And they worshipped the dragon which gave power unto the beast: and they worshipped the beast, saying, Who is like unto the beast? who is able to make war with him?

5. And there was given unto him a mouth speaking great things and blasphemies; and power was given unto him to continue forty and two months.

15. Ane he had power to give life unto the image of the beast, that the image of the beast should both speak, and cause that as many as would not worship the image of the beast should be killed.

16. And he causeth all, both small and great, rich and poor, free and bond, to receive a mark in their right hand, or in their foreheads:

17. And that no man might buy or sell, save he that had the mark, or the name of the beast, or the number of his name.

18. Here is wisdom. Let him that hath understanding count the number of the beast: for it is the number of a man; and his number is Six hundred threescore and six.

19:20. And the beast was taken, and with him the false prophet that wrought miracles before him, with which he deceived them that had received the mark of the beast, and them that worshipped his image. These both were cast alive into a lake of fire burning with brimstone.

21. And the remnant were slain with the sword of him that sat upon the horse, which sword proceeded out of his mouth: and all the fowls were filled with their flesh.

SETTING THE SCENE

One of the first events after the rapture of believers will be the revelation (the sudden appearing) of "the man of sin" (2 Thessalonians 2:3). The apostle John names him as the Antichrist. John, of course, was less concerned about the future Antichrist than he was about the many antichrists who were already in the world. He indicates that those to whom he wrote had heard correctly that

Begin class today with a chalkboard or overhead projector activity like the one you used to discuss "tribulation" last week.

Write ANTICHRIST on the chalkboard or overhead. After the students enter the room, draw attention to the word and ask them to suggest what they understand about *Antichrist* from the Bible.

If their responses center exclusively on the Antichrist (one), help them develop the connection in the New Testament between "antichrist" as present evil and *the* Antichrist as a coming world ruler. (The "Setting the Scene" section will help with this. Use the Scripture references given there from 1 and 2 John as your time permits.)

Clarification

Beast—wild animal, dangerous monster.

The name of blasphemy—blasphemous names.

Dragon—serpent; the devil.

Seat—throne, dominion, sovereignty.

Wondered after—followed the beast, full of wonder and admiration.

Power was given—authority was given. (See verse 2.)

Tabernacle—dwelling (in heaven).

TEACHING TIP 1

If you have PATH, use the agree-disagree sheet given for today as you start the class session.

You may wish to use it in conjunction with or in addition to the above "Getting Started" activities. The PATH instructions suggest ways of using the sheet's statements.

TEACHING TIP 2

Prepare a comparison-contrast of the vision here in Revelation 13:1-7 and Daniel's vision of a beast with 10 horns in Daniel 7:7, 8. The simplest

the Antichrist would indeed come. But in that day the many false Christs were what believers had to face. These present antichrists deny that Jesus is the divine Son of God come in the flesh (1 John 2:18, 19, 22; 4:3; 2 John 7). The Antichrist who is to come will also deny that Jesus is the real Christ. He will claim that he fulfills the Second Coming. (See Teaching Tip 1.)

BIBLE COMMENTARY

I. His Power

Revelation 13:1-7

Revelation 13:1. I stood upon the sand of the sea, and saw a beast rise up out of the sea, having seven heads and ten horns, and upon his horns ten crowns, and upon his heads the name of blasphemy. 2. And the beast which I saw was like unto a leopard, and his feet were as the feet of a bear, and his mouth as the mouth of a lion: and the dragon gave him his power, and his seat, and great authority. 3. And I saw one of his heads as it were wounded to death; and his deadly wound was healed: and all the world wondered after the beast. 5. And there was given unto him a mouth speaking great things and blasphemies; and power was given unto him to continue forty and two months. 7. And it was given unto him to make war with the saints, and to overcome them: and power was given him over all kindreds, and tongues, and nations.

A. Satan's Agent

In this vision John sees a great monster rise suddenly from the sea. Ten horns with ten royal crowns appear first, then seven heads, each with a name inscribed on it that claimed divine honor and was therefore blasphemous to God. Then as the monster emerged, its body was like a leopard, its feet like those of a bear, and its mouth like a lion's.

The language is like that of Daniel 7, where Daniel saw a sequence of four beasts, the last one having ten horns with a little horn coming up among them and plucking up three of the other horns. (See Teaching Tip 2.)

As always, the Book of Revelation uses Old Testament language to describe a new revelation. In Daniel 7, the little horn represents the Antichrist. But here this monster, this beast from the sea, that is, from the midst of confused and suffering humanity, is himself the Antichrist. In him we see the consummation of all the evil of the former world systems that Daniel describes.

Guideline for Living 1

Would "good" people follow someone so evil as the Antichrist? How will he gain control over the nations of our 20th-century, sophisticated world?

History—even the 20th century—is full of evil rulers who were welcomed by good people as national heroes and saviors. Adolf Hitler is one example. When he began his rise to power, most of the populace found him odd at worst, at best a deliverer from the ills that were hurting the nation. Before he was finished, the course of human history was altered as never before.

approach might be to make headings such as this:
TERRIBLE BEAST
(Daniel 7)
SEA BEAST
(Revelation 13)

Using some Bible commentaries and reference Bibles, plus the "Bible Commentary" in the Adult Teacher, list some similarities and differences between these two beasts.

Use your chart by asking two students to read Daniel 7:7, 8 and Revelation 13:1-7, then doing a mini-lecture on your chart. Display the chart on posterboard or simply sketch it on the chalkboard or overhead.

Be sure to incorporate the "Bible Commentary" questions and student responses as you go along.

Question.
What will be the source of his power and authority?

TEACHING TIP 3
Ask a student to read 2 Thessalonians 2:1-4, where Paul refers to the "man of sin." If possible, read the verses in a variety of versions and compare their designation for the Antichrist. As you discuss what this title tells us about him, you may wish to jump ahead to "Guideline for Living 2" and discuss his power to deceive and mislead the nations into worshiping him by his showing evil in a good light.

(If you have class members who lived through the period leading up to World War II, you might ask them to share any testimony they have about initial world reaction to Hitler.)

Question.
Is there any limit on his power?

Also, deception by the Antichrist will be made easier because God's people will be gone from the world when he appears.

Because Revelation 17:9 speaks of the seven heads as seven hills, many writers identify the beast with Rome and its emperors or with the papal system and its popes. Next week's study will deal further with Revelation 17. Suffice it to say here that 2 Thessalonians 2:3 makes it very clear that the Antichrist is a man, a real human being, not a system.

The *anti* could mean "against," but the more common meaning of *anti* in the Greek New Testament is "instead of" or "in place of." We know that the Antichrist who comes at the end of the age will be an enemy of our Lord Jesus Christ. But he may not say that he is, at least not at first. Neither will he call himself the Antichrist. He may say that Jesus was only a forerunner, and he will deny the claims of Jesus. In other words, he will claim to be, not the Antichrist, but the real Christ. (See Teaching Tip 3.)

Paul also refers to him as the "man of sin." This fits in with this description of the beast who embodies all the evil of past empires. Some ancient Greek manuscripts call him the man of lawlessness. He will put himself above law and make his will supreme as an absolute dictator.

Satan himself, here called the dragon or serpent, and who is further identified as the devil (Revelation 20:2), gives his power, his throne or dominion, and his authority to him.

To draw attention to the beast one of his heads appears to be mortally wounded. Then this apparently fatal wound is healed. The Bible does not explain how this was done or what trickery is involved. But it does cause the whole earth to follow the Antichrist with amazement, wonder, and admiration. Then this wonder leads to worship, and they give him divine honor, forgetting that God is still on the throne, still in control.

Those who worship the Antichrist are really worshiping that old serpent, the devil, Satan, who gave his power to the Antichrist.

B. Power Over All Nations
Daniel 7 indicates the Antichrist will pluck up or take power by force over three kingdoms or nations. Then seven others will delegate their powers to him, so he will control a ten-nation confederation. But Satan will then extend the Antichrist's power, dominion, and authority over the whole world. Many other passages show the Antichrist will be the leader over all nations during the Tribulation. (See Daniel 7:23; Joel 3:2; Zephaniah 3:8; Zechariah 14:2; Revelation 19:19.)

There is no limit to Antichrist's power with respect to people. Even the saints (here probably used in the Old Testament sense of Israel) will suffer defeat at the Antichrist's hands. But his power will be limited by time. After 42 months it will come to an end. This shows that the Antichrist will be in full power for the 3½ years before Jesus comes in power and great glory to put an end to his rule. All the big speeches and all his blasphemies of God and Christ Jesus will then reap their just reward.

Clarification

Power—authority.

Great wonders—great signs.

Miracles which he had power to do—signs which were given him to do.

He had power to give life unto the image—it was given to him to give spirit (or, breath, Greek, *pneuma*) to the image.

Question.

What is the one thing that will keep us from coming under the influence of the Antichrist?

Question.

What is the purpose of these miracles?

II. His Influence

Revelation 13:8-15

Revelation 13:8. And all that dwell upon the earth shall worship him, whose names are not written in the book of life of the Lamb slain from the foundation of the world. 11. And I beheld another beast coming up out of the earth; and he had two horns like a lamb, and he spake as a dragon. 12. And he exerciseth all the power of the first beast before him, and causeth the earth and them which dwell therein to worship the first beast, whose deadly wound was healed. 13. Ane he doeth great wonders, so that he maketh fire come down from heaven on the earth in the sight of men. 15. And he had power to give life unto the image of the beast, that the image of the beast should both speak, and cause that as many as would not worship the image of the beast should be killed.

A. The Lamb's Book of Life

Our names must be written in the Lamb's Book of Life. That is, we must be born again. We must have placed our faith in Jesus as our Saviour and Lord. This is in line with what the Bible says in 2 Thessalonians 2:10-12. Those who will be deceived by the Antichrist are those who "received not the love of the truth [the gospel], that they might be saved." Therefore God will send them strong delusion so that they might believe, not merely "a lie," but literally, "the lie," the big lie, that is, the pretensions and claims of the Antichrist.

B. The False Prophet

Revelation 19:20 identifies this second beast as the false prophet. He has the same power as the Antichrist, and his power has the same source. He does many miracles, and, in imitation of Elijah, even makes fire come down from heaven.

Their one purpose is to deceive. He has the people make an image of the beast. And it was given to him to give breath or spirit to the image so that the image would speak. It was given to him also to put to death those who refuse to worship the image of the beast.

This also fits in with what the Bible says in 2 Thessalonians 2:9, 11. The Antichrist's appearance is also called a "coming," (Greek, *parousia*). Satan will energize all sorts of deeds of power, miraculous signs, and amazing wonders. But every one of them is a lie, a deception. Satan knows how to use his power, but he is a liar. He is also the father or source and promoter of lies (John 8:44). He will use these lying signs and lying wonders to get the attention of the people of the world and make them worship the Antichrist. It may be also he will use them to make the people forget the rapture of the Church.

Guideline for Living 2

Satan doesn't tempt the "common man" with open, wicked displays of evil. Just as the serpent appealed to Eve's love of beauty and wisdom (Genesis 3:1-6), the devil's attacks are usually subtle appeals to reason—a sort of friendly persuasion to go our own way. In similar fashion, the Antichrist will come with signs and wonders that thrill the world. He will probably be seen at first as a powerful and good leader.

Are we alert to the terrible nature of sin now—even when it looks attractive, even perfectly innocent? Perhaps as we learn of the coming great deception of the Antichrist, we will be more careful to evaluate our interests, involvements, and behavior anew in the light of Paul's words: "Test everything. Hold on to the good. Avoid every kind of evil" (1 Thessalonians 5:21, 22, *New International Version*).

The Antichrist will appeal to those who have made pleasure or money their god. The unrighteousness mentioned in 2 Thessalonians 2:10, 12 involves the seduction that comes from wealth (Matthew 13:22), reveling that involves riotous sin (2 Peter 2:13), and other deceitful lusts and deceptive desires (Ephesians 4:22). In other words, those who follow the Antichrist and yield to his power will be those who are already perishing, already on the broad way leading to destruction (Matthew 7:13). It is no wonder that when they are given the choice between following the Antichrist or being killed, they will choose the Antichrist.

III. His Mark

Revelation 13:16-18

Revelation 13:16. And he causeth all, both small and great, rich and poor, free and bond, to receive a mark in their right hand, or in their foreheads: 17. and that no man might buy or sell, save he that had the mark, or the name of the beast, or the number of his name. 18. Here is wisdom. Let him that hath understanding count the number of the beast: for it is the number of a man; and his number is Six hundred threescore and six.

A. A Mark Upon All

The Antichrist will further extend his power by gaining economic control over all the business, all the buying and selling all over the world. This will be monitored through a mark or brand everyone will be forced to take either on their right hand or on their forehead. This will probably not be a problem, for all those who refuse to worship the image of the Antichrist will already have been killed. It is probable, however, that this demand to take the mark will bring further martyrdoms. (See Revelation 20:4.)

B. The Number of His name

The mark of the beast is either the name of the Antichrist or the number of his name. But even though the number of his name is given, the meaning of that number, 666 (or possibly, 616) is still very controversial. (See Teaching Tip 4.)

1. Some say the 666 should be taken literally. They suggest that 666 will be the actual number put on the right hand or forehead and will in some way be worked into the economic system.

2. It has been popular since ancient times to add up the numerical equivalents of the letters of names to try to identify the Antichrist. Some have taken the name of Nero Caesar and put it into Hebrew letters. But a Jewish student in the Hebrew University did the same for Richard Nixon in Hebrew letters. (Actually, there is no reason for putting it into Hebrew since the Book of Revelation is in Greek.)

Question.
What else will encourage the world to accept the Antichrist?

Clarification
Bond—slave.
Mark—stamp or brand (could be engraved, cut, printed, etched, branded, etc.).
Count—calculate. The ancient Greeks used letters of the alphabet for numbers. Each letter represented a number, and the sum of these numbers would be the number of the name.
A man—a human being or mankind.
Six hundred threescore and six—a few ancient writings give 616 instead of 666.

Question.
What is the mark of the beast?

TEACHING TIP 4
During the week before class, contact three students to prepare 3- 5-minute oral reports on the mark of the beast. Give each student one of the three interpretations suggested in the "Bible Commentary." Suggest various Bible commentaries, Bible encyclopedias, prophecy books, and reference Bible sources that you have available.

Clarification

Him that sat on the horse— Jesus, the Living Word of God (verse 13), the King of kings and Lord of lords (verse 16). He is followed by the armies who were with Him in heaven.

Taken—seized and taken into custody.

Miracles—the signs.

Brimstone—sulfur.

Fowls—birds, especially unclean birds, scavengers.

Question.

What will bring about the defeat of the Antichrist and the rulers of this world with their armies?

TEACHING TIP 5

Use the overhead transparency, "God's Coming Kingdom," from PATH study 4 as a visual review of Daniel 2 in discussing the above "Bible Commentary" parallels.

Question.

Who are the armies of heaven who are with Jesus?

Question.

What is meant by the sword of our Lord's mouth?

Some take the Greek word for *Latin* and show it adds up to 666. This they take to mean the Roman Empire or a revived Roman Empire at the end of the age.

3. Others take the number 6 as the number of man or mankind. The Threefold repetition would then refer to the Trinity. This would simply mean then that the Antichrist will be a man who pretends to be the full expression of the Trinity. In other words, he will be a false Christ.

IV. His Defeat

Revelation 19:19-21

Revelation 19:19. And I saw the beast, and the kings of the earth, and their armies, gathered together to make war against him that sat on the horse, and against his army. 20. And the beast was taken, and with him the false prophet that wrought miracles before him, with which he deceived them that had received the mark of the beast, and them that worshipped his image. These both were cast alive into a lake of fire burning with brimstone.

A. The Final Battle

Revelation 19 describes two great feasts. The first is the Marriage Supper of the Lamb. What a celebration that will be!

The other feast is one for the birds as they flock around the dead bodies of the armies of the Antichrist.

Jesus will return riding a white horse. This speaks of His coming as the triumphant, conquering King of kings and Lord of lords. Since He administered the partial judgments of the seven trumpets and the more complete judgments of the seven vials or bowls of God's wrath, He is seen as treading "the winepress of the fierceness and wrath of Almighty God" (verse 15). Now He comes to smite or strike down the nations with the sword of His mouth, even to rule them (act the part of a shepherd against them) by destroying them with a rod of iron. This is parallel to what we see in Daniel 2 where the stone cut out of the mountain without hands smites the image representing the world system and destroys it totally. (See Teaching Tip 5.)

Some other passages use the term "armies" of heaven to describe angels. But in this chapter it speaks of the wife of the Lamb, the Church, as those who are clothed in fine linen, clean and white (verse 8). Thus it is clear that the Church will be already with Christ when He comes to destroy the Antichrist and his armies. However, angels will also be with Him.

Second Thessalonians 2:8 calls this sword the spirit (that is, the breath) of His mouth. All Jesus will need to do is speak the word, and the Antichrist and his armies will be defeated. The same passage also says Jesus will destroy him "with the brightness of his coming." (See also 2 Thessalonians 1:7, 8.)

Guideline for Living 3

How important is the Word of God? Revelation 19:21 gives some indication of the power of Christ's words at the last battle. Taken together with many New Testament passages, it reinforces the might available to give us spiritual victory as the Holy Spirit uses the Word in our lives.

TEACHING TIP 6

As you close your class, emphasize again the correct perspective your students should have about Bible prophecy. There are great, awesome mysteries about coming events which we cannot know in detail from the revelation God has given us. But we *can* know God through our faith in Christ. Use your closing prayertime to invite unsaved students to come to Jesus.

Indeed, we have a detailed description of the Word's power to meet our needs: "All Scripture is given by inspiration of God, and is profitable for doctrine, for reproof, for correction, for instruction in righteousness: that the man of God may be perfect, thoroughly furnished unto all good works" (2 Timothy 3:16, 17). The Word is also our source of power to combat the devil as the Spirit wields it: "And take the helmet of salvation, and the sword of the Spirit, which is the word of God" (Ephesians 6:17).

B. The Lake of Fire

Before the armies of the Antichrist are killed, the Antichrist and his false prophet are taken into custody and then cast alive into the lake of fire and sulfur that was prepared as the final judgment for Satan and his angels. Thus, because they both became willing agents of Satan, they go to Satan's place. Revelation 20:10 adds that they will be tortured there forever and ever.

What a contrast this is to the glory shared by the armies of the true Christ! Not only will we share His glory, He will be glorified in us (2 Thessalonians 1:10). Thank God, we can share a little of that glory now as we worship, serve, and glorify Jesus, the true Christ, the real Christ. May we reach out in love to bring others to Jesus that they too may share the glory which is ours as sons and heirs of God and joint heirs with Christ (Romans 8:17). (See Teaching Tip 6.)

LIVING THE TRUTH

There are many things about the Antichrist which remain a mystery. But there are in the Word specific truths about him which God has shown us for our profit now.

First of all, the Antichrist is the ultimate concentration of the Christ-denying evil which has been in the world since the Fall. We would do well to guard against all who seek to deny Christ's reality and the truths of the gospel.

Daily Devotional Guide

M. Defeat Foretold.
Daniel 2:31-35
T. Week of Antichrist Predicted.
Daniel 9:24-27
W. Day of Antichrist Discussed
Matthew 24:15-28
T. Coming of Antichrist Foretold.
2 Thessalonians 2:3-10
F. Christ Comes With the Saints.
Revelation 19:11-16
S. Christ's Victory.
Revelation 19:17, 18

Secondly, just as the Antichrist will receive many and make them believe lies, there are insidious forms of evil which pervade our society and seek to lead us away from serving the Lord loyally. We must ask the Spirit to deliver us from such snares of the devil.

Finally, we have the Word, which is the sword of the Spirit, to help us triumph each day over the forces and efforts of evil to enslave us. We do well to turn to it again and again for guidance, strength and comfort.

EVANGELISM OUTREACH

Apart from a personal walk with Christ, we are open prey for Satan. Allow Christ to save you today. He will make His Word come alive in your life and give you the ability to resist the snares of the devil. He will enable you to detect and escape the deceptions which even now are preparing the way for the Antichrist.

MYSTERY OF BABYLON

SEEING THE SCRIPTURES

Revelation 17:5, 15-18; 18:16-20

5. Upon her forehead was a name written, MYSTERY, BABYLON THE GREAT, THE MOTHER OF HARLOTS AND ABOMINATIONS OF THE EARTH.

15. And he saith unto me, The waters which thou sawest, where the whore sitteth, are peoples, and multitudes, and nations, and tongues.

16. And the ten horns which thou sawest upon the beast, these shall hate the whore, and shall make her desolate and naked, and shall eat her flesh, and burn her with fire.

17. For God hath put in their hearts to fulfil his will, and to agree, and give their kingdom unto the beast, until the words of God shall be fulfilled.

18. And the woman which thou sawest is that great city, which reigneth over the kings of the earth.

18:16. Saying, Alas, alas, that great city, that was clothed in fine linen, and purple, and scarlet, and decked with gold, and precious stones, and pearls!

17. For in one hour so great riches is come to nought. And every shipmaster, and all the company in ships, and sailors, and as many as trade by sea, stood afar off,

18. And cried when they saw the smoke of her burning, saying, What city is like unto this great city!

19. And they cast dust on their heads, and cried, weeping and wailing, saying, Alas, alas, that great city, wherein were made rich all that had ships in the sea by reason of her costliness! for in one hour is she made desolate.

20. Rejoice over her, thou heaven, and ye holy apostles and prophets; for God hath avenged you on her.

SETTING THE SCENE

Isaiah prophesied the first destruction of Babylon (Isaiah 13:19-22; 14:22, 23; 47:1-15; 48:14, 20). Most versions treat the verbs in the first part of 13:20 as passives because the translators did not know Babylon was leveled to the ground and a swamp made of it by Sennacherib in 689 B.C. Actually, the verbs are active and mean that Babylon will not sit forever, nor will it continue from generation to generation. Then the thought is continued in the end of verse 22: "Her time is near to come, and her days shall not be prolonged." They were not.

Isaiah 21:9, 10 tells how Isaiah received the news of that destruction. He speaks of it as his threshing, that is, the harvest, the fulfillment of his prophecies. But it points ahead to a great fall of a greater Babylon.

PREPARING TO TEACH

Study Text
Revelation 17:1 through 18:24

Outline
I. Babylon Described
   A. An Apostate World System
   B. The World's Self-Destruction
II. Babylon Judged
   A. Babylon and Its Wealth Destroyed
   B. A Sudden, Unexpected End
III. Heaven Rejoices
   A. Deserved Judgment
   B. A Total End

Golden Text
The world passeth away, and the lust thereof: but he that doeth the will of God abideth for ever. 1 John 2:17

Central Truth
Though evil forces will have sway over man for a period, God's judgment will destroy every evil power.

Learning Goals
1. To examine what Revelation tells us about the fall of the present evil world system.
2. To renew our commitment to Spirit-led holiness.

Start your class session with
a general discussion of
Babylon. Ask several of the
students to tell you what
they remember learning
about Babylon from various
parts of the Old Testament.

Lead from this into a general
discussion bolstered by some
pre-class research in a Bible
dictionary, encyclopedia, and/
or Bible archaeology book.

When you have put Babylon
in perspective, direct the class
to Revelation 17, 18, and 19.
Using the "Setting the Scene"
and "Bible Commentary" material, get started on this week's
study.

Clarification

The wilderness—a desolate place.

Mystery—secret; that is, the
name has secret or allegorical
meaning and is not to be taken
literally.

Perdition—destruction,
eternal loss.

Power—authority.

Desolate—waste, depopu-
lated.

TEACHING TIP 1

Ask one of the students to
prepare a short report on the
suffering and/or persecution of
believers for their faith in a current area of the world. If you
have access to missionary reports and church event magazines, you might find
something suitable there.

If you are unable to get current information, ask the student to prepare a 3-5 minute
oral report on instances of persecution of believers from
church history.

BIBLE COMMENTARY

I. Babylon Described

Revelation 17:1-18

Revelation 17:3. He carried me away in the spirit into the wilderness: and I saw a woman sit upon a scarlet-covered beast, full
of names of blasphemy, having seven heads and ten horns. 4. And
the woman was arrayed in purple and scarlet color, and decked
with gold and precious stones and pearls, having a golden cup in
her hand full of abominations and filthiness of her fornication: 5.
and upon her forehead was a name written, MYSTERY, BABY-
LON THE GREAT, THE MOTHER OF HARLOTS AND
ABOMINATIONS OF THE EARTH. 6. And I saw the woman
drunken with the blood of the saints, and with the blood of the
martyrs of Jesus. 9. Here is the mind which hath wisdom. The
seven heads are seven mountains, on which the woman sitteth.
10. And there are seven kings: five are fallen, and one is, and the
other is not yet come; and when he cometh, he must continue a
short space. 11. And the beast that was, and is not, even he is the
eighth, and is of the seven, and goeth into perdition. 12. And the
ten horns which thou sawest are ten kings, which have received
no kingdom as yet; but receive power as kings one hour with the
beast. 14. These shall make war with the Lamb, and the Lamb
shall overcome them: for he is Lord of lords, and King of kings:
and they that are with him are called, and chosen, and faithful.
16. And the ten horns which thou sawest upon the beast, these
shall hate the whore, and shall make her desolate and naked, and
shall eat her flesh, and burn her with fire. 17. For God hath put
in their hearts to fulfil his will, and to agree, and give their kingdom
unto the beast, until the words of God shall be fulfilled.

A. An Apostate World System

The Book of Revelation often introduces something at one point
or from one point of view and then gives more details later. The
fall of the great Babylon is first introduced in 14:8 in a context of
divine judgment. Then it is mentioned again in 16:18, 19 in connection with a great earthquake where Babylon is divided into
three parts and the cities of the nations fall. Finally, in chapters
17 and 18 more details of Babylon's fall are given.

The angel who shows John the vision of chapter 17 calls Babylon
the great prostitute who sits on many waters. These waters are
explained to be peoples, crowds, nations, and languages. Thus,
this great Babylon dominates the population of the world.

What John actually sees in the vision is a woman dressed in
royal robes, adorned with gold, jewels, and pearls. She is sitting,
not on waters, but on the beast with seven heads and 10 horns,
only now the beast is seen to be scarlet in color. Scarlet here
probably speaks of sin. The vision probably means Babylon is
controlled by the spirit of the Antichrist and shares the sin of
denying that Jesus is the Son of God manifest in the flesh. As a
prostitute she promotes false worship and idolatry, the same spir-

itual adultery that the prophets spoke against so often. The golden cup in her hand shows how she uses wealth and power to get men to share in the abominations which so deserve the wrath of Almighty God. Then the woman herself John saw drunk with the blood of the saints, the martyrs (literally, the witnesses) of Jesus. (See Teaching Tip 1).

The beast has its source in the bottomless pit, the abyss, the place of Satan's captivity. He is headed for perdition, destruction, eternal loss. This would further identify him with the Antichrist as the embodiment of the present world system.

The seven heads have two secret or symbolic meanings. First, they represent seven mountains or hills on which the woman sits. Some have tried to identify the seven hills with Jerusalem. But in John's day seven hills could only mean the great city of seven hills, Rome.

The seven heads also represent seven kings or kingdoms—five fallen, one in operation in John's day, another still to come. Then the beast is himself an eighth kingdom, but he belongs with the seven and is headed for destruction.

No sequence of Roman emperors makes any sense here, so it is better to take these kings as kingdoms or empires at least in part parallel with the kingdoms of the great image of Daniel 2. They would thus represent godless world governments which have rejected God's promise and persecuted God's people. Many see them as beginning with Egypt, followed by Assyria, Babylon, Medo-Persia, Greece, and Rome. The reason, then, for saying first that the woman sits on all nations and then that she sits on seven hills is that in John's day this apostate world system was in the Roman stage. The seventh kingdom would then be what Daniel explained was of iron and clay. This would include the Roman Church in the days of the Dark Ages. It tried then to fill the void after the city of Rome fell, and became involved in the politics and government of Europe with all its corruption.

But today the territory of this kingdom is dominated by secular states, some strong, some weak, like iron and clay. The beast himself would then represent the Antichrist's kingdom. It will be an eighth. That is, it is not part of the sequence that parallels the Babylon image in Daniel 2. Yet it is of the seven. That is, its character and nature is like those that preceded it. The Antichrist will not bring in a really new world order. It will be just as full of corruption as those of the dictators who preceded him.

Guideline for Living 1

What is "worldliness"? How can we know if we are being "worldly"? Is it a danger (or what is the danger) for a Christian in worldliness? How can we avoid it?

One glimpse at the awful wickedness of "Babylon" as the apostle John saw it in Revelation 17, 18, convinces us that the believer has no business being involved with sin. But is that possible?

Someone has said that "worldliness" or "worldly" refer to any person, place, activity, or thing which becomes so important to us that it distracts us from Jesus. This is a powerful truth. And it covers even those things and/or activities which may be good in themselves but keep us from Him.

Yes, we can avoid worldliness, even though we cannot avoid the

TEACHING TIP 2

Contact three students 2 weeks ahead of time to form a discussion panel on the current economic-social-political state of the world.

Ask one student to clip and bring two or three short newspaper or magazine articles showing current economic trends which might be identified with the world economic system portrayed as "Babylon." Have the second and third students do the same with social and political trends. Allow a few minutes for class discussion following the reports.

Your reports and discussion will probably uncover trends and alliances which demonstrate how easily the current world system could fully blossom into the "Babylon" depicted in the Scripture passages for this week's study.

Question.
How will the destruction of the great Babylon begin.

Clarification
Costliness—that is, the great amount of her costly things.

In one hour—that is, in an unbelievably short period.

Question.
Is the Babylon of Revelation 18 the same as the Babylon of Revelation 17?

"world," because we are required to live in it (but not be of it: John 17:14). We can avoid worldliness by refusing to love the world and making our goals heavenly goals: "Set your affection on things above, not on things on the earth" (Colossians 3:2).

B. The World's Self-Destruction

This vision puts the 10 horns into the future, so they represent 10 kingdoms at the end of the age. They receive power or authority as kings or kingdoms for 1 hour, that is, for a short time, with the beast. But they delegate their power and authority to the beast. By becoming subservient to him, they are drawn into the final battle. They, along with the Antichrist, will be defeated by God's Lamb who will have the called, the chosen, and the faithful (the faithful believers who make up the true Church) with Him. (See Teaching Tip 2.)

The 10 kings will delegate their power to the Antichrist. They will suppose the Antichrist's kingdom is something new, and they will be destructive of the present world order. No doubt we can connect this with the vision of the first four seals. That is, conquest, war, famine, and death will lay waste and depopulate much of the earth. In this, without realizing it, these kings will be carrying out part of the judgments of God, for God will put it in their hearts and minds to do so. In other words, God will use them, just as He used the ancient Assyrians and Babylonians (Isaiah 10:5-12; Habakkuk 1:6). But, like modern dictators, they will not realize until too late that they are really destroying themselves.

II. Babylon Judged
Revelation 18:16-19

Revelation 18:17. For in one hour so great riches is come to nought. And every shipmaster, and all the company in ships, and sailors, and as many as trade by sea, stood afar off, 18. and cried when they saw the smoke of her burning, saying, What city is like unto this great city! 19. And they cast dust on their heads, and cried, weeping and wailing, saying, Alas, alas, that great city, wherein were made rich all that had ships in the sea by reason of her costliness! for in one hour is she made desolate.

A. Babylon and Its Wealth Destroyed

Some believe it is not. They distinguish two Babylons, the one in chapter 17 as an ecclesiastical or religious Babylon which will culminate in an apostate ecumenical world church. They point out that some ecumenicals are trying to bring in Hinduism, Buddhism, and other heathen religions along with an apostate "liberal" church, both Catholic and Protestant. Certainly we need to avoid any such association. It can only play into the hands of the Antichrist because it is already full of the spirit of Antichrist.

Those who distinguish two Babylons see in chapter 18 a political or commercial Babylon, full of material wealth and at the same time full of moral sin and corruption.

Actually, the majority of writers throughout church history have seen these chapters as presenting different aspects of the one Babylon. Many of the earlier commentators took it to be pagan Rome, for it was the commercial and religious center in their day. But

Rome never suffered the kind of devastation described here. Neither did its commerce cease when it ceased to be pagan or when it fell to the barbarians. Rome gave way to what followed it just as did Babylon, Medo-Persia, and Alexander the Great's Greek Empire.

After the Protestant reformation, most Protestants believed this Babylon represented papal Rome or the hierarchy of the Roman Church. They argue that harlotry in the prophetical books of the Old Testament almost always speaks of spiritual unfaithfulness, that is, of turning away from the worship of the one true God to the worship of idols. They argue also that the contrast with the woman of Revelation 12 points to Babylon's being a religious system, at least in chapter 17.

Several things, however, point to the Babylon of chapter 18 as the same in chapter 17. All nations have drunk of the wine of the wrath of her fornication (verse 3). The kings of the earth (that is, all the kings and kingdoms or realms) have committed fornication with her. All the merchants of the earth have become rich through the abundance of her delicacies, that is through the wealth expressed in sensuality and luxury. The call to come out of her is not merely a call to leave pagan Rome or papal Rome. Clearly it is a call to have no fellowship with the sins of the world. The sins of the world are pictured as piled high on top of each other like a tower reaching to heaven and demanding the judgment of God (verse 5).

Guideline for Living 2

Once we have identified "worldliness," we are compelled to "come out" from any share in the world's sins. Much of the success of our Christian lives depends upon how we solve this problem. We are specifically commanded regarding the world's sinful traps, "Wherefore come out from among them, and be ye separate, saith the Lord, and touch not the unclean thing; and I will receive you" (2 Corinthians 6:17).

In a word, we are called to *holiness*—a conscious, daily separation from the sinfulness of this world's motives, actions, and desires so we may walk close to Christ. And the closer we walk with Him, the more our lives will be avenues of service and blessing to those who are trapped by the world. In this way we fulfill God's call to evangelize.

Question.
What is the immediate result of the fall of the great Babylon?

With Babylon's fall comes a worldwide economic collapse. The kings (including all the rulers) of the earth mourn its fall, even though they helped to bring it. The merchants of the whole earth mourn because no one buys any of their merchandise. The mention of ships and sailors also shows that world trade comes to a sudden halt.

Some note that language used here in these chapters is similar to that used of the Fall of Babylon in Isaiah's day. He lived to see his prophecies fulfilled when Sennacherib destroyed Babylon in 689 B.C., leveled it to the ground, and made a swamp of it as Sennacherib's own records declare. But, as we have seen, the Book of Revelation often used Old Testament language to describe something different, something beyond what the Old Testament prophets saw. Thus, the fact that the Babylon in Isaiah's prophecies was the city on the Euphrates River does not necessarily mean that the great Babylon in these chapters is a city, whether Rome or a rebuilt Babylon. Just as the Babylon image with the head of gold in Daniel 2 represents the world system in history, so this Babylon the Great seems to represent the whole historical world system which is soon to come to an end.

B. A Sudden, Unexpected End

The great mourning, symbolized by the throwing of dust on their heads, will be more intense because it is so sudden and unexpected. Even though many of the world leaders today say a nuclear war is inevitable, most people do not let themselves think about that possibility too much. But here is pictured the smoke of burning that involves the whole world system and brings total worldwide economic collapse, so no one is able to buy or sell.

Question.
How long will it take to bring this collapse?

The words "one hour" are repeated in verses 10, 17, and 19. This phrase is used frequently in the New Testament to mean either a single hour or an unbelievably short time. We have seen that the Antichrist's kingdom is an "eighth" and is thus distinguished from the great Babylon, though it is "of it." This seems to mean that Babylon falls before the Antichrist takes over. Perhaps the worldwide economic collapse pictured here could become the occasion for the Antichrist to rise up and say, "I have a plan," and to use this collapse as grounds for instituting the mark of the beast. (We have already noted that the Book of Revelation, like most of the prophetical books of the Old Testament, is not in strict chronological order, but does some jumping back and forth.)

III. Heaven Rejoices

Revelation 18:20-24

Revelation 18:20. Rejoice over her, thou heaven, and ye holy apostles and prophets; for God hath avenged you on her. 21. And a mighty angel took up a stone like a great millstone, and cast it into the sea, saying, Thus with violence shall the great city Babylon be thrown down, and shall be found no more at all. 22. And the voice of harpers, and musicians, and of pipers, and trumpeters, shall be heard no more at all in thee; and no craftsman, of whatsoever craft he be, shall be found any more in thee; and the sound of a millstone shall be heard no more at all in thee; 23. and the light of a candle shall shine no more at all in thee; and the voice of the bridegroom and of the bride shall be heard no more at all in thee: for thy merchants were the great men of the earth; for by thy sorceries were all nations deceived. 24. And in her was found the blood of prophets, and of saints, and of all that were slain upon the earth.

Clarification
  Holy apostles—rather, saints (holy ones, consecrated ones; true believers) and apostles.
  God hath avenged you on her—God has judged her with the judgment she wanted to put on you.
  Harpers—singers who accompany themselves on a harp or guitar-like lyre.
  Pipers—flute players
  Craft—skill, trade.
  Candle—lamp.
  Great men—magnates, politically great men.
  Sorceries—magic arts, drugs, poisons.
  Slain—butchered, murdered, slaughtered violently.

A. Deserved Judgment

This vision of the fall of Babylon the Great concludes with a call for a response of rejoicing from those in heaven, including the saints (that is, the believers, the true Christians, the apostles,) and the prophets.

Question.
Why are believers to rejoice and be glad?

They see that a holy God has acted in justice. The ungodly world system has always wanted to hurt and destroy the people of God, especially those who actively proclaim the gospel. Now we see that God has pronounced judgment on the whole Babylonish way of life. They will receive the judgment they wish now to put on the people of God. (See Teaching Tip 3.)

The Babylonish world system actually has brought about the murder of prophets who spoke for God and of saints, believers who lived for God. It is also responsible for all the violent deaths of God's children have been murdered and slaughtered throughout history.

B. A Total End

The description of total destruction given in verses 21-23 parallels the picture in Daniel 2. Even the good things of the present world order must be destroyed before Christ can bring in the better things of the Kingdom.

TEACHING TIP 3

Ask a student well ahead of time to prepare a mini-lecture on the question, "Why must the Christian suffer persecution?" Suggest the following guidelines as he or she prepares the mini-lecture:

1. Can a Christian ease his relationship with the world in such a way that he can remain popular, successful, and avoid persecution for his faith?

2. If so, why must a Christian ever suffer persecution? If not, why aren't faithful Christians suffering constant persecution?

3. If, as believers, we encounter only "smooth sailing" in our lives, are we failing to stand up properly for holy living?

4. What are some positive ways we can overcome persecution and still remain faithful to the Lord?

TEACHING TIP 4

Distribute copies of the HOLY LIVING self-evaluation sheet from PATH. Instructions in PATH suggest options for using the sheet.

Guideline for Living 3

On one occasion when Jesus spoke of demons, He explained a principle of good and evil (Luke 11:24-26). In essence, He said that a life which has been freed from demonic influence may be cleaned up and purified, but there is a spiritual vacuum if that life is not filled with the presence of God.

So it is with holiness. Being separated from the world is only the first step. Putting away sin and evil is a beginning. Filling our lives with the fullness of the Spirit and devoting ourselves to God's interests is next: "Fill your minds with those things that are good and that deserve praise: things that are true, noble, right, pure, lovely, and honorable" (Philippians 4:8, *Good News Bible).*

Daily Devotional Guide

M. Prophecy of Destruction.
Isaiah 13:19-22

T. Worldly Pride.
Isaiah 14:3-11

W. The Apostate Church.
Jude 11-19

T. Fall of Babylon.
Revelation 14:6-13

F. Return of Christ.
Matthew 25:1-13

S. Reward of the Saints.
Matthew 25:31-36

LIVING THE TRUTH

The days are coming when God will bring judgment upon the evil, false religious-political-economic system of the world— "Babylon." The Book of Revelation indicates these terrible, destructive judgments will come after the rapture of believers. In God's gracious plan, we will escape this outpouring of His wrath.

But the Bible teaches that we have a share in God's plans for the evil world system which Babylon represents. In a sense, we must seek God's grace and "police" our lives daily to shun the world's efforts to mire us down in the sins of our present-day "Babylon."

This means holy living. We must allow the Spirit to keep us strong to remain unspotted by the world's evil and dedicated to the good things of God's kingdom.

EVANGELISM OUTREACH

If you have never opened your life to Christ, it is impossible for Him to give you this holiness of life to keep you safe from Satan's sin traps in this evil world system. Why not ask Christ into your heart right now?

9 | MARRIAGE OF THE LAMB

PREPARING TO TEACH

Study Text
Revelation 19:1-10

Outline
I. The Triumphant Christ
   A. Triumphant in Judgment
   B. Triumphantly Reigning
II. The Bride of Christ
   A. A Prepared Bride
   B. Clothed in Shining Garments
III. The Marriage Supper
   A. A Happy People
   B. True Words

Golden Text
Let us be glad and rejoice, and give honor to him: for the marriage of the Lamb is come, and his wife hath made herself ready. Revelation 19:7

Central Truth
The bride of Christ is now in preparation for the great Marriage Supper.

Learning Goals
1. To increase our understanding of the "Marriage Supper of the Lamb."
2. To let this increased understanding of God's future blessings of us expand our praise for Him.

SEEING THE SCRIPTURES
Revelation 19:1-10

1. After these things I heard a great voice of much people in heaven, saying, Alleluia; Salvation, and glory, and honor, and power, unto the Lord our God:

2. For true and righteous are his judgments; for he hath judged the great whore, which did corrupt the earth with her fornication, and hath avenged the blood of his servants at her hand.

3. And again they said, Alleluia. And her smoke rose up for ever and ever.

4. And the four and twenty elders and the four beasts fell down and worshipped God that sat on the throne, saying, Amen; Alleluia.

5. And a voice came out of the throne, saying, Praise our God, all ye his servants, and ye that fear him, both small and great.

6. And I heard as it were the voice of a great multitude, and as the voice of many waters, and as the voice of mighty thunderings, saying, Alleluia: for the Lord God omnipotent reigneth.

7. Let us be glad and rejoice, and give honor to him: for the marriage of the Lamb is come, and his wife hath made herself ready.

8. And to her was granted that she should be arrayed in fine linen, clean and white: for the fine linen is the righteousness of saints.

9. And he saith unto me, Write, Blessed are they which are called unto the marriage supper of the Lamb. And he saith unto me, These are the true sayings of God.

10. And I fell at his feet to worship him. And he said unto me, See thou do it not: I am thy fellow servant, and of thy brethren that have the testimony of Jesus: worship God: for the testimony of Jesus is the spirit of prophecy.

SETTING THE SCENE

At the opening of the fifth seal, the martyrs under heaven's altar cried out for vengeance, that is, for vindication with justice. They were given white robes and told to remain quiet for a little season until other martyrs would be added to their number. Then their vindication would come. This vindication is seen in the visions of the destruction of Babylon the Great in chapters 17 and 18. In contrast to the picture of the great harlot, chapter 19 turns our attention to a tremendous contrast. We now see the Church as the pure and spotless Bride of Christ who will reign with Him during the Millennium.

What assurance this gives us! God has a plan that will climax in Christ's victory and Christ's kingdom.

During the week before class, ask two or three students to be prepared to share some memories of their weddings. Ask them to limit their remarks to 2-3 minutes—just one or two special memories.

As you begin your class session, call on these couples.

If you are teaching a singles class, you could assign one or two students (well ahead of time) to research wedding customs in different parts of the world and report briefly on this subject.

Use the activity to move into your discussion of the events of Revelation 19:1-10 related to a wedding as the picture of God's special praise—reward time for the Church.

Clarification

Alleluia—another spelling of *hallelujah,* Hebrew for "Praise the Lord."

Power, unto the Lord—mighty powers are of the Lord. He manifests them. He is the source.

Whore, which did corrupt the earth with her fornication—the prostitute who seduced and ruined the earth with her habitual immorality (including both sexual sin and turning from God to false religions and cults).

Avenged—vindicated with justice.

Amen—truly!

Praise—keep on praising.

Omnipotent—the Almighty (used to translate *El Shaddai* and "the Lord of hosts").

BIBLE COMMENTARY

I. The Triumphant Christ

Revelation 19:1-6

Revelation 19:1. After these things I heard a great voice of much people in heaven, saying, Alleluia; Salvation, and glory, and honor, and power, unto the Lord our God: 2. for true and righteous are his judgments; for he hath judged the great whore, which did corrupt the earth with her fornication, and hath avenged the blood of his servants at her hand. 3. And again they said, Alleluia. And her smoke rose up for ever and ever. 4. And the four and twenty elders and the four beasts fell down and worshipped God that sat on the throne, saying, Amen; Alleluia. 5. And a voice came out of the throne, saying, Praise our God, all ye his servants, and ye that fear him, both small and great. 6. And I heard as it were the voice of a great multitude, and as the voice of many waters, and as the voice of mighty thunderings, saying Alleluia: for the Lord God omnipotent reigneth.

A. Triumphant in Judgment

The call in Revelation 18:20 was for all heaven and the saints, apostles, and prophets to rejoice. They responded with four great hallelujahs, giving continued praise to the Lord.

The first two hallelujahs come from "much people," literally, a great crowd. Some take these to be the martyrs who are now glorified. Others take them to be the innumerable company of angels who are described in Revelation 5:11 as surrounding the throne, the living creatures, and the elders. Hebrews 12:22 also speaks of an innumerable company of angels, and the Bible often speaks of the heavenly hosts.

The first hallelujah actually begins a great song of praise. By it the people recognize that God is the one true source of salvation (including healing and deliverance), of glory (including true honor and the radiant, sublime majesty we shall share with Christ when we reign with Him), and of supernatural power. Then they honor God for His true and righteous judgments by which He punished the great prostitute Babylon and brought justice for the shed blood of His servants, the martyrs who died for their witness to Jesus. Then, like the last group of psalms in the Book of Psalms, they not only began with hallelujah, they ended with hallelujah. At the same time it is noted that the smoke of the destruction of the Babylonish world system goes up forever. That is, the punishment is eternal for those who were involved in sins here.

Guideline for Living 1

Can the terrible wrath of God's judgment become a motive for our praise? It would seem that the heavenly voices (verses 1-3) called John to praise the Lord for His outpouring of judgment upon the world.

Perhaps we should reevaluate our image of God if praise for His judgment upon wickedness troubles us. One Bible commentary suggests we are so often satisfied with an "anemic" Jesus that we lose sight of the Christ who is triumphant over evil.

The heavenly throng is simply expressing the pent-up cry of the ages for ultimate justice to right all the wrongs of the world. It is that reality—when justice is done for all—that calls us to praise God!

B. Triumphantly Reigning

The next response comes from the living beings (representing all creation) and the elders (probably representing the Church). To the hallelujahs of the heavenly hosts they add an "Amen" and then shout out their own hallelujah or "Praise the Lord!" as they join in worshiping the One on the throne.

Then a voice comes from the throne. This is probably not the voice of Jesus, since He never includes himself when He tells others to say "our Father" or "our God." Some take it to be the voice of one of the elders or of one of the living beings. But it is more likely an angelic voice.

Question.
To whom is this call to praise God given?

It is addressed to all God's servants (slaves, love slaves) who are further identified as all who fear, reverence, and worship God. The angelic voice calls for them to keep on praising God, and their response is the fourth hallelujah.

Some writers identify these servants with a special group distinct from the Church. But the call here is clearly to all God's servants. Then we are told that they include both the small and great, the humble ones, and those in high office or leadership. In other words, none of God's servants, none of God's people are left out. It should be noted here also that these four hallelujahs are all part of heaven's praises. There is no room for any of the true Church, the born-again believers, to be left on earth at this point. They have all already been raptured.

Question.
For what does the fourth hallalujah give praise?

We give praise because God the Lord is our God, and because He is omnipotent. He is the Almighty, and He reigns; that is, He has taken over the rule. God is about to establish the millennial kingdom of Christ on earth.

Clarification

Be glad—rejoice with joy and delight.

Rejoice—be overjoyed, jump for joy, shout for joy.

Give honor—give the glory.

Marriage—wedding banquet celebrating the marriage.

Granted—given (by God). A reference to the gift of His Son who died on Calvary and rose again that we might stand in His righteousness.

Clean and white—pure, bright.

Righteousness of saints—righteous acts of the holy (dedicated) ones; that is, of all believers.

II. The Bride of Christ
Revelation 19:7, 8

Revelation 19:7. Let us be glad and rejoice, and give honor to him: for the marriage of the Lamb is come, and his wife hath made herself ready. 8. And to her was granted that she should be arrayed in fine linen, clean and white: for the fine linen is the righteousness of saints.

A. A Prepared Bride

These verses are the continuation of the fourth hallelujah and its song of praise. Like the other songs, it celebrates the vindication of God's people. Only this time it is the final vindication.

Question.
What will be our final vindication?

It will be not merely the judgment of our enemies, not merely the destruction of the anti-God world system, but the Marriage Supper, the wedding banquet of the Lamb. This will demonstrate and bring into full view that the Church is what the Bible says she is, the Bride of Christ. (See Teaching Tip 1.)

TEACHING TIP 1

The display of the Church as Christ's body, as God's completed workmanship, is a theme which runs throughout the New Testament. As you discuss this section of the "Bible Commentary" and seek responses to the above question, you might have students read the following Scripture passages on the subject: Colossians 1:21, 22; Ephesians 2:4-7; 4:11-13.

(If classtime permits, provide paper and pens or pencils to the students, write the above references on the chalkboard, and use them as a Scripture search activity on Christ's plan for His church.)

Question.
What is the important point concerning the wife in verse 7?

Question.
Does the Church have any part in this?

TEACHING TIP 2

Using the "Bible Commentary" material and a good Bible dictionary or encyclopedia, prepare a 3-5 minute mini-lecture on Biblical marriage customs. After the lecture, allow 2-4 minutes for questions. (Be careful not to let this activity bog down the flow of the study or distract from the central truths of the Church's relationship to Christ.)

TEACHING TIP 3

Divide the class into two buzz groups to explore the relationship between God's judgment and the praise of the saints.

Provide paper and pencil for each group to record its conclusions. Ask each group to choose a leader and scribe to record its work.

Give the two groups the following guidelines and topics to discuss and respond to:

Group One: Since God's

Some point to the ancient Hebrew custom which used the word *man* or *lord* for "husband" and the word *woman* for "wife." Actually, "wife" here is the ordinary Greek word for woman. Thus, in view of this custom, the wife is the one who acknowledges the Lamb, Christ, as her Lord.

Others point to the ancient marriage customs where the betrothal took place sometime before the marriage. Then, when the appointed time came, the husband would go to the house of his bride and claim her as his wife. He would then take her as his wife to his house, where the wedding banquet would be celebrated. Thus, the Church after the Rapture could be called the Lamb's wife, and then would remain with Him and take part in the Marriage Supper of the Lamb in heaven. (See Teaching Tip 2.)

We see also that the word *wife* in the Bible is often used as a symbol of a close, loving, personal relationship. Paul compares marriage to the relationship which the Church enjoys with Christ now (Ephesians 5:22-33). The same relationship between Christ and the Church is also symbolized by the "Head" and the "Body" 1 Corinthians 12:12-27; Ephesians 1:22, 23; 4:15, 16). What closer relationship could there be than that!

It is not the terminology of verse 7 that is important, but the fact that the Lamb's wife has made herself ready.

B. Clothed in Shining Garments

Verse 8 explains how the Lamb's wife has prepared herself. She is only ready when she is clothed in fine linen, clean and white; that is, pure, shining bright, and radiant.

"Righteousness" here is in the plural and means the righteous acts of the saints. Because clothing ourselves in fine linen is a privilege given us by God, this means we stand not in our own righteousness, but in Christ's. However, the robes themselves do not represent the righteousness of Christ in which we stand. They represent rather the deeds we do as the result of our relation to Christ and as a result of the gift of salvation and the gifts of the Spirit. We cannot accomplish these righteous acts without the help of the Holy Spirit. But we cannot sit around waiting for the Spirit to push us. We must cooperate with Him freely and willingly. We thus have our part to do. (Compare Matthew 25:35-40, which shows we shall be judged by our works that flow out of our love for Christ and our love for those for whom He died.) (See Teaching Tip 3.)

Guideline for Living 2

God has given us the responsibility of doing "good works." Good works, of course, will never save us—we are saved by grace, through faith in Christ's ultimate "good work" when He paid sin's penalty through His death on the cross.

Rather, good works are at the heart of God's purpose for creating us: "God has made us what we are, and in our union with Christ Jesus he has created us for a life of good deeds, which he has already prepared for us to do" (Ephesians 2:10, *Good News Bible*).

In the light of this basic plan for our lives, we can ask the Holy Spirit to overflow with the love of Christ in us and through us to others. That is the source or power at work that prepares the "fine linen" (Revelation 19:8) with which we will be clothed at the Marriage Supper of the Lamb.

judgment is always righteous, we can feel only gladness at the destruction of the evil world system and those who are at the heart of it.

Group Two: It is callous to rejoice in any way over the suffering and punishment of the wicked. Therefore, Revelation 19:2, 3 cannot really mean we are to praise God over His judgment and punishment of the wicked.

Allow about 10 minutes for the groups to work. Emphasize that these topics are open ended. They have no quick or easy solution—there are no "right" or "wrong" answers to the questions they pose.

Reassemble the class and ask the leaders to share the group findings with the entire class. Take as much time as your session allows to discuss these.

Clarification

He saith—Probably the angel of 17:1 is speaking.

Blessed—happy because full of blessings.

Called—have been called and still are the called. That is, those who have accepted the inviation and now actually take part.

True—genuine and dependable.

I am thy fellow servant, and of thy brethren that have the testimony of Jesus—I am a fellowservant who serves both you and your brothers who have the testimony of Jesus. (See Hebrews 1:14.)

TEACHING TIP 4

Take time to discuss and plan a class service activity. This could be something related to work which needs doing around your church (check with the pastor and/or church board before class for suggestions) or a group visitation activity. Make definite plans to execute the project during the coming week.

What a contrast there is between the false woman Babylon and the true woman the Church. Babylon corrupts the earth with her morally and spiritually depraved acts. The Church prepares herself by her good works that glorify God and bear witness to Christ in the power of the Spirit (Acts 1:8). (See Teaching Tip 4.)

III. The Marriage Supper

Revelation 19:9, 10

Revelation 19:9. And he saith unto me, Write, Blessed are they which are called unto the marriage supper of the Lamb. And he saith unto me, These are the true sayings of God. 10. And I fell at his feet to worship him. And he said unto me, See thou do it not: I am thy fellow servant, and of thy brethren that have the testimony of Jesus: worship God: for the testimony of Jesus is the spirit of prophecy.

A. A Happy People

The first command to write was given in connection with messages given to the seven churches in the Roman province of Asia. This new command to write could indicate that here is a special word, a further word for those churches. They were in danger of persecution. They had no social standing. The wealthy and great ones of this world were not inviting them to their banquets. But actually, the believers were the happy ones, for they had accepted the invitation to the Marriage Supper of the Lamb.

The Marriage Supper celebrates the fact that the Church will "ever be with the Lord" (1 Thessalonians 4:17). It expresses a marvelous fellowship brought about by Christ's love for us and our love responding to His. It will be full of joy, delight, and glorious consummation and victory. However, we do not get into this relationship as a body or group, but as individuals. Each one must personally respond to the invitation.

Some writers make distinctions on the basis of terminology here. But when we examine the parables of Jesus, we see He uses different terms in different parables to bring out different aspects of our relation to Him.

For example, in Luke 14:16-24, Jesus told of a man making a great supper and sending out many invitations. When the supper was ready, he sent his servants to notify those who were previously invited, but they all had excuses. He then sent the servant into the city to bring in the poor, the maimed, the lame, and the blind, but still there was room. So he sent the servant into the highways and hedges and filled the house with guests. The context shows that those with previous invitations were the religious Jews. Those from the city were the poor, the tax collectors, and the sinners who were despised by the Pharisees but who heard Jesus gladly. Those from the highways and hedges were the Gentiles. Thus, in this parable the guests included all the Jews and all the Gentiles.

On another occasion Jesus referred to His own disciples as "the children of the bridechamber," that is, the friends of the bridegroom, the bridegroom's attendants (Luke 5:34). But referring to Jews and Gentiles as guests and apostles as friends of the Bridegroom clearly does not exclude them from the Bride. The Bible simply does not uphold the idea of two classes, one the Bride, and the other, less favored, the guests. Neither does the Bible uphold the idea that only "super" believers will make the Rapture. Paul told the Thessalonians that there will not be two classes, but all who are in Christ, whether dead or alive, will be joined together in one Body and rise for that meeting in the air (1 Thessalonians 4:16, 17). Thus the terms, *the Body, the Bride, the Church,* are completely synonymous in the Bible. We must not make artificial distinctions on the basis of terminology. The important thing is that we accept the invitation and make ourselves ready.

Guideline for Living 3

Fellowship is at the heart of God's ultimate, heavenly goals for us: "Then we which are alive and remain shall be caught up together with them in the clouds, to meet the Lord in the air: and so shall we ever be with the Lord" (1 Thessalonians 4:17).

What will God have for us to do and to be throughout all eternity? We don't know. But the glimpses we have of God's heavenly city in Revelation—and of this great Marriage Supper—indicate that enjoying the presence of the Lord and the fellowship of the other believers is at the center of His eternal working. The late scholar-writer C. S. Lewis had a special feeling for this idea. He saw this life as a training ground or workshop in which we are being shaped and equipped as creatures who will live in fellowship with God and each other for eternity.

This truth is reflected in the angel's words to John: We are readied to share with God and each other as we let the "testimony of Jesus" mold our lives in His service.

B. True Words

The angelic messenger then declared that what he had just pronounced was the true sayings, the genuine, dependable words of God. This message so overwhelmed John that he fell down before the angelic speaker in an attitude of worship. This the angel rejected.

Question.
Why did the angel reject worship?

Only God is worthy of worship. As Hebrews 1:14 points out, angels are spirits who are holy servants of God sent forth to serve God for the sake of those (the believers) who are the heirs of salvation. That is, God sends them on His behalf to promote the interests of those who are to inherit Christ's kingdom. Thus they are servants of God who serve us who are also servants of God, for we have the testimony of Jesus. God depends on us, not on angels, to spread the gospel in this present age. The angel also in rejecting worship from John, wanted John to give all his attention to Jesus.

Question.
What is meant by the statement that the testimony of Jesus is the spirit of prophecy?

The angel brought a prophecy that was a witness to Jesus and should have made John think only of worshiping Him. The Holy Spirit as the Spirit of prophecy was working in and through the angel to bring testimony to Jesus. The same Spirit of prophecy wanted John to bear witness to Jesus and He wants us to bear witness to Jesus. Prophecy was never given merely to satisfy idle curiosity but to point men and women to our Lord.

In fact, as we go through the entire Bible, both Old and New Testaments, we find the Spirit of prophecy focusing His attention on Jesus. It begins in Genesis 3:15 with the promise that the Seed of the woman would crush the head of the same old serpent that tempted Eve. It continues in the promises to Abraham and to David. It is unfolded more and more through Isaiah and the rest of the prophets. It is central in all the New Testament. The whole Bible thus encourages us to keep our eyes on Jesus and follow Him. He himself is the hope of all true believers.

No wonder, then, the festivities of the great Marriage Supper, the great wedding banquet of the Lamb will be so joyous. At the Rapture we are united with Jesus forever; we will find nothing hindering our fellowship and joy. And because these are the real, genuine, dependable words of God, we can be sure they will be fulfilled. As Romans 5:5 indicates, our hope in Christ will never disappoint us, never cause us to be ashamed of our faith and trust in Him. Those who have put their trust in the Napoleons, the Hitlers, and in multitudes of other leaders of this world have already come to shame. Those who put their trust in the Antichrist will come to shame. But those who put their trust in Jesus will rise with Him and go on to shout with joy around the heavenly banquet table at the Marriage Supper of the Lamb. (See Teaching Tip 5.)

LIVING THE TRUTH

"The Marriage Supper of the Lamb" is cloaked in a great air of mystery. What will the event be like? How will we take part? Will it involve a literal banquet or is this just symbolic of the fellowship we will share? The Bible leaves these questions veiled in mystery.

But God conveys His truth about this great occasion: It will be the ultimate reward, the time of great rejoicing for His people the Church. We will gather for worship and for sharing our praise that God has destroyed the evil world system in preparation for setting up the new heaven and new earth.

Above all, the Marriage Supper of the Lamb will be a time of special union with Christ. It will be the time and place when we will worship our triumphant Saviour and know the fullness of joy only looking upon His face can bring.

EVANGELISM OUTREACH

Have you joined yourself to Christ by faith? Apart from Him, there is no place in the great Marriage Supper. Why not make that connection by faith today? Even before you reach heaven, you will enjoy fellowship with Christ and experience His joy in your heart.

Daily Devotional Guide

M. The Bride in Preparation.
Matthew 25:1-10
T. The Betrothal.
2 Corinthians 11:1-3
W. The Bridegroom Calls.
1 Thessalonians 4:16, 17
T. The Bridegroom's Love.
Ephesians 5:25-27
F. The Invitation.
Matthew 22:1-9
S. The Participants.
Matthew 22:10; Revelation 7:13-17

BATTLE OF ARMAGEDDON

SEEING THE SCRIPTURES

Revelation 19:11, 16-21; 20:1-3

19:11. I saw heaven opened, and behold a white horse; and he that sat upon him was called Faithful and True, and in righteousness he doth judge and make war.

16. And he hath on his vesture and on his thigh a name written, KING OF KINGS, AND LORD OF LORDS.

17. And I saw an angel standing in the sun; and he cried with a loud voice, saying to all the fowls that fly in the midst of heaven, Come and gather yourselves together unto the supper of the great God;

18. That ye may eat the flesh of kings, and the flesh of captains, and the flesh of mighty men, and the flesh of horses, and of them that sit on them, and the flesh of all men, both free and bond, both small and great.

19. And I saw the beast, and the kings of the earth, and their armies, gathered together to make war against him that sat on the horse, and against his army.

20. And the beast was taken, and with him the false prophet that wrought miracles before him, with which he deceived them that had received the mark of the beast, and them that worshipped his image. These both were cast alive into a lake of fire burning with brimstone.

21. And the remnant were slain with the sword of him that sat upon the horse, which sword proceeded out of his mouth: and all the fowls were filled with their flesh.

20:1. And I saw an angel come down from heaven, having the key of the bottomless pit and a great chain in his hand.

2. And he laid hold on the dragon, that old serpent, which is the Devil, and Satan, and bound him a thousand years,

3. And cast him into the bottomless pit, and shut him up, and set a seal upon him, that he should deceive the nations no more, till the thousand years should be fulfilled: and after that he must be loosed a little season.

SETTING THE SCENE

The Bible speaks of the whole general period of the Great Tribulation as the day of wrath. This week's study takes us to the climax and conclusion of that day of wrath. Beginning with Revelation 19:11 John sees a new vision of the victorious, all-powerful Christ.

The preceding verses gave a picture seen from the standpoint of heaven with the 24 elders and the living creatures in view. Beginning with verse 11 the standpoint changes back to the earth. From the point of view of the earth John looks up and sees heaven opened. Only this time John is not called up. Instead, he sees Christ coming down to win the final victory over the Antichrist.

PREPARING TO TEACH

Study Text
Revelation 19:11 through 20:3

Outline
I. The King of Kings
   A. Coming in Triumph
   B. A Harvest of Judgment
II. The Great Conflict
   A. A Supper for Birds
   B. The Final Battle
III. The Devil Bound
   A. Bound a Thousand Years
   B. Three Interpretations

Golden Text
He hath on his vesture and on his thigh a name written, KING OF KINGS, AND LORD OF LORDS. Revelation 19:16

Central Truth
The Battle of Armageddon will culminate in the exaltation of Christ as King of kings.

Learning Goals
1. To investigate what the Book of Revelation says about the Battle of Armageddon.
2. To renew our commitment to the written Word of God as our contact point with the Living Word, Jesus.

Begin today's class session by familiarizing your students with Armageddon. The "Bible Commentary" material below under "The Final Battle" presents an excellent overview of what the Bible says of the battlefield.

You can also find information about this coming battle in a Bible dictionary or encyclopedia. Many regular encyclopedias have interesting material under the "Armageddon" entry which would be of use to you.

Either contact a student during the week before class or do it yourself and prepare a 3-5 minute oral presentation about Armageddon, using these source ideas.

Clarification

True—genuine, real, in contrast to the false christ, the Antichrist.

Crowns—royal crowns.

Knew—or understood. Many ancient manuscripts have "names" in the plural, perhaps indicating there was a name written on each of the crowns.

Vesture—long robe.

Dipped in blood—rather, spattered with the blood of His enemies. (See Isaiah 63:1-6.)

Sharp—also means swift.

Rule them—do the work of a shepherd against them.

The fierceness and wrath of Almighty God—the wrathful outburst of the hostility of Almighty God (against sin). The winepress indicates a harvest of judgment.

On his thigh—that is, on the robe as it was spread out over His thigh.

TEACHING TIP 1

Duplicate and distribute copies of today's PATH work sheet. It is intended to give an in-depth study of Revelation 19:11-16. PATH instructions suggest ways it can be used.

BIBLE COMMENTARY

I. The King of Kings

Revelation 19:11-16

Revelation 19:11. I saw heaven opened, and behold a white horse; and he that sat upon him was called Faithful and True, and in righteousness he doth judge and make war. 12. His eyes were as a flame of fire, and on his head were many crowns; and he had a name written, that no man knew, but he himself. 13. And he was clothed with a vesture dipped in blood: and his name is called The Word of God. 14. And the armies which were in heaven followed him upon white horses, clothed in fine linen, white and clean. 15. And out of his mouth goeth a sharp sword, that with it he should smite the nations; and he shall rule them with a rod of iron: and he treadeth the winepress of the fierceness and wrath of Almighty God. 16. And he hath on his vesture and on his thigh a name written, KING OF KINGS, AND LORD OF LORDS.

A. Coming in Triumph

As John looks again he sees a new vision with heaven already opened. Out of heaven he sees Christ coming seated on a white horse. The white horse of the conqueror indicates His coming is in triumph. He is called Faithful because now He will prove His faithfulness by bringing in the promised Kingdom on earth. He is called True because He is the real Christ, God's anointed One, the Messiah promised long before. His eyes are as a flame of fire because of His penetrating wisdom and His righteous judgment. The many royal crowns show He comes as King to make David's throne eternal and to fulfill the many prophecies that He will reign on the earth over the entire world, over all nations. The name that no man knows speaks of His divine nature and the inner glory He shares with the Father. This is something that none of us as finite beings will ever fully understand. When John sees Him, His long outer robe is already spattered with the blood of His enemies, indicating that the previous judgments of the Book of Revelation were also part of His triumph. (See Teaching Tip 1.)

This Jesus who is coming back is the same Jesus who existed in past eternity as the Living Word, the Word who was with God and who was God (John 1:1). He is the same Living Word who became flesh and unfolded the nature of God while He ministered here on earth (John 1:14, 18). He is the same Jesus who went away and of whom it was promised He would come again (Acts 1:11).

B. A Harvest of Judgment

Some say those on white horses are angels. But they ride white horses, indicating they share in the Saviour's triumph. Surely they are the overcomers, the winners, those who have been made more than conquerors through Him who loves us. Then, who are those in white linen? They have already been identified as the saints, the bride of Christ (verse 8). They have already had the promise that they will be with Him and share in the judgment of the nations. (See Teaching Tip 2.)

Guideline for Living 1

With the stress of everyday battles against sin and temptation it is easy to forget that we as believers truly are overcomers in Christ. Lest we lose sight of this reality, the Book of Revelation gives us a vivid picture of our final triumph with Christ over Satan and his forces (Revelation 19:11-16). (See Teaching Tip 2.)

Elsewhere in Scripture, we are told how to live as overcomers:

1. *By our faith.* "Everyone born of God has overcome the world. This is the victory that has overcome the world, even our faith" (1 John 5:4, *New International Version*).

2. *By Using the spiritual weapons of victory God has given us.* "Put on the full armor of God, so that when the day of evil comes, you may be able to stand your ground, and after you have done everything, to stand" (Ephesians 6:13, *New International Version*).

3. *By the salvation and newness of life which is ours through the blood of Christ.* "They overcame him by the blood of the Lamb and by the word of their testimony" (Revelation 12:11, *New International Version*).

This judgment is pictured first as a terrible, swift sword that will smite and destroy the nations, so swift and sharp that none will escape it. Because it issues from His mouth, this means all Jesus will have to do is speak the word and the judgment will be accomplished.

Second, it is pictured as a shepherd taking an iron rod and breaking the bones of the enemies of the sheep. This is another reference to the Second Psalm where the Hebrew word can also mean break, and it is compared with the shattering of a potter's vessel. Once again we see a parallel to the picture in Daniel 2:34, 35, 44, 45, where the stone, representing Christ and His kingdom, breaks and shatters the present world order into a powder that the wind blows away. (See Teaching Tip 3.)

Third, it is pictured as treading the winepress of God's wrath in a fierce outburst of judgment. This is parallel to the picture in 2 Thessalonians 1:8, 9 where Jesus appears in flaming fire taking vengeance (bringing just retribution) on those who know not God and who obey not the gospel.

Second Thessalonians 1:7 does indicate that Christ's mighty angels will be with Him when He is revealed here, but this does not mean they are the ones on white horses. The Bible is full of assurance that when Jesus returns in glory to judge the nations and destroy the present world order, every faithful believer will be with Him. We also have the plain statement that those caught up for the meeting with the Lord in the air will "ever be with the Lord" (1 Thessalonians 4:17).

The name written across the lower part of the robe covering His thigh is clear for all to see. He comes as King of kings and Lord of lords. As the living Word of God He is the one Mediator in creation (John 1:3). He is also the one Mediator between God and man in our redemption. He will also be the one Mediator in judgment. As Jesus himself said, "The Father judgeth no man, but hath committed all judgment unto the Son" (John 5:22). But His purpose in judgment is to remove the godless world system that has rejected Christ. Because of the exceeding sinfulness of sin, the kingdom can only be brought in through judgment. Yet God's purpose is good, as His purpose has always been. Even in judgment He is still King of kings, bringing in the better things of the millennial kingdom.

II. The Great Conflict
Revelation 19:17-21

Revelation 19:17. I saw an angel standing in the sun; and he cried with a loud voice, saying to all the fowls that fly in the midst of the heaven, Come and gather yourselves together unto the supper of the great God. 19. And I saw the beast, and the kings of the earth, and their armies, gathered together to make war against him that sat on the horse, and against his army. 20. And the beast was taken, and with him the false prophet that wrought miracles before him, with which he deceived them that had received the mark of the beast, and them that worshiped his image. These both were cast alive into a lake of fire burning with brimstone. 21. And the remnant were slain with the sword of him that sat upon the horse, which sword proceeded out of his mouth: and all the fowls were filled with their flesh.

A. A Supper for Birds

Once again John looks toward the heavens and sees another vision. This time he sees an angel standing in the sun. That is, the brightness and glory of the sun is focused on him.

Most of the heathen nations of that day considered the sun god to be their chief god. They considered the sun to be a chariot in which the sun god rode. But what John sees in the sun is not some god intent on protecting the heathen nations. It is an angel who comes as a messenger of judgment, calling the birds of the midheaven to God's great feast. It is God's judgment on the Antichrist and his armies.

Guideline for Living 2

Just as the angel standing in the sun is a messenger to the world of God's judgment, so we are messengers to our world of God's coming judgment upon sin. This presents us with a problem as we witness for Christ: In our testimony how do we strike a proper balance between His abundant love and His coming judgement upon sin?

On the one hand, we risk spiritually "assaulting" the unsaved with a heavy load of doom and gloom. Everyone knows well-meaning saints who have alienated the unsaved needlessly because they have been unwilling or unable to let Christ's love show through their zeal.

On the other hand, we may risk imparting a "witness" which is little more than portraying God as a cosmic "happy face," whose main goal is to see that everyone has a nice day! In this lies the danger of failing to call men to repentance—which Jesus never failed to do (Mark 1:14, 15).

The answer lies in prayerfully letting the Holy Spirit guide each witnessing situation. He can give us the words and deeds to show Christ in a real way to each person in our world.

This great supper for the birds is also a deliberate contrast to

Clarification

Fowls—birds.

The supper of the great God—the great supper of God.

The beast—the wild beast; the Antichrist.

Miracles—signs.

Brimstone—sulfur.

The remnant—the rest of the armies of the Antichrist.

TEACHING TIP 4

Review the "Getting Started" presentation on Armageddon. You may wish to ask one or two students to look up and read key verses given here on Armageddon if you were unable to include that activity in your original presentation.

TEACHING TIP 5

One of the fascinating teachings of the Bible is that creation itself has somehow shared in the Fall and will in some fashion share in ultimate redemption from sin.

If time permits, ask students to look up and read the following verses and state in one or two sentences what they think the passages teach: Genesis 3:17, 18; Isaiah 11:6-9; Romans 8:19-22.

These Scripture passages give details on the nature and purpose of Christ's millennial reign. They are among those which Bible scholars see as requiring a special reign of Christ on earth to fulfill God's promises to Israel at some point before the new heaven and new earth.

Clarification

The bottomless pit—the abyss, that is, the depths of *sheol* or hades; translated "the deep" in Luke 8:31 and Romans 10:7. It is recognized here as the abode of demons and Satan's headquarters.

Dragon—serpent.

That old serpent—the original or ancient snake. (See Genesis 3:1, 15; 2 Corinthians 11:3, 14.)

The Devil—a slanderer.

Satan—the adversary.

Shut—locked.

Set a seal upon him—marked with a seal over him or above him, that is, identifying the fact that Satan is shut up by God's authority.

the Marriage Supper of the Lamb. It puts the choice before us. Do we want to prepare ourselves for the Lamb's wedding banquet or would we rather choose to have our bodies become a banquet for the birds?

B. The Final Battle

John in vision then saw the Antichrist and the kings or rulers of the earth and their armies joined together in mass defiance of Christ and His army of saints and angels. (See Teaching Tip 4.)

The place has already been designated in Revelation 16:16. It is Armageddon, the hill of Megiddo. Megiddo probably means the place of rebellious banding together. Others take it to mean the city or hill of slaughter. Joel 3:12 gives it the name of the Valley of Jehoshaphat, that is, the valley where Jehovah judges. Zechariah 14:4, 5 show that when Jesus returns in glory, His feet will touch the Mount of Olives and it will split in two, half moving toward the north and half toward the south, leaving a great east-west valley between. Megiddo is also the name of the Emek Valley, the Biblical Plain of Esdraelon. There Deborah and Barak defeated the Canaanites. There Josiah was slain by Pharaoh-necho. Many battles in ancient times were fought in the Valley of Megiddo.

Revelation 19 does not describe the battle. Undoubtedly, the appearance of Christ on the white horse overwhelms the armies of the Antichrist in the manner already described in the opening of the sixth seal (6:15-17). The battle is soon over. The Antichrist and his false prophet are thrown alive into the lake of fire prepared for the devil and his angels. Their armies do not have time to contemplate the terror of this, however. For Jesus speaks, the word and all the birds are soon gorged with their flesh. It is a sad and terrible judgment on those who have rejected the truth of Christ and been deceived by the pretensions of the Antichrist.

III. The Devil Bound

Revelation 20:1-3

Revelation 20:1. I saw an angel come down from heaven, having the key of the bottomless pit and a great chain in his hand. 2. And he laid hold on the dragon, that old serpent, which is the Devil, and Satan, and bound him a thousand years, 3. and cast him into the bottomless pit, and shut him up, and set a seal upon him, that he should deceive the nations no more, till the thousand years should be fulfilled: and after that he must be loosed for a little season.

A. Bound a Thousand Years

The destruction of the Antichrist and his armies is not all that is necessary before Christ can bring in the millennial kingdom with all it glory, peace, and blessing. The real battle between God and Satan is over the souls of men. Satan here is identified with the ancient serpent who tempted Eve and brought about the fall of man. He is also the devil, the slanderer, who spreads lies and false charges about God's people, just as he did about Job (Job 1:9-11; 2:3-5). He is Satan, the chief adversary, who opposes us in all our battles for the Lord and for truth and right (Ephesians 6:12, 16; 1 Peter 5:8). The earth cannot be free to enjoy the Kingdom until Satan is put out of the way. (See Teaching Tip 5.)

There is a great deal of confusion or misunderstanding about the three terms *postmillennial, amillennial,* and *premillennial.*

Using the material summarizing these three interpretations of the Millennium, ask three students to present a panel discussion. Try to contact them at the end of last week's session or during the week before class. (They may wish to consult various Bible dictionaries, encyclopedias, etc., for added information.)

Seat the panel members at a table in front of the class if you can. Start with the postmillennial position, then amillennialism, and finally, the premillennial viewpoint.

Ask each panel member to present his material with no break between speakers. Allow 10-15 minutes for this. Then open the session to questions from the class. Limit this according to the amount of time you have and the level of student interest.

(Important: Next week's study deals with Christ's millennial reign. You may want to limit your discussion here to handle it in more detail then.)

To accomplish this, an angel binds Satan and throws him into the abyss for 1,000 years. There, locked up and shut in by the seal of God's authority, he will not be able to deceive the nations anymore at all for the entire period of 1,000 years that we call the Millennium (from the Latin words *mille* meaning "thousand," and *annus* meaning "year"). Thus the Millennium will be completely free from all the lies and impulses that come from the one who is the father or author. of lies (John 8:44).

Guideline for Living 3

The Millennium will be the experience of living a sinless life in a totally sin-free world. This should be a comfort and motivation to us as we seek to live sin-free lives in this marred, sin-tainted world. We know God is in control and the present condition of sin will not last permanently. God will restore His creation to the kind of beauty and order He intended.

B. Three Interpretations

It may be worth noting here that there are three main schools of interpretation with regard to the Millennium. Their adherents are known as premillennialist, postmillennialist, and amillennialist. (See Teaching Tip 6.)

The postmillennialists include many of the old Methodist and holiness groups. They look at the Millennium as an extension of the Church Age. They believe the power of the gospel will bind Satan and there will be a great period of revival and successful missionary endeavor that will bring the salvation of all or almost all the people of the world. Then at the close of this Millennium (which they spiritualize to mean however long it takes), the forces of evil will make a final attempt at defiance and Christ will come to bring in His eternal kingdom and the new heaven and the new earth. They tend to disregard Christ's warnings that "iniquity shall abound," and that it will take endurance to remain faithful to the end.

The "a" in *amillennialist* means "no." Some people simply ignore the Millennium altogether. Others say there will be no Millennium on earth. Most take the binding of Satan to be the defeat of Satan at Calvary, saying that the gospel binds Satan in this age. But we are warned that Satan still goes about as a roaring lion, seeking whom he may devour (1 Peter 5:8). The purpose of the binding of Satan is that he should deceive the nations no more. Certainly Satan is still at work among the nations today. Some amillennialists also take the word "souls" in Revelation 20:4 to mean souls in heaven. Thus they say the Millennium is going on in heaven now and explain away the plain statement that we shall reign with Christ on the earth (Revelation 5:10).

Like the postmillennialists the amillennialists spiritualize the number 1,000 and teach that when Jesus comes there will be a general resurrection and a general judgment of both the righteous and the wicked at the same time. Neither postmillennialists nor amillennialists have room in their system for any restoration of national Israel. Both tend to spiritualize the unfulfilled prophecies concerning Israel and apply them to the Church. They fail to

Music plays a key role in learning as well as worship in the Church. If you don't use songs, tapes, and records much in your class, consider doing so more often.

This week's Scripture passage provides the basis for one of the most majestic pieces of music in Church history: Handel's "Hallelujah Chorus" from "The Messiah."

Find a record or tape of this chorus and bring it to play for your students as you close the class session.

recognize that the restoration of Israel and the land is based on the promise to Abraham and is demanded for the honor of God's name (Ezekiel 36:22-28).

While amillennialism is popular among many of the Reformed or Calvinistic churches, premillennialism is the common view among fundamentalists and many other conservative, Bible-believing churches. The premillennialist takes Revelation 19 and 20 in sequence and sees that Christ will come before the Millennium to establish a kingdom on earth that will fulfill the prophecies of the Bible. Premillennialists tend also to take these prophecies literally unless the context clearly shows they are to be taken spiritually or symbolically. They also recognize that the symbols in the Book of Revelation, such as the beast, represent realities. That is, the beast will be a real Antichrist, a world ruler, not merely some vague spirit of evil.

The premillennialist also sees that the 1,000 years of the Millennium come between the resurrection and judgment of the believers and the resurrection and judgment of the unbelievers. This is the simplest interpretation and the one accepted in this study. It is also the only interpretation which fits in with the imminence of the coming of Christ. This emphasis on the coming of our Lord is one of the key things emphasized by the Holy Spirit from the beginning of the Pentecostal revival at the turn of the century until today. (See Teaching Tip 7.)

LIVING THE TRUTH

Christ is coming to earth in triumph as "King of kings and Lord of lords," bringing us along to share in His final victory over evil. This will be a great battle, but one which He is equipping us to have a part in as we trust Him each day.

This daily trust not only prepares us to enjoy heaven's perspective of ultimate triumph over sin and the devil. It gives us the resources to live overcoming lives right now through daily application of our faith in Christ. We have the resources, and the Holy Spirit can motivate us to use them so we may live the victorious life today.

In so doing, we draw others to Christ through our lives. In addition, we have the insight and strength we need through Him to share His message of judgment and salvation with the world.

Daily Devotional Guide

M. Gathering for Battle.
Revelation 16:12-16

T. Confident Foes.
Psalm 2:1-3

W. The Triumphant Christ.
Psalm 2:4-12

T. Sword of the Lord.
Isaiah 34:1-7

F. Day of Vengeance.
Isaiah 34:8-15

S. Conqueror Hailed.
Revelation 5:8-12

EVANGELISM OUTREACH

What will your decision be? You can choose today whether you want to have part in the Marriage Supper or the "supper for the birds." God's wrath is not a pleasant subject, but it is taught in the Bible and is something we must face. It cannot be ignored. Christ bore God's wrath in His own body on the cross, but those who reject Him must experience that wrath for their sin.

THE MILLENNIAL REIGN

Study Text
Psalm 72:1-19; Isaiah 65:20-25; Revelation 20:4-6

Outline
I. Reigning With Christ
  A. Thrones
  B. Priest-Kings
II. A Restored Earth
  A. Long Life
  B. The Rewards of Labor
III. Peace Everywhere
  A. Changed Behavior
  B. A Greater Than Solomon

Golden Text
They shall be priests of God and of Christ, and shall reign with him a thousand years. Revelation 20:6

Central Truth
God will reveal His glory more fully when Christ reigns on earth for 1,000 years.

Learning Goals
1. To explore what the Bible teaches about the nature of Christ's millennial reign.
2. To suggest ways we can make the benefits of the Millennium more real in our lives today.

SEEING THE SCRIPTURES

Isaiah 65:20-25

20. There shall be no more thence an infant of days, nor an old man that hath not filled his days: for the child shall die a hundred years old; but the sinner being a hundred years old shall be accursed.

21. And they shall build houses, and inhabit them; and they shall plant vineyards, and eat the fruit of them.

22. They shall not build, and another inhabit; they shall not plant, and another eat: for as the days of a tree are the days of my people, and mine elect shall long enjoy the work of their hands.

23. They shall not labor in vain, nor bring forth for trouble; for they are the seed of the blessed of the Lord, and their offspring with them.

24. And it shall come to pass, that before they call, I will answer; and while they are yet speaking, I will hear.

25. The wolf and the lamb shall feed together, and the lion shall eat straw like the bullock: and dust shall be the serpent's meat. They shall not hurt nor destroy in all my holy mountain, saith the Lord.

Revelation 20:4-6

4. And I saw thrones, and they sat upon them, and judgment was given unto them: and I saw the souls of them that were beheaded for the witness of Jesus, and for the word of God, and which had not worshipped the beast, neither his image, neither had received his mark upon their foreheads, or in their hands; and they lived and reigned with Christ a thousand years.

5. But the rest of the dead lived not again until the thousand years were finished. This is the first resurrection.

6. Blessed and holy is he that hath part in the first resurrection: on such the second death hath no power, but they shall be priests of God and of Christ, and shall reign with him a thousand years.

SETTING THE SCENE

Ever since man fell and was cast out of the Garden of Eden, God's great purpose for mankind has been redemption, restoration, and blessing. He is a good God and He gave good promises to Abraham for the blessing of all the families of the earth. He gave a good promise to David that there would always be a man for the throne. Then when David's descendants proved a disappointment, the prophets reemphasized the promise to David and focused attention on David's greater Son, the messianic King to come. Isaiah also saw brand-new heavens and brand-new earth. But in contrast to this, he saw that the present Jerusalem will also have its fulfillment. This fulfillment takes place in Christ's millennial kingdom.

Write the words *GOLDEN AGE* on the chalkboard. When your class begins, ask, "What does this mean to you?"

Responses may vary. Some will know that the Greeks often spoke of a "Golden Age" of special glory on earth. Others will associate the term with nostalgic "good-old-days" feelings. Still others may think of literary references to a coming utopia on earth longed for by many writers.

After the students have talked about it for a while, write the word *MILLENNIUM* on the chalkboard beside *GOLDEN AGE*. Ask: "What do you understand by this word, and how does it differ from *GOLDEN AGE?*

Use the discussion of the Millennium to proceed into your discussion of the "Bible Commentary."

Clarification

Judgment—authority to judge.

Souls—persons. These are not disembodied souls but living persons, since they are included with those who live and reign.

Reigned—reigned as kings.

Blessed—happy (because of the fullness of blessing).

Question.

Why are these martyrs given special attention here?

Question.

What does the first resurrection include?

BIBLE COMMENTARY

I. Reigning With Christ

Revelation 20:4-6

Revelation 20:4. I saw thrones, and they sat upon them, and judgment was given unto them: and I saw the souls of them that were beheaded for the witness of Jesus, and for the word of God, and which had not worshipped the beast, neither his image, neither had received his mark upon their foreheads, or in their hands; and they lived and reigned with Christ a thousand years. 5. But the rest of the dead lived not again until the thousand years were finished. This is the first resurrection. 6. Blessed and holy is he that hath part in the first resurrection: on such the second death hath no power, but they shall be priests of God and of Christ, and shall reign with him a thousand years.

A. Thrones

The Bible does not tell us here who are the ones sitting on the thrones. Some suggest they are the 24 elders. This may be true if they are taken as representatives of the entire body of the redeemed. But John usually names the 24 elders when they are in view. Actually, the promise to reign with Christ is part of the message of the Spirit to the churches (Revelation 3:21, 22). This is Christ's promise to those who are overcomers, winners of victories through faith. Among them will be the 12 apostles judging or ruling the 12 tribes of Israel (Luke 22:30).

Some say those seated on the thrones will spend time in the millennium reviewing cases and drawing attention to the righteous judgment of God. Others take the word *judge* in the Old Testament sense of "rule." Though the outpouring of God's wrath during the Great Tribulation will bring death to many, the final destruction seems to apply primarily to the armies of the Antichrist. If so, there will probably be millions still left alive. Just how many will be permitted to remain during the Millennium we are not told. But there will be many for the saints to rule as agents of Christ. (See Teaching Tip 1.)

In addition to the overcomers from the Church Age, John sees souls, that is, living individuals, who had been martyred during the Tribulation because they did not worship the Antichrist or his image or take the mark of the beast.

The martyrs live (because they are resurrected) and reign with the rest of the believers during the Millennium. They are given special attention because of the mention of the first resurrection. Their resurrection completes the first resurrection and brings it to an end. There is no further resurrection until after the Millennium when the wicked dead are brought before the Great White Throne.

The first resurrection has many interpretations, but a key may be found in the words of Jesus. He does not speak of the 1,000 years between the two resurrections. The Bible gives a step-by-step revelation, and the 1,000 years was not revealed until Revelation 20. But Jesus does clearly indicate two distinct resur-

First Corinthians 6:1-3 is an interesting Scripture passage which indicates some ruling function believers will have in God's future. Ask a student to read that passage and take time to discuss its possible relationship to the thrones in Revelation 20:4-6.

Question.
Why are they called "blessed" or happy?

TEACHING TIP 2

Duplicate and distribute the PATH work sheet for in-depth Bible personalization of 1 Peter 2:9.

The PATH instructions suggest ways of using the sheet for individual or small group study.

(If you do not have the PATH material, ask the students to turn to 1 Peter 2:9 and read and discuss it in connection with God's priest-king role for the believer.)

rections: one the resurrection of life; the other the resurrection of damnation or judgment (John 5:29). The first resurrection, then, is the resurrection of life. Jesus also calls it "the resurrection of the just" (Luke 14:14).

The apostle Paul gives us a little more insight when he compares the resurrection of the believers to a harvest. Christ's resurrection was the firstfruits. Then the main body of the harvest comes with the resurrection of the believers at Christ's second coming, that is, at the Rapture, which is the first phase of His coming (1 Corinthians 15:23; 1 Thessalonians 4:16, 17). Now Revelation gives us further insight by showing us that these martyrs of the Tribulation will be part of the same harvest. We might call them the gleanings of the harvest. Thus we could define the first resurrection as the resurrection of which Christ's resurrection is the firstfruits. All who live because He lives will be part of this resurrection.

B. Priest-Kings

Those on the thrones are further identified here to include all who have part in the first resurrection, all who are priests of God, and all who reign as kings with Christ for the 1,000 years. (See Teaching Tip 2.)

The word *blessed* is the opposite of the word *miserable* (1 Corinthians 15:19). Some who were under the influence of Greek or possibly Sadducee ideas tried to deny that Christians will rise, though they may have accepted Christ's resurrection. But the Bible emphasizes that our resurrection and Christ's are tied together. If we will not rise, then Christ did not rise; our faith is vain or empty and our sins are not taken away. Then those who died with their faith in Christ perished and are eternally lost. Moreover, "if in this life only we have hope in Christ, we are of all men most miserable." The meaning is not that we feel miserable but that we are to be pitied, for we are building our lives on a falsehood. "But," the Bible goes on to say, "now is Christ risen from the dead." His resurrection is a fact of history. We have solid ground for the assurance of our resurrection.

Guideline for Living 1

"Well, after all, I'm only human." How often do we offer that excuse for our shortcomings and failures? And as long as we live in our sin-marred world, there is a measure of truth in the statement.

But as believers we are not *only* human. Our humanity has been changed by the Spirit of God when we received Christ and now we share in the divine nature (2 Peter 1:4). We partake of the same quality of resurrection life which Christ released when He rose up from the tomb.

It is this "more than human" nature which we have in union with Christ that can bring the foretaste of the glories of the millennial reign into our daily living: "Ye are a chosen generation, a royal priesthood, a holy nation, a peculiar people; that ye should show forth the praises of him who hath called you out of darkness into his marvelous light" (1 Peter 2:9).

Clarification

Infant of days—a baby who lives only a few days.

Be Accursed—be declared accursed.

Elect—chosen ones.

Long enjoy—enjoy fully.

Bring forth for trouble—bear children for terror.

Question.

What is the first thing Isaiah emphasizes (verse 20)?

TEACHING TIP 3

At least two weeks ahead of time, assign two students to give reports to the class about advancements in medical science and health problems that continue despite these advances. One student should report on the various diseases that have virtually disappeared from American life because of vaccines and other treatment. This student should also find statistics that show how life expectancy has increased through the years. The other student should bring information about such medical problems as heart disease, cancer, arthritis, etc., that still persist. This student's report should also include information about other countries where all kinds of disease runs rampant and where health care is very poor.

Use these contrasting reports to show the best this life can offer as opposed to the quality of life mankind will enjoy during the Millennium. (See "Guideline for Living 2.")

II. A Restored Earth

Isaiah 65:20-23

Isaiah 65:20. There shall be no more thence an infant of days, nor an old man that hath not filled his days: for the child shall die a hundred years old; but the sinner being a hundred years old shall be accursed. 23. They shall not labor in vain, nor bring forth for trouble; for they are the seed of the blessed of the Lord, and their offspring with them.

A. Long Life

The Book of Revelation does not give any details of living conditions during the Millennium, probably because the prophecies given in the Old Testament are sufficient. This passage in Isaiah is one example. The passage actually begins with verse 17, which tells us there will be brand-new heavens and a brand-new earth. Isaiah, however, does not describe that new heaven and earth. The word *but* at the beginning of verse 18 is a strong adversative and shows a contrast with the previous verse. It emphasizes that though there will be a new heaven and a new earth, the present Jerusalem will also have its fulfillment. Isaiah then goes on to describe conditions which do not fit the new earth or the new Jerusalem at all. (See Revelation 21, 22.) But they do fit millennial conditions.

Over much of the world before the advent of modern medicine, as much as 50 percent of the babies died in the first year of life. Even now babies die all too often, sometimes for no apparent reason. But in the Millennium this will not happen. If a person dies at the age of 100 it will be like a baby's dying today. (See Teaching Tip 3.)

Then, over much of the world's history men (and women) did not live out a long life. The spiritual giants in the godly line of Seth did live long lives, but even Methuselah did not complete a thousand years. After that life spans gradually shortened, probably as a result of the accumulation of the effects of the Fall. By the time of Saul and David, history shows that the average life expectancy in Israel was 31 years, and in much of the rest of the world was even less. Modern medicine has increased this. It is said that our hearts could go on for a thousand years if it were not for disease. Yet in spite of all modern science can do, heart disease is still the number one killer. But in the Millennium anyone who dies at even 100 years will be recognized as a sinner who has been declared cursed.

Guideline for Living 2

What is death to the believer? Death is simply passing from this life into the glorious presence of our Lord (2 Corinthians 5:6-8).

The work of modern medical science which lengthens and improves the quality of life is a tremendous blessing when used by God. But more exciting still than extended or better quality life here on earth is the quality of life we will share in the Kingdom: "We, however, are citizens of heaven, and we eagerly wait for our Saviour, the Lord Jesus Christ, to come from heaven. He will change our weak mortal bodies and make them like his own glorious body, using that power by which he is able to bring all things under his rule" (Philippians 3:20, 21, *Good News Bible*).

Distribute small slips of paper to the class members with one of the following Scripture references written on each: Luke 24:37-43; John 20:26; Romans 8:11; 1 Corinthians 15:37, 38, 1 Corinthians 15:42-44, 49.

Allow 2-3 minutes for the students to look up and study their passages. Then ask each one to read the verses on his slip.

As the verses are read, take time to write the reference on the chalkboard.

Stop between readings and invite students to discuss what that passage tells about the resurrection body of the believer. Write key word or key phrase summaries on the chalkboard underneath each reference.

Question.

How will this affect the believers who are reigning with Christ?

Question.

What happened to Adam's work as a result of the Fall?

For us, possessed by this "living hope" (1 Peter 1:3, GNB), death may hold uncertainty—because we have not experienced it before—but it holds no terror.

Other passages show there will be many changes in the surface of the earth. The splitting of the Mount of Olives when Jesus returns in glory will surely involve an earthquake that will change the entire topography of Palestine. This will probably prepare for the kind of redivision of the land in' east-west strips described in Ezekiel 48. The same chapter shows that land which was desolate will become like the Garden of Eden. The implication is also that the Lord will clean up the pollution that is now destroying natural life on the land, in the sea, and in the air. We can be sure also that all those things which contribute now to the shortness of human life will be removed.

This blessing of long life is something man has always desired. Men in the past have dreamed of finding some fountain of elixir of life. Our bodies have tremendous God-given abilities for healing, restoration, and regeneration. But as we grow older we gradually lose these abilities. Some have suggested there must be accumulations of substances which cause this. In the 1930s when heavy water was discovered some said perhaps the accumulation of heavy water in our tissues brought on the signs of old age. Today scientists are experimenting with genes, hoping to find some way to extend life. But in the Millennium, God, who is the Giver of life, the Creator, and who knows our bodies, will remove the causes of old age and restore long life to all who are living in natural bodies during this period.

Believers will already have new bodies which are immortal and incorruptible, no longer capable of being touched by sin, sickness, decay, or death. Though these bodies are called spiritual bodies, the meaning is that they are Spirit-dominated, the perfect instruments to enable believers to do the work of the Holy Spirit. They will be like Christ's resurrection body and thus will be suited for life both on earth and in heaven. After His resurrection Jesus' body was real but no longer subject to all the limits our present bodies have. He could eat with His disciples. Yet He could rise into the heavens without a space suit. (See Teaching Tip 4.)

B. The Rewards of Labor

Some people think of work as part of the curse. But Adam was given work to do when he was first placed in the Garden of Eden. He did his work as unto the Lord, and it was a joy.

The Fall brought a curse on the ground. Thorns and thistles hindered Adam's attempts to raise good crops. His work became toil. Much of his labor was filled with frustration. Later on, the Israelites were placed in a land that was at the crossroads of the ancient world. Armies swept back and forth through the land, taking the fruits of Israel's labor as spoils of war for themselves. They had to live in walled cities and walk long distances to their fields in order to find protection from raiding parties and from desert tribes who would sweep in and steal their crops. Children came into a world filled with terror. There will be nothing like that in the Millennium. God's elect (here meaning the restored Israel) will fully enjoy the fruit of their labor. In line with the blessing of Abraham, all nations will share the same blessings.

Also, as Ezekiel 47:22, 23 indicates, even Gentiles will be able to share the same inheritance with the restored tribes of Israel.

Clarification
The bullock—cattle.

Hurt—or do evil, behave badly, cause damage.

Fall down—bow in worship.

Sheba—in southwest Arabia, now called Yemen. In ancient times they were famous for their trade in gold and gold objects.

Prayer also shall be made for him—He shall make intercession for the poor and needy.

His name shall be continued as long as the sun—let His name increase or spread before the sun (that is, everywhere).

III. Peace Everywhere
Isaiah 65:25; Psalm 72:11-19

Isaiah 65:25. The wolf and the lamb shall feed together, and the lion shall eat straw like the bullock: and dust shall be the serpent's meat. They shall not hurt nor destroy in all my holy mountain, saith the Lord. Psalm 72:11. Yea, all kings shall fall down before him: all nations shall serve him. 12. For he shall deliver the needy when he crieth; the poor also, and him that hath no helper. 15. And he shall live, and to him shall be given of the gold of Sheba: prayer also shall be made for him continually; and daily shall he be praised. 17. His name shall endure for ever: his name shall be continued as long as the sun: and men shall be blessed in him: all nations shall call him blessed. 19. And blessed be his glorious name for ever: and let the whole earth be filled with his glory. Amen, and Amen.

A. Changed Behavior

The ideal conditions of the Millennium will also affect the animal world. By His creative power God will bring a change in them that will alter their behavior completely.

Isaiah 11:1 speaks of the new branch from the roots of Jesse, that is, from the line of David. He is the divine messianic King who brings righteousness to the earth. It is His reign that brings peace in the animal world as well as in the world of men. Violence as we know it today will be no more.

In some passages this phraseology refers to Jerusalem, which will be the capital of the worldwide millennial kingdom. But this passage seems to be talking about universal conditions. It seems to fit with Daniel's description of the Messiah's kingdom which becomes a mountain that fills the whole earth (Daniel 2:35). It also fits with Isaiah 11:9 where the Bible adds, "For the earth shall be full of the knowledge of the Lord, as the waters cover the sea."

Question.
To whom does Isaiah 11:6-9 connect this change?

Question.
What is meant by God's holy mountain?

Guideline for Living 3

"Peace now! Peace now!"

The world and its protesters cry out in passionate pleas for peace. At the same time, history records millions who have died to bring about peace.

But will there ever be peace apart from Christ's visible reign upon the earth? No. Apart from Christ there will never be true, full peace. In fact, He warned us not to expect any real or lasting peace apart from Him as long as we are living in the present world system: "Peace I leave with you, my peace I give unto you: not as the world giveth, give I unto you" (John 14:27).

Nevertheless, we are called by Christ to be peacemakers (Matthew 5:9) and we are told that we will have a special blessing as we strive to bring about peace. But the peace we share is the peace that comes to individuals who give their lives to Jesus. The total-harmony, absence-of-strife sort of peace comes about as the kingdoms of the world are replaced by His kingdom.

Review the Scripture passages in Isaiah 65:17-29 and Isaiah 11:6-9.

If you have farmers (or avid gardeners!) in your class, encourage them to speculate about the sort of crops that could be grown in a world where the ground has been freed from the curse caused by the fall.

Use the discussion—which, for lack of Biblical detail, must be very speculative—to stir your students' sense of excitement over the coming millennial kingdom and our share in it. Let this enthusiasm carry over into your closing prayer and praise time. Close the class session with favorite choruses of praise.

Daily Devotional Guide

M. Praise the True King.
Psalm 72:12-19
T. Trust in Christ.
Psalm 91:1-13
W. Worship Him.
Psalm 92:1-5
T. Honor Him.
John 5:19-24
F. Watch for Him.
Matthew 25:1-13
S. Serve Him.
Matthew 25:14-23

B. A Greater Than Solomon

Jesus said of himself, "a greater than Solomon is here" (Matthew 12:42). Psalm 72 in its superscription is ascribed to Solomon. But the psalm looks beyond Solomon to the messianic King. Verse 8 prophesies, "He shall have dominion also from sea to sea, and from the river unto the ends of the earth." The mention of the river (the Euphrates) is a reference to the promise to Abraham that His descendants would inherit the land from the River Euphrates to the River of Egypt (Genesis 15:18). Israel was never promised more than that, and even Solomon did not quite fulfill it. But the Messianic King will reign over the whole world. Zechariah 9:9, 10 also connects this prophecy directly to the Messiah-King. Verse 9 was fulfilled in Christ's first coming. Verse 10 will be fulfilled in His second coming.

The rest of Psalm 72 goes on to show how wonderful the reign of the Messiah will be. The poor and the needy will find Him to be their Helper, their Redeemer, and no more will they be the victims of violence and oppression. He will still be the Intercessor, continuing the ministry He now has at the right hand of the Father. People will honor His name. That is, they will recognize His true character and nature and give Him praise. They will be blessed in Him and call Him blessed, praising His glorious name, for the whole earth will be filled with His glory. (See Teaching Tip 5.)

LIVING THE TRUTH

When we read in the Bible of Christ's coming reign, we must remember that His people will reign with Him. Our position in this present life may be obscure, and we may even be persecuted for our faith at times. But in Christ we are destined to be rulers! This should not only comfort us but inspire us to live holy lives. Those who are preparing for kingship do not live like others. They engage in special training and learn to exercise discipline not expected of average citizens. All the self-denial and hard work is seen in a different perspective when the future king knows its purpose. When he finally assumes the throne, he will realize that the schooling and labor are not to be compared with the glory of being king.

EVANGELISM OUTREACH

What sort of life will you choose? You can share this resurrection-quality life right now by accepting Christ as Saviour and be born again by His divine power. Eternal life begins now for those who accept Jesus Christ.

JUDGMENT

SEEING THE SCRIPTURES

Daniel 7:9-14

9. I beheld till the thrones were cast down, and the Ancient of days did sit, whose garment was white as snow, and the hair of his head like the pure wool: his throne was like the fiery flame, and his wheels as burning fire.

10. A fiery stream issued and came forth from before him: thousand thousands ministered unto him, and ten thousand times ten thousand stood before him: the judgment was set, and the books were opened.

11. I beheld then, because of the voice of the great words which the horn spake: I beheld even till the beast was slain, and his body destroyed, and given to the burning flame.

12. As concerning the rest of the beasts, they had their dominion taken away: yet their lives were prolonged for a season and time.

13. I saw in the night visions, and, behold, one like the Son of man came with the clouds of heaven, and came to the Ancient of days, and they brought him near before him.

14. And there was given him dominion, and glory, and a kingdom, that all people, nations, and languages, should serve him: his dominion is an everlasting dominion, which shall not pass away, and his kingdom that which shall not be destroyed.

2 Corinthians 5:10

10. We must all appear before the judgment seat of Christ; that every one may receive the things done in his body, according to that he hath done, whether it be good or bad.

Revelation 20:11-15

11. I saw a great white throne, and him that sat on it, from whose face the earth and the heaven fled away; and there was found no place for them.

12. And I saw the dead, small and great, stand before God; and the books were opened: and another book was opened, which is the book of life: and the dead were judged out of those things which were written in the books, according to their works.

13. And the sea gave up the dead which were in it; and death and hell delivered up the dead which were in them: and they were judged every man according to their works.

14. And death and hell were cast into the lake of fire. This is the second death.

15. And whosoever was not found written in the book of life was cast into the lake of fire.

SETTING THE SCENE

Old Testament prophets prophesied judgment on Israel and Judah for their sins. They also looked ahead and saw a greater day

PREPARING TO TEACH

Study Text
Daniel 7:9-14; 1 Corinthians 3:10-15; 2 Corinthians 5:9-11; Revelation 20:11-15

Outline
I. The Judge
  A. The Ancient of Days
  B. The Son of Man
II. Judgment Seat of Christ
  A. Building on the Right Foundation
  B. Christ's Award Throne
III. Great White Throne Judgment
  A. The Final Judgment
  B. The Second Death

Golden Text
He hath appointed a day, in the which he will judge the world in righteousness by that man whom he hath ordained. Acts 17:31

Central Truth
All men must stand before God, the Judge of all the earth.

Learning Goals
1. To explore the role judgment will play in the believer's future.
2. To explore the role of judgment in the unbeliever's future.
3. To seek the Holy Spirit's help in letting predicted judgment motivate us to greater efforts in winning the lost.

GETTING STARTED

Before class starts, draw a cross on the left side of your chalkboard (or use an overhead projector), and a large throne on the right side. Under the cross, write "JOHN 3:16." Under the throne, write "REVELATION 20:15."

As you begin class, refer to the cross drawing. Ask: "What does this tell us about the Christian and judgment?" Ask someone to read or quote John 3:16 and John 5:24 as you discuss the question.

Next, refer to the throne drawing. Ask: "What does this tell us about the unbeliever and judgment?" Have someone read Revelation 20:11-15. Use this discussion to lead into this week's "Bible Commentary."

Clarification

Cast down—set up, placed.

His wheels—the wheels on His throne.

Ministered unto—served.

Judgment was set—the council of judges sat down.

Dominion—lordship.

A kingdom—kingship, royal power and sovereignty.

TEACHING TIP 1

This week's PATH item is a sheet of topical questions to be used for buzz group study and discussion of the "Bible Commentary" material. You may wish to divide the class into the same groups you used earlier in the quarter, but don't hesitate to form new groups.

The PATH instructions suggest two options for using the buzz group sheet. Depending on which option you choose, you will want to handle the activity differently from the beginning of class.

1. If you use it as your major class activity, allow 15 minutes for preparation in groups at the beginning of the session. Then call on each group to lead your discussion time for each of the major sections of the study outline.

2. If you use the sheet as

of judgment in the distant future, a day that will involve the judgment of both the righteous and wicked. The apostle Paul sees it will mean "glory, honor, and peace, to every man that worketh good" (Romans 2:10). But the chief emphasis of the Bible is on the judgment of sinners.

Sinners do not like to hear about the coming judgment. But the Bible intends to disturb them in order to open their eyes to the consequences of their sin and bring them to salvation. God wants to show mercy to all. He does not will that any should perish. He wants all to come to repentance (2 Peter 3:9). (See Teaching Tip 1.)

BIBLE COMMENTARY

I. The Judge

Daniel 7:9-14

Daniel 7:9. I beheld till the thrones were cast down, and the Ancient of days did sit, whose garment was white as snow, and the hair of his head like the pure wool: his throne was like the fiery flame, and his wheels as burning fire. 10. A fiery stream issued and came forth from before him: thousand thousands ministered unto him, and ten thousand times ten thousand stood before him: the judgment was set, and the books were opened. 13. I saw in the night visions, and, behold, one like the Son of man came with the clouds of heaven, and came to the Ancient of days, and they brought him near before him. 14. And there was given him dominion, and glory, and a kingdom, that all people, nations, and languages should serve him: his dominion is an everlasting dominion, which shall not pass away, and his kingdom that which shall not be destroyed.

A. The Ancient of Days

Daniel 7 takes us back to the time when God is judging the Antichrist and his kingdom. A number of thrones are set up and God's judgment throne is in the midst. The council of judges sits down. The books are opened. Judgment on the beast then takes place and he is destroyed.

Some say the council of judges which sits down on the thrones is composed of angels. Others say they are the 24 elders. But the picture is quite different from the picture in Revelation 4, so it is difficult to say who they are. (See Teaching Tip 2.)

The Ancient of Days, the Eternal God, the Father, is the center of attention. The whiteness of His hair points to His wisdom. The whiteness of His garment points to His holiness and absolute purity and righteousness. But there is another emphasis. He is surrounded by fire and flame. His throne is like fire. Its wheels, unlike the wheels in Ezekiel's vision, are like burning fire. A stream, literally, a full-sized river of fire, flows out before Him. This is clearly a scene that speaks of judgment. The thousands of thousands who serve Him and the myriads of myriads who stand before Him are probably angels who do His bidding as the heavenly hosts, the armies of heaven.

supplemental discussion, allow the same 15 minutes for preparation at the beginning of class. Simply limit the emphasis and time you spend on each group's presentation as you come to the appropriate section.

Question.
What is the purpose of this judgment?

TEACHING TIP 2
Call for the first buzz group presentation. If you are using the supplemental option (See Teaching Tip 1, #2), call for the group's responses to their three topics as you discuss the section of the outline headed "I. The Judge." If you've chosen the major activity option (#1), turn the majority of your classtime spent on "The Judge" over to the first buzz group and its leader.

Clarification
The day—the day of judgment (specifically, when we appear before the judgment seat of Christ after the Rapture).

Declare—reveal and explain; make it clear.

Try—test.

Abide—remain unhurt by the fire of testing.

He shall suffer loss—the Greek may mean either he will be punished, or he will forfeit the reward for his works. The context calls for the latter.

By fire—through a fire; again implies loss.

Labor—make it our ambition; strive eagerly.

Accepted of him—well-pleasing to Him.

Guideline for Living 1
How reliable is God? What difference does that make to our belief in the future?

Daniel's picture of the Ancient of Days gives great emphasis to His wisdom as well as judgment. We know that the One who will judge us with perfect wisdom (only He is omnipotent and omniscient) is the One who holds our future. Because of this, we can have confidence as we face even the hardest circumstances which come our way. As the song says, "I don't know about tomorrow, but I know who holds my hand!"

This gives us not only great confidence for ourselves, but great confidence to reach out boldly with the gospel. Nothing can truly "harm" us, for it must first pass His loving hand. He has a purpose for everything that happens to us as we live faithfully in service for Jesus.

This judgment prepares the way for Christ to take over His kingship and manifest His royal rule on earth. The Antichrist (the false beast who deceives the nations and who is the great enemy of the true Christ) is the one upon whom judgment is pronounced.

B. The Son of Man
In the Book of Ezekiel God calls Ezekiel "son of man," meaning a representative man. It is true that Jesus came to be the representative of all mankind as He took our place on the cross. But that is not what Jesus meant by this title. Since it did have more than one possible meaning, the people may not have understood what He meant. Actually, Jesus used it without defining it publicly during most of His ministry. It was not His purpose to identify himself to the rulers before God's time for His crucifixion.

Jesus did identify himself privately to His own disciples when He prophesied, "Then shall appear the sign of the Son of man in heaven: and then shall all the tribes of the earth mourn, and they shall see the Son of man coming in the clouds of heaven with power and great glory" (Matthew 24:30). This is a very clear reference to Daniel 7:13, 14 where one like the Son of Man comes with the clouds of heaven and is given kingship and sovereign power over all people, nations, and languages, a kingship that will last forever and ever.

Then when Jesus was brought before the Sanhedrin, He clearly declared himself as the heavenly Son of Man of Daniel 7. That was enough for the Jewish leaders to condemn Him.

II. Judgment Seat of Christ
1 Corinthians 3:10-15; 2 Corinthians 5:9-11
1 Corinthians 3:11. Other foundation can no man lay than that is laid, which is Jesus Christ. 12. Now if any man build upon this foundation gold, silver, precious stones, wood, hay, stubble; 13. every man's work shall be made manifest: for the day shall declare it, because it shall be revealed by fire; and the fire shall try every man's work of what sort it is. 14. If any man's work abide which he hath built thereupon, he shall receive a reward. 51. If any man's work shall be burned, he shall suffer loss; but he himself shall be saved; yet so as by fire. 2 Corinthians 5:9. Wherefore we labor,

Seat—throne. (See Romans 14:10.)

Done—the Greek emphasizes the motive that caused him to make these deeds his business.

Good—useful, beneficial.

Bad—worthless, low, paltry, unworthy, as well as evil, wicked.

TEACHING TIP 3

Call for the second buzz group's presentation. You will want to vary the emphasis you give to this and the amount of control you give the group based on the option you use.

Question.
What makes the difference between gold, silver, precious stones, and wood, hay, stubble?

Question.
Why does Paul emphasize that the worker himself shall be saved?

that, whether present or absent, we may be accepted of him. 10. For we must all appear before the judgment seat of Christ; that every one may receive the things done in his body, according to that he hath done, whether it be good or bad. 11. Knowing therefore the terror of the Lord, we persuade men; but we are made manifest unto God; and I trust also are made manifest in your consciences.

A. Building on the Right Foundation
(See Teaching Tip 3.)

Turning now to 1 Corinthians, we see that we are given the privilege of being responsible sharers in the work of the Lord. We can trust His promises and see results in His work because He has given us the right foundation in His Son, our Lord Jesus Christ.

Paul gave himself as an example to encourage us to work wisely and well. He built as a wise masterbuilder lays the foundation by his preaching of the gospel of Christ.

Paul also encourages us to build wisely and well by reminding us there is a judgment day coming, a day of testing and reward for all believers. We are pictured as workmen in charge of building a particular part of a great building. The building, of course, is the Church. God is the Owner. Our work is all the service we do as members of the body of Christ.

The difference is in the nature and quality of our motives. If we do our work in the spirit of the apostle Paul with all the love, consecration, and devotion to one another that Romans 12 talks about, our work will be gold, silver, and precious stones. It will stand the fires of God's testing. If we do it in a selfish spirit, looking for the praise of men or trying to build a kingdom for ourselves without any real consecration to Jesus, then it will be wood, hay, and stubble and there will be no reward. This is brought out also in 1 Corinthians 13:3 where Paul says, "Though I bestow all my goods to feed the poor, and though I give my body to be burned, and have not charity [*agape*, high, holy, selfless Calvary love], it profiteth me nothing." Giving our goods to the poor may help a great many people. Giving our body to be burned (as a martyr) might inspire others to serve the Lord. But unless we have the right motive, the works will be burned up as far as reward is concerned.

Only the saved, the born-again believers, appear before the judgment seat of Christ. Salvation is ours because of our faith in Christ and because of His work in His death and resurrection. But we are saved to serve. Thus rewards are ours because of our faithful service done in response to His love. (See Teaching Tip 4.)

B. Christ's Award Throne

In 2 Corinthians 5 Paul recognizes the fragile and temporary nature of this body. But he is comforted by the assurance that to be absent from the body is to be present (at home) with the Lord. This assurance brought Paul to a wonderful realization. It did not really matter to him anymore whether he lived or died. All he wanted was to be acceptable or well-pleasing to his Master and Lord. Later he told the Philippians his hope was that "in nothing I shall be ashamed, but that with all boldness, as always, so now also Christ shall be magnified in my body, whether it be by life,

Question.
Did the judgment seat of Christ hold any terror for Paul?

TEACHING TIP 4

Ask two students to roleplay for the class. You will want to arrange this before class time. If not, allow 2-3 minutes in a separate room for the students to prepare the activity based on the following situation:

Student One is a successful athlete. (Running and jogging are very popular among many adults. If you can select someone who does some running, so much the better for realism.) He has just earned an award or medal for his running achievements.

Student Two is a sports reporter for a local TV or radio station. He is here to interview Student One about his success. He is interested in how One got started, what One likes most about the sport, how One attained his success, and any "secrets" of success which he wants to pass along to listeners.

Provide whatever chairs, tables, prop microphones, etc. you are able to bring to class.

When the students are done with the roleplay, relate this to the non-judgmental, "achievement award" nature of the judgment seat of Christ, as discussed in the section, "Christ's Award Throne."

Clarification

Throne—royal throne (Greek, *thronos*); a different word from the judgment throne (Greek, *bema*).

Hell—hades; in the New Testament this is always the intermediate place for the wicked dead.

TEACHING TIP 5

Call for your final buzz group presentation according to the option you have chosen to use for the previous two groups.

or by death. For to me to live is Christ, and to die is gain" (Philippians 1:20, 21). That is, since life meant Christ, death could only mean more Christ.

Again Paul used the coming day when we must all appear before the judgment seat of Christ as a motive to live for the Lord.

Paul was looking forward to that "far more exceeding and eternal weight of glory" that would be his reward. The word "appear" also suggests rewards, not punishments, so the judgment seat of Christ is basically an award throne.

Guideline for Living 2

We have been freed from fear of judgment if we are believers. Jesus said, "Verily, verily, I say unto you, He that heareth my word, and believeth on him that sent me, hath everlasting life, and shall not come into condemnation; but is passed from death unto life" (John 5:24). So we need never fear the judgment which leads to the condemnation faced by those outside of Christ.

Since we are free from condemnation through Christ, we are also released from the fear which leads to guilt and defeat. We are open to the power of the Holy Spirit in a way which the unsaved can never know. He pours the love of Christ through us to make our lives creative and godly.

What is our responsibility concerning this freedom in Christ? Paul said, "For the love of Christ constraineth us. . . . Now then we are ambassadors for Christ, as though God did beseech you by us: we pray you in Christ's stead, be ye reconciled to God" (2 Corinthians 5:14, 20).

Freedom from condemnation in Christ motivates us to share the gospel with those who still face judgment and the second death.

Paul does recognize, however, that some things we do contribute in a beneficial way to the work of God and will receive rewards. Other things are worthless and will receive no reward. The Bible also indicates that this judgment or award throne will take place before the 1,000 years of the Millennium, while the Great White Throne will take place after the Millennium.

III. Great White Throne Judgment
Revelation 20:11-15

Revelation 20:11. I saw a great white throne, and him that sat on it, from whose face the earth and the heaven fled away; and there was found no place for them. 12. And I saw the dead, small and great, stand before God; and the books were opened: and another book was opened, which is the book of life: and the dead were judged out of those things which were written in the books, according to their works. 14. And death and hell were cast into the lake of fire. This is the second death. 15. And whosoever was not found written in the book of life was cast into the lake of fire.

A. The Final Judgment
(See Teaching Tip 5.)

After the Millennium, Satan is released for a short time. Some wonder why God would allow this. But the Book of Revelation is very much concerned about the justice of God. It is a terrible thing to cast people into the lake of fire which was prepared for the devil and his angels and was never intended for mankind. Some might say that if people could only know how wonderful the reign of Christ will be, they would all believe in Him and follow Him. But the release of Satan shows that even after the world has seen peace and blessing for 1,000 years under Christ's rule, some will still follow Satan when they get the opportunity to do so. Clearly they are rebels. They say to God, "Leave us alone!" There is nothing God can do but separate them from His presence forever.

Satan's rebellion after his release ends with his followers' being consumed by fire from heaven. Then Satan is cast into the lake of fire forever. After that the Great White Throne appears.

Question.
Who is seated on the throne?

Some say it is God the Father. But Jesus declared, "The Father judgeth no man, but hath committed all judgment unto the Son" (John 5:22). Thus, Jesus, the one Mediator between God and man, becomes the Mediator in judgment. So He will be the One actually seen sitting on the throne.

So great is His majesty in judgment that the present earth and heaven flee away and no place is found for them. That is, they go out of existence. Peter prophesied this would be done by fire that will make the very elements of the universe (the stars and planets) disappear in fervent heat. In other words, the same thing will happen to them as happens when matter and antimatter come together. There is a flash of energy which goes off as heat, and then nothing. This will prepare for the creation of a brand new heavens and earth where there will be no more sun or moon.

Question.
Who are the dead who appear before the Great White Throne?

Since the righteous who take part in the first resurrection already have their new bodies which are immortal and incorruptible, they are the living, not the dead. Thus, the dead here must mean "the rest of the dead" (verse 5), that is, the wicked dead, plus those who were killed after the Millennium when they chose to follow Satan.

Some suppose that those who are brought into the Millennium plus those who are born during the Millennium will have an opportunity to be saved and follow Christ and will then come before the Great White Throne to receive rewards. But the Bible does not tell us this. Only the "dead" appear in this second resurrection, which is the resurrection to judgment (John 5:29). Those saved during the Millennium will probably receive new bodies immediately.

Question.
Why, is the Book of Life opened?

Though the wicked are judged by their works, salvation is not by works. Their works are simply the evidence of their unbelief. Thus, the Book of Life is opened as a witness to the fact that they were not among those who had placed their faith in Jesus.

B. The Second Death

After the witness from the Book of Life that their names are not included, the wicked are cast into the lake of fire, the second death. In the Bible death most often means separtion. Thus, the second death is a final separation from God and from the inheritance of the saints. The wicked will miss the glories of the new heavens and the new earth as well as the new Jerusalem.

Question.
Why are death and hades cast into the lake of fire?

Jesus refers to the final punishment of the wicked as "outer darkness." Revelation 22:15 also indicates that the wicked dead will be "without" (literally, outside), not only the New Jerusalem, but outside the whole new creation of the new heavens and the

Too often our age loses sight of the fearfulness of eternal punishment. Draw special attention to the above discussion question about the lake of fire. Be sure to read or have a student read the "Bible Commentary" section on the fire of divine judgment.

Question.

How long will the lake of fire last?

new earth. That is, death and hades will have no part in the new creation but will be merged with the second death, the lake of fire in outer darkness, and be forever separated from the light of Christ. In this way "the last enemy," death, will be destroyed (1 Corinthians 15:26), for in the new heavens and the new earth there will be no more tears, no more dying. Only in the outer darkness of the lake of fire will there be weeping and gnashing of teeth (Matthew 8:12; 13:49, 50; Luke 13:28). It will be full of remorse, bitterness, frustration, and raging lusts that cannot be fulfilled. Death and judgment will not change a sinner's nature. Only the blood of Jesus can do that. (See Teaching Tip 6.)

Some would tell us that the word *eternal* means only "age-lasting." This is a case where a little knowledge of Greek is a bad thing. The Greek word translated "eternal" or "everlasting" is used of eternal life, eternal death, and the eternal God. We are all in trouble if God is only "age-lasting." Moreover, the Bible describes the fires of divine judgment in ways that have nothing to do with time. By its very nature the fire is unquenchable (Matthew 3:12; Luke 3:17) and therefore endless.

We should note also that God's promise of life to the obedient believer means more than a gift of bare existence. All men already have that. The gift of eternal life brings blessings and eternal fellowship with God and Christ. So the second death as a penalty does not mean mere loss of existence. It means everlasting punishment and everlasting separation from God and from the faith, hope, and love which remain for the believer. Let us remember also that it is not God's will that any should perish. God has put many things in mankind's path to turn us from sin. But the choice is up to us.

LIVING THE TRUTH

Although the subject of judgment is not universally popular, it reminds us basically of man's accountability to God. This is a theme totally missing from life in today's society. Just as the auditor comes in to examine the company's books, the Almighty Judge will examine every life down to the finest detail. His judgment will be absolutely fair and without any favoritism. As believers we must remember that although we will not face judgment for sin, our works will be subject to the intense scrutiny of our Lord. On that judgment will depend whether we are rewarded or lose our reward. Certainly this should have a strong influence on our daily behavior as well as our motives. Our knowledge of the judgment awaiting sinners should motivate us to be about the business of soul-winning every day.

EVANGELISM OUTREACH

If you are an unbeliever, you can escape facing God as your Judge by receiving Christ right now. It is not God's will for anyone to be lost. Those who are lost must trample on God's love deliberately. The Holy Spirit is pleading with you now not to pursue such a path.

Daily Devotional Guide

M. Judged Righteously.
Genesis 18:23-29
T. Judged Severely.
1 Samuel 2:1-11
W. Judged by Fire.
Numbers 21:5-9
T. Judged at the Cross.
Luke 23:39-43
F. Judged by Conscience.
Acts 24:10-16
S. Judged by the Lord.
2 Timothy 4:1-3

PREPARING TO TEACH

Study Text
Revelation 21:1-27; 22:1-5

Outline
I. New Conditions of Life
   A. New Heavens and New Earth
   B. God Dwells With Mankind
II. New City
   A. Possessing God's Glory
   B. Gates and Foundations
III. New Environment
   A. The Light of the Lord
   B. The River of Life

Golden Text
God shall wipe away all tears from their eyes; and there shall be no more death, neither sorrow, nor crying, neither shall there be any more pain: for the former things are passed away. Revelation 21:4

Central Truth
God's plan of redemption will culminate in the establishment of a new heaven and earth.

Learning Goals
1. To see what the Bible shows us of the glories of our heavenly home.
2. To focus on the presence of God as the ultimate glory of heaven.
3. To let this study increase our sense of praise and worship.

SEEING THE SCRIPTURES

Revelation 21:1, 2, 10-14; 22:1-5

1. I saw a new heaven and a new earth: for the first heaven and the first earth were passed away; and there was no more sea.

2. And I John saw the holy city, new Jerusalem, coming down from God out of heaven, prepared as a bride adorned for her husband.

10. And he carried me away in the spirit to a great and high mountain, and showed me that great city, the holy Jerusalem, descending out of heaven from God,

11. Having the glory of God: and her light was like unto a stone most precious, even like a jasper stone, clear as crystal;

12. And had a wall great and high, and had twelve gates, and at the gates twelve angels, and names written thereon, which are the names of the twelve tribes of the children of Israel:

13. On the eat three gates; on the north three gates; on the south three gates; and on the west three gates.

14. And the wall of the city had twelve foundations, and in them the names of the twelve apostles of the Lamb.

22:1. And he showed me a pure river of water of life, clear as crystal, proceeding out of the throne of God and of the Lamb.

2. In the midst of the street of it, and on either side of the river, was there the tree of life, which bare twelve manner of fruits, and yielded her fruit every month: and the leaves of the tree were for the healing of the nations.

3. And there shall be no more curse: but the throne of God and of the Lamb shall be in it; and his servants shall serve him:

4. And they shall see his face; and his name shall be in their foreheads.

5. And there shall be no night there; and they need no candle, neither light of the sun; for the Lord God giveth them light: and they shall reign for ever and ever.

SETTING THE SCENE

When Adam and Eve sinned, they lost spiritual life and fellowship with God. When they heard His voice, their consciences, instead of helping them, made them run and hide. Then they were condemned to pain and sorrow and driven out of the Garden.

Jesus shed His blood and died on Calvary to pay for a full restoration of all that was lost in the Fall. When we take Him as Lord and Saviour, our fellowship with God is restored. If we keep walking in the light, we keep enjoying that fellowship (1 John 1:7). At the Rapture we shall receive the redemption of our bodies, new bodies that are immortal and incorruptible. Then in the new creation and the New Jerusalem, we shall have something even better than the Garden of Eden. (See Teaching Tip 1.)

GETTING STARTED

Put this final study of the quarter in perspective by asking the students to recall some of the high points of each of the studies about "Things To Come." Keep this opening unstructured, simply asking for those truths which have special meaning or were especially memorable for the students.

Move into the "Bible Commentary" with a transition such as: "This week's study touches the high point of all the themes we have seen developed—we look at the new heavens and new earth."

Clarification

New—brand-new, not previously present. The word has the connotation of marvelous, unheard-of, remarkable, something not known before.

Passed away—gone,

Tabernacle—tent, dwelling, the place where God manifests His glory.

Pain—including fruitless toil and hard, unrewarding labor.

Overcometh—keeps on winning victories.

All things—these things.

TEACHING TIP 1

Prepare the "Thought Provoker" slips according to PATH instructions. After you have distributed them, allow 2-3 minutes for each slip holder to collect his thoughts, then call for responses.

(*Important:* This activity is designed to stimulate thinking, not develop lengthy discussion. Avoid the temptation to let it take too much classtime.)

TEACHING TIP 2

As your time and class arrangements permit, call on several students to look up and read the various Scripture references from the "Bible Commentary" which deal with a discussion of the new heavens and new earth.

BIBLE COMMENTARY

I. New Conditions of Life

Revelation 21:1-8

Revelation 21:1. I saw a new heaven and a new earth: for the first heaven and the first earth were passed away; and there was no more sea. 2. And I John saw the holy city, new Jerusalem, coming down from God out of heaven, prepared as a bride adorned for her husband. 3. And I heard a great voice out of heaven saying, Behold, the tabernacle of God is with men, and he will dwell with them, and they shall be his people, and God himself shall be with them, and be their God. 4. And God shall wipe away all tears from their eyes; and there shall be no more death, neither sorrow, nor crying, neither shall there be any more pain: for the former things are passed away. 5. And he that sat upon the throne said, Behold, I make all things new. And he said unto me, Write: for these words are true and faithful. 6. And he said unto me, It is done. I am Alpha and Omega, the beginning and the end. I will give unto him that is athirst of the fountain of the water of life freely. 7. He that overcometh shall inherit all things; and I will be his God, and he shall be my son.

A. New Heavens and New Earth

As we have seen in chapter 20, the present heaven and earth go out of existence. Satan, death, hades, and all the wicked are separated forever in the lake of fire. Now in chapter 21 John sees brand-new heavens and a brand-new earth, an earth as Peter prophesied, "wherein dwelleth righteousness" (2 Peter 3:13).

Some people say the new earth will be the present earth renovated or restored. They base their theory on the word "regeneration" or rebirth (Matthew 19:28), which is also used of spiritual rebirth (Titus 3:5), and "restitution" or restoration (Acts 3:21). These passages, however, refer to the restoration which must take place after the Tribulation to bring in the millennial kingdom of Christ. (See Teaching Tip 2.)

Others point to passages such as Ecclesiastes 1:4; Psalms 93:1; 96:10; and 104:5 which speak of the earth's abiding or not being moved. But the same phraseology is used of people's not being moved and of Zion's not being moved (Psalms 10:6; 16:8, 46:5). In their context the passages which speak of the earth mean either that the earth will remain for a long time in contrast to temporary things, or else they mean there will always be an earth though not necessarily the same earth.

This is confirmed by passages like Psalm 102:25, 26; Isaiah 51:6; and Hebrews 1:10-12 which clearly state that the heavens will vanish away like smoke and the earth will grow old like a garment. Moreover, God will change them in the same way we change clothes. When we change old, worn-out clothes, we do not just shake them out and put them on again. We put on a new set. Hebrews 1:11 says further that the present heavens and earth will perish.

This fits also what we read in 2 Peter 3:10-12. Some do say that

Give each student a pencil or pen and slip of paper. Ask everyone to read Revelation 21:4 at least four times, then write a paraphrase of this verse on the slips.

You may wish to review the paraphrase definition: restating the verse in their own words.

Allow 5 minutes or so for the students to work. It might be good for you to do your own paraphrase before classtime so you will be better prepared to answer questions and make suggestions for those who need help.

When most of the class members appear to have finished, call on two or three to share their thoughts with the rest of the class.

You can relate this work on Revelation 21:4 to the "Guideline for Living 2" discussion of 1 John 3:2, 3.

Question.

Why does the Bible tell us there will be no more sea?

"pass away" in 3:10 means "to pass from one condition to another without passing out of existence." But one of the old Greek translations of Daniel 7:14 uses the word "destroyed," and it is often used of time passing away or coming to an end or of things that disappear. Revelation 21:1 uses a different word which means "they are gone." This word is used in Revelation 9:12 to say one woe is past, over, done with, and two more woes (not the first woe renovated) will come. It is clear from the context that both words mean that the first heaven and earth will disappear and go out of existence.

Some also take the word "melt" in 2 Peter 3:10 to mean "untied, loosed, broken up," and say the elements of the present creation will only be broken apart in a superficial way and rearranged without a really new creation. But 2 Peter 3:12 uses a different word for "melt" that can only mean "to be melted away" in this context.

Some still question whether the new earth will be brand new because some of the passages go on to talk of millennial conditions. But as we have seen, these are presented in contrast to the new heavens and earth. It should be noted also that the Old Testament often mentions the first and second comings of Christ in the same breath. It also includes what happens both before and after the Millennium within "the day of the Lord." (Compare Isaiah 61:1, 2; Luke 4:17-19; Daniel 12:2; Malachi 4:5, 6.) The important thing is to realize we have something better ahead of us than can be found on the earth, better than any astronaut could find in outer space as it is today.

Guideline for Living 1

The single most popular theme in our society's entertainment media is science-fiction/fantasy-speculation about other, more exciting worlds out there somewhere in the universe. Films and books on extraterrestrial beings and fantasy creatures are best-sellers.

Have we believers been so caught up in the glamour and charm of such things that we have gotten our eyes off looking forward to heaven's glories which the Bible encourages? We face the danger of replacing heaven's glory with an imaginary space-world fantasy drama.

Perhaps we need to rethink our purpose and let the words of Paul rekindle our enthusiasm for heaven as the only worthwhile "obsession": " 'Everything is permissible for me'—but not everything is beneficial. 'Everything is permissible for me'—but I will not be mastered by anything" (1 Corinthians 6:12, *New International Version*).

The ancients often looked on the sea as something restless, unstable, and full of danger (Isaiah 57:20; James 1:6). The new earth will lack this (though the millennial earth will not). But the ancients did not always look on the sea as bad (Isaiah 11:9; 48:18; Habakkuk 2:14). Actually, since water coves the major portion of the present earth, lack of oceans and seas would be quite noticeable. In fact, microorganisms in the present ocean are responsible for replacing much of the oxygen in the atmosphere. The Bible wants us to know here that the new earth is not only new but quite different from the present earth. The whole economy and life patterns will thus have to be different as well.

Question.

Why doesn't John tell us more about the new earth?

Question.

What is the real reason the New Jerusalem comes to the new earth?

Clarification

Jasper—a name used of various stones in ancient times. This was probably like a blue-white diamond.

Furlongs—the 12,000 furlongs would be about 1,378 miles or 2,119 kilometers.

Equal—some see this to mean the city is in the shape of a cube. Others take it to be in the form of a step pyramid.

Cubits—about 17.9 inches each, making the wall about 215 feet or 65.5 meters high.

Of a man—though measured by the angel, the angel used human measuring standards that John could understand.

Street—wide street. The singular may be used collectively for all the streets of the city.

In John's vision his attention is drawn immediately to the New Jerusalem coming from God out of heaven. This is the city Abraham caught a glimpse of, the city "whose builder and maker is God" (Hebrews 11:9-16).

Because of the mention of the bride, some suppose this picture is symbolic of the Church, and that no real city is intended. But the Bible often identifies a city with its inhabitants. When Jesus wept over Jerusalem, He was weeping over its people, but He was not denying a real city was there. So here the bride is mentioned to draw attention to the way the city is adorned. God will not disappoint the faith of His ancient patriarchs and saints like Abraham. "He hath prepared for them a city" (Hebrews 11:16). The city is real and will be the home and headquarters for Abraham and the Old Testament saints as well as for the Church in the eternal state.

B. God Dwells With Mankind

Next John hears a loud voice announcing God's purpose.

At present, God manifests himself in a special way in what Hebrews calls the true or real tabernacle, the heavenly temple where John saw the throne. But now God moves His "headquarters," the place of His primary manifestation of His presence, to the new earth where His throne will be in the New Jerusalem. Thus, the glory that is known in its fullness only in heaven will now be known and experienced by all in the New Jerusalem. Nothing will ever again break our relationship with Him. (See Teaching Tip 3 on preceding page.)

To make sure of this, God says He makes all things new. This does not mean He takes the old things of the present heaven and earth and makes them over. God's words could well be translated here, "I am making new things, all of them brand new." In God's providence and purpose this is settled, as good as done. Therefore we know the prophecy is true and faithful.

II. New City

Revelation 21:9-21

Revelation 21:10. And he carried me away in the spirit to a great and high mountain, and showed me that great city, the holy Jerusalem, descending out of heaven from God, 11. having the glory of God: and her light was like unto a stone most precious, even like a jasper stone, clear as crystal; 12. and had a wall great and high, and had twelve gates, and at the gates twelve angels, and names written thereon, which are the names of the twelve tribes of the children of Israel. 14. And the wall of the city had twelve foundations, and in them the names of the twelve apostles of the Lamb. 16. And the city lieth foursquare, and the length is as large as the breadth: and he measured the city with the reed, twelve thousand furlongs. The length and the breadth and the height of it are equal. 21. And the twelve gates were twelve pearls; every several gate was of one pearl: and the street of the city was pure gold, as it were transparent glass.

A. Possessing God's Glory

John's first vision of the New Jerusalem was very brief. Now one of the same angels who heralded God's wrath shows him a

Question.
What is the significance of the great, high mountain?

TEACHING TIP 4

One of the primary goals of the study this week is to stimulate increased praise and worship as students consider the glories of heaven.

Rather than spending a lot of time on specific discussion of the physical characteristics of John's vision of the heavenly city, you may wish to try a class "testimony" activity to stimulate worship and praise.

Starting at the front of your class—or next to you in the circle, if you have a circular seating arrangement—ask each student to state, in two or three sentences, what he/she wants to do in heaven.

This activity should be kept loose and open in nature. Encourage the students to think of people they want to see, questions they would like to ask, etc.

As you go around the class, jot down key words or phrases on the chalkboard or overhead projector. When each person has responded, lead the class in a time of prayer and praise for the wonderful things we have to look forward to in heaven.

Question.
What is the significance of giving these names such prominence?

Clarification

Temple—inner sanctuary.
Light—lamp, source of light.
Nations—peoples; often translated "Gentiles," but frequently includes both Gentiles and Jews, as it does here.

Tree—some picture a small stream with a large tree towering over it with roots on both sides of the stream. It seems

new vision of the city. Again, as so often in the Old Testament, the city is identified with its inhabitants. This city is the home city of the saints for all eternity.

That this is a new vision is confirmed by the fact the angel carried John away in the Spirit.

Satan took Jesus into a high mountain and showed Him all the kingdoms of this world and their glory. Jesus rejected that temptation (Matthew 4:8-10) and went on to win for us something far better. From that mountain John saw a city far more wonderful than all this world can offer. He saw a glory far greater too. The New Jerusalem was so radiant with the glory of God that it was like a scintillating gem, the ancient crystal jasper, what we would call a giant blue-white diamond.

Guideline for Living 2

Why is the heavenly city described in such elaborate detail? How can we possibly hope to understand the symbolism and meaning of each picture?

We probably won't understand everything this detailed description of the indescribable glories of heaven is meant to give us. But we can understand this: God wants us to know that He is the God of the indescribably glorious.

Throughout the Scriptures, God challenges His people to trust Him for great things: "Call unto me, and I will answer thee, and show thee great and mighty things, which thou knowest not" (Jeremiah 33:3). It is this great, glorious God who is our Father. This wonderful Lord is preparing a marvelous, unspeakably perfect place for us (John 14:3)—where we will be forever with Him: "Eye hath not seen, nor ear heard, neither have entered into the heart of man, the things which God hath prepared for them that love him" (1 Corinthians 2:9).

B. Gates and Foundations

There is controversy about the shape of the city. Because the wall was only about 215 feet high, many take it that the city was in the form of a pyramid. But the attention is given rather to the gates and the foundations. The gates of pearl had the names of the 12 tribes of Israel inscribed on them. The foundations, or rather, foundation stones, had the names of the twelve apostles of the Lamb inscribed on them.

There is no wall between Israel and the Church anymore. There is one city open to all of God's people. (Compare Ephesians 2:11-22.)

III. New Environment
Revelation 21:22 through 22:5

Revelation 21:22. I saw no temple therein: for the Lord God Almighty and the Lamb are the temple of it. 23. And the city had no need of the sun, neither of the moon, to shine in it: for the glory of God did lighten it, and the Lamb is the light thereof. 24. And the nations of them which are saved shall walk in the light of it: and the kings of the earth do bring their glory and honor into

better to take the singular here as a collective (as often used in the Old Testament). This would mean that the river would be lined on each side with trees.

Healing—health. This word originally meant serving, service, or care. There is no implication that there will be any sick. The fruit promotes the health, well-being, and happiness of the inhabitants of the city.

Serve—serve in worship or as priests, or in devotion to God.

Candle—lamp.

Reign—reign as kings.

Question.
Will there be any unsaved people present?

Question.
What does the river signify?

Question.
Will anything hinder our joyful service to the Lord?

it. 22:1. And he showed me a pure river of water of life, clear as crystal, proceeding out of the throne of God and of the Lamb. 2. In the midst of the street of it, and on either side of the river, was there the tree of life, which bare twelve manner of fruits, and yielded her fruit every month: and the leaves of the tree were for the healing of the nations. 5. And there shall be no night there; and they need no candle, neither light of the sun; for the Lord God giveth them light: and they shall reign for ever and ever.

A. The Light of the Lord

There are several ways the environment of the New Jerusalem will be different from millennial conditions First, there is no temple. God's glory was manifest in the Holy of Holies in Solomon's Temple. But in the New Jerusalem the whole city will be *the* Holy of Holies. That is, the manifestation of God's presence and glory will be everywhere, and we will dwell in the midst of it, everyone of us in direct contact with God and the Lamb who saved us.

There will be no sun nor moon to give light. In this present world most of the energy needed for light and life comes from the sun. In the New Jerusalem, Christ will be the immediate source of all the energy we need for our life and for all our activities throughout eternity. Our glorified bodies will be like His and will be able to stand the full impact of God's glory, so no intermediate source will be needed. (Compare Exodux 33:20-23; 1 John 3:2.) So energized, we shall never be tired or weary. Thus, we shall no longer need the succession of day and night. (See Teaching Tip 4 on preceding page.)

Revelation 21:26, 27 are addressed to the readers of the Book of Revelation. Only the nations of the saved, only people whose names are written in the Book of Life will be present in the new heaven and the new earth. All others will be in the lake of fire.

B. The River of Life

Inside the city, the angel shows John a clear, beautiful, flowing river coming from the throne of God and the Lamb.

The millennial river sweetened the waters of the Dead Sea (Ezekiel 47:1-12). But there is no sea in the new earth.

This river is a reminder that even in the New Jerusalem we will always be finite beings. We will still be as dependent on God and the Lamb as we ever were. The Father has given to Christ to have life in himself as the Father has life in himself, that is, by His own right and nature (John 5:26). But the Father has never given this to anyone else. We can never be a source of life as He is. We have life only as it continues to flow from Him (John 15:5). This river means the water of life is always there, always sufficient.

The tree of life has a similar meaning. Even though our new bodies will be immortal and incorruptible, they will not have life in themselves. All we have or ever will have is what we receive. Thank God, the leaves of the tree guarantee we shall always be in health. They provide a fullness of happy well-being.

There will be no more curse, no more cursed thing. This includes the curse of Genesis 3:17-19 that cursed Adam with fruitless toil and unrewarding or disappointing labor. In the New Jerusalem we will enjoy serving and worshiping the Lord without any hindrance or encumbrance.

TEACHING TIP 5

If you did not do it during the Scripture paraphrase activity above, call special attention at this point to the "Guideline for Living 3" discussion of 1 John 3:2, 3. Reemphasize the close connection between our joy of basking in the actual presence of the Lord and all that is the very essence of heaven.

If you wish, this would be an excellent point to invite any unsaved visitors or class members to make a commitment to Christ. (See "Evangelism Outreach" for suggestions.)

TEACHING TIP 6

Distribute copies of the Quarter's Review Quiz from PATH as you near the close of your classtime today. You may wish to use this as a "take-home" quiz and ask the students to bring it back to discuss at the start of the new quarter next Sunday.

Suggested answers for the quiz are given in the PATH instruction sheet.

Surely our worship of the Lord will be one of the most wonderful things in the New Jerusalem. When Solomon was making preparations to build the temple, he recognized that no temple he could build would be sufficient for the full manifestation of God's glory, "seeing the heaven and heaven of heavens cannot contain him" (2 Chronicles 2:6). Isaiah saw the same thing (Isaiah 66:1; 57:15). God is so much greater than the heavens that they are but His throne, and the earth His footstool (Acts 7:48-50; 17:24, 25). Now our worship and service is limited to what we can stand in these present mortal bodies. What joy when we are in the full light of His presence to reign, all of us with the full joys, benefits, and privileges of kings forever. (See Teaching Tip 5.)

Guideline for Living 3

What is the most exciting truth, the most important reality about heaven? It is not the place—it is the Person. Heaven will be heaven because our Lord will be there.

The apostle John, no doubt remembering the glory and joy he had walking and talking with Jesus (1 John 1:1-3) when He was still on earth, linked the joy of seeing God face to face with the essence of our sonship in Christ. "Beloved, now are we the sons of God, and it doth not yet appear what we shall be: but we know that, when he shall appear, we shall be like him; for we shall see him as he is" (1 John 3:2). But more than a source of exciting hope, John sees this expectation of glory as motivation which should change our whole life-style. "And every man that hath this hope in him purifieth himself, even as he is pure" (1 John 3:3).

LIVING THE TRUTH

The Book of Revelation is the great prophetic book of the New Testament. However, it is not written merely to satisfy our curiosity. Its message challenges, inspires, and comforts God's people. Sin has plunged our world into problems that are becoming increasingly agonizing. We see possibilities of food shortages, fuel shortages, water shortages. There seems to be no end to the acceleration of violence, terrorism, crime, and war. If we did not have the Bible, we would have no hope that all of this will ever end. But the Book of Revelation shows us that the present order is not permanent. God has a purpose in letting the work of sin go on without intervention. But that intervention will come, and after God has dealt with Satan and those who have served him, believers will experience the consummation of their redemption. They will know how God intended things to be when He created the universe. (See Teaching Tip 6.)

EVANGELISM OUTREACH

Today is the last session of the quarter. You have seen and heard many things from God's Word about the future God has for the world and for His people. Today may be the best time you will ever have to become one of His people and gain a share in those coming joys. Why not ask Jesus into your heart right now?